Small Business

Small Business

CREATING VALUE THROUGH ENTREPRENEURSHIP

Vishal K. Gupta

VP AND EDITORIAL DIRECTOR	Mike McDonald
PUBLISHER	Lise Johnson
EDITOR	Jennifer Manias
EDITORIAL ASSISTANT	Kali Ridley
ASSISTANT MARKETING MANAGER	Jessica Spettoli
SENIOR MANAGING EDITOR	Judy Howarth
PRODUCTION EDITOR	Umamaheswari Gnanamani
COVER PHOTO CREDIT	© Arpad Benedek / Getty Images

This book was set in 10/12 pts STIX Two Text by Straive™.

Founded in 1807, John Wiley & Sons, Inc. has been a valued source of knowledge and understanding for more than 200 years, helping people around the world meet their needs and fulfill their aspirations. Our company is built on a foundation of principles that include responsibility to the communities we serve and where we live and work. In 2008, we launched a Corporate Citizenship Initiative, a global effort to address the environmental, social, economic, and ethical challenges we face in our business. Among the issues we are addressing are carbon impact, paper specifications and procurement, ethical conduct within our business and among our vendors, and community and charitable support. For more information, please visit our website: www.wiley.com/go/citizenship.

ISBN: 978-1-119-59177-1 (PBK)
ISBN: 978-1-119-79136-2 (EVALC)

Library of Congress Cataloging-in-Publication Data:

Names: Gupta, Vishal K., author.
Title: Small business : creating value through entrepreneurship / Vishal K. Gupta.
Description: First Edition. | Hoboken : Wiley, 2021. | Includes index.
Identifiers: LCCN 2021009905 (print) | LCCN 2021009906 (ebook) | ISBN 9781119591771 (paperback) | ISBN 9781119791331 (adobe pdf) | ISBN 9781119591696 (epub)
Subjects: LCSH: Small business—Management. | Small business—Finance. | Business planning. | Entrepreneurship.
Classification: LCC HD62.7 .G866 2021 (print) | LCC HD62.7 (ebook) | DDC 658.02/2—dc23
LC record available at https://lccn.loc.gov/2021009905
LC ebook record available at https://lccn.loc.gov/2021009906

The inside back cover will contain printing identification and country of origin if omitted from this page. In addition, if the ISBN on the back cover differs from the ISBN on this page, the one on the back cover is correct.

SKY10027570_061621

To my nephew, Leonardo David da Costa Cabral Mortal (1998–2020)

Inside us there is something that has no name, that something is what we are.

Dentro de nós há uma coisa que não tem nome, essa coisa é o que somos.

José Saramago, *Portuguese writer, recipient of the 1998 Nobel Prize in Literature*

PREFACE

Over the years, I have found it very rewarding and exciting, yet also quite challenging, to teach small business management. Although there are some students who take courses in small business management because they want to start, and run, their own firm someday, there are lots of other motivations that bring students to small business management courses. For those students who don't have immediate plans to create a startup, while the "idea" of having their own business is appealing, they know that ultimately they would prefer to have a regular job following graduation. An entirely different group of students, who have not necessarily systematically contemplated beyond graduation, may find themselves in a small business course because it looks like an interesting elective to add to their schedule. There are also some students who have grown up in a small business, where they had direct experiences with one or both parents (and sometimes, grandparents) working hard to grow and develop the business. It is clear that there are often vast differences across students in regards to how much experience, knowledge, and information they bring to the classroom, or how much they care about small business management. While some students know and care a lot, others are likely to be much less motivated about the topic. My principal goal while writing this book was to encourage student learning and, perhaps more importantly, their engagement with the core ideas and nuanced perspectives that characterize small business courses, regardless of (oftentimes) substantial differences in students' motivations and reasons for signing up for the course.

Distinctive Features

Conventional wisdom in business tells us that a good product should meet customers' needs and wants. However, two American entrepreneurs – Henry Ford and Steve Jobs – famously challenged this seemingly straightforward understanding of business, arguing that good products offer features that are both novel and useful – features that customers may not even know they want. From this perspective, a good product is not one that meets customers' needs and wants, but rather exceeds customers' expectations and generates novel expectations, including those latent desires and wants that have yet to be recognized, articulated, or verbalized. The textbook industry is no exception to the customer (read: professors' and students') needs approach, for both expressed and latent needs. To address the learning needs of today's increasingly sophisticated, worldly, diverse students, and to enrich the teaching experience of their professors, this book incorporates many novel features that are intended to enhance learning both within and outside of the classroom:

1. Opening Examples: Each chapter starts with an example of a vignette featuring a business owner whom students are likely to find relevant to their own experiences both within and outside of school. For instance, we begin Chapter 1 with a discussion of Koel Thomae, founder of Noosa Yogurt. These featured entrepreneurs are pioneers in their domains and serve as role models who were successful at starting or managing a small business.

2. Interactive Exercises: Each chapter includes interactive activities that provide students the opportunity to gain hands-on, practical learning connected to the concepts and principles discussed in the chapter.

3. "What Do You Think?" boxes that put students in the role of a small business decision-maker. The core aim we seek to accomplish with this feature is to get students to think actively about what they "would do" – or will do...! – if they were making decisions that had real-world consequences for a small business.

4. Current research on small firms, blended with the practice of business ownership. Each chapter judiciously combines academic insights and evidence relating to management practices within small businesses with real-world, practical knowledge.

5. In the Movies: Small firms have often appeared in movies over the years, sometimes as made-up ventures (remember *Risky Business*?) or as real ventures started by real people (*Tucker*, anyone?). Each chapter provides an example of a movie that students can watch as a way to connect to principles and concepts related to small firms in an entertaining way.

6. World of Books: Thousands of new books are published every year, making it difficult for professors and students to keep track of relevant books that can add real value to our knowledge of concepts and topics in small business management. Each chapter suggests some books that students can read to improve their understanding of various aspects of small business management.

In addition, there are several other features included with each chapter to facilitate student engagement with the text. My primary objective for incorporating these distinctive features was to enrich the chapters, helping to make them come alive, and make students' experiences in their small business management courses more engaging. It is my hope that these novel features will enable both students and instructors to anchor concepts in a compelling way.

Target Audience

The primary audience for this book is undergraduate and graduate students interested in business, economics, and entrepreneurship. Students in liberal arts (e.g. music, theatre) and professional schools (e.g. engineering, medicine) who are interested in small business also should find this text useful, as there are numerous points of conceptual and empirical intersections between these disparate domains and the focal content and ideas highlighted in the book. Other audiences that should find the book engaging and instructive include small business owners seeking structured guidance related to decision-making or taking an entrepreneurship course, as well as a range of additional stakeholders (e.g. loan officers, regulators) looking to expand their knowledge of the operation of small firms.

Instructor website: www.wiley.com/go/gupta/smallbusiness1e Resources: Instructor Manual; Test Bank, Computerized Respondus Test Bank, Power Point Slides, and an Image Gallery.

Acknowledgments

During the two-year period over which I developed this project, and the several years that went into building and iteratively delivering the materials discussed above, I benefited tremendously from colleagues, students, and business owners. My colleague, Daniel Bachrach, encouraged me to write this book from the moment he heard about it, and introduced me to the right people to get started on the path to bring this book to publication. I am very grateful for his support and help throughout the process. Dan Turban of the University of Missouri has been a mentor throughout my academic career, whose advice and counsel have been instrumental in helping me become a better researcher and teacher.

I also very much appreciate the numerous sections of students who became the sounding board for the material covered in this book. I feel that having been able to discuss the material in the text with my students over the years provided an invaluable opportunity for me to learn from them and to incorporate their insights. I am fortunate to count many successful business owners among my close friends and relatives, who are too numerous to mention here by name. These business owners have always been very open about their professional lives with me, and generously answered my numerous probing questions about the work they do. During the writing of this book, some of them even took the time to visit with my students to share their experiences and insights. I continue to count on them to enrich my students' learning experience in the future.

My wife (Sandra Mortal, PhD in Finance) and sister (Alka Gupta, PhD in Management) are two people I often turn to for advice and support in my academic endeavors. Not surprisingly, I needed their counsel many times during the writing for this book, and they were always there. My father was my first business teacher, as I learned my initial lessons about starting and running a small firm from him, in the business he had started before I was born. He was also an enthusiastic cheerleader for this project, and did not hesitate to remind me about the deadlines I needed to meet to complete the manuscript on time. In her youth, my mother was an avid reader, and I credit her with nurturing and encouraging my love for reading. Mom, without you, I would not be where I am today!

My special thanks go to Nedah Rose for her fine editing and guidance throughout the writing of this book. I also appreciate the understanding and patience of Lise Johnson, Publisher at Wiley, as the book took longer to write than we initially expected. The Wiley team, including Jennifer Manias, Judy Howarth, and Umamaheswari Gnanamani were very professional throughout the process. One important lesson learned during the past two years: It does indeed take a village to take a book from an idea in one's head to a finished product ready for the market.

Several professors across the country generously made the time to review the material discussed in the book: Dominic Bartola, Paradise Valley Community College; Erick Chang, Arkansas State University; Gloria Cockerell, Collin College; Dev Dutta, University of New Hampshire; A. Banu Goktan, University of North Texas at Dallas; April Hearne, University of Arkansas Pulaski Technical College; Golshan Javadian, Morgan State University; Noureddine Lalami, Chabot College; and Theresa Torres, Central New Mexico University. Ethne Swartz, Montclair State University, provided an expert review with a focus on diversity and inclusion. I am very thankful to y'all (as we say in our part of the country) for your critical insights and suggestions that helped improve the book.

About the Author

Professor Vishal K. Gupta is on the faculty of the Department of Management at Culverhouse College of Business of The University of Alabama. His previous academic positions were at University of Mississippi, State University of New York at Binghamton, and University of Nebraska at Omaha. He also has been a visiting professor at Bahrain Institute of Banking and Finance, and the Indian Institute of Management (at Kashipur and Shillong). He has published 2 academic books and over 75 research articles. His work is regularly discussed in the popular press, including the *Wall Street Journal*, *New York Times*, and *Business Insider*, among others. Before embarking on an academic career, Professor Gupta worked in the family business (YESCO), making industrial grinding machines. He earned a PhD in Business Administration (concentration in Strategic Management with an emphasis on Entrepreneurship) from University of Missouri. His pedagogical approach combines theory and practice, which also informs the way the material in this book is presented.

One More Thing

I made every effort to write an error-free text. Yet, it is possible that some mistakes and flaws made it into the book, and I take full responsibility for these. I hope that readers, including students and instructors, will share with me any errors they find, or suggestions they may have to strengthen the quality of the text for the next edition. My email is vkgupta@cba.ua.edu. I look forward to hearing from you. Thank you!

BRIEF CONTENTS

CONTENTS

10   Ethics and Social Responsibility   230

15 Strategic Thinking for Small Firms   358

CHAPTER 1

Understanding Small Business

LEARNING OBJECTIVES

This chapter will help you to:

LO 1.1 Discuss the importance of small business to the economy

LO 1.2 Define small business management and explain the role of entrepreneurship in managing a small business

LO 1.3 Recognize the common myths about and various benefits of small business entrepreneurship

LO 1.4 Identify various forms of small business entrepreneurship

Small businesses are the backbone of our economy and the cornerstones of America's promise.

BARACK OBAMA,
Former President of the United States

It makes sense to have the small businesses at the cornerstone of a pro-growth economic policy.

GEORGE W. BUSH,
Former President of the United States

1.0 Introduction

Small businesses are ubiquitous in the modern world. From the United States to Japan, and everywhere in between, small businesses play an important role in economies world-wide. Some believe that the history of small business is as old as human civilization, with evidence of business activity found in all ancient civilizations of the world. Today, there is no country in the world where small business is completely absent. Small businesses are often rightly described as engines of the economy for the important role they play in the economic growth of any country.

Small business has long been an integral part of American society. Even as far back as 1835, the French diplomat Alexis de Tocqueville wrote in his book *Democracy in America*: "What astonishes me in the United States is not so much the marvelous grandeur of some undertaking as the innumerable multitude of small ones." Whether numbers translated into respect is, however, debatable. Edith Wharton, American novelist and short story writer, shares in her autobiography: "A Backward Glance' that the person who 'kept a shop' was more rigorously shut out of polite society in the original thirteen states than in post-revolutionary France."

SPOTLIGHT | Noosa, a Trendy Yogurt

Koel Thomae, cofounder of Noosa Yogurt, had no idea that a spoonful of yogurt with passion fruit puree would change her life. Born in Australia to an American mother and a Canadian father, Koel moved to Boulder, CO, as a young adult and dabbled in information technology, before working for the beverage company Izze. While visiting her mom in Australia one year, she chanced upon a little corner shop in the beach town of Noosa that sold a yogurt that grabbed her taste buds in a special way. When she returned to Colorado, she couldn't get the yogurt out of her mind. She reached out to the family that ran the yogurt shop in Australia, and after much cajoling, convinced them to license her their recipe for the American market.

Koel Thomae, cofounder of Noosa.

Desiree Navarro/Getty Images

Despite the licensing agreement, Koel still had a problem: She had zero dairy experience. Around this time, she stumbled upon a flier for a family farm in northern Colorado. She cold-called Morning Fresh Dairy, and was connected to a fourth-generation dairy farmer Rob Graves, who was skeptical at first. Koel's persistence – and a sample (or two) of the Australian yogurt – convinced Rob to agree to sign on. Koel became responsible for designing the packaging and branding, and Rob was in charge of production. The pair started making Noosa in small batches, introducing just four flavors at first: honey, blueberry, raspberry, and mango.

At the time, when low-fat and no-fat yogurt was center stage, Noosa offered yogurt made with whole milk (translation: it was rich in fat). Chunks of fresh fruit lined the bottom of each container. The yogurt was only available in 8-ounce transparent containers. "No one else was in a clear tub," Koel remembers. The transparent packaging allowed Noosa to show off the freshness of the product and let people see what they're eating, especially the fruit.

Noosa debuted at the Boulder Farmers Market, which Koel believes was instrumental in creating a loyal following and viral word-of-mouth. "Colorado is a mecca for the natural foods industry, and I think people here are more open to trying products that might be a bit unconventional," Koel says. Whole Foods became Noosa's first retail customer, but balked at the 8-ounce tubs. An 8-ounce tub takes up a lot of shelf space – and retailers are very protective of shelf space. Koel and Rob, however, were not open to changing the packaging. They had already purchased equipment specifically for those packages without doing a retail presentation, and changing everything would need the kind of money they didn't have.

Like many new businesses, Noosa got off to a slow start. The founders couldn't pay themselves for the first two-and-half years. All the money they were earning went back into growing Noosa. Rob was still managing his dairy and Koel had a consulting gig, so they were financially okay even without an income from Noosa. Fortunately, a local banker heard about them, loved the product, and offered to lend them money to grow the business. Soon, other retailers started selling Noosa: Target, Rite Aid, Walgreens, and Walmart. Noosa is now a nation-wide yogurt brand, selling coast-to-coast.

"I knew I was going to have to work hard and I wasn't afraid of that," Koel says. "I think it was the intersection of all these things and timing, and that's something you can't predict. But it's amazing what you can do when you find these things and are willing to work hard."

Discussion Questions

1. Who would you say were key players in helping Koel get her start in business?

2. Who do you think benefitted from Koel starting a new business and its success?

3. Koel liked a product, and decided to start a business based on what she liked. Do you think that is a good approach to starting a business?

Today, American society has an impressive diversity of small business, and together these small businesses are a powerful driving force in the American economy. Some estimates suggest that there are about 31 million small businesses in the country, which together employ about 64 million workers (about half of America's private-sector employment). Most small businesses, about 80%, are single-person firms with no employees. In recent years, the Internet has played an important role in fostering a new generation of small businesses. Many of these small firms, like Apple and Netflix, have been so successful that they have become among the largest corporations of our times.

Module 1.1 Describe Small Business

The first issue we want to understand is the meaning of the term *small business*, as it lies at the heart of this book. The US Congress defines a **small business** as "one that is independently owned and operated and is not dominant in its field of operation." Most common definitions of small business are based on size. Firms with less than 500 employees are usually considered small, though even here things are more complicated than they seem. For the **Small Business Administration** (SBA), the two most widely used criteria to consider a business as small are 500 employees for most manufacturing and mining industries and $7.5 million in average annual receipts for many nonmanufacturing industries. There are however several exceptions to these criteria as size standards vary by industry and change with time; so it is best to go directly to the SBA website and check whether a business qualifies to be classified as "small."

What Do You Think?

P. F. Chang's is an American-based, Asian-themed restaurant chain founded by Paul Fleming and Philip Chiang. The company has more than 300 restaurants worldwide, including more than 200 in the United States. The company is valued by private equity investors for at least $1.5 billion. Do you think it's a small business? According to the SBA, it is. The SBA counts employment at the establishment level, not at the firm level, to classify a firm as a small business, as long as each establishment has its own identification number. What do you think are the pros and cons of counting employment at the establishment level, rather than the firm level, for classifying a firm as a small business?

Pedego Electric Bikes, based in Fountain Valley, CA, is a prominent example of a successful small business in America. Started by Don DiCostanzo and Terry Sherry in 2008, Pedego is now the largest electric bike retailer in the country.

When the novel Coronavirus pandemic hit in 2020, small businesses were at the forefront of our country's crisis response. Frank Timberlake, owner of Rich Square Market in North Carolina, worked extra hours to keep his grocery store open, as it is the main source of fresh food in an economically challenged rural county. Phil Cai, who runs Cai Dentistry in McLean (VA), used a 3-D printing machine in his lab that typically makes surgical guides for dental implants to instead produce N95 protective masks. Audrey Zimmerman of Kepner Scott Shoe Co. retooled her production line to make cotton masks for donating them to healthcare workers who could wear them over the N95 respirators, extending their lifespan. Neil Thanedar, chief executive of the technology startup Labdoor, teamed up with Silicon Valley investor Sam Altman and other technology ventures on an ambitious project to produce a million low-cost ventilators in three months ("mass-produced and made in a decentralized way by individuals and small businesses," he says). Alisha Crossley, who runs a photography business in Mountain Brook, AL, offered free

Pedego Inc.: America's largest retailer of electric bikes.

Pedego Electric Bikes

front-porch portraits to families riding out the outbreak at home (while keeping a safe distance, consistent with federal guidelines), in part as a way to give back during the pandemic. These are just some examples of the ways in which small business owners responded to the pandemic.

Companies such as Nike, Alibaba, and Zara are now household names. But they were once small businesses managed by growth-oriented individuals with dreams in their hearts (who probably struggled initially to meet payroll). What helped them go from such humble beginnings to becoming so successful? While many people attribute the success of such companies, and countless others like them, to the mystic influence of luck, the entrepreneurial efforts of enterprising individuals who start and manage these companies often go unnoticed.

Of course, few small businesses ever manage to scale the towering heights that companies like Nike and Zara reach. A large proportion of new businesses remain small forever. Yet, even businesses that remain small can be a good source of wealth for their owners. Professors Thomas Stanley and William Danko observed in their blockbuster book *The Millionaire Next Door*:

> Self-employed people make up less than 20 percent of the workers in America, but account for two-thirds of the millionaires . . . Many of the businesses [they] are in could be classified as dull-normal: welding contractors, auctioneers, rice farmers, owners of mobile-home parks, pest controllers, coin and stamp dealers, and paving contractors.

It is worth remembering here that just because a large proportion of affluent people are small business owners, it does not mean that a large majority of small business owners end up in the ranks of the affluent. Indeed, many small businesses fail, and we will return to this topic later in the chapter. Moreover, it is not completely clear whether the wealth creation potential of small businesses is due simply to the income they generate or the positive desirable habits that people running these businesses develop over time (such as meticulous budgeting).

KEY TAKEAWAY

Many everyday millionaires (successful people who build wealth) are business owners.

There is much to celebrate about small business:

1. They comprise more than 99% of the employers in the country.
2. They employ half of all private sector employees and generate a good proportion of new employment annually.
3. They are a fertile source of new innovations, with some suggesting that small firms file more patents per employee than large corporations.
4. There is an increasing trend of small businesses going international (with some "**born global**"), so that small firms are a large part of the American exporter pool.
5. Anyone can be a small business owner as there are no minimum or maximum legal age requirements for starting a new business (Michael Dell famously started his first business at age 9 selling collectible stamps through the mail).

A healthy capitalist society encourages small businesses, helping enterprising actors start new firms and supporting the growth of existing companies. Some small firms grow to become large corporations. As such, small and large firms are both important for a thriving economy. Countries that favor one or the other risk getting left behind as small firms and large corporations have a symbiotic relationship.

During the 2020 Coronavirus pandemic, small businesses around the country had to close for an indefinite period. To help small business owners stay afloat, the federal government launched the Paycheck Protection Program (PPP) to distribute more than $500 billion to around 5 million businesses. Firms that met conditions such as spending most of the money on payroll would be forgiven the loans, effectively turning them into tax-payer funded grants. Table 1.1 provides some examples of small firms that received the PPP funding during the COVID-19 pandemic.

Not all small firms, however, qualified for the PPP loan program, which required that the money largely be spent on payroll within a specific time period. Many such firms were able to borrow money from the Main Street Lending Program, which were aimed at helping pandemic-hit firms not serviced by the PPP. March Epstein of Milk Street Café in Boston, MA, focusing heavily on corporate catering, was able to get a Main Street loan, and plans to reopen when workers return to downtown offices.

TABLE 1.1

Many Small Firms Benefited from the PPP Loans During the COVID-19 Pandemic

Firm name	Location	Owner	PPP funding
Sand & C Travel Inc.	Parkland, FL	Alan and Cathy Rosen	$92,400
Bluebird Lanes	Chicago, IL	William Brennan	$70,900
Suwana's Thai Orchid	Asheville, NC	Suwana Cry	$72,126
Nubian Hueman	Washington D.C.	Anika Hobbs	$26,000
Little Jumbo	Asheville, NC	Chall Gray	$52,000
Chirokei Consulting	Washington D.C.	Keita Vanterpool	$14,000
Cold Spring Construction	Akron, NY	Richard Forresetel Jr	$2,200,000
DemandMaven	Atlanta, GA	Asia Orangio	$10,000
Dazzle Estate Sales	Lawrence, KS	Gretchen Wilson	$6,700
Massage Envy Franchise	San Jose, CA	Aditi and Jaymin Patel	$125,000
Highland Yoga	Atlanta, GA	Elspeth Brotheron	$143,000
County Kitchen	Big Pine, CA	Jackie and Nick Nersesian	$40,600
Warehouse of Fixtures TNG	St. Louis, MO	David Singer	$600,000
Starlite Lanes	Flagstaff, AZ	Ronald and Karen Getto	$142,000

The SBA is a federally funded agency tasked with helping Americans start, build, and grow businesses. It provides assistance and loans to small firms, as well as helps them with federal contract procurement.

Small Business Owners Are Underdogs

Small business owners are often underdogs. They are running a business where they may be competing with large, well-established firms. A business owner running a small restaurant competes with local restaurants affiliated with large chains that have much deeper pockets and immediate brand recognition. Hear Malcolm Gladwell talk about what entrepreneurs can learn from David and Goliath, the classic story about an underdog winning against a large well-established incumbent.

Wikimedia Commons

View the video online at https://www.youtube.com/watch?v=jqx37yjCaJs.

Does it matter if a business is considered big or small? The short answer is "it sure does." There are two major reasons why the classification as small business is so important:

1. Businesses recognized as small are eligible for SBA's small business programs, including financial assistance.
2. Businesses that qualify as small are eligible to sell to the set-aside programs of the federal government.

Firms that meet SBA's criteria for small business can get the agency's assistance, which comes in four forms: financial support, education and training, government contracting, and advocacy. Over the years, thousands of small businesses have benefited from SBA assistance. American college students reading this book will be familiar with Under Armour, the athletic-wear company started by University of Maryland football player Kevin Plank. Most people, however, do not know that Under Armour received considerable support from SBA in its early days, which helped the small company transform itself into a global multimillion-dollar corporation in less than 15 years from founding. In 2016, Kevin Plank and Under Armour received SBA's inaugural Hall of Champions Award.

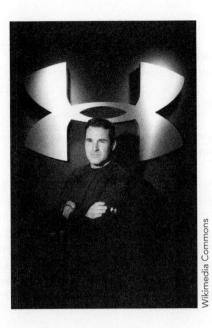

Wikimedia Commons

Kevin Plank of Under Armour appreciates the support he received from SBA when he first started out. He later became SBA's first Hall of Champions Awardee.

Comprehension Check

1. How would you define small business?
2. What does the Small Business Administration (SBA) do?
3. What makes it difficult to have one universal definition of small business that applies across all firms?

Module 1.2 Define Small Business Management

This is a book about managing small businesses. But, what does one mean when one uses the term *small business management*? For the purpose of this book, **small business management** refers to the deliberate administration of a small firm with the goals of survival and improvement. Survival is a necessary condition for small business management. After all, in the absence of survival, there is no business left to manage. Consider Pebble Technology, a smartwatch maker that ran three of the top Kickstarter campaigns of all times, including the largest at $20 million in 2015. The company was started by University of Waterloo engineering student Eric Migicovsky and managed to sell two million watches through Kickstarter and retailers before the watch-making business ceased in 2016. Four years after its birth, the small company with lots of promise was gone. No business then remained to manage!

Improvement is the highly desirable condition for small business management; without attention to improvement, the business risks getting left behind by aggressive rivals and eventually dying. Some people may resist making improvement a part of small business management, arguing that many small firms are simply lifestyle endeavors producing a decent income for their owners to maintain the quality of life they want. Their logic is that these **lifestyle businesses** may not want to improve, so it does not make sense for improvement to be part of the definition of small business management. It is true that there are thousands of businesses that exist simply to provide an additional income for their owners (as we discuss later), but it would be incorrect to infer that owners of such firms do not need to think about improving their operations and/or product offerings.

It is useful to think here of what is sometimes called the *Red Queen effect*. Inspired by Lewis Carroll's *Alice's Adventures in Wonderland*, the **red queen effect** refers to the idea that in a world of intense competition, increasing globalization, and rapid-fire product and technological innovation, a firm needs to constantly think of improving, even to remain where it is at a given time. Consequently, firms that want to expand need to be doubly focused on improving themselves. We often do not realize that the inability to improve and become better at what they (can) do leads to the demise of many firms in our towns and cities every year (think Blockbuster and Borders for two prominent examples of now-dead firms that once were the leading players in their industry). As the Queen observed in Carroll's popular book:

> Here, you see, it takes all the running you can do to keep in the same place. If you want to get somewhere else, you must run at least twice as fast as that.

Noosa's story illustrates the red queen effect quite well. Had Koel not continually improved Noosa's product and operations, she would have soon found her business come under attack from Dannon, Yoplait, or other incumbents and even upstarts. In such a situation, she could have chosen to remain a small player focused on the customers in her local area of Boulder, CO, which may have given her a good lifestyle income. Yet, she would still need to constantly come up with creative ways to keep her existing customers coming back for more yogurt (and to find new customers for the ones getting pulled by other yogurt makers). Either way, Koel would need to think of continuous improvement for her business to survive.

KEY TAKEAWAY

Small businesses need to constantly work to improve even if they want to stay in the same place. When small firms stop improving, it's the beginning of the end.

There are many ways to manage a small firm well. Regardless of how a business is run, following the law and making ethical decisions is a cornerstone of good management. Sometimes people forget that flouting the law and behaving unethically may hurt the firm, and even lead to its untimely demise. The life of a business owner is filled with temptations to do wrong in pursuit of short-term gains. Running a business brings with it constant pressure to stretch the truth, manipulate the financial accounts of the firm, violate the law, and otherwise engage in unethical or immoral behaviors. Figure 1.1 illustrates some common ethical violations reported by employees at small firms.

The Ethical Picture

A look at what employees at the smallest companies (2 to 24 workers) said about their experiences

ON THE LOOKOUT
35%
of employees at the smallest companies (two to 24 workers) observed misconduct.

BOSSES' BEHAVIOR
58%
of misconduct involved someone with managerial authority.

A LIMITED SCOPE
10%
of observed misconduct was characterized as a companywide behavior

RECURRING BEHAVIOR
32%
of rule breaking was represented as isolated incidents

A SOLID FOUNDATION
65%
characterized their workplaces as having a strong or strong-leaning ethics culture

A STRONG COMMITMENT
75%
believe their top management is committed to ethics and ethical conduct. Supervisors and co-workers also got high marks (72% and 68%, respectively)

Most common forms of misconduct observed:

15%
Anticompetitive practices
- - - - - - -
13%
Lying to employees
- - - - - - -
12%
Abusive behavior
- - - - - - -
10%
Lying to customers
- - - - - - -
10%
Conflicts of interest
- - - - - - -
10%
Violations of health/safety regulations

FIGURE 1.1 Ethical Issues in Small Firms
Source: Adapted from 2013 National Business Ethics Survey by the Ethics Resource Centre, the Research Arm of the Ethics & Compliance Initiative, *The Wall Street Journal.*

Students of small business will frequently encounter the word *entrepreneurship* in their readings. It is therefore useful to understand how the two concepts – small business and entrepreneurship – are related. We have already defined small business earlier in the chapter. Many different definitions of **entrepreneurship** exist. A common definition of entrepreneurship is new venture creation. From this perspective, anyone starting a new business is an entrepreneur, whether it is Jeff starting a barbershop or Jane starting an e-commerce company. Another definition of entrepreneurship is about identifying and pursuing new opportunities to introduce novel goods and services to the market. Seen in this way, firms that introduce new offerings are behaving entrepreneurially.

Interactive Activity

What do you think when you hear the word *entrepreneurship*? Interview 10 people (no more than three of them students) on what entrepreneurship means to them. Do they have a favorite entrepreneur? If yes, what do they like about this entrepreneur? Be prepared to share with the class what you find.

Every business starts small, but only some firms are able to continue behaving entrepreneurially over time by constantly pursuing new profitable opportunities to introduce novel products and services in the market. Such firms are called "entrepreneurial small businesses" (see Figure 1.2). Of course, businesses that continue to grow (as Chobani did) will someday manage to break through the size threshold to be considered "small" and eventually become large corporations such as Walmart and Amazon. Did you know that both Walmart and Amazon started as very small businesses?

Consider the case of George Washington, America's first president. Mount Vernon was the center of Washington's business endeavors. Washington experimented with as many as 60 different grain crops before abandoning tobacco, the soil-depleting crop that had been the foundation of the Chesapeake economy since the first English settlers arrived in the early seventeenth century. He not only raised large quantities of grain but also ground it into flour in his own state-of-the-art grist mill, packaged it in sacks marked with his "G. Washington" brand, and marketed it throughout North America, the Caribbean, and Britain. Washington also made sure much of the flour left Mount Vernon's wharf aboard his own oceangoing transports. The business side of George Washington seldom gets much attention but is quite informative and inspiring. Interested? Take a look at John Berlau's short but lively book *George Washington, Entrepreneur* to read about the first president's many business endeavors.

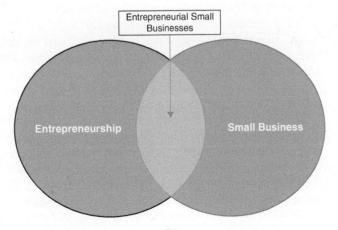

FIGURE 1.2 Small Business and Entrepreneurship Are Complementary

First Entrepreneur

It has long been discussed that George Washington, first President of the United States, was first in war and first in peace. Many books have been written about Washington's success before and after the American war of independence. In recent years, some researchers have turned to understanding Washington's work as a business owner. Hear Professor Edward Lengel of University of Virginia talk about George Washington as First Entrepreneur.

View the video online at: https://www.youtube.com/watch?v=XYyyDBa37LI

Mass media makes it seem that entrepreneurial small firms are the most common form of business in society. If you believe that the typical business is a growth-oriented enterprise always on the lookout for a new product or service that will revolutionize the world, you are mistaken! The typical business in our society does not look anything like what is portrayed in the media and most how-to books. In fact, most small businesses, perhaps as many as 70%, are tiny and their owners make little effort to grow. These lifestyle businesses are a way for the owners to earn additional income, much like a part-time job (we call such businesses *turtles*). Tracy Obolsky is the owner of Rockaway Beach Bakery in Queens, NY, a lifestyle business that she closes whenever she feels an urge to go surfing. The way Tracy sees it, the purpose of her business is to fund the living expenses and lifestyle ambitions she has.

Traditional small firms, ones that generate enough income for the owners to provide a living for the family (and perhaps, save some), are next with about 20% of the business population in this category (we refer to such businesses as *goats*). Red Barn Technology in Binghamton, NY, is one of the thousands of traditional small businesses that are the backbone of the American economy. Jon Layish started Red Barn when a friend complained there was nowhere locally to get computer parts and service. Over time, the company gradually expanded to offer high-end servers and technology for research universities around the nation.

Turtles and goats usually do not get much attention in popular media and academic discussions. David Sax's *The Soul of an Entrepreneur* is a rare book that draws attention to the interesting stories of lifestyle ventures and traditional firms, providing us a renewed appreciation of the daunting challenges faced by small businesses.

Finally, **entrepreneurial small firms**, those that have high rates of growth and stand to benefit from professionalization, are the smallest proportion of the business population (no more than 10% overall). These are *gazelles*, fast runners who will outperform most everyone else in their market when it comes to growth. When the American economist David Birch used the label gazelle to describe high-growth firms, he reserved it for young, fast-growing companies with revenues of at least $1 million and four years of sustained revenue growth (around 20% annually). He estimated that gazelles comprise only 4% of all US companies, but account for 70% of all new jobs. Inc. magazine is popular for its annual rankings of the fastest-growing small firms in the country. Vegetable "pasta" maker Cece's Veggie Co. is a gazelle based in Austin, Texas, ranking #3 on Inc. Magazine's 2019 list of fastest-growing American small firms, with a three-year revenue growth of a whopping 23,880%. The company started as a kitchen experiment by Mason Arnold, when doctors advised him and his two sons to adopt a gluten-free diet for health reasons, growing quickly to become a major player.

What happens when "entrepreneurial small business" become highly successful and no longer remain small? They become large firms, some of which can still be entrepreneurial. **Corporate entrepreneurship** refers to the practice of large firms seeking to grow through entrepreneurial actions and behaviors. We call such firms *whales* for their large size and aggressive marketplace behaviors. The online retail giant Amazon, founded by Jeff Bezos as an online book seller, has $280 billion in revenues and employs about 800,000 people. Even when it is so big, the company is well known for its aggression and ambition.

There are also large firms that stop growing at some point. We call them *elephants*, for their large size and slow, limited movements. GE, HP, and Xerox are prominent examples of large corporations that have struggled to grow and maneuver in a highly competitive place.

What Do You Think?

Chobani is America's largest Greek-yogurt company. Founded by Hamdi Ulukaya, a Kurdish immigrant to New York, it started as a very small company that received an SBA loan for buying a plant to make yogurt in upstate New York. Gradually, Chobani grew and finally became a large company. At a certain stage in its growth, Chobani ceased to qualify for SBA assistance and guidance. Conversely, had Chobani not been able to grow, it could have continued to look toward SBA for help. Do you think it is fair that companies that manage to grow are no longer eligible for support from SBA? Do companies like Chobani end up being penalized for success?

1.2.1 Problems with (Rapid) Growth

Is growth always good? For most people, the answer to this question would be a resounding yes. Unfortunately, they would be wrong. Firms that grow rapidly are sometimes, but not always, in a good position. Indeed, the business world is full of companies that failed because of rapid growth that was not properly managed. As a result, growth can be healthy for the firm (e.g. it allows for economies of scale), but it can also be unhealthy for the firm. Here are some situations when rapid growth becomes very problematic for the firm:

1. Reckless spending or spending money you don't have: You've probably never heard of Webvan, the online grocery delivery company. Founded in 1996 by Louis Borders (cofounder of the eponymous retail chain Borders), Webvan is considered one of the largest flops of the dot-com bubble era. The company had raised about $600 million, which it spent lavishly and recklessly.

2. Taking on too much debt: Some businesses take up too much debt, which they then find difficult to repay or even service (because of high interest payments), particularly when the economy turns. Steve & Barry's was a prominent American retail clothing chain, cofounded by University of Pennsylvania student Barry Prevor, and famous for selling low-priced clothes. It met its end during the 2008 financial crisis when it was deficient in paying back its debt and defaulted on payments.

3. Premature investment in scaling: Many small business owners want to grow, and some try to grow before they have a profitable or sustainable business model in place. Such efforts, unfortunately, usually end up in failure. Wise Acre Frozen Treats, a maker of organic popsicles from unrefined sweeteners, expanded quickly to increase production capacity, but then came crashing down just as quickly when they could not finance the growth.

4. Extending too much credit: Did you know that quite a number of small businesses fail because they extend too much credit to customers? These business owners forget that growth is not too difficult when it is done on the back of selling on credit. Credit, they say, can make or break a small business. A credit policy that is too lenient can cause collection and cash-flow problems later, whereas a carefully designed credit policy can attract (new) customers.

5. Hoarding too much inventory: Firms that try to grow rapidly often stock up on inventory to either avoid the problem of lost sales or gain from economies of scale. This poses two problems: Too much money gets tied up in inventory or the inventory becomes dated. The problem with inventory is that it rarely sells for as much it is worth on the surface. Astute business owners are able to figure out how to grow without hoarding too much inventory.

6. Inadequate understanding of the market and its future trends: Crumbs, founded in 2003, was once considered the world's largest cupcake business. In 2016, the company closed down permanently. So, what went wrong? Management kept expanding, even as consumer tastes were shifting and competition was intensifying.

7. Lack of skills to manage a bigger business: It is common knowledge that Steve Jobs got fired from his own company in 1985. It is, however, not well understood why it happened. Steve Jobs was a directionless college student at 20, founded Apple when he was 21, became a millionaire at 25, and was unceremoniously kicked out of Apple at 30. While Jobs was good at starting the business, he had been a failure at managing the complexities of a rapidly growing company. Not everyone has the skills to manage a business that is growing rapidly. When the business owner lacks the skills needed to manage a large business, things can go bad, sometimes very quickly.

What Do You Think?

It is said that no firm goes from a small business to a large corporation without hiccups. Chobani, America's dominant player in the Greek-yogurt business, is not as large as Walmart (2019 revenue: $514.4 billion) and Amazon (2017 revenue: $280.5 billion), but it is certainly not the small business it once was (its estimated revenues are about $1.5 billion). Unlike Walmart and Amazon, Chobani also still remains a private company (meaning, Chobani continues to be owned by Hamdi and its ownership is not in public hands). What "hiccups" or challenges do you think Chobani faced as it transitioned from a small business to a large company?

When rapid growth kills a business, it is often not because of lack of "hard work." On the contrary, most business owners who find themselves at the helm of a rapidly growing business are already working hard. It is therefore useful to understand the seven common problems associated with rapid growth. In their own way, each of these "sins" can lead to the downfall of a growing business (see Table 1.2).

There are many successful companies that forego growth in favor of excellence. These companies focus not on revenue growth or geographical expansion, but they pursue other

TABLE **1.2**

Seven Deadly Sins of Fast Growth

Seven Sins of Rapid Growth	
1 Reckless spending	Spending money without carefully thinking about where it will come from or why it is being spent
2 Taking on too much debt	Growing by taking on debt that the firm is unable to service
3 Premature scaling	Growing before the business model has been worked out
4 Extending too much credit	Growing by selling on credit, so that customers are buying without actually paying for it
5 Hoarding inventory	Buying too much in anticipation of sales that may not happen in the future
6 Inadequate market knowledge	Growing without truly understanding the product you are selling or the customer you are serving
7 Lack of management skills	Inability to manage the complexities of an expanding business

goals that they consider more important than getting as big as possible, as fast as possible. These companies are sometimes called *small giants*, firms that are great at what they do, which includes creating a desirable place to work, providing excellent service to customers, having developmental relationships with their suppliers, making productive contributions to their communities, and finding positive ways to lead their lives. Bo Burlington's book *Small Giants* first brought these companies to the public's attention.

KEY TAKEAWAY

Growth is often mistakenly seen as the ultimate sign of success. It is not! Growth can be good for a firm, but firms can also be great without focusing on growth.

Comprehension Check

1. How would you define small business management? In what ways does small business management differ from, and yet is similar to, entrepreneurship?
2. Name and explain the different types of small businesses. Can you come up with some examples for each type?
3. Is growth always desirable for small firms? Explain.

Module 1.3 Myths About and Benefits of Small Business Entrepreneurship

Most new ventures fail! Pretty much everyone agrees on this issue. Most small businesses never manage to grow. Almost everyone agrees on this too. Where people differ is what can be done about the risk of **failure** and the problem of **dwarfism**. For small businesses, failure usually means not being financially viable, because either you are not attracting enough paying customers or you are spending more than you are earning. Dwarfism refers to a firm's inability to grow despite intentions and desire for growth. Even though business owners generally launch their ventures with the best of intentions and plan to work hard for long hours, some businesses either fail or are unable to grow. The financial research firm Dun & Bradstreet defines **business failure** as when a firm closes due to bankruptcy, foreclosure, or voluntary withdrawal from the firm with a financial loss to a creditor or investor.

Most professors believe that with the right education and training the risk of failure can be significantly decreased and students can acquire the skills to nurture and grow their business. Starting and running a small business is a skill, akin to riding a horse or driving a car. Everyone can learn how to do it; some learn it quickly, but for others it takes longer. Some become good at it, while others barely get by. A common myth is that entrepreneurs are born, and entrepreneurship is innate. Nothing could be further from the truth. Starting and running a business is a skill that can be learned and mastered. How good you are at it, will depend on how seriously you take it.

Interactive Activity

Interview people you know about whether they think entrepreneurs are born or made. In other words, can entrepreneurship be learned or are you born with it? Compile what you learn, and share it with the class.

It is worth remembering that the risk of failure is part of everyday life. In 2018, the divorce rate in the United States was 45% (which is still not the highest the world), but that does not stop people from getting married (and also spending lots of money on their wedding). Only about 58% students who start college manage to finish in six years, and yet college enrollment is at a record high. The issue here is not that business can fail, but that with good preparation one can significantly reduce the chances of failure. Successful people in every field understand that failure is a real option, and success comes from learning from setbacks. Even in situations where one fails despite their best efforts, it is important not to get discouraged. Thomas Edison famously said when asked about his unsuccessful efforts to invent the light bulb, "I didn't fail a thousand times. I found a thousand ways that don't work." From Henry Ford to Jack Ma (of Alibaba), the world is full of entrepreneurs who refused to get discouraged by setbacks and went on to become highly successful.

There are also many other myths about entrepreneurship and small business. You have probably heard that to be successful in business, you need to forget everything else. Many, including some entrepreneurs, believe that running a business leaves little time for **work–life balance**. While it is good to be passionate about your business (or for that matter any career you choose), it is not healthy to completely sacrifice your personal life to advance your business. No point becoming a successful business owner only to find you have no family or good friends to share your success with! Successful business owners (like successful people in any field) need to find a work–life balance that does justice to both their work and their family. Perhaps, a better way to think about how many small business owners are able to do well in their venture as well as their personal life is to shift the focus away from balance between work and family to integration between the two. Entrepreneurs who are able to constructively integrate their work and family life will be able to find synergies across the two spheres. Consider Sam Walton, the founder of Walmart, who started as a small business owner in Arkansas. He got married when he was in the military before he started his business, had four children, and by all accounts was a loving husband and doting father all his life. For business owners, balancing the needs of their work and life may not be easy, but those who are able to integrate the professional and personal demands are likely to be happier than those who do not.

Another common myth is that "entrepreneurs are a rare breed," and a "kind of genius who is born, not made." Nothing could be further from the truth! Anyone can learn how to start and manage a business as long as they have the right attitude to learn and develop themselves. Researchers have found that a **growth mindset** (as opposed to a **fixed mindset**, which stipulates that one's skills and qualities are largely immutable) is essential for anyone who wants to perform well at unfamiliar tasks (see Figure 1.3). About 11% of American households own a business. Good management of business results not from "being born with it" but from learning the tools and practices of management (which is what this book will teach you).

"This is not a good time to start a new venture" is another myth about small business entrepreneurship. In fact, when it comes to starting a business, anytime is a good time. Many famous businesses of today – FedEx, CNN, and Krispy Kreme – started during economic recessions. The best time to start a business is whenever you feel ready. While lean economic times may foster a general climate of despair and gloom, businesses started during periods of busts have as good of a chance at success as those started during boom times.

Would it surprise you to learn that each year more people in the United States start a business than get married or have children? Clearly, these enterprising individuals are not discouraged by the prevailing myths about entrepreneurship and small business discussed above. So, what are some of the benefits of managing your own business? Of course, every entrepreneur has their own reasons for why they want to manage their own firm, ranging from the highly ambitious "to make great wealth" to the humbler "continuing a family tradition." But what benefits do we find to small business ownership when we look at entrepreneurs as a whole? (See Figure 1.4.) The most common benefit people perceive in working in their own business is independence. It seems that

What Kind of Mindset Do You Have?

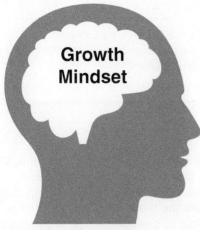

Growth Mindset

I can learn anything I want to.
When I'm frustrated, I persevere.
I want to challenge myself.
When I fail, I learn.
Tell me I try hard.
If you succeed, I'm inspired.
My effort and attitude determine everything.

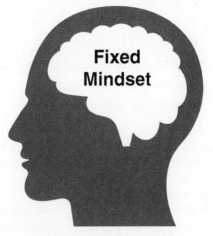

Fixed Mindset

I'm either good at it, or I'm not.
When I'm frustrated, I give up.
I don't like to be challenged.
When I fail, I'm no good.
Tell me I'm smart.
If you succeed, I feel threatened.
My abilities determine everything.

FIGURE 1.3 Fixed Versus Growth Mindset
Source: Adapted from Reid Wilson, Fixed vs. Growth Mindset for Elementary (https://getrawenergy.co/?s=mindset#.XyxilW5FyRs)

FIGURE 1.4 Various Rewards of Having Your Own Business

people often start businesses because they do not want to work for someone else. The **independence reward** does not mean that business owners are free to do whatever they want, but that they do not want to always be looking at their boss to define what to do and how to do it. Kim Jordan, founder of New Belgium Brewing, shares that she loves "having the freedom to make decisions" about the company with no one telling her "No, you can't do that."

Independence rewards should not be taken to mean full unconstrained autonomy. Having your own business does not mean you do not answer to anyone. For a small business owner, customers are like bosses, as they expect their needs and wants to be fulfilled. Employees and suppliers are also like bosses, as you will need to work with them to keep the business going.

Three other common rewards for small business owners are learning, flexibility, and income. **Learning rewards** are the countless opportunities to improve their existing

Interactive Activity

As you look forward to planning your own career, what rewards are important to you? In other words, what career rewards do you seek? Rank order the six rewards covered here, from your highest preference to lowest for your own career at this stage in your life. Find another student in class and compare your ordering of the rewards. Be prepared to share with the class where the two of you agree and disagree.

What Do You Think?

If Hamdi Ulukaya of Chobani were asked what he hoped to achieve from starting a business, what rewards do you think he would have considered most highly? It is worth remembering that Hamdi never expected Chobani to achieve the kind of success it ultimately did. Could he have foreseen the tremendous financial success that came his way when he started the feta cheese company or Chobani?

skills and gain new ones that comes with managing one's own business. Reid Hoffman, founder of LinkedIn, thinks that starting a business allows you to "be an infinite learner, constantly breaking new ground, innovating and building upon your ideas." **Flexibility rewards** refer to the ability of business owners to organize their lives in ways that best suits their needs. **Income rewards** capture the money-making potential of small business ownership as the overwhelming majority of business owners generate some or all of their annual income from the business they own.

Business owners also recognize two other benefits of having their own business. Business ownership is an ideal platform to bring a new product-service idea to the market (**idea rewards**). Steve Jobs and Steve Wozniak first offered the personal computer they had designed to Wozniak's employer Hewlett-Packard, but when the large corporation refused their offer, the Steves decided to start a company to sell it themselves. Business ownership also offers a chance to build wealth (**wealth rewards**). As Professor Thomas Stanley and William Danko reported in their seminal book on the affluent in America, more than 50% of America's millionaires are self-employed people running small businesses. Table 1.3 describes some of the joys and miseries of owning a small business.

KEY TAKEAWAY

There are many myths about small business. Reading and learning about small businesses can help you separate the chaff from the wheat, the myth from the truth.

TABLE 1.3

Successful Business Owners on the Joys and Miseries of Being Their Own Boss

Founder	Company Started	What I love most about what I do	What I hate most about what I do
Kim Jordan	New Belgium Brewing	Having the freedom to make decisions	Having so much weight on my shoulders
Tope Awotona	Calendly	Pursue my crazy ideas even when others are saying it will not work	The business took over every aspect of my life
Tim Brown	Allbirds	Choosing the people who I work with	Always thinking about the business, even when I don't want to
Reid Hoffman	LinkedIn	Getting to be an infinite learner, constantly innovating and building upon my ideas	Starting and growing a business brings constant anxiety
Neil Blumenthal	Warby Parker	Love that my work and life can be fully integrated	Letting go of someone who works for me
Payal Kadakia	ClassPass	The impact you can have on employees' lives as the company grows	There's no blueprint to guide you as you struggle to build the company

Comprehension Check

1. What are the various rewards for small business ownership?
2. In your view, why are small business owners so highly represented among American millionaires?
3. Which are the various myths associated with running your own business?

Module 1.4 Identify Various Forms of Entrepreneurship

The focus of this book is on **commercial entrepreneurship**, defined as small businesses that sell goods and services with the goal of turning a profit. But there are several kinds of entrepreneurship (see Figure 1.5). When people think of owning a business, they usually want to derive financial benefits for themselves. For some business owners, the personal rewards go hand-in-hand with doing something for society, such as providing employment or supporting the community. People interested in addressing pressing social needs or environmental problems were historically expected to work at (or start) a nonprofit or find employment with the government. This is now beginning to change as some people launch small businesses with the primary goal of addressing a fundamental social or environmental problem. **Social entrepreneurship** occurs when the social purpose is not only an integral part, but also the most salient aspect, of the firm. While the United States does not rank very high on global indicators of commercial entrepreneurship (Canada, Iceland, and United Kingdom are just some of the countries that have greater rates of self-employment and new business ownership than the United States), Americans lead the world in their drive to pursue social entrepreneurship. Does it surprise you that the desire to become a social entrepreneur is strongest for Americans between the ages of 25 and 45? Universities and colleges are recognizing the growing trend toward businesses that want to make a difference and are offering courses focused on social entrepreneurship skills and practices.

It is said that the typical American business owner is a married white man in his forties who started the business by himself. While this may be statistically true, such descriptions of business ownership obscure many interesting facets of entrepreneurship: entrepreneurial teams, women and minority entrepreneurship, student entrepreneurship, and silver entrepreneurship. **Entrepreneurial teams** consist of two or more individuals coming together to start or manage a business venture. This is how Apple got started when three men – Steve Jobs, Steve Wozniak, and Ronald Wayne – got together to incorporate the company, though Wayne soon sold his part of the company to the two Steves for $800 and walked away. Some funding teams may be mixed-sex, that is, men and women come together to start a business. The yogurt company Noosa, for example, was started by Koel Thomae and Rob Graves in Colorado.

Women entrepreneurship refers to the tendency among women to start and manage their own business. Vanessa Raptopoulos, for example, is owner of Awesome Brooklyn, a

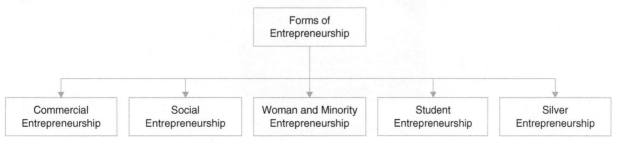

FIGURE 1.5 Main Forms of Small Businesses in the United States

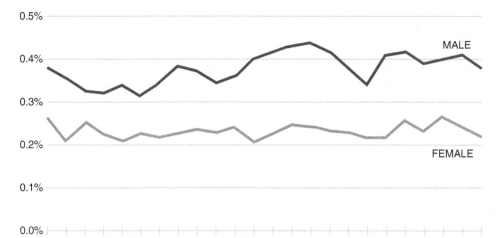

FIGURE 1.6 Rate of New Business Startup by Sex
Source: Adapted from 2019 Kauffman Foundation Report on Early-Stage Entrepreneurship in the United States

gift shop in New York. Currently, about 36% of all US firms are women-owned, employing about 9 million people and generating upward of $1.5 trillion in sales. In 2019, 230 of 100,000 female adults, or 0.23%, created businesses, compared to 0.27% in 2017 and 0.23% in 2016 (see Figure 1.6). Spanx is a woman-owned company that achieved tremendous success within a short time. Do you know who was America's first self-made millionaire female business owner? Her name was Madam C. J. Walker (or Sarah Breedlove), and she was in the hair care industry.

MADAM C. J. WALKER

Do you want to know more about the fascinating story of Madam C. J. Walker, born Sarah Breedlove, to newly freed slaves soon after the Civil War? You can watch the Hollywood movie "Self-Made" available on Netflix. Or, you can watch the documentary "Two Dollars and a Dream" about America's first self-made millionairess, who started making products for women's hair at home on her stove, selling them door to door, and then city to city. Her tireless efforts ultimately led to a company that was worth a million dollars by the time of her death in 1919.

David Cannon/Getty Images

View the video online at: https://www.youtube.com/watch?v=WrpVozNIHds

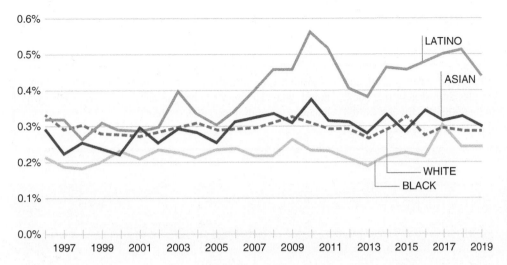

FIGURE 1.7 Rate of New Business Startup by Race and Ethnicity
Source: Adapted from 2019 Kauffman Foundation Report on Early-Stage Entrepreneurship in the United States

The term **minority entrepreneurship** is generally used to describe racial minorities who have their own businesses. Robert Johnson became America's first black billionaire on the back of the media company, Black Entertainment Television (BET), he founded. There are also minority entrepreneurs like Jerry Yang (Yahoo founder), Manoj Bhargava (5 Hour Energy), and Hamdi Ulukaya (Chobani). According to recent data from the Kauffman Foundation, 300 of every 100,000 Asian-American adults, or 0.30%, started businesses, as did to 0.24% African-Americans and 0.44% Hispanic Americans (see Figure 1.7).

Barbara Gardner Proctor, owner of Chicago-based firm Proctor & Gardner Advertising Inc., was a famous woman entrepreneur who was also a racial minority. "If someone were to tell me a glass ceiling was standing in my way," she once said, "I would open a window, fly out and continue to soar." When she applied for a SBA loan to start an advertising firm, she was asked what her collateral was. "Me," she replied, and got the loan. Barbara, like many small business owners, did not get discouraged by problems and challenges. Instead, she found a way around obstacles and barriers to achieve her goals.

Interactive Activity

Consider the five forms of entrepreneurship discussed here. Which do you find the most interesting? Use the internet to find three interesting examples of entrepreneurs who fit the form of entrepreneurship you like the most. Gather enough information about them to explain to the class what they did, how they did it, and what some of the challenges they faced were. Be prepared to share the information you find with the class.

Student entrepreneurship is about students running their own business. Michael Dell started his eponymous venture in his college dorm at University of Texas at Austin and so did Mark Zuckerberg (Facebook) at Harvard and Seth Borkowitz (Insomnia Cookies) at University of Pennsylvania. Sue Zimmerman, a watercolor artist (you can check out her work at www.sue-zimmermann.pixels.com), shares that her first venture was selling hand-painted barrettes at recess in grade school. "The passion I had for art and painting turned into a nice side hustle," she says and "eventually gave me the confidence and validation to do what I loved at a very young age."

What Do You Think?

Many businesses are started by students. Facebook, Dell, and Insomnia Cookies are some examples discussed in this book. Can you use the internet to find five other businesses started by student entrepreneurs? Identify the advantages and pitfalls of students starting their own business. Would you recommend your younger brother or sister to start their own business when they are still a student?

KEY TAKEAWAY

Anyone can own a small business, regardless of their age, race, gender, or socio-economic status.

Silver entrepreneurship is defined as entrepreneurial activity pursued by people after retirement or resignation from work at age 50 or later. Interestingly, about a third of retirees who return to work pursue self-employment. For most Americans, Harland Sanders, the founder of KFC, popularly known as "Colonel Sanders" is the quintessential late-career entrepreneur. Some estimates suggest that the rate of silver entrepreneurship may be as high as about 50%, so that nearly half of those over 50 try to start a business at some point in their life. Valerie Green is a good example of someone who became a small business owner after a long corporate career. After graduating from Stanford University's Hasso Plattner Institute of Design, she worked at consulting firms where she helped clients formulate new products. After two decades in the corporate world, she decided to start an organizing business. Her company, Pivot Organizing (www.pivotorganizing.com), leverages her expertise in "making smart use of space" to help clients.

What Do You Think?

It is human nature to want to categorize people: he is a racial minority, she is a woman, and so on. Hamdi was a commercial entrepreneur, but he was also a racial minority. His company also started investing in social causes as it became successful, including and perhaps most notably, in hiring refugees. Can you think of business owners you know who can be categorized in more than one bucket?

Comprehension Check

1. Define the various forms of entrepreneurship we see in society.
2. What is student entrepreneurship? Discuss the opportunities and challenges of being a student entrepreneur?
3. What is an entrepreneurial team? What benefits do you think someone could get from starting a business as a team rather than by themselves?

Summary

Think about all the things you do when you drive a car: Not only do you start the car (by turning the key, or increasingly by pressing a button), but you also run the car on the road, take it to the destination, and park it when you get to where you want to go. Of course, if you are on the highway, you can (sometimes) turn on the cruise control, but you still need to keep your eye on the road and your hands on the steering wheel, in case something unexpected happens. Similarly, entrepreneurs launch new firms as well as "drive" them: that is, they manage the running of the firm. As such, this book will cover the entire entrepreneurial process of small business management.

There are four major ways people get into business for themselves: De novo start-ups, family business, franchising, and acquisition. Think of Koel Thomae who you met in the opening vignette of this chapter. Many people start their own business as Koel did, which will be discussed in Chapter 2. For some, the path to business ownership is through the family firm. Audrey Zimmerman, a fourth-generation owner of Kepner Scott Shoe Co., a specialty shoe manufacturer in Orwigsburg (PA), is one such business owner. The business was founded in 1888, and came to the Zimmerman family in the time of Audrey's grandparents. Family firms are discussed in Chapter 3. What do McDonalds and Days Inn have in common? They are both franchises, a popular American path to having your own business discussed in Chapter 4. Jersey Mike's CEO Peter Cancro took a different path to being his own boss. He bought an existing small business, which we discuss in Chapter 5.

Interactive Activity

There are four major ways to have your own business. Interview the owners of some small businesses in your community. Ask them about how they got into business. What were the challenges they faced and how they managed those challenges?

Live Exercise

At a recent party at your parent's house, you met Johnny Gold and started talking about career plans. He had some good advice for you, and then he mentioned something that got you thinking. Johnny lives in Memphis, TN. A graduate of Vanderbilt University, he has been an institutional bond salesman all his working life, selling bonds to institutional investors. One of his mentors in the company grew up on a farm in Kentucky; as a kid this mentor used to plow fields with a mule, and he'd tell Johnny that "staring at the ass-end of a mule for 10 hours is hard work. We sit in air-conditioning and talk on the phone. This isn't too hard." Johnny's wife founded a very successful dance nonprofit that has become a leader in the creative youth development space – they have a national profile and are doing many things for students in Memphis. You enjoyed talking to Johnny and hearing about his wife's nonprofit. As you looked each other up on LinkedIn to connect, he asked if you thought 60 was too late for him to become a small business owner. You see, Johnny is thinking of having his own business. He is trying to assess how his children and grandchildren will react if and when he decides to move ahead with his entrepreneurial endeavor. Any advice you can give him would be greatly appreciated.

World of Books

To delve deeper into some of the ideas discussed in this chapter, we recommend the following books:

- *The Soul of an Entrepreneur* by David Sax
- *Leapfrog: The New Revolution for Women Entrepreneurs* by Nathalie Nino and Sara Grace

In the Movies

We have all seen Mickey Mouse onscreen, visited Disneyland, and read the story of Snow White and the Seven Dwarfs. Few of us, however, pause to think about the visionary entrepreneur who brought all these, and much more, to life for us: Walt Disney. The movie *Walt Before Disney* is the highly relatable story of the man who struggled financially and had to work hard to convince others to believe in his dream.

Things to Remember

LO 1.1   Discuss the importance of small business to the economy
- Most common definitions of small business are based on size.
- Small businesses together make up more than 99% of the employers in the country and employ about half of all private sector employees.
- The SBA's mandate is to help small businesses in four key areas: financial support, education and training, government contracting, and advocacy.
- Most independent businesses start small. This includes companies like Nike and Walmart, which are now dominant players in their business.
- When the novel Coronavirus pandemic hit, small businesses were at the forefront of our country's crisis response.
- Even businesses that remain small can be a good source of wealth for their owners.

LO 1.2   Define small business management and explain the role of entrepreneurship in managing a small business
- Small business management involves running the firm in a way that increases the chances of survival and continuously improves the firm as a whole.
- Companies that do not try to continually improve themselves will eventually fail.
- Very few firms are able to continuously search for new profitable opportunities to bring novel offerings to the market.
- Academics, policy-makers, and mass media are generally fascinated with small businesses that grow rapidly. However, growth can be healthy or unhealthy, and businesses that do not grow in a healthy fashion are destined for early death.

LO 1.3   Recognize the common myths about and various benefits of small business entrepreneurship
- A common myth is that because most new businesses fail, going to work for yourself is a risky undertaking.
- Managing a small business is mistakenly associated with sacrificing your family and personal life, focusing only on work.
- A common myth is that either you are born to be a business owner or you are not. Indeed, entrepreneurship is learnable, if you have the right mindset for it.
- There is no right time to pursue entrepreneurship.
- More Americans start businesses every year than get married or have children.
- People often become an entrepreneur because they do not want to work for someone else.
- More than 50% of America's millionaires work for themselves.

LO 1.4   Identify various forms of small business entrepreneurship
- Some businesses focus on the profit motive, others are driven by altruism, and yet some tend to have a hybrid orientation.
- The typical American entrepreneur is white, married, male, and in his forties, who started the business by himself.
- Many businesses are started by two or more entrepreneurs.

- More than one-third of American businesses are women-owned.
- Many racial minorities have their own businesses.
- There is a growing focus on entrepreneurship among students.
- For many, entrepreneurship is a second career, in which they start a business after retirement or dismissal from a previous job.

Key Terms

small business
red queen effect
entrepreneurship
small business management
turtles (lifestyle
    businesses)
goats (traditional
    small firms)
gazelles (entrepreneurial
    small firms)

corporate
    entrepreneurship
whales
elephants
born global
Small Business
    Administration
small giants
failure
dwarfism

business failure
work–life balance
growth mindset
fixed mindset
independence rewards
learning rewards
flexible rewards
income rewards
idea rewards
wealth rewards

commercial
    entrepreneurship
social entrepreneurship
entrepreneurial teams
women entrepreneurship
student entrepreneurship
minority entrepreneurship
silver entrepreneurship

Experiential Exercise

This exercise can be done by an individual or people working in teams of two.

Pick up the latest issue of a business newspaper like *The Wall Street Journal*. Alternatively, you can also get the business section of a national newspaper like *The New York Times*. The current issue of Bloomberg's *BusinessWeek* will also work. Identify at least 8–10 companies discussed in the newspaper and try to classify them into the different types of businesses: *turtles*, *goats*, *gazelles*, *whales*, and *elephants*. Search the web for who started the business and when it got started. Be prepared to answer the following questions:

1. What is the most dominant type of business in your list?

2. Who started most businesses in your list: men or women? Individuals or teams? Students or seniors or others?

3. When and where was each of the business in your list started?

4. Is there any business in the list that you wish you had started? Why?

Select any one of the businesses that you have identified in the previous step and search its history on the internet. Your goal is to find as much information as you can about how it got started. While you may start your search from Wikipedia, you need to read some of the source articles that Wikipedia cites and also others not cited on Wikipedia. Put together a timeline of important milestones in its historical evolution so far or as long as it remained a small business (whichever is earlier). What do you think were some of the challenges this business faced in its early years?

CHAPTER 2

Starting a New Business

A lot of people have ideas, but there are few who decide to do something about them now. Not tomorrow. Not next week. But today. The true entrepreneur is a doer, not a dreamer.

NOLAN BUSHNELL,
founder of Atari

LEARNING OBJECTIVES

This chapter will help you to:

LO 2.1 Identify motives for starting a new business

LO 2.2 Distinguish between part-time and full-time entrepreneurship

LO 2.3 Explain how ideas turn into startup opportunities

LO 2.4 Describe the universal startup model

LO 2.5 Analyze the current state of startups in the United States

2.0 Introduction

Millions of people around the world are running their own business. The majority of them become business owners by starting their own venture. The U.S. Small Business Administration estimates that about 700,000 new businesses are created annually, with the actual number of startups varying per year. In 2019, 774,725 small firms in existence were started within the past year. Starting your own venture is the most common path to becoming an entrepreneur and having your own business.

Starting a business from scratch is fun and challenging. There is high uncertainty as one has absolutely no idea how the venture will turn out. Yet, the process of starting with an idea and then taking it through the various steps to make it a viable business can be very exciting. Many entrepreneurs thrive on the challenge of launching a new venture from the ground up and take pride in creating something that did not exist before.

Anyone can start their own business. Michael Dell started his first venture when he was 12 years old, making thousands of dollars in mail order sales to stamp collectors. Brian Chesky and Joe Gebbia were unemployed and had no money when they started Airbnb (back then, it was airbedandbreakfast). Sara Blakely was working at a local stationary company when she decided to start Spanx using all her savings. Jan Koum was a college dropout who started the messaging service WhatsApp, while Larry Page and Sergey Brin were in a computer science PhD program when they started Google. Indeed, one can start a business at any time in their life.

SPOTLIGHT | Drew Houston and Dropbox

Drew Houston grew up in Acton, a suburb outside Boston, the oldest of three children of an engineer father and a librarian mother. He got a perfect score on the SAT and attended the Massachusetts Institute of Technology. At M.I.T., he joined the Phi Delta Theta fraternity, which helped him learn about corporate culture. "My first management experience was being rush chairman for my fraternity, and I learned a bunch of things," he shares. "You deal with a lot of the same broad questions – who do we want to be as an organization, what kind of culture do we want, what kind of people are we looking for? – that you do when you're starting a company."

At M.I.T., like most students then, Drew worked on multiple desktops and a laptop. He would often forget to keep his USB drive with him. When he shared files with himself as email attachments, he found it difficult to keep track of them. One day, the power supply on his home desktop exploded, destroying one of his hard drives, for which he had no backup. After that bad experience, he tried several solutions to store his files but wasn't satisfied with anything he could find.

On a bus one day from Boston to New York, Drew realized he had forgotten his USB stick. Frustrated, he started coding a solution for himself and then realized it could solve file storage problems for a lot of other audiences. Incorporating as Evenflow Inc., Drew's product, which let people store and access their files in the cloud, was originally aimed at the consumer market. He also entered the company into the Boston program of Y Combinator, the Silicon Valley startup incubator. He released a demo video of the company to Hacker News in the hope of attracting the attention of the right audience. One impressed viewer Arash Ferdowsi paired up with Houston as a partner. The video also helped Drew receive immediate and valuable feedback about the company. When asked if he was worried about copycats stealing the concept at the time, Drew responded, "It is easy for me to explain the idea; it is actually really hard to do it."

The New York Times

Drew Houston of Dropbox

Soon after, Drew moved the company from Cambridge to San Francisco to get closer to the startup scene. A month later, Sequoia Capital invested in the company. Drew changed the company's name to Dropbox. The company's business also evolved, when its products started getting used primarily for work, with businesses paying a subscription fee for the platform. "From Day One, Dropbox has been an incredibly user-friendly product – which is a big reason why it spread virally – but it also took the company too long to realize the money was in being a business-focused company, not a consumer-focused one," said Ben Thompson, the analyst behind the influential tech newsletter Stratechery. At the time, investors valued the company at $10 billion.

About 11 years after the fateful bus trip to New York, Drew took Dropbox public. Not bad for a company that Steve Jobs had famously said didn't have much of a future. "You are a feature, not a product," Jobs declared about Dropbox.

Discussion Questions

1. How did Drew Houston get the idea for starting Dropbox?

2. What were some of the things Drew did that helped him succeed?

3. What business is Dropbox in?

Module 2.1 Motivations for Starting a New Venture

Why do people start their own business? The Global Entrepreneurship Monitor (GEM), an international survey of business owners, asks people to share reasons for their entrepreneurial ventures. Based on the responses of tens of thousands of business owners, the GEM researchers distinguished between two major reasons for starting a business: necessity (push) or opportunity (pull). **Necessity entrepreneurship** refers to people starting a business because there are no desirable alternatives. It often describes low-skilled entrants forced by adverse circumstances into starting a business. **Opportunity entrepreneurship** refers to people who start a business to bring a new product idea to market. It tends to describe high-ability entrants attracted by a promising idea to start their own venture. Economists generally see opportunity entrepreneurship as more desirable than necessity entrepreneurship. People who start a new business because they had a great idea or because they truly wanted to be their own boss are celebrated. Conversely, people who go to work for themselves because no one else will hire them are generally viewed unfavorably.

Entrepreneurship by Necessity

The public and popular media give little attention to necessity entrepreneurship. Professor Jagdish Sheth, a well-respected thought leader, talks about the critical role necessity entrepreneurship plays in the American economy.

Watch the video online at: https://www.youtube.com/watch?v=1h9VgV_SSnE

The total rate of entrepreneurial activity in a society is the sum of necessity and opportunity entrepreneurship. In other words:

Total Entrepreneurial Activity (TEA) = Necessity Entrepreneurship (NE)
+ Opportunity Entrepreneurship (OE)

The share of necessary entrepreneurship is usually higher when the economy is weaker (and unemployment is high), whereas the share of opportunity entrepreneurship goes up when the economy is stronger (and unemployment is low). The GEM project found that necessity entrepreneurs make up about 21% of the **total entrepreneurial activity** in the United States, similar to many other countries such as Greece, Spain, Ireland, Japan, and South Korea.

The COVID-19 pandemic forced many people to start their own businesses, after being laid off from their regular jobs. Necessity entrepreneurs are starting businesses, ranging from in-home personal training to mobile car-washing. Consider the case of Danielle

TABLE 2.1

Examples of Small Firms Started During the Covid-19 Pandemic

Name	Location	Work before COVID-19	Nature of business
Damien Johnson	Paramus, NJ	Personal trainer	Offers training sessions for people working from home
Ramona Wilmarth	Sonoma County, CA	Hair stylist	Bought a wagon, a collapsible salon chair, and a long extension cord to see clients outside their homes and on her front porch
Aaron Thomas	Athens, OH	DJ	Turned himself into a one-man distanced-wedding planner
Jorge Paredes	Silver Spring, MD	Food runner	Launched his own mobile car wash and knife-sharpening business
Madison Schneider	Haviland, KS	Baker	Rented commercial space to start a new bakery
Danielle Payton	Miami, FL	Publicist	Launched an online workout-class platform
Janizze Masacayan	Monterey, CA	Nursing home director	Makes and sells customizable reusable masks online
Ian Oestrich	Madison, WI	Fitness trainer	Started a mobile bike-repair shop
Nic Bryon	Tampa, FL	Sous chef	Launched a local meal-kit delivery service
Leigh Altshuler	New York City	Communications director	Used her savings to start a bookstore
Joyre Montgomery	Chattanooga, TN	Therapist	Started her own therapy practice

Payton, who saw her publicist business dry up when fitness studios, a core client base, had to close to comply with shelter-in-place orders. In response, Danielle launched kuu-dose, an online workout-class platform, where trainers receive monthly commissions for the members they bring to the platform. "We're using the pandemic as the stepping-stone to really launch us," Danielle says.

If you want to know more about what kinds of businesses entrepreneurs have been started out of necessity, Table 2.1 provides some examples.

The Wall Street Journal

Danielle Payton launched Kuudose during the COVID-19 pandemic to provide workouts for people working from home.

While the distinction between necessity and opportunity entrepreneurship is quite popular among entrepreneurship researchers, many entrepreneurs report a combination of push and pull factors to explain their reasons for starting a new business. They start a business both because they have an idea and also because they think the paid labor market does not adequately reward their skills and abilities. Dal LaMagna, founder of Tweezerman, is one such entrepreneur who graduated from Harvard Business School, worked minimum wage job at an electronics company, where he stumbled upon a chance to sell tweezers to remove splinters until a female friend suggested that they could be modified to remove ingrown hairs. His friends thought the name Tweezerman was "the height of silliness." LaMagna's engaging autobiography *Raising Eyebrows* describes his entrepreneurial journey from an unemployed college graduate to a successful multimillionaire entrepreneur.

Interactive Exercise

Interview ten people who have started their own business. Ask them what motivated them to start their business. List the reasons you hear and classify them as either necessity or opportunity.

Everyone who starts a business from scratch is beginning their entrepreneurial journey with a clean slate on which they can write whatever story they want. In other words, they can mold the new venture into the form that they see as appropriate. The fact that the startup is all new can be an advantage in itself, as there is no carryover baggage of someone else's mistakes, location, employees, or products. Consider, for example, Jim Senegal, a cofounder of the wholesale retailer Costco, who wanted to create a company with an egalitarian culture where the working environment would be informal and unintimidating so that there is no jockeying for position and no one is afraid of making mistakes. He also wanted to run a company where the markups were low, quality was good, and workers were paid well. That was the genesis of the first Costco store in Seattle. There are also other advantages of beginning from scratch, including deciding what the venture's unique capabilities will be and who it would like to serve.

KEY TAKEAWAY

Starting a new business from scratch means the entrepreneur has a clean slate to write whatever they want and create the type of business they envision.

For some, starting a new venture from scratch can be quite daunting because there is no existing template onto which the business may simply be overlaid. It is also difficult to make prospective customers aware of the new business, especially when it is in a highly competitive market with lots of sellers. There are also thousands of details, many of which are difficult to foresee, such as where to find motivated employees, whether to furnish the company's officers in a fancy fashion, and how to choose the right suppliers. The time-to-market is also higher for *de novo* **startups**, as there are many little pieces that need to be put in place before the business can officially be launched (whether it is a brick-and-mortar store or a virtual business).

The success rate of startup businesses is a matter of some debate. The SBA estimates that about two-third of new businesses (with employees) survive two years or more, half survive at least four years, and about 40% last more than six years. Yet, businesses that get help have a longer life. There are many sources where aspiring and nascent entrepreneurs

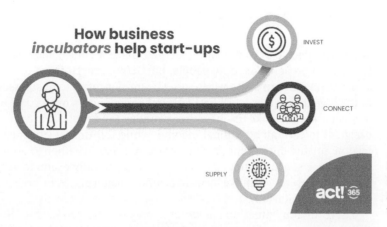

FIGURE 2.1 Business Incubators Provide Critical Help for Startups
Source: https://www.act365.com/what-is-a-business-incubator

can get help. Jason Grill, cofounder of Sock 101, turns to his father for advice. Some entrepreneurs look toward other successful business owners for guidance. SCORE, which stands for Service Corps of Retired Executives, is a nonprofit organization that seeks to help small businesses get off the ground and grow. You can visit their site at https://www.score.org. Many new firms, especially in the technology industry, get help from **business incubators**, which are private organizations that offer startups shared space and mentoring. You may recall from the Spotlight story that Drew Houston of Dropbox found early help from the Y Combinator (YC), a privately owned business incubator that has helped the launch of many tech-oriented firms such as DoorDash, Airbnb, and Instacart. More than 80% of ventures that begin in business incubators are still running five years later (see Figure 2.1).

It is worth remembering that for many businesses that come to an end, it is not failure per se, but because the owner(s) got other, significantly better, opportunities. Whether the business fails or succeeds, the effort of the enterprising individual(s) who chooses to start a new business is admirable.

Interactive Exercise

Identify four or five people you consider your mentors. Clearly articulate the reason(s) why you consider them mentors. Did you make a conscious effort to set up your advisory board or did it develop on its own? Going forward, how would you like to change the composition of your advisory board?

What Do You Think?

Yasmine Khater shares that she felt "dead inside" working at her corporate job, but "was too scared to leave." She didn't want her boss's job, any of the other senior management roles, or to work more 12–14 hours days. If Yasmine asked you for advice, would you suggest that she continue the job that gives her security (in the form of stable paycheck) or try to start her own business?

Comprehension Check

1. What is the difference between necessity and opportunity entrepreneurship?
2. What is total entrepreneurial activity and how is it calculated?
3. What are some advantages of starting your own business?

Module 2.2 Part-time and Full-time Startups

When you decide to start a business, you make a choice about pursuing a part-time or full-time approach. For some people, **part-time startups** make more sense. For others, a **full-time startup** is the way to go. The former refers to businesses that are in addition to the owner's regular work and take only a few hours of the day, while the latter refers to businesses that take up the entire workday (and more). Part-time startups are usually designed to earn an additional income, while full-time startups are the main source of income for the entrepreneur. The choice between whether to go for a full-time startup or part-time startup is not easy. The key is to carefully evaluate your situation and then decide the best way to move forward (without being biased by preconceived notions about either form of startup).

There are four situations in which it may be better to start with a part-time business. One is when you are new to business and need to gain basic experience. Those who have never been involved in basic business behaviors, such as buying, selling, and pricing, sometimes struggle with these seemingly simple tasks in the beginning. For such people, learning these types of skills before they start on their business journey full-time makes a lot of sense. It is useful to have good experience before starting a full-time business of your own, including experience in the industry, experience in the specific market you plan to serve, or even experience talking to or dealing with customers and employees.

Interactive Exercise

Poll entrepreneurs that you know to ask if they started their business part-time or full-time. Ask them the reason(s) for their decision. Be prepared to share your findings with the class.

Another situation is when you lack resources to pursue a full-scale business. Money and time are probably the ultimate resources for new business owners. Depending on what business it is, starting a business can require a huge investment in money and/or time. If you are not able to commit the time or money needed to start a business full-time, it makes a lot of sense to make a part-time commitment. Some entrepreneurs choose the part-time option because they lack the contacts needed to succeed in the business they are considering. Going part-time allows them to build their network, one step at a time.

A third type of situation arises when there is a narrow or limited window of opportunity for a new product or service. Perhaps you really have good language skills and are able to help students and professionals looking for someone to edit their writing. Part-time businesses can be created quickly and cheaply, allowing you to test the market for your offering.

A final situation to start a part-time business is when you want to hedge your bets. You want to go into business for yourself but are not sure how it will work out. You do not mind working hard but are not inclined to change the direction of your career without having something concrete in hand.

It may surprise you that a very high proportion of entrepreneurs in the United States start out working part-time on their new businesses. The Panel Study of Entrepreneurial

Dynamics (PSED), which surveyed thousands of business owners in the country, has estimated that 75% of new ventures start on a part-time basis. The ease and low cost of entering into part-time entrepreneurship make it a great way to try starting a new business.

KEY TAKEAWAY

You can start a new business part-time or full-time. In some situations, part-time is better. In other situations, full-time is better.

Working on your own business part-time after a regular job is called **moonlighting**. As you can imagine, moonlighting poses particular risks for the persons trying to start their own business. Three major concerns are worth discussing here: conflict of interest, poisoning the well, and cannibalizing. **Conflict-of-interest** refers to the interests of the part-time venture being different from those of the full-time job or when outsiders are not sure which firm you are representing at a particular time. It happens when the boundary is blurred between the part-time business someone is starting and his or her full-time job.

Poisoning the well refers to leaving a negative impression – intentionally or unintentionally – among the customers or suppliers of the existing employer. If someone dips into the contact list of their current employer to generate business for the new part-time venture, there is likely to be a problem with those customers or suppliers (or other stakeholders) who do not want to have to deal with the new venture. If because of the sales pitch, they become less likely to do business with the current employer, the part-time venture ends up hurting the full-time business.

What Do You Think?

Jane is young woman who graduated from an entrepreneurship program. She is thinking of starting an 'Uber for dog-walking' business, offering one-on-one dog walking service that includes live GPS tracking of the walk and video feed from the body camera used by the walker. She is looking for investors who want to be part of her entrepreneurial journey. Do you think the business has potential? If you could invest in it, would you invest? Would your decision change if Jane was running the business part-time or full-time?

Cannibalizing involves taking business away from the employer. It can happen because people put in less hours into their existing job when they are trying to start a part-time business or because they are taking some sales from the current employer. While concerns about cannibalization are real for anyone starting a part-time business, they become particularly salient when the new business is very similar to that of the current employer. When the part-time venture and the employer business engage in different kinds of work or have separate clients that do not overlap, the existing employer may even provide referrals to help get new clients for the startup. However, when there is a considerable overlap between the offerings, clients, or activities of the part-time venture and the existing employer, it will likely lead to cannibalization.

From Part-time to Full-time

If you've ever bought eyeglasses, you know the pain of spending lots of money for a product based on a technology that is hundreds of years old. Four students of Wharton School came together to start Warby Parker, the company that sells $95 eyewear (with prescription glasses) online. Demand quickly outstripped expectations. Warby Parker became known as the Netflix of eyewear.

Watch the video online at: https://www.youtube.com/watch?v=AWRF2wvUDxQ

Comprehension Check

1. Define full-time and part-time entrepreneurship.
2. What are some situations in which it is better to start a part-time business than a full-time business?
3. What are some problems that part-time entrepreneurs should try to avoid?

Module 2.3 From Idea to Opportunity

There is no shortage of ideas for new and improved products and services. However, not every idea makes for a good opportunity. A **business opportunity** is an attractive and timely idea anchored in a specific product or service that creates or adds value for its buyers or end users. Many ideas for new products and services do not add value for customers or users. Sometimes an idea can be way behind the times, and sometimes it may be ahead of the times. In business, as they say, timing is important.

> ### KEY TAKEAWAY
> We all have plenty of ideas for new businesses, but not all ideas offer a good opportunity for a business.

What if someone had the idea to set up a place near campus where college students could go to type, print, and copy their essays and assignments? There would be computers and copy machines, and students could also buy other school-related items such as pens, pencils, notebooks, and writing pads. Such a place did once exist – remember Kinko's? But, as desktops became commonplace on campuses and students had ready access to high-powered computers and copiers in school (as well as in their own homes), such places did not add much value to potential customers. One could make them really high end if they wanted with all the luxuries and trappings you could think of, or strip them to the basics to focus just on the essential services, and it is still unclear what value college students could get today from a place that allows them to print and copy their work. Kinko's may be an interesting idea, but as a business opportunity, it would be about two decades late.

There is a common saying in the startup world: The only thing worse than being wrong is being early. Why would "being early" be a problem? For starters, sometimes the market or technology is not where it needs to be for an idea to be a good opportunity. Same-day delivery was the premise of famous startups such as Webvan, which lost a billion dollars of investor money. Today, many companies are trying to make same-day delivery work, both logistically and financially. But in the 1990s when it was first tried, less than 40% of Americans were using the Internet and the speed to access the web was slow (compared to the speeds we have now, and it's still not where it needs to be). Two decades later, about 90% of the American public is using the Internet, consumers have the Internet in their hands, and people communicate almost in real time using the Internet. When it comes to same-day delivery, the issue is not if it will work out, but only when it will work out. What the crash of Webvan and others taught was that even startups with substantial resources cannot make an idea work whose time has not come yet.

What Do You Think?

Dodgeball, a mobile-based social networking company, was founded by Dennis Crowley and Alex Rainert in 2003. Crowley and Rainert worked on the concept of Dodgeball for their Master's degree thesis at New York University. Joining Dodgeball involved completing a profile, posting photographs of yourself on the company's website (www.dodgeball.com), and listing your friends and their cellphone numbers. The target demographic of the people who use the Dodgeball service were those who aged 21–35, who had lots of friends, would like to go out, and were very social. When Dodgeball users checked in at a given locale by sending a text message to the service, it went to all their preselected friends, as well as any friends of friends within a ten-block radius. Users who texted their location via a mobile phone to the service were notified of friends, friends' friends, crushes, and interesting venues nearby. Crowley and Rainert sold the company in 2005 to Google, which considered Dodgeball as a novel experiment and investment (not a revenue generator). Google discontinued the service in 2009. Recall that the best-selling mobile phones from 2003 through 2005 were by Nokia, and the iPhone wasn't introduced until 2007. As a result, the social networking model of Dodgeball was based on text message via the service. Some believe Dodgeball was a company ahead of its time. What do you think?

A useful tool that can be used to help identify new business ideas was developed by Robert Eberle, based on the work of Alex Osborne. While Eberle was an education administrator and author, Osborne is well known as a pioneer in the field of creativity. It was Osborne who coined the word **brainstorming**, a popular group creativity technique to generate ideas on particular issues. The tool that Eberle developed, called **SCAMPER**, started with many of the questions that Osborne came up with to increase creativity. The key insight that underlies SCAMPER is that most of what is considered new is actually a revision of things that already exist.

What Do You Think?

Elyse Kaye is founder of Bloom Bras, offering sports bras without underwire. In her view, the major brands in the $1.5 billion sports-bra category – Victoria's Secret, Athleta, Lululemon, and Nike – do not cater to the 90% of the active female populace in the country. Elyse brought together folks from NASA, shipping industry experts, and a celebrity corset maker to address what she saw as an engineering challenge: how to distribute weight throughout the back and sides, rather than putting pressure over the shoulders and across the ribs. What do you think about Elyse's business idea?

SCAMPER (see Figure 2.2) can be a very effective method for coming up with new ideas. Its value lies in helping you step outside the usual thinking processes to come up with new ideas. It offers simple cues that take you outside your traditional areas of expertise, so as to consider what other things may be out there that you could try. When you see a highly innovative product or idea, do not simply think there is something especially magical or lucky about the entrepreneur who started it. The entrepreneur simply thought of a creative way of doing things that many others had ignored so far.

Shaping eyebrows is a regular part of many people's daily beauty routine. A good pair of tweezers is useful in plucking eyebrows, ingrown hairs, and facial hair. The story behind Tweezerman provides a good illustration of how SCAMPER can be helpful in coming up with creative ideas. LaMagna was walking through the assembly line of an electronics factory when he noticed workers using needle-pointed tweezers to pick up tiny capacitors

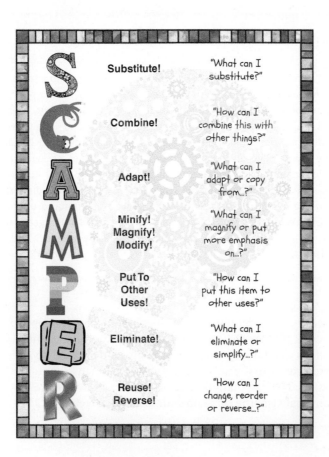

FIGURE 2.2 SCAMPER.
Source: Redrawn from Creative Thinking "SCAMPER" Posters, https://www.teacherspayteachers.com/Product/Creative-Thinking-SCAMPER-Posters-3051349

and diodes. He thought the tweezers could be used to remove splinters people might get from sunbathing on a wooden deck (*put to other use*). To display the tweezers professionally, LaMagna decided to package them in a transparent plastic bubble (*combine*). He found one used for packing pens, had yellow Splinter Remover cards made, which he then glued over the plastic cases with 3M adhesive (*adapt*). He started selling the tweezers at hardware stores, until a female friend suggested that they could be modified to remove ingrown hairs (*put to other use*). He found another type of tweezer that jewelers used to handle diamonds (*put to other use*), repackaged them as Precision Eyebrow Tweezers (*modify*), and started selling them to beauty salons.

What Do You Think?

Katrina has always loved orange juice. As a child, she would drink several cups of OJ a day, much of it squeezed fresh. She absolutely loved the taste of freshly squeezed OJ. When other children her age were setting up lemonade stands, or selling home-baked cookies, Katrina would opt for an OJ stand instead. So, it was no surprise that when she got to college, Katrina thought of selling fresh OJ to students, faculty, and the community. When she discussed the idea with her small business management professor, he cautioned her about the difficulties she would face in selling OJ due to stiff competition. Her professor advised Katrina to use SCAMPER to come up with some creative and novel ideas to offer OJ in a crowded marketplace. Can you help Katrina?

Let's say you have a business idea. What do you do next? Conventional wisdom suggests that you build the idea into a new venture and then market it. Unfortunately, going directly from idea to new venture skips an important step: opportunity evaluation. In effect, is there a business opportunity for the idea you have? To gauge if your idea is actually a business opportunity, you must take three steps:

1. Clearly articulate the value of the idea: what does it offer to potential customers, what pain-point does it address, and so on. This takes the following form: I will help (*customers*) solve (*problem*) by (*solution*). In describing the customer, problem, and solution, be as specific as you can. The shorter and tighter your description, the more clearly you understand what you are offering. This is your initial idea.

2. Explain how you know the customer and problem exists. You claim that there is market demand for your proposed offering, but the basis of this claim needs to be made clear. At this stage, you answer the following questions:
   a. My customers are _____.
   b. Their problem is _____.
   c. They are currently solving their problem by _____.
   d. Other solutions they have tried in the past include _____.
   e. On a scale of 1–5, the seriousness of the problem can be rated as _____.
   Notice that none of these questions say anything about the idea you are offering. Instead, the focus here is on making sure that the customer and problem you believe exists is actually there. Most entrepreneurs try to answer these questions based on their experience and gut-feel. A better way to address these questions is by talking to potential customers to better understand their position. The bigger the problem the customer has, the better for the entrepreneur.

3. Identify reasons for believing customers will use your proposed solution. Most entrepreneurs think customers would enthusiastically buy what they are offering. However, what is the base for thinking that if you build it, they will come? The key questions here are whether customers will actually buy your product as a solution and how much would they be willing to pay for it. Every business has a

specific action it wants from the customer, such as sign up (Facebook), make a purchase (Modsy), browse around (Pinterest). You can survey customers to determine whether they would engage in that action if were your product available in the market. It is even better if, with a small bet of time and money, you can get the customer to actually take that action. You have then shown that the customer is actually open to using your proposed solution.

Answering these three questions helps turn an idea into an opportunity. While these three questions are presented here in a linear manner, they are anything but. Figure 2.3 shows the three-stage process of turning an idea into an opportunity. Diana Kander's book *All in Startup* provides an engaging account of an entrepreneur's initial struggles and eventual success in thinking about his or her business idea and transforming it into a viable venture opportunity.

Say, you have found a problem that your customers agree exists. What do you do next? Not all problems are the same. Some customer problems are **headaches**; they exist, the customers want them solved, but they are not that a big deal. Headache problems are usually associated with businesses that do not grow much. Other problems are **migraines**; they are a big deal and the customer really needs them solved. Migraine problems are associated with businesses that have good growth potential. You can start a venture based on headache problems or migraine problems, but you will probably struggle less to gain traction in the market if you are helping solve a migraine problem.

What if you have a solution you think the customer wants, but you can't find a problem that it solves. Sort of like a solution looking for a problem. You may still start a venture to offer your solution in the market, but it will likely take you much money and effort getting customers to buy your product. It will also increase your chances of failure as in the absence of a problem, no real business opportunity exists, but you are hoping to create a new opportunity. "No market need" is the #1 reason why new ventures fail. Stephanie Burns, who started Chic-CEO.com to help female entrepreneurs, shares that she hears a lot of ideas that are really just solutions looking for problems. Apps are built, prototypes are made, websites are created, but because the market doesn't want or need it, disappointment inevitably follows. It is much easier to succeed if your idea solves an existing problem (**opportunity discovery**) than if it tries to generate market need where none currently exists (**opportunity creation**).

Generally, opportunity discovery relies on the human facility of **alertness**, while opportunity creation on **imagination**. Alert individuals discover opportunities that exist, but others miss or ignore. Imaginative individuals create new opportunities seemingly out of nothing. In his book *Zero to One*, the famed entrepreneur Peter Thiel shares his experiences about creating a new opportunity based on envisioning a new future. Figure 2.4 presents the decision flow chart that you can use to see if your idea involves opportunity discovery or opportunity creation.

It is not widely recognized that most business ideas are a lot like the others in the industry, with the caveat that they are not exactly like the others. Entrepreneurs who imitate existing players still need to have something that makes them a little different from the others. Although the distinction between **imitation** and **innovation** is truly important and often overlooked, the truth is that imitation is the preferred approach for most new businesses. The vast majority of people starting businesses plan to imitate existing businesses. In his book *Start It Up*, Luke Johnson observes that most new businesses do something pretty similar to many others – they provide familiar services or products, fulfilling a definite demand – with an incremental improvement.

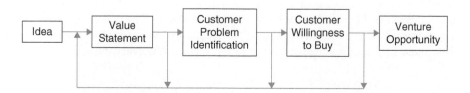

FIGURE 2.3 Three Steps from Ideas to a New Opportunity

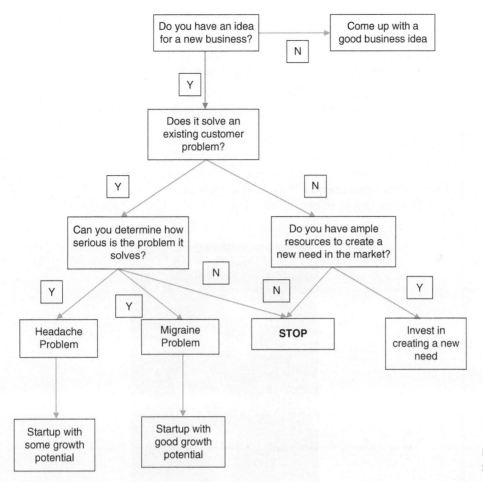

FIGURE 2.4 Decision Tree to Move from Business Idea to Startup

Interactive Exercise

Most students use one or more of social networking sites: Facebook, Snapchat, LinkedIn, Instagram, and Pinterest. Can you use SCAMPER to come up with an idea for a new social networking site that offers a twist on one of the popular sites?

There are several advantages to taking an imitative approach for starting the business. One can buy existing technologies, such as Web servers for a hosting service or an industrial fryer for a restaurant kitchen. Service providers, from banks to architects (and everyone in between), are likely to understand the new business and its industry, which makes it easier for them to do transaction with you. In imitative business, you can buy cheaper used items (e.g. furniture) and hire experienced workers for your venture. In practice, most imitative businesses are not a replica of an existing business, so that it is more useful to consider **degree of similarity** (which refers to the extent to which one venture – or its offering – is similar to another). An entrepreneur looks at one or more existing businesses and patterns the new business after them, with the exception of one or two key areas where things can be done in different ways.

Entrepreneurs that select an innovative strategy for their startup have the benefit of customizing the business precisely for their ideas and preferences. The challenge is that the novelty may make it difficult for others to understand the business. Highly innovative businesses also demand a lot of energy and effort from entrepreneurs in creating the processes and markets as well as in educating the suppliers, customers, and employees about the new product or service.

KEY TAKEAWAY

Most new businesses are imitative. They imitate an existing business but add a new twist to it.

Do Entrepreneurs Innovate?

Most businesses imitate. Can imitation help a firm become very successful? Peter Thiel of PayPal thinks that it is best to pursue a one-in-a-kind business that has no competition anywhere.

Wikimedia Commons

Watch the video online at: https://www.youtube.com/watch?v=JqxzLUE6pP8

What Do You Think?

Do the names Linio, Zalora, or CityDeal ring a bell? Linio is Amazon cloned for Mexico, Zalora is Zappos for Malaysians, and CityDeal is GroupOn for Germany. All three companies were founded at the Berlin-based startup incubator Rocket Internet, which itself is a brainchild of German brothers Marc, Oliver, and Alexander Samwar. Rocket's claim to fame: It takes promising Internet-based business ideas from the United States and clones them abroad for the international market. Since starting their first dot-clone in 1999 (Alando, which copied eBay), they have duplicated (or helped duplicate) eharmony, Pinterest, Airbnb, and Uber, among many others. The brothers grew up in Cologne (Germany), developing a love for business and commerce from their corporate lawyer parents, who would routinely bring clients home for meetings and discussions. As Oliver, who later completed his college thesis on US startups, recounts, "before we started university, we were thinking of starting an airline or a shipping company." When eBay bought Alando in late 1999 for $53 million, the Samwar brothers became Germany's first Internet millionaires. The brothers, who were then in their mid-20s, had built and sold the startup in less than 100 days. Today, Rocket Internet has a market capitalization of over three billion Euros, and the brothers have a 65% stake in the company. The Samwar brothers do not see themselves as just a copycat machine. Their argument: Every successful business idea is borrowed from others in some way, and the ability to take a proven business idea from one market to another is a skill unto itself. As Oliver observed, "The internet moves at Formula One speed; execution is the most important component of a successful business." If the Samwar brothers asked you for advice, what new American startup would you recommend they imitate in Europe?

Comprehension Check

1. What is SCAMPER? What are the different elements that constitute SCAMPER?
2. Distinguish between imitation and innovation.
3. What are the advantages of starting an imitative business?

Module 2.4 The Universal Startup Model

In order for a new startup to become a reality, four elements need to fall in place: boundary, resources, intention, and exchange (see Figure 2.5) – we refer to this as the BRIE model (yes, spelt like the cheese, but with a different meaning). Until these four factors come together, the new business exists only in the entrepreneur's head.

A new business needs to have a **boundary**, something that demarcates it as a distinct firm, and sets it apart from the buying, selling, or bartering we all do occasionally. Have you ever sold things on Amazon or Etsy? If you are like most of us, you have probably sold your used textbook online. Even though you made some money selling the used book, would you consider yourself a business? Of course, not! You were just a college student looking for some extra cash. To be considered a business, you would need to set up a company. This can be something as simple as coming up with a name for the venture, identifying a specific location dedicated to the business (physical or on the Internet), registering with the appropriate authorities, or even just a phone number and email address dedicated to the business.

Resources include the various inputs into the business, the materials and processes that go into the products or services the business wants to provide. It also includes financial resources (e.g. bank account or credit card) and human resources such as the time and effort of people who will be working in the business, including yourself. No matter how strapped the business, there are always some resources that need to be considered.

Intention is a basic element of a new business, as it captures the desire or inclination to venture on your own. It is important to remember that new ventures are neither coerced into existence nor random byproducts of environmental conditions. Instead, new ventures are a direct outcome of the intentions and consequent actions of some individuals. New businesses start with intention and advance through execution. Without intention, therefore, there is no business.

Exchange refers to the process of transferring resources, goods, or ideas into or from the business. An exchange occurs when the business makes its first sale for money or when it buys from another seller. Until the firm starts exchanging with other entities,

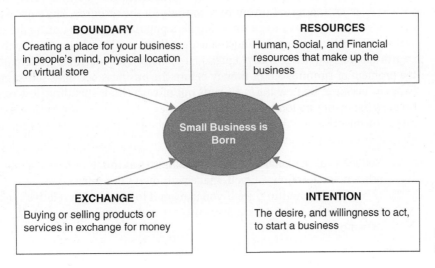

FIGURE 2.5 BRIE Model for Startups

there is really no "business" happening. Firms that maintain a consistent flow of exchange over time achieve stability and are able to survive longer.

> ### KEY TAKEAWAY
>
> Four elements need to come together – Boundary, Resources, Intentions, and Exchange – for a small business to get started.

The value of the BRIE model lies in helping you deal with the biggest hurdle to starting a business: **inertia** (or simple inaction). You may recall the principle of inertia from your basic science classes. Inertia is the property of a body to continue in its existing state unless acted upon by an external force. Because of inertia, things at rest tend to remain at rest. It may surprise you that inertia is also a major obstacle to starting your own business because people have a tendency to continue in the same state as they were even when they know they would be better off doing things differently. As a result, it is useful to consider small steps that will take you in the direction you need to go. The BRIE checklist shown in Figure 2.6 summarizes the various steps that help you make progress toward having your own startup.

What Do You Think?

Sam had been selling home-made fabric face masks with quirky motivational messages like Try + Oomph = Triumph before the federal government recommended that people wear face masks in public to slow the spread of the novel Corona virus. As a growing number of states mandated face masks, Sam's sale slowly grew to about 10,000 face masks a month. Almost everyone in Sam's extended family was making masks for her, and making good money doing so. She sold mostly on Etsy, but Amazon customers also bought some masks. One day Sam's grandfather asked her if she wanted to grow her business more. "What business?" Sam replied, "this is just a summer thing." Her grandfather advised her to think carefully saying, "You've a good thing going here." Should Sam turn her summer gig into a business? If yes, what steps should she take to do so?

As an entrepreneur works through the BRIE model to start his or her venture, it is useful to remember two specific activities that help increase the chances of having a successful business. The first important activity is **bootstrapping**, which refers to "getting by with less," or arranging to borrow, rent, or trade for the resource. The emphasis on finding a no-cost or low-cost way to do something is a popular approach during the startup phase and is part of the culture for most startups. Bootstrapping helps deal with the **undercapitalization** challenge that plagues a large majority of startups. Undercapitalization is the problem of running out of money before the business becomes self-supporting. This happens because the new business runs out of cash (high spending, low cash intake) or because the owner no longer has enough money left to put in the business (for new ventures, the business and the owner are often relying on the same pool of money). The key ideas of bootstrapping are simple:

1. Reduce your personal and business expenses as much as possible (e.g. do the office manager's job yourself, make your own sales pitch).
2. If you need something, see if you can get it for free (e.g. a relative's used phone for the office) or get it for a discount (e.g. a used car instead of the latest new model).

BRIE Checklist		
Boundary: A place for your business in time, in space, and in people's minds		
Number of boundary actions done	o	Came up with a name for your business
	o	Registered the business name with the appropriate authorities
	o	Created business cards and/or official stationery for the business
	o	Created an email address to be used solely for business purposes
	o	Bought a domain name and created a website for the business
	o	Obtained a telephone number to be used by the business
	o	Identified appropriate office space for the business
Resources: The things that make up the business		
Number of resource actions done	o	Identified the start-up team
	o	Participated in training programs, classes, or workshops on starting a business
	o	Marshalled the raw materials, supplies, and equipment you will need to get started
	o	Identified the minimum employees you will need to get started
	o	Talked with potential customers about their needs and desires
	o	Gained a good understanding of the product or service you will be offering
Intention: Determination to get a successful business going		
Number of intentions actions done	o	Decided that you want to get into business for yourself
	o	Identified the market opportunity you will be pursuing
	o	Developed the product or service you will be offering
	o	Worked out a 1-minute, 3-minute, and 5-minute value explanation for your business (what will you be doing, why are you doing it, and how you will do it)
	o	Begun your part-time (less than 35 hours per week) or full-time (more than 35 hours per week) commitment to the business
	o	Considered how you will run the marketing and promotion efforts for your business
Exchange: Transacting with external stakeholders		
Number of exchange actions done	o	Saved money to invest in the business
	o	Invested money in the business
	o	Explored if family or friends will lend you money, when needed
	o	Identified suppliers who will extend credit
	o	Identified customers who will pay cash for your offerings
	o	Made a sale
	o	Made 4–5 sales to customers outside your friends and family

FIGURE 2.6 BRIE Checklist
Source: Based on Katz, J., & Gartner, W. B. (1988). Properties of emerging organizations. *Academy of Management Review*, *13*(3), 429–441

3. Look for lower-cost alternatives to make-do instead of the best you want to get (e.g. do you really need the fancy MacBook for the office or will a low-end laptop do the work?).
4. Make-do with limited means as long as you can.
5. If you need to borrow money, first dip into your own pockets, then turn to family and friends, and only then to banks, credit cards, and credit companies.

The second important activity is **aggrandizing**, which involves making the new business look bigger, more substantial, and more capable than it really is. For a new business, aggrandization can be important to achieve legitimacy with potential customers and suppliers, but it can also undermine the trust others have in the firm and its owner. In today's Internet age, it is easy to aggrandize by having a nice website that makes the business looks much more established than is truly the case. Unfortunately, the Internet also makes it easier for people to check up on new firms without much effort, such as by obtaining credit reports or business directories with the company's information. Some aggrandization behaviors are relatively straightforward and generally acceptable:

1. Have a nice website that makes the business look professional and trustworthy, especially if people will be making online payments.

2. Have professional-looking office stationery (e.g. business cards) and talk about your new venture in professional terms. If you see your venture as a frivolous undertaking, it is unlikely others will take it seriously.
3. A board of advisors comprising well-known people can be an invaluable asset to the firm. When Stefanie Strack decided to leave her corporate job at Nike Inc., she consulted with A. K. Pradeep, an adviser whom Stefanie refers to as her "Jedi master" because of his wise entrepreneurial candor. The company she launched in June 2020, VIS Holdings, includes a member-only website, advisory podcasts, and a digital mentorship program, all of which are geared toward supporting female athletes aged 12–22. She has a four-person advisory board.
4. Seeking and obtaining (free) ad space for the company, either as airtime on the local radio or a column in a trade publication will give good visibility to the business and you.
5. Have someone else answer the office phone, perhaps a family member or student intern.

It is worth noting that aggrandization does not mean you lie outright about the business or its capabilities. For example, while you may exaggerate the number of employees that work for you if you are willing to do the work of multiple people to make the business work, one should not lie about things that can be easily checked and verified (e.g. product capabilities). The dark side of aggrandization should be avoided as much as possible.

Secrets of Startup Success

William (Bill) Gross has founded several companies. He also started Idealab, a business incubator, where he is CEO and chairman of the board. At a TED talk, Gross shared what he found when he compared companies that became successful with those that fail.

CTV News

View the video online at: https://www.youtube.com/watch?v=bNpx7gpSqbY

Comprehension Check

1. What is the BRIE model for startups? What are the various elements of BRIE?
2. Define inertia and explain how it relates to starting a new business
3. What is bootstrapping?

Module 2.5 Analyze the State of Startup in the United States

A discussion of business startups is incomplete without discussing the current state of new venture creation in the country. Several researchers have noted that new businesses make up a steadily shrinking portion of companies in the United States and generate a declining fraction of new jobs. As shown in Figure 2.7, the **startup rate** in the country has declined consistently over the last 40 years. For most people, the word "startup" conjures up images of small technology firms in Silicon Valley vying to become the next Facebook, Square, or Twitter. But such companies are actually just a small, rarefied strata of new ventures – one that seems to be doing okay. To better understand the problem of declining startups, one needs to consider the full array of new companies, including what most of us just think of as small firms: new businesses in industries like retail or construction. According to the Roosevelt Institute, most industries "are now more concentrated and less competitive than at any point since the Gilded Age." American strip malls and yellow pages used to be filled with new firms. Now, where several small stores might once have opened, big-box chains dominate.

Imagine a day in the life of a typical American and ask: How long does it take for her to interact with a small startup? The average person wakes up to use toiletries from one of the large fast-moving consumer goods companies, like Proctor & Gamble. She browses the Internet through a browser for a giant corporation (Google or Microsoft), brought to her through a local monopoly. She buys food at a superstore such as Whole Foods or Walmart, sleeping and relaxing on furniture bought at a large big-box retailer. If she needs medication, she will go to a pharmacy, likely owned by one of three companies controlling that market. If she wants to step outside the shadow of an oligopoly, she'll have to stay away from music, ebooks, and beer; two companies control more than half of all sales in each of these markets. For eyewear, her only real option is Luxottica, a company that the business periodical *Forbes* called "the four-eyed eight-tentacled monopoly." To escape, she can try boarding an airplane, but four corporations control 80% of the seats

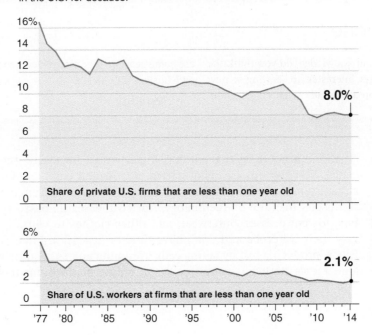

Start Me Up

The rate of startup formation has been declining in the U.S. for decades.

FIGURE 2.7 Decline in Startup Rates of Small Businesses
Source: Adapted from Commerce Department, *The Wall Street Journal*, https://www.wsj.com/articles/sputtering-startups-weigh-on-u-s-economic-growth-1477235874

on domestic flights. The truth is you could go through an entire week, or a whole month, and never cross paths with a startup firm. As one commentator, America seems to have become the land of the big and the home of the consolidated.

The state of new venture creation is even worse among millennials (defined by the Pew Research Center as those born between 1981 and 1996). The share of millennials who own a business has fallen to almost a quarter-century low, according to one analysis of Federal Reserve data. A 2016 survey of 1200 millennials by the Economic Innovation Group found that more millennials believed they could have a successful career by staying at one company and attempting to climb the ladder than by starting a new firm. When EIG's president and cofounder, John Lettieri, testified before the US Senate, he shared that "Millennials are on track to be the least entrepreneurial generation in recent history."

KEY TAKEAWAY

The startup rate for small businesses in the United States has steadily gone down over time. Interest in starting a new business is really low among the millennial generation.

There is also a common misconception that America has the highest startup rate in the world. Comparing countries on their startup rate is difficult because different countries have different population demographics. China and India with their billion-plus population will certainly have more startups than tiny Portugal with a population of about 10 million. Furthermore, countries also seem to measure startups differently, which makes cross-country comparisons confusing. One popular approach among economists to measure national startup rate is to count how many new businesses with paid employees are created in a year, then divide them by the number of companies that are already up and running. The Organization for Economic Cooperation and Development (OECD), an international research organization that specializes in side-by-side comparisons between different countries, calls this percentage the "**employer enterprise birth rate**." Many others just call it the startup rate. But whatever you name the measure, the United States scores fairly low on it. The United States is second to last, for instance, on the OECD graph below, which looks at the years 2007 through 2009 (see figure 2.8).

Interactive Exercise

Based on your experience and knowledge, do you think the millennial generation is less interested in starting a new business than having a corporate career? What do you think are some reasons that discourage people from starting their own business?

All this is not to say that enterprising actors are not starting companies in the United States. New startups are being started on a regular basis, even under the most adverse circumstances. Ambika Singh, a graduate of the electrical engineering program of Massachusetts Institute of Technology, started the Seattle-based company Armoire Style Inc., to rent dresses, outerwear, and other clothes to working women who want to vary their wardrobe and don't have time to dry-clean. Mike Seldon founded Finless Foods, producing fish by taking cells from tuna and cultivating them in the laboratory. Matt Pierce started Trusted Health, an online platform for travel nurses to find jobs

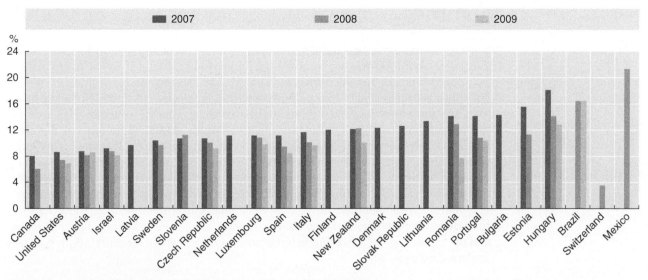

FIGURE 2.8 Birth Rate of Firms as a Proportion of the Total Economy of a Country

Source: Entrepreneurship at a Glance 2012, OECD library, https://doi.org/10.1787/entrepreneur_aag-2012-en

and build career skills, helping meet demand for nurses in hospitals responding to a surge in patients during the COVID-19 pandemic. Sidekick is a startup that offers an always-on tablet aimed at small firms and other teams that want constant and spontaneous communication among coworkers, as if they were sitting together all day long. As the COVID-19 pandemic spread through the country, hundreds of men and women launched new firms to get into the mask-making business. Michael Hubbard started Texas Mask Inc., procuring a mask-making machine from China for his facility in North Texas. "When you have these kinds of events there ought to be some opportunities that don't normally exist," he says.

Ambika Singh is an electrical engineer who started Armoire Style Inc., a clothing rental service for professional women.

Comprehension Check

1. Explain the employer enterprise birth rate.
2. How has the new startup rate in the United States trended over time?
3. Compare the state of entrepreneurship in the United States with other countries.

Summary

Starting your own business is the most popular path to becoming a small business owner. Every year, about 700,000 new ventures are launched in the United States, many of them part-time businesses that the owner starts on the side. New businesses begin with an idea, but only some ideas actually offer a good opportunity to start a business. Not all business ideas are worth pursuing, and it is important to consider whether a business idea is timely and relevant for starting a new venture. In other words, does the idea one has represent a good business opportunity? This does not mean that the idea needs to be highly innovative; indeed, most small businesses tend to be quite imitative (that is, they are based on imitation-with-a-twist). A big hurdle to starting a new business is inertia. The BRIE model provides a handy tool for those who need some guidance in getting started on creating a new venture. Although there is much more emphasis on entrepreneurship now than was the case in the past, the actual startup rate in the United States has gradually gone down, and we are now at risk of falling behind other countries where far more new businesses are launched every year.

Live Exercise

Your parents are not the party kind, but they decided to throw a big graduation party when your sister graduated from college. You were surprised to see Johnny Gold at the party. You liked him when you met him last time, but you didn't know your parents had gotten so close to Johnny and his wife. Johnny was also happy to see you and asked lots of questions about how college was going for you. Just when you thought the conversation was about to finish, he blurted, "I've an idea for a business, you know." Now, he had your full attention! "Like so many good ideas," he continued, "this idea also came to me in the shower." You wanted to hear more. Johnny shared that he used to play basketball, and suffers from a bad hip, probably the result of too many dives onto gym floors. "That makes one daily chore very painful – retrieving a bar [of soap] from the shower floor," Johnny admitted somewhat sheepishly. You found yourself wondering where this was going. You also wanted to ask why he was still using bar soap when there were so many other options on the market, but you didn't want to sound rude. His idea, Johnny explained, was to create a device that would keep soap from slipping out of one's hands. Before you knew it, Johnny popped the question: "So, what do you think about my idea? And, how do I go from this idea to having my own dream business?"

World of Books

To delve deeper into some of the ideas discussed in this chapter, we recommend the following books:

- *All in Startup* by Diana Kander
- *Zero to One* by Peter Thiel

In the Movies

The child day-care industry in the United States is about $58 billion. It is one of the largest in the world, owing mainly to the prevalence of a culture where both parents work. How does one start a day-care business? The Hollywood movie *Daddy Day Care* stars Eddie Murphy in the role of an out-of-work father who decides to start a child day-care to provide for his family.

Things to Remember

LO 2.1 Identify motives for starting a new business
- Necessity entrepreneurship refers to people starting a business because there are no desirable alternatives.
- Opportunity entrepreneurship refers to people who start a business to bring a new product idea to the market.
- The total rate of entrepreneurial activity in any society is the sum of necessity and opportunity entrepreneurship.
- Many entrepreneurs report a combination of push and pull factors to explain their reasons for starting a new business.
- The share of necessary entrepreneurship is usually higher when the economy is weaker (and unemployment is high), whereas the share of opportunity entrepreneurship goes up when the economy is stronger (and unemployment is low).

LO 2.2 Distinguish between part-time and full-time entrepreneurship
- Those who start a business from scratch are beginning their entrepreneurial journey with a clean slate on which they can write whatever story they want. New startups do not have the carryover baggage of someone else's mistakes, location, employees, or products.
- There are also other advantages of beginning from scratch, including deciding what the venture's unique capabilities will be and who it would like to serve.
- Starting a new venture from scratch can be quite daunting. This is because there is no existing template onto which the business may simply be overlaid. The time-to-market is also higher for *de novo* startups as there are many little pieces that need to be put in place before the business can officially be launched.
- When you decide to start a business, you make a choice about pursuing a part-time or full-time approach. A part-time business today can become a full-time business tomorrow, or vice versa.

LO 2.3 Explain how ideas turn into opportunities
- There is no shortage of ideas for new and improved products and services. However, not every idea makes for a good opportunity.
- The first idea a potential entrepreneur has is not necessarily the best opportunity to pursue.
- Each of us can use creative methods to help take a simple idea to an opportunity that has the potential to build a viable business.
- SCAMPER can be a very effective method for identifying new ideas. Its value lies in helping you step outside the usual thinking processes and providing a new way to think differently.
- Most small business ideas are a lot like the others in the industry, with the caveat that they are not exactly like the others

LO 2.4 Describe the universal startup model
- In order for a new startup to become a reality, four elements need to fall in place – boundary, resources, intention, and exchange. Until these four factors come together, the new business exists only in the entrepreneur's head.
- A boundary is something that demarcates a distinct firm, and sets it apart from the buying, selling, or bartering we all do occasionally.
- Resources includes the various inputs into the business, the materials and processes that go into the products or services the business wants to provide.
- Intention is a basic element of a new business as it captures the desire or inclination to venture on your own.
- Exchange refers to the process of transferring resources, goods, or ideas into or from the business.

- Inertia is a major obstacle to starting your own business because people have a tendency to continue in the same state as they were even when they know they would be better off doing things differently.

LO 2.5   **Analyze the current state of startups in the United States**
- New firms make up a steadily shrinking portion of companies in the United States and generate a declining fraction of new jobs.
- The average American could go through an entire week, or a whole month, and never cross paths with a startup firm.
- The millennial generation shows more interest in working for a large firm than starting a new firm.
- A common misconception is that the United States is the most entrepreneurial nation in the world.
- Enterprising actors are starting new businesses even under the most adversarial circumstances.

Key Terms

necessity entrepreneurship	full-time startups	imitation	inertia
opportunity entrepreneurship	moonlighting	innovation	bootstrapping
total entrepreneurial activity	conflict of interest	degree of similarity	undercapitalizing
de novo startup	poisoning the well	boundary	aggrandizing
part-time startups	cannibalizing	resources	startup rate
	brainstorming	intentions	employer enterprise
	SCAMPER	exchange	birth rate

Experiential Exercise

This exercise is designed for students working in groups of two or three. Use of the Internet (via laptops or hand-held devices like the iPad or smartphone) during the exercise is very desirable.

Pick up the latest issue of either the *Inc.* or the *Entrepreneur* magazine. Identify businesses that started from scratch. In other words, identify *de novo* startups from the magazine of your choice. You may need to use the Web to look for the story of the origins of the businesses you encounter.

When you have a list of 10 startup businesses, search for relevant information that allows you to answer the following questions about the business:

1. Where, i.e. in which country, was the business started?

2. Is this business an example of necessity or opportunity entrepreneurship?

3. When the business started, would it be considered a part-time startup or a full-time startup?

4. On a scale of 1–7 (where 1 = highly imitative and 7 = highly innovative), how would you classify this business?

5. Using SCAMPER as a diagnostic tool, can you classify what type of idea was at the core of this business? In other words, was it an example of "substitute" or "rearrange" or something else?

When you have answered the five questions above for all the 10 businesses you identified earlier, can you spot some dominant trends and themes in the information you gathered?

Family Business

It's something that's really fun to do. It's a family business.

RON WHITE

3.0 Introduction

Small businesses often become family enterprises. Although a significant other or even a parent may have helped a founder in the early stages of starting a new business, the real transition to a family enterprise happens when the next generation of the family joins the business. The participation of the founders' siblings in the company may also lead to a family business. Regardless of what actually leads a small business to become a family enterprise, it is a fact that the joining of family members in the business changes the nature of the firm, as well as alters the challenges it faces.

This chapter introduces you to family firms. It presents the basic concepts and principles related to family firms and also provides a diverse collection of real-life cases and exercises to help you become familiar with the complex issues that family firms confront. The goal is to pass on the accumulated knowledge about family firms. It should come as no surprise that there is much to learn about family businesses than can be covered within one chapter. Many universities offer dedicated courses focusing on family firms. One chapter, no matter how thorough and detailed, cannot rival a complete course in the amount of material that can be covered in a rich area like family firms. Nevertheless, this chapter should provide you a good strong foundation, and hopefully whet your appetite, for further learning about family firms. At the minimum, this chapter should equip you with the knowledge and tools you need to have an informed conversation about family firms.

SPOTLIGHT | George R. Ruhl & Son: As Young as the American Presidency

Search for @GeorgeRRuhl on Facebook and you land on the page of a family firm that has existed for as long as this country. At about the time that George Washington was taking the presidency of the young republic in 1789, Henry Ruhle – a German immigrant – first began milling flour in Fells Point, Maryland. The Ruhles were among the hundreds of German immigrants who flocked to America in the eighteenth century, many of whom got their start as millers and grain handlers. Flour became Baltimore city's first major export. At some point in the mid-1800s, the Ruhles closed their milling operation and began distributing flour to bakers in Baltimore City. Horse-drawn wagons carrying sacks of Ruhle grain and processed flour became a familiar sight on the local roads.

Then came the Great Baltimore Fire of 1904, raging for two days. At the family enterprise of Ruhl & Son, a feed-and-flour shop located on the edge of Baltimore Harbor, proprietor Conrad Jr. and his son George worked deliberately and expeditiously, rolling barrel after valuable barrel of flour off the pier into the frigid choppy river waters. As the Ruhle's expected, the flour around the edge of the wooden barrels swelled to seal the spaces between the slates. When the fire finally stopped burning, the Ruhles and their employees rowed out with a hook and brought back a good amount of the company's product. The flour in the middle of the barrels was still good, so they scooped it out, repackaged it, and saved the company.

During World War I, anti-German sentiments were common in the United States, so the family slightly Americanized its name, dropping the umlaut and the final "e." After the war ended, consumer tastes changed and new competition came from regional and national brands. When George Ruhl Sr. died suddenly, his 18-year-old son George Jr. was forced to abandon his plans of attending the U.S. Naval Academy and instead take over the family enterprise. The Ruhls added sugar to the product line in 1950 and mixes in 1960. But George Jr. was not optimistic about the bakery supply business and advised his son Bob to make his life somewhere else. For many years, Bob worked at a steel company in Baltimore.

A few years later, Bob rejoined the family business, and despite his father's reluctance, began to bring

George R. Ruhl & Son is a 250-year-old family business in its sixth generation.

some big changes. "I fought with my father like cats and dogs. He and I fought over putting a forklift in, putting a computer in, and then he just finally gave up, I argued so much," Bob recounts. Bob's efforts led the company to diversify their product line to service the new wave of donut shops, supermarkets, and other retailers. The Ruhl family business expanded, while the steel company where Bob had worked earlier (and which his father thought had more job security and was a safer bet) declared bankruptcy and shut down.

Today, Bob, or George Ruhl III, is the sixth-generation owner of the independent family-owned business that distributes a wide variety of dry and frozen goods throughout the Mid-Atlantic states. The seventh generation has Bob's children Erin and Bill Ruhl, both of whom are involved in the business. As Bob gets older, he sometimes finds himself wondering about the future of the firm that dates back to Washington's first presidential inauguration.

Discussion Questions

1. What do you think helps a family business survive and grow for 250 years?

2. Why did George Ruhl II not want his son to join the family business?

3. What do you think pulled Bob (George Ruhl III) to rejoin the family business despite his father's objections?

Module 3.1 The Basics of Family Business

Although they do not get much attention in our popular media, family businesses are ubiquitous in the United States as well as in many other countries. Some estimates suggest that more than two-thirds of all incorporated firms in the United States may be considered family businesses. George R. Ruhl & Son is an example of a long-lived family business. Another such example is Schoedinger Funeral & Cremation Service in Ohio, which started in 1865 and is now in its sixth generation of family ownership.

Family businesses are also not uncommon among the largest corporations in the country: Almost 35% of the S&P and Fortune 500 firms are family-controlled firms. A large majority of family businesses are small businesses, but more than 100 family firms in the United States are billion-dollar enterprises. The Walton family, which owns about half the retail giant Walmart, are the wealthiest family in the country. The Koch (majority owners of the conglomerate Koch), Mars (owners of their namesake candy giant that owns M&Ms and Snickers), Cargill (owners of the largest privately held business in America), and Cox (in the media business) families make up the other four in the America's Wealthiest Families list. Family businesses also make nontrivial contributions to economic output and job creation, with estimates suggesting about 40–50% of the GDP and more than 80% of private-sector employment comes from family firms. Consider Lifeway Foods, a publicly traded manufacturer of tart and tangy cultured milk smoothies. The family matriarch Ludmila Smolyansky is chairperson of the board, while her daughter Julie Smolyansky is Chief Executive Officer and son Edward Smolyansky is Chief Operating Officer. With about $93 million annual revenues and nearly 400 employees, the company has a large footprint nationally, but especially in Illinois where it is headquartered.

KEY TAKEAWAY

From small businesses in your neighborhood to some of the largest corporations in the country, family businesses are everywhere.

Family firms are often praised for their resilience, the ability to successfully withstand crisis and problems. Consider Eastman Machine of Buffalo, New York. The company, which has been in the family for four generations, makes fabric-cutting machines. In its 132-year history, Eastman has survived several crises: World War I, the Spanish flu pandemic of 1918, the Great Depression, and World War II. When the COVID-19 pandemic swept across the country, the fourth-generation owner Robert Stevenson had this to say to his employees: "We survived those episodes, and we'll survive this one. We're a family business, and we will take care of everybody." Demand for the cutting machines that Eastman makes went down by half during the pandemic, and the company needed to take out a $2 million loan under the government's Paycheck Protection Program to keep workers on the payroll. Yet, Trevor, who is preparing to one day run the business, shares his father's upbeat attitude. "I know we can weather the storm. We're ready for when the spigot gets turned back on."

3.1.1 Definition of Family Business

What does the term *family business* mean? At a simple level, it is clear that the concept of family business combines two important entities of modern society: family and business. One may say that a family business happens when the family and business come together. In other words:

$$\text{Family Business} = \text{Family} + \text{Business}$$

Trevor Stevenson is poised to be the fifth-generation owner of Eastman Machine. The portrait of his great-great-grandfather who founded the company hangs in the boardroom.

Consider the luxury giant Cartier, once described as "the jeweler of kings and the king of jewelers." In 1847, Louis-François Cartier founded Cartier in Paris, France. The business passed on to his son Alfred Cartier in 1874. Over time, Alfred's sons Louis, Pierre, and Jacques joined the firm, relocating the Paris store and setting up new stores in New York and London. After the three Cartier brothers passed, the next generation sold the firm to outside investors. The company Cartier still exists, but it is no longer a family business as it once was.

Despite the apparent simplicity of the conceptualizing family firms, you may be surprised to know there is no consensus on the meaning of the family business designation. Given the tremendous heterogeneity of family businesses nation-wide (which is even greater when we look at family businesses internationally), it is clear that no one definition of family business will be acceptable to everyone. For the purpose of the discussion in this book, we adopt the following definition of **family business**:

> *A family business is one in which multiple members of the same family are involved as major owners or managers, either contemporaneously or over time.*

The definition adopted here is broad enough to allow for a number of variations in the generation of key family members, level of ownership and control, and the managerial roles of family members. Despite its breadth, the definition is specific enough to exclude firms that are not really family businesses. Consider, for example, the distinction between **lone founder firms** in which there is one founder with no relatives in the business and **family firms** in which there are multiple major owners or executives over time or contemporaneously from the same family.

The definition of family business includes the following salient characteristics:

1. Strategic influence by family members on the management of the firm, whether by being active in management or ownership or by serving on the board of directors.
2. Significant ownership control by two or more members of the family (the actual threshold for significant ownership depends on whether the firm is privately held or publicly owned. For private firms, significant ownership usually means 50% or higher, whereas for publicly held firms, significant ownership may mean 5% or more of the firm).
3. The possibility or dream of **business continuity** across generations.

Thus, these three things need to come together for a business to become a family firm: influence of the family, ownership of the family, and a possibility to continue the business in the next generation. Take out one of these three characteristics, and the business can no longer be considered a true family firm.

Interactive Exercise

Check out the website of Community Coffee in Baton Rouge, LA. It is a fourth-generation family business. See if you can find the page that tells the story of the family that runs the business. After reading the Web pages "Story" and "Family," what are the first words that come to your mind to describe this family business?

Family Business: An American Tradition

Would you like to learn about a successful American family firm that has been in operation for more than 100 years? Meet Community Coffee of Baton Rouge, LA. Matt Saurage, fourth-generation owner of Community Coffee, shares his family recipe for success as a business owned by a family and dedicated to serving the community.

Watch the video online at: https://www.youtube.com/watch?v=e6KEkpVW-7g

3.1.2 Family Business System

A common theoretical approach often used in academic studies of family firms is systems theory. In the systems theory approach, the family business is made up of three independent yet overlapping subsystems: family, business, and ownership. Any individual in a family business can be placed in one of the seven sectors that are formed by the overlapping circles of the subsystems (see Figure 3.1). For example, owners (whether partners or shareholders) will be somewhere in the top circle. Similarly, all family members will be in the bottom-right circle and everyone who works in the business in the bottom-left circle. One's placement in the model will depend on how many connections he or she has to the family business. Individuals with only one connection to the firm will be in one of the outside circles. Individuals with two connections will be in the sectors formed by the overlap of two systems. Only individuals with three connections will occupy the center (or the heart) of the model.

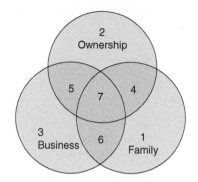

FIGURE 3.1 Three Subsystems of a Family Business

Depending on where someone is placed in the interconnected subsystems influences their authority in the family firm as well as the responsibility they owe to the survival and longevity of the business. A family member with no ownership and no involvement in the business will be placed in sector 1 to the extreme right. Family members who have ownership and work for the business will be placed in sector 7 of the model. One's placement in the model helps understand the biases and prejudices the person brings to his or her decision-making. It also helps understand how important someone is to the family business. A person who checks all three boxes (is a member of the family, has ownership in the business, and works in the firm) has a much more direct impact on the survival and success of the business than someone who checks only one or two of the boxes.

What Do You Think?

Pete Smith has a bachelor's degree in engineering from Penn State and an MBA from New York University. After receiving his MBA, he joined the family real-estate business, which his grandfather had started about 40 years ago. Pete's father, mother, and older brother were already in the family business, which had seen impressive growth over the past two decades. Over the next few years, Pete got married and had two kids. Lately, Pete has begun drinking heavily and can be seen leaving work early to go socializing with his friends. Pete's proximity to his former secretary is also a topic of gossip among the employees at the company. She had been fired by Smith Sr. two years earlier for some accounting irregularities and is now among Pete's close group of friends outside of work. Pete's parents are bothered about his behavior, which they think is affecting his family and the business. His older brother has raised Pete's inappropriate behavior with the parents a few times, although he has not confronted Pete directly about it. Do you think it is appropriate for the other family members to worry about what Pete does outside of work?

Comprehension Check

1. Define family business.
2. What is the difference between lone founder firms and family firms?
3. What are the salient attributes of a family business?

Module 3.2 Two Sides of the Family Business

When the psychologist Sigmund Freud was asked what he considered to be the secret of a full life, he responded with three words: *Lieben und arbeiten* (English translation: to love and to work). Most people would probably agree that family and work are two most important things in their life. As such, the family firm is a unique organizational form that brings together two things most people consider to be most important in their lives.

The specialness, however, has both a dark-side and a bright-side to it. Let us see some of the advantages and challenges of family business.

3.2.1 Positives of a Family Business

> **KEY TAKEAWAY**
>
> Family firms are a unique type of organization, combining two things central to our life: family and work.

Imagine making decisions about a company founded by your great-great-grandfather and where your siblings work in the office next to yours. The role of the CEO is different when you hope to someday pass on the company to your children and expect the firm to live longer than any family member working in it now. To be honest, even walking through the door every day for work is different when the name on the building is your own. Think, for example, Ford Motor Company started by Henry Ford in 1903, where his great-grandson William Clay Ford Jr. is now the executive chairman (having also served as CEO, COO, and president). It seems reasonable to assume that William Ford is mindful of the **family legacy** when making decisions about the firm that was founded by his larger-than-life great-grandfather and is closely associated with his family. J. Willard "Bill" Marriott, Jr., whose father founded the Marriott hotels, proudly declares that he wants everyone at the hotel chain "to know that there really is a guy named Marriott who cares about them."

Personal commitment. Because the needs and wants of the family are served from the business, family firms encourage a high level of personal commitment and accountability. The high level of personal commitment that a family business fosters is almost impossible to find in nonfamily business. For example, when the management of Hines, a privately owned global real-estate investment, development, and management firm, met to discuss the challenges posed to their business by the upstart WeWork, they were assured that "it's not too late for us [yet]" by 94-year-old Gerald Hines, who is the family patriarch and the founder and chairman of the company.

Long-term perspective. Generally speaking, family firms tend to have a long-term view of the business. The leadership is likely to have already seen ups and downs in the business, gone through economic booms and busts, and so understand that they are not to overreact to momentary challenges to the business. Take Kongo Gumi, the world's oldest continuously family-owned company (although it has now been sold to the Takamatsu Construction Group). Founded in 578 AD in Japan, the company is in the temple restoration business, and made it to the 40th generation. Masakazu Kongo, the last of the family to own the business, observed: "I have a responsibility to the company, of course, but also to society, because we are so old." The Kongo group was there before World War I, the Japanese reformation, the discovery of the new world, and even before the crusades.

Flexibility. Family members who work for their business wear several different hats and take on tasks outside of the formal job description (if there is one) to ensure that work gets done. Many family businesses find it hard to recruit good employees, so the flexibility of family members becomes critical for the survival of the company.

Leadership stability. In a family business, the position in the family typically determines who leads the business, so the leader tends to stay in the position for several years until retirement, death, or illness forces a change in the organizational hierarchy. There are also family businesses like the Mellerio dits Meller of France (makers of the cups of the French Open tennis tournament and the Ballon d'Or awarded to the best French soccer player annually), where the policy is for family leaders to step aside at the age of 65 (though, as we discuss later, such policies are uncommon in family businesses). Founded in 1613, Mellerio may be the oldest manufacturing company in Europe.

Ballon d'Or, the most prestigious individual award for soccer players, is made by a French family firm that is more than 400 years old.

Proven systems. A family business, especially if it has been in existence for a few years, already has a business model and systems that have been proven to work. Working for a family business that is already proven to work alleviates the uncertainty typically associated with running one's own business. For most people, funeral homes may be a difficult business to get into (with the growing trend of cremation and consolidation in the industry), but for John and Norman Bachmann, eighth-generation owners of the Bachman Funeral Home in Strasburg (Pennsylvania), the business has been in their family since 1769.

Interactive Exercise

Identify five business owners who either inherited their business or plan to pass on their business to family members. Ask them about the challenges and opportunities of working in and owning a family business. Be ready to share your findings with the class.

3.2.2 Negatives of a Family Business

The preceding discussion may give you an impression that everything is good with family businesses. Indeed, many people only see good things in family firms. Consider what Karen Mills, the 23rd Administrator of the SBA, had to say about family businesses (www.jaylucas.us):

> I grew up in a family business . . . that really has provided the core of my belief in American small business, and in America's ability to grow and operate important businesses that can compete and be successful.

Unfortunately, it is not the case that everything about a family business is good. As anyone who has ever worked in a family business knows, there are also many problems that can occur when the family and business come together. These problems if not addressed properly can doom the family business to mediocrity, or even early demise.

Weak or misguided leadership. Often family businesses do not have adequate checks-and-balances to keep the whims and fancies of the leader in check. Because the leader of the business is also the head of the family, other family members may be unable to raise legitimate questions about his or her ability to provide effective or ethical leadership for the business. Samsung, the family-held Korean conglomerate, found itself in the news for the wrong reasons when its chairman Lee Kun-hee was indicted for tax evasion and criminal breach of trust. When the legendary Henry Ford retook the reins at his namesake company after the death of his son, he was widely considered unfit for the job, and yet he was accepted as the president of the company he had founded.

Family conflict. No firm is completely free from conflict, but add in familial rivalries, long histories, and relationship issues, and the family business becomes a fertile ground for conflict. Many experts believe it was family squabbles that inflicted irreparable damage to Robert Mondavi Corp., Napa Valley's best-known winery that had once put California and the United States on the world's wine map.

Lack of interest among family members. There are times when some or all family members have no interest in joining the family business. They may be officially associated with the business because it's expected of them or that's where their monthly paycheck comes from. As a result, the business is burdened with unengaged employees who are apathetic to the needs of the company. Outside of family businesses, such disinterested workers would be fired. But how do you fire your family members who are not fully engaged with the business?

Nepotism. In many family businesses, the top rungs of the corporation, and many of the choice positions, are reserved for family members. Consequently, outsiders with knowledge, skills, and abilities find themselves excluded from positions that they truly deserve, while family members make it to positions for which they have no training or experience.

Succession planning. As will be discussed later, **succession planning** is the Achilles heel of family business. Most family firms lack good succession planning, often because the leader does not want to deal with the difficult issues that arise from thinking about how the business will transition to the next generation. That's what happened at Johnson Security Bureau, Inc., when Charles Johnson Sr., a second-generation owner was diagnosed with terminal cancer and given months to live. Suddenly, his daughter Jessica Johnson and son Charles Jr. were scrambling to learn everything before they had to take the helm at the firm their grandparents founded. In many firms, once the founding generation has retired or passed, the business either crumbles quickly or lingers on as growth sputters and the family lives off the wealth accumulated by previous generations. The family either ends up pouring more and more money into the failing enterprise or treats the business as a life-style rather than something to be nurtured. It is therefore not surprising that most family-owned businesses lose the entrepreneurial spark in subsequent generations.

The professional-services firm PriceWaterhouseCoopers surveyed family business owners in 30 countries and found that a quarter of their respondents believed the next generation lacked the skills or aptitude to manage the family firm (see Figure 3.2). Only about 40% respondents reported that they will pass on the management of the family firm to the next generation.

Succession planning is a perennial issue for family firms through the generations. Remember the Cartiers you met earlier in this chapter? The small family firm really took off in the third generation under the three brothers when it expanded worldwide. The fourth generation, however, lacked the knowledge and dedication needed to sustain and grow the business, so the different branches of the family decided to sell their share of the business to outside investors.

Family Matters

A look at attitudes among family-business owners

Plans for Succession

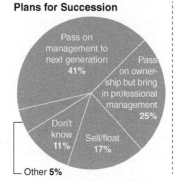

- Pass on management to next generation **41%**
- Pass on ownership but bring in professional management **25%**
- Don't know **11%**
- Sell/float **17%**
- Other **5%**

Concerns About Passing the Business On

No concerns	**47%**
Next generation would be under too much pressure	**7**
Next generation won't want to get involved	**8**
Next generation won't be ready in time	**8**
Next generation won't have skills/aptitude	**24**

Reasons/Concerns for Bringing in Outside Management When Passing Business On

No concerns	**51%**
Next generation won't want to get involved	**8**
Difficulty integrating family/external management	**6**
Difficulty finding external management	**6**
Next generation won't be ready in time	**6**
Next generation won't have skills/aptitude	**18**
Conflict between family and management	**8**

Reasons for Selling the Business

Never intended to pass it on	**14%**
No family to pass it on to	**8**
Worry about the pressure	**5**
Next generation won't have skills/aptitude	**17**
Next generation won't be ready in time	**19**
Next generation won't want to get involved	**24**

FIGURE 3.2 Attitudes toward Succession among Family Firm Owners
Source: Wall Street Journal

Source: PriceWaterhouseCoopers survey of 1,952 family-business owners in over 30 countries, conducted largely by telephone between May and September 2012

What Do You Think?

Jessica joined Fusion Automobiles, a large family-owned multistore automobile dealership, right after finishing an engineering degree from Lehigh University. Jessica was hardworking and over the next 10 years rose to become General Manager of Operations at the dealership. She was well-respected by the employees and customers, who found her friendly and approachable when they needed her. She was compensated well and had flexible working hours consistent with the company policy of "Employees First." Jessica was expecting to become President of the company. The company had been doing very well financially, when suddenly, without any advance warning, Jessica found herself fired by Ed Sullivan, son of the company patriarch, who had recently started taking an active role in the family business. When some family members asked Ed about his unceremonious firing of Jessica, he remarked, "Sometimes you just don't like somebody." What do you think Jessica should do now? If you were the family patriarch, how would you deal with this situation?

Sages Family Business: Opportunities and Challenges

All family businesses face some common problems, some sooner than others. This tale of a fictional family firm highlights key issues and challenges as the business transitions across generations.

Watch the video online at: https://www.youtube.com/watch?v=cCbRanMtkLo

Comprehension Check

1. What are some positives of family firms?
2. What are some negatives of family firms?
3. Discuss the pros and cons of **nepotism** in family businesses.

Module 3.3 Types of Family Businesses

There is a wide variety of family businesses in the United States as well as worldwide. As such, any attempts to classify family businesses into a few distinct types may be criticized for ignoring the rich heterogeneity that makes family firms unique. And yet, typologies are popular because they provide an efficient way of making sense of the large variety of firms that we see around us.

A popular typology of family businesses seeks to understand them on two dimensions: simplicity versus complexity of the family and the business. Crossing the two dimensions of simplicity–complexity and family–business yields four types of family firms (see Figure 3.3):

Simple family, simple business. Recall the George R. Ruhl & Son company you met in the opening case of this chapter? It is the oldest family-owned firm in Maryland

	Simple Family Complex Business (e.g. TATA)	Complex Family Complex Business (e.g. Hyundai)
Complex **Business** **Simple**	Simple Family Simple Business (e.g. George R. Ruhl & Son)	Complex Family Simple Business (e.g. Robert Mondavi Corp.)
	Simple	Complex

Family

FIGURE 3.3 Four Types of Family Firms

and advertises itself as "America's Oldest Bakery Supply House." Run by the same family for seven generations, it has remained fairly simple by focusing on its core business (though the product line has evolved with changing times) and keeping the transition simple from one generation to another.

Simple family, complex business. These are family businesses where the business is highly diversified, but ownership stays within the same family over the years. Consider the Indian conglomerate TATA, which is famous for its salt-to-software diversification, and yet ownership and control has historically passed from one generation of the family to the next. In such firms, the family structure is quite simple, but the business has become complex, requiring professional managers to run it.

Complex family, simple business. These are firms where many family members are involved in the business, but the family is too large or complicated to keep the various factions together simply by love and trust. Experts tracking the rise and fall of the Robert Mondavi Corp. attribute the decline in the company's fortunes in part to Robert pitting his two sons, Michael and Timothy, against each other on numerous occasions, even publicly criticizing them, and then forcing them to fight for his approval against the backdrop of their shared desire to keep the winery in family hands.

Complex family, complex business. A multifaceted family and a sprawling business, such as is the case for South Korea's Hyundai group. The founder, Jeong Ju Young, started the company as a construction business in 1947 in the aftermath of World War II. Upon his death in 2001, Hyundai was split up among his sons and brothers. The various Hyundai firms were interconnected via a convoluted cross-shareholding pattern. With three generations in the family business, including some deceased descendants replaced by heirs, the family has little common ground and frequently finds itself fighting its battles in court.

As you can imagine, the family and the business becomes more complex as time passes. More generations become part of the family over time, which makes it hard to maintain the familial bonds especially as one moves beyond the third generation. For the firm, success usually brings about diversification in the business, which makes the company more difficult to manage. As the family and the business becomes more complex, there is a higher likelihood of something going wrong. Of course, neither the family nor the business needs to be complex for things to go awry. The troubles at the Redstone family – owners of an American media empire that includes CBS, Viacom, and Paramount Pictures – seem straight from a Hollywood movie. There, the father, Sumner Redstone, and his daughter, Shari Redstone, are publicly feuding for control over National Amusement, the family-holding company that Sumner's father Michael Redstone founded.

An alternative way to think of family businesses is based on combinations of family, ownership, and business development stages: the founder-owned company with

The Redstone clan, father Sumner Redstone and daughter Shari Redstone, are fighting for control of the family firm.

involvement of next generation, family-owned company, complex family enterprise, and publicly owned family corporation. Recall that at the outset of this chapter the family business was defined as one where "multiple members of the same family are involved as major owners or managers." Following such a definition, a firm led by a single person is not a family business until another member of the same family joins the enterprise. The simplest family business, therefore, is one where the founder owns the firm, and other members of the family are involved in the firm as employees (paid or otherwise). Working in the family business is not simply a way to fill their time for non-founder family businesses, but they have a part-time or full-time commitment to the business. Thus, these are **founder-owned family-involved businesses**. One may also consider this as the first stage of a family business.

As the business grows, it may transition from a founder-owned family-involved company to a **family-owned business**. Here, two or more members of the family, most likely across two generations, have ownership in the business. By the time a business reaches this stage, it has developed an entry process for the next generation. Only about 30% of businesses ever make it to this stage. As such, this is a critical stage for family firms that survive and thrive.

The next stage in the evolution of the family business is the **complex family enterprise**. The business is now a multigenerational, cousin-involved company. Unfortunately, such firms are a rarity among family businesses. Some estimate that not more than 5% of all firms in the United States ever reach this stage of development. Firms that make it to this stage have to deal with considerable complexity in all three dimensions of family businesses.

The ultimate stage in the life of a family business is the **public-owned family corporation**. At this stage, the family firm has become so large that it is efficient to let its ownership be in the hands of the public, with the family holding significant stock in the public corporation. Family members serve on the board of the firm and influence the strategy and direction of the firm by their ownership stake and board involvement. Consider Marriott International, founded by J. Willard Marriott and then managed by his son Bill Marriott; the firm went public in 1953. Bill's children worked in the business, with his sons starting out in the kitchen and his daughter at the front desk. As they moved up in the company, they found that running a big company like Marriott International requires meetings, speeches, and other things they did not really like to do. So, after 90 years of being managed by the family (Bill and his father), a nonfamily member was made CEO.

What Do You Think?

Theresa didn't have much money when she was growing up, but she always knew she wanted to start a business that the next generation could call their own. When she was 30, Theresa started a small machine shop that grew at a steady pace for the next 20 years. The business provided well for the family, with all three of Theresa's kids going to college debt-free. Like most self-made people, Theresa had much confidence in her abilities, and until now did not have to share authority with anyone in the company. Everyone either did what Theresa asked them to do, or they were asked to leave. Now, Theresa's two sons Patrick and John want to join her in the business. What advice would you give to Theresa? Is there any advice you would offer John and Patrick? Should there be concerns about three owners from the same family in the business?

The Marriott family is still on the board, but the strategic and operational responsibilities of the firm are now in the hands of someone who is not a family member.

We consider here two ways to think of family firms: (a) based on simplicity or complexity of the family and the business and (b) based on ownership and development stage of the firm. These two typologies should give you a good sense of the rich diversity of family businesses in the country. Of course, many other typologies are possible too, but no one typology will fully capture the rich heterogeneity of family businesses in society.

> **KEY TAKEAWAY**
>
> There are many different types of family firms.

Comprehension Check

1. Explain the two-dimensional typology of family business based on the simplicity (or complexity) of families and businesses.
2. What is a publicly owned family corporation?
3. What is a founder-owned family-involved business?

Module 3.4 Succession Planning in Family Business

A common problem in many family firms is succession planning, either because the founder is reluctant to accept the fact that one day he or she will need to step down, or because there is too much trust within the family to address this issue when it becomes necessary. The absence of sound succession planning means that few family businesses are passed down to the next generation. Some estimates suggest that only 30% of successful businesses (defined as those that survive after five years of operation) are transferred to the next generation. The situation of Donley's Wild West Town is quite typical of family firms. Located 60 miles northwest of Chicago, Donley's is a popular theme-park owned by an octogenarian couple Larry and Helene Donley who have run the place for more than 40 years. Their sons, Randy and Mike, are in their early 60s and have helped manage the park, but are keen to pursue other opportunities. The three Donley grandchildren grew up playing cowboy games at the 23-acre amusement park, and are already living their own lives elsewhere. Similar family-owned theme parks once dotted the country, benefiting from Americans taking their vacations after the opening of the Interstate

System of highways. Most closed over the years. The Donleys have also been trying to find a buyer, one that would not be looking to close the theme park to use the land in other ways. None of the younger generations of the Donleys sees their future in the theme park.

Even when a family firm successfully transitions from the first generation to the second, subsequent transitions can be challenging. The odds of successful transition worsen in the subsequent generations: about 12% from the second to the third generation and about 4% from the third to the fourth generation. Indeed, family businesses worldwide are said to be afflicted with the **three-generation syndrome**. In North America, the common adage on the subject is "from shirtsleeves to shirtsleeves in three generations." Other countries have similar popular sayings: *Della Stalle a la stella a la stalle* (meaning, from the stable to stars and back to the stable) in Italy, *Padre bodeguero, hijo caballero, nieto pordiosero* (or, father-merchant, son-gentleman, grandson-beggar) in the Spanish-speaking world, and *Pai rico, filho nobre, neto pobre* (or, rich father, noble son, and poor grandson) in Portuguese. The Chinese expression *Fu bu guo san dai* and the Indian adage *Dada banaye, beta badhaye, pota bigaadey* are unequivocal about the tragedy that befalls the third generation.

What Do You Think?

Claude Cartier grew up in money. His father Louis Cartier headed the family firm of Cartier, and was its creative heart. The Cartier family had once been poor, struggling to make ends meet, but by the time Claude came of age, the family was well known throughout the world for their exquisite jewelry. Unfortunately, Louis's love for the business and keen eye for design did not pass on to his son Claude, who was more interested in the good life that came with the wealth and status of his family. After the death of his father, Claude sold the flagship Cartier store in Paris, and exited the family business. Many blame Claude Cartier for the ultimate demise of the famed family firm his great-grandfather had started. Do you think Claude made the right decision in selling the family firm?

Some experts use the term **corporeuthanasia** to refer to a business owner's act of unwittingly killing off the business he or she loves by failing to provide in their lifetime for a viable organization with clear continuity. Some businesses are never intended to be passed on. The dry cleaning business in your town may simply be a place for the owner's to earn enough money to provide for their family and send their kids to an ivy-league college. Other businesses are to be passed on to the next generation, but the owner does not plan well. Leon Danco, president and founding director of The Center for Family Business in Cleveland, Ohio, observes:

> too often the owner who had the ability, vision, and guts to build his business from nothing, does not have the courage to face the problems of the future, then his banker and attorney will do it for him on the way back from his funeral, four cars back from the flowers.

There are five major reasons why succession has been problematic for many family firms:

1. Owner is so occupied with running their firms that they neglect to plan their own exit.
2. Confidence in the offspring(s) is lacking.
3. Business perpetuity is not seen as an important concern at an early stage.
4. Facing one's own mortality is difficult.
5. The business is run like a monarchy, the oldest son is the next leader president and succeeding sons (or sons-in-law) assume roles based on order of birth. In case you are wondering about the daughter(s), we will discuss them later in this chapter.

Interactive Exercise

Imagine your family had a successful business that was 150 years old and had been through six generations. How would your growing-up years have been different? Would you have wanted to join the family business, working with your parents, siblings, and cousins? Would it matter what business your family was in? Be prepared to share your responses with the class.

Despite the succession problems that plague family businesses around the world, there are also those family firms that manage to survive and thrive hundreds of years (such as the one profiled in the opening case of this chapter). The Tercentenarian Club in Britain is the most exclusive private organization in the world, as membership is open only to companies that have survived more than 300 years and are still owned by the same family that started them. It has only a dozen members. The membership of the France-based Les Henokiens (or, the Henokiens Associations) is based on company longevity (firms should be at least 200 years old), permanence (founding family must be owner or majority shareholder and one member of the family must still manage the company or be a member of the board), and financial health (the company should be in good financial shape). The Association currently has 49 members, with 15 French, 12 Italian, 9 Japanese, 4 German, 3 Swiss, 2 Dutch, 2 Belgian, 1 Austrian, and 1 English family firm.

> ### KEY TAKEAWAY
>
> Succession is the biggest challenge faced by family firms. For most family firms, it is never too early to start thinking about succession.

The book *Centuries of Success* discusses 20 enduring family businesses from around the world. As mentioned earlier in this chapter, the oldest of the family business in the world is from Japan: The Kongo Gumi founded in 578 AD working in the temple restoration business (although it ceased independent operations in 2006). The tradition of family businesses – *dozoku geisha* in Japanese – is an ancient one in Japan. The oldest European business in the book is Marchesi Antinori, an Italian winery, founded in 1385 and currently under the 25th generation of the family. The oldest American family business discussed in the book is Avedis Zildjian Company, a cymbal manufacturer that passed across the Atlantic Ocean from Constantinople to Massachusetts in the early 1900s and is now under the ownership of the 13th generation. Given the succession problems discussed earlier, how is it that some firms are able to survive for so long? The Wirsching winery of Germany, for example, has been in business since 1630.

3.4.1 Enduring Family Firms

Three core principles characterize enduring family businesses: (1) family unity, (2) commitment to continue the legacy, and (3) products that cater to basic human needs. Given the central role of the family in family firms, it is no surprise that **family unity** is a bedrock principle for those that want the business to survive for the long term. There is respect for the family's traditions and values in such family firms. Harmony is maintained in the family through judicious allocation of resources. While it is expected that there will be some "bad apples" and "sour grapes" in the family, especially when one considers the long time span, they are encouraged to seek opportunities elsewhere rather than contaminate the family values and traditions.

Succession Tips for Family Firms

The Family Business Institute considers succession planning as being "the toughest and most critical challenge" many family firms face. While there is no easy solution to the succession problems, experts do offer some suggestions for families struggling with figuring out how to pass on the business in a way that enhances the company's longevity.

Watch the video online at: https://www.wsj.com/video/family-business-succession-tips/1C9B5391-2D3A-4B20-89E5-9928410D63E9.html

When asked why they started the business, many founders responded that they wanted to create something that they could pass onto the next generation. Yet, as evident from the low rates of successful intergenerational transfers, it seems few founders truly have the commitment to *continue the legacy*. Enduring family firms show a strong commitment to continuing the business over the next generation, involving young family members in the business at an early age. Adam Pitel, chief executive of Magna-Power Electronics Inc., in Flemington, NJ, recalls being involved, from a young age, in nightly dinner conversations with his parents about the day's achievements and struggles – whether it was a new contract, a nonpaying customer, challenges with a vendor, or new prospects for business growth.

As much as possible, the values and traditions of the family are instilled in the younger generations, without forcing them. A study of multigenerational wineries in Europe found that the "entrepreneurial legacy" was passed down through the generations: stories about the family's achievements and how it survived tough times, such as the great-great-great-great-grandfather who went on horse to Paris to repurchase the family winery at auction. Stories of the family's past experiences overcoming natural disasters, theft, financial hardship, revolution, and war are repeatedly shared at family gatherings.

As the business makes successful transitions across generations, each new generation becomes increasingly responsible for maintaining the continuity. No one wants to be the one responsible for bringing down the dynasty! When the Bingham family sold the *Louisville Courier-Journal* to the Gannett Company, each member of the third generation went off on his or her own. Years later, several fourth-generation members openly regretted the decision to sell the firm and the loss of identity and legacy that it represented for them.

Enduring family businesses tend to offer products and services that satisfy basic human needs or are essential for life, such as food, clothing, and shelter. Perhaps this is because, even as consumer tastes and product trends evolve over time, the need for life's essentials never really goes away (although it may change with time). Consider Confetti

Mario Pelino, a small Italian confetti manufacturer with annual sales of only $4 million, founded in 1783. They make confetti for weddings, graduations, anniversaries, and engagements, among other life celebrations. While the exact taste, shape, and form of their offerings can certainly be expected to change, there will always be demand for their basic products as long as people feel the need to celebrate life events.

3.4.2 Best Practices for Family Firms

There are several practices that are essential for the longevity of family businesses: (a) **conflict resolution**; (b) business first, family second; (c) strong obligation to customers, employees, and communities; and (d) planning for the future. Around the world, one can find countless examples of family businesses that met their demise when family members were at war with one another. Family businesses survive longer when they adopt intentional practices to avoid or resolve conflicts: direct communication, regular meetings, and mediation involving influential unbiased outsiders.

It is never easy to place the business before the family, especially as emotional ties between parents, siblings, and other relatives loom large for most people. Yet, when the challenges and problems of the family clash with the needs of the business, family firms that want to survive for the long term need to prioritize the business over the family. Failure to do so often results in destroying both the family and the business. When Susan Groth, whose family owns Groth Vineyards & Winery in Napa Valley, decided that she wanted to leave her post-college hospitality jobs to come back to the family firm, she was told to first get a job with a local distributor to learn the sales side of the business as she had no experience in the wine industry. After working at the distributor for five years, Susan was able to join the family firm, where she now reports to her parents who are currently managing the business.

Family firms that survive over generations tend to be closely associated with the local community. Not only employees but also suppliers and customers come from the community where the firm is located. Family businesses distinguish themselves by responding favorably to the needs of their communities and stakeholders.

For a family business to survive over the long term, it is essential to keep an eye on future contingencies related to the family and to the business. As the family and the business grow, such planning is even more necessary to ensure there is buy-in from all the important constituents. Unfortunately, many family firms fail to plan for succession in time, which ultimately leads to the demise of the business.

What Do You Think?

In his early 60s now, Shane found himself at a crossroad: He started Max Electricals when he was in his 30s and had grown the company to impressive heights. It was now the largest dealer in the United States for GE motors and Otis elevators. It also took on turnkey projects for local and state governments. Both his kids, son Jason and daughter Judy, had joined the business about 10 years earlier. Both were hardworking, had finished their engineering degrees, worked overseas for a year after graduation, and gained at least two years of work experience in leading American firms before joining the Max group.

Shane's lawyer was now advising him to decide on a succession plan. One option was to divide the business equally between Jason and Judy, giving them about 50% of the business each. Another option was to give 100% of the business to one, so that the business would not be broken up. But, how would he decide who should get the business? Another option was to sell the business to a corporate buyer and give Jason and Judy shares from what he could make by selling the company. What should Shane do? What other options does he have? What are the pros and cons that Shane should weigh?

3.4.3 Next-Generation Challenge

For a family firm to successfully transition to the next generation, several pieces need to fall in place. Many companies are sold to outsiders either because there are no heirs or because the available children made other career decisions. Some children are not interested in their parent's business. Some children have the interest, but lack the aptitude. Some are not well motivated. Two things need to fall in place for succession to go smoothly.

First, the incumbent generation should have the interest and foresight to pass on the business. While many entrepreneurs believe they want to create a business for the next generation, this is easier said than done. Consider the divergent fortune of the Bingham family of *Louisville Courier-Journal* and the Blethens of *The Seattle Times*. Both firms were getting ready to transition to the next generation around the same time, from the first to the second generation for the Binghams and the fifth to the sixth generation for the Blethens. Barry Bingham Sr. seemed to lack confidence in his son and heir, and relationships in the Bingham family were characterized by emotional distance and distrust. Among the Blethens, on the other hand, Frank Blethen emphasized the need to appreciate the extended value over the individual or family branch and encouraged the family members involved in the business to assume stewardship responsibility.

Second, the next generation must have the interest and ability to manage the business. How does one steer the next generation to be interested in the family business and have the ability to manage it well? Passing along the family history, getting the youngsters involved early in the business, emphasizing quality education and practical training, and communicating clearly about the future of the business. Seems simple? Consider the case of a successful business owner who informed his sons a few years before he intended to retire that it was time for them to start thinking about joining the family construction business. Neither son, who had their own careers by that point, wanted it – which surprised their father, who had made a fortune from nothing. The father, who was in his 70s, will probably need to continue working, which was never his intent. After he retires, the business will probably be sold or liquidated. Had he spoken to his sons when they were still in college and contemplating their career path, perhaps things may have turned out differently. Better still, maybe he could have involved his sons in the business when they were still teenagers, so they had a deeper, stronger connection with the business their father founded. Table 3.1 summarizes some best practices for parents who want to pass on the family business to the next generation.

TABLE 3.1

Best Practices for Family Business Succession

Dos	Don'ts
Involve children in the business as they grow up.	Let the family business dictate your young child's life.
Make joining the business optional (gently encouraging them).	Put your children in roles they aren't well suited for.
Let your children help determine what roles might be right for them.	Criticize the business for limiting your life choices.
Pass along your family history, highlighting the high points and learning from the low points.	Lack pride in their ancestors' achievements or confidence in the next generation's capabilities.
Encourage education that is relevant to the business, and emphasize practical learning.	Tell children that taking over the business is an "obligation" they have.
Multiple generations learn from each other.	Only one-direction learning from parent to children. Parents know all.

Even when the succession occurs smoothly, it is possible that the successor is not able to manage the firm effectively. Researchers have identified three forms of ineffective succession:

1. *Conservative.* The parents have exited the business and are no longer involved in decision-making. Yet, the parental shadow remains, and the firm and its decision-making are locked in the past, unable to accommodate the changing times.
2. *Rebellious.* The next generation rebels against the established ways of doing business. Perhaps an overreaction to the previous generation's control of the firm, the next generation wants to wipe the slate clean. In ignoring the legacy and tradition that has helped the firm succeed so far, there is a risk of the "secret of success" is destroyed or discarded.
3. *Wavering.* The next generation is unsure of what to do and paralyzed by indecisiveness. As a result, the firm is 'lost at sea' and is unable to respond to competitive conditions.

For a firm to thrive when transitioning from one generation to next, family firms will have to surmount these challenges without causing a rift in the family or a disruption in the business. The company Alberto-Culver, best known for its Alberto VO5 hair conditioner, was founded by Leonard Lavin. His daughter, Carol, joined the business after graduating from college, working in the consumer division, where she dreamed up and developed blockbuster products such as Static Guard fabric spray and Mrs. Dash seasoning. Despite the successes, her father was reluctant to turn over the reins of the company. Carol remembers that his desire to maintain tight control was extremely frustrating. "It was impossible . . . he would call me 14 times in a given day," she shares.

3.4.4 Role of Offspring Gender

In family businesses, succession has historically been biased by gender. Daughters have almost always been excluded from taking over the business. In her book on women in family business, *From the Other Side of the Bed*, Katy Danco writes that the idea that a daughter could inherit and run a family company – other than a boutique or some other frilly business – has seldom been entertained by business owners. Consider the owners of one successful family-run business who simply decided that their sons were going to inherit the company. The parents were well-meaning and intended to financially remunerate their daughter. They assumed the daughter was not interested in being involved in the business. When the daughter found out after the parents had transferred the business to the sons, the family relationships were "seriously fractured" and took a long time to be repaired.

When there are no sons, many families chose the son-in-law as a potential heir for the business. Noting that wealthy families who have only daughters frequently look for suitable sons-in-law to run their businesses, feminist Gloria Steinem observed that family firm "is like hemophilia – it passes through women and men get it." Son-in-law succession is quite common in Japan, where it is referred to as **mukoyōshi**. The history of Japanese businesses, from the automobile company Suzuki to the Tofu-maker Sagamiya Foods, is replete with succession through sons-in-law. The practice is so commonplace in Japan that some business families seek professional help to identify potential sons-in-law interested in taking over the business someday. Such an arrangement is "like mergers and acquisitions," believes Chieko Date, a professional matchmaker who runs the Tokyo-based Mukoyoshi Support Centre, which introduces business families to potential son-in-law candidates.

Until about two decades ago, there was virtually zero preference for women for succession in family business. This aversion has now begun to change. Walter Kuemmerle, president of Boston-based Kuemmerle Research Group, runs annual meetings for young executives in family businesses. He shares that he sees "more women interested and more older generations receptive to the idea of the best person taking over, rather than

Father, Daughter, Son Together in Business: Red Apple

John Catsimatidis, head of the Red Apple Group, a privately owned company of diverse businesses, son, John Jr., and daughter, Andrea, talk candidly about working together in the family business.

Watch the video online at: https://www.youtube.com/watch?v=I-gCLZ5tw24

having a gender bias." Frank Venegas Jr. has both a daughter, Linzie, and a son, Jesse, working at the Ideal Group, a Detroit manufacturing and construction services company that now has four divisions and employs hundreds of workers. Linzie is vice president for marketing, finance, and human resources, while Jesse runs one of the divisions. Frank has not yet decided who will lead the company after him, believing that it could be either of them.

Interactive Exercise

Identify three businesses that are proudly "& Daughter". What industry are they in? Be prepared to share your findings with the class.

Just as "& Son" businesses have been commonplace in history, there are now also a growing number of "& Daughter" firms. Some examples include the trucking company G.L. Williams & Daughter in South Carolina and the window-design firm of Henderson & Daughter in Washington, D.C. Then, there are also family firms where there are no sons in the next generation, only daughters. Sweet Potato Sensations is a 15-employee bakery in Detroit founded by Jeff and Cassandra Thomas. Their daughters – Jennifer and Espy – worked in the bakery as children, lugging potatoes and smelling like pie. Both sisters thought they would pursue other challenges, until they felt drawn back to the family business. Now the sisters work in the family business, working on ways to expand it and help their parents step back from day-to-day work. "Even though it's a challenge working with my parents every day, I like it," Espy Thomas says. "I feel like our parents have tried to create a legacy for us. I am passionate about that legacy. I don't want to see what they created just go away."

Julie Smolyansky was 27 when she took over as CEO of her family's Lifeway Foods Inc. after her father died suddenly. She has been working for the kefir yogurt maker for years, but it was her father's senior advisers who presented the biggest obstacles to her ascension. Leah Klein is part of Chicago-based Klein Tools, which has been in her family since 1857. "I think a lot of women think it's a barrier if it's a male-dominated business, but I think it's more about them," said Klein, who is among the sixth generation working at her company. "If a woman is interested, they have to make their choices about what they want to do for their life."

What Do You Think?

Dating back to 1515, butchers R. J. Balson & Son, based in Bridport, Dorset, is Britain's oldest family firm, selling everything from meat and poultry to game. Richard Balson is the 26th-generation owner of the family at the helm of a business that was founded only 23 years after Christopher Columbus reached the New World. "I see myself as the current custodian holding the fort at the moment, until either my son or his sons or my nephew or somebody else takes the reins," he says. Richard's son works in London, but his daughter sometimes helps out her father in the business. Richard also has several nieces who live nearby and have shown an interest in the business. What do you think are the pros and cons of handing over the 500+ years old business to his daughter or nieces?

The Ringling Bros. and Barnum & Bailey Circus is not only an American pastime, it is also a family business that has successfully transitioned to the next generation of only daughters. Most people know Feld Entertainment as the Florida company that produces the Ringling Bros. and Barnum & Bailey Circus and Disney On Ice. Feld also produces as many as 5000 other performances a year, including Disney Live, Monster Jam, Marvel Universe Live, and Feld Motor Sports. Kenneth Feld took over the company after his father died. As he got closer to retirement, his three daughters – Nicole, Alana, and Juliette – were finding their place in Feld Entertainment. Feld had strict rules about how and when his daughters could join the company. He required them to finish college and work elsewhere first, believing that working elsewhere would give them a better understanding of how to work with people. "I think a lot of the obstacles I faced were the result of not having work experience. People who were there before I was had no reason to respect me other than my name," he says. Nicole says she, her sisters, and her father see each other often, call regularly to update each other. "Each of us has a different perspective on situations, but we are all clear on what is best for the company," she says. "It's nice to feel like we're in it together. Each of us understands that we all live the risks and the rewards."

Like with everything else, it is easy to attribute the longevity of some family businesses to luck. Many family themselves attribute their success to luck. Consider William Clark & Sons, the oldest family-owned linen company in the world, founded in 1736. Wallace Clark is fond of saying when speaking of the family firm, "I am a great believer in luck. We undervalue the importance of luck in anything." And yet, it is helpful to remember that some men and women seem to always be luckier than others.

What Do You Think?

John Marcus is frustrated with his seven brothers and sisters. Their family firm Marcus Supply had saved enough cash for a bold acquisition that John saw as a strategic imperative for the company, but his siblings vetoed the acquisition and voted dividends for themselves. Marcus Supply, a machine tool manufacturer, has annual revenues of about $50 million and is owned equally by the Marcus siblings. John became president after his Dad suddenly died 10 years earlier, and has done a commendable job managing the firm. He even organized an outside board of directors to provide strategic oversight and advice. All his siblings have good careers outside the company. While they are glad to have John in charge at the company where sales have quadrupled over the past decade, some of them think he is overpaid. The siblings meet regularly to share their thoughts and ideas, and the next family council meeting is coming up soon. John finds himself dealing with siblings who do not want to hear that the world around Marcus Supply is changing. He knows he needs to do something, but he is not sure what his options are. Can you help John identify his options?

Comprehension Check

1. Explain the three-generation syndrome.
2. What core principles characterize enduring family businesses?
3. Why are so many family businesses poor at succession planning?

Summary

Mars, Cargill, Walmart. And, TATA, BMW, and Honda. This chapter focuses on businesses owned by the families that started them. It is also about the families that own successful businesses that survived over the years. Some of the best-known names in the world are family firms, and so are countless other small businesses that are also family owned. As one may expect, the term *family business* encompasses firms of different sizes and forms. Some industries seem to be more conducive to family firms than others, such as wineries and breweries. Family businesses also seem to be more common in specialty trades, such as glass blowing and fireworks, passing the business down through the generations. However, only a very small percentage of new firms created each year actually manage to survive the transition across generations. Succession planning is therefore one of the most important, albeit underappreciated, facets of family businesses.

Live Exercise

"We are very proud of you," your parents told you when they came to see you get the best student award from the college. You've been looking forward to your parents' visit, not only because of the award you were getting but also because you wanted to share with them about the job offers you have. You were also hoping to introduce them to someone special you had met in college. "And guess, who's here with us?" your father announces. That's when you see that your parents didn't come alone. With them is their friend Johnny Gold, who you've met before, but you weren't expecting to see him there. At dinner that evening, you learn why Johnny came with them for the visit. "Remember my business idea I told you about?" Johnny asks. Of course, you remember the idea: a device to keep soap from slipping out of one's hands. "Well, my son is in marketing and my daughter is an engineer. I am thinking perhaps they can join me in this business. If all three of us are in this together, we get to see each other often and then they can take over the business someday." Last time you talked to Johnny, he had mentioned this idea that seemed a little crazy to you. This time he tells you he wants to involve his grown-up children with him. "What do you think of Johnny's idea?" your father asks you. This is going to be a long dinner, you think as you dig into the cheese board your mother ordered as an appetizer for the table.

World of Books

Interested in reading more about family firms? Take a look at the following books:

Centuries of Success by William T. O'Hara
Lessons from Century Club Companies by Vicki Tenhaken

In the Movies

Many family businesses face a typical rich-person's problem: Their success and wealth produce a sense of entitlement in younger generations. The next generation does not understand the values that made the business successful in the first place, resulting in mean reversion across generations. The movie *Christmas Inheritance* is the story of spoiled heiress Ellen Langford who needs to prove that she's capable of running the toy business her father started. The father is rightly worried about the company's future when it passes to his daughter living the fast life.

Things to Remember

LO 3.1   Explain what a family business is
- A family business happens when the family and business come together.
- Family business is made of up of three independent, yet overlapping systems: family, business, and ownership.
- People related by blood, marriage, or adoption have strategic influence in a family business.
- There is a strong possibility or dream of business continuity across generations in a family business.

LO 3.2   Identify the advantages and disadvantages of joining a family business
- The specialness of family businesses comes with both positive and negative consequences.
- The high level of personal commitment that a family business fosters is almost impossible to find in a nonfamily business.
- Family members who work for their business often wear several different hats and take on tasks outside of the formal job description (if there is one) to ensure that work gets done.
- Often family businesses do not have adequate checks-and-balances to keep the whims and fancies of the leader in check.
- No firm and no family are completely free from conflict, but add in familial rivalries, long histories, and relationship issues, and the family business becomes a fertile ground for conflict.

LO 3.3   Distinguish between different types of family firms
- There is a wide variety of family businesses in the United States as well as worldwide. Attempts to classify family businesses into a few distinct types get criticized for ignoring the rich heterogeneity that makes family firms unique.
- A popular typology of family businesses seeks to understand them on two dimensions: simplicity versus complexity of the family and the business. Of course, neither the family nor the business needs to be complex for things to go awry.
- An alternative way to think of family businesses is based on combinations of family, ownership, and business development stages.
- The founder-owned family-involved business is the first stage of a family firm.

LO 3.4   Describe succession planning in family firms
- A common problem in many family firms is succession planning.
- The absence of sound succession planning means that few family businesses are passed down to the next generation.
- Despite the succession problems that plague family businesses around the world, there are also those family firms that manage to survive and thrive hundreds of years.
- There are three core principles that characterize enduring family businesses: (a) family unity, (b) commitment to continue the legacy, and (c) products that cater to basic human needs.
- Family businesses survive longer when they adopt intentional practices to avoid or resolve conflicts.

- It is never easy to place the business before the family, especially as emotional ties between parents, siblings, and other relatives loom large for most people.
- Family business succession has historically been through male heirs, but increasingly many families are also considering female heirs for succession.

Key Terms

family business	simple family, simple business	founder-owned family-involved firm	family unity
lone founder firms			conflict resolution
family firms	simple family, complex business	family-owned business	business first, family second
business continuity		complex family enterprise	
family legacy	complex family, simple business	public-owned family corporation	mukoyōshi
family conflict			
nepotism	complex family, complex business	three-generation syndrome	
succession planning		corporeuthanasia	

Experiential Exercise

This exercise is designed for students working in groups of two or three. Use of the Internet (via laptops or hand-held devices like the iPad or smartphone) during the exercise is necessary.

The oldest surviving family business in the world was Japan-based Kongo Gumi, founded in 578 AD, and briefly discussed in the text. In 2006, when the company was in its 40th generation, the business was sold to a large corporation. The oldest-surviving family business in the world was now gone. Search the Web for information on what helped the business last 14 centuries, and also what finally caused the business to cease operations.

1. Do you think there were some special practices that allowed the business to survive for 40 generations in the same family?

2. Do you think the demise of the business was inevitable or avoidable?

3. Does Masakazu Kongo, the 40th generation scion of the Kongo Group, has a responsibility for the company's demise under his watch?

4. Imagine you were the 41st generation of the Kongo Group. How would you react to the news that your parents were considering the sale of the family firm?

5. Based on your research and class discussion, what advice would you give to Masakazu Kongo when he was still considering the future of the company?

CHAPTER 4

Franchising for Small Firms

For some, the structure that franchising offers is a godsend. Someone else has blazed a trail that you can now follow.

CHRIS MYERS

LEARNING OBJECTIVES

This chapter will help you to:

LO 4.1 Explain the meaning and history of franchising

LO 4.2 Identify the advantages and disadvantages in franchising

LO 4.3 Distinguish between different types of franchises

LO 4.4 Decide whether franchising is a good option for you

4.0 Introduction

Franchising is an attractive means of starting and operating a small business in many countries, including the United States. Walk through any college town in the country, and you will see several successful franchises around you, such as McDonald's, Great Clips, Dairy Queen, and Orange Theory, to name a few. Worldwide, the largest franchisor in terms of number of locations is 7-Eleven, the convenience store chain founded in 1946 in Dallas, TX. The largest franchisor globally in revenue is McDonald's, the fast-food giant started in 1940 in San Bernardino. Ever heard the expression "as American as apple pie"? While apple pie may not be truly American (apples are native to Asia and pies are European in origin), franchising is a truly American invention. It is, you might say, even more American than the apple pie.

This chapter introduces you to franchising, providing the basic concepts and principles related to franchising. Several examples and real-life cases are presented to illustrate the basic ideas underlying franchising. It is useful to keep in mind that many colleges and universities offer majors and certificate programs in franchising, so there is much more to learn about franchising than can be presented in just one chapter. Nevertheless, the material presented in this chapter should provide you with a good foundation to learn more about franchising. Of course, nothing in this chapter should be taken as an offer to sell, or the solicitation of an offer to buy a franchise. The information presented in this chapter is solely for educational purposes (as we will see later, such disclaimers are widespread in franchising).

SPOTLIGHT | Franchising Her Way to Success

When Susan Smith heard that she had been selected as the Franchisee of the Year by Fish Window Cleaning, she could not believe it. She had definitely worked hard to grow the business and it had succeeded beyond anyone's expectations. Yet, to be considered the top performer among the company's more than 200 franchisees nation-wide was an honor she had not expected.

Founded in Tampa (Florida), Fish Window Cleaning ranks among *Entrepreneur* magazine's Top 500 franchises nationwide. FISH calls itself "the world's largest window cleaning company." Unlike many other franchise systems, FISH does not accept part-time franchisees, requiring its owners to be full-time in the business (Monday–Friday during normal business hours only, no nights or weekends or holidays). The company's CEO says, "If anyone wants to be a window cleaner, they don't need a franchise. FISH only awards franchises to candidates who want to be business owners and benefit from our 40+ years of knowledge and be a part of niche, recession-resistant market with fragmented competition and unlimited potential."

When Doug Smith was downsized from his corporate job, he decided to use the severance money to start a FISH franchise in Traverse City, MI. Doug and his wife Susan together signed the franchise contract with FISH, and Susan helped out in the office during the early days before she stepped back to spend time with the family. Doug and Susan used to joke that if anything were to happen, she wouldn't even know "how to print out the next week's work orders." Things were going well for their small franchisee company, when Doug had a fatal heart attack on his way to meet a cleaning team. The business was still young, so there was little time to grieve. Customers' orders needed to be completed and cleaning crews needed work and pay. After the funeral, a FISH executive helped Susan for about a week and the FISH district manager from Grand Rapids, MI, would drive over to provide hands-on help. Susan recalls that "because the business was a franchise, lots of systems were in place and I could call headquarters with all my questions."

Soon, and by investing much time and effort, Susan got a good handle on the business. Within a

FISH is the world's largest window cleaning franchise.

(continued)

few years, Susan was recognized by FISH not just for the performance of her franchisee but also her work guiding and advising prospective franchisees. The franchise that Susan and Doug had started together became one of the top performers for FISH under Susan's leadership, serving both residential and commercial customers.

Discussion Questions

1. What do you think the Smiths got from joining a franchise business?

2. Why do you think FISH does not accept part-time franchisees?

3. Do window cleaners need a franchise?

Module 4.1 Meaning and History of Franchising

What is franchising? In simple terms, **franchising** is a legal agreement that allows one business to be operated using the name and procedures of another business that already exists. The company that offers the agreement is a **franchisor** (the parent company of the product, service, or method) and the company that accepts the agreement is a **franchisee** (a business that pays fees and royalties for exclusive rights to local distribution of the product or service). Franchising allows the franchisor to sell the benefits of its expertise, systems, and reputation to the franchisee in exchange for payment. In franchising, franchisors are able to expand by leveraging the capital and resources of franchisees. Academic articles usually define franchising as a business system that enables one firm (the franchisor) to sell the right to market specific goods and services under its brand name and using its business practices to a second firm (the franchisee).

Four elements need to be in place for an agreement to be considered franchising:

1. It should allow the franchisee to use a brand name, trademark, logo, and/or other commercial symbols legally owned by the franchisor.
2. It should provide the franchisee the legal right to engage in the business of offering, selling, or distributing goods or services.
3. It should allow the franchisee to engage in the business using a marketing plan or system offered by the franchisor.
4. It requires the franchisee to pay a fee (or royalty) for the right to do business.

Unless all four of these elements are in place, it is not really franchising. This is important to remember because the term *franchising* is sometimes used loosely in media and everyday language.

KEY TAKEAWAY

Even though the term franchising is used loosely in popular language, it has a specific legal meaning that is important to understand.

Many franchises have a hefty price tag. To open a McDonalds or Taco Bell, for example, one has to have at least $750,000 in liquid assets. To open a KFC restaurant, one's net worth has to be at least $1.5 million. The IFA estimates average initial franchise investment to be around $250,000, excluding real estate, and average royalty fees paid by franchisees range from 3 to 6% of monthly gross sales.

TABLE 4.1

Low-cost Franchising Options

Franchise name	Service offered	Startup cost	Number of US locations
Dream Vacations	Vacation travel	$9,800	1200+
Complete Wedding + Events	Wedding and event solutions	$10,000	~200
Showhomes Home Staging	Staged houses for sale	$10,000	50+
TSS Photography	School and team photos	$10,500	175+
Cruise Planners	Vacation planning	$10,995	2500+
Motto Mortgage	Mortgage shopping	$12,500	100+
Help U-Sell Real Estate	Flat fee real-estate sales	$15,000	100+
Rhea Lana's	Children consignment clothing	$15,000	~90
United Country Real Estate	Lifestyle real estate	$15,000	400+

Source: Data from 10 low-cost franchises you can start with $15,000 or less and reap a six-figure salary, SMALL BUSINESS PLAYBOOK; 21 September 2019. © 2020 CNBC LLC

Yet, there are also other franchise choices that cost a lot less to start. Franchise Business Review is a leading market research firm that is like the "Consumer Reports" for the franchise industry. It identified several low-cost franchises that let you get started for $15,000 or less in cash (see Table 4.1). "Many people think you need hundreds of thousands of dollars to buy a franchise business, but the reality is that there are some great low-cost franchises that can provide a very high return on your investment in the long run," shares Eric Stites, CEO and managing director of Franchise Business Review.

Franchising: Expert Speak

Do you understand what franchising is? Hossein Kasmai, a successful franchisor, explains what franchising means to him. Kasmai now consults companies on how to expand through franchising. You can read more about him at https://franchisecreator.com/about-us.

Watch the video online at: https://www.youtube.com/watch?v=p9BcY3ctyLY

Cost is a major factor for many people interested in getting into franchising. After a 20-year career as a sales manager for an electric tool company, Bob Caramusa of Chicago was looking for a low-cost franchise option when he signed up with the cleaning-service company Image One as a way to have his own business and to make some extra money. For $15,000, Caramusa says, he bought "a complete turnkey business," which included equipment, training, ongoing technical support, and two accounts to get started. "The financial risk was pretty minimal, so I knew I could make my money back even if I didn't stay with the business," he says. Caramusa did stay, quitting his corporate job after a few years to work full-time at Image One. The business now books annual revenues of about $1 million. Caramusa now wishes: "I would have done this [become part of a franchise] the day I graduated from college."

Many franchises involve businesses that can be started from home. The appeal of these businesses, which offer everything from cleaning services to baby-sitting, is their low cost as one does not need to spend on commercial office space. Stephanie Harbour, a former investment banker in New York, bought into Mom Corps, a home-based franchise that helps companies fill nontraditional jobs with professionals, many of them mothers, who seek more flexible schedules. Joining the Mom Corps staffing service business costs about $25,000. SeekingSitters, a Tulsa, OK, baby-sitting chain, says people can buy into the system for less than $45,000. Table 4.2 shows how pervasive home-based franchises are in different sectors.

Working from home usually, but not always, goes hand in hand with online franchising where the business operates primarily in cyberspace. It may provide services

Interactive Exercise

Your sister wants to be part of the Two Maids franchise system (www.twomaidsfranchise.com), which advertises itself as "the most talked about maid service in America." She has asked for your help in deciding if this is the right path for her. What questions should you ask her to help her make the decision?

TABLE **4.2**

Sweet Home Franchises

Your Home, Their Plan

A look at which types of businesses have the most home-based franchisees, and the number of home-based brands in various industries.

SECTOR	FRANCHISE UNITS	INDUSTRY	NO. OF BRANDS
Commercial/residential cleaning	**24,860**	Maintenance services	**197**
Tax services	**14,680**	Business-related	**165**
Carpet/upholstery cleaning	**6,212**	Building/construction	**94**
Financial services	**6,189**	Services-general	**62**
Maid services	**3,128**	Decorating/home design	**58**
Property-inspection services	**1,819**	Real estate	**20**
Plumbing/electric services	**1,751**	Child-related	**18**
Restoration products/services	**1,389**	Party-related goods/services	**17**
Window treatments	**1,344**	Computer products/services	**13**
Exterior improvements	**1,316**	Health/fitness	**10**
Source: FRANdata		Pet-related products/services	**4**
		Automotive	**2**

Source: Adapted from The ins and outs of home-based franchises, *The Wall Street Journal*

physically, but it can be run from anywhere through its presence online. Some prominent companies that operate online franchise systems are CMIT Solutions (information technology services for small businesses), WSI (Internet marketing), and ActionCOACH (business advising services). Figure 4.1 presents the advantages and disadvantages of participating in an online franchise system.

ActionCOACH claims to be the world's #1 business coaching franchise. Its franchisees provide business coaching, leadership training, and executive development. It promises low-cost startup and the freedom to work from anywhere. Founder Brad Sugars started ActionCOACH in Australia and built it into a successful international company through franchising. You can learn more about ActionCOACH and its franchising model by watching their promotional video (https://www.youtube.com/watch?v=4fIGgD8TyYA).

4.1.1 Historical Evolution

The word *franchise* comes from the Middle French word *franchir*, meaning "to be free." The French term *Francis* means bestowing rights or power on a peasant (or serf). The English term *enfranchise* refers to empowering people with no rights. The predecessor of the word *royalties* is "Royal Tithes," which originated from the practice of certain Englishmen receiving a share of the land fees paid by peasants to nobility. The term *franchising* is therefore of Anglo-French origin and signifies freedom.

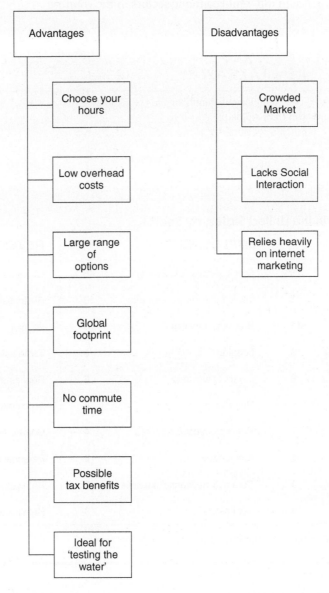

FIGURE 4.1 Pros and Cons of Online Franchising

As is the case with most business practices, it is difficult to definitely identify the origins of franchising. Despite what you may have heard, McDonald's was not the first franchisor in the United States. The credit for the first use of franchising as a business practice is usually given to Isaac Singer, founder of the Singer Sewing Machine Company. When Singer had trouble marketing the sewing machine because of lack of money and absence of public awareness about his offering, he turned to franchising by recruiting agents to sell and service the machines on commission. By doing so, Singer was able to use agents to build a vibrant sales network quickly at little cost. His use of exclusive commissioned agents laid the groundwork for modern-day franchising. When President Eisenhower decided to build the Interstate Highway System (based on what he had seen in Germany during the war), automobile travel took off in the United States, and with it came the golden age of franchising. Given this history, it is not surprising that franchising is widely celebrated as a particularly American invention. Today, franchising has become an international phenomenon, spanning more than 160 countries worldwide.

Examples of franchising can be found in almost every industry today. In 2017, there were 745,290 franchise establishments in the United States, with an economic output of about $713 billion. About eight million people in the country work for a franchised business. According to the International Franchise Association, almost 4% of all small businesses in the United States are franchises. The most famous American franchisor may be McDonald's, bringing in about $90 billion in 2018 sales, followed by 7-Eleven at about $85 billion in annual sales. Table 4.3 presents a quick summary of franchise prevalence in different economic sectors in the country.

KEY TAKEAWAY

The birthplace of franchising is the United States. As such, franchising is even more American than Apple pie.

TABLE 4.3

Make-up of Franchises in the United States, by Sector

OUTLETS		EMPLOYMENT		REVENUE	
Quick-service restaurants	26%	Quick-service restaurants	46%	Quick-service restaurants	34%
Personal services	15	Table/full-serve restaurants	13	Business services	13
Business services	14	Business services	8	Lodging	10
Comm. & residential services	9	Lodging	8	Table/full-serve restaurants	10
Real estate	8	Personal services	6	Real estate	7
Retail products & services	8	Retail food	6	Automotive	6
Retail food	7	Retail products & services	4	Comm. & residential services	6
Automotive	5	Automotive	3	Personal services	5
Lodging	4	Comm. & residential services	3	Retail food	5
Table/full-serve restaurants	4	Real estate	3	Retail products & services	4

Source: Adapted from As Franchising Takes Off, These Businesses Are Hottest, *The Wall Street Journal*

4.1.2 Forms of Franchising

The value of a franchise is based on (a) the rights granted to and (b) the cash flow potential of the franchise. Both factors vary from one franchise to another. There are four basic forms of franchising:

1. *Trade name franchising.* **Trade name franchising** includes only the rights to use the franchisor's trade name and/or trademarks. An example of this is True Value Hardware, which covers about 4400 stores worldwide with retail sales totaling about $5.5 billion.

2. *Product distribution franchising.* **Product distribution franchising** has the franchisor offering specific brand name products that are then sold to franchisees in a specific territory. An example is Snap-On Tools, founded in Milwaukee, WI, and having net sales of about $3.7 billion in 2017.

3. *Conversion franchising.* **Conversion franchising** brings together independent businesses combining resources under a well-known corporate umbrella. A prominent example is REMAX, which started with a single office in Denver, CO, and is now a global real-estate franchisor.

4. *Business-format franchising.* **Business-format franchising** is based on the right to adopt the way the franchisor does business, including operational procedures, marketing strategy, physical building and equipment, and full business services. Franchisees usually pay both an up-front fee to obtain the franchise rights and a percentage of gross sales. Cold Stone Creamery, cofounded by Donald and Susan Sutherland in Tempe, AZ, is an example of business format franchising.

Cold Stone Creamery is an example of business-format franchising, the most popular form of franchising in the country.

When most people think of franchising, the type of franchising they tend to consider is the turnkey approach of business-format franchising. Such franchising is commonly used in quick-service restaurants (think McDonald's and Subway), but also lodging, retail food, and full-service restaurant businesses. Some franchisors, such as Subway (the sandwich company), prefer to sell **master franchises** that require assuming responsibility for opening multiple stores in a specific region through sub-franchisees. Franchisors may also differ in the number of stores they want the franchisee to manage, such as Chick-fil-A, where the average franchisee has one store, or Moe's, where the franchisee has to commit to at least three stores. Applebee's, the Kansas-based bar-and-grill chain, has 1873 restaurants in the United States run by 31 franchisees.

Franchising is a common mode of entrepreneurship in the United States. Estimates suggest that anywhere from 1 in 8 to 1 in 10 businesses operating in the country are franchised operations. What makes franchising such a popular choice for entrepreneurship? When it works out well, franchising can be a "win–win" situation for both the franchisor and the franchisee. Franchising gives franchisors the ability to achieve rapid growth and fast market penetration without investing huge amounts of capital and hiring a large workforce. Franchisees are able to start a small business rather quickly by learning a proven "recipe" of success from an established business. Figure 4.2 presents general information about a typical franchisee in the United States.

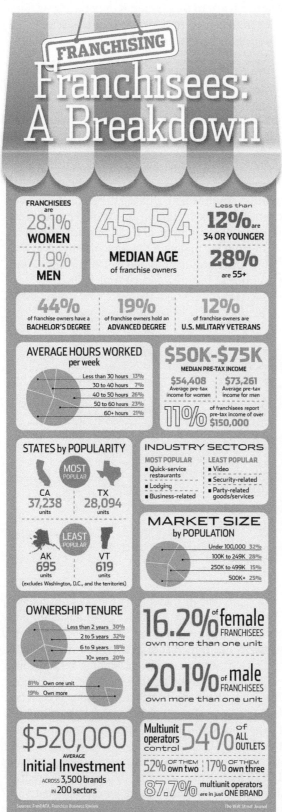

FIGURE 4.2 Franchising in the U.S. at a Glance
Source: The vital statistics on franchisees.

Let us meet some successful franchisees. Consider Greg Flynn of San Francisco. Greg was an overeducated 33-year-old commercial real-estate investor when he first realized that the Burger King restaurant his father owned was a proverbial gold mine. His father, Donald Flynn, was a tax lawyer who had gotten into franchising when he saw his formerly underachieving younger brother make money from a successful McDonald's franchisee. After getting his bachelor's degree from Brown and an MBA from Stanford, Greg founded a real-estate fund that was doing well when he started thinking of getting into the franchising business. In early 1999, Greg bought his first Applebee's locations for $14 million (eight outlets in the Seattle area), borrowing $12.8 million. His goal from the beginning: Become the #1 Applebee's franchisee. Over the years, Flynn went on an acquisition spree, snapping up restaurants cheap, especially when the economy was faltering. By 2012, Greg owned 438 Applebee's franchises. Greg then began looking to diversify beyond Applebee's, first buying Taco Bell's franchises and then Panera Bread's. Today, Greg owns more than 25% of Applebee's 1800+ restaurants (the other 75% are owned by 30 franchisees, making Greg the largest Applebee's franchisee). The Flynn Restaurant Group is now the largest restaurant franchisee in the United States, with over 800 Applebee's, Taco Bell, and Panera Bread outlets and annual revenues of about $2 billion. If you are curious about how he succeeded, you can hear him share his experience in his acceptance speech (https://www.youtube.com/watch?v=F-mc-eqMCbc&app=desktop) when he received the Restaurant Leader of the Year award in Phoenix, AZ.

Greg is in a brick-and-mortar business with heavy investment in real estate. Franchising can be equally attractive for asset-light service businesses. Dan Gagne is plumber, but he is no ordinary plumber. It has been years since he actually held a wrench. His plumbing business, which is a franchisee of the national chain Benjamin Franklin Plumbing, generates $20 million a year in revenue and employs 100 people. The money his business brings in allows him and his family to pursue other interests. "The income is more than I'd ever imagined," Dan shares. "I own several homes. We've invested in eight acres in Costa Rica and are going to build a health spa. We live there about six months of the year."

Comprehension Check

1. Define franchising.
2. What are the different forms of franchising?
3. What needs to be in place for business systems to be considered franchising?

Module 4.2 Considerations in Franchising

As with all business decisions, astute students should consider both the advantages and disadvantages of franchising (see Figure 4.3). Before making the decision to purchase a

	Advantages	Disadvantages
Franchisor	Expansion with low capital investment	Reduced influence
	Controlled expansion	Limited point-of-sale control
	Multiple sources of revenue	Management disputes
	Quantity purchasing	
Franchisee	Proven business model	Risk of fraud or misunderstanding
	Brand reputation	Cost of franchising
	Advertising and marketing	Decision-making constraints
	Professional guidance	Termination or transfer issues
	Financial assistance	Other franchisees (shadow effect)
	Potential for growth	

FIGURE 4.3 Franchising Has Its Advantages and Disadvantages for the Franchisor and the Franchisee

franchise, one would also do well to understand the benefits and risks of starting a new business or buying out an existing non-franchise business (explained in other chapters of this book). It is also useful to consider whether the unique attributes of franchising fit your own needs and desires. Remember, while franchising allows you not to have to fully reinvent the wheel (as there is a proven system provided by the franchisor), it also constrains the franchisee within the boundaries set by the franchisor.

4.2.1 Advantages of Franchising

The advantages of franchising can be considered in terms of both the franchisor and the franchisee. For the franchisor, there are several benefits as we discuss below.

Expansion with lower capital investment. Franchising allows the franchisor to expand its market footprint with limited financial investment. The investment toward fixed assets and movable assets come largely from the franchisee. Franchisors therefore need not borrow from lenders or attract outside investors for growth. Thus, franchisees share the financial burden of the franchisor's growth.

Controlled expansion. For growth-oriented companies, franchising allows opportunities to expand with a simpler management structure than would be needed to grow without franchising. The biggest impediment to growth is often management's inability to effectively manage the growing company. In franchising, the franchisor is responsible for managing growth at the corporate level, with management responsibilities for the operations of the stores delegated to the franchisees.

Multiple sources of revenue. Franchisors often have multiple sources of revenue built into their franchising agreements. Most everyone is familiar with franchising fee, which is paid when the agreement is signed, and royalties, which are paid from gross operating revenues. But franchisors are sometimes also able to add an annual fees as well that the franchisee needs to pay to renew the agreement. The agreement may also include revenue for the franchisor from selling products and supplies to the franchisee. The sandwich company Quiznos has an up-front franchising fee, plus 7% royalty on sales, plus 4% advertising fee per year (and they also sell food to their franchisees at profit, prohibiting them from buying food from anyone else).

Quantity purchasing. Franchisors that sell products and supplies to franchisees are able to take advantage of volume discounts from the economies-of-scale that come from buying for all their locations. This quantity purchasing can increase profit margins, which ideally may be passed on to the franchisee.

The franchisee also has several benefits from being part of a franchise:

Proven business model. Remember from our discussion about business models that it can be challenging for companies to know whether the idea they have in mind can make money. A key benefit of franchising for the franchisee is that someone has already worked out a successful business model that works.

Brand reputation. It can take years for a new company to build a reputation. With franchising, however, the franchisee is able to capitalize on the reputation of the franchisor. Consider a new hotel coming up in a tourist destination like Destin, FL. Tourists interested in visiting Destin are unlikely to know much about the new hotel, but if the hotel has a Marriott sign on the front, customers will come in based on Marriott's reputation. Hotel operators are aware that customers are more likely to stay at properties associated with brand names they trust rather than at an unknown property.

Advertising and marketing. Companies spend millions of dollars annually on advertising and marketing. The hamburger chain Wendy's alone spent about $372 million on advertising in the United States in 2017. To put this in perspective, Wendy's annual ad spend is more than the entire GDP of more than 30 countries in the world. The 6500 Wendy's franchisees enjoy the recognition such spending brings. While most franchisees need to contribute to local advertising and marketing (e.g. around their location), they are able to benefit from the national branding that only a large franchisor can afford. Further, franchisees should also be able to capitalize on the advertising and marketing expertise of the franchisor.

KEY TAKEAWAY

All else being equal, it is better to join a franchisor with a proven business model and a strong reputation in the market.

Professional guidance. Many franchisors provide training to their franchisees, both in preparation for running the business and for instructing them in the finer points after the business is in operation. Good franchisors also provide professional guidance and day-to-day assistance in crisis situations. Franchisors are also often able to hire skilled professionals to provide technical assistance with location, store layout and design, and equipment purchase. Thus, franchisees can benefit from the experience and knowledge that franchisors have acquired over the years.

Financial assistance. Some franchisors, though not all, provide financial assistance to new franchisees. This assistance can take the form of help with getting loans to start the business or inventory credit or overhead reduction.

Sweet and Sour Taste of Franchising

Before you consider franchising as an option, it is helpful to understand the various advantages and disadvantages of franchising. Hear Kim Taylor of Next News Network talk about some of the major benefits and pitfalls of owning a franchise.

Sira Anawong/123RF

Watch the video online at: https://www.youtube.com/watch?v=LUK_2HJNUBc

Potential for growth. Successful franchisees are able to expand to other territories once the franchisor sees they are successful with one location. As a result, if you are successful with a franchise, you are in the enviable position of multiplying that success rapidly. According to the trade publication *Franchise Times*, 10 US restaurant franchisees have more than $500 million in annual revenues, making their owners multimillionaires several times over.

4.2.2 Disadvantages of Franchising

Every approach to starting a small business has its challenges, and franchising is no exception. The business world is littered with many franchises that failed. For some, the failure comes after years of success, and for others, failure comes before they taste real success. Sbarro and RadioShack are examples of once-successful franchises that fell on hard times. Super Suppers (meal prep kitchens) and The Right One (dating) are examples of franchises that crashed quickly after getting off the ground.

Some of the key problems that franchisors encounter in franchising are described below:

Reduced influence. You have probably heard the popular saying "Change is the only constant in the business world." Businesspeople are encouraged to think about managing for change. The franchising agreement, however, limits the franchisor's discretion to alter or eliminate products even in response to external changes. As a result, it becomes difficult for franchisors to test new offerings in the market. To deal with this problem, some franchisors maintain company-owned stores where they can test-market new products and services. This allows them to adapt to customer needs as well as to present their units as examples to franchisees.

Limited point-of-sale control. While the franchisor controls the organization to the extent specified by the franchise agreement, the individual franchises are under the day-to-day management of the franchisee. Franchisors, therefore, have limited visibility on the strategy and operations of the individual franchisees. When franchisees do not maintain their business well, it reflects poorly on other franchises as well as on the franchisor.

Management disputes. Disagreements between the franchisor and its franchisees may arise over many issues, such as hours of operations, range and cost of offerings, expansion plans, and royalties. These disputes can make it difficult to manage the company. Subway, for example, had to discontinue the $5 foot-long when many franchisees protested that it hurt their profitability. Because operating costs differed by location (say, Los Angeles versus Arkansas), Subway corporate management had to deal with franchisees who wanted the flexibility to price their own products based on the vagaries of their local market.

Of course, all is not good for the franchisees either. The pitfalls faced by franchisees are as follows:

Risk of fraud or misunderstanding. It is not uncommon to come across franchisors that mislead potential franchisees by making exaggerated promises. To reduce the problem of misrepresentation by franchisors, it is advisable for new franchisees to talk to existing established franchisees. However, franchisors are not always forthcoming with information about existing franchisees, making it difficult for new entrants to talk to them. NY Bagel, started by Joe Smith and Dennis Mason, was sanctioned in early 2019 for failing to disclose to potential franchisees the several pending state enforcement actions, civil lawsuits, judgments, and penalties as required by law.

Interactive Exercise

Identify entrepreneur business owner who owns a franchisee. Reach out to them to schedule an interview, so you can ask them about the opportunities and challenges they see in becoming part of a franchise system. Be prepared to share your answers with the class.

Cost of franchising. Every franchise comes at a price, and this eats into the profitability for the franchisee. As mentioned before, franchisors usually charge a fee and a percentage of sales revenue. Thus, franchising requires hefty initial investment and profit sharing with the franchisor. Because most franchisors take their cut from gross or net sales, it can drastically reduce profitability for the franchisee.

Decision-making constraints. While franchisees are independent business owners, franchisors place constraints on the decisions that the franchisees can make on their own. For example, franchisees generally have to follow corporate policies and procedures. When the COVID-19 pandemic spread in 2020, McDonald's issued a 59-page dine-in reopening guide for its franchisees to follow. The guide included commitments to clean bathrooms every half-hour and digital kiosks after each order, turning off dining-room soda fountains or assigning an employee to operate them, and installing foot-pulls to allow customers to open bathroom doors without using their hands. Franchisees were required to spend on things like a $310 automatic towel dispenser and a $718 touchless sink to increase hygiene in stores even as some of them were struggling to meet payroll. Franchisees are also expected to limit their territorial aspirations to the geographical area specified in the agreement. Even if franchisees feel that the policies, products, or promotions offered by the franchisor are not appropriate for their market, there is little they can do to opt out without violating the franchising agreement.

Termination or transfer issues. An important issue that gets little consideration in the run-up to the franchising agreement is the problem of termination or transfer. Carefully read the section of the agreement that describes how the franchisee can get out if they need to. What provisions does the agreement have for franchisees who want to cease operations, transfer their rights to family or friends, or sell the franchise to someone else? Also, look for whether the agreement specifies the grounds on which the agreement can be terminated by the franchisor. A franchising agreement is a contract, and as with most contracts, it is best to read it carefully before proceeding.

Other franchisees (shadow effect). Franchising brings together different individuals within the umbrella of one company that is viewed as a single corporation by customers. Consequently, poor performance or quality concerns at one location can lead to problems for other franchisors. The "we are all alike" message of franchising works well under some circumstances, but can be counterproductive in other situations.

For those interested in reading more ongoing issues with existing franchises, the website www.UnhappyFranchisee.com is worth visiting.

What Do You Think?

A famous sandwich chain decided to give away food as a promotion. The sandwiches were to be free for customers, but the franchisees had to buy all ingredients from Corporate at above-market prices. As per the franchise agreement, franchisees were barred from buying food from any other sources except Corporate. The promotion was wildly successful with customers. More than a million people signed up for the free sandwich within three days of the promotion announcements. The company's restaurants saw lines of hungry patrons stretching around the block. However, many franchisees revolted and refused to offer the promotion, or offered it in limited manner. Signs saying "We're not participating" appeared outside many locations. Their grievance: Corporate expects them to pay above-market to buy food and then hand it out to customers without charge. Who do you think should bear the cost of such promotions in a franchisee?

Comprehension Check

1. What are the advantages of franchising for a franchisor?
2. What are some things that franchisees need to be careful about when franchising?
3. Can franchising pose some problems for the franchisor? Discuss with some examples.

Module 4.3 Types of Franchise

Given the diversity of franchising companies, people who study franchises (yes, there is such a thing as a franchising researcher!) have put forth various typologies of franchising. Franchises are not homogenous in their structure and operations. One way to identify different types of franchises is based on the stage of franchising. In this typology, there are four types of franchises: the **beginners**, the **developers**, the **growers**, and the **maturers**. You may call this the *BDGM* typology of franchising.

The beginners are early-stage franchising companies. These firms are both young and small. They have low entry requirements for new franchisees and few established outlets. In effect, the beginners are still establishing their franchising identity, so they either have low recall in the consumer's mind or don't have an established track record yet. At this stage, the franchises' geographical footprint is very small – they are a local player limited to a certain area.

The developers are moderately established, though they are still not national players. For these developer franchises, the format has been established and the franchise enjoys a growing reputation. Growth allows them to increase the up-front payment and royalty fee, but some franchises reduce their charges to fuel growth. The franchise is still geographically concentrated, though the footprint is larger than regional at this stage.

> ### KEY TAKEAWAY
>
> The vast range of franchise systems can be organized into four types, each of which offers some benefits to those interested in becoming a franchisee.

The growers are companies that have already spent a substantial time in the franchise business and yet continue to expand at a healthy rate (in terms of number of establishments and total revenues). They have fully developed systems and good brand name recognition. They open several new outlets annually. They tend to have a national footprint, though their physical density is still low. They have a healthy number of both company-owned and franchised locations, so the business is not reliant on just the income coming from the franchisees.

Interactive Exercise

Are you familiar with hot yoga? Visit Hot Yoga Plus at https://www.hotyogaplus.com. What type of franchise system do you think they are? If you could, would you consider becoming a franchisee?

The mature franchisors are companies that have already peaked. At these companies, growth has slowed considerably, so they open very few new stores. Maturers charge a very high up-front payment from new franchisees, which makes it difficult for small new firms to buy into their system. They have a national footprint with high store density. Franchisees who want to associate with mature players generally do so by buying out existing franchisees. The franchise's business model is already established and brand recognition is very high, but their business may be facing turbulence because of new trends and tastes in the industry.

Feel the Burn

Burn Boot Camp is a women-focused fitness franchisee. They can be visited at www.burnbootcamp.com. The husband- and-wife team of Morgan and Devan Kline started Burn after thousands of hours of experience with personal training.

Watch the video online at: https://www.youtube.com/watch?v=etAjTjurhck

4.3.1 Legal and Institutional Environment for Franchising

All franchise systems, irrespective of their growth stage, are required to operate within a legal and institutional framework that can have a critical impact on their success. Franchising is a highly regulated path to business ownership. There are federal and state laws that govern the operation of franchise systems. Conforming to federal or state regulatory requirements is imperative to avoid legal trouble, financial penalties, or even jail time. The Federal Trade Commission (FTC) is authorized to seek both preliminary and permanent injunctions against companies that violate franchising rules, and many even bar you from franchising in the future. The FTC can freeze assets at the corporate and personal levels, impose civil penalties, and seek monetary redress on behalf of those injured by rule violations.

Companies can inadvertently create franchising relationship, even when they have no intention of becoming a franchisor. In some cases, this happens because the companies want to avoid being subjected to strict regulations. In other cases, firms do not like the idea of calling their relationship a "franchise," thinking that if they call it something different, they would not be violating franchise regulations. Sperry Van Ness International Corporation is a full-service commercial real-estate franchisor under the SVN brand.

In *LASVN #2 v. Sperry Van Ness Real Estate*, a jury awarded more than $6 million even when both parties had agreed in writing that the relationship was not a franchise. Some firms simply have no idea that there are regulations that even govern this type of contractual relationship. A common reaction to being told that a business is a franchisor is: "Who? Me?"

Since 1979, FTC has required all franchisors to provide prospective franchisees with information about the company franchising and its principals in a document at least 10 days before the signing of a franchise agreement. Franchisors who sell franchises only internationally are exempt from this requirement. The FTC rule defines an arrangement as a "franchise" if it (1) requires the buyer to pay at least $500; (2) for the right to operate a business under the seller's trade name or to sell the seller's branded products; and (3) the franchisor provides significant assistance to the buyer or can exercise significant control over the buyer's operating methods. Experts in franchising law recommend that firms ask themselves three questions to determine if they are covered by FTC franchising rules:

1. Does the relationship involve a common trademark or format?
2. Does the relationship involve significant control or assistance from the seller? Conditions such as only the seller's products can be sold, the seller will train the buyer to perform the service in question, or the seller will show the buyer how to market the products are relevant factors here.
3. Is there a required payment of $500 or more to the seller or its affiliates during the first six months of the relationship? This may be in the form of a denominated franchise fee, or may include required payments for "other than reasonable quantities of wholesale goods purchased for resale," a minimum order of supplies, a required purchase of goods for more than the cost of similar goods elsewhere, or a requirement to buy services.

The FTC rule makes it unlawful for a franchisor not to provide written disclosures to prospective franchisees before (a) the first face-to-face meeting between the franchisor and the prospective franchisee for discussing the possible sale of a franchise or (b) 10 business days prior to executing the franchise agreement. The FTC rule does not require any governmental filings – just disclosure in the prescribed way.

KEY TAKEAWAY

Franchising is highly regulated at federal and state levels. To ensure that you comply with the FTC rules and myriad other regulations, make sure to work with a lawyer with expertise in franchising law.

To meet federal requirements, franchisors can use the FTC version of the standard offering circular or a Uniform Franchise Offering Circular. This document, first produced by the Midwest Securities Commissioners Association in 1975, is the form preferred by most franchisors. In 2008, the FTC changed the name to the **Uniform Franchise Disclosure Document** (UFDD). Despite the name change, the purpose remains the same as before: Identify the information all franchisors must provide before they can sign up franchisees. Table 4.4 lists the items that franchisors are required to share with potential franchisees.

Franchisors deal with two broad categories of state laws. The first involves requirements for registration and dissemination of information and consists of laws regarding what franchisors can and cannot do to sell franchisees. The second covers issues such as franchisee termination and consists of laws governing relationships between franchisors and franchisees. Not all states have registration laws. States that regulate how franchisors sell franchisees may or may not have relationship laws. As a result, understanding which laws apply to which states is important in making sure you stay on the right side of law.

TABLE 4.4

Items That Franchisors Are Required to Share with All Potential Franchisees

1	The franchisor and predecessors
2	Business experience of persons affiliated with franchisor
3	Litigation history
4	Bankruptcy history
5	Initial fee
6	Other fees
7	Initial investment
8	Restrictions of franchisee sourcing
9	Franchisee's obligations
10	Financing
11	Franchisor's obligations
12	Territory
13	Trademarks and service marks
14	Patents and copyrights
15	Obligation of the franchisee to participate in the business
16	Restrictions on franchisee sale of goods and services
17	Renewal and termination
18	Arrangements with public figures
19	Earnings claim
20	Information on the system
21	Audited financial statements
22	Contracts
23	Acknowledgement of receipt

States with registration laws and relationship laws are listed in Table 4.5. The Internet multiplies the likelihood of trouble, as a business that inadvertently "offers" a "franchise" under a state's laws triggers that state's registration and disclosure requirements.

Registration states are the US states that require a franchisor not only submit presale disclosures but also register the franchise within the state before any sales can be made. These states also require franchisors to file reports with state regulators at least annually, and in some cases, quarterly. Franchisors are able to furnish necessary documentation to all states simultaneously and in electronic form. Yet, only about half of the franchisors in the nation choose not to operate in registration states. This is in part because they want to avoid the additional regulations of the registration states. It must, however, be remembered that the purpose of these regulations is to provide some modicum of protection to franchisees.

Registration requirements provide additional scrutiny of the information that franchisors provide to franchisees, which makes it more likely that inaccurate information is filtered out before it gets to the franchisee. Franchisors may also be required to update their offering document on record with the state authorities whenever there is a "material change" to the franchise system. A material change refers to changes made to things such as fees charged to franchisees, their obligations, the operating system, the legal structure of franchisors, financial information, or a program for interacting with franchisees. Such requirements make it difficult for franchisors to differentiate in the contracts offered to different franchisees, reducing the chances of discrimination and fraud.

Brief Legal Primer

Anyone interested in being part of franchising in the United States should learn the basics of franchising law. Nancy Lanard is a franchise lawyer with Lanard and Associates, P.C., a "legal boutique" that provides customized solutions for individuals seeking a franchise and businesses looking to expand into franchising.

Billion Photos/Shutterstock.com

Watch the video online at: https://www.youtube.com/watch?v=FK9K4FgtajY

TABLE **4.5**	
List of States with Franchise Registration or Relationship Laws	
States with registration laws	**States with relationship laws**
California	Arkansas
Hawaii	California
Illinois	Connecticut
Indiana	Delaware
Maryland	Florida
Michigan	Hawaii
Minnesota	Illinois
New York	Indiana
North Dakota	Iowa
Rhode Island	Kentucky
South Dakota	Maryland
Virginia	Michigan
Washington	Minnesota
Wisconsin	Mississippi
	Missouri
	Nebraska
	New Jersey
	Oregon
	Virginia
	Washington
	Wisconsin

Many registration states require that the franchisor put any fees paid by the franchisees into escrow until the franchisor has provided the services that the fees are to cover. If regulators assess the franchisor's balance sheet to be weak, they may require the franchisor to post a bond to guarantee that franchise fees are used for the opening of outlets (rather than diverted elsewhere). Franchisors deemed to be **undercapitalized** (that is, franchisors with net worth less than the franchisee's initial investment) are seen as risky for franchisees. These regulations help protect franchisees from franchisors that are in precarious financial condition. Some states also regulate franchisor advertisements to attract franchisees, so that unsupported claims about anticipated performance and success are not included in the advertising materials.

For franchisors, operating in registration states is a way to signal quality to potential franchisees. The oversight from regulators helps weed out bad franchisees and also signals to franchisees that the franchisor is willing to submit to the extra oversight. Registration states are generally concentrated in an arc running along the coasts and industrial Midwest. In contrast, many Southern states do not require registration (see Figure 4.4). Many franchisors thus adopt a regional expansion strategy by focusing on the non-registration states. After they have saturated the market in non-registration states, they consider moving into registration states. For a new franchise offering, the registration fee can vary between $250 and $750 for each registration state.

Relationship states are US states that have laws governing the interaction between franchisors and franchisees. The purpose of these laws is to protect franchisees by ensuring that franchisors have "good cause" to terminate franchisees and by allowing franchisees to address contract violations before they are terminated. The good cause clause means that the contract can be terminated if the franchisee has engaged in some type of breach

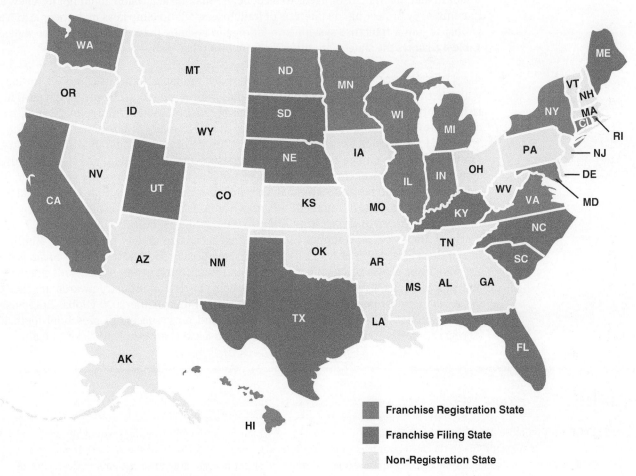

FIGURE 4.4 Franchise Registration and Filing States
Source: From The Franchise Registration States, ©2020 The Internicola Law Firm, P.C., All Rights Reserved.

> **TABLE 4.6**
>
> **States with Franchise Relationship Laws**
>
> | States that require cause for termination | States that allow cure in termination |
> | --- | --- |
> | Arkansas | Arkansas |
> | California | California |
> | Connecticut | Hawaii |
> | Delaware | Illinois |
> | Hawaii | Michigan |
> | Illinois | Minnesota |
> | Indiana | Washington |
> | Michigan | Wisconsin |
> | Minnesota | |
> | Nebraska | |
> | New Jersey | |
> | Virginia | |
> | Washington | |
> | Wisconsin | |

of contract. By requiring good cause for termination, franchise relationship laws raise the standard that the franchisor needs to meet before making a decision about not to renew a franchisee. By protecting the interests of franchisees, relationship laws make people more willing to join a franchise system in relationship systems than they are in other states. Table 4.6 shows the states with different franchise relationship provisions.

4.3.1.1 Franchisor certification Certification by reputable authorities and institutions is another way for franchise systems to enhance their reputation. The media is a particularly important source of certification for firms because magazines, newspapers, and periodicals provide information on the legitimacy and desirability of businesses. *Franchising Today* and *Franchising Times* are two publications dedicated to the franchising industry. Franchise systems ranked highly in such magazines are more likely than other franchise systems to survive over time. Companies featured in trade magazines are generally considered more reputable and legitimate. One such franchisor is The Simple Greek, a quick-service dining restaurant founded in Pennsylvania. It began franchising in 2016. By the time it was featured in *Franchising Today* in 2019, it had 33 locations in operations.

There are also several reputable awards that recognize quality franchisors. Winning one of these awards not only brings additional legitimacy and positive media coverage to the franchisor, it also brings more scrutiny and monitoring of the franchisor's practices and processes. As a result, franchisors that win prestigious industry awards are likely to be better performers than others. The overall winner of the 2020 Global Franchise Awards was Little Kickers, the world's biggest and most successful preschool football (soccer) academy. You can read more about Little Kickers at www.littlekickers.co.uk.

Interactive Exercise

The 2020 Global Franchise Awards were given in eight different categories for franchisors. To see the 2020 awardees, you can visit https://www.globalfranchisemagazine.com/awards/winners. If there was a popular choice overall winner award category, which of these eight awardees would you vote for? You can also vote NOTA (None of the Above), if you do not think any of these eight franchise systems is deserving of your vote.

The Simple Greek is a fast-growing company that combines quality ingredients, open kitchens, and Mediterranean food in a fast-casual setting. It was featured in Franchising Today in 2019.

Membership in trade associations also serves a critical certification function. The International Franchise Association (IFA), headquartered in Washington D.C., is the world's largest membership organization for franchisors, franchisees, and franchise suppliers. Membership in IFA requires franchisors to abide by a code of conduct and adhere to certain standards. Failure to follow the code of conduct can be serious for both franchisors and franchisees.

What Do You Think?

Soccer is the most popular sport in the world. Little Kickers is a successful franchise that targets preschool children and young kids to help them learn to play soccer. Currently, Little Kickers does not have a presence in the United States. Why do you think that is the case? If someone was looking to get into franchising, would you recommend that they try out a Little Kickers franchisee in the United States? What kind of challenges or competition would they face in the United States?

Franchising is a legally regulated mode of business ownership. Federal and state laws affect the operation of franchise systems. Companies need to conform to these laws if they want to make the franchise system successful. It is highly recommended that aspiring franchisors and franchisees consult with a lawyer specializing in franchising law before making any major decisions.

Comprehension Check

1. Explain the differences between beginners and developers.
2. What would one gain from joining a mature-type franchise? What are some challenges in joining a mature franchise?
3. What is a registration state?

Preparing Future Ronaldo

Started in 2002 by a mother who was looking for play options for her young child, Little Kickers is today a successful worldwide franchisor. It runs programs that combine high-quality football skills with important preschool learning concepts such as color and number recognition, sharing, following instructions, and using imagination.

Watch the video online at: https://www.youtube.com/watch?v=4EfqMB0mtwQ

Module 4.4 Decision to Become a Franchisee

The decision to consider franchising can be studied from either the franchisor's perspective or the franchisee's perspective. When we talk of franchisors like McDonald's and Burger King, we are talking about large, multinational corporations (they are all maturer-type franchises). Not all franchisors, however, are like them. When Marc Shuman decided to start franchising GarageTek, his garage makeover company was just one year old. His business was small, and he wanted to start franchising so he could grow quickly with the goal of preventing imitators from driving him out of the market. Thus, the discussion of franchising as relevant for a book about small business management can be done from both sides of the franchising agreement: the franchisor and the franchisee. Many issues are common for both, such as the need to make sure the franchise creates value for investors and customers. The decision to franchise is not an easy one for the franchisor. The decision to buy a franchise is also difficult for the franchisee. Many franchisors rush too fast into franchising after the first unit takes off. Many franchisees are hasty about buying a franchise, so impatient are they to run their own business.

> ### KEY TAKEAWAY
>
> Do not rush into buying a franchisee. Good research early on can save you lots of trouble later.

The remainder of this section focuses on the prospective franchisee's perspective in getting started. Investing in a franchise, whether for a new entrant like Profile by Sanford (founded 2011) or an established player like Subway, is a major commitment of time and money. Consequently, choosing the right franchise is an important decision that deserves serious consideration. Before signing the franchise agreement and committing yourself, it is helpful to think about your business needs and weigh the pros and cons of the various franchising options.

4.4.1 Assess Your Situation

Any potential franchisee should start with a careful assessment of their own situation, thinking about their interests, skills, and needs. Here are some questions that can help you decide whether franchising is a suitable path to small business ownership for you.

- Why do you want to franchise? What do you see as the advantages you will get from franchising (as opposed to starting your own independent venture)? In other words, what do you hope to get from the franchisor that you cannot do yourself?
- How much capital are you willing to invest to buy the franchise and run it until the business starts to break even (that is, gets to a point where income equals expenses)?
- Who will be operating the franchise once you set it up? Do you have the time to invest in the day-to-day management of the new business or will you be partnering with someone?
- Are you ready to work within the constraints laid down by the franchisor?

4.4.2 Start Your Research

The first step is to seek franchising opportunities in business periodicals and trade publications. When Marc Shuman decided to franchise GarageTek, he took out ads in the *Wall Street Journal* looking for prospective franchisees. *Inc.*, *Fast Company*, and *Entrepreneur* are other general publications where you can find articles and advertisements related to franchising. Trade publications specializing in franchising include *Franchising Opportunities World* and *Quarterly Franchising World*. The major trade association for franchising is the International Franchise Association, which puts together an annual conference where you can learn about the latest developments in franchising (what's hot, what's not!). The Web address for IFA is www.franchise.org. You can also sign up for the monthly newsletter from *The Franchise Handbook* (www.handbook.franchisetimes.com) to get some information about fastest growing franchise brands and other franchising trends.

Interactive Exercise

Of all the franchise systems mentioned in this chapter, seek out a franchisee who runs a local store. Share with them that you are a college student doing research on what makes a franchisee successful in picking the right franchise and doing well in the business. Also, ask them about the opportunities and challenges they face. Be prepared to share your findings with class.

There are several other franchising-related associations worth knowing about when you start your research. The American Franchisee Association (AFA), headquartered in Chicago, IL, promises to represent the franchisees' interests. Their website is www.franchisee.org. There is also the American Association of Franchisees and Dealers (AAFD), which is based in San Diego, CA, and seeks to improve the franchising climate (www.aafd.org). The AAFD developed a Franchisee Bill of Rights for ethical business conduct for franchised businesses. The World Franchise Council (NFC) is another source for franchising information (www.worldfranchisecouncil.net). The Federal Trade Commission also publishes a consumer's guide to buying a franchise, which is helpful for those new to franchising. The guide can be found at https://www.ftc.gov/tips-advice/business-center/guidance/consumers-guide-buying-franchise.

What Do You Think?

Your friend is debating between two franchises: Clean Juice or Hammer and Nails. It's either one or the other. Can you use the concepts learned in this chapter to advise them as to which option would be better for them? If you have another possibility in mind, you can suggest that as an option too, but it should be better than the two your friend is already considering. The websites for the two companies are www.cleanjuicefranchising.com and www.hammerandnailsgrooming.com. Which do you think is a better option for your friend?

Make a list of the franchises that interest you. Ask the following questions about these franchisors:

1. In what year was the firm founded? When did they start offering franchising?
2. Does the firm have certified financial statements that you can examine?
3. Is the firm willing to introduce you to existing franchisees? What do the existing franchisees say about the firm?
4. What kinds of support does the firm provide its franchisees? Capital, location assistance, employee training, capital and credit, or advertising and marketing support?
5. What kind of managerial talent does the franchisor have?

Once you find a franchise that appeals to you (or better still, if there are a few options from which you would choose), evaluate these prospects carefully by asking the following questions:

- Have you read the franchise contract carefully and tried to understand it as best as you can?
- Does the contract have an exit clause? What is the cost to exit for the franchisee if you wish to get out of the business?
- Are there conditions that restrict your ability to sell your franchise?
- Will you have an exclusive territory as a franchisee or can the franchisor sell other franchises in the area?
- Does the franchisor have other companies that franchise a similar product or service? Franchisees should be careful about protection from other franchise systems associated with the same franchisor.

Remember, franchising is not cheap and it is not for everyone. Franchising seems like a simple and straightforward path to small business ownership: Find a company like Sports Clips or Planet Fitness, take advantage of the pretested business model, leverage their name-recognition and reputation to bring in customers, and make a tidy profit after paying a startup cost and a cut of the money that comes in. Ever heard of the expression "if it sounds too good to be true, it probably is"? If you are interested in franchising, make sure you carefully study the franchisor, their business model, and the industry before you sign on the dotted line.

Table 4.7 presents a checklist of nine main questions that you can use to determine whether you are ready to move ahead with franchising.

TABLE **4.7**

Are You Ready to Be a Franchisee?

What you are trying to figure out?	Questions to ask yourself	Why is this important?
1. Who are you?	What are my skills and interests? Can I follow a system or do I like to march to my own tune? Do I prefer to work independently or manage people? Am I willing to pull 12-hour days or am I looking for a part-time gig that allows me to keep my day job? What kind of a business am I interested in?	Nick Bibby, a franchise consultant in Shreveport, LA, says his first advice to clients comes from an ancient Greek aphorism: "Know thyself." Unfortunately, many people become enamored with the dream of business ownership and fail to ask simple questions that determine whether franchising is a good fit.
2. Should you hire experts?	Who do I need to make the business work? Do I have the expert advice I need? If I run into trouble, do I know people who I can turn to for help?	Don Sniegowski, editor of Blue MauMau, a franchise news site, recommends that would-be franchisees hire experts in three areas: marketing, accounting, and legal.
3. What is the best business opportunity?	Does this business satisfy a need or a trend? How many potential customers live in my area? What is the competition? The goal of all these questions is to collect hard data about the business.	Jim Denney, an experienced business owner in Scotia near Albany, NY, spent six months investigating his market before satisfying himself that he had a viable business opportunity for his concrete-raising franchise. He looked at census data, information on the housing stock and talked to people throughout the industry.
4. Who is your franchisor?	What is the reputation of the franchisor? Is the brand well established? Is the product or service unique? How is this company different from competitors? Does it have hidden profit centers, like rents or annual meetings? Does the franchisor provide support like marketing and training? Does the company have a history of litigation? What is the background of top management? How long have they been in the business? What is their reputation, and have they had any personal bankruptcies or litigation?	Investigate your potential franchisor thoroughly. Nick Bibby, a franchise consultant, is blunt: "Most — I'll say a minimum of 70 percent of all franchises — are not worth the powder it would take to blow them up." "Not all franchises are created equal," says Jim Coen, president of the Dunkin' Donuts Independent Franchise Owners. "It's incumbent on the franchisee to really drill down and figure out the potential to make money."
5. What do other franchisees say?	Have I visited with the existing franchisees? Have I spent time hanging out at other franchisees? Was I able to track down some franchisees who left the system and ask about their experiences?	Every franchisor is required to provide you the business contact information (names, addresses, and telephone numbers) of all of its franchisees located in your state. If the number of franchised units in a state is fewer than 100, the company also must include the contact information for franchisees based in contiguous states, and then the next closest states, until at least 100 franchised outlets are listed.
6. Can you afford it?	What is the total cost of starting with this franchise? Where will you get the capital to start? What is the break-even point for the business? How long does it take to reach break-even?	Many first-time franchisees make the mistake of underestimating working capital requirements and buy a franchise at the upper range of their affordability. As they say: It will cost twice as much and take twice as long. "It's not uncommon at all for a store to open and still be struggling a year or two later," says Peter Birkeland, a small business consultant in Chicago and author of *Franchising Dreams.* "You have to have a lot of working capital."
7. What are the legal terms?	Have I been provided with the franchise agreement and the disclosure document? Have I discussed the legal terms with a lawyer who represents me and understands franchising?	The franchise agreement serves as the primary and most important legal document that will govern and define the legal relationship between the franchisor and franchisee. Franchise law varies by state, so what matters is a how a particular law applies in your state.

(continued)

TABLE 4.7		
(Continued)		
What you are trying to figure out?	Questions to ask yourself	Why is this important?
8. Could you do better as an independent?	What specific benefits do I get from running this business as a franchisee, rather than as an independent? Will the franchise provide continuing value for the life of the franchise agreement?	When Timothy Bates, a professor at Wayne State University, studied a sample of more than 20,000 new businesses, he found that 35% of franchise units had gone out of business compared with 28% of independents. Franchisees can have high failure rate, because franchisors vary in the amount of support they provide to help succeed.
9. Can you negotiate?	Are there things I would like to negotiate? Have I asked the franchisor, if we can change the things I think are not fair or reasonable?	Terms may be less negotiable with strong franchises, especially on items that might dilute the integrity of the brand and/or create inequalities among franchisees. Some franchisors flatly refuse to budge from the standard template. Aspiring franchisees should ask their franchisor a simple question: Are you willing to negotiate the franchise agreement? If their answer is "no," consider walking away.

Comprehension Check

1. Franchising is a good option for everyone who wants to start a business. Do you agree?
2. Some firms are hasty in franchising. Explain.
3. What support does a new franchisee need from the franchisor?

Summary

Some franchises are very successful: McDonald's, The UPS Store, and 7-Eleven. Some franchises do not work out well: Golf Etc. and Planet Beach, for example. While the history of small businesses is quite old, franchising is a relatively recent American invention. In modern society, there is tremendous heterogeneity in franchising around the world. One simple typology of franchising identifies different types of firms based on their growth and expansion. Of course, other typologies are possible too. Despite the tremendous growth in franchising worldwide, franchising is no easy, sure-shot path to success. Some fail because of lapses on the part of the franchisor, while others fail because of problems on the part of the franchisees. It is useful to think through the opportunities and challenges of franchising before you decide to move forward in this direction. Franchising is also a heavily regulated mode of doing business. It is important that both franchisors and franchisees pay careful attention to the legal issues involved in franchising.

Live Exercise

"Johnny could use some of your advice," your mother says when you call her to share that you are thinking of going on a study abroad trip next year. "What's going on, Mom?" you ask. "Call him, and you will find out" is all your mother says before she disconnects. When you call Johnny, he is as upbeat and enthusiastic as always. "We are now doing $200,000 in annual sales, so things are pretty good with the business," he tells you. "I am so excited that the business is working out well. You know, soap has been around for 4000 years, but there has been nothing like this before." You wanted to tell him that entrepreneurs often show optimism bias, but you bite your tongue. Johnny and his wife are such good friends with your parents, and you don't want to say anything that would upset your parents. You do need them to pay for the study abroad trip that everyone in school has been talking about. "I have plans for new colors and materials, as well as a travel case and additional distribution channels," he continues. "Mom said you wanted my advice on something," you respond. "Ah, yes! I want to ask you about franchising," he says. "They say franchising is a way to expand your business without incurring much cost. Do you think franchising could work for us?" Johnny asks.

What would you advise Johnny to do? Can you prepare a short memo preparing your recommendation for Johnny and the reason(s) for your recommendation?

World of Books

There is much more to learn about franchising than can be covered in just one chapter. If you want to learn more about franchising, you may find the following books useful:

From Ice Cream to the Internet by Scott Shane
The Economics of Franchising by Roger Blaire and Francine Lafontaine
From French Fries to a Franchise by Michele Layet

In the Movies

Isaac Singer may have been the father of franchising, but it was Ray Kroc of McDonald's who defined franchising the way it is understood today by the public. The true story how a struggling salesman used franchising to transform McDonald's from a single-restaurant business to the largest fast-food franchise in the country is captured in *The Founder*.

Things to Remember

LO 4.1   Explain the meaning and history of franchising
- Franchising is a legal agreement that allows one business to be operated using the name and business procedures of another business that already exists.
- Franchising allows the franchisor to sell the benefits of its expertise, systems, and reputation to the franchisee in exchange for payment.
- The franchisee is required to pay a fee (or royalty) for the right to do business.
- Franchising is widely celebrated as a particularly American invention.
- Franchising does not always require heavy investment in infrastructure as there are many successful franchise systems that can be run from home or online.
- There are four basic forms of franchising.

LO 4.2   Identify the advantages and disadvantages in franchising
- While franchising allows you not to have to fully reinvent the wheel (as there is a proven system provided by the franchisor), it also constrains the franchisee within the boundaries set by the franchisor.
- Franchising allows the franchisor to expand its market footprint with limited financial investment.
- For growth-oriented companies, franchising allows opportunities to expand with a simpler management structure than would be needed to grow without franchising.
- Many franchisors provide training to their franchisees, both in preparation for running the business and for instructing them in the finer points after the business is in operation.

- Disagreements between the franchisor and its franchisees may arise over many issues, such as hours of operations, range and cost of offerings, expansion plans, and royalties.
- Some franchisors mislead potential franchisees by making exaggerated promises.

LO 4.3   **Distinguish between different types of franchises**
- Franchises are not homogenous in their structure and operations.
- Beginners are early-stage franchising companies.
- Developers are moderately established, although they are still not national players.
- Growers have already spent a substantial time in the franchise business and yet continue to grow at a healthy rate.
- Maturers are companies where growth has slowed considerably, so they open very few new stores.
- All franchisors have to follow federal and state laws that regulate franchising.
- Franchisors that win awards or positive media coverage enhance their credibility and legitimacy.

LO 4.4   **Decide whether franchising is a good option for you**
- The decision to consider franchising can be studied from either the franchisor's perspective or the franchisee's perspective.
- Many franchisors rush too fast into franchising after the first unit takes off; many franchisees are hasty about buying a franchise.
- Read the franchise contract carefully and try to understand it as best as you can.
- Before signing the franchise agreement and committing yourself, it is helpful to think about your business needs and weigh the pros and cons of the various franchising options.
- Franchisees should be careful about protection from other franchise organizations associated with the same franchisor.

Key Terms

franchising	conversion franchising	growers	undercapitalized
franchisor	business-format	maturers	franchisors
franchisee	franchising	uniform franchise	relationship state
trade name franchising	master franchise	disclosure document	
product distribution	beginners	registration state	
franchising	developers		

Experiential Exercise

This exercise is designed for students working individually. Use of the Internet (via laptops or hand-held devices like the iPad or smartphone) during the exercise is necessary.

There are several websites that list upcoming franchises. One such website is Franchise Opportunities (https://www.franchiseopportunities.com/hot-and-trendy-franchises), which lists hot, trendy, and new franchises. Pick any one such list that provides 10–20 franchises. Which business sectors do you see

most represented in the list you chose? Which of these franchises seem suitable for someone who is just starting out in business?

From the list you picked, identify three specific franchises that interest you most. What is it about these franchises that interest you? What stops you from going forward with any of these franchising opportunities? If you had a chance to ask questions to the franchisor about taking one of their units for your business, what would you ask them?

CHAPTER 5

Small Business Ownership Through Acquisition

LEARNING OBJECTIVES

This chapter will help you to:

LO 5.1 Define the meaning of business acquisition and outline its pros and cons

LO 5.2 Provide a bird's-eye view of the acquisition process

LO 5.3 Distinguish between different types of business acquisitions

LO 5.4 Describe how to value a business

The key to making acquisitions is being ready because you never know when the right big one is going to come along.

JAMES MCNERNEY

5.0 Introduction

Many enterprising individuals take conventional routes to becoming small business owners. They pursue their own startup, perhaps join a family business, or even consider a franchise opportunity. Another path to small business ownership that is gaining traction in recent years is buying an existing business, or business acquisition. The online marketplace BizBuySell, which lists small businesses for sale, reports over one million monthly visits from people interested in buying or selling businesses. Of course, not everyone sees value in acquisitions. Louis Gerstner Jr., the former CEO of IBM and the best-selling author of *Who Says Elephants Can't Dance*, was adamant that "Successful enterprises are built from the ground up; you can't assemble them with a bunch of acquisitions."

Acquisitions show up in a small business owner's life in two ways. The first way, and the one that will be the focus of this chapter, is getting into business by buying out a venture that is already in operation. The second way, not discussed in this chapter, is selling a business to a well-established corporation. Consider Ryan Smith, who as a student at Brigham Young University in Utah created a research tool for academics with his father and a college classmate. The Web-based business they started, Qualtrics, now counts among its customers every major US university and many blue-chip companies, including FedEx and PepsiCo. In 2018, the German enterprise software giant SAP acquired Qualtrics for $8 billion in cash. Many business owners sell their ventures to other companies. Exiting the firm through selling your firm to a larger, more-established company is also a well-trodden path for many business owners, but it will not be the focus of this chapter. The purpose of this chapter is to look at acquisitions as a path to small business ownership.

SPOTLIGHT | Kevin Taweel: Finding Success by Acquiring a Small Business

Kevin Taweel was in the last quarter of the MBA program at Stanford University, but he still didn't know what he wanted to do after he got his degree. Kevin had an undergraduate degree in mechanical engineering from McGill University, after which he had spent three years in mergers and acquisitions (M&A) at the now-defunct Salomon Brothers, a financial services firm. While working there, Kevin was exposed to several different industries, but he did not feel passionate about any particular business. Kevin avoided on-campus recruiting because he couldn't see himself working for someone else. What really excited him was the possibility of running his own business someday. Unfortunately, none of the startup ideas he generated or encountered interested him much.

After talking to his professors and visiting entrepreneurs at Stanford, Kevin identified an emergency road services company, Road Rescue, that could be bought for about $8 million. At the time, Road Rescue was a small, Texas-based company that offered roadside assistance through local wireless carriers. The company was for sale, but there was one major problem: Kevin had no money. In fact, Kevin found it difficult to cover his living expenses at the time. Kevin and Jim Ellis, a fellow graduate of the Stanford Graduate School of Business, reached out to investors and raised the money to buy the company.

Four years later, Kevin and Jim also bought Nashville-based Merrimac Group, which provided specialty insurance for cell phones. By 2001, their business had reached over $200 million in sales. That same year, Kevin and Lee received the Ernst & Young Entrepreneur of the Year Award. Kevin had arrived!

More acquisitions followed. The company, now called Asurion LLC, employs about 19,000 employees and brings in about $9 billion in revenues. It provides insurance for a broad range of products, including consumer electronics, appliances, and jewelry. The company is considered a leading device insurance and support services provider. The Tennessee-based insurance giant is the "white label" provider of smartphone insurance for the big four wireless carriers: AT&T, Verizon, T-Mobile, and Sprint. If you own or lease a smartphone, there is a decent chance you also carry an Asurion insurance plan.

Kevin is now the chairman of the board of directors at Asurion. He is also a faculty member at the Stanford Graduate School of Business where he teaches entrepreneurship courses in the MBA program. He is a member of the school's advisory council and has served on its management board. He is also on the board of trustees for the California Institute of Technology (Caltech). He lives in the ultra-ritzy Silicon Valley town of Atherton in California on a 2.5 acre, $30+ million property located on what is often considered the wealthiest residential street in town.

Discussion Questions

1. What benefits do you think Kevin got from acquiring Road Rescue as opposed to starting a similar firm?

2. How did Kevin raise the money to buy Road Rescue?

3. Do you think Kevin could have foreseen the success he had with Road Rescue? How far in the future can one be reasonably expected to think when acquiring an existing business?

Module 5.1 Business Acquisition and Its Two Sides

Becoming a business owner through acquisition means buying out an existing venture. One can define **business acquisition** as taking over a company that is already in operation. The payment can be in cash or stock or a combination of the two (cash and stock). When WhatsApp was acquired by Facebook in 2014, the social networking behemoth paid about $4 billion in cash and the rest in stock for the test messaging app used widely across the globe (albeit mostly outside the United States). Every acquisition has two parties: (1) the party interested in buying, or the **bidder**; and (2) the firm on the market, or the **target**. In the Facebook–WhatsApp example, Facebook was the bidder (and the acquirer) with WhatsApp the target (and, ultimately, the acquired).

At this stage, you may be thinking "Well, I don't have much money, so buying an existing business is not an option for me". Before you make that decision, there is something else you should know. Several people have been successful at business acquisition without spending much money. They have – you may find it hard to believe – bought the business for free (or almost free). An unusual route to small business ownership is through sweepstake-style competitions where you can buy a small firm for a negligible amount. Some owners sell their business by organizing a contest that has a small entrance fee and a challenge like a photo submission. If enough people enter, the entry fees add up to something close to the desired sale price for the seller. If too few people enter, the contest is usually canceled and contestants get refunds. For the buyer, the transaction can be a bargain as he or she gets an attractive property for close to nothing. However, any contest to sell a business in such a way cannot completely be one of chance, as it would be an illegal lottery. For this reason, the entrance fee is matched with a challenge like an essay submission. Let's call it **Janice-style business acquisitions** in honor of Janice Sage, who became the first small business owner in the United States to purchase an existing business through a challenge-based public contest.

KEY TAKEAWAY

A Janice-style acquisition involves buying a business through an essay-based contest for practically no cost. It is legal in some states, but not everywhere.

At the foothills of White Mountains in Western Maine on the border with New Hampshire is a small boutique hotel: Center Lovell Inn. The CLI is a Georgian-style historic farmhouse built in 1803 and located on Main Street in Lovell, Maine. Bill and Susie Mosca had been married only 10 months when they decided to buy a mansion featured in the "House for Sale" section of *Yankee* magazine. They paid the owner's asking price: $39,500. Transforming the house into a beautiful inn, the Moscas built a successful lodging business on a shoestring budget and lots of old-fashioned sweat (living and working without central heating for the first five years). After running the business for about 20 years, they sold the inn to Janice Sage in an essay contest for $100 and a 250-word essay on why the person wanted to own an inn in Center Lovell, becoming the first successful business buyout through a contest. The Moscas' contest drew more than 7000 entries, but they returned 2000 because they had set a limit of 5000 entries. "The person who writes the best essay wins something they would probably never own," Bill shares. "The others know going in what the chances are. And the owner gets to sell his or her property." Janice Sage ran the

CLI for over two decades, before she sold it to Rose and Prince Adams in another essay-style contest with a $125 entry fee. She received 7255 entries for the contests and asked two independent judges to pick from the 20 finalist essays.

Interactive Exercise

For four years, the Adams family of the US Virgin Islands ran the CLI they bought from Janice Sage. The property is now valued at $1.5 million. The Adams family is ready to sell CLI to the next buyer. Identify the advantages and disadvantages of selling through an essay-based contest.

As you can imagine, Janice-style acquisitions are uncommon. They are also not allowed everywhere. Maine does, Massachusetts does not, for example. Yet, it is fully legal to buy an existing business for a dollar (yes, just one dollar!). When businessman and philanthropist Sidney Harman bought the venerable, but struggling, news magazine *Newsweek* from *The Washington Post*, he paid $1 for it. There are several other such business acquisitions: The magazine *TV Guide* was sold for $1, and so was Doctors Hospital in Perry Township, OH. The catch in such acquisitions is that outstanding liabilities of the business (that is, the money the firm owes to others) are the responsibility of the buyer. Carl Taylor, a young Australian entrepreneur, even runs a website for those interested in buying firms for "little to no money," which you can check out at https://www.howto buyabusinessforadollar.com.au.

What Do You Think?

Many business owners have found that essay-based contests do not work for them. Paul Spell of Northern Alabama (goat cheese farm) and Carole Kelaher of Vermont (cupcake shop) found out, to their dismay, that sometimes there are not enough paying contestants to make the buyout happen (despite much media attention). Why do you think that is the case? What are some steps they can take to address the problems they face?

Think of a business as a horse already running around the track. What happens if you change the jockey? If the new jockey is talented and motivated to succeed, the horse may run even faster than before. For those who believe that acquisition of an existing business is a good path to business ownership, a good horse and good jockey are both critical factors (and also a good trainer). When investors were asked what they thought was important when acquiring a business, the general sentiment was 50% horse, 30% jockey, and 20% trainer. Clearly, the business to acquire is the most important factor when making the acquisition decision. Some like to quote Warren Buffet on this issue: "When a management team with a reputation for brilliance tackles a business with a reputation for bad economics, it is the reputation of the business that remains intact." The quality of the target firm is therefore paramount when considering an acquisition.

At this stage, you may be wondering how common it is to buy an existing business as a path to small business ownership. Once you start looking around, you will find many businesses where the owner bought a venture already in operation. We discuss only two examples here, but they will help you understand how commonplace acquisitions are a way to become a small business owner. Tanasi Brewing is a boutique brewing and supplier of home-brewing materials in Chattanooga, TN. The current owner Clinton Salle

> **TABLE 5.1**
>
> **Buying an Existing Business Has Advantages and Disadvantages That Need to Be Seriously Considered**
>
> | Thinking of buying a business? | |
> |---|---|
> | **Advantages** | **Disadvantages** |
> | Existing customer base | Considerable investment |
> | Established processes | Expensive search |
> | Proven and tested market | Honor prior commitments |
> | Short return on investment | Lack of clarity about reasons for sale |
> | Reputation | |

was an investment banker with an interesting hobby: brewing beer. When he learned that the owner of Tanasi was looking for a buyer, he made an offer and bought the place. Another owner who acquired an existing business is Patrick Jacks who bought a gym (Tru-Fit 24/7) in Tuscaloosa, AL. Patrick used to work out at the gym when he learned that the owners wanted to sell. Although he was already working full-time in a paid position and managing a part-time venture on the side, he decided to buy Tru-Fit as something he could run together with his daughter. For more examples of acquisitions as a path to small business ownership, you can check out Ryan Moran at https://www.youtube.com/watch?v=EuC1AXha9RY&app=desktop discuss what it takes to buy a business, give examples of successful buyouts, and interview entrepreneurs who prefer buying a business over starting one from scratch.

One needs to carefully think through the pros and cons of becoming a small business owner through buying out an existing firm (see Table 5.1). Like with every other path to small business ownership, acquiring an existing business has its advantages, but it also has some disadvantages.

5.1.1 Bright Side of Acquisitions

Existing customer base. Perhaps the most attractive aspect of buying out an existing business is that there is an existing customer base ready to buy the company's offerings. As a result, businesses with a loyal customer base, preferably customers who buy often and on terms favorable to the business (e.g. on a cash basis), should be prioritized over businesses where the customer base is more fickle and transitory.

Established processes. Another attractive feature of buying an existing business is that the processes through which the offerings are produced and brought to the market are already in place. Because of established processes, the new owner does not need to think about how to sequence operations or deliver goods to the customer. Things are already in place in an operational business (though there may be a need for improvement).

Proven and tested market. Every new business has to grapple with the question of whether there is a large enough market to support its business. When buying an **established business**, the question of market viability has already been affirmatively answered. The fact that the business exists and is operating profitably shows that there is a proven market for its offerings.

Short return on investment. An established business will have some revenues with some expenses, and, hopefully, the revenues exceed the costs. As a result, when one buys such a business, there is a positive return on investment from day one.

Reputation. Businesses come with their reputation, that is, how the business is viewed by suppliers, customers, and other stakeholders. If the business has a good reputation, then the new owners also benefit from the positive image the business has built in the market.

5.1.2 Downsides of Acquisition

Despite the benefits of acquisitions, there are also some disadvantages one needs to consider when making an acquisition decision. In effect, buying an existing business also has some pitfalls that limit its appeal to a prospective owner.

Considerable investment. Buying out an existing business is not a cheap proposition, especially if the business is doing well. One needs to pay not only for the physical assets of the business (which can be priced in the market), but also for the reputation of the business (which cannot be readily priced).

Expensive search. How does one find a business available for sale? Often, the process of finding a business to buy can be expensive. The prospective buyer needs to budget for lost wages, due diligence, legal fees, and other expenses. There are likely to be many wrong turns on the way, and each of these wrong turns has its costs.

Honor prior commitments. When one buys an existing business, he or she needs to honor or renegotiate contracts and commitments already in place. Perhaps the current owner has made certain commitments to employees, suppliers, and customers that are financially burdensome. There may also be verbal commitments one is expected to honor. While verbal commitments may not be legally binding, they do create a psychological contract between the parties, the violation of which can cause one party to feel aggrieved about how they were treated by the new owners.

Reasons for sale. Buying a business involves seeing a positive future in a venture in which someone else does not see a future. Why is the current owner selling the business? Ideally, the buyer knows why the seller wants to sell the business. Practically, the buyer does not always know the real reason(s) the existing owner is selling. The seller has little incentive to fully disclose why they are selling the business, especially if the reasons for sale are not conducive to the seller (e.g. lawsuits or penalties that are likely to come in the future).

Economists talk about the challenge of **information asymmetry**, where one party in an economic transaction has greater material information than the other party. In business acquisitions, the seller generally knows more about the business than the buyer. This creates two problems for the buyer – **adverse selection** and **moral hazard**. A seller is more likely to offer the business for sale when he or she knows they can get a good price that is more than the market price of the different parts of the business. The buyer, of course, does not fully know how much the business is worth, so the less the buyer knows about the business, the better the price the seller will be able to get. This is the problem of adverse selection. After the buyer and seller agree on the sale of the business, the seller is usually allowed a period of time to cease their involvement in the business. Unfortunately, this creates a perverse incentive for the seller to behave recklessly. This is the problem of moral hazard. When buying a business, prospective buyers need to carefully watch out for adverse selection and moral hazard problems. While these problems can never be fully eliminated from the acquisition transaction, astute buyers will try to reduce or minimize the problem.

Like all business decisions, the decision to buy an existing business has its advantages and disadvantages. One should weigh the pros and cons and think through the problems that come up in acquisitions to boost the chances of success. Aspiring entrepreneurs looking to buy a company tend to make some common mistakes. Professor

Timothy Bovard of INSEAD Business School in France has spent years studying entrepreneurship through acquisition. In this short interview at https://www.youtube.com/watch?v=EMzf54ne7Oc, he shares his views on misunderstandings about entrepreneurship through acquisition and the common mistakes entrepreneurs make when they pursue this path.

Fast Company is a New York–based magazine focused on business-related issues. In an article projecting "a booming business-for-sale market," with restaurants, retail, bars, and Internet services as some of the top sectors for business buyers, the magazine recommended eight things for aspiring buyers to keep in mind before they take over an existing business:

1. Research, research, research. Obtain as much information as you can about firms you may consider buying and their owners.
2. Find good matchmakers. Identify competent people to introduce you to the target firm.
3. Do your due diligence. There is no substitute for in-depth examination of the performance and financials of the target firm.
4. Understand potential customers and competitors. Buyers need to understand who they will be competing to and who they will be selling to once they acquire a firm.
5. Think through how you will add value to the business. What will you bring to the firm that is currently missing?
6. Develop the pitch you will make to the existing owner. Why should the owner sell the firm to you rather than to someone else?
7. Be patient through the closing process. Do not try to rush things through, especially as the deal comes close to the finish line.
8. Have a 100-day plan. Before you step into the CEO's role, think carefully about how you will navigate the first 100 days at the wheel. Kevin Hudson, Managing Director at Grant Thornton LLP, notes that the "first 100 days will ultimately determine whether the transaction evolves from promise to performance." As Figure 5.1 shows, about half of the acquirers always have a **100-day plan** when they buy an existing company.

Comprehension Check

1. Define business acquisition.
2. What are some of the advantages of business ownership through acquisitions?
3. Identify the disadvantages or challenges associated with business ownership through acquisitions.

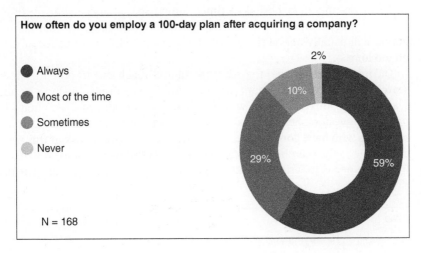

FIGURE 5.1 A 100-day Plan Can Be Critical for Success After an Acquisition
Source: Grant Thornton 2013 Report "What Can Be Done in 100 Days?" © 2013, Grant Thornton LLP

Module 5.2 The Acquisition Process

As you may guess, buying an existing business is not as straightforward as going out to buy a new car. One needs to proceed forward thoughtfully and considerately, keeping in mind that when it comes to acquiring a business a bad deal is worse than no deal. While the exact trajectory of every business acquisition will differ, some steps are common to all buyouts. Of course, before someone embarks on the long journey of buying out an existing business, it is helpful to put in a significant amount of forethought and self-reflection. Some people view business ownership through a **parenting metaphor**: "My business is my baby," they say. Brian Smith, the Australian surfer credited with bringing Ugg boots to the United States, wrote the book *The Birth of a Brand* in which he talks about how expecting your business to take off right away is like expecting your two-year-old to head off to college tomorrow. Brian is not exaggerating when he likens growing a business to raising a baby. Many people use the parenting metaphor to describe the work that business owners do in nurturing their ventures. Seen from this perspective, a business acquisition is like taking on the responsibility of someone else's child. Not everyone is ready for such a major responsibility.

> **KEY TAKEAWAY**
>
> From a parenting metaphor, running a business bought from someone else is like taking care of someone's child.

Most people see the acquisition process as involving four stages: raising capital, identifying targets, funding the buyout, and operating the business to create value (see Figure 5.2). These four stages are what may be called a formal acquisition. An informal acquisition may skip a stage (e.g. raising capital), change the order in which some stages occur (e.g. identify targets and funding the buyout). Despite these variations, the four-stage business acquisition process described here provides a useful framework to help understand how some people acquire existing firms.

5.2.1 Step 1: Raising Capital

Searching for a business to buy costs money, so one starts with thinking about how to obtain the capital to conduct the search. The capital is needed to pay the searcher's salary (personal expenses) and cover expenses such as office space, travel, and due diligence costs for an uncertain period of time. Some experts advise **searchers** to budget their capital requirements for two to three years, because searches that go longer than this period will usually not be fruitful. Perhaps the search is not headed anywhere, if it goes on too long.

During this first stage, the searcher should reach out to potential investors, former searchers, or current searchers who successfully acquired a business or abandoned their search. Such outreach brings with it valuable knowledge and also helps build a pool of potential investors. Searchers should spend as much time as they can, and learn from searchers who have gone before them. The first question to ask at this stage is: Who will contribute to the search fund? If one expects several investors to contribute to the search fund, one needs to write up a **Private Placement Memorandum** (or PPM). The PPM

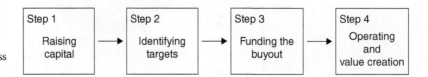

FIGURE 5.2 Four Steps of Business Acquisition

is a formal document that describes the searchers' background and motivation, how the search fund will be structured, and how much money is being sought. The completed PPM is then sent out to potential investors, so that both parties (the searchers and the investor) can assess each other and make an informed decision about fit. Searchers typically sell "units" of their search funds to investors. There are typically 10–20 units in each fund, each valued between $20,000 and $40,000 (so that a search fund can be as small as about $200,000 or as large as about $800,000). Investors who decide to buy one or more units in the search fund get two main benefits. First, when the buyout happens, they get preferred equity in the acquired business proportional to their investment in the search fund. Second, they get the right of first refusal to invest additional capital in the acquired business. When all fund units are sold, the searcher is ready to move to the next stage.

For those who expect the search fund to be supported fully or primarily through informal personal loans or by one's family business (or another existing business), then a formal PPM may not be needed (unless the investing family asks for it to balance the interests of different family members). Nevertheless, it is still advisable to put together a short document summarizing one's background and goals before embarking on a search. Many entrepreneurs look toward professional investors who specialize in working with young entrepreneurs interested in owning a business through acquisition. Pacific Lake Partners, with offices in Boston (MA) and San Mateo (CA), is one such investor that has worked with over 200 entrepreneurs to raise money for business buyouts.

5.2.2 Step 2: Identifying Targets

Once a search fund is in place, one can begin the arduous, and often time-consuming, task of identifying and evaluating targets. There are two paths one can follow here: proprietary and brokered. The difference between the two paths is that one identifies targets either through one's own network (proprietary) or through an intermediary with prior experience in this area (broker). **Proprietary deals** are not actively circulating in the market, so they are more difficult, but also tend to be more lucrative. **Brokered deals**

Some buyers and sellers advertise in the newspaper when they have a business to sell or want to buy a business.

are being actively marketed, so the competition is greater for these deals, which generally makes them more expensive. Take a look at two advertised opportunities from The Marketplace section of the *Wall Street Journal*. One is an **advertised deal** to buy a Florida-based company from the owners. The other is a buyer seeking deals, probably directly from sellers.

KEY TAKEAWAY

The ideal business to buy is a profitable company in an attractive stable niche where the owner wants to exit for personal reasons.

What kind of target should one acquire? The ideal acquisition target is a profitable company in an attractive stable niche where the owner wants to exit for personal reasons. The worst acquisition target: a poorly performing company in a declining industry segment where the owner is exiting because she does not see many prospects. Peter Cancro was a high school quarterback in Point Pleasant Beach, NJ, when he became interested in buying Mike's Subs, a local sandwich shop where he'd worked for the past four years. The owners were asking for $125,000, and another buyer was willing to pay. Peter went to his coach (who was also a banker) to raise the money for the buyout, laying out the business's gross profits and earnings potential. In the four years he had worked at the shop, Peter had noticed that winters were quiet, but business exploded during summer, when the town's population quadrupled as people came for the beach, with lines regularly snaking out the door. The coach loaned him the money with a seven-year payback plan. Over time, Peter parlayed the one sandwich shop he bought into Jersey Mike's Subs, a national chain with more than a billion dollar in annual sales.

Chris Henriksen, who bought a small health-care business that offers remote patient monitoring for keeping people home from hospitals, shares that searching for a business to buy is like kissing a lot of frogs to find your prince. He remembers calling up companies to see if the owner was interested in selling. "Cold calls were the worst part of the process, mentally, emotionally, and satisfaction wise . . . it was brutal. Every day you're going to work, to make twenty phone calls, research stuff and probably get no output. No one calls back, or if they do, they tell you you're an idiot. Once in a while you get a meeting, only to find out that the company is terrible." There is also the risk of fraud. Many people are scammed when trying to identify target firms. Such fraud can happen because either the seller or the broker makes up fictitious information about the business. It is therefore important to be careful in your quest to identify suitable targets. In this video at https://www.youtube.com/watch?v=p8fDN2QkgoQ, David Barnett, an expert in managing small- and medium-sized firms, shares how you can avoid scams when searching for businesses to buy.

During the search phase, it is important that the searcher proactively communicates with investors to make sure that they are aware of what is going with the search. There are two channels of communication between investors and searcher: formal communication (which is quite standard) and informal communication (varies depending on investor and searcher). Formal communication takes the form of periodic updates that summarize the progress made in that time period. Of the different investors, there are some with which the searcher speaks regularly, perhaps even multiple times a week. These investors serve as coaches, mentors, and advisors to the searcher.

5.2.3 Step 3: Funding the Buyout

After preliminary discussions with the target firm, if the searcher wants to move ahead with the deal, a formal investment proposal is sent to the investors. Favorable response from the investors moves the process forward to due diligence, where all information is vetted and questions answered. After due diligence is completed, one goes back to the investors for final approval and signing the letter of interest. It is worth remembering that the investors are not obligated to provide capital; they simply have the right of first refusal. Consequently, it is the searcher's responsibility to obtain the capital needed to close the deal.

5.2.4 Step 4: Operating and Value Creation

The deal has closed. What's next? Some searchers get so occupied with the search process that they forget that closing the deal is not the goal (although it may seem like it is), but an important means to an end. Transitioning into the CEO role – where you are your own boss – is an altogether different beast, requiring very different skills that not everyone has. Just take a look at the list of well-known CEOs who had to give up the top spot because they were found undeserving of leading their firms: Adam Neumann of WeWork (who famously considered himself as just the right combination of Mark Zuckerberg and Sheryl Sandberg of Facebook) and Travis Kalanick of Uber (who found himself in one controversy or another throughout his time at the helm), to name just two. Those who transition into a CEO role through acquisition need to embrace it wholeheartedly and start behaving like a leader who others in the company can look up to for advice and mentorship.

In some situations, the new CEO may need to work alongside the previous CEO during a transition period. Having a transition period to work with the previous CEO allows the search-turned-CEO to get a better handle on the business and build positive relationships with key partners (such as suppliers and customers). However, the previous CEO should not overstay, so that it is optimal to phase his or her out at most over a 6–12 month period. There are few successful examples of previous CEOs who have been happy in the firm under new management. This is because, sooner or later, the new CEO and the old CEO will disagree about the direction of the firm. Case in point: Within five years of the Facebook's much-hyped acquisition of WhatsApp, founders Brian Acton and Jan Koum departed after running into disagreements with their new bosses.

Interactive Exercise

Do you know anyone who bought their business? If not, ask your professors and parents for help identifying someone who became a business owner through acquisition. Interview this person on how they identified the business to buy, the sources from which they raised money, and the post-acquisition challenges they faced.

For incoming owners, experienced people in the acquisition business suggest three best practices to be successful at his or her new job:

Ask questions. Incoming owners should be willing to ask questions, reaching out to employees about why and how things are done in the company the way they are. This does two things: Existing employees will feel valued and the answers give the new owner an insider view of the business.

Be patient. No matter how tempting it is for new owners to begin changing things immediately, it is worth being patient and not making major changes over the first few months. Avoiding the urge to change things immediately to put their own imprint on the business, new owners need some time to gain a nuanced understanding of the business. Patience allows the new owner time to learn the business well.

Choose comfort. When an acquisition happens, employees, customers, and suppliers get concerned about what will happen to the company. Anyone who is reading this book has definitely heard the popular phrase "Change is the only constant in this world." A more uncommon saying tells us "Change is scary." As a result, when a new CEO comes in, he or she needs to assure stakeholders to make them feel comfortable and secure.

It's good for the new owner to learn the A, B, C of what he or she should be doing in the first few weeks after the acquisition. For this reason, budget appropriately when doing an acquisition: There is no point expecting that revenues will suddenly go off the charts and costs will readily shrink to nothing in a short time after transition. Once the new owner has settled in and has a good grasp of the business, then he or she can work on gradually redirecting the firm in the way he or she wants to take it.

What Do You Think?

Joe Schneider is a serial entrepreneur, focusing on the food and beverage industry. Over the years, Schneider has acquired and grown a variety of small companies, including a bakery and a confectioner. His first acquisition was a candy company, and it taught Schneider many things he had not considered before. On his first day in his new office, Schneider noticed employees waiting in long lines to use the two lunchroom microwaves to heat up lunches they had brought from home. He found that one customer accounted for about 55% of the company's sales and revenue growth was quite weak. Only 60% of the orders were being shipped complete on time. He was surprised to see that some employees were happy with the status quo, though there were others who were ready for someone to shake things up. He also noticed that the company's production line had not been maintained well in recent years, and many of the facilities looked run down and overused. What should Schneider do now? Can you develop a plan for Schneider?

Comprehension Check

1. Explain Private Placement Memorandum (PPM).
2. What are the four main stages of the acquisition process?
3. What are some advantages and challenges of incubated search for the aspiring business owner?

Module 5.3 Possible Acquisition Paths

The growing popularity of acquisition as a path to small business ownership has spawned several options for prospective business owners. Prospective searchers need to consider whether acquisitions are an appropriate path for them to have their own business. At the same time, they also need to think through which of the available paths will work well for them. There are four main paths to acquiring a small business: (1) **self-funded search**, (2) **traditional search fund**, (3) **sponsored search**, and (4) **incubated search**.

What is the best source of information to learn about the pros and cons of each path? The answer: members of the search community, which comprises current and former searchers, CEOs, and investors.

5.3.1 Self-funded Search

As the name suggests, self-funded search (SFS) involves the searcher(s) funding their own search. Searchers who are self-funded may be dipping into their savings (or taking out informal personal loans) or being backed by their family resources. The benefits of SFS are that it gives a searcher the autonomy to search in the direction of their choosing and at the pace that they are comfortable with. The searcher can focus on small companies or large, in a particular industry or geography (perhaps in the general area where they have family), and in sectors overlooked by investors (say, dating services for married folks). Searchers also may prefer SFS if they want greater equity in the business or want to make sure they have majority control after the acquisition is complete. However, SFS can make it difficult for the searcher to signal credibility and get mentorship from experienced investors (unless the searcher already has the investors in place).

He Went SFS!

Austin Hall, founder and director of Brick Hall Partners, reflects on his journey as a self-funded searcher. He discusses his initial motivation to pursue entrepreneurship through acquisition and why he chose a self-funded search. His search led him to buy Greenwise Organic Lawn Care and Landscape Design.

Wikimedia Commons

Watch the video online at: https://www.youtube.com/watch?v=rnMvUWGT5Zo

5.3.2 Traditional Search Fund

The traditional search fund (TSF) model got its start in 1984 when Professor Irving Grousbeck and Harvard graduate Jim Southern launched Nova Capital. In brief, TSF involves a searcher bringing together a group of 15–20 investors to raise search capital for about two years. The investors are essentially buying the right to invest significantly more capital in an eventual acquisition. If the investors choose not to invest in the deal, their initial capital is rolled over into the acquisition. If an acquisition is not made, the search capital is lost (so investment in the search fund is not risk free).

When a single searcher succeeds in making an acquisition, they usually receive up to 25% carried interest (30% for a team of two) on the gains from the acquisition. The searcher invests time and effort in finding a company to buy and acquire but is not expected to invest money in the deal. Therefore, the searcher's equity is structured as carried interest with the initial search capital, the acquisition capital, and a preferred return on investment payable to investors before the searcher enjoys the split of capital gains. The right to carried interest, or capital gains, is split into three parts: one-third at acquisition, one-third over a specified period of time (say four to five years), and the remaining third at exit (in order to incentivize the searcher to maximize investor returns).

After forming Nova with investments from professors and former associates, Southern searched for businesses that were open to being acquired. He eventually came across Uniform Printing, a $43-million, 750-employee specialty insurance documents division of a publicly traded printing company. With the mentorship and guidance of his investors, Southern was able to grow the company over the next 10 years, selling the business in 1994 for a 24 times the return on investment.

TSFs typically target companies in the $5–$30 million price range – requiring $2–$10 million of equity capital – in fragmented industries, with stable market positions, histories of consistent cash flows, and opportunities for improvement and growth in the long term. Principals start by raising about $500,000 to fund the search. Once a target firm is identified, and a letter of intent signed, the principals will go to the original investors and other sources to raise the equity needed to get the deal done. Anneke Jong, a startup veteran who writes on entrepreneurship, has documented that in the more than 30-year history of TSFs, all but one were led by male searchers. The one exception: Karen Moriarty, CEO of Carillon Assisted Living, has been the only female entrepreneur to pursue the TSF route, but she later decided to start the business herself rather than acquire one through the search fund. David Dodsen, a lecturer at Stanford Graduate School of Business, sees the gender imbalance among TSFs as "a source of embarrassment and discomfort" for the search fund community at large.

Some research has found that female entrepreneurs lag behind male entrepreneurs in accessing external funding for their entrepreneurial endeavors, though there is considerable debate about the exact reasons for this pervasive and glaring gender gap. The Diana Project has documented that women often face more challenges than do men in obtaining growth capital to scale and expand their businesses.

Though TSFs have been around for more than 30 years, and there has been much growth in the number of entrepreneurs taking the TSF route, they still remain a relatively less traversed path for entrepreneurship through business acquisition. A study done by Stanford University found that there were 51 new TSFs and 18 acquisitions in the United States in 2019. While 2019 was a down year compared to 2018, the overall trend since the 1980s has been increasing activity in the number of TSFs and the successful business acquisitions through this route (see Figure 5.3).

5.3.3 Sponsored Search

The growing popularity of the search fund model has attracted other sponsors to support and fund searchers looking for companies to acquire. **Private equity** (PE) firms are one

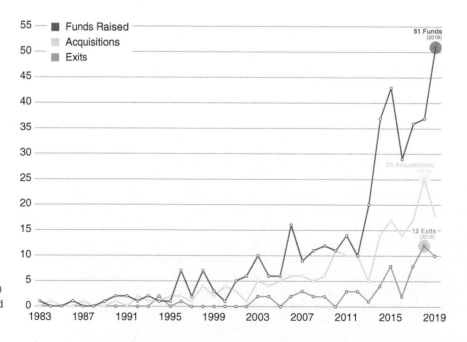

FIGURE 5.3 TSF Activity by Year
Source: Redrawn from Stanford Graduate School of Business 2020 Search Fund Study © 2020 Stanford Graduate School of Business

such player. PE firms sign exclusive agreements with searchers, paying higher compensation than other search sponsors, but also restricting searchers to lower equity in the acquired company. Searchers that associate with a reputable and well-known PE firm benefit from a "halo effect" that could help them successfully consummate the business acquisition. Searchers partnering with a PE firm may also be able to pursue an acquisition of a larger size than they would otherwise be able to do, which should balance out the lower equity share. The PE firm may also have its own sourcing team, so that the searchers are not just relying on their own network for finding deals.

Once the deal closes, the PE firm is also able to help with management support, such as recruiting expertise and marketing advice. Of course, searchers still need to take ownership of the search process, and any deals that come through the PE sponsor should be considered upside (or bonus, or the proverbial cherry on the cake). The searcher is still the one in the driver's seat for the search process, no matter how experienced the PE sponsor is.

5.3.4 Incubated Search

The idea of accelerators for acquisition search, or incubated search, is quite new in the United States (and almost completely absent overseas). The goal of incubators is to provide a structured environment for searchers, which will then increase the odds of a successful search and lower the chances of a failed search. The accelerator provides some training on search techniques and best practices. There is also the necessary infrastructure in place: office space, administrative services, information systems, and so on. Every industry and deal that the searcher comes across is documented in a software system, which can be quite useful for the next cohort of searchers who move into the incubator. The incubator may also provide interns for the searchers, with the recruitment, hiring, and onboarding all handled by the incubator (reducing the administrative load on the searcher). The goal is for the searcher to be able to focus on sourcing proprietary deal flow and finally closing a transaction. The principles of the accelerator provide mentorship and varying levels of investment capital. The various resident searchers may collaborate with each other, depending on their interests, although they do not have to work together. A typical incubator houses three to five searchers at a given time. Incubator managers generally have some search experience, which can be useful for first-time searchers.

One such accelerator is Broadtree Partners, founded by David Slenzak, who sees his firm as a half-way option between a TSF and a PE-sponsored search. "I came up with the model for Broadtree based on the pains I experienced when I was a searcher. I had to recreate the wheel — create my own CRM system, develop my own list of contacts and targets, contact people my colleagues had already contacted who were not useful, make the mistakes my friends had already made." At the same time, David found other searchers – many of who became his friends – to be highly collaborative. "It's not a competitive dynamic. Everyone wanted to share their experiences and best practices. I saw an opportunity to formalize some of that."

Another incubator is the Search Fund Accelerator, founded by INSEAD professor Timothy Bovard, based on the problems he identified after doing extensive research on search funds. Since its founding, SFA has recruited a class of four to five searchers annually, and has a pool of committed capital to fund searchers' acquisitions.

Interactive Exercise

Check out the website of Search Fund Accelerator: www.searchfundaccelerator.com. What are the main elements of their pitch to prospective entrepreneurs interested in buying a company?

Some accelerators focus on entrepreneurs from underrepresented groups. For example, Women's Startup Lab runs an accelerator for women-owned technology ventures. You can learn more about them at https://www.womenstartuplab.com. NewME was one of the first accelerators for entrepreneurs of color. NewME's coworking space, Roam, is located in the Little Havana neighborhood of Miami, FL. Indeed, there are now several gender-focused and race-focused accelerators, which one can consider.

The value proposition of accelerators lies in helping searchers optimize their processes and find companies that are the right fit for their skill set. "We put them through a three-week bootcamp where we teach them how to search and get the search up and running at full speed. For a traditional searcher, it may take months of trial and error to get to the same level."

The things that they go over range from basic activities like best practices for executing a direct marketing email campaign in a proprietary search process to more abstract lessons on how to think like an investor says Bovard. "Often searchers find a company and become infatuated with it, but what they really need to do is think dispassionately and put themselves in the shoes of a third-party investor. It may be a great business if you're the owner, but is it a good business to invest in?"

KEY TAKEAWAY

Traditional search funds are a more popular option for business acquisition than sponsored search and incubated search, though self-founded search is the most common path to identifying a target to acquire.

What Do You Think?

Nick Hardy is finishing up his business degree. He wants to run his own small business but hasn't been able to come up with any ideas that excite him. His friend Callie, who has just taken a class where she learned about buying an existing company as a possible path to business ownership, suggests that Nick look into acquisition rather than start from scratch. Nick is intrigued by the idea, but he has no idea where and how to start. Can you help Callie come up with a list of questions for Nick to consider that would help them see if buying a business is a viable possibility for him? If it is, what questions does Nick need to consider to identify which of the search routes are most suitable for him? If you can, flesh out a decision tree that Nick can use to decide whether business acquisition is right for him.

Comprehension Check

1. Explain traditional search fund.
2. What are some advantages of SFS?
3. Explain incubated search.

Module 5.4 Valuing a Business

A critical step in acquiring a new business is **valuation**. Stated simply, valuation is about assessing how much a business is worth monetarily. In this step, the buyer needs to value the target company so that it can be determined how much to pay for the business. If the target firm is priced too low compared to what it is worth, the seller is unlikely to agree to the deal. If the target firm is priced too high compared to what it is actually worth, the buyer will most likely end up losing money. The valuation has to be just the right amount, but how does one determine how much a company is worth?

Firms have a **life cycle**. Whether it is an established corporation like Walmart or a unicorn like WeWork, firms start as young idea companies and work their way to high growth, maturity, and eventual decline (yes, all firms die at some point, making way for new players!). As firms go through the different stages of the life cycle, the difficulties associated with valuation will vary. The time a firm spends in each of the stages will also vary for individual firms. Some, such as Apple and Amazon, speed through the early phases and quickly become a growth firm (the so-called hockey-stick type of firms). For others, the growth stage comes much slower. Some firms, like Nike and Walmart, are able to stretch their growth periods over a long period, but others get only a few years of growth before they mature up. There are also those who come back from decline and reinvent themselves, such as IBM did under Louis Gerstner, Jr. At each phase, some companies never make it because they run out of money, are unable to access capital, or have trouble repaying debt.

As you can imagine, valuation is most difficult for startups or growth companies and is relatively easier for mature and declining firms (never easy though!). This is because for young **startups** and **growth firms**, future growth is a major part of the valuation. The future, as they say, is hard to predict, so that there is high uncertainty about the growth potential of a firm that is not yet mature. In fact, the more the value of the firm rests with future growth, the more difficult it becomes to accurately determine the value of the firm. The current financial statements of the firm in the early stages of the life cycle provide no or little information about margins and returns that will be generated in the future. By the time a firm is mature, its revenue growth becomes steady and profit margins have settled into a pattern, so that the financial statements are now more informative, making it easier to forecast earnings and cash flow.

Apart from the challenges described above, there are certain types of firms that are more difficult to value if you want to buy them:

1. **Cyclical or commodity firms.** For such firms, earnings are quite volatile, either because of the ebbs and flows of the economy or the underlying commodity. Consider, for example, a firm in the business of constructing and selling housing. If you value it using information gathered during an economic downturn, you risk undervaluing it, but if you value it using data from the peak of the economic cycle, you risk overvaluing it. The price for oil-based businesses not only changes based on economic conditions but is also affected by revelations and news about drilling rights as there is only a finite amount of oil under the ground.

2. **Financial services firms.** You would think financial service is a mundane business that makes for a stable investment. However, financial services tend to be a highly regulated business, so that changes in rules can drastically affect the value of a business. Moreover, the assets of such companies are primarily financial, which makes it difficult to value them.

3. **Emerging market companies.** Firms that are headquartered in emerging markets or have significant exposure to them (perhaps because of their exporting practices) are exposed to considerable risk because of political instability and monetary fluctuations. Expectations about the future growth of these companies will rest not only on the firm's own prospects but also on how the emerging market where the company is located will evolve.

4. **Firms with intangible assets.** Many times, the value of the business comes not from physical assets (e.g. land and building) but from intangible assets. What exactly is an intangible asset? It can be a secret formula (think Coca Cola), technological know-how (Google), or maybe human capital (e.g. McKinsey). The value of intangible assets does not appear in the balance sheet as is the case with tangible assets (for example, a new factory or a warehouse), making it difficult to assess how one would value them.

Some companies are more difficult to value than others. Companies with solid earnings, consistent growth history, and predictable futures are relatively easier to value. When a company has no earnings, little history, and unpredictable future, buyers tend to invent new principles, violate established practices, and come up with unsustainable values for the company, which may seal the future of the new business even before it has taken off.

KEY TAKEAWAY

Estimating what a target firm is worth is challenging, and it is even more difficult for firms with unstable or unclear revenue and profits.

What Do You Think?

Adam Neumann, the founder of WeWork, was raised in Israel on a kibbutz. When he was 22, he moved to the United States, where he attended Baruch College and tried to start businesses. Many failed, but a small co-working space he started on the side during the recession that followed the financial crisis worked. In 2010, Neumann started WeWork by leasing an office in the long term, renovating it to make it hip and inviting, and sublease smaller desks and offices in the short term. WeWork's leases run about 15 years on average, much longer than the average two-year commitments its customers make to the company. By 2019, the company had leases valued at over $18 billion. In exchange for rent payments from its leasers, the company promises workers entrée to a vibrant community where they will work in fun communal spaces with organized social events, many points of connection and all the latest technology – or what the company describes as a "physical social network." The company wanted to be valued at about $47 billion, the public markets did not want to go more than $10 billion. From 2016 through 2018, the provider of trendy office space more than quadrupled its revenue to $1.82 billion. Its annual loss also mounted to $1.61 billion. Where is the remainder of the value coming from?

Comprehension Check

1. What makes a new business difficult to value?
2. What types of businesses are difficult to value?
3. Why is accurate valuation important in a business acquisition?

Summary

Acquisitions are growing in popularity as a path to small business ownership, both in the United States and overseas. Despite their growing popularity, acquisitions remain a less common path to having your own business compared to starting from scratch, joining a family business, or franchising from an established business. Even when the business can be bought for little to no cost (as in the case of Janice-style business acquisitions discussed in the first part of this chapter), buying a business already in operation is not for everyone. Like any other path to small business ownership, acquisitions have their advantages and disadvantages that aspiring business owners should carefully weigh when making their acquisition decision. There are several different ways an aspirant may go about to acquire an existing business, depending on the circumstances that they are in and the resources they have. The acquisition process can be long and arduous, so it is good to be patient. An acquisition decision made in haste can be counterproductive going forward. When making an acquisition, it is critical to carefully assess the value of the target firm, resisting the temptation to overpay to make the deal happen. Remember that a well-priced acquisition made with careful consideration can help avoid a lot of trouble in the future.

Live Exercise

"I am considering buying a plastic die-casting factory," your father shares during your family's recent trip to Disneyland. He had been driving for two hours while you were on the phone checking Facebook. If he wanted to get you off the phone, this certainly was a good move. You look up, and he continues. "You know, Johnny's SoapStandle has taken off. More than 50 retailers in the country are selling it, and so is Amazon. He thinks he is going to have problems getting enough of the product to sell." You are still wondering where your father comes into the picture, so you ask him to explain what led him to think of buying a business in an industry about which he knows nothing. "Well, there is a factory with plastic injection molding machines for sale in Lewisburg, TN. They are a small family-owned operation with about 10,000 sq. ft. of space. The owner wants to retire, and his son is a successful investment banker up in New York, so he is not interested in the business. We could use one of the machines to make soapstandles. Johnny says the way his sales are, he thinks he will be able to buy whatever we make for him." You put away your phone, ready to ask more questions. "The challenge is if we buy the factory, we probably cannot pay for the rest of your time in college. So, you will have to take out a loan. On the other hand, if the business works out as well as some people think it can under new leadership, we would be in a much better financial situation in five years." Before you could say anything, your mother chimes in, "We will not make any decision that you disagree with, so you can think more about this." Should your parents consider buying this business? What questions should they be asking in order to make the right decision?

World of Books

Passing Along Our Dream by Bill and Susie Mosca
Buy Then Build: How Acquisition Entrepreneurs Outsmart the Startup Game by Walker Deibel
HBR Guide to Buying a Small Business: Think Big, Buy Small, Own Your Own Company by Richard S. Ruback and Royce Yudcoff

In the Movies

What if you entered an Internet contest and won ownership of a historic inn? The Janice-style acquisition of a crumbling inn located in New Zealand is the subject of the movie *Falling Inn Love*. A romantic comedy, the film traces the transformation of a washed-up designer into a small business owner committed to running the inn she accidentally bought for free.

Things to Remember

LO 5.1   Define the meaning of business acquisition outline and its pros and cons
- Becoming a business owner through acquisition means buying out an existing venture.
- The merit of the business to acquire is the most important factor when making the acquisition decision.
- Acquisitions allow the buyer to draw the benefits of an existing customer base, established processes, proven and tested markets, and strong reputation of the seller.

- Acquisitions pose challenges for buyers in the form of considerable investment, the high cost of searching for a suitable firm, the risks associated with honoring prior commitments, and figuring out the reasons for the sale.
- The problem with business acquisitions is that the seller usually knows more about the firm than the buyer.

LO 5.2 **Provide a bird's-eye view of the acquisition process**
- If a business is the owner's baby, acquiring a business means willingly taking the responsibility to raise someone else's baby.
- Business acquisition is a four-step process, involving raising capital, identifying targets, funding the buyout, and creating value through effectively operating the firm.
- Searchers would do well to budget capital requirements for two to three years because of how long it can take to find a business that meets their needs and is available at a good price.
- The searcher needs to proactively communicate with investors to make sure that they are aware of what is going with the search.
- Investors who contribute to the search fund are not obligated to provide capital; they simply have the right of first refusal in deals that flow from the search fund.
- Managing and running a business requires different skills and qualities compared to starting a new business.
- Sooner or later, the new CEO and the old CEO will disagree about the direction of the firm.

LO 5.3 **Distinguish between different types of business acquisitions**
- Prospective acquirers need to carefully consider which of the available paths will work well for them when launching their search for a firm to buy.
- There are four main paths to acquiring a small business: (1) self-funded search, (2) traditional search fund, (3) sponsored search, and (4) incubated search.
- Members of the search community, which comprises current and former searchers, CEOs, and investors, are the best source of advice for those who are seeking to identify which search path is best for them.
- Regardless of what acquisition path one chooses, prospective acquirers need to take ownership of the search process. The searcher is still the one in the driver's seat of the search process, no matter what path they chose.

LO 5.4 **Describe how to value a business**
- The buyer needs to value the target company so that they can determine how much they should pay for the business.
- If the target firm is priced too low compared to what it is worth, the seller is unlikely to agree to the deal. If the target firm is priced too high compared to what it is actually worth, the buyer will most likely end up losing money.
- Valuation is most difficult for startups or growth companies, and relatively easier for mature and declining firms.
- Some companies are more difficult to value than others.

Key Terms

business acquisition	moral hazard	Brokered deals	valuation
bidder	100-day plan	advertised deal	life cycle
target	parenting metaphor	self-funded search	startups
Janice-style acquisitions	searcher	traditional search fund	growth firms
established business	private placement	sponsored search	commodity firms
information asymmetry	memorandum	incubated search	financial services firms
adverse selection	Proprietary deals	private equity	firms with intangible assets

Experiential Exercise

This exercise is designed for students working individually. Use of the Internet (via laptops or hand-held devices like the iPad or smartphone) during the exercise is not needed for the first part but is required for the second part.

When Lasse Rheingans acquired a small technology consulting firm, he immediately implemented a radical idea: Reduce the workday to five hours, from the standard eight, while leaving worker salaries and vacations at the same levels as before.

Why did Rheingans introduce the shorter workday at his new company? Several reasons, he says. First, personal experience: At his last employer, Rheingans initially took a salary cut so he could spend two afternoons a week with his daughters. When he realized that he was still producing as much as work as before, Rheingans asked for his original salary to be reinstated, which the owners agreed to, but they were not too happy about it. Second, research findings he had seen: Some studies seem to find that most workers are only productive for four to five hours of the workday, so reducing working time should not lower the productivity of the company. Third, economic situation: The labor market is tight, making it difficult for small technology companies to hire and retain good employees.

To successfully achieve a short workday, Rheingans made several other rules: Small talk during work hours is discouraged; social media is banned in the office; phones are to be kept in backpacks; company email accounts are checked just twice a day; most meetings are scheduled to last no more than 15 minutes.

Part I (Internet not needed):

1. Rheingans made all these changes immediately on acquiring the company. Is it too much too soon?

2. If you were an employee at such a company, how would you react to working under new management?

3. What do you think are some advantages and disadvantages of the changes Rheingans introduced at the company?

Part II (Internet needed):

1. Rheingans Digital Enabler operates in Germany. Can you find other firms worldwide where shorter workdays were introduced?

2. Do you think cultural values and norms of German society make it more conducive for such policies?

3. How do you think American employees would react to new management coming in and drastically transforming the work culture in the company they bought?

CHAPTER 6

Small Business Marketing

> *Marketing takes a day to learn, but a lifetime to master.*

PHILIP KOTLER

6.0 Introduction

Imagine a small firm that has identified and developed a unique product or service to offer. What do you think needs to be done next? The answer to this question is so simple that we usually do not think about it: Potential customers need to be informed about the available offerings. Unless the public knows about what a firm is offering, little has been accomplished. Regardless of how much effort the business owners have put in the firm, all that effort is wasted if the firm fails to become known to its potential customers. Witty slogans like "if you build it, they will come" may sound good to the ear, and may even make you popular with friends, but the reality is that a business must do quite a lot of work to make potential customers aware of its offerings. As Scott Kirby, CEO of United Airlines, observed, "in the real world, if you build it, and they don't come, you go bankrupt."

Large, well-established companies create awareness for their new offerings by running expensive marketing campaigns such as advertising on TV, in print, and online. Citibank's *Live Richly* marketing campaign, for example, cost about a billion dollars over a five-year period to encourage potential clients to trust the bank. Small firms, including many banks and credit unions that compete with Citibank, would be fortunate to have even 1% of a billion dollars for marketing. Furthermore, people are not waiting for a new product or service to come to the market. Humans are creatures of habit, preferring to use what they are already familiar with rather than change their behavior to use a new product. As a

SPOTLIGHT | OCJ Jeans: Marketing on a Budget

Greg Adams was an entrepreneurship major at Texas Christian University. During college, Greg toyed with many business ideas, but the one that seemed most appealing to him was school-branded jeans. Greg believed that while there were lots of clothing options using university logos, most were not suitable for nicer settings, such as after-game parties. The challenge Greg faced was how to test his hunch. After some thinking, Greg came up with a plan: He designed some jeans with the University of Kansas logo (his sister was a student there) and recruited sorority members to wear the jeans after a game. In exchange for a free pair of jeans, the sorority models were to take notes on how many people noticed the Jayhawk logo and the comments they got. Greg's hunch proved right. The models reported people stopping them to ask where they could buy the jeans. For a free pair of jeans and a little money, Greg had his market research. The sorority sisters, Greg's models, thought there was a market for college-branded jeans.

Like many business students majoring in entrepreneurship, Greg didn't have much technical knowledge. In college, he had learned about the business side of things but had remained oblivious of the technical aspects. Now, he needed to know about apparel. Greg quickly began reading up on the apparel industry and started to develop designs for jeans. He found that approvals for products branded with a university logo needed to come from a clearinghouse. For the most part, schools outsource the approval process for the commercial use of their logos to select clearinghouses, although at times the institution does retain the final approval of a particular product. The approval process can take some time because the applicant has to be approved both as a vendor and for each specific product category.

After Greg got clearinghouse approval, he set out to source a key input in jeans: denim. A problem in the jeans-wear business is that there are not many suppliers of quality denim for the American market. Once Greg found a good denim supplier, he was able to start OCJ Apparel and launch the jeans with logos for six major universities. College students loved the jeans, and Greg expanded to 26 schools the next year and more than 50 schools the year after. Arkansas Razorbacks, Alabama Tide, Florida Gators, Missouri Tigers, and Texas Aggies were just some of the schools OCJ covered. The company was now selling the jeans in two colors, deep indigo and victory-blue, and two types of leg fit, skinny and boot cut. The design of the jeans was so good that Neiman Marcus – a leading national high-end retailer – asked the company to develop products for its stores.

Blair Staky is a Chicago-based alumna of TCU. Blair also runs the popular blog The Fox & She, which "celebrates the stylish, healthful, colorful, and abundant life that's enviable, yet attainable." When she received a promotional sample of OCJ jeans, she featured it on her blog, noting that "the game day apparel I've purchased in the past has been poorly made and less than flattering, but not OCJ." Staky found the jeans "comfortable, stylish, and perfect for showing your team spirit on game day without sacrificing style." Riding on the success of its jeans, OCJ was able to expand its product line to shorts, T-shirts, and other related products.

indira's work/Shutterstock.com

Discussion Questions

1. What was novel about Greg's approach to testing the market for the product he had in mind?

2. What other products could one test using Greg's approach, or another similar approach? You may come up with product suggestions for college campuses or for the broader market.

3. Would a large well-established jeans company, say Levi's or Wrangler, have come up with a Greg-like approach to testing the market for a new line of jeans? How would an established jeans company test the market for its new product?

result, a small business must take active steps to convince potential customers that it has an offering that can address problem(s) they have. This chapter focuses on how to market your business and how to write a marketing plan for your firm. Think of this chapter as Marketing 101 for small firms.

Module 6.1 What Is Small Business Marketing?

At a basic level, marketing is about engaging customers and managing profitable customer relationships. The twin goals of marketing are (1) attracting new customers and (2) retaining and strengthening the loyalty of existing customers. Small business marketing, therefore, deals with the topic of how resource-constrained firms retain their existing customers and attract new customers. Marketing thus deals directly with a firm's interactions with its customers.

There was a time when marketing was understood simply as "telling and selling." At the time, marketing was all about making a sale, or more technically, customer acquisition. Boastful marketing professionals would pride themselves on their ability to sell ice-cream to Eskimos or hair-combs to bald people. Such an approach to marketing is longer in vogue (though many business owners continue to follow it, arguably to their long-term detriment). Nowadays, marketing is about understanding and satisfying consumer needs. Modern marketing focuses not on merely making a sale but also on meeting customer needs. Firms that engage consumers, understand customer needs, and develop offerings that provide superior customer value will generally do better than those who are not as interested in their customers (everything else being equal). When firms satisfy customers (both potential and actual) in an effective manner, sales will follow, sooner or later. There is even a name for this modern approach to marketing. It's called **relationship marketing**, and it focuses on a firm focusing on developing mutually beneficial relationships with customers.

Most people think they already know a lot about marketing, perhaps because they are surrounded by some form of marketing every minute of their waking life. Walk into a mall, pick up a magazine, go online, or open your mailbox, either way one is struck by the pervasiveness of marketing. At school, at home, at work, and in the playground, marketing seems to be everywhere. And yet, there is much more to marketing than what the casual customer sees. Marketing is definitely not as simple as it often seems. Every year, thousands of new products are introduced and thousands of new businesses are launched in the United States alone. History tells us that about 70–80% of new ventures and new products fail within a short time of launch. Like with failure in other things, there are many reasons for why a majority of new firms and new offerings fail to take off. The fact that many small business owners do not give enough consideration to how they will sell their product is just one of the many possible reasons for failure, but it is an important one.

Conversely, keeping the customer in mind from the very beginning helps the company be better at understanding and satisfying what the market needs. Consider the case of Nike, a company with annual sales of more than $25 billion. There was a time when Nike was a (very) small business, the brainchild of a young MBA graduate Phil Knight and his college coach Bill Bowerman. In Nike's early days, Knight got athletic shoes made from Japan to sell in the United States. Knight then faced a challenge that would be familiar to every small business owner: When you have limited funds, how do you bring your product to the attention of potential customers and get them to buy it? Knight came up with an innovative solution to his problem: He loaded up the trunk of his car with several pairs of sneakers, and went around to high school track events, where he gave away free shoes to the winners. Subsequently, other students wanted the same shoes that winning athletes were wearing. Because no other company was pursuing this approach at the time, Nike soon cornered the local high school market for high-quality sneakers suitable for running track events.

When Sheri Poe (www.sheripoe.com) founded Ryka to offer athletic shoes designed for women, she emphasized that Ryka shoes were "by women" and "for women," which helped her make inroads in a business dominated at the time by large corporations. The company, which most footwear industry pundits expected to fail, turned out to be phenomenal success story as Sheri cultivated celebrities like Princess Diana who were photographed wearing Ryka shoes in public.

Building relationships with customers is a serious issue. Marketing efforts targeted at bringing in new customers can leave existing customers feeling neglected and ignored. Consequently, keeping existing customers happy should be a high priority for small businesses. There are several ways in which small firms benefit from maintaining good relationships with existing customers:

1. The cost of acquiring a new customer is usually greater than the cost of keeping an existing customer.
2. Satisfied customers refer their friends and colleagues, possibly leading to more sales.
3. The nonfinancial cost of selling to existing customers is less because they already know how to buy from you.
4. There is a history with existing customers, which helps with setting reasonable expectations.
5. Existing customers appreciate the value proposition offered by the seller and tend to be less price-sensitive.

Firms that are effective at managing their existing customer base will be at a competitive advantage. Of course, because a firm's next sale can come from only one of two sources – an existing customer or a new customer – it is important that firms target their marketing efforts to both groups.

KEY TAKEAWAY

Most firms prioritize either acquiring new customers or retaining existing customers, forgetting that both customer acquisition and customer retention are equally important for a firm to thrive and grow.

Many entrepreneurs consider customer relationships to be the secret weapon of small firms, one that can help them compete with the most deep-pocketed and entrenched rivals. Mary Liz Curtin, owner of Leon & Lulu, a destination lifestyle store in Detroit, advises that small business owners should consider their customer base to be their most important asset. "The relationships we build with our customers, the service we offer and the careful selection of offerings keeps us in business," she shares. Table 6.1 summarizes what marketing means to some successful business owners.

TABLE 6.1

What Does Marketing Mean to Me?

Name	Firm	Marketing means. . .
Joanne Chang	Flour Bakery + Café; Myers + Chang	Listen to customer requests; connect on a more personal level with customers
Sharon Hadary	Center for Women's Business Research	Offer more personalized service, customize to meet the customer's needs, and respond to the customer's needs more quickly
Henry Elkus	Unlimited Ltd. Clothing	I always found joy in writing personal letters to our customers
David Kalt	Chicago Music Exchange; Reverb.com	Focus on connecting with customers on a personal level; build a user experience that others find difficult to match
Richard Duncan	Rich Duncan Construction	Adjust more quickly to the market and customer needs; meet your customers where they are
Mary Liz Curtin	Leon & Lulu	Profile your customers so you can serve them better; understand your clientele, know who they are and what they need from you; stay in touch with your clients and keep them aware of your products and services

Source: Adapted from How Can Small Businesses Compete With Big Competitors? 25 December 2013, *The Wall Street Journal*

128   **Chapter 6** Small Business Marketing

Interactive Exercise

Interview five business owners and ask them what marketing means to them. Share what you have learned with the class.

Comprehension Check

1. Define and explain small business marketing
2. How has marketing changed over the years?
3. Why should firms try to build relationship with existing customers?

Module 6.2 Products: Goods and/or Services

The first lesson in small business marketing involves understanding what exactly is it that a firm is offering to its customer, or in other words, what is it that a customer is getting from the seller. Anything that a firm offers in the market is called a **product**, and is targeted at satisfying one or more customer needs, wants, and demands. Products may include **goods** (the t-shirt a customer bought at a local store or the burrito from the small Mexican restaurant in town) or **services** (haircut, dental work, and legal services). Most people think in terms of either goods or services, but most of the things we buy and use tend to be some combination of both goods and services. For example, when you go to a neighborhood deli for lunch, you are usually concerned not just with the quality of the food you buy but also the service you get.

> **KEY TAKEAWAY**
>
> Any product a company sells is a combination of goods and services. Some products can be pure goods or services, but most products are a combination of a good and a service.

A common small business in many American cities and towns is the auto dealership. When customers buy a car, one would think they are getting a pure good, but that is generally not the case. If the customer is like most Americans, the purchase of the car is accompanied with a loan originating at the dealership (about 90% of American buyers take out a loan to purchase a car). The car is tangible (it is something you can touch), but the loan is intangible (so it's a service). **Tangibility** is a key difference between goods and services.

The monthly check from the customer will partly cover the cost of the car and the cost of the loan. Cars come with some warranty, which again is intangible, and so it is a service. If the customer bought an extended warranty on the car, there is even more service. The vast majority of what most customers pay goes for the car itself, so car purchasing is an example of a good-dominated product.

A growing trend in the United States is car leasing. When customers lease a car, the company owns it and the customer gets to use it (for a fee), which is now a service. The customer is responsible for gas and maintenance, so the tangible item (the car) is still in the care of the customer, but it is on the terms of a lease. The leased car is a hybrid, a sort of mid-way point between goods and services (see Figure 6.1).

What happens when the customer rents a car? The customer pays and drives. The rental company takes care of maintenance. Most students will be familiar with rental

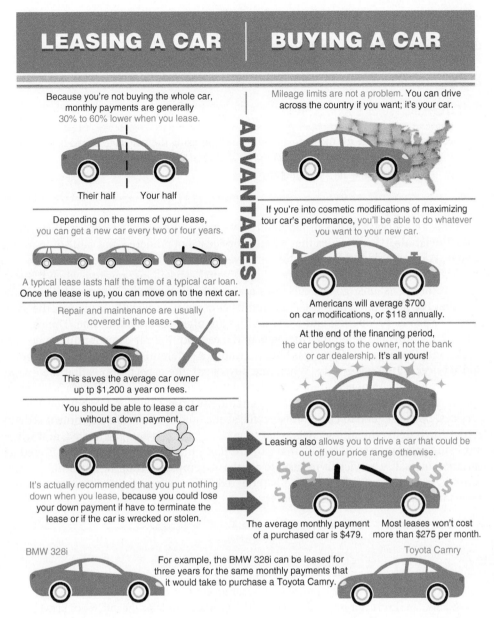

LEASING A CAR | BUYING A CAR

ADVANTAGES

Because you're not buying the whole car, monthly payments are generally 30% to 60% lower when you lease.

Their half   Your half

Depending on the terms of your lease, you can get a new car every two or four years.

A typical lease lasts half the time of a typical car loan. Once the lease is up, you can move on to the next car.

Repair and maintenance are usually covered in the lease.

This saves the average car owner up tp $1,200 a year on fees.

You should be able to lease a car without a down payment.

It's actually recommended that you put nothing down when you lease, because you could lose your down payment if have to terminate the lease or if the car is wrecked or stolen.

BMW 328i

For example, the BMW 328i can be leased for three years for the same monthly payments that it would take to purchase a Toyota Camry.

Mileage limits are not a problem. You can drive across the country if you want; it's your car.

If you're into cosmetic modifications of maximizing tour car's performance, you'll be able to do whatever you want to your new car.

Americans will average $700 on car modifications, or $118 annually.

At the end of the financing period, the car belongs to the owner, not the bank or car dealership. It's all yours!

Leasing also allows you to drive a car that could be out off your price range otherwise.

The average monthly payment of a purchased car is $479.   Most leases won't cost more than $275 per month.

Toyota Camry

FIGURE 6.1 Buying Versus Leasing a Car
Source: Redrawn from https://www.mikeandersonchevymerrillville.com/leasing-vs-buying

companies, such as Avis and Enterprise, which are large national chains. The Big Three companies in this sector – Enterprise, Hertz, and Avis – together account for 95% of the auto rental industry in the country. Yet, many towns and cities across the country also have small, local rental companies, which are mom-and-pop owned. There are also new startups like ZipCar, where cars can be rented on an hourly basis. Such rentals include all services (including insurance). Consequently, customers are now being offered a service-dominated product.

When you look at the transportation business, is there a pure service product? Cabs, whether through medallion-based providers (as is the case in New York City) or through online apps like Lyft or Uber, are pure service. Sure, a car is involved, but the customers are in no way responsible for the vehicle. The driver is responsible for maintaining and running the car, and customers pays for the convenience of using it whenever they want. Here, the offering is like a pure service. After the customer has paid, there is nothing tangible they get to show for it (except the receipt).

As you can see, in the same business of personal transportation, various types of products may be on offer, and each product may be marketed in different ways to strengthen its appeal for the customer. The marketing for Toyota or Honda is different from that for Uber or Lyft, even though these companies are all in the same business of transporting the customers from point A to point B.

Interactive Exercise

Check out the website for the company Fire Features (https://www.firefeatures.com/). Explain to the class what the company is selling using the language of goods and services learned in this section.

Goods and services differ in tangibility, as discussed earlier, but also in three other ways. **Perishability** is the idea that when a service is not rendered, the value of that time is gone. A car can sit at the dealership for a week or a month and will eventually be sold for close to its sale price, but a car operating as a taxi-cab will lose revenue when it is idle. Cars are nonperishable goods, cab-rides are perishable services. **Inseparability** is the idea that the production of the service and its consumption usually happen at the same time. For goods, production and consumption are often separated in time. The cab ride can only be provided when the rider gets in the cab, but the car can continue to be used weeks, months, or years after it was bought. Another differentiating factor between goods and services is **heterogeneity**. When one buys a car, the expectation is that the quality of the car is quite homogenous or consistent across time and place. A Honda is a Honda, and the customer expects the same consistent quality from each Honda when it is bought. Services, however, tend to be heterogeneous, as the quality changes every time it is delivered. Who is delivering the service, what time of the day it is being delivered, and where it is being delivered are all factors that can influence the quality of the service. To reduce variation in quality, service firms need to emphasize employee training and strict internal controls so that every time a service is rendered, it is as close as possible to the quality expectation of the firm and its customers.

Good Or Service?

The difference between goods and services can be difficult for people to understand. Matthew Alanis, an instructor of business and entrepreneurship at Clovis Community College in California, founded the Alanis Business Academy to provide universal access to a quality business education. In this video, Professor Alanis explains the difference between a good and a service.

Watch the video online at: https://www.youtube.com/watch?v=AyyvFASW6Nw

A product is not only what the firm offering it thinks it is, but also how customers think about it. From this perspective, a product has three levels: core goods-services, augmented goods-services, and total goods-services. The **core product** is the most basic, fundamental description of what the firm is offering. It is the most general description of the business and does not really capture the special or unique aspects of a particular offering. For Toyota and Mercedes, the core product is the same: a car. The fact that the two companies may not see their product in the same way is a moot issue here. When a customer buys from Toyota or Mercedes (or Fiat or BMW), she is buying a car. The **augmented product** is the one that has features differentiating it from competitors such as quality, packaging, reputation, brand name, or other specific features. Here, Toyota and Mercedes diverge, with the former offering a more basic, less luxurious product than the latter. The **total product** goes further to include the entire bundle of offerings and is based not just on what the business owner things but also what the customer thinks about it. Here, Toyota and Mercedes need to try to get into the customer's head to figure out why people buy their product, what they see in the product, and how they use the product.

What Do You Think?

Ever heard of a small business that had to beg people not to come shop there? Well, that is exactly what happened in 1987 when Jordan's Furniture opened their Avon (MA) location. The opening created such a traffic jam on Route 24 that owners Barry and Eliot Tatelman had to go on air to tell people not to come to the store. Customers waited for hours just to get into the new showroom. Jordan's sells furniture, but each of their stores offers a unique array of interactive, sensory features that makes shopping an entertainment. One of their stores once featured a spectacular liquid firework show called Splash with thousands of nozzles shooting water up to the ceiling mixed with colorful laser lights. At their Natick (MA) stores, the Tatelmans created a Mardi Gras celebration featuring amusement rides, animatronic characters, and refreshments stands reminiscent of Bourbon Street. A furniture store with great entertainment, now that's a combination you don't hear very often! What part of the Jordan's business do you think is goods and what part is service? Do you think the investment in entertainment at the Jordan's is justified? Can you find other examples of small businesses that provide such a "shoppertainment" experience to draw customers?

Comprehension Check

1. What are the ways in which goods and services differ?
2. Explain how leasing a car is part good and part service.
3. Can you think of a pure "goods" business?

Module 6.3 Capturing the Attention of the Market

For customers to purchase from a small business, they must first know that a firm exists that sells the product that will address some need, want, or desire they have. Some firms have a captive market. For example, perhaps you make shoelaces that you then sell to your brother-in-law's shoe company. In this case, you have one customer who probably knows you from when you started the business. Perhaps your customer was the one who encouraged you to start the shoelace business in the first place, promising to buy all your production as long as it meets certain criteria. A **captive customer**, therefore, is one that does not change their buying preferences even if other options are available because of past association with the seller. But what if your brother-in-law, the captive customer you had, decides to sell the business or close it for some reason? Alternatively, maybe you are no longer satisfied with selling the shoelaces to just one customer and want to grow the business, perhaps even sell to other customers.

6.3.1 The Marketing Funnel

All businesses, at one point or another, need to reach out to potential customers to gain some new customers, if they want to remain in operation and achieve even a modicum of growth. To get people interested in your offerings and convince them to buying it, you first need to contact them, so they know who you are and what you bring to the market. The contacts can be established passively or actively. **Passive contacts** are people who form an impression of your business and you based on your public outreach without directly talking to you or meeting with you. Conversely, **active contacts** are people whose impression of your firm and you stems from direct interactions with you, whether verbally or visually.

A common example of passive contacting is using billboards that showcase your products or service. If you do not live in Alabama (or the neighboring states of Florida and Mississippi), you have probably never heard of Alexander Shunnarah, but his name is very familiar to millions of Alabamans. He is a personal-injury lawyer who needs new clients to come to his law firm rather than his competitors'. To get his name out, Shunnarah relies on billboards with his name, trade, and face plastered all over the state of Alabama, including on the major freeways. Advertising on billboards is not cheap, and Shunnarah spends a handsome budget on billboards every year (he even made a video (ABANDONED BILLBOARDS? NOT ON MY WATCH that you can watch on You-Tube) poking fun at his unparalleled billboard empire across Alabama). It is worth mentioning here that when Shunnarah, who probably spends more money on billboards than any other lawyer in the country, started his law firm, his marketing efforts were initially limited to "handing out business cards to family and friends and fellow church members."

Alexander Shunnarah of Alabama was named "Master of Marketing" by the *National Trial Lawyer Magazine.*

An example of active contacts is the bread-sellers who set up shop every Saturday in your local farmer's market. They give each visitor a free sample of bread, along with some conversation, their card, and a (big) smile. That is how Graison Gill built his bakery business. When he was 25, Gill "got to New Orleans on the Greyhound bus with 20 dollars on me." He read up on baking in the public library, then began selling his experiments at the farmers' market one customer at a time. Seven years, and some ups and downs later, Gill owned Bellegrade Bakery in New Orleans, employing 15 people and selling mostly wholesale to other businesses (e.g. restaurants).

Only a subset of contacts will be interested in buying from you. These people, called **leads**, will be open to your efforts to interact further with details of your product. When you reach out to the leads, a few will maintain interest in your product. They are **prospects**. Of all the prospects you may have, you would be lucky to make some **sales**. In doing the sales, you will be able to foster loyalty in some customers, who will return to you as **repeat customers**. Because the cost of retaining an existing customer is lower than the cost of acquiring a new one, companies have an incentive to make it easy for customers to stay with them. Look at the business model of companies like Netflix. The streaming video giant charges you every month for watching movies and shows, and most of us don't even notice it. It assumes you are a repeat customer unless you take specific tangible steps to stop payment to the company. Of course, few small businesses have the luxury of such repeat customers.

The idea that it takes considerably more contacts to land one sale or have a repeat customer is called the **marketing funnel**. Figure 6.2 graphically shows how to promote your product and how the marketing funnel fits into it.

Promotion is essential to gaining the attention of people who you think may buy your product. A good entrepreneur should always be on the lookout for novel ways to promote their product. Because promotion is not cheap and the cost of promoting is borne by the seller, resource-constrained firms will try to come up with novel ways to promote their products inexpensively. As the marketing funnel shows, you need to be known to hundreds and thousands of potential customers to make one sale; likewise, one loyal customer saves you from having to reach out to hundreds of contacts.

To better understand the marketing funnel, it is helpful to take a look at a few more concepts: value proposition, target market, advertising, public relations, personal selling, and **customer retention**.

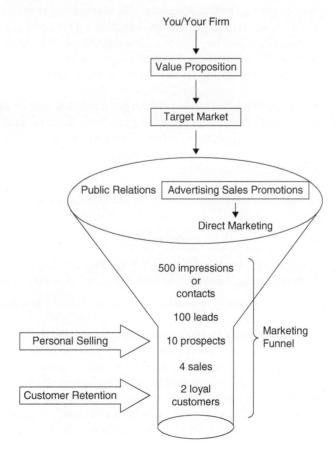

FIGURE 6.2 Understanding Marketing as a Funnel
Source: Redrawn from Wiley marketing book (or database)

When you take a new product to the market, you need to think about its value proposition. Simply stated, **value proposition** is the answer to the question of why someone should buy your product. If you are introducing a new hairbrush to the market, you may be tempted to think that your value proposition is that the hairbrush you are offering is the cheapest on the market. Sometimes low prices are the value proposition – for example, when the product is undifferentiated (that is, rival offerings are all alike) or when customers are unappreciative of particular features of a product. Oftentimes, however, the value proposition for a product relies on specific parameters, such as style, quality, service, delivery, ease-of-buying, technology. Consider Red Barn Technology, a boutique computer seller, in upstate New York. Jon Layish, founder of Red Barn, is clear that his company does not compete with computer giants like Dell and Lenovo on price. Instead, the small company focuses on high-performance computer systems for industry and academia. When a customer walks into a Red Barn store, the sales pitch does not emphasize price, but quality and performance.

KEY TAKEAWAY

Before launching the marketing efforts for your firm, it is important to figure out *why* customers should buy your offering.

Many business owners struggle with identifying who their target market is. When asked the question "Who is your target market?" they tend to respond "everyone." The inability to identify a target market shows that the business owner does not really understand who would be the best buyer and user for their product. The identification of a target market starts with **segmentation**, the process of dividing the market into smaller portions of people who share common characteristics. Segmentation can be based on any number of factors, including geographic (in or near specific cities), demographic (race, gender, age, or socioeconomic status), or activity (for example, yoga, golf, or football). A target market is the segment or segments that a business selects to concentrate its marketing efforts. Firms can choose as many target segments as they want, but small businesses usually start by concentrating on one target market and add secondary markets later. After the target market is defined, the focus shifts to identifying information the customers need to make a decision and ways to get that information to them. It is tempting to think that a business owner does not care who actually buys their product, as long as it's sold. But, in many businesses (e.g. fashion, luxury), the user of the product also matters.

Interactive Exercise

Check out the website for Hot Yoga Plus (www.hotyogaplus.com). Who do you think is their target market? What value proposition does the company offer to its customers?

Perceptions about your product may be shaped by what kinds of people use them. Ask yourself: If you are the designer Jimmy Choo, celebrated for your high-end range of luxury women's shoes, does it matter who is wearing your shoes? Indeed, many companies that sell to high-end customers prefer to destroy unsold goods rather than allow them to be sold at a discount. Customers who spend thousands on a designer dress or bag tend to get angry when they see the same item a year later at a discount store selling for a fraction of the price. Many brands "don't want their unsold products winding up at flea markets or on Craigslist," said Matt Connelly, Chief Executive of Good360, a nonprofit that collects excess merchandise from companies to distribute to charities.

6.3.2 Digital Marketing

There are about 315 million Internet users in the United States, which is about 95% of the country's population. Worldwide, about 59% of the global population or nearly 4.5 billion people use the Internet. When the Pew Research Center began tracking social media adoption in 2005, just 5% of American adults used at least one of social media platforms. By 2011 that share had risen to half of all Americans, and today 72% of the public uses some type of social media. Internet usage in the United States is quite frequent, with 43% of surveyed adults saying that they used the Internet several times a day and only 8% who access the Internet about once a day. The average American spends about 142 minutes per day on social media.

Given this information, it should come as no surprise that the Internet and social media have become major venues for a company's promotion activities. Some estimates suggest that 97% of marketers use social media and 78% of sales people outsell their peers by using social media for their business. Yet, about 50% of small firms do not promote their business on the Internet and an additional 25% have no plans to use it in the future. Clearly, some business owners either are not able to see the benefits of using the Internet to promote the business or are struggling to get started. Such entrepreneurs are missing an important venue to grow their business.

KEY TAKEAWAY

The Internet and social media have become major avenues for a company's promotion activities.

While it may seem daunting at first, Internet promotion involves two basic activities: (1) building and promoting the company website and (2) social media campaigns. Take the case of Silly Goats Soap Company, first of upstate New York and now South Central Kentucky. The company owes its start to the founding husband-and-wife team of Chris and Sandy, who had a desire for good high-quality milk for drinking (and for the coffee too!) They bought some goats, and then realized exactly how much milk they were going to have left over and thought of ways to use it. Their own skincare issues, combined with the need to do something with the excess milk, led them to making and selling goat milk soap. Their presence on the Web helps them sell their product all over the country, and possibly even around the world, if they wanted. Or, consider Pompanoosuc Mills Corp., a contemporary furniture manufacturer and retailer in Vermont, with eight showrooms. When the COVID-19 pandemic spread, founder Dwight photographed dining tables, chairs, and desks in his flagship showroom at the company headquarters, offering them online with immediate delivery and discounted pricing. He sold about $210,000 of deeply discounted furniture in three weeks and closed the first Facebook Messenger order in its history. One customer snapped up a king-size bed and two night tables he had photographed just two weeks earlier. Dwight expects online to play a bigger role in the future. "Some of these things are exciting," he admits about his company's online efforts. "We are so far behind."

Figure 6.3 shows the most effective marketing approaches for small firms as revealed by a survey of business owners in the United States.

6.3.2.1 Small Business Websites At the time of this writing in 2020, there were about 2 billion websites on the Worldwide Web, of which about 400 million were actually active. For a firm, the website is its virtual location, a sort of Web-based office where people can

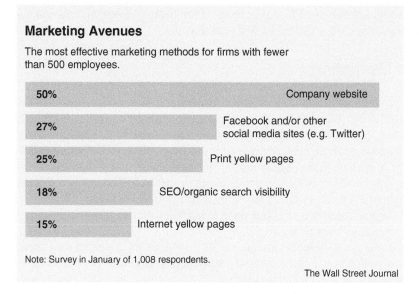

FIGURE 6.3 Marketing Approaches for Small Firms *Source:* Adapted from Thrive Analytics, *The Wall Street Journal*

visit any time. When you read about a company in this book (or elsewhere), what is the first thing you do? Like most people, you probably start by searching for it on the Web. After the search engine finds the company, you click on the link, and reach its website. In the virtual world, each company's website has an address, which is technically called a **domain name**. The domain name can have a maximum of 63 characters, and must begin and end with a letter or number (no space can be included). The domain name is followed by a suffix (for example, .com, .net, .biz, .edu) that specifies the kind of website it is. A nonprofit organization (Internet Corporation for Assigned Names and Numbers) manages all domain names globally.

Since the domain name is the company's address on the Web, it's helpful to identify an appealing name that people remember. It is tempting to use the name of one's business as the domain name, but it may already be taken. When Anu Menon and her cofounder were getting ready to launch their Brooklyn, NY company, they struggled with what to name it. As Anu began designing packaging – with luggage tags that denote the origins of the coffees and the sense of ritual – they decided on Driftaway Coffee. The problem was that the domain name was already taken in the most popular dot-com url. It was then that Anu learned ICANN had expanded the list of suffixes to include more generic names such as .business, .life, .company, and .movie as well as more specific ones such as .coffee, .clothing, .florist, and .farm. Lions Gate, the film company behind The Hunger Games franchise, had already launched TheHungerGames.movie. Anu decided to use driftaway.coffee for her website. "We didn't want to make the url too long, but we wanted to be sure to include the word coffee, so this was perfect," says Menon. "It looked better on the packaging, too."

Interactive Exercise

If you were to start a company today, what would you name it? Using the Internet, determine if the domain name for your company is available. If not, see if you find a suitable domain name for your company that is available. What do you learn in this process? You can use godaddy.com or 1and1.com or another portal to search for available domain names.

Once you have a domain name, the next step is to build a high-quality website. At this stage, you have two options. You can either go to a technical specialist to help design and build the site or you can design and build it on your own using website-building services. Joanna Stern, Senior Personal Technology Columnist for the *Wall Street Journal*, tested four services (Wix, Weebly, Jimdo, and Squarespace) that enable users to build their own website. Weebly and Squarespace were considered the best options in terms of ease-of-use and high-quality tools and templates (if you want to hear her talk about her experience building her own website, visit https://www.wsj.com/video/how-and-why-to-build-a-website/229553F7-130F-4CC8-8416-AD03CE416942.html). Both services can be tried for free and allow users to create a secure storefront and manage payments. Table 6.2 compares the four services.

Once the website is up and running, it needs to be promoted to existing customers and possible prospects. There are many ways to promote your website, such as including the url of the domain name (e.g. www.soul.camp) in direct mail letters, radio campaigns, and banner advertisements. The idea is that the user sees or hears the firm's name and clicks on it to visit there. The traffic to a particular site can be increased through **search engine optimization** (SEO). The logic for SEO is that the higher your firm ranks in search engine results, the more visitors it will attract. Google accounts for roughly 90% of all searches globally (Bing is a major competitor, but other options include DuckDuckGo and Neeva), and where a website ranks in the Google search results impacts the number of people visit it. The goal of SEO is to make your website as friendly for the search engine, primarily Google, as possible.

6.3.2.2 Social Media Digital tools that allow users to quickly create and share content with the public constitute **social media**. For marketing, social media includes social networking and blogging sites as well as other means of online communication where users can share messages, information, or other content. The rapid diffusion of mobile devices such as smartphones and tablets has helped make social media a popular way for entrepreneurs to reach customers and prospects. At the same time, social media makes it more

---

TABLE 6.2

Comparison of Four Major Website Managers

The Battle to Build

Don't entrust your personal website to just anyone. Pick wisely.

	Squarespace	Weebly	Wix	Jimdo
What's Good	Best-looking templates of the bunch	Most user-friendly interface and tools	Strong business, résumé tools	Nice-looking templates
What's Bad	Some tools are too hard to find	Domains can be expensive	Templates look outdated	Cluttered, out-of-date interface
Customer Service	Email, live chat	Email, live chat, phone	Email, phone	Email, live chat
Pricing (per month)	No free option; $8 and up for hosting with custom domain	Free option; hosting $4 and up (waived if you buy custom domain)	Free option; hosting starts at around $4 (with ads)	Free option; custom domains start at $7.50
Domain (per year)	$20 (private registration included)	$40; $10 extra for private registration	$15; $10 extra for private registration	Included with a yearly plan

Source: Adapted from Forget Social Media! Build Your Very Own Website, *The Wall Street Journal*

difficult for business owners to control how their business is viewed by customers. Kevin Williams is the cofounder of a Utah-based seller of water-powered cleaning brushes to clean vehicles. A retailer declined to give him a large contract for the patented Brush Hero product, made in the United States and United Kingdom, because the "Amazon reviews are terrible." Sometimes, entrepreneurs accidently stumble in their social media activities. When John Pepper tweeted that his chain of burrito restaurants would remain open during Hurricane Sandy, there was a severe backlash about putting his employees at risk, forcing him to close well in time for the employees to get home. Not every business owner is so responsive to social media. When a customer of Marc Orfaly's restaurant in Boston did not like the pumpkin pie served to her for thanksgiving dinner, she made a comment to that effect on the restaurant's Facebook page. The owner-chef responded by unloading on the woman with profanity, name-calling, and insults, which likely didn't earn him any favors with other customers.

In the early days of social media, **email promotion** wherein the firm's message is delivered electronically to the consumer's inbox provided a low-cost way to reach customers. The popularity of email marketing has declined over time for several reasons: (a) customers inbox became cluttered with marketing messages; (b) recipients are reluctant to open email messages from unknown senders; (c) the Can-Spam Act of 2003 established federal standards around the use of commercial email; and (d) anti-spam software blocks some emails from reaching the inbox of the intended recipient. Many small firms use social networking sites like YouTube, Facebook, Pinterest, Snapchat, Twitter, LinkedIn to promote their offerings. Popular sites also offer businesses the opportunity to run paid advertisements. Lauren Pohl, founder of KidzCentralStation.com, pays Facebook to advertise her online platform for parents to find and book children's classes. She first tests her ad free of charge in her company's newsfeed. For example, her newsfeed included ads with slightly different images (a drawing of three kids, versus a photo of just one) and marketing language ("NYC top class providers" versus "classes for kids in NYC"). After seeing which ads generated the most 'likes' – such as the photo of the one child with the words "NYC top class providers" – she pays for just the better-performing ad to appear inside and to the right of users' newsfeeds. Using Facebook's built-in menu options for targeting users based on their age and location, gender, if they have children, and the ages of their children, she focuses on parents of children ages 12 and below in two New York City boroughs, instead of moms throughout New York City with children any age.

Small firms may also use blogs or apps for marketing. The word **blog** is a contraction of the term weblog, which refers to online journals offering writers' experiences, opinions, and views. For Ree Drummond, blogging was a way to share her personal experiences raising and home schooling four kids with her rancher husband in rural Oklahoma, which gradually evolved into a successful business that includes a restaurant, housewares brand, magazine, cookbooks, and food network show.

Entrepreneurs can start their own blog focusing on their companies and products, by using such websites as WordPress or Blogger.com. When Kate Peterson, owner of baby-gifts retailer Baby Bella in Fish Creek, WI, opened her online store, she started her own blog and began checking and posting comments on other baby-related blogs. Alternatively, entrepreneurs may reach out to established bloggers to talk about their products. Robert Yonke, a 65-year-old watercolor artist, wanted to promote his paintings of bluegrass musicians; he pitched to three online bluegrass hubs, the Bluegrass Blog, the Mandolin Cafe, and the Cybergrass Bluegrass Music News, asking them to review or post photos of his art. All three sites wrote about his work, and he began receiving orders overnight.

For some entrepreneurs, marketing on blogs may not be as easy as the examples discussed so far. Andrew Milligan started Los Angeles–based Sumo Lounge International to sell bean-bag chairs. He had spent $60,000 on trade-show exhibitions and magazine advertising, but sales were languishing at a couple of bean bags a day. He sent an email to the technology blog Engadget.com, asking the editors to review his product. They declined his request, but agreed to trade three months of advertising on their site for 20 Sumo bean bags to outfit their new office. Within 48 hours of the ad's appearance on Engadget, an editor at *Playboy* magazine clicked on the ad and liked what he saw. He featured the bean bags in the magazine, and within about a week, Sumo had sold 500 bean bags. Pleased with the results of that effort, Andrew began to regularly pitch his bean bags to bloggers, sending them emails with links to the company's website and offers to send bean bags to review. Two years later, after more than 250 blogger endorsements or posts about Sumo's bean bags, the company's annual profit had tripled. "This approach saved my business," Andrew shares. "It took Sumo from nothing to a fairly large and profitable company."

The increasing popularity of smartphones means that mobile software or **apps** are fast becoming a quick way to connect with the business or learn more about it. Short for application, an app is a specialized software program that can be used as a marketing tool. Danny Abrams, owner of Mermaid Inn restaurants, thinks that any business not using apps for marketing is shortchanging itself. When Danny was looking to educate and excite seafood lovers about oysters – potentially confusing food with lots of different varieties, he launched Oysterpedia, an app that lets users learn the taste profiles of specific oysters, from beausoleil to bluepoint, and note the ones they've tried. The app has been a hit, with thousands of downloads. Diners even created a game – trying to eat their way through the app's database. "Even if only 1% of our customers download the app, it's a lot of great word of mouth," Mr. Abrams says.

The soaring usage of smartphones has also motivated many companies to use **quick-response (QR) codes** to connect with customers on the go. A QR code is a small bar code that connects to a website, a video, or another Web content, making it easy for people to access your site without having to type in the full domain name. QR codes can be placed in ads, direct mail, in-store displays, and product packaging and linked to a host of features such as discounts or deals. Ethical Bean Coffee Co., a three-store chain in Vancouver, British Columbia, used QR codes to stand out in a competitive market. The company started putting QR codes in train ads. When customers scan the little squares with their smartphone cameras, a coffee menu pops up on their screens. Then they can order a cup of coffee on the train – and have it waiting when they arrive at one of Ethical Bean's shops. Business has doubled since then, says Chief Executive Lloyd Bernhardt. "We catch people who are on the go and don't have a lot of time," he says.

Comprehension Check

1. What is a captive customer?
2. Distinguish between active contacts and passive contacts.
3. Define public relations. Provide some examples of public relations activities.

Module 6.4 Locating Your Business in the Right Place

A business owner needs to consider two basic where questions. The first one is "Where are my customers?" and the second one is "Where should I be?" These two questions are related, but their answers may vary. In some businesses (e.g. restaurants), the firm most likely needs to be located where the customers are (unless your clientele mostly orders "delivery," in which case you have more flexibility in deciding where to locate). In other businesses, the firm may locate at a distance from the customers, preferring instead to locate wherever it is most advantageous to do so (either because of cost or convenience). The guiding principle in location decisions is what makes most sense to get products and services to the customers so that they are able to buy it if and when they are interested. Sometimes location decisions may also be influenced by competitors. If your rivals are locating close to your target market, or your customers are buying from your competitors that are located close to them, you will need to come up with solutions to counter your locational disadvantage.

6.4.1 Is Your Customer the User?

Some businesses sell directly to the end consumer. Other businesses sell to intermediaries who help move the product to the end consumer. There are also businesses that sell directly to both the end consumer and intermediaries. Consider the local pizzeria in your town. It sells directly to customers, and so its marketing efforts need to be focused on how to generate a demand for its product among consumers. The pizzeria will focus on marketing directly to customers. The local brewery in your town is an example of a firm that needs to sell through intermediaries. In the United States, breweries, with some exceptions, advertise to consumers, but sell to intermediaries because of the legal restriction on selling directly to consumers. Coffee roasters, like Toomer's Coffee, are businesses that sell to both end users and intermediaries. Depending on the nature of the link between a business and its customers, firms will choose whether to invest in **direct** or **indirect marketing**.

6.4.2 Getting Through to the User or Customer

There are several things a business can do to break through the cluttered marketplace to get in the line of sight of its users or customers.

Advertising is the presentation of your company's products, services, and image to potential customers and the public. It is the major approach for most businesses to convey their message to potential customers. The goal of advertising is to create a positive impression of the company among the target market. Advertising can be done in print outlets (e.g. specialty magazines, newspapers), electronically (such as through Facebook), or via signs from billboards to aerial banners. **Direct response advertising** involves placing something with a phone number and email or regular mail address with the intent of soliciting immediate orders from customers. The ad may be placed in a magazine or newspaper or on radio or TV or billboard, depending on how much money the owner is willing to spend. For many business owners, the dream is to get their product on a home shopping channel and sell out in minutes. Faced with the problem of keeping her kids' lacrosse gear smelling clean, Krista Wood came up with GloveStix, an odor suppressor shaped like a pair of nunchucks designed to inhibit bacterial growth and absorb moisture from sports equipment. She managed to sell 2000 GloveStix from distribution tents at lacrosse tournaments over eight months, but an appearance on QVC led to selling 5000 units in eight minutes.

Advertising can be paid for (e.g. commercials on radio or TV), but it can also be free (e.g. car sticker, passing out cards at the local fair). These days you will hear people talk about **viral marketing**. A company posts a video or photo that people start sharing, so much so that thousands or millions of people are seeing and sharing the content. Viral marketing refers to the quick and wide diffusion of a message created to showcase a company's offering through unpaid sharing on social media platforms.

Direct mail involves informational materials in the form of postcards, catalogs, videos, sales letters, brochure, emails, and many others. There are several advantages to this approach: selling on your own schedule, low startup costs (especially, if you manage to place your goods in others' catalogues or online store), avoiding major inventory

What Do You Think?

What would you do if you got an oversized UPS envelope in the mail? A company accidently mailed several empty UPS envelopes with the 1-800 number printed on the return address label. To the company's surprise, their phones started to ring. The prospects wanted to know: "What were you trying to send me?" The company's executives soon realized their accidental tactic worked, and the stealth campaign became its core direct-mailing strategy. Can you come up with some novel ideas to get people to respond to direct mail campaigns?

investments, and potentially reaching a large market. Of course, there are also challenges to this approach. Every one of us is familiar with the problem of junk mail. If your direct mail can reach the right decision-maker at a good time when she needs your product, you avoid joining the daily wastebasket of junk mail. Find the right market for your offerings, and chances increase that your mail will land on the desk of someone who is interested. The Direct Marketing Association estimates the typical direct mail prospecting campaign motivates 1% of the recipients to take action.

One of the areas for explosive growth in marketing on the Internet has been daily deal sites. Groupon.com, founded by Andrew Mason (with Eric Lefkofsky and Brad Keywell), was the first to make it big in this space, but there are now hundreds of similar sites. There are two major types of daily deal sites. One is **coupon sites**, where a small business can make available a coupon that gives customers a substantial discount on a product or service. The other daily deal type is a **group buying site** where potential customers can buy a product at a deep discount. Businesses use these sites, such as www.1sale.com, to get rid of excess inventory. For both types of sites, make sure you are allowed to limit your discounted offerings as there can sometimes be a major spike in customer demand immediately after the sale goes live.

Telemarketing is another form of marketing your offerings. Telemarketing refers to contacting potential customers via phone for selling a product or service. While most consumers report being annoyed with telemarketers, the continued popularity of tele-marketing suggests that it does work. Companies sell everything from aluminum siding to timeshare vacations using telemarketing. Currently, many states have do-not-call lists, and there is also a national do-not-call list.

Guerilla marketing can be a startup company's best friend. It involves the use of creative and relatively inexpensive ways to reach your customer, including T-shirts, bal-loons, sidewalk messages, flyers under windshield wipers, door-knob hangers, and funky roadshows. Julia Enthoven, cofounder of video-editing startup Kapwing, publicly shared her experience of chalking her company's name and cartoon kitten logo on the streets of San Francisco on her blog (https://www.kapwing.com/blog/what-happened-when-we-chalked-sf). While her chalking didn't draw attention, the subsequent blog post about it continues to draw readers. Have you heard of the Meow Mix Mobile? Cat food manu-facturer Meow Mix developed the Meow Mix Mobile to cruise around spreading brand awareness on local streets and highways. When it comes to guerilla marketing, think cre-atively and be ready to push the envelope.

Direct sales is often the primary way of selling to customers without going through intermediaries. A salesperson directly contacts other businesses (or schools or any other organization likely to use your products). The salesperson tries to meet with the

The Meow Mix Mobile is a head-turner.

Interactive Exercise

Wild Earth is a company that sells vegan dog food. One of your classmates wants to start a company that will compete with Wild Earth, which will sell all-natural vegan pet food. How do you think the new company should market its offerings?

decision-maker, presents the product, negotiates the terms and conditions, and perhaps, makes a sale. Direct sales methods can also include door-to-door sales ("We knock on doors and set up appointments": Kirby Vacuum Cleaners), party sales (think Mary Kay or Tupperware), and vending machines (think Redbox). **Door-to-door selling** used to be very common in the United States. However, most neighborhoods now have anti-soliciting ordinances that allow people to call the police if someone is knocking on doors. Despite this challenge, door-to-door selling is invaluable for products that need demonstrations or detailed explanations, as consumers get to see how the products work in their homes.

Another way is **personal selling**. In a small firm, no one will know more about the various product features than the business owners themselves. Thus, business owners are expected to be a good salesperson for their offerings. Personal selling has two parts to it. First, business owners should learn as much as they can about their products, the industry, and how the product is used. Second, business owners should engage enthusiastically with potential customers to exchange information and knowledge about the product with them.

Public relations, or PR, pertains to activities that help increase or influence the market perceptions of a business or its products and services. These activities can be targeted to the public or to specific groups such as industry or trade associations, neighborhoods or lines of business. PR draws media coverage to your business, including newspaper, magazines, blogs, radio, and television. Media will be attracted to things that are new and newsworthy, from people and products to solutions and services.

Do-It-Yourself Public Relations

Many small business owners have very limited resources to invest in public relations. For entrepreneurs who find themselves in this situation, one option is to do their own public relations, or DIYPR. Angela Mastrogiacomo (www.angelamastrogiacomo.com) is a business coach who has some useful advice for small business owners doing their own PR.

Watch the video online at: https://www.youtube.com/watch?v=RB34hsePGys

TABLE 6.3		
How Can You Become Smarter About Trade Shows?		
Entrepreneur	**Business name**	**What they say**
Andy Birol	Birol Growth Consulting Inc.	Conventions and trade shows will always be one of the most valuable things you can do. There's simply a consolidation of buyers in one place. They have money to spend and buying authority to exercise.
Jayme Broudy	Contractor's Business School LLC	Do some research to find out which shows are likely to offer the best prospects. Review sales figures from events you have attended in the past, including transactions that resulted from leads you obtained. For new events, ask the registrars what kind of crowds they normally attract and how many of the attendees are actually buyers. Also request referrals to past exhibitors and buyers from within your industry and ask them about their experiences.
Cesar Vargas	Rocket USA Inc.	Once you know which shows you want to attend, consider offering to split the cost of an exhibit space with another firm in a different market. Contact trade associations, small-business groups and other organizations that cater to entrepreneurs and using networking sites such as LinkedIn.com to get the word out that you want to share a space.
Aaron Rasmussen	Harcos LLC	When it comes to outfitting your booth, consider used display materials. Buy furniture for your booth from a discount store such as Ikea instead of renting it from the show operator. Not only are you likely to spend less, but you'll be able to use whatever you buy more than once. Be creative.
Rebecca Morgan	Fulcrum Consulting Works Inc.	Offering to be a guest speaker at an exhibition is another effective way to win the attention of potential buyers without having to incur steep expenses related to exhibiting. My business is all about having credibility and being respected by people who are authorized to spend money. Before landing paid speaking gigs, you may need to get some experience doing it at no charge.

Sometimes a firm will get a booth at a trade fair, local event, cultural show, or flea market, where it showcases its products to potential buyers. The key is to pick the event most likely to attract your target market with the least dent on your pocketbook. If you pick the wrong event, there is little return on your marketing investment. Many experts believe that exhibiting at – or at the very least attending – trade shows and exhibitions is one of the smartest things that a business owner can do. Not only do exhibitions provide critical exposure to potential buyers, they also are essential for learning about unfamiliar markets, building personal relationships, and getting an up-close look at the competition. When going to a trade show, it is helpful to bring some product that you can give away to "anyone with a camera or microphone," says Aaron Rasmussen, cofounder of Harcos LLC, Santa Monica, CA, the maker of Mana Energy Potion, an energy drink for gamers. At one comic-book industry convention he attended, Aaron handed a sample of his company's energy drink to video producers for The Review Zoo, an entertainment website. The crew responded with an on-the-spot interview request, to which he happily obliged. Table 6.3 shares insights from some entrepreneurs on how to use trade shows effectively for promoting your business.

Comprehension Check

1. What is public relations?
2. Explain direct response advertising.
3. What is guerilla marketing?

Module 6.5 Pricing Is Crucial!

Pricing is a critical consideration for any business. When a business prices its products at a level consistent with what the market is willing to accept, the product sells better. Most firms want to charge a premium for their offerings, which then prices the product higher than its worth in the market. The higher the price of a product seems to be, the faster the rivals will try to challenge the firm.

How should a business go about pricing its product? The simplest approach is **cost-plus pricing**, where the firm determines its costs and then adds onto that some level of profit it believes to be appropriate. The most common approach is simply adding a given percentage – whether 10% or 50% or 500% – as profit to the costs incurred by the business. The percentage that can be added to the cost depends on what the market can bear. When there is more competition, the plus part of pricing is lower; less competition allows the firm to expand the plus part. Because the firm is adding a profit mark-up to the cost, it is also called **mark-up pricing**.

The total cost of the product to the firm is the **pricing floor**, since the firm should not price below its costs (when a firm prices below the pricing floor, it incurs a loss). When calculating the floor price, the estimated overheads (such as marketing expenses, administrative expenses) should also be included. Because the overheads are just estimates, firms will need to go through the pricing process several times to arrive at their true floor price. Beware of those who advise you to sell below the floor price in the hope that a higher volume will make up for the difference (it almost never does!).

Sometimes, firms do sell at a loss. **Penetration pricing** is selling at a loss to attract customers to new offerings for a specific time period (see Figure 6.4). In such cases, the firm sells below the cost, so that the more the firm sells, the more money it loses. A product that is sold at a loss to get customers to buy other products from the firm is called a **loss-leader**. Small businesses should refrain from relying on loss-leaders until the firm has good momentum and is on solid financial ground (in other words, until the firm is doing well financially).

Another way to determine the price for a product is to look at what rivals are charging. This approach is called **competition-based pricing**. Here, the firm focuses on obtaining pricing information from the market, using the prices of competitors as a benchmark. Once the firm knows the prices rivals charge for their products, it may decide to sell above or below the benchmark price. For consumers, there will be a comparison effect, as they evaluate different firms' products and make decisions based on the value they expect to get from buying that product. When two companies offer very similar products, it is difficult for one company to deviate much from the competitor's price.

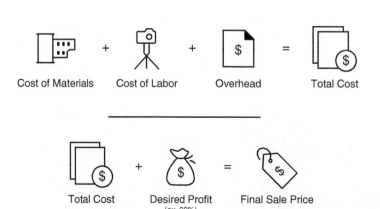

Cost of Materials + Cost of Labor + Overhead = Total Cost

Total Cost + Desired Profit (ex. 20%) = Final Sale Price

FIGURE 6.4 How Cost-plus Pricing Works?

FIGURE 6.5 Surge Pricing

In some industries, companies are able to set flexible prices that rise and fall with market demand. When demand is high, prices will go up, and when demand is low, prices are reduced, as is common in the airline industry. This approach is called **dynamic pricing**, or **surge pricing** (see Figure 6.5). Ride-share companies such as Uber have embraced dynamic pricing, so that riders pay more for trips taken during busy hours and less for trips during non-busy periods. Computer algorithms are used to automate price increases in periods of high demand and limited supply and to lower prices when demand is weak.

Regardless of the pricing strategy one uses, it is important for a firm to break even, which means there is no financial loss to the firm. The **break-even price** is the point at which revenues and costs are equal. At the break-even point, the firm is not making money, but it is not losing money either.

KEY TAKEAWAY

When a business prices its products at a level consistent with what the market is willing to accept, the product sells better. The higher the price of a product seems to be, the faster rivals will try to challenge the firm.

Interactive Exercise

Surge pricing, or dynamic pricing, is popular in ride-sharing and air travel. What other industries lend themselves well to dynamic pricing? Search the Internet for what people say are the pros and cons for surge pricing. Do you think surge pricing is a good approach?

Pricing a service is more complicated than pricing a tangible good. With goods, the firm has a potential floor based on how much the product costs in the first place, but there is no similar reference point for a service. In service industries, the principal inputs are education or experience, which are difficult to convert into costs. For many small business owners, competition-based pricing is the preferable approach for services. The price charged by rivals is crucial information in determining the price of one's offerings. In some situations, for example, auto repair, services are charged based on a **flat-rate price** that comes from an industry manual or computer software. Flat-rate pricing is based on the average time it takes an experienced employee to perform a given task multiplied by the shop's hourly rate (which itself depends on location of the store, overheads, types of clients serviced, and skill level of employees) to calculate the total price for the service.

When pricing a product, it is useful to keep in mind that pricing is also a tool to balance customer demand with the supply a firm can bring to the market. The link between price and sales is called **price elasticity** (see Figure 6.6). When the demand for a product does not fluctuate very much with changing prices, it is an **inelastic product**. Basic needs – e.g. utilities or gasoline – tend to be price inelastic. Products for which demand fluctuates heavily with price changes are **elastic products**. Clothing is an example of an elastic product: The demand for jeans rises and falls considerably with changes in prices.

When the price of an inelastic product increases, demand may reduce, but only by a little. What do you think happens when gas prices go up sharply? People drive less, but not by much. Our driving needs stay about the same regardless of gas prices. When the price of an elastic product increases, people buy a lot less. If the cost of a pair of jeans doubles, demand will reduce by about half, maybe even a little more. Figure 6.7 shows the change in demand for elastic and inelastic products with changing prices. The difference in the slope of the lines can help think about the impact of dropping or raising the price. When money is tight, price increases for elastic products will be more hurtful to demand than increases for inelastic products.

Price elasticity is closely associated with the **law of supply and demand** (see Figure 6.7). When the supply of a product or service is generally sufficient to meet the customer demand for it, the price is stable, and, over the long term, quite average. If demand suddenly grows (say, Alabama Crimsons make it to the national championship game there is greater demand for Alabama-branded jeans), prices are likely to go up (if supply remains constant). If supply suddenly shrinks (if, for example, a trade embargo

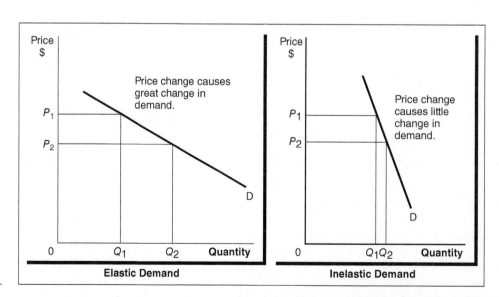

FIGURE 6.6 Price Elasticity
Source: Adapted from A Primer
on the Price Elasticity of Demand.

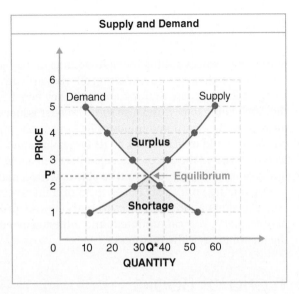

FIGURE 6.7 Law of Supply and Demand

increased the cost of importing denim), prices will go up. Firms can adjust their prices based on supply and demand, but they also need to be mindful of the competition. If a bottle of water sells for a dollar in one store, few would be willing to pay more for it in the store next door. But, if you were to set up a kiosk to sell ice-cold water at a football game on a hot day across the stadium, even $2 for a water bottle may seem like a bargain to thirsty patrons. The heat, or more broadly, the weather conditions, will have altered the relationship between supply and demand. The principle of supply and demand is one of the most important concepts in microeconomics.

Elasticity is an important concept, but there are things for which customers will pay extra based on perceived value and cost. When customers see value in a product (e.g. fine wine), they will readily pay more for the product. Does the company benefit by enhancing the price even further? Probably, if they can do it without the customer thinking, it is just price gouging by the company. The term **price gouging** refers to the practice of suddenly and exorbitantly increasing the price of goods or services in anticipation of or in the event of an external shock to either the demand or supply of the product.

What Do You Think?

Jackie Smith is a guest speaker in your class who runs a popular local restaurant. She just shared with the class that she is considering adopting dynamic pricing where the prices of drinks and foods go up and down with demand and supply. Things will be more expensive on Friday nights, game weekends, Valentine's day and cheaper on weekdays and during holidays. "A well-known London restaurant called Bob Ricard is already doing this," she says. "And, that's how many other industries work, like airlines." As you are a student in a small business management class, and the kind of customer her restaurant targets, she is asking for your feedback on the idea. What would you advise her?

Comprehension Check

1. Identify three types of pricing models.
2. Explain the concept of price elasticity.
3. What is break-even price? Illustrate with an example.

Summary

Marketing involves putting the right product in the right place at the right price at the right time. In a small business, marketing efforts start with the idea for the company's offerings and builds from there to think about the key benefits that customers will want, the price they are willing to pay, and also some broader issues as to how the firm will make a place for itself in the hearts and minds of its target customers. To do well in the market, a small business should understand who its target customer is, the cost of making and delivering its products, and the prices that customers will agree to pay. Now that you understand the basics of marketing, you should be able to write a marketing plan (see Table 6.4).

Organizing your ideas in the form of a marketing plan will help you make important decisions about how best to market your product. Once you have a marketing plan in place, you can update it and adjust as needed based on what you learn about the customer and the business.

World of Books

The 1-Page Marketing Plan: Get New Customers, Make More Money, and Stand Out from the Crowd by Allan Dib

Traction: How Any Startup Can Achieve Explosive Customer Growth by Gabriel Weinberg and Justin Mares

The Lead Machine: The Small Business Guide to Digital Marketing by Rich Brooks

---

TABLE 6.4

Roadmap to a Marketing Plan

No.	Question to ask	Things to consider	Estimated length
1	What is the company selling?	Describe the product, its benefits, and how does it stack up against others in the market? Consider your total product offer and the benefits customers will seek from using it.	300 words
2	Who is the target customer?	Describe the specific market segment that will be targeted for this product. What is the potential size of this customer segment? What do you know about the preferences and beliefs of this segment?	500 words
3	How will the company promote its product, both in the real world and virtually?	Make sure the promotional strategies are consistent with the target market. Discuss each and every promotional strategy to be used. Identify the time frame in which each promotional activity will be implemented (remember, a small business cannot do everything at once). In effect, include a complete list of every effort that will be implemented in a one-year time frame.	1000 words
4	How will the product be priced?	Discuss the approach you will use to price the product and why you think it will appeal to your target market. Will your pricing be static or dynamic? Do you plan to sell at a loss to attract customers?	300 words
5	What resources do you need to implement your marketing plan?	Identify financial and human resources that you will need to put your promotional activities in practice. Consider also the "time" resources you will need, such as how many hours will you need for a particular activity? Remember that small firms are resource-constrained, so you will need to be thrifty in allocating the resources needed for marketing.	500 words

In the Movies

In the movie *Baby Boom*, the protagonist J. C. Wiatt didn't want to start a new business, but circumstances forced her to start selling baby food applesauce she had concocted for her adopted daughter. The applesauce is made from fresh ingredients, but it initially struggled to gain traction in the market. Fortunately, customers loved her product, and she soon has a gourmet baby-good company that a national company wants to buy.

Live Exercise

As you sat through the lectures on small business marketing, you cannot help think about Johnny Gold and his innovative product SoapStandle. You find yourself wondering if you can use the principles and concepts learned in this class to come up with a marketing plan. Tired of thinking all day, you decide to call Johnny first thing next morning. If Johnny was surprised to hear from you, he didn't let you notice it on the phone. When you told him you were hoping to put together a marketing plan for his business, he was clearly happy. "Well, let me send you a picture of the SoapStandle," he says. "I will also text you some other information to help you get started. Of course, you should feel free to ask me for anything else you may want to know to come up with a marketing plan," he continues. True to his words, within 10 minutes of finishing the call, your phone lit up with messages. Here are the notes you have based on the information you got from Jimmy:

1. A device that keeps soap from slipping out of hands in the shower
2. No similar product in the market
3. New colors and materials, as well as a travel case, coming soon

Can you put together a marketing plan for the SoapStandle?

Things to Remember

LO 6.1 Explain the basics of small business marketing
- The twin goals of marketing are (a) attracting new customers and (b) retaining and strengthening current customers.
- Modern marketing focuses not just on making a sale but also on meeting customer needs.
- Managing customer relationships can be very useful for small firms.
- Keeping existing customers happy should also be a high priority for small businesses.

LO 6.2 Distinguish between products as goods and services
- Anything that a firm offers in the market is called a product and is targeted at satisfying one or more customer needs, wants, and demands.
- Products may include goods (the t-shirt a customer bought at a local store or the burrito from the small Mexican restaurant in town) or services (haircut, dental work, and legal services).
- *Tangibility* is a key difference between goods and services.
- *Inseparability* is the idea that the production of the service and its consumption usually happen at the same time.
- *Perishability* is the idea that when a service is not rendered, the value of that time is gone.
- Heterogeneity refers to change in the product based on who is delivering it and when. Goods are highly homogenous, whereas services tend to be heterogeneous.

LO 6.3 **Recognize different ways in which a small business can attract market attention**

- A *captive customer* is one whose buying preferences, because of past association with the seller, do not change even if other options are available.
- All businesses, at one point or another, need to reach out to potential new customers, if they want to remain in operation and achieve even a modicum of growth.
- When you take a new product to the market, you need to have a clear value proposition.
- Many business owners struggle with identifying who their target market is.
- Promoting your business on the Web has become an entrepreneur's important marketing toolkit.
- Many small businesses fail to build a user-friendly website that attracts good traffic.

LO 6.4 **Describe the important role of locating your business in the right place**

- A business owner needs to consider two basic where questions: (a) Where are my customers? and (b) Where should I be?
- The guiding principle in location decisions is what makes most sense to get products and services to the customer so that they are able to buy it if and when they are interested.
- Sometimes location decisions may also be influenced by competitors.
- Small firms need to be mindful of how potential customers and the public perceive them.
- Small firms need to be proactive in trying to break through the cluttered marketplace to get in the line of sight of potential users and customers.

LO 6.5 **Explain why pricing is a crucial decision for small businesses**

- When a business prices its products at a level consistent with what the market is willing to accept, the product sells better.
- In cost-plus pricing, the firm determines its costs and then adds onto it some level of profit it believes to be appropriate.
- Sometimes, firms sell at a loss to get customers to buy their products.
- A product that is sold at a loss to get customers to buy other products from the firm is called a loss-leader.
- In some industries, companies are able to set flexible prices that rise and fall with market demand.
- At the break-even point, the firm is not making money, but it is not losing money either.
- The demand for some products does not fluctuate very much with changing prices, but for others demand fluctuates heavily with price changes.

Key Terms

relationship marketing	captive customer	domain name	viral marketing
product	passive contacts	search engine optimization	direct mail
goods	active contacts	social media	coupon sites
services	leads	email promotion	group buying site
tangibility	prospects	blog	telemarketing
perishability	sales	apps	guerilla marketing
inseparability	repeat customers	quick-response (QR) codes	direct sales
heterogeneity	marketing funnel	direct marketing	door-to-door selling
core product	customer retention	indirect marketing	personal selling
augmented product	value proposition	advertising	public relations
total product	segmentation	direct response advertising	cost-plus pricing

mark-up pricing
pricing floor
penetration pricing
loss-leader

competition-based pricing
dynamic pricing
surge pricing
break-even price

flat-rate price
price elasticity
inelastic products
elastic products

law of supply and demand
price gouging

Experiential Exercise

Jackie loves milk! Because she lives on a farm in rural Arkansas, Jackie gets her milk from the goats that graze freely on her family farm. Now, Jackie wants others to enjoy her organic goat milk as well. She wants to start a business selling goat milk.

The US milk market is worth about $47 billion (market size), dominated by cow's milk. However, there are some signs that America's love for cow milk is on the decline. Americans seem to be slowly moving away from dairy-based milk. Almond milk is the most popular alternative, followed by soy milk and coconut milk in the distance. Goat milk comes from animals but is believed to be healthier than cow's milk.

Develop a marketing plan for Jackie to sell goat milk (and possibly, other products derived from goat milk) as a small business owner with (very) limited resources. You can assume that Jackie has all the regulatory approvals she needs to sell goat milk commercially. Feel free to use the Internet to search about the benefits of goat milk, possible competitors, and the milk industry. Come up with a name that helps distinguish Jackie's goat milk from the other offerings in the supermarket. Your goal is to help Jackie figure out where to locate her business, who her target market is, how to price her product, and how to draw market attention to her product(s). It's a challenging assignment, but ARE YOU UP TO THE CHALLENGE?

CHAPTER 7

Small Business Accounting

Accounting is what generally provides the clearest picture of the business' success.

OSMOND VITEZ

7.0 Introduction

Accounting is probably the most underappreciated aspect of managing a small business. It has a reputation of being difficult and tedious. Many students and business owners would readily admit that accounting is not their favorite subject. In fact, accounting may even be their least favorite subject. Popular media recognize this problem, as evident, for example, in the observation by the *New York Times* that "the term *accounting* (and its partner *financial analysis*) tends to put many business owners to sleep or send them screaming from the room."

A standing joke among many business owners, and often students, is "Why should I learn accounting; I can always hire someone to handle that for me!" Nothing could be further from the ideal for a small business owner. A basic understanding of accounting is essential for anyone who wants to successfully manage a business. Unfortunately, for many business owners, the value of accounting becomes obvious only after it is too late. When business owners do not understand the accounts of their firm well, they are more likely to make bad decisions, regardless of how good of an accountant they have.

The purpose of this chapter is to discuss the basics of accounting. As such, the material is covered at a level suitable for those who want a working knowledge of accounting. Think of this chapter as a starting point for your accounting knowledge. For a small business owner, there is much to learn about accounting, and this chapter should get you started on that journey. There are many good books on the market to help you on the journey, but for now, let's get started.

SPOTLIGHT | The (Hidden) Story That Numbers Tell

Peloton is a New York–based indoor fitness company. Founded in 2012, Peloton was the brainchild of John Foley, an avid cyclist and a fan of spin studios. As a parent of two children, Foley found it difficult to get to spin classes, which motivated him to start Peloton to bring the SoulCycle vibe into people's homes. Investors were initially skeptical of Peloton, questioning how successful the company could be selling expensive hardware.

In 2014, Peloton began shipping its Internet-connected stationary bikes with attached screens, enrolling customers on a monthly subscription plan for accessing streaming classes. The company opened showrooms in shopping centers with attractive and fit instructors working out on pricey exercise bikes, so that people could try the bikes and streaming classes. In 2018, Peloton expanded its product offerings by introducing a treadmill that sold for $3995. Analysts believe that Peloton bikes and treadmills are so expensive at $2000–$4000 apiece that paying an additional $39 in monthly subscription fee is a footnote for its mostly affluent customer base. For its backers, Peloton's attraction is that it combines an Apple-like high-margin hardware business with a Netflix-like subscription revenue. Peloton's success

(e.g. The Obamas are fans, and so are Richard Branson, Kate Hudson, and Jimmy Fallon) has led many other startups to imitate Peloton's model of combining different kinds of fitness equipment with monthly streaming subscription.

"We are profitable," Foley said in a CNBC interview in 2018. The audited financial statements Peloton was required to release ahead of its October 2019 IPO, however, told a different story. Peloton lost $195.6 million in 2018 and $47.9 million in 2017 against annual revenues of $915 million and $435 million, respectively. In fact, the company has been losing money every year since its founding. The company's IPO filing also noted that management expected to continue to incur losses "for the foreseeable future."

The audited financial statements show that the only measure on which Peloton makes money is gross profit, which is revenue minus the cost of its exercise bikes (and other products). When the cost of running the company (e.g. marketing expenses) is added in, the profit disappears, and the company is in the red. Peloton is not the only young technology company that shows negative profitability despite management's claim to the contrary. Lyft, another tech unicorn, adjusts EBITDA (earnings before interest, taxes, depreciation, and amortization), a common measure of operating profit, to exclude many of the costs of running the business. We Co., the popular office-sharing company, claims that it has a "proven profitable business model . . . with locations (that) operate with average margins greater than 40%," but reported an annual net loss of $1.6 billion in 2018, $884 million in 2017, and $430 million in 2016.

Lynn Turner, a former Securities and Exchange Commission chief accountant, noted that profit means only one thing – the bottom line – and all other definitions are misleading.

Discussion Questions

1. What do you think is happening – financially speaking – at Peloton?

2. The Peloton CEO insists that the company is profitable, but the company seems to be losing money every year. Why do you think there is a mismatch between what the CEO is saying and how the company is actually doing?

3. Many well-known new companies (e.g. Peloton, We, and Lyft discussed here), but also others like Uber and DocuSign are losing money year after year, despite bringing in hundreds of millions in revenues annually. Why do you think this happens?

stokkete/123RF

Peloton has become a phenomenon, drawing fans where many others have failed.

Module 7.1 Why Accounting Matters

Many small business owners are intimidated in thinking about accounting, scared of dealing with row after row and column after column of numbers. Being frightened by, or dreading, the numbers of your business is, however, not helpful. **Accounting** is the practice of organizing and communicating the quantitative information pertaining to the financial conditions and activities in a business. The only way a business owner knows for sure, and can prove to others, that the firm is doing well is through maintaining a careful account of the business. Numbers, they say, are the language of business. Clayton Oates, a successful entrepreneur in the accounting technology industry, has this to say on this issue (3 Things You Should Never Ask Your Accountant | Inc.com):

> As a business owner and operator, you need to take ultimate responsibility for every aspect of your business, including the finances. Your accountant can help you plan and interpret the numbers, but you should still develop a thorough understanding of how to independently read the data.
>
> When asked, "Where is your business, financially?" some entrepreneurs say, "Oh, my accountant handles that," or "My bookkeeper handles that." And that *is* a real issue. If you want your business to be successful, take the time to know your finances and implement systems to ensure this information is always at hand.

There are at least five reasons why accounting is important to small business:

1. It reveals how well the business is doing financially.
2. It shows the worth of the business.
3. Regulators (e.g. IRS), development agencies, and investors require it.
4. It provides information necessary for planning.
5. It provides a summary of business performance.

Accounting pulls together all the information presented in the other parts of the business. It quantifies the varied assumptions and historical information concerning business operations. Some of the questions that accounting helps answer are as follows:

- What is the total annual income for the business?
- What profit does the business make?
- What is the break-even point for the business?
- What is the monthly cash flow for the business?
- What does it cost to keep the business open?

When business owners understand accounting, they can make better use of the information at hand to figure out how to run the firm better. Yet, many owners either ignore accounting information or do not understand it well enough to make intelligent decisions, which can put their business at risk. Table 7.1 provides some examples of small firms that were at risk of failing because they did not understand the accounting information. "Small-business owners tend to hate accounting because it's boring," notes Brian Hamilton, chief executive of Sageworks, a company in Raleigh, NC, that tracks financial data for private firms. "The mistake they make is not thinking about how they can use certain numbers as tools to better manage where their business is headed tomorrow."

When most people hear the word "accounting," they think of tax accounting, which is used for calculating and reporting taxes. At the same time, accounting also includes managerial accounting and financial accounting. The former involves the

> **TABLE 7.1**

Accounting Information Is Vital to Survival of Small Firms

Owner	Company name	Problem	Lesson learned
Bart Justice	Secure Destruction Service (Huntsville, AL)	Kept borrowing money from the bank, not realizing that the more he grew, the more he needed to borrow because his revenue was not covering his expenses. The loans meant he had money in his accounts – but it was borrowed money	Don't mistake debt for earnings
Paul Burns	Fireclay Tile (San Jose, CA)	Didn't realize that the substantial accounts receivable balance (more than $100,000) included a lot of stale accounts that were more than six months overdue where the customers had gone out of business	Proactively manage accounts receivables
Daniel Gershburg	Gershburg Law, P.C. (New York City, NY)	Thought he needed to spend money on advertising. Even though his revenue was only $5000 a month, he was spending as much as $4000 monthly on advertising. The result: the more revenue he took in, the more compelled he felt to buy more ads to land additional clients. Expenses were increasing faster than his revenue	Understand your expenses and don't ignore profits
Lara Hodgson	Nourish (Atlanta, GA)	Large customers promised to pay her company anywhere from 30 to 90 days after receiving the bill, but actually paid much after that time. Frustrated with the cash flow situation, Lara later started Now Corp to help other small firms facing similar problems.	The small business with a high cost of capital was essentially funding the big players with more capital and much lower cost of capital
Todd Campbell	E.B. Capital Markets (Durham, NH)	Focused on building and marketing his product. Paid attention to numbers only at tax time. Didn't have a good handle on how his company was performing, including whether he would be able to make payroll	Track the break-even, the point at which revenue for a given period equals expenses

use of accounting by managers for planning and control, while the latter entails the use of accounting by banks and investors. **Managerial accounting** understands and predicts the results of management's decisions and actions. **Tax accounting** is used to ensure that the business is always in compliance and calculate how much money the firm pays in taxes. **Financial accounting** is a formal rule-based system for absentee owners, bankers, and investors.

Think of the many piles of checks, invoices, receipts, and other sundry papers a running business generates in any given month. These papers contain lots of information about the financial health of the business, but they are not in a form that can be used easily. Accounting systems transform the piles of data into usable information by first recording every business transaction in journals, then taking the entries into ledgers. From here, information is taken to financial statements like a balance sheet, income statement, cash flow statement, and so on. These statements show how the business is doing much better than do the stacks of papers with which this paragraph started. The information in the financial statements can be used to compute key ratios for comparison with industry averages, historical information from the business itself, and rivals (if their information is accessible).

KEY TAKEAWAY

To run a business effectively, business owners should have some understanding of their company's accounting.

When the federal government launched the $660 billion Paycheck Protection Program for small businesses to cope with the COVID-19 pandemic, less-populated states like Nebraska, Kansas, and North Dakota received a much larger share of federally backed loans than densely populated states such as New York and California (see Figure 7.1). Why was this the case? The answer lies in the financial statements of the companies located there. The PPP required that 75% of the funds go for employee salaries, and no more than 25% on rent, mortgage interest, and utility payments. The goal of the 75% rule was to ensure that the millions of Americans who work for small companies continue to get a paycheck. Unfortunately, it also meant that many small businesses with modest payrolls and high rent costs, such as restaurants, salons, and shops in urban areas including New York, Los Angeles, and Chicago, were unable to access the PPP aid and were forced to close. Andrea Hans and Josie Sanchez co-own the Broome Street Society, an upscale Manhattan hair salon. They applied for a $174,000 loan through the federal program, but only $43,500 could go to nonpayroll expenses – much less than they needed to cover nearly $60,000 in rent for the two-month period covered by the PPP plan. "We put our life savings, every moment of our time and any financial resources we had toward opening this business," shared Andrea when she was two months behind on rent. "It feels like a funny joke if we had to close because of this," she said.

An important issue in accounting concerns the role of creativity. Is there a place for creativity in accounting? It is commonly believed that creativity can be bad in accounting. In fact, too much accounting creativity can doom your firm and even land you in jail (as the top people at Enron found out). As Sherron Watkins, the much-lauded Enron

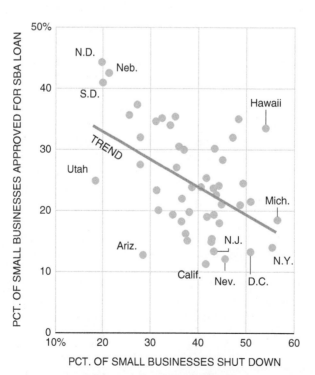

FIGURE 7.1 Small Business Closure and PPP Loan Recipients by State
Source: Based on University of Chicago Booth School of Business; Homebase; Small Business Administration

Note: SBA loan data are for April 3–15. Data on businesses shut down are for the week of March 29.

whistleblower famously said about the financial shenanigans at her once-storied employer, "accounting doesn't get that creative."

Interactive Exercise

Interview five entrepreneurs you know about their approach to accounting in the business. Ask them if they understand their accounting system and how much time they spend on accounts every week.

But must creativity always be bad for accounting? As long as creative ideas meet legal expectations (e.g. generally accepted accounting principles, GAAP), and are consistent with prevailing ethical standards, some creativity can be helpful for good accounting. Some folks consider the "Balanced Scorecard," created by Robert Kaplan and David Norton in the 1990s, as an example of praiseworthy creative accounting (see Figure 7.2). The Balanced Scorecard includes standard accounting metrics (e.g. profitability), but also incorporates intangibles such as customer satisfaction and organizational learning. As a result, the Balanced Scorecard allows firms to link various aspects of their business activities to the overall strategy. Of course, as you can imagine, few accounting innovations are so useful and constructive.

Consider the creative accounting practice of showing a large quantity of reserves from an economically successful year on the books as a way of boosting earnings results, while incurring them against losses during weaker quarters. This practice is called "cushion" or "cookie jar" accounting and is fraudulent. Edward DiMaria, chief financial officer of Bankrate Inc., a financial services and marketing company, was sentenced to 10 years in prison when he was found guilty of conspiring and directing a scheme to artificially inflate the company's earnings.

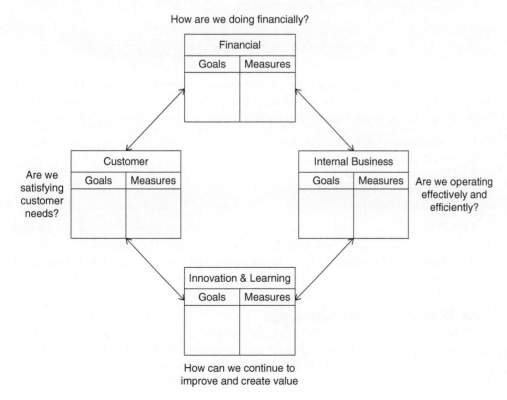

FIGURE 7.2 Balanced Scorecard Is Used as a Good Example of Creative Accounting

Curious About Balanced Scorecard?

Would you like to learn more about the Balanced Scorecard? In simplest terms, the Balanced Scorecard is a management system that employs various criteria to measuring organizational performance, criteria that extend beyond traditional accounting benchmarks captured in earnings reports and include relationships with consumers, employees, and so on. You can watch the video online at https://www.youtube.com/watch?v=O71daIs6x_M.

What Do You Think?

Jumio is a mobile-payments startup founded in 2010 by Daniel Mattes, an Austrian citizen who worked in Silicon Valley. He is alleged to have personally prepared Jumio's 2013 and 2014 financial statements, making it appear as if the revenue was $100 million instead of the $9.5 million it actually was. Profits were reported as $1.2 million when the company actually lost $10 million. Mattes personally benefitted from the misstatement because he sold Jumio stock worth $14.6 million in 2014 and 2015. The Securities and Exchange Commission (SEC) observed that "Mattes enriched himself at investors' expense by making false claims about Jumio's financial results . . . Company executives must provide investors with accurate information irrespective of whether their companies are publicly or privately traded." Are accounting shenanigans acceptable if (a) the founder does it? (b) the perpetrator doesn't personally benefit from it?, and (c) there is a low risk of getting caught?

Comprehension Check

1. What are the different types of accounting that small business owners need to be familiar with?
2. Why should business owners care about accounting?
3. Explain how creativity affects accounting.

Module 7.2 Basic Accounting Concepts

What should a small business owner do to learn about accounting? As is the case with most things, starting with the basic concepts is helpful. The fundamental accounting concepts that everyone needs to understand are as follows:

1. Business entity concept
2. Going concern concept
3. The accounting equation
4. The notion of revenues and expenses
5. The idea of cash flow

Each of these concepts will now be covered in more detail. Many business owners may have learned some or all of these concepts from experience. The discussion here should help everyone become familiar with the concepts that are foundational to a business owner's work.

7.2.1 Business Entity Concept

The **business entity concept** makes it possible to separate business transactions from your own personal transactions. In other words, the money that the firm spends or borrows can be legally distinguished from the money spent or borrowed for the personal needs of the business owner. The business entity concept is the foundation for the legal existence of different forms of businesses, such as limited partnerships and corporations. Failure to adequately appreciate the business entity concept and comply with it can be very harmful for a firm and its owner. Texas-based builder Mauro Padilla learned this lesson the hard way when he was found guilty of commingling his own funds with payments and loans received by his company. The judge noted that Padilla diverted part of the money from the customers and the banks "for personal expenses, including a million-dollar mansion, TV-shopping purchases, a son's wedding and funding for his brother-in-law's car dealership."

7.2.2 Going Concern Concept

The **going concern** concept refers to the assumption that a business once started will remain in existence for the foreseeable future. For accountants, the going concern concept implies that the business intends to make money over many years, and this year's business performance will affect next year's results. Even if the business is sold to other owners, the business may continue to exist independently. When an auditor issues a negative or unfavorable going concern opinion for a firm, the implication is that the business will have to close for financial reasons within the next 12 months. Sears' 2016 annual report illustrates the going concern concept well, as it accepted that "substantial doubt exists related to the company's ability to continue as a going concern." As the *Wall Street Journal* observed in its coverage of Sears' annual report, such "language is typically used when there are doubts about the business' ability to meet obligations for the next 12 months." Companies that receive a going concern audit opinion may be subjected to more rigorous covenant terms or downgrades in their credit ratings.

The number of going concern filings has steadily been declining since the 2008 Great Financial Crisis (see Figure 7.3). According to regulators and accounting experts, the decline in going concern filings is expected to reverse as many companies struggle to deal with the economic pressure from the COVID-19 pandemic.

7.2.3 The Accounting Equation

The accounting equation may be the simplest, but least understood, concept in all of accounting. The entire accounting system is built on this simple equation. A primary value of accounting for owners and managers is that of keeping records. The accounting equation is the method to place these records into specific categories useful for managing the business.

The accounting equation is based on the need to keep track of everything the business owns, while also tracking what the business owes to others and its worth to the owners. So, what is the **basic accounting equation**? It is expressed as

$$\text{Assets} = \text{Liabilities} + \text{Owner s Equity}$$

The accounting equation can be better understood with an example. Suppose you decide to start a business assembling and selling personal computers. Since you were little, you have always liked tinkering with things and putting them together. Now you decide to turn your hobby into a business. To get started, you put $10,000 of your own money in the business. Your Dad, who always wanted you to run your own business, has agreed to loan money, say $40,000, to the fledgling enterprise. How would these transactions be recorded using the accounting equation?

First, you invest $10,000 in the business by transferring the money from your bank account to the account of the company.

What the Business Owns		What the Business Owes	
Cash	$10,000	Capital Provided by Owner	$10,000

You will note that the business has the cash of $10,000. The owner, you, has a claim on the business equal to the amount you gave. If you change your mind about the business at this time, you can get the money back from the business. Or, if someone else was to buy the business, they would be expected to pay no less than the cash already in the bank.

Next, your Dad, who everyone calls Mr. Sam, comes through with the $40,000 loan he promised:

What the Business Owns		What the Business Owes	
Cash	$50,000	Loan Payable to Mr. Sam	$40,000
		Capital Provided by Owner	$10,000
		Total Claims	$50,000

Now the business owns more cash than it had before. The total cash it has is $50,000. At the same time, the business also owes $40,000 to your Dad, and once this debt is paid off, there will be $10,000 left for you, the owner. The value of everything that the business owns is equal to the sum of what the business owes to others plus the claim the owner has on the business. This is the crux of the accounting equation.

If we were to rewrite the above example using accounting terms, we can set it up as follows:

Assets		Liabilities + Owner's Equity	
Cash	$50,000	Loan Payable to Mr. Sam	$40,000
		Capital Donated by Owner	$10,000
		Total Liabilities and Equity	$50,000

This is now a good time to understand the terms such as "assets," "liabilities," "equity," and so on. An **asset** is something of value the business owns. A **liability** is a legal obligation to pay off something (or to give up products or services) at a specific time in the future. **Owner's equity** is whatever is left in the business after all liabilities are paid off. Assets and liabilities can be current or long term. *Current* means that the value of the item can be realized or can be paid in cash within one year. *Long term* means that the asset will be valuable more than one year in the future or that the firm may take longer than one year to pay the amount it owes. Thus, businesses have **current assets** and **fixed assets** (also called **long-term assets**) as well as **current liabilities** and **long-term liabilities** (also called noncurrent liabilities).

The accounting equation is the basis of the balance sheet where assets must be equal to the sum of liabilities and owner's equity.

Any entry made on one side of the accounting equation must also be entered on the other side to maintain a balance. For example, suppose the business had a good year and you are able to return $10,000 of the loan from your Dad. You would credit your cash account (an asset) by $10,000 and debit your notes payable account (a liability) by $10,000. The balance sheet remains in equilibrium.

KEY TAKEAWAY

The accounting equation is based on the need to keep track of everything the business owns, while also tracking what the business owes to others and its worth to the owners.

When you understand the account equation, it can be rearranged as needed. For example, you can write it as

$$\text{Owner's Equity} = \text{Assets} \quad \text{Liabilities}$$

This can also be rewritten as

What you have = What you own   What you owe

7.2.4 Revenues and Expenses

Suppose the business purchases $3000 of PC consumables, $2000 of supplies, and $1000 of tools using some of the cash it has. What does this do to the accounting equation? As you can see, the basic equation does not change, but the cash gets allocated to other use. The situation of the business can be summarized as below.

Assets		Liabilities + Owner's Equity	
Current Assets		**Current Liabilities**	
Cash	$44,000	Loan Payable to Mr. Sam	$40,000
Inventory	$3,000		
Supplies	$2,000		
Long-Term Assets		**Owner's Equity**	
Working Tools	$1,000	Capital Provided by Owner	$10,000
Total Assets	$50,000	Total Liabilities and Equity	$50,000

Suppose that, having started the business and purchasing the necessary tools and parts to assemble computers, you manage to produce and sell two PCs to a local mom-and-pop store. In making the two computers, you use $1000 of your own inventory and pay someone $50 to deliver it to the customer (as you don't yet have a car). When you give the invoice for the two PCs worth $1500 each to the customer, he promises to pay you in a week. How do you record these transactions in the balance sheet?

The inventory that has been used to produce the computers already belonged to the business. The business hasn't been paid the $3000 for the PCs yet, but there is a promise to pay. Fifty dollars were paid out in cash. Here is how things look like now:

Assets		Liabilities + Owner's Equity	
Current Assets		**Current Liabilities**	
Cash	$43,050	Loan Payable to Mr. Sam	$40,000
Accounts Receivable	$3,000		
Inventory	$2,000		
Supplies	$2,000		
Long-Term Assets		**Owner's Equity**	
Working Tools	$1,000	Capital Provided by Owner	$10,000
		Revenues Earned	$3,000
		Inventory Expenses	($1,000)
		Wage Expense	($50)
Total Assets	$51,050	Total Liabilities and Equity	$51,050

Revenue is an increase in owner's equity that is the result of selling your products or services. **Expenses** are reductions in owner's equity based on the value of goods and services used to produce your offerings. When the PCs were sold, the customer promised to pay within a week, which is considered accounts receivables. In return, the business gave up the value of the inventory and labor used.

Imagine that the business takes off, and you make hundreds of transactions that now need to be recorded. What if the hundreds of transactions all happen in the same month? If all transactions continue to be recorded in the balance sheet, pretty soon it will become unreadable. Consequently, all transactions are not recorded directly onto the balance sheet but are recorded in what's called an **account**. Simply stated, an account records similar transactions. One may have an account for revenues where each sale is recorded as it is made. There may also be an account for wage expenses to record them as they occur. At the end of the accounting period, whether it is a week or month or year, simply add up all revenues and expenses and subtract the latter from the former to obtain profits (or loss, if it is a negative number).

Interactive Exercise

What do you think happens when expenses exceed revenues for a business? How would an owner meet the shortfall?

7.2.5 Cash Flow

The inward and outward movement of actual money to and from the business is referred to as **cash flow**. When a business has more money coming in than going out, it is said to have a positive or favorable cash flow. Conversely, businesses where less money comes in than goes out have a negative or unfavorable cash flow. The saying "in business, cash is king" conveys how important it is for a business to have a positive cash flow. The importance of tracking and forecasting the cash flow in a small business is difficult to overstate because a positive cash flow is usually more critical than profits to the survival of the business. Many small businesses are profitable on paper, but have troubles paying their bills because they have an unfavorable cash flow. While it is not uncommon for a new business to have a negative cash flow in its early days, firms that regularly have more cash going out than coming in have a chronic problem that needs serious treatment.

> **KEY TAKEAWAY**
>
> For small firms, cash is king. Many small businesses are profitable on paper, but struggle to pay their bills because they do not maintain good cash flow.

Keeping an eye on the cash flow is very important for businesses that provide substantial credit to customers. Why do some businesses give significant customer credit? A benefit of providing credit is that it can increase sales (revenue), as it is far easier to sell on credit than on cash. However, there are also several downsides of selling on credit (see Table 7.2). First, providing credit naturally delays the receipt of cash. When cash receipts are delayed, small businesses find it difficult to meet payroll and make payments to suppliers and vendors. To avoid cash shortfall, the business owner is forced to borrow money, which creates the second problem. Borrowing is expensive, both in terms of time (you need to convince others to loan you cash) and money (interest is owed on borrowed money). A third problem with extending credit is that, sooner or later, one (or more) customer will default and not pay for the products they bought. Small business owners who provide credit generally express confidence in the creditworthiness of the customer and resolve to engage in careful monitoring and collection efforts, but soon find themselves chasing a defaulter. There may be many reasons why someone defaults and does not pay, ranging from lack of money to ethical issues and outright fraud. Even if one could pursue legal channels against defaulting customers, the law is not always a viable option because of the high cost and the time it may take. Thus, when customers do not pay, the business loses. If the cash flow in the business is tight, as is the case for most small businesses, defaulting customers may doom the business to the point of no return.

TABLE 7.2

Extending Credit Has Some Risks That Need to Be Considered

Problem	Example
Providing credit naturally delays the receipt of cash	A home repair company allows customers to pay later for repairs during the COVID-19 pandemic. The company still needs to pay employees, vehicle insurance, parts suppliers, and all usual expenses.
When customer payments are delayed, the business may be forced to borrow to meet its commitments	A manufacturer of aluminum die casting components decides to extend credit to customers to increase sales. When customer payments are delayed, the manufacturer is forced to borrow to make payments to suppliers and meet payroll. The interest on borrowed money increases costs for the manufacturer.
Sooner or later, one (or more) customer will default and not pay for the products they bought	A commercial cleaning firm finds that many companies that owed it money were unable to pay. Some of the companies had already closed.

What Do You Think?

Vanessa Baltazar is CEO of Black Hills Restaurant Supplies in Sioux Falls, South Dakota. She grew up in Argentina, received an undergraduate degree in Restaurant and Hospitality Management, and started working at a popular restaurant in Buenos Aires. Fast forward to coming to America and becoming a food truck owner. From there she started a restaurant supply business. At the end of her second year of operations, Vanessa was surprised to see that even though her company grew by 15% and made a lot of profits, she still had no money left. What was even worse is that she didn't even have money to pay the taxes she owed on the profits her business made.

Comprehension Check

1. Explain the going concern concept.
2. What is the basic accounting equation?
3. How does extending credit affect a firm's cash flow?

Module 7.3 Accounting System and Financial Reports

The specific accounting needs of a small business are determined by the nature of the work it does and its industry. Some very small businesses (actually, micro businesses) may not need very much in the way of accounting records beyond an accurate cash register. As the business grows, it becomes impossible for one person to remember all relevant financial details. Firms that have one or more employees almost always need to keep formal accounting records. It is worth remembering that good accounting can help avoid many problems that may occur later.

The output of any accounting system is a set of financial statements and reports. Although a small business owner can customize financial reports in many ways, the presentation of financial statements is actually quite standard by convention. Stakeholders, such as bankers and IRS, are most comfortable with standard financial statements. Small business owners are expected to present financial statements in the format and with the content that is standard for the industry.

There are five common financial statements:

1. Income statement
2. Cash flow statement
3. Balance sheet
4. Statement of retained earnings
5. Statement of owners' equity

The important thing about the financial statements is that information flows from the income statement through the statement of retained earnings, the statement of owner's equity to the balance sheet. Information from the income statement and the balance sheet informs the cash flow statement.

7.3.1 Income Statement

The **income statement** is the primary source for information on the profitability of a firm. For this reason, it is also called the profit-and-loss (P&L) statement. The income statement shows the amount of net income (or profit), which is calculated as the amount of revenues earned minus the expenses incurred. It summarizes the income and expenses of the company over a specific period of time.

$$\text{Net Income (or Profit)} = \text{Revenues} \quad \text{Expenses}$$

All income statements follow the same general format. When read top-down, the income statement presents answers to several key questions that are of interest to a business owner. There are two formats for income statements: (a) single-step format listing all revenues together, all expenses together, and computes an overall income value and (b) multiple-step format clearly identifying the various sources of revenue and avenues of expenses. Because the multiple-step format provides greater details, most business owners prefer it over the single-step format.

Not only does the income statement present an itemization of the company's sales, cost of goods sold, and expenses, it also allows for calculating the percentage relationship of each expense item to sales. Including these percentages on the financial statements produces a common-size financial statement, which is a valuable tool for checking the efficiency trends of the business by assessing and managing specific expense items.

KEY TAKEAWAY

The income statement is the primary source for information on the profitability of a firm.

The income statement is widely used to analyze the effectiveness of a business. **Gross profit** provides a quick summary of management's proficiency in efficiently running the business. Most experts consider **net profits** as the litmus test for how well a firm is managed. Figure 7.3 depicts the relationship between revenue, various expenses, and different types of profit.

7.3.2 Cash Flow Statement

The statement of cash flow documents the cash coming into and going out of the business. A business is in a good position when more cash comes in than goes out, which is **positive cash flow**. When a business has more cash going out of the business than coming in, it is called **negative cash flow**. Such a condition is acceptable only as long as it happens sporadically or during the early days of the business.

```
        REVENUE
   —    Cost of Goods Sold
   _____
        Gross Profit
   —    Operating Expenses
   _____
        Operating Profit
   —    Taxes and Interest
   _____
        Net Profit
```

FIGURE 7.3 Basic Income Statement

The cash flow statement generally comprises six elements:

1. Cash flows from operating activities
2. Cash flows from investing activities
3. Cash flows from financing activities
4. Net effect of foreign exchange rates
5. Net change in cash balance
6. Noncash investing and financing activities

Operating activities pertain to all activities performed to create the product or service. Thus, the receipt of cash from customers is an operating activity, but the receipt of funds associated with bank loans is a financing activity (not an operating activity).

Investing activities pertain to the procurement and sale of property, plant, and equipment, and securities of other firms. The inflows result from disposal or sale of noncash assets acquired from prior investments. The outflows are cash investments made by the business to acquire noncash assets.

Financing activities relate to actions taken by management to fund the ongoing operations of the business. Cash inflows come from investments by owners and borrowed money. Cash outflows from financing activities involve capital repaid to owners and prepayment of principal amount of borrowings.

Net effect of foreign exchange rates was once only for large corporations but is now becoming increasingly important to small businesses also, as the Internet has opened up foreign trade to firms of all sizes. Because of exchange rate variations, the value of sales and contracts made in other currencies may fluctuate drastically.

Net change in cash balance simply reconciles the net increase or decrease from the beginning cash balance to the ending cash balance.

Noncash investing and financing deals with transactions in which an exchange of value other than cash occurs. An example of a noncash transaction is when a small business barters with another entity.

7.3.3 Balance Sheet

The **balance sheet** is sometimes also called the **statement of financial position**. You may recall that the income statement presents the financial condition of the business over time. The balance sheet, on the other hand, provides an instant snapshot of the business at a given moment in time. A balance sheet is made up of two main sections – one showing the assets of the business and one showing the liabilities and owners' equity of the business. Do you remember the accounting equation discussed previously? If yes, you will appreciate that the two sides of the balance sheet must be equal to each other.

The usefulness of a balance sheet is determined by the detail it includes. The general trend is to report both assets and liabilities in two categories of current (those that produce or use cash within the short term, or a year) and long term (which involves time periods longer than one year).

The information presented in the balance sheet does pose several challenges that also need to be recognized. First, the balance sheet presents historical values that reflect the cost of the asset when it was acquired. In the case of long-term assets, such as land, buildings, and equipment, the value captured by the accounting records can be widely different from the asset's current value. Land can have high appreciation over time, whereas equipment may depreciate over time. Consequently, the value of such assets in the balance sheet does not reflect their true worth. Cash, of course, is always current. So, when calculating ratios that have both cash and asset values (such as *Return on Assets*), the result is an approximation at best.

Second, balance sheets report some estimated amounts, such as warranty costs and uncollectible accounts receivables. Because these items are estimates, they may turn out to be incorrect, for example, when unexpected product defects increase the projected warranty expenses.

Interactive Exercise

SCORE offers some free workshops for those interested in learning more about accounting-related issues. You can take a free online workshop on preparing an income statement (https://www.score.org/event/creating-profit-and-loss-statement), balance sheet (https://www.score.org/event/preparing-balance-sheet), and other such topics. Take one of the virtual accounting workshops offered by SCORE and share your experiences with the class.

Finally, balance sheet items do not do justice to the qualitative nature of some assets and liabilities. For example, established well-regarded customers like Department of Defense and blue-chip corporates would be valued highly by most firms, but the balance sheet does not distinguish high-status customers from low-status ones. When such assets are critical to the success of the company, the balance sheet underreports the firm's financial strength.

7.3.4 Statement of Retained Earnings

Retained earnings refer to the accumulated net income earned by the firm after paying out any dividends to the owners. A common mistake many students make is to believe that retained earnings represent surplus cash available in the firm, which IT IS NOT. Say, a firm has positive net income. In other words, it makes a profit overall (as opposed to making a loss). The profit can be paid out to the owners, but it can also be reinvested back into the company for expanding the business. This amount, which is not paid out to the owners, counts as retained earnings.

The statement of retained earnings captures the changes in retained earnings for a specific reporting period. The beginning balance in the retained earnings account is the starting point for the statement, with additions and subtractions for profits and dividends, respectively, all of which lead to the ending retained earnings balance. Mathematically, one can write as follows:

Ending Retained Earnings = Beginning Retained Earnings + Net Profit   Dividends

7.3.5 Statement of Owner's Equity

Owner's equity, stated simply, is the monetary value of the owner's share of the business. It is also the measure of a company's net worth as it is calculated by subtracting the total liabilities owed by the firm from the total assets owned by the firm. Owner's equity represents the owner's investment in the firm plus the net income since the firm began minus the withdrawals from the firm. It is viewed as a residual claim on the firm's assets, since liabilities have a higher claim. It is sometimes also referred to as the book value of the firm, because it is mathematically equal to the asset amounts minus the liability amounts. Recall the basic accounting equation discussed earlier:

$$\text{Owner's Equity} = \text{Assets} - \text{Liabilities}$$

The statement of owner's equity captures the changes in the equity section of a balance sheet during the reporting period. In the statement, owner's equity increases when the business makes a net profit or the owner contributes monetarily to the business. Owner's equity decreases when the business makes a net loss or the owner draws from the business.

What Do You Think?

Under Armour, the sportswear company that Kevin Plank, a former University of Maryland football player, founded in his grandmother's basement, was doing really well. It had been taking market share away from Nike and Adidas, and it had 26 straight quarters of at least 20% year-on-year revenue growth. The winning streak came to a sudden halt in the last quarter of 2016 when the company missed its sales targets. Shares plunged as the company scaled back its growth forecasts for the next year. In November 2019, news came out that the company's accounting practices were under investigation by the Justice Department and the Securities and Exchange Commission. The question being investigated: Did the company shift sales from quarter to quarter to look healthier? The investigation, which had started in 2017, was not revealed to the public until 2019. When companies are accused of improper revenue recognition practices, authorities generally focus on whether companies record revenue before it is earned or defer the dating of expenses to make earnings appear stronger, among other possible infractions. Under Armour reported flat sales in the third quarter of 2019. Why do you think a successful company like Under Armour would consider engaging in improper revenue recognition practices?

Comprehension Check

1. What is the difference between gross profit and net profit?
2. Explain retained earnings.
3. When does a firm have positive cash flow?

Module 7.4 Key Ratios for Financial Statement Analysis

The ability to make good financial decisions depends on how well one can understand, interpret, and use the information contained in the company's financial statements. This section provides an overview of ratio analysis, which is the most common form of analyzing financial statements.

A good grasp of the state of the business requires understanding the relationship between differing financial accounts of the firm. The relationships that capture the relative magnitude of some economic quantity to another economic quantity of a firm are called **financial ratios**. There are at least four important categories of financial ratios: *profitability*, *leverage*, *activity*, and *liquidity*. When analyzing a company, it is useful to look at more than one ratio from each of the four categories and to use various categories. Each of the categories of ratios and the types of comparison provide differing insights into the financial workings of the business.

To make sure we understand how to use these ratios to analyze a company, we will use the financial statements from two competing food truck businesses: Gabriella runs Adega, a Portuguese food truck and Ebony runs Kateh, a Persian food truck. Key information from their income statement and balance sheet is presented in Table 7.3.

Quick Financial Primer

Do you want to watch a quick video to walk you through financial ratio analyses? Phillip De Vroe is a Netherlands-based finance expert (www.devroe.org) who likes to tell stories through finance. In this short lecture, he shows you how to calculate 10 key financial ratios.

Watch his video online at: https://www.youtube.com/watch?v=MTq7HuvoGck

TABLE 7.3

Select Information from Financial Statements of Two Food Truck Businesses

		Adega	Kateh
Income statement	Revenue	362,438	250,967
	Cost of goods sold	225,591	168,033
	Labor	25,152	20,851
	Advertising	53,397	42,661
	Gas and parking	10,525	9,527
	Depreciation	7,270	10,057
Balance sheet			
Assets	Cash on hand	18,859	12,742
	Accounts receivable	90,610	50,000
	Inventories	8,873	14,750
	Fixed assets	288,024	224,912
Liabilities	Accounts payable	18,619	13,914
	One-year loan (0% interest rate)	24,892	17,724
	Long-term loan (2% interest rate)	55,528	72,000

7.4.1 Profitability Analysis

The purpose of *profitability ratios* is to measure the ability of a company to derive profits from sales and to transform its assets into profits. Profitability ratios also cast light on the overall efficiency with which the business is managed. There are four important profitability ratios: **gross profit margin** (GPM), **net profit margin** (NPM), **return on assets** (RoA), and **return on equity** (RoE).

7.4.1.1 Gross profit margin GPM measures the percentage of the sales dollars available in profits after the full costs of goods sold are considered (but before expenses are paid). GPM is often also used as a quick indicator of the profitability of the industry as a whole.

For example, one might say that the average GPM in this industry is 50%. GPM is calculated as follows:

$$GPM = (\text{Gross Profit} / \text{Total Sales}) \times 100$$

where Gross Profit = Total Sales   Cost of Goods Sold

To compute GPM, therefore, we need two pieces of information: total sales (or revenue) and cost of goods sold (COGS). The respective values for Adega are $362,438 and $225,591 and for Kateh are $250,967 and $168,033. Subtracting COGS from sales gives gross profit of $136,847 for Adega and $82,934 for Kateh. Plugging these values in the equation above gives GPM values of 37.75% and 33.05% for Adega and Kateh, respectively.

7.4.1.2 Net profit margin NPM captures the proportion of each sales dollar that remains as profit after all expenses have been paid. This ratio is widely used as a measure of the efficiency with which the firm is managed. High NPM indicates the firm is able to keep expenses low relative to sales. Mathematically, NPM can be calculated as follows:

$$NPM = (\text{Net Profit} / \text{Total Sales}) \times 100$$

To compute net profit, all expenses are subtracted from sales. We find that expenses total $321,935 for Adega (sum of $225,591, $25,152, $53,397, $10,525, and $7270) and $251,129 (sum of $168,033, $20,851, $42,661, $9527, and $10,057) for Kateh. This gives us net profit of $40,503 for Adega and −$162 for Kateh. The NPM then for the two companies is 11.18% and −0.06%.

7.4.1.3 Return on assets RoA captures the effectiveness with which a firm converts its existing assets into profits. High RoA usually suggests management is effective at running the firm. Conversely, low RoA raises concerns about management's ability to run the firm effectively. RoA can be computed as follows:

$$RoA = (\text{Net Profit} / \text{Total Assets}) \times 100$$

To compute ROA, we need net profit (which we have above) and total assets (sum of all assets the firm has). Total assets are $406,366 (sum of $18,859, $90,610, $8873, and $288,024) for Adega and for $302,404 (sum of $12,742, $50,000, $14,750, and $224,912) for Kateh. The ROA for Adega is 9.97% and for Kateh is −0.05%.

7.4.1.4 Return on equity The RoE measures the return the firm earns on its owner's investment in the firm. It is calculated as follows:

$$RoE = (\text{Net Profit} / \text{Owner s Equity}) \times 100$$

We already have net profit calculated earlier. To obtain owner's equity, liabilities are subtracted from assets. In the present situation, owner's equity for Adega is $307,327 ($406,366 − $99,039) and Kateh is $198,766 ($303,404 − $103,638). Thus, RoE for Adega is 13.18% and for Kateh is −0.08%.

7.4.1.5 Return on investment RoI assesses the return a firm earns on the financial investment made in the company. It is computed as under:

$$RoI = Net\ Profit / (Debt + Owner\ s\ Equity) \times 100$$

We already have net profit and owner's equity calculated earlier. To obtain debt, we add the one-year loan and long-term loan the company has taken. For Adega, debt is $80,420 ($24,892 plus $55,528). For Kateh, debt is $89724 ($17,724 plus $72,000). Thus, RoI for Adega is 38.46% and for Kateh is −0.001.

For all profitability ratios, higher values are generally better (all else being equal).

7.4.2 Leverage Ratio

The goal of leverage ratios is to gauge the extent to which a firm uses debt as a source of financing and assess its ability to service the debt. The term **leverage** refers to the magnification of risk and potential returns associated with using other people's money to generate profits. Two important leverage ratios are **debt-to-asset ratio** and **times-interest-earned (coverage) ratio**.

7.4.2.1 Debt-to-asset ratio The debt ratio captures the percentage of a firm's total assets acquired with borrowed funds. Total debt includes both short-term and long-term debt. If a company has a total debt to total assets ratio of 0.6, this shows that 60% of its assets are financed by creditors, with owners (shareholders) financing the remaining 40% with equity. A high debt ratio suggests an aggressive approach to financing and a high-risk, high-return managerial strategy. Conversely, a low ratio is evidence of a more conservative approach to financing. To calculate debt ratio, the following formula may be used:

$$Debt\ Ratio = Total\ Debt / Total\ Assets$$

As this formula shows, debt-to-asset ratio is based on two different values: total debt and total assets. We already have total assets (see above). Total debt comes from adding up the money the firm has borrowed: $80,429 (sum of $24,892 and $55,528) for Adega and $89,724 (sum of $17,724 and $72,000) for Kateh. This gives us the debt-to-asset ratio of 0.20 for Adega and 0.30 for Kateh.

7.4.2.2 Times-interest-earned ratio The times-interest-earned ratio, also called *coverage ratio*, reflects the firm's ability to meet its interest requirements. It reveals how far operating income may fall before the firm will begin to face financial difficulties in meeting its debt commitments. High ratio suggests low-risk approach but may also be indicative of inefficient use of leverage. Low ratio is usually worrying as it suggests that immediate action needs to be taken to prevent any debt payments from going into default status.

$$Times\ Interest\ Earned\ (coverage\ ratio) = Operating\ Income / Interest\ Expense$$

Here, we first need to compute operating income (or profit). To obtain operating income, we subtract all operating expenses from total sales. In the present case, operating expenses are $89,074 (sum of $25,152, $53,397, and 10,525) for Adega and $73,039 (sum of $20,851, $42,661, and $9527) for Kateh. Interest expense here is $1110.56 for Adega (2% of 55,528) and $1440 for Kateh (2% of 72,000). Thus, coverage ratio is 80.20 for Adega and 50.72 for Kateh.

7.4.3 Activity Ratios

Activity ratios are used to assess the speed with which various assets are converted into sales or cash. These ratios reveal how efficiently a firm uses the assets it has. Four important activity ratios are of interest here: **inventory turnover, fixed assets turnover, total asset turnover,** and **average collection period.**

7.4.3.1 Inventory turnover The inventory turnover ratio captures the liquidity of the firm's inventory – how quickly goods get sold and replenished in the company. The greater the inventory turnover, the more times the firm is selling, or "turning over," its inventory. High inventory ratio signals good inventory management. Inventory turnover is computed as follows:

$$\text{Inventory Turnover} = \text{Cost of Goods Sold} / \text{Inventory}$$

We have 25.42 for Adega (dividing \$225,591 by \$8873) and 11.39 for Kateh (dividing \$168,033 by \$14,750).

7.4.3.2 Fixed assets turnover Fixed assets turnover ratio measures how efficiently the firm is using its asset to generate sales. This ratio is particularly important for firms with considerable immovable assets (e.g. equipment and/or buildings) since it captures their effectiveness in generating sales. A high ratio indicates that the firm is making optimal use of its assets, successfully deriving good sales from the asset base it has. Fixed assets turnover is calculated as follows:

$$\text{Fixed Assets Turnover} = \text{Sales} / \text{Fixed Assets}$$

We have 1.26 for Adega (dividing \$362,438 by \$288,024) and 1.12 for Kateh (dividing \$250,967 by \$224,912).

7.4.3.3 Total assets turnover The total assets turnover ratio captures how effectively the firm deploys all of its assets to generate sales. This ratio is particularly important for asset-heavy firms. A high ratio generally indicates good marketing strategy and/or appropriate capital expenditures. Total assets turnover can be calculated as follows:

$$\text{Total Assets Turnover} = \text{Sales} / \text{Total Assets}$$

We have 0.89 for Adega (dividing \$362,438 by \$406,366) and 0.83 for Kateh (dividing \$250,967 by \$303,404).

7.4.3.4 Average collection period The average collection period measures how long it takes a firm to convert credit sales (where the firm gives credit) into a usable form (cash). Firms that sell on credit (which includes most firms) should compute this ratio to determine the effectiveness of their credit policies. When the average collection period is high, it suggests the presence of substantial uncollectible receivables, but a low average collection period suggests restrictive credit-granting policies. The average collection period is computed as follows:

$$\text{Average Collection Period} = \text{Accounts Receivables} / \text{Average Sales per Day}$$

The first step here is to compute average sales per day by dividing total annual sales by 365 (for days in a year), which comes to \$992.98 for Adega and \$687.58 for Kateh. Once you have these values, calculating average collection period is straightforward: 91.25 (dividing $90,610 by $992.98) for Adega and 72.72 (dividing $50,000 by $687.58) for Kateh.

7.4.4 Liquidity Ratios

The purpose of **liquidity ratios** is to assess a firm's ability to meet its short-term obligations toward creditors as they become due. *Liquidity* refers to the ease with which an asset can be transformed into the cash equivalent – the more quickly it can become cash, the more liquid it is. Generally, high liquidity is considered good for the firm. There are two important liquidity ratios for the firm: **current ratio** and **quick (or acid-test) ratio**.

Current ratio. The current ratio captures the extent to which the firm can cover its current liabilities with its current assets. The assumption here is that accounts receivables and inventory can be readily converted into cash (which may not always hold true though). Firms with current ratio lower than 1.0 may be in financial troubles. Current ratio can be calculated as follows:

$$\text{Current Ratio} = \text{Current Assets} / \text{Current Liabilities}$$

Current assets are $118,352 (sum of $18,859, $90,610, and $8873) for Adega and $77,492 (sum of $12,742, $50,000, and $14,750). Current liabilities are $43,511 (sum of $18,619 and $24,892) for Adega and $31,638 (sum of $13,914 and $17,724) for Kateh. The current ratio of Adega and Kateh then is 2.72 and 2.45, respectively.

Quick ratio. The quick (acid-test) ratio reflects the firm's ability to meet current obligations without assuming that the inventory can be readily converted into cash. The logic is that quick ratio provides a conservative estimate of the firm's liquidity by considering only the most liquid of its current assets. Quick ratio is calculated as follows:

$$\text{Quick Ratio} = (\text{Current Assets} - \text{Inventory}) / \text{Current Liabilities}$$

We start by subtracting inventory from current assets: $109,469 (from $118,352 − $8873) for Adega and $62,742 (from $77,492 − $14,750) for Kateh. We then divide these values by current liabilities to obtain quick ratio = 2.52 (from $109,469 divided by $43,511) for Adega and 1.98 (from $62,742 divided by $31,638) for Kateh.

Interactive Exercise

Obtain the income statement and balance sheet of a company. You can either obtain them from a business owner you know, your professor can provide it for you, or you can download one for a company that went public in the last two years. For example, Smile Direct Club, a DIY teeth straightening company, went public in 2019 and its financial statement is available on the company's website. Use the income statement and balance sheet to conduct a financial ratio analysis for the company.

Table 7.4 summarizes the financial ratios we analyze here for the two food truck companies, Adega and Kateh.

Financial ratios tell us very little by themselves. In the analysis of a firm's condition, financial ratios are most useful when used comparatively. Comparisons can be made across firms (say, competitors or relative to industry averages) or within the same firm across time. Thus, three types of ratio comparisons are used in practice: trend analysis, where the firm's present performance is compared with its past performance (preferably for more than two years), industry-average analysis, where the firm's financial ratios are

---

TABLE 7.4

Financial Analysis of Adega and Kateh

Financial ratio	Formula	Adega	Kateh
Gross Profit Margin	(Gross Profit / Total Sales) × 100	37.75%	33.05%
Net Profit Margin	(Net Profit / Total Sales) × 100	11.18%	−0.06%
Return on Assets	(Net Profit / Total Assets) × 100	9.97%	−0.05%
Return on Equity	(Net Profit / Owner's Equity) × 100	13.18%	−0.08%
Debt-to-Asset	Total Debt / Total Assets	0.20	0.30
Coverage Ratio	Operating Income / Interest Expense	80.20	50.72
Inventory Turnover	Cost of Goods Sold / Inventory	25.42	11.39
Fixed Assets Turnover	Sales / Fixed Assets	1.26	1.12
Total Assets Turnover	Sales / Total Assets	0.89	0.83
Average Collection Period	Accounts Receivables / Average Sales per Day	91.25	72.72
Current Ratio	Current Assets / Current liabilities	2.72	2.45
Quick Ratio	(Current Assets − Inventory) / Current Liabilities	2.52	1.98

compared to industry averages, and benchmarking analysis, where a firm is compared to peers or industry leaders.

Trend analysis involves comparing a firm's current financials with their financial from past years, usually two or three years in a row. Sometimes, companies may want to compare over quarters rather than over years. The idea behind tracking financial performance across time is that if there is trouble in any of the four key areas (profitability, activity, leverage, and liquidity), it can be detected in time for correction. The key to potential solutions lies in a sound understanding of the ratios themselves. For example, when the trend analysis shows that profitability is going down over time, managers will want to take actions to improve profitability. Consider the following discussion of the ride-hailing unicorn Uber in Uber Books Another Quarterly Loss as Revenue Climbs, the *Wall Street Journal*:

> The San Francisco-based company reported a net loss of $1.2 billion for the three months ended Sept. 30, better than analysts expected but still the third-largest since the company started reporting earnings as a private company in 2017. The record was a $5.2 billion loss in the second quarter of 2019 . . . . Excluding interest, taxes, depreciation and amortization, Uber's loss widened on an adjusted basis to $585 million, compared with a loss of $458 million in the year-earlier quarter.

Clearly, the profitability trend for Uber is not very encouraging. Very likely, the company's management will come under pressure from investors to improve its profitability. **Industry-average analysis** compares a firm's financials against the standard financials for the industry in which the firm operates. Most firms prefer to be somewhere in the vicinity of the industry averages. Where does one find industry averages? One possible source is the *Financial Studies of the Small Business*, which provides financial information for more than 3000 small private firms making less than a million dollars annually. Media coverage of businesses also sometimes includes industry averages that can be used to compare a company's performance with the industry as a whole.

KEY TAKEAWAY

Financial ratios are most useful when used comparatively, whether across firms or within the same firm across time.

If one looks at the bottled-water industry, which has long been criticized for packaging and selling something readily available free, sales growth in the United States was 8.3% in 2015 and 4% in 2018. Globally, sales growth was 7.2% in 2015 and 6% in 2018. Let's say a small company in the bottled-water business had 20% sales growth in 2015 and 2% in 2018. Comparisons with the industry average can help inform if they need to revisit their strategy or they are heading in the right direction.

Benchmarking involves comparing the firm to industry leaders or major competitors. The astute reader would have noticed that financial ratios are agnostic about firm size. As a result, firms of all sizes can compare themselves to major players in the industry (and identify their strengths and weaknesses). Let's say you run a restaurant that serves Chinese, Mexican, or Italian cuisine (by the way, those are the top three cuisines in the United States). You can compare your financials against leading players in these segments by finding publicly traded firms that are closest to what you are offering. Such comparisons can allow you to identify where your costs may be higher than other companies in the same business, whether you are spending more compared to established players, or if you are paying more to your employees than others. While the financial information necessary for benchmarking is not always easy to obtain, some industries have systematic formal sources to which firms can turn when they need data against which to benchmark themselves. Health care and retail are two examples where firms share information that individual players can use to benchmark. Poultry firms in the United States, for example, can obtain detailed information about their industry from Agri Stats, a private service that gathers data from poultry processors, which it then uses to produce confidential weekly reports that are then sold to companies paying for subscription.

Comprehension Check

1. Why should entrepreneurs examine profitability ratios for their firm?
2. What is the purpose of financial ratio analysis?
3. What is benchmarking?

Summary

The only way a business owner knows, or can prove to others, that a firm makes money is through maintaining careful accounting records. The purpose of this chapter is to present readers with the basics of small business accounting. While specific accounting needs of a small firm will be determined in large part by the industry in which the firm operates and the complexities of the business, the underlying accounting concepts and financial

What Do You Think?

McDonald's, the global fast-food giant, has about 38,000 stores across the globe, of which 93% are operated by franchisees. In the United States, McDonald's has 14,146 stores, operated by about 2000 owner-operators. The typical McDonald's restaurant in the United States generated about $360,000 in annual cash flow in 2018, which is down roughly $30,000 from 2016. The company is asking its franchisees to remodel stores and introduce new equipment such as self-ordering kiosks. Some 9000 restaurants in the United States have been renovated, but the franchisees are complaining they haven't seen much return on investment amid declining customer visits. McDonald's offered to pay 55% of the cost for the changes with operators paying the rest. The company estimates that restaurant modernization would cost it and the franchisees about $6 billion. Let's say you are Geraldine Herald, a franchisee with 20 restaurants in the Phoenix area. What financial information would you like to look at before you started the renovations? Remember, you may delay starting the remodeling, but you will not be able to defy McDonald's very long.

reports are broadly the same for all businesses. These days most small businesses use complex accounting programs to ensure the accuracy of their record keeping. Small business owners also often get accounting help from outside professionals. Nevertheless, it is useful to have a good understanding of the basic accounting concepts and standard financial statements. At the very least, some accounting awareness helps business owners have informed discussions with their accountants and ask intelligent questions on why and how the financial reports are being prepared the way they are. When entrepreneurs have a good understanding of accounting, it helps them better manage the business and remain in compliance with legal or regulatory requirements.

World of Books

Accounting for the Numberphobic by Dawn Fotopulos
The Accounting Game by Darrell Mullis and Judith Orloff

In the Movies

When Uncle Billy misplaces the cash he was asked to deposit in the bank, the family business Building and Loan and its owner George Bailey are in trouble. George seeks a loan, offering his life insurance policy as collateral, but is turned down. As he is pursued by law enforcement for embezzlement of funds, George wonders about the choices he has made in life. The American Film Institute considers *It's a Wonderful Life* to be number one on the list of the most inspirational Hollywood films of all times.

Live Exercise

After finishing the small business accounting chapter in class, you reached out to Johnny Gold to ask where he thinks the firm will be in three years. When you looked at your phone after your evening run, you had a stream of messages from Johnny with some financial information. You write them all on paper, and here is what you have:

Revenues: $1,119,521; COGS: $498,451; Advertising and Marketing Expenses: $164,264; Warehousing Expenses: $64,234; Administrative Expenses: $26,416.

Cash on Hand: $26,943; Accounts Receivables: $279,880; Inventory: $36,218; Plant and Equipment: $22,835; Accounts Payable: $47,932; One-year Bank Loan: $26,190; Long-term Bank Loan: $189,340.

The last message you have from Johnny reads "Hey, this is all I was able to salvage from the computer after my accountant quit last month and the computer crashed on me. Can you make some sense of this information? Will I be profitable in three years? I have already invested $250,000 of my own money in the business."

Can you help Johnny make sense of the information he has? Are you able to tell him where his company may be in three years?

Things to Remember

LO 7.1 **Outline the importance and uses of accounting records**
   - A basic understanding of accounting is essential for anyone who wants to successfully manage a business.
   - Accounting is the practice of organizing and communicating the quantitative information pertaining to the financial conditions and activities in a business.
   - Managerial accounting understands and predicts the results of management's decisions and actions.

- Tax accounting is used to ensure that the business is always in compliance and calculate how much money the firm pays in taxes.
- Financial accounting is a formal, rule-based system for absentee owners, bankers, and investors.
- Creativity in accounting can be very bad for the firm, but when one can use accounting information creatively to make more informed business decisions, creativity in accounting can be good for the firm.

LO 7.2   Describe the basic accounting concepts
- The business entity concept makes it possible to separate business transactions from your own personal transactions.
- The going concern concept allows for the assumption that a business once started will remain in existence for the foreseeable future.
- The accounting equation is the basis of the balance sheet where assets must be equal to the sum of liabilities and owner's equity.
- The inward and outward movement of actual money to and from the business are referred to as cash flow.
- Revenue is an increase in owner's equity that is the result of selling your products or services.
- Expenses are reductions in owner's equity based on the value of goods and services used to produce your offerings.

LO 7.3   Explain the format and content of common financial statements
- The income statement, also called the profit-and-loss (P&L) statement, is the primary source for information on the profitability of a firm.
- The statement of cash flow documents the cash coming into and going out of the business.
- The balance sheet provides an instant snapshot of the business at a given moment in time, focusing on the assets and liabilities a business has.
- Retained earnings refer to the accumulated net income earned by the firm after paying out any dividends to the owners.
- Owner's equity is the monetary value of the owner's share of the business.

LO 7.4   Identify the key ratios used to analyze financial statements
- Profitability ratios measure the ability of a company to derive profits from sales and to transform its assets into profits.
- Leverage ratios gauge the extent to which a firm uses debt as a source of financing and assess its ability to service the debt.
- Activity ratios assess the speed with which various assets are converted into sales or cash.
- Liquidity ratios assess a firm's ability to meet its short-term obligations toward creditors as they become due.
- In the analysis of the condition of a firm, financial ratios are most useful when used comparatively, whether within the same firm across time or across firms.

Key Terms

accounting	assets	revenues	negative cash flow
managerial accounting	liabilities	expenses	balance sheet
tax accounting	owner's equity	account	statement of financial
financial accounting	current assets	cash flow	position
business entity concept	fixed assets	income statement	retained earnings
going concern	long-term assets	gross profit	financial ratios
basic accounting	current liabilities	net profit	profitability
equation	long-term liabilities	positive cash flow	analysis

gross profit margin	debt-to-asset ratio	fixed asset turnover	quick ratio
net profit margin	times-interest-earned	total asset turnover	trend analysis
return on assets	(coverage) ratio	average collection period	industry-average analysis
return on equity	activity ratios	liquidity ratios	benchmarking
leverage	inventory turnover	current ratio	return on investment

Experiential Exercise

This exercise is designed for students working individually. Use of the Internet (via laptops or hand-held devices like the iPad or a smartphone) during the exercise is not necessary.

Café Du Monde is a New Orleans institution that is a must-visit on any tourist itinerary. It has a simple menu: beignets (squared pieces of fried dough covered with a generous topping of powdered sugar), dark-roasted coffee with chicory (served black or latte style), milk, hot chocolate, and fresh-squeezed orange juice. So popular is the company's original location in the French Quarters neighborhood that even though it is open 24 hours a day (and 7 days a week), it is not uncommon to see a waiting line stretching more than a hundred yards to get into the seating area (takeout has its own separate line). What makes the Café Du Monde experience particularly interesting from an accounting perspective is that all sales are cash (no receipts are given; no credit and credit cards are accepted). If you don't have cash, you will not be served. What do you think are the benefits and challenges of running an all-cash operation with no receipts given to customers? If you were the company's accountant or auditor, what concerns would you raise with management?

If you have access to the Internet, search for other popular places around the country that only take cash and do not provide receipts for customers. Do some only take cash, but also give receipts? If yes, how does it differ from the only-cash, no-receipt model?

CHAPTER 8

Small Business Finance

If you're an average person with an average great idea, then you're like the rest of us: your idea is worth nothing if you can't manage the funding to get it running.

ANONYMOUS

LEARNING OBJECTIVES

This chapter will help you to:

LO 8.1 Explain the meaning of small business finance

LO 8.2 Identify the different types of financing

LO 8.3 Recognize personal sources of financing

LO 8.4 Distinguish between various formal funding sources

LO 8.5 Describe crowdfunding and its appeal as a source of financing

8.0 Introduction

A widespread belief held by many people is that vast sums of money are needed to start a new business. It is not uncommon to hear people say, "I can't start a business because I don't have the money I need." Many well-intentioned folks believe that the key to success as a business owner is to raise as much capital as possible as quickly as you can, but this is simply not true! Very few people manage to convince others to invest in their business idea, especially when they lack a track record that would give confidence to potential investors. Even in cases where enterprising individuals are able to raise money, there is little guarantee that the business will succeed.

The truth – which few are willing to admit – is that lack of money seldom stops people from starting or growing their business (although it may discourage them from trying to become a business owner or from starting their dream business or growing the business at the speed they want or need). Consider U-Haul, the ubiquitous trailer rental company, started by L. S. Sham Shoen and his wife Anna Mary Carty Shoen. The Shoens started U-Haul with $5000 and some help from friends and family. How U-Haul and other similar businesses manage the finances to get started and grow before they become a large corporation is the topic of this chapter. This chapter should get you thinking more deeply about how business owners manage to obtain the money and resources to start and grow.

SPOTLIGHT | Exploding Kittens: Success with Other People's Money

Exploding Kittens Inc., founded in 2015, is the company behind the eponymous popular card game that combines quirky cat drawings with cut-throat strategy. It is a brainchild of former Xbox designer Elan Lee, cartoonist Mathew Inman of webcomic *The Oatmeal*, and Shane Small, who all came together to make games that would get players away from TV screens and have them to interact in person. Lee, who had previously worked on "Halo" for Microsoft, later recounted that "I have nieces and nephews that play 'Halo' a lot. They're just staring at the TV, and they're not talking and they're not laughing, and their siblings are sitting right next to them, and it started to feel like this very lonely experience. I started to feel responsible for that, because I was the one who put those pixels on the screen." That's when Lee decided to come up with an old-fashioned card game that lets people interact and enjoy being together around a table.

Exploding Kittens started as a Kickstarter project on January 20, 2015, with a hilarious video. The goal: raise $10,000 to print 500 card decks. So fascinated were people with the idea of dangerously naughty felines that the initial goal was met within 20 minutes of the game's debut on the crowdfunding site. When the Kickstarter campaign finished a month later on February 19, a staggering 219,382 backers had pledged more than $8 million, making it the fourth most-funded campaign on the site and the one with the most backers to date. Supporters started receiving the product in July 2015. The company also reached out to Amazon about featuring the game on the retailer's wildly popular Prime Day, where it "broke the record for preorders." At Comic-Can, the company distributed cheap urinal cakes with the Exploding Kittens characters in the men's room. People loved the seemingly absurd idea! In its first year of operations, the company shipped 2.5 million card decks at $20 apiece, bringing in about $50 million in revenues. Over the next five years, the 24-person company sold over eight million units of its card games (the original, plus three others), with the namesake game still the best-seller by a wide margin.

Elan Lee launched Exploding Kittens as a Kickstarter campaign.

In October 2019, Exploding Kittens sold a $30 million minority stake to the Chernin Group affiliate TCG, although the company revealed neither the total valuation nor the exact percentage the venture fund bought. Jesse Jacobs, a partner at the Chernin Group, believes the rapidly growing tabletop game industry is quite fragmented, which makes it a good target for strategic investment. With the new financial backing in place, Exploding Kittens hopes to publish three games annually and make its games the basis for television shows, movies, interactive media, theme parks, or other entertainment. The games, at least some of them, will still launch on Kickstarter, probably even before they are fully finished as happened with the original five years ago. The company sees Kickstarter as a marketing channel as well as the source of financial backing, plus Kickstarter allows audience input into the final product. Win–win all the way!

Discussion Questions

1. How did Exploding Kittens get its initial startup funding?
2. How did Exploding Kittens get the funding to expand and grow?
3. What did Exploding Kittens have to give in return for the funding it received?

Module 8.1 Introduction to Small Business Financing

There are many definitions of *finance*, but the original meaning of the word relates to management of money. The word *finance* seems to have French origins and was later adopted by English speakers in about the eighteenth century. Over time, the term was used in many different fields, and has come to be defined in many ways, depending on who is using it.

At a broad level, finance relates to obtaining money, investing money, and understanding the cost and use of money. It is used for individuals (as in **personal finance**), for companies (**corporate finance**), and also for governments and countries (**public finance**). Financing is a critical issue at all stages of a company life (see Figure 8.1).

The seed stage of a company begins with an idea for introducing a new offering in the market. In most cases, there is no formal venture yet, but the founders will have identified a specific opportunity and be willing to devote time to it. Sometimes reaching the market and getting the first paying customer may be quite quick (as happened to both Microsoft and Apple when they first started). At other times, successfully reaching the market may take a very long time (as, for example, happens to biotechnology firms where the process of product validation and approval can take years). The seed stage, therefore, varies based on the activity of the business and its specific attributes. Depending on the type of business they are in, the founders will need funding to finance the venture until they start selling. What will they do with the funding? Salaries need to be paid, assets need to be acquired, and suppliers need to be compensated. At this stage, we are squarely in the realm of personal finance.

Consider Ken Deckinger, who avoided asking others for money to grow his fledgling online dating service Jess Meet Ken. During the first year of the company, Ken put in more than $100,000 in personal savings into the business. His website accumulated roughly 10,000 users, women who pay monthly fees of $9–$23 to be introduced to potential dates. "We basically hustled to bring this to market," Ken shares.

By the time a company gets to infancy, it already has some customers buying and/or using the product offerings. This stage lasts until the company reaches break-even, which is the stage at which the startup is able to cover all its costs. After the break-even point, the company should be self-sustainable (though it still may need additional funding for growth). However, before break-even the company is still consuming financing, as the income is not yet sufficient to cover expenses. At this stage, we may be dealing with both personal finance and small business finance.

The adolescence stage of a company starts once it has reached break-even and is becoming profitable. In this stage, the company may not be generating much profit, but the important thing here is that the company is no longer losing money. The ongoing operations, and possibly its growth, are funded by the cash generated from paying customers. By this time, banks may also agree to provide credit, as the firm will be able to meet the requirements of traditional financial institutions. At this stage, the company is fully in the realm of small business finance.

The maturity stage of a firm begins once the expansion of the company or its market has stabilized. At this stage, large investments are no longer needed, unless the company decides to jumpstart growth again. The guiding mantra in the maturity stage is "business as usual" with a focus on maintaining current market share. Regular

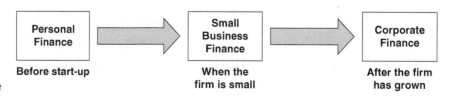

FIGURE 8.1 Types of Finance

financing, from operations and creditors, should be enough to keep the company running at the pace suitable for a mature firm. A mature firm can be small or large (e.g. Nike or Ford). When a small firm is at a mature stage, we are still dealing with small business finance. If the firm is large by the time it is mature, then it is the domain of corporate finance.

Interactive Exercise

Identify three business owners. Interview them to understand (a) what stage their business is in, and (b) how they finance the business? Be prepared to share your findings with the class.

Typically, small business finance involves mainly private funding, as opposed to public funding, which is the case for large corporations. Of course, some small businesses grow and reach the stock market, and at that point they go from private to public funding. Corporate finance focuses on established business and the challenges they face in delivering healthy returns to their investors. The ultimate objective of corporate finance is to increase shareholder value. The assumption: The business already has value, and the key task of managers is to figure out how to increase it. Small business financing, on the other hand, typically pertains to raising and investing the money to identify and generate new value in a relatively small firm. The challenge here starts way before the generation of value, during the opportunity phase as enterprising owners start to think about and hone their ideas.

Often, a key difference between small business financing and corporate financing is that in the latter one will most likely have reliable historical information that can be used to make forecasts for the future. Of course, there is still no guarantee of accurate forecasting, and future projects do go wrong more often than people to admit. For startups, there is no previous history, and the future is largely unknown. Many small businesses do not keep good historical information, making it difficult to rely on history to plan for the future.

KEY TAKEAWAY

Small business financing typically pertains to raising and investing the money to identify and generate new value in a relatively small firm.

Corporate finance theories are based on an important assumption: Investors are (economically) rational. In finance, rationality means that decision-makers carefully consider the risk of each opportunity available to them and either select the option with the lower risk, given the same expected return, or the one with the higher return, given the same level of risk. For small business owners, other factors often interfere with economic rationality. What if the firm is based on something that is socially beneficial or that is related to one of your hobbies? Rationality here gets comingled with some passion, a bit of fun, and a lot of uncertainty. Elena Colombo's Fire Features is a typical small business. Elena started the business after a personal crisis in her life (work challenges post–9/11) by combining her childhood pastime (sit in front of a fire) with her work experience (director of TV commercials). When people responded favorably to the improvised fire design she built in front of her cottage, she founded Fire Features to sell "fire bowls."

What Do You Think?

Your school has started a new initiative to encourage students to start businesses. Under this program, you could apply to the school's entrepreneurship incubation center for help starting your business idea. If you are selected, you will receive $100 to get your business off the ground within a month. If you achieve that milestone with a functional business, you can then get $5000 to grow your business over the next six months. You also get shared office space for your business in a dedicated part of the business school. Those who successfully cross the six-month milestone can then get $50,000 to expand the business over the next year. At this stage, if you want, you can also get dedicated office space from the school that comes with secretarial support. The program is part of the school's "let a thousand flowers bloom" approach to entrepreneurship. If you had this option at your school, do you think would you avail it? If yes, can you come up with a business idea (or two) that you would like to explore?

Comprehension Check

1. Explain the meaning and importance of finance for small businesses.
2. What is the difference between small business financing and corporate financing?
3. What is the difference between private funding and public funding?

Module 8.2 Types of Funding

There are three types of funding a business can access: debt, equity, and profits from operations. Debts are funds borrowed from a creditor and must be repaid. Equity is money received in exchange for selling a part of the business. Debt and equity funding require the business to look outside for financing. The particular combination of debt and equity that make up the financing of a company is referred to as **capital structure**. Many businesses, however, prefer to fund the business internally from the profits generated from their operations.

> **KEY TAKEAWAY**
>
> A firm can be financed through the profits it generates, by taking on debt, or selling to others.

8.2.1 Debt Funds

Debt funds are provided by a creditor with the expectation that they will be paid back with interest in the future. This type of funding is also called a loan. The benefit of debt funding is that it allows a company to access additional funds based on the investment already made. Using debt to finance a business creates **leverage**, which is defined as the ratio of a company's loan capital (debt) to the value of its ordinary shares (equity). High leverage reflects the growth orientation of a small business, but it also increases risk of failure (as discussed below).

Caroline Keefer, a clothing designer in Los Angeles, is owner of apparel maker River + Sky. Her company sells directly to merchants like boutiques, department stores, and hotel spa shops, doing about $2 million in sales in 2019. As the COVID-19 shutdown spread throughout the country in March 2020, she lost nearly $700,000 in orders, all of her spring and summer seasons. She sought about $500,000 in loan, partly to retool her business so she could sell directly to customers.

Debt funding places a cost on the future earnings of a business in the form of interest payments. Creditors provide debt in the expectation of receiving interest. For a small business, the interest payment becomes a fixed cost that must be paid out over time. If the payment is not made on time, the business risks becoming financially insolvent. When a firm does not pay its debt on time, it is said to be in **default**. Unable to pay back his loans on time, Eric Brown, owner of Brown Bros Telecom & Utility in Dalton, GA, constantly worried about one of his lenders arriving at his worksite to repossess a piece of heavy machinery he uses to lay utility cables underground.

Repeated non-repayment of debt will ultimately lead to bankruptcy of the business. Debt can be problematic for a small business, particularly during an economic downturn. For this reason, many business owners try to repay their creditors as soon as possible and become debt-free, but this is not always possible. Nicole O'Brien, owner of the Pandering Pig restaurant in Upper Manhattan, received a $29,000 no-interest loan from the city that helped cover her rent, utilities, insurance payments, and taxes at a time when she was bringing in negligible revenue due to the COVID-19 pandemic as well as looting that occurred after the racial justice protests. However, when the business failed to pick up, she found herself struggling with repaying the six-month loan.

The New York Times

Caroline Keefer's apparel maker, River + Sky, saw almost $700,000 in orders disappear after the pandemic struck. She sought $500,000 in debt to weather the crisis.

Advantages of debt financing

- Lenders have no say in how the company is managed. If loan payments are made on time and contracts are not violated, lenders have little influence over management.
- Repayment of loan generally does not change with business conditions, so managers can plan in advance.
- Loan payments can be structured to match the seasonal sales of the business.
- Lenders have no claim in the profits of the business.

Disadvantages of debt financing

- Lenders can force the firm into bankruptcy when the loan is not repaid on schedule.
- Depending on how the loan contract is written, the lender may have claim on the personal possessions of the owner – the house, for example – if the loan is not repaid.
- Loan repayments are fixed costs for the business, thereby dampening profits.
- Debt payments reduce the cash available to the firm.
- Lenders expect compliance with loan contracts even under adverse business conditions.

8.2.2 Equity Funds

Equity funds are provided by investors in exchange for ownership interest in the business. As such, they need not be repaid in the form of required regular payments for principal or interest. Equity providers are able to share in the profits of the business. Consequently, equity funding does not impose demands on the future earnings of the business. However, equity providers expect a voice in the management of the firm, which dilutes the entrepreneur's discretion to manage the business as she or he sees fit. Sometimes, firms may sell too much ownership to outsiders, so that the owner may lose control of the business to investors. When ownership in Apple was sold to outsiders to raise money, the new owners gradually accumulated enough clout to fire the cofounder Steve Jobs from the company he founded.

Equity funds are a common source of capital for successful small firms. Blooom Inc., a 16-person startup in Leawood, KS, that helps manage retirement accounts. When chairman and cofounder Chris Costello wanted to raise money, he reached out to investors such as Commerce Ventures and QED Investors, who provide money in exchange for equity in the company.

Advantages of equity financing

- Investors get paid only when the business makes a profit.
- No regular payments are to be made to investors in the form of principal or interest.
- Equity investors cannot force the firm into bankruptcy in order to recoup their investment.
- Equity investors may offer helpful advice, valuable mentoring, and new contacts to the firm as they have an interest in seeing the business succeed.

Disadvantages of equity financing

- The owner may lose control of the business when too much ownership is sold to outside investors.
- Even investors with small amounts of equity may try to interfere with the management or direction of the business.
- Because investors get paid only if the business does well, equity financing is riskier for the investor, due to which investors expect a higher rate of returns.
- All investors have claims on the firm's profits.

The **Pecking Order Theory** (POT) provides some guidance on how small businesses can prioritize their sources of financing. According to POT, the cost of financing depends on the information one has about the workings of the business. The difference between the information two parties to an economic transaction have about the matter at hand is called information asymmetry. Because of information asymmetry, it is preferable for small firms to rely on internal operations for financing (where available), then debt, and lastly, equity. POT considers equity funding to be most expensive (because of high information asymmetry) and internal financing to be cheapest (because of low information asymmetry). POT is based on two key assumptions: (1) business owners are better informed about the issues faced by their firms than are outside investors (an asymmetric information assumption); and (2) business owners always act in the best interest of the firm (an appropriate steward assumption).

Another theoretical perspective, **trade-off model**, posits that the observed capital structure of a small business is the result of individual firms trading off increased debt usage against the increasingly severe agency costs that result as debt goes higher than critical levels. As debt increases, it dampens profitability, reduces cash flow, and ultimately increases the chances of bankruptcy in the firm.

8.2.3 Funding Growth Internally

Of course, many small businesses choose to grow without issuing debt or equity. Instead, they fund growth from the profits generated from within the firm. Consider Anant Kale of Sunnyvale, CA, and his cofounder who developed AppZen, a software tool for detecting fraud in expense reports. Their goal was to have a "real product we could show off" to investors, he shares. Within months, AppZen was bringing in revenue, which the founders reinvested in the business so it could hire developers and rent office space.

Savvy business owners try to accumulate capital reserves to fund growth projects without looking toward others. The challenge is to build up capital quickly so that (a) revenue outpaces liabilities and (b) incoming cash flow exceeds outgoing cash flow. As a general rule, entrepreneurs who finance their companies internally, rather than outside capital, are more likely to be attuned to financial issues, according to Katia Beauchamp, cofounder of online cosmetics seller Birchbox Inc. Katia relied entirely on internal financing for the first year of the company's operations. "It made us scrappy," she said. "We were incredibly focused on every single dollar we spent."

It is not always possible to keep revenues higher than expenses and maintain a positive cash flow. Lara Hodgson learned firsthand how much capital it takes to grow a business while bootstrapping her manufacturing company. She and her business partner were selling patented bottled water for children to small retailers and using the proceeds to fund the next order. Cash flow worked well while the company was growing slowly, but everything changed when they received their first big order from a national retailer. Instead of cases of product, they were suddenly selling pallets and their customer wanted net-30 terms (where the customer pays after 30 days). So, they negotiated 60-day terms with their suppliers to help with cash flow. But on the 30th day after shipping their first truckload, Hodgson looked for a check from the customer. It didn't come, and weeks later, still no check. Instead, they received another order. They needed capital.

"More companies *grow* out of business than *go* out of business," believes Hodgson, who, at the time, was advised to take out a bank loan. As a new mother, Hodgson was not eager to put up her home as collateral. She also knew she would soon need more money to purchase additional equipment. "Debt capital, such as bank loans and lines of credit, work well when you're investing in your business–making strategic purchases for equipment, inventory, or real estate," says Hodgson. Borrowing money to then lend to customers in the form of an invoice – a free loan – is generally not an effective way to manage cash flow. "The problem is the more you grow, the more capital you need," she explains. "So, if you're using debt to fund growth, you've got to keep taking out more loans or growing your line to fund new sales." Furthermore, securing a bank loan can be difficult and time-consuming, especially for new businesses without years of financial documentation, or for service businesses without assets that can be used as collateral because they walk out the door every night.

Millions of small business owners around the world face the same problem as Hodgson. How they respond to the problem will depend on three factors:

1. Potential profitability of the business. Every owner wants to run a profitable business that provides a good return on their investment. Both absolute profits and returned earned on the investment made in the business are important

outcomes. Making $50,000 in profit sounds wonderful, but whether that profit is made on an investment of $500,000 or $10,000,000 changes the whole picture. In one case, the return is 10% on the investment made, but in the other case it is 0.5% on investment (less than what one could make on a certificate of deposit).

2. The financial risk the owner is willing to take. Because debt reduces the owner's investment in the firm, issuing debt can help generate a higher rate of return. If debt is so beneficial, one may ask, why shouldn't business owners take on as much debt as possible – even 100% – if they can? The rate of return would be so much higher if the owner had no direct investment in the business. The problem is that debt is risky. Regardless of how the firm is doing at any time, interest on debt still needs to be paid. If the firm fails to earn profits, creditors still insist on being repaid. In dire cases, creditors can force firms into bankruptcy if they fail to honor their financial obligations. And not every business owner is willing to use their personal house as collateral to get a loan.

3. The voting control the owner wishes to retain. Business owners can raise money for their business through selling equity. Raising new capital through equity financing would mean giving up a part of the firm's ownership, and most owners of small firms resist giving up control to outsiders. Many business owners do not want to be responsible to outside equity holders, and certainly do not want to lose control of their business.

What Do You Think?

Vanessa needs $4500 to remodel her coffee shop in Hot Springs, AR. Her plan is to add outside seating to accommodate customers in the new zeitgeist of social distancing. On the one hand, she is concerned about another lockdown because of the COVID-19 pandemic. On the other hand, she sees many other coffee shops in the town set out outside seating. Do you think this is a good idea at this time? If yes, what options do you think are available to her?

Comprehension Check

1. Explain debt funding, equity funding, and gift funding.
2. What are the three major considerations in deciding the funding for one's venture?
3. What does the term *capital structure* mean?

Module 8.3 Financing from Personal Resources

Popular wisdom suggests that the transformation of a novel business idea into a new venture occurs when **venture capitalists** – people who provide money in exchange for equity – enter into the picture. From this perspective, enterprising individuals who want to start a business reach out to venture capitalists for funding. The reality of fundraising for new and small businesses is much different. The number one source for most new businesses is the owners themselves (or potential owners). The personal resources of the business owner are often the first source of financing for most new and small firms. Many people mistakenly believe that, in the modern economy, entrepreneurs do not need to invest their personal resources in the business. An entrepreneur's investment in his or her business is considered his or her commitment to the business. Consequently, most new businesses are started with personal investment from the owner. While the use of personal resources such as the house or car is obvious, new businesses also rely on financial capital from the entrepreneur's savings.

You have probably heard that about 40% of US adults do not have enough savings to cover a $400 emergency. Or, you may have heard that 29% of US households have less than $1000 in savings. Clearly, many people struggle with saving money, which can then constrain their ambitions to start a business. Therefore, when starting a new business, it is important to be aware of how much money you have saved, and how much of it can be used for investing in a business.

Figure 8.2 presents the results of research conducted by the Kauffman Foundation on the funding sources of the fastest growing firms in the United States. As you will see, about two-thirds of *Inc.* magazine's fastest growing firms relied on personal savings to finance their business.

Related to personal savings is another common source of startup funding: friends and family, or the 2Fs. It may come as a surprise, but friends and family tend to be major investors in new and small businesses. Estimates put 2F funding at over $70 billion annually, with about 40% of startup founders reporting raising money from their friends and family (average 2F investment is about $25,000). Friends and family often overlook the weak points of a new business, provide flexible terms, and may even offer zero percent interest rate. Liza Deyrmenjian, founder of ShopToko.com, an online fashion and accessories wholesaler for independent retailers, raised $250,000 from friends and family to get her site up and running. Max Belenitsky started Text-A-Cab smartphone reservation system for taxis and limousines after raising $100,000 from friends and family.

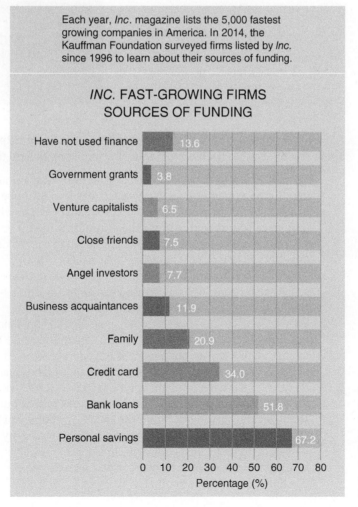

FIGURE 8.2 Common Financing Sources for Fast-Growing Companies
Source: Redrawn from https://www.kauffman.org/wp-content/uploads/2019/12/how_entrepreneurs_access_capital_and_get_funded.pdf

For many new ventures, both personal savings and family and friends come together to help get started. When Mary Blackett and Deborah Zwick decided to start a day spa in Chicago for stressed-out women, they put in $900,000 of their own money (far more than they expected), with family and close friends giving an additional $600,000. Gary Casimir, cofounder of BK9, a Caribbean restaurant in Brooklyn, started with his personal savings and the rent-free use of a building his mother owned.

Gary Casimir and his eight partners in BK9, a Caribbean restaurant, have his mother to thank for helping them when no one else was willing to invest in their idea.

How does one ask for 2F money though? Here are seven helpful tips for those thinking about reaching out to friends and family for financing to help them get started:

1. Be realistic about who you are asking and for what amount. Your parents or grandparents may love you very much, but it may not be a good idea on your part to ask them for so much money that they will need to take out another mortgage to finance your dream. Ask for the minimum amount you may need, perhaps with some buffer for the unknown, rather than the maximum amount you can possibly squeeze out of them.
2. Ask for a specific amount based on a specific milestone. Offers that come with no strings attached or unlimited refills are tempting, but a better move is to ask for just enough money to meet a particular objective.
3. Thank them, but also offer a formal agreement. People that love you get happy when you show your appreciation for their kindness and support. Yet, it is advisable to offer them a written agreement after you have received the money. The vehicle of choice in many cases is a convertible note, which is really a loan with a specified duration and interest, with an option to convert it into equity at a later stage.
4. Show them what you got. Do your homework with industry experts and potential suppliers and customers. Then, use the information you have collected to convince your loved ones that you are not asking for charity or a donation.
5. Be willing to first invest your own time and money. Every good founder should invest some money of their own, as well as sweat equity, to show credibility and personal commitment to others.

6. Communicate your plan and the risks up front. An investment opportunity with no risk? They rarely exist, and most likely, yours is not one of them either. Be honest with your trusting family members and naive friends, since the vast majority of startups fail in the first five years.

7. Tie payback to revenue rather than a fixed date. When you borrow money from friends and family, you also need to return it. One approach is to set a date-driven repayment schedule, and some may prefer it for the certainty it brings. From a borrower's perspective, it may be better to tie repayments to revenue-and-profit targets, though it may not always be acceptable to the lender.

For many external investors (which will be discussed in what follows), founders who have no skin in the game and are unable to find friends or family willing to take the plunge with them at an early stage are simply not worth risking any money on at a later stage. "If you don't have any skin in the game, how can you expect others to put up their own money," asks Katherine O'Neill, executive director of JumpStart New Jersey Angel Network.

Not everyone, however, supports the idea of 2F financing. In *The Startup Founder's Guide to Fundraising*, Justin DiPietro, cofounder and COO at SaleMove, who comes from a long line of entrepreneurs, expressed his reservations about seeking 2F investment, "I would rather not take friends and family money. It would add a massive amount of personal awkwardness and stress." Indeed, asking friends and family for money can be one of the most stressful and awkward parts about raising money.

When filmmaker Lisa Ebersole, of Venice, CA, wanted to raise money from family and friends to fund a new Web series, she turned it into a fun game. She contacted friends and family by sending personalized requests for money. To motivate contributions, Lisa promised to perform a humiliating task if she got to a certain dollar amount, such as eating raw eggs with shells or walking Venice Beach Boardwalk in an egg costume, and shared a video of it with her audience. When people gave her money, she posted tailored public thank-yous on her Facebook page. One read: "Valerie was my doubles partner in 7th grade. She definitely looked better in a tennis skirt. All these years later, she's an amazing lawyer and Mom and I couldn't be more grateful for her contribution." The notes also included a discreet link to her fundraising site, so that friends of friends would see it. Her creative efforts paid off, with Lisa raising $37,080, enough to make her series *37 Friends*.

Lisa Ebersole promised family and friends that she would do dares (like dressing as an egg) if they helped her reach specific funding milestones.

Source: Asking Friends and Family for Startup Cash on Social Media, *The Wall Street Journal*.

The Panel Study of Income Dynamics found about one-third of the small businesses reported receiving unpaid labor from family members. This unpaid labor may not always be a gift from your family members, but sometimes it is.

> ## KEY TAKEAWAY
>
> The number one source of funds for most new firms is the owners themselves or their family and friends.

Personal gifts seem like an easy way to fund the business. Capital without strings, what could be better? When one is trying to start or expand a business, a personal gift may be the boost you need to get going. However, before you accept a gift from a family member, ask the following questions:

1. Is the gift in cash or in kind? A cash gift is straightforward to quantify. Your grandmother is willing to give you $10,000, so that's her contribution to getting you started. But when the gift is in kind, it is hard to figure out its worth. Let's say your grandmother offers to manage your office for a year without charging you anything. You know that you need this help, as your budget does not allow you to hire an office manager with the experience and knowledge your grandmother has. The problem is you have no idea how her gift is worth.

2. Is it truly a gift? Sometimes, a gift is truly a gift. At other times, you may think it is a gift, but your aunt who seemed so generous when you accepted the gift may think she extended a loan or made an investment in your business. If offered a gift, especially when it is in cash, make sure the nature of the transaction is clear on both sides.

3. Who is the giver of the gift? It is important to consider the relationship you have with the person giving the gift. When it is a cash gift, the Internal Revenue Service will want to evaluate whether the relationship between the gift giver and recipient justifies the amount gifted. It is reasonably understandable that a grandmother wants to give a generous gift to help her grandchild start a business, but it seems difficult to explain to the taxman why the grandmother's cousin gifted the money for the business. For in-kind gifts, it is useful to ask if your relationship with the giver merits the type of gift given to you. Remember that gifts create a future obligation, such that the giver may want you to do something for them in the future when they need your help.

4. Will the gift impose a hardship on the giver? When offered something to help with the business, ask yourself if accepting the gift may create significant problems for the giver. As an example, consider that you are moving to Silicon Valley to start a new business. The median rent in Mountain View is more than $4000 a month and the median house is about $2 million. As a new business owner, you are in no position to pay for housing, rental or otherwise. Your Dad's brother – your favorite uncle – has lived in the area for years. If he offers you the guest bedroom in his house until your business takes off, should you take it?

5. What is the motivation for the gift? Whether you believe that humans are mostly altruistic or that they are largely selfish, it goes without saying that accepting a gift creates an obligation of sort. At a minimum, the giver would want the taker to be grateful for what has been given to them. In some cases, the giver may want you to do something for them in the future when they need your help. Consider that when you move to Silicon Valley to pursue your dream of starting a business, your uncle offers to let you use a desk in his office as your temporary workspace. Should you be grateful to your uncle for such help? Absolutely. But, when accepting such a gift, you should also ask yourself if you would help your uncle when the shoe is on the other foot.

Personal gifts can be a wonderful way to finance the business, at least partly.

Interactive Exercise

If you had to ask your family for help starting a new business, what would be your concerns. Be prepared to share your three top concerns with the class.

Comprehension Check

1. Why is personal investment critical to starting a business?
2. Why are friends and family willing to invest in an unproven venture?
3. What are some of the things to keep in mind when asking family and friends for investment?

Module 8.4 Formal Sources of Financing

As the business becomes more established, owners may need to look outside toward formal funding sources. To launch Netflix, cofounder Reed Hastings invested $2 million of his own money. His cofounder Marc Randolph borrowed $20,000 from his mother to invest in the company. As the company grew, it needed more money to stay afloat as it was losing money in its early years. The company then looked outside to formal sources for financing. External financing is not easy for small business owners, especially women and minority business owners. Malene Barnett, an African-American, is owner of custom carpet maker, Malene B Carpets LLC. She was forced to continue funding the company out of her own savings when she couldn't obtain external financing. A Federal Reserve survey found that black- and Latino-owned businesses and very small businesses were roughly half as likely to receive financing through banks compared with white-owned small firms and those with larger revenues.

8.4.1 Financing from Debt

Borrowed funds are the most common source of external capital for established small businesses. This was the finding of researchers Alicia Robb (founder and CEO of Next Wave) and Professor David Robinson, who looked at the financing structure of 3972 US-based newly established firms tracked by the Kauffman Firm Survey. Federal and local governments in the United States also encourage borrowing by small businesses, either by direct cash loans, guaranteeing loans made by commercial banks, and allowing interest payments to be deducted from cash. However, not all firms have equal access to borrowed funds. Ongoing businesses with valuable assets that are readily tradable in the market and separable from owners are able to borrow money more easily than startups or businesses with few assets. To get a loan, firms and their owners need to be willing to pledge **collateral**, assets that a bank can claim if the loan is not repaid as per schedule. When banks asked Kenneth MacKinnon for collateral in exchange for funding his tapas wine bar in Los Angeles, he offered his house. Of course, many business owners are reluctant to borrow money for the business against their house in case things go south.

When considering debt financing, three parameters merit consideration: amount of borrowing (also called the **principal**), **interest rate** on the borrowing, and the duration of the loan (or **maturity period**). These three elements together determine the size and extent of the obligation to the creditor. Until the debt is repaid, the creditor has a legal claim on the cash flow of the business. In extreme cases, creditors can force a business into bankruptcy because of overdue payments.

The principal is the original amount of money to be borrowed. Keeping the loan size smaller reduces leverage and financial risk. The interest rate captures the cost of the borrowed funds. It is generally based on current **prime rate of interest**, which is the rate that banks charge their best customers – those with the lowest risk. Interest rates for small business loans are usually the prime rate plus some additional percentage points. For example, if the prime rate is 6%, small businesses may be offered loans at prime plus three, or 9%. Interest payments are a fixed cost for the business that must be paid to the creditor. When an interest payment is missed, the business is in default of the loan conditions and the entire loan becomes due. Thus, it is important to consider timely interest payment when deciding to take out a loan.

The interest that a business pays to the creditor is usually higher than the stated rate of interest. There are several reasons why this happens. First, some lenders may require borrowers to maintain a minimum deposit at all times, which is referred to as compensating balance. This requirement reduces the amount of accessible funds for the borrower and increases the actual rate of interest. Second, interest may be computed at different frequencies, which is called compounding. For example, semiannual compounding involves two interest periods within a year as half of the stated interest rate is paid every six months on the cumulative outstanding balance. The more compounding periods, the higher the effective rate will be.

Third, rate of interest may also be affected by whether the loan has a fixed rate or variable rate of interest. A fixed-rate loan retains the same interest rate for the entire duration of the loan; a variable-rate loan fluctuates over time as the interest rate is pegged to an external benchmark (e.g. prime rate or federal funds rate).

Finally, the maturity of a loan also impacts the interest rate. Generally speaking, the longer the maturity, the higher the rate of interest. Maturity refers to the length of time for which a borrower obtains the use of funds. Short-term loans typically have a repayment period of one year, intermediate-term loans must be repaid within 1–10 years, and long-terms loans are for 10 or more years. The business owner will choose the maturity period of the loan depending on the purpose for which the money is needed. To buy inventory that is likely to be sold within the year, one would use short-term loans. A long-term loan would be suitable when one wants to finance a building, which is an asset that would serve the business for a considerable length of time. The interest rate of the loan depends on the maturity period, such that loans with longer maturity have a higher interest rate. One exception to this is **overdraft loans** or emergency loans that are of short duration and have high interest rates. The reason loans with a longer maturity period have a higher interest rate is that the lender is committing to forego the use of the funds for other purposes for a considerable period. To compensate, lenders charge a premium to borrowers for loans with long maturity periods.

From the perspective of a business owner taking a loan, the key is to seek as much flexibility as possible. A loan with shorter maturity will usually have a lower rate of interest, but it must be repaid sooner than a loan with longer maturity, which can create cash flow problems and liquidity issues in the business. To have flexibility, business owners should seek loans that have longer maturity, but with the option of repayment before the maturity date and without penalty.

8.4.1.1 Where does one get debt financing? There are several places where one can go for debt capital. Understanding the nature and characteristics of the various debt sources will help ensure that the business owner is knowledgeable about the requirements for each source.

- *Commercial banks.* These banks are the backbone of the US credit markets, offering a wide assortment of loans to creditworthy small businesses. Bank loans can be short term (e.g. for purchasing inventory) or long term (e.g. for land procurement). Many short-term loans may be unsecured, that is, no collateral is required by the bank as long as the entrepreneur has good creditworthiness. Loans may also be self-liquidating, which means that the loan will be repaid directly from the revenues flowing to the asset under the loan. When Maurice Brewster, the African-American owner of RM Executive Transportation Inc. in Redwood City, CA, was looking for financing for his limousine, sedan, and shuttle business, he reached out to Wells Fargo for a loan of $250,000. The company had 44 employees and provided transportation to corporate clients in more than 400 cities, but was rejected by the bank because of the lack of collateral and no profits for several years. As a result, the company was unable to take on new clients who wanted to be billed for payment as that would put excessive strain on the company's cash flow.

- *Commercial finance companies.* These are nonbanking organizations, also called nonbanking financial corporations (NBFCs), that provide debt capital to firms. Commercial finance companies (CFCs) generally cater to firms that are unable to obtain credit elsewhere, so small businesses that have yet to establish their creditworthiness turn to such companies for loans. Because CFCs extend credit to riskier firms, their interest rates tend to be higher. Three types of loans are commonly provided by CFCs: floor planning, leasing, and factoring accounts receivable.
- *Insurance companies.* For some small firms, life insurance companies are a principal source of debt financing. Here, the most common type of loan made to small businesses is based on the amount of money paid in premiums on an insurance policy that has a cash surrender value. A typical arrangement is that the insurance company lends up to 90–95% of a policy's cash surrender value. The collateral for the loan is the cash that the entrepreneur has already paid into the policy. The interest rate for the loan is usually favorable to small businesses because the insurance company is essentially lending the entrepreneurs their own company.
- *Federal loan programs.* Small firms can also get loans from government lending programs designed to stimulate economic activity. The underlying rationale for such lending programs is that when companies become profitable, they will create jobs, which in turn creates more tax dollars for the local region. The most active government lender in the United States is the U.S. Small Business Administration (SBA), a federal agency.

In addition, there are other sources such as nonprofit loan funds catering to small firms that typically have trouble securing debt capital from traditional financial institutions. Mountain BizWorks in Asheville, NC, is one such *Community-Development Financial Institution* (CDFI), providing loans to 350 small businesses, many of which are led by women, minorities, or people from rural areas. CDFIs typically have the express mission of lending to low-income and disadvantaged borrowers.

8.4.1.2 Different forms of debt capital Debt capital can take on many different forms. To make an informed decision, it is helpful to know the various forms of debt capital. *Line of credit* is an agreement between a business and a financial institution that specifies an unsecured short-term fund that will be made available to the business. The business is then able to borrow up to the maximum amount specified in the agreement, which then has to be repaid. Interest is due only on the funds actually borrowed at a given time, although there may also be a setup fee or handling charge. For businesses with volatile or unsure cash flow, the line of credit can make a difference between survival and failure.

Cathy LaCognata is owner of a boutique gym, Training For Warriors Brooklyn, in New York. For years, she struggled to find affordable financing for her business, often turning to friends and family when she needed money. When she heard that New York's Department of Small Business Services had started a program to provide up to $100,000 at about 12% interest to women-owned firms, she applied and was approved for $75,000 line of credit. She planned to use her new line of credit to renovate and buy equipment for her gym. *Demand note* is a loan taken out by a small business for a predetermined period to be repaid at maturity. The catch here is that the bank can demand the repayment of the loan at any time. For example, say a bank issues a demand note to a new business for $100,000 for one year at 10% interest. At the end of the year, the business will owe the bank the total interest of $10,000 (product of 0.10 and 100,000) and the principal amount (of $100,000).

Banks can also provide long-term loans, such as unsecured term loans, balloon loans, and installment loans. Unsecured term loans are provided to established businesses that have a strong overall credit profile. To be eligible for unsecured term loans, businesses need to show excellent creditworthiness so that the lender sees that repayment is certain. These loans are made on specific terms with restrictions on the use of the borrowed money.

Balloon notes are long-term loans that require only small periodic payments over the life of the loan, with a large lump-sum payment due at maturity. The interest may be covered through monthly payments, and the entire principal is due at the end of the loan's term. The balloon loan is conducive to cash flow of the business. If you are unable to make the final payment, the loan may be refinanced by the bank for a similar or longer period of time, with the provision that the business continues to make interest payments.

Installment loans are for businesses to purchase fixed assets such as real estate and equipment. These loans are to be repaid in periodic payments that cover part of the outstanding principal balance and interest. For real estate purchases, banks will typically lend between 75 and 85% of the value and allow repayment over 15–30 years. For fixed assets, the principal amount loaned will range from 60 to 80% of the value, and repayment will be made over the life of the asset. The bank will claim a lien on the asset until the loan is fully paid.

Floor planning is a loan geared toward businesses that need financing for high-priced inventory items, such as new automobiles and boats. A business can borrow money to finance inventory that then can be displayed on the premises for customers, with the ownership of the inventory held by the CFC. When one of the inventory items is sold, the proceeds of the sale will be used to repay the principal amount. The interest is paid monthly by the business for the loan, so that the longer it takes for the business to sell each item, the more the business pays in interest expenses. The loan here is secured, so that the assets purchased with the loan proceeds serve as collateral.

Leasing is a loan arrangement in which a finance company purchases durable goods needed by small businesses and rents them to a small business for a specific period. The rent payment includes the interest on price of the goods.

Factoring is another source of financing. Under this arrangement, a small business either uses the accounts receivable as collateral for a loan (referred to as *pledging*) or sells the receivables outright to a finance company. Some accounts receivables may never be collected, so the amount of the loan needs to be discounted for potential losses. Also, the finance company will not receive full repayment of the accounts receivables until sometime in the future, so the loan amount will need to be discounted for the time period in which receivables will be collected. Historically, factoring has been viewed as one of the least desirable approaches to financing, although recent trends in the industry may be changing that perception.

8.4.2 Financing from Equity

Equity financing involves obtaining money from external providers in exchange for ownership rights in the business. The benefit of equity support is that it does not need to be repaid and there is no interest due on the funds. As a result, no payments are made by recipients of equity financing. Those who provide equity financing are looking for returns other than in the form of repayments: (a) receiving dividends, (b) having a say in how the business is managed, and (c) acquiring ownership in a business that is going up in value. Each of these is now discussed in turn.

Dividends are payments made to equity providers based on the financial condition of the business. These payments are made based on a specific temporal cycle, such as quarterly, semiannual, or annual basis. Generally, the dividend amount depends on the profitability of the business.

Having a say in the management of the business is a key consideration for some providers of equity capital. Not all equity providers are interested in becoming involved with the management of the business, but for some it is important to have a direct influence in a business to which they have extended financing. The business too can benefit from the expertise of the equity provider.

Successful businesses see an increase in value, which is beneficial to those who own a "piece of the action." The value of their equity increases in direct proportion to the increase in the value of the business. Equity providers are able to sell all or part of their investment for a sizable profit on their initial investment.

The source of equity financing that has received more attention from the media is the *venture capitalist*, more commonly called VC. A VC is a wealthy private investor willing to provide capital to companies with high growth potential in exchange for an equity stake. VCs expect to take substantial ownership in the business and receive a high rate of return (20–50%). More than 600 VC firms operate in the United States, of which about 90% are private independent firms. A 2019 ranking found that of the top five VC firms in the world, four are based in California – Accel, Andreessen Horowitz, Benchmark, and Sequoia Capital. The only top five VC firm located outside the United States is Index Ventures in London (England).

Most VCs have investment policies that specify their preferences in terms of desired industry, investment size, and geographic location. VCs rarely invest in retail operations, rather looking for businesses that have the potential for high profitability and robust growth. They provide firms with funds in exchange for an equity position, which they then like to sell off within a few years for a substantial profit. Over the years, many successful firms have been supported by VCs, including Amazon, Apple, Facebook, Google, Netflix, and Starbucks.

Obtaining capital from VCs is not easy. An excellent business plan is essential when approaching a VC firm. It is also critical to obtain a referral from a credible source, such as an attorney, banker, or entrepreneur familiar to the VC. It can take an average of six to eight months to receive a potential investment decision. The average sum invested by VC firms is about $2 million per business, with an overall range of about $20,000 to more than $50 million. Estimates suggest that roughly 50% of all true initial public offerings (IPOs) in America are VC-backed, even though fewer than one-quarter of 1% of companies receive venture financing. In 2018, nearly 9000 companies around the country received VC funding totaling about $75 billion.

There is some evidence that women-owned businesses are underrepresented in VC funding. In 2010, only 7.6% of all VC financing went to female-owned startups, which increased to about 16% in the period 2015–17, and is now at nearly 12% (see Figure 8.3).

Small business investment companies are VC firms licensed by SBA to invest in small firms. In 1958, Congress authorized SBA to provide equity financing to qualified businesses. The SBA, in cooperation with the Department of Commerce, created minority enterprise small business investment companies (MESBICs) to provide equity financing to minority entrepreneurs. Businesses that are more than 50% owned by African Americans, Hispanic Americans, Native Americans (including Alaska Natives), or other predefined groups of socially and economically disadvantaged Americans are eligible for funding. SBICs and MESBICs may be formed by individuals, corporations, or financial institutions, although a few are publicly owned. These investment companies must be capitalized with at least $500,000 of private funds. Once capitalized, they are eligible to receive as much as $4 from the SBA for each $1 in private money invested.

SBICs and MESBICs can be good sources of startups and expansion capital. Like VC firms, however, they tend to have investment policies regarding what types of firms to invest in and where. Currently, about 300 SBICs and MESBICs are in operation in the United States. Walk into any SBA office and obtain the Directory of Operating Small Business Investment Companies for a list of SBICs and MESBICs nation-wide.

You have probably heard the term *angel investor* in the context of financing for small businesses. An angel is a wealthy, preferably experienced individual desirous of investing in early-stage ventures. The use of the word *angel* may be derived from its use to describe financial backers for theatrical productions (plays, operas, etc.), also called angels. Throughout history, wealthy individuals (often the royal family) sponsored and

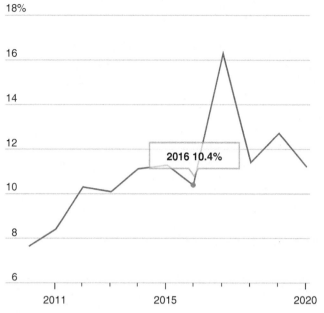

The percentage of all venture funding in the
U.S. raised by startups founded by women

2016 10.4%

FIGURE 8.3 Percentage of All
Venture Funding in the United
States Raised by Women-
founded Startups

Notes: Data includes U.S.-based companies that have
at least one female founder. Data for 2020 is through
Sept 1.
Source: Crunch base.

funded new ventures. The funding of Christopher Columbus' fifteenth-century venture
by Queen Isabella of Castile (Spain) is a familiar example.

In the modern world, the target of angel investments is usually growth-oriented startups.
There may be more than 250,000 angel investors in the United States. Typical angel investments range from $20,000 to $50,000, although a large proportion are for more than $50,000.
The value provided by angel investors goes beyond their monetary support though. The
know-how and contacts provided by the angel investor can also be valuable to business success.

Not all angel investors are the same. Based on the investors' investment activity and competence, there are four types of angels: (a) lotto investors (low activity, low competence), (b)
traders (high activity, low competence), (c) analytical investors (low activity, high competence), and (d) engaged investors (high activity, high competence). The activity level indicates
the extent to which an angel investor has used and plans to use his or her financial resources
for investment in entrepreneurial ventures. The competence of angel investors refers to their
knowledge, skills, and experience related to founding and running entrepreneurial ventures.
Figure 8.4 presents a visual summary of the different types of angel investors.

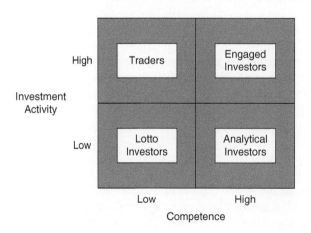

FIGURE 8.4 Types of
Angel Investors

Considerable differences are found between the four categories of investors:

1. Lotto investors are characterized by a low investment activity level and low competence in founding and running entrepreneurial ventures. They, therefore, make very few informal investments and have only limited knowledge and skills to add value to the firms in which they invest.
2. Traders show a high investment activity level with a low competence level in founding and running ventures. They seem to be willing to invest, but they have limited competence to add value to the firms in which they invest. Their contribution, thus, may be rather constrained beyond providing financial resources.
3. Analytical investors have a low investment activity level and fairly high competence. They are labeled analytical because they seem to possess the competence, but they are either not able or not willing to commit themselves to substantial investment activity in the informal capital market.
4. Engaged investors are characterized by a very high investment activity level with high competence. They can contribute both knowledge and skills to the firms in which they invest, and they generally engage in many informal investments.

Finding a good angel investor is not easy. For an entrepreneur to find an appropriate angel investor, they should network widely and seek referrals.

8.4.3 Other Financing Sources

There are other financing sources that a small firm can pursue. Three specific sources are discussed here: private placements, public offerings, and institutional gifts.

8.4.3.1 Private placements Some ventures opt for **private placement**, wherein the stock is sold to a selected group of individuals. This stock is not for the public. Stock sales can be in any amount, with placements less than $500,000 subjected to fewer governmental restrictions and less onerous disclosure requirements than those greater than $500,000. When the company selling the stock is located and it does business in only one state, and the stock is also sold within the same state, it is considered an intrastate stock sale subjected to the regulations of that state. When the stock sale crosses state boundaries, then it is an interstate stock sale, so that the conditions of the federal Securities and Exchange Commission will apply.

8.4.3.2 Public offerings A public offering occurs when a firm sells its stock to the public. These sales are regulated by the Securities and Exchange Commission. The first time a company offers its stock to the public is called an initial public offering (IPO). Companies that go for an IPO need to be in good financial health and be able to attract an underwriter to help sell the stock offering. Why do some companies choose to raise money through public offerings? Three main reasons are important:

1. When market conditions are favorable, it is better to raise funds through public offerings than through alternative methods of raising money.
2. Companies find that their image improves when they have an established (and stable) stock price.
3. Owners who are able to sell shares in the market may find their wealth greatly magnified.

A critical prerequisite of public stock offerings is that companies need to make financial disclosures to the public. This draws public scrutiny to the company, bringing the chief executive officer (CEO) and other managers into the limelight.

Not All Investors Chase IPOs

Some investors stay away from IPOs. Warren Buffett, also known as the Oracle of Omaha, is one such investor. He says he prefers to invest when others are not investing, which is certainly not the case for IPOs.

CNBC

Watch the video online at: https://www.youtube.com/watch?v=CVzv7liXfFU

8.4.3.3 Institutional gifts The most common form of institutional gift is government support, either in the form of subsidies or reduced taxes. *Subsidy* refers to the sum of money given by a public body or state to help an industry or business lower the price of a commodity or service. Tax credits are deductions that lower the tax liability by reducing taxable income. The rhetoric about the free market in the United States often obscures the fact that businesses across different sectors receive billions in subsidies and tax breaks every year. You have probably never heard of *Y'allywood*, the new nickname of Georgia, which has spent billions to attract movie makers to shoot films in the state.

Interactive Exercise

Many states in the United States offer subsidies (and other support) for film-related work within their state. You can do either of the following: (1) Visit the website of Georgia Film Office to understand the various incentives the state offers to filmmakers; (2) identify the American states that offer some incentives to filmmakers.

Grants are another form of institutional support for businesses. There are two large governmental grant programs that are targeted specifically at small businesses: (1) Small Business Innovation Research (SBIR) program and (2) Small Business Technology Transfer (STTR) program. Both these programs require every US grant-making agency to provide a minimum of 2% of its grant budget to small businesses, as defined by the SBA. You may not think much of 2%, but it should be considered in light of the $850 million given out in SBIR grants in 2018. The SBIR and STTR programs each have a three-phased procedure. When a proposal is selected, it receives about $100,000 to conduct a feasibility study, as detailed in the grant proposal. Upon successful completion, additional funds (which can be in millions of dollars) can be provided for the second and third stages.

There are also private foundations that seek to address pressing social needs not adequately met by market forces. Foundations are private organizations to which private wealth is contributed with the intent of allocating money for public purposes. The largest private foundation in the United States is the Bill & Melinda Gates Foundation. Most foundations are started by successful entrepreneurs and business executives, but they do not generally support the creation, growth, or sustenance of for-profit ventures. Most private foundations explicitly stipulate that grants will be made only to nonprofit organizations.

Comprehension Check

1. What kind of small firms are in the best position to get funding from commercial banks?
2. What is IPO?
3. Define subsidy, and explain its purpose.

Module 8.5 Crowdfunding and Its Appeal

Given the challenges in attracting external financing from traditional sources, some business owners are now tapping large, online communities of consumer-investors for financial support. Called *crowdfunding*, this new form of financing allows founders to appeal directly to the public (i.e. the crowd) for help in getting their ideas off the ground. Crowdfunding can be defined as a "method of financing, whereby an aspiring or existing business owner seeks financial resources to support specific initiatives through an open call for funding on Internet-based platforms." When founders use crowdfunding, they are able to tap the "ordinary crowd" for money instead of specialized investors.

At a basic level, crowdfunding involves collecting small amounts of money from a large number of people, a method that has a long history. Mozart and Beethoven, for example, financed new compositions and concerts with money from interested patrons. The Statue of Liberty in New York was funded by small donations from American and French people. The idea of crowdfunding is rooted in the broader concept of **crowdsourcing**, which refers to obtaining ideas, solutions, and feedback to develop corporate activities by using the crowd. In the specific case of crowdfunding by new and small businesses, the objective is to raise money to fund a specific endeavor, generally by using online social networks. In other words, crowdfunding helps ambitious business owners avoid raising money from a small group of sophisticated financiers in favor of large audiences in which each individual provides only a small amount. The advent of crowdfunding websites, also called platforms, has fueled rapid growth in crowdfunding. People who finance initiatives through crowdfunding platforms are called crowdfunders. Table 8.1 presents the major advantages and disadvantages of crowdfunding.

The first platform for crowdfunding was probably Kiva (www.kiva.org), where crowdfunding is used to finance small loans for poor business owners, largely in low-income countries. Crowdfunding has seen a rapid expansion over the last few years, with some enterprising individuals raising millions of dollars within a short period. One of the largest crowdfunded projects to date is Eric Migicovsky's Pebble Watch, which raised more than $10 million in 37 days from over 65,000 backers, even though its original goal was only $100,000. Most crowdfunding campaigns are more humble. The amounts that entrepreneurs typically raise via crowdfunding are usually less than $10,000. Regan Wann raised more than $4000 in 45 days from 60 people through RocketHub.com to expand her Shelbyville, KY, tea shop, Through the Looking Glass LLC. "I did not know what the response would be," Regan says. "Every day until the day I hit my goal, I worried I wouldn't make it. The day I achieved my goal, I was so excited."

TABLE 8.1

Pros and Cons of Crowdfunding

Advantages	Disadvantages
It can be a fast way to raise money with no upfront fees.	Not all projects that apply to crowdfunding platforms are accepted to get onto them.
Ideas struggling to get conventional funding can often get financed more easily.	A lot of work needs to be done to build up interest in the project. Significant resources (time and/or money) may be required.
Investors may become loyal customers through the financing process.	Failed campaigns may damage the reputation of your business. Remember, a majority of crowdfunding campaigns fail to meet their financing goals.
Pitching on the online platform can be a valuable form of marketing and result in media attention.	Once an idea is shared on a public platform, others may copy it.
Sharing the idea with strangers often gets feedback and expert guidance on how to improve it.	One has to be careful about giving away too more rewards for funding, which could hurt the business in the long term.
Offers a good way to test the public's reaction to the product/idea. If people are willing to invest, it is a good sign that the idea could work well in the market.	Crowdfunding platforms take a substantive bite from the money raised, so make sure it is included in the budgeting.

Different forms of crowdfunding now exist. Most discussions of crowdfunding center on **reward-based crowdfunding**, which is currently the most prevalent one. In this approach, funders receive a reward for financially supporting a project. Rewards can include material items (e.g. tumbler or coffee cup) or psychological benefits (e.g. movie credits or meeting with the product creators). Supporters of Regan Winn's crowdfunding campaign for her tea shop got a combination of gifts, depending on the amount pledged, including free tea samples and the honor of naming one of the tea rooms. The most prominent example of reward-based crowdfunding platform is Kickstarter, founded in 2008 and headquartered in New York. Kickstarter is the brainchild of Perry Chen and Yancey Strickler, who had crossed paths when Strickler was a customer at a bar where Chen was a part-time waiter and bartender at the time.

KEY TAKEAWAY

Many different forms of crowdfunding exist, so that those who want to raise money through crowdfunding should carefully consider which form of crowdfunding will work best for them.

Another crowdfunding model, generally called **donation-based crowdfunding**, follows a patronage model, placing funders in the position of philanthropists, who gift money to a new initiative without expecting a tangible benefit in return. Donation-based platforms dominated in the early days of crowdfunding, though their relative representation has gone down over time. The goal of donation-based crowdfunding is generally to support humanitarian and artistic projects. Fundraisers rely on voluntary contributions to a public good, and do not offer monetary returns or in-kind payments other than recognition within a community and the satisfaction of the giver of having helped a cause of one's own choice. An example of a donation-based crowdfunding platform is GoFundMe, where fundraisers can ask for money for a particular project or for help in times of difficulty.

On some crowdfunding platforms, funds are offered as a loan, with the expectation of some rate of return on capital invested (if the project works out). Here, lending bypasses traditional banks. Different from a traditional bank, lending-based platforms do not screen between different projects. Instead, funders decide for themselves if a particular project should be funded. As such, the financing that occurs on such platforms is also called peer-to-peer lending. An example for a lending-based platform is Prosper, which hosts campaigns that "help hardworking families escape the credit card trap, fund an entrepreneur's dream, or finance a dream wedding" as advertised on their platform (www.prosper.com). This is lending-based crowdfunding. Bronson Chang used ProFounder to create a private fund-raising Web page, showcasing the business plan of Uncle Clay's House of Pure Aloha LLC. Nineteen people invested a total of $54,000 in exchange for a 2% cut of the store's revenue over a four-year period.

Crowdfunding may also involve funders as investors, giving them equity stakes or similar consideration (e.g. royalty) in return for their financial support. Funders assess the risk of the investment by weighing the expected performance of a successful campaign. Fundraisers typically specify a target that has to be reached. This "all-for-nothing" approach means that if a project does not reach its target then it does not receive any of the money that has been pledged, which is a way of protecting funders and encourages projects to have realistic funding targets that match the amount of money they really need. From the funder's perspective, the uncertainty is whether the project will actually lead to an offering that caters to the tastes of a sufficiently large number of potential customers who will be motivated to buy. Equity-based crowdfunding, which had already been legal in many countries (e.g. the United Kingdom and France), was legalized in the United States by the 2012 Jumpstart Our Business Startups (JOBS) Act. As is the case with equity investments in general, equity-based crowdfunding tends to be heavily regulated. Consequently, *equity crowdfunding* is still relatively rare worldwide, making up less than 5% of all crowdfunding investment. In the absence of offering an equity stake, investor-based crowdfunding can take other forms, including royalties or shares of future profits, a portion of returns for a future acquisition or planned public offering, or a share of a real estate investment, among other options. Some examples of equity-based crowdfunding are UK-based Crowdcube and France-based Smart Angles.

Interactive Exercise

Google the phrase "successful crowdfunding campaigns." Identify three most successful campaigns that you find most interesting. Use the Internet to obtain more information about these campaigns and find out how they eventually turned out.

Once thought of as a fad, crowdfunding has grown at a fast pace. The global crowdfunding marketplace was valued at about $10 billion in 2018 and is expected to almost triple by 2025. "We're at the beginning of a huge crowdfunding movement that will disrupt the traditional channels for funding," says Bo Fishback, vice president of entrepreneurship at the Ewing Marion Kauffman Foundation, a research organization in Kansas City, MO, dedicated to startups. He reasons that entrepreneurs prefer the idea of pooling small amounts from ordinary people, rather than "trying to say the right things to get a rich guy to cut a check."

Despite the growing popularity of crowdfunding, it is useful to remember that it is not for everyone. Crowdfunding generally works best for glamorous projects that require small amounts of capital. While artistic-minded investors may be drawn to funding art exhibitions or documentary films, financial support from strangers for working capital for a traditional business is likely to be lackluster. Crowdfunding is also not a desirable option for professionals like doctors and lawyers as posting their business plans online in search of funding may affect their legitimacy. For business owners who need a rapid infusion of cash, waiting for their idea to catch fire on a crowdfunding site may not be a viable option.

When New York–based chef Anton Nocito used Indiegogo to raise money to build a kitchen where he could make soda syrups, he received only $3796 of the $18,000 he needed. Unable to afford his own kitchen space, Anton used the funds to buy bottles and labels for the syrups. He continued to run P&H Soda Co. out of shared kitchen space in Brooklyn. "I wouldn't do it again," he says, "It was worth the try, and it was a good learning experience, but for me, I may end up going other [funding] routes the next time."

What Do You Think?

The first time Juana Lopez used crowdfunding, she set up a private fund-raising Web page and invited 75 family members, friends, and customers to view the plan and asked them to contribute money. In exchange for 2% cut of the store's revenue for four years, 21 people donated a total of $65,000. Now, she wants to raise another $50,000 for Auntie Fernanda's Mexican Grill, where she is a partner. She could follow the same path as before. She is toying with an alternative approach: Create a public campaign, allowing strangers to invest as little as $100 in exchange for a 2% revenue share for four years – but only until they are repaid. Any additional returns they receive would be donated to charities. Which option do you think is better for Lopez? Is there another approach you want her to consider?

Comprehension Check

1. What is crowdfunding?
2. What are some disadvantages of crowdfunding?
3. Explain different types of crowdfunding.

Summary

Learning as much as you can about small business finance is crucial for people who want to run their own business as well as those who wish to advise enterprising individuals who are already running a business. There are two common misconceptions related to finance about starting and running your own business. The first is that you need tons of money to be a successful business owner. The second is that one only needs to come up with a business idea, which can then be pitched to an angel investor or VC who will fund it to stupendous growth. Hopefully, this chapter puts to rest these two misconceptions. It is very important for business owners to have skin in the game or to invest their own resources in the business, both as a way to get their ideas off the ground and to signal their commitment for the firm. Many business owners rely on the profitability of the firm to fuel further growth. For others, sources of external funding – debt, equity, and gift – are needed to start and grow the firm. Crowdfunding has also emerged as a popular source of financing for many small businesses. Despite the impressive diversity of funding sources, business owners need to carefully consider the emphasis on debt and equity (or the capital structure) of the firm. Those who are unable to judiciously manage the financing needs of their firms will find themselves stumble, and even fail, as has happened with many well-known companies over the years.

World of Books

Raising capital: Get the money you need to grow your business by Andrew Sherman
The startup game: Inside the partnership between venture capitalists and entrepreneurs
   by William H. Draper III
What every angel investor wants you to know: An insider reveals how to get smart funding for your billion dollar idea by Brian Cohen
Crowdstart: The ultimate guide to a powerful and profitable crowdfunding campaign
   by Ariel Hyatt

In the Movies

Start.up is a documentary about an Internet startup called GovWorks.com, which seeks to tap into a 600-million-dollar market in the uncharted arena of "atomic democracy" (translation: pay government bills – from parking tickets to taxes – through the site). The founder CEO Kaleil Tuzman is a Harvard graduate, who leaves his job at Goldman Sachs to start the firm with his childhood friend Tom Herman. Together, they raise $60 million from venture capitalists. How did they convince people to finance their entrepreneurial venture? A critic noted that "It's not every day, or every decade, that you get to see a film as eye opening in its timeliness as Startup.com."

Live Exercise

"You know, I have already put in $250,000 of my own money to get this business off the ground," Johnny shares with you when you interview him for a class project. You had decided to interview Johnny for one of your class assignments that required you to have an in-depth interview with an entrepreneur managing a small business. With about $125,000 in revenues from selling the SoapStandle at $4.99 apiece, Johnny's company seemed like a good candidate for the interview. When you ask Johnny where he expects the company to go in the future, he asks you for your advice. "I want to grow the company. I really believe in the idea of this simple device for securing the soap bar. I think we can do a lot here. New colors, other sizes, and travel options. But I am not sure how to go about it. I could mortgage my house and invest more money in the company. Or, I could try to get a business loan. Another option is to get an investor who believes in the mission of this company. I also want someone else to manage the day-to-day operations, so I can focus on the creative side of the business. Which direction do you think we should take?" You were not expecting to be asked for your input on the financing needs of the upstart firm, so you ask Johnny for some time to think about the various options. "Yes, certainly!" Johnny replies. "Why don't we do this? You can put together a one-to-two-page memo that outlines the pros and cons of each of these options. That would give me something tangible to chew on. Of course, if you think of any new funding methods that I haven't considered, feel free to share those too. I can definitely use some fresh thinking on this issue." Well, there goes the weekend, you think.

Things to Remember

LO 8.1   **Explain the meaning of small business finance**
   • Finance relates to obtaining money, investing money, and understanding the cost and use of money.
   • Small business finance involves mainly private funding, as opposed to public funding, which is used for large corporations.

- Small business financing typically pertains to raising and investing the money to identify and generate new value in a relatively small firm.
- Corporate finance theories are based on an important assumption: Investors are (economically) rational.

LO 8.2 Identify the different types of financing

- Debts are funds borrowed from a creditor and must be repaid. Debt funds are provided by a creditor with the expectation that they will be paid back in the future with interest.
- Equity is money received in exchange for selling a part of the business. Equity funds are provided by investors in exchange for ownership interest in the business.
- Using debt to finance a business creates leverage, which is the ratio of a company's loan capital (debt) to the value of its ordinary shares (equity).
- Pecking Order Theory (POT) suggests the cost of financing increases with asymmetric information.
- Many small businesses choose to grow without issuing debt or equity.

LO 8.3 Recognize personal sources of financing

- Personal resources of a business owner are often the first source of financing for most new and small firms.
- Friends and family tend to be major investors in new and small businesses.
- Asking friends and family for help with funding can be stressful and awkward.
- Financial support from some family and friends may come in the form of personal gifts.
- Accepting gifts from family and friends creates a personal obligation of sorts.

LO 8.4 Distinguish between various formal funding sources

- Borrowed funds are the most common source of external capital for established small businesses.
- When considering debt financing, three parameters merit consideration: amount of borrowing, interest rate on the borrowing, and the duration of the loan.
- Dividends are payments made to equity providers based on the financial condition of the business.
- The source of equity financing that seems to get more attention from the media is the venture capitalist.
- Angel investors are wealthy, preferably experienced, individuals desirous of investing in early-stage ventures. Based on the investors' investment activity and competence, different types of angels can be identified.
- A public offering occurs when a firm sells its stock to the public.
- Personal gifts include not only money but also goods and services that may be of value to small businesses.
- Given the challenges in attracting external financing from traditional sources, some business owners are now tapping large, online communities of consumer-investors for financial support.

LO 8.5 Describe crowdfunding and its appeal as a source of financing

- Crowdfunding allows founders to appeal directly to the public (i.e. the crowd) for help in getting their ideas off the ground.
- Crowdfunding generally involves collecting small amounts of money from a large number of people.
- Crowdfunding has some advantages and disadvantages that need to be carefully considered before a campaign is launched.
- Reward-based crowdfunding is the most common form of raising small amounts of money from several people.
- Once thought of as a fad, crowdfunding is growing in popularity around the world.
- Crowdfunding does not work well for all types of business endeavors.

Key Terms

personal finance	principal	pledging	subsidy
corporate finance	interest rate	venture capitalist	tax credits
public finance	maturity period	angel investors	crowdfunding
capital structure	overdraft	Small Business Invest-	reward-based
debt	line of credit	ment Companies	crowdfunding
equity	demand note	lotto investors	loan-based crowdfunding
gift	balloon notes	traders	equity-based crowdfunding
leverage	installment loans	analytical investors	donation-based
Pecking Order Theory	floor planning	engaged investors	crowdfunding
trade-off model	leasing	private placement	
collateral	factoring	public offering	

Experiential Exercise

There are two parts to this exercise. The first part of the exercise is to be done individually. The second part of the exercise is to be done with your classmate.

Exercise I

Contact a business owner that you know, either directly or through someone else. Arrange an in-person interview. After understanding from him or her what the business does, ask the owner how he or she arranged for startup financing and how he or she funded subsequent growth of the business. Try to understand how the financing sources differed or overlapped for the owner between the startup phase and the growth phase. Share your findings with the professor and the class.

Exercise II

Every year hundreds of firms have their IPOs in the United States. Identify one firm that had its IPO event in the last calendar year. Use Web-based sources to read as much as you can about the firm you identified. From the information you have gathered, can you tell how the firm was financed at startup and in subsequent years? How did the financing needs of the firm change post-IPO? Write a one-page memo explaining the initial funding of the firm and its evolution over the years.

CHAPTER 9

Small Business and the Law

No organic law can ever be framed with a provision specifically applicable to every question which may occur in practical administration. No foresight can anticipate nor any document of reasonable length contain express provisions for all possible questions.

ABRAHAM LINCOLN

LEARNING OBJECTIVES

This chapter will help you to:

LO 9.1 Distinguish between the various legal forms of small businesses

LO 9.2 Explain the basics of contracts

LO 9.3 Identify the fundamentals of intellectual property

LO 9.4 Describe various types of bankruptcy laws

9.0 Introduction

Would you like to live in Baracas? Or, perhaps, visit there? It is a place with no laws. Yes, that's correct, absolutely no laws at all! You can drive as fast as you want. There is no age limit to buy or drink alcohol (or smoke). No laws for drugs either. In short, you could do whatever you want, anytime and anywhere you wish. And so can other people. How do you think life is in Baracas? Would you like to run a business there? No laws there means your suppliers, customers, and employees can behave whatever way they want. So can you.

Business and law are inseparable. Laws help ensure fair competition between businesses, to protect the rights of employees and customers, to protect the revenues and profits booked by the business, to enforce contracts and agreements, and so on. Any way you look at it, when business owners understand the law, they can be better prepared for the problems that come up (and, maybe, even avoid some problems altogether). This chapter introduces you to basic legal concepts and principles relevant for small firms. Before we go further, a legal disclaimer is in order:

> The information provided in this chapter does not, and is not intended to, constitute legal advice; instead, all materials and content in this chapter are for general informational purposes only. If you want legal advice, please contact an attorney authorized to practice in your jurisdiction.

SPOTLIGHT | Intellectual Property Law, in a Two-Piece Suit

Ipek Irgit's swimwear business started when, on the beach one day, a friend complimented her on the bikini she was wearing. That flattering comment motivated Irgit, who had previously worked as a waitress and bartender in New York City, to ask a friend in the fashion industry to develop a prototype. Irgit placed an order to a factory in China for a batch of 300 bikinis at a cost of about $29 apiece and marked up the retail price to $285, landing her swimwear into the high-end luxury market. She paid careful attention to branding, playing around with the word "bikini" and her initial "I.I.I," before deciding to call it Kiini. The new venture consisted of one product: a bright, colorful bikini with triangular panels, contrast color stitching, and vibrant elastic straps threaded through loops of crochet. The bikini was sexy, sporty, bohemian, and sophisticated – a reflection, Irgit believed, of herself.

Sales were lackluster until the model Dree Hemingway posed provocatively by a surfboard in a bikini with dark panels and green-and-orange detailing. Captioning the picture "Thank you for my kiini!!" she posted on Instagram. "I was, like, bombarded," Irgit said, "That was it." The bikini was featured on Vogue.com, *Vogue UK*, *Women's Health*, and *Elle Italia*. *People Magazine* called it "the hottest bikini this summer." Within a year from the launch, Kiini was available at Barneys, the Valhalla of upscale boutique brands. Bringing in $9 million, Kiini's sales had exploded.

Success brought copycats. When Irgit complained about knockoffs, her lawyer advised her to apply with the United States Copyright Office for protection. She also hired a company to scrub the #kiini hashtag from Instagram images erroneously referring to other brands as the real deal. When Victoria's Secret introduced a faux Kiini, Irgit filed a federal lawsuit accusing the lingerie retailer of copyright violation. Lawsuits against Neiman Marcus, Bloomingdales, Lord & Taylor, Macy's followed. The accusation: unfair competition, misleading the consumers about the origin of the colorful swimsuit, and infringing on Kiini's "trade dress." In lay terms, Irgit was saying that any consumer who saw a crochet-and-exposed-elastic bikini would assume it was a Kiini.

Maria Ferrarini lives in Trancoso, a small beach town in Brazil's Bahia state. She describes herself as a street artist, but most Trancosans know her simply as the "bikini lady." For more than 20 years now, she has been selling handmade crochet-and-elastic

Ipek Irgit with her colorful crochet bikini.

swimwear on the beach, walking along with her creations dangling off a hula hoop. In 2009, the Trancoso tourist economy was booming, with the *Vogue* calling it Brazil's hottest beach town. Around this time, Irgit visited Trancoso.

When a Neiman Marcus lawyer reached out to Ferrarini, she negotiated a nonexclusive deal for using her crochet-and-elastic design and her name. Neiman Marcus and other retailers were now able to legally sell swimwear under the name "Platinum Inspired by Solange Ferrarini." Ferrarini received about $5100 for her creative design, with an annual four-figure fee every year. Ferrarini then sued Irgit and Kiini in federal court for unfair business practices and asking for a public apology.

Jeanne Heffernan is a partner in the law firm Kirkland & Ellis. As she sees it, "The role of the truth in our judicial system is central. Here you have a woman who appears to have the IP (intellectual property) of someone else and registered it as her own and then, it seems, had the audacity to sue an industry over something she did not create and may have stolen. If true, it's breathtaking."

Ferrarini still sells her colorful bikinis on the Trancosan beach, but now she hears from customers that

(Continued)

they had already seen her designs. "I'd see people in bikinis, and foreigners doubted that I was the creator," she said. "They said the bikini was from the United States. To my face." It stung. To an artist, Ferrarini believes, it is about creative integrity. And, what does she think of Irgit? "*Eu quero que ela se ferre verde e amarelo.*" English translation: "I want her to get (expletive) in green and yellow."

Discussion Questions

1. How did Ipek react when she found that major retailers were copying her Kiini?

2. How did Ferrarini find out that someone had copied her bikini design?

3. What interest did Neiman Marcus have in negotiating an agreement with Maria Ferrarini?

Now that you've read the legal disclaimer, and you know that only a lawyer in the relevant jurisdiction can provide accurate and appropriate legal advice on a particular matter, it is time to move forward.

Module 9.1 Legal Structures for Small Businesses

One of the first decisions a business owner makes is about how to structure the company. The type of legal structure affects various aspects of the way the business is managed: the authorities that need to be notified of developments in the business, the records and documentations that need to be maintained, and the taxes and other dues that the business is required to pay. Legal structures vary from country to country, so that the legal framework for small businesses will be different in Germany or Brazil than it is in the United States. The law also may vary from state to state within the country (as it does in the United States), so it is useful to do as much research as possible before deciding on a particular legal structure for the business.

Three general legal forms for businesses are in the United States: proprietorships, partnerships, and corporations (see Figure 9.1). The legal form one selects is not set in stone

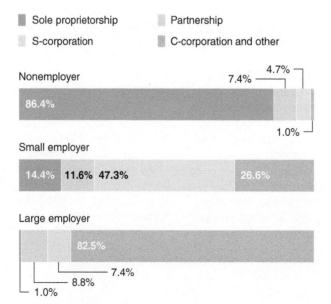

FIGURE 9.1 Business Forms of US-based Companies
Source: Adapted from U.S. Small Business Administration Office of Advocacy, U.S. census Bureau Data

and can be changed in the future as and when needed. The online auction giant eBay, for example, started as a sole proprietorship owned by Pierre Omidyar, then became a partnership, and finally a public corporation.

> ### KEY TAKEAWAY
>
> The three general legal forms for businesses in the United States are proprietorships, partnerships, and corporations.

9.1.1 Proprietorship: Most Common Legal Form for American Businesses

For small businesses, the most popular form of legal structure is the **sole proprietorship**, perhaps because it is the most inexpensive and simplest to set up. A sole proprietorship involves a person who fully owns his or her business but has not formed a separate legal entity for it. The vast majority of new and small businesses start out as sole proprietorships, with the entrepreneur owning all the assets in the business and the profits that come from the business. The owner is also responsible for all liabilities and debts of the business. In the eyes of the law, there is no distinction between a proprietor and his or her business – they are one and same. Proprietorships are also taxed at the owner's personal tax rate, which gives them a comparative advantage relative to other forms of business (see Figure 9.2).

However, sole proprietorships have some downsides that should also be considered. As mentioned earlier, the owner is solely responsible for any problems the firm faces. If the firm does not have enough funds to pay its obligations, the owner must use personal assets to pay them. Because the business and the owner are inseparable in the eyes of the law, the legal existence of a proprietorship ends when the owner passes, so that legal action is then needed to restart it.

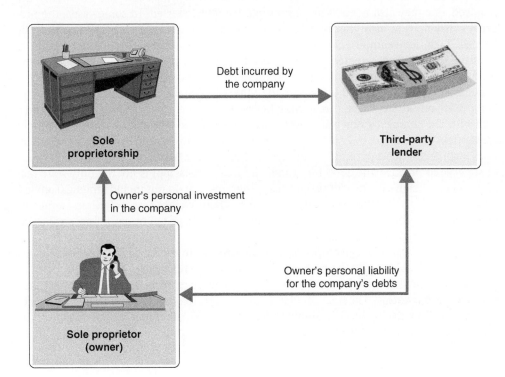

FIGURE 9.2 In Sole Proprietorships, the Owner Is Solely Responsible for the Company's Debt
Source: Redrawn from http://graffitisoldiers.org/business-ownership

Starting a sole proprietorship is quite straightforward. In many industries and across many jurisdictions, no legal filing is required to set up a proprietorship. Simply come up with a **trade name**, which is a fancy way of saying that you need to think of what you want your business to be called. You may use your name (e.g. The Jane Smith Company) or something other than your name. If you do not use your own name for the business, think of an **assumed name**, or a **doing business as (DBA) name**. For example, the metal refiner Libertas Copper LLC is registered as doing business as Hussey Copper. Register the name in the state where you want to run the business (assumed name filing). The SBA website provides information on registering your new business. For more details, visit https://www.sba.gov/business-guide/launch-your-business/register-your-business.

Katharine O'Moore-Klopf is an experienced board-certified editor in life sciences, doing business as KOK Edit. When she started her business in the 1990s, she had to drive a 70-mile round trip to the county clerk's office to file the paperwork for a DBA – or a "doing business as" – certificate for her sole proprietorship. Katharine needed the DBA documentation to open a bank account for her new business. At the time, DBA applications and completed certificates for the entire county were physically filed in a large bank of filing cabinets in the county clerk's office. In order to get the county to complete the certificate, one had to search, by hand, through the filing cabinets to ensure that no one else had already claimed the business name that you wanted. Much has changed since then as today the paperwork for a business certificate can be filed online sitting in front of your computer at home.

Interactive Exercise

What name would you use for DBA if you were to start a business today? Google "DBA filing [your state name]" and go to the Secretary of State website that opens up (it will have a Web address that finishes in .gov). What are the steps needed for the DBA filing in your state?

If the business is in an industry and/or a jurisdiction where licenses or permits are required, one may also need to pay a nominal fee to get started. In some cases, the proprietor may need to have the right academic credentials and work experience to get the license. Take, for example, Donna Harris of Mississippi. Donna, a personal trainer at Madison County Gym, created an eight-week program for otherwise-healthy adults who want to slim down. Clients would pay $99 for one-on-one weight-loss coaching and other perks. Seventy clients signed up, before the Mississippi State Department of Health sent her a cease-and-desist letter, threatening her with jail time, fine, criminal charges, and a civil suit. The charge: Donna was working as an unlicensed dietician. Without the proper credentials, Donna was only allowed to redirect clients to government-approved guidelines such as the food pyramid. A dietician's license in Mississippi requires 1200 hours of supervised practice and $300 for exams and fees. Mississippi is not the only state that requires a dietician's license for weight-loss programs that do not include medical advice. There are at least 15 other states in the Union where weight-loss programs cannot be offered with appropriate licensing. Donna did not want to go jail or pay a fine, so she had to cancel the program and issue refunds.

The taxman treats the sole proprietor and the firm as one entity, so the business income and expenses are filed with the owner's personal income tax return. Because the taxes of the business are filed with the tax return of the individual owning the business, it is called **pass-through taxation**. The finances of the firm are reported on a separate form, Schedule C. The income from the business is simply added to whatever other income the owner (or the spouse) may have and is taxed at the personal income tax rate.

9.1.2 Partnerships: Formed by Many, Hated by Many

A **partnership** is a voluntary association of two or more people who make a conscious decision to co-own a business together. As with proprietorships, the law does not distinguish between a partnership business and its owners. AmyLynn Keimach and her business partner, Kenneth Tran, founded Border7 Studios, a Web-services firm in Simi Valley, CA, after getting laid off without severance pay. They are operating the company as a partnership and hoping none of their 20 clients give them any legal trouble. "If they sue our company, they could take everything me and my partner own," says AmyLynn. "It's scary."

Each partner reports income and losses on individual tax returns (pass-through taxation), and taxes are paid at the personal income tax rate. The partnership does not protect against personal liability. Also, partners are held responsible for the actions of the other partners.

A partnership is required to inform the IRS by filing a Form 1065. The IRS may challenge the status of a partnership and require that it be taxed as a separate legal entity.

Partnerships may be general or limited. A **general partnership** involves two or more "visible" partners, all of whom are liable for the acts of all partners. Such partnerships are common in retail or service businesses. A **limited partnership** involves general partners plus one or more "anonymous" partners whose identity is not known to the public at large. The general partners are responsible for managing the firm and also bear personal responsibility for the firm's liabilities. The limited partners are not engaged in active management of the firm, and their liability may not exceed their capital contribution to the business. A limited partnership may be appropriate for a small but growing business that wants to raise money by selling limited partnership interests in the company.

Partnership arrangements can be quite flexible. It is advisable (though not required) for partnerships to have a formal legal agreement, called the **articles of copartnership**, which lays out the terms and conditions for the smooth running of the business. Ideally, the agreement spells out, as clearly as possible, the rights, duties, and responsibilities of the partners. It includes things like how decisions will be made and how profits (or losses) will be shared, the preferred approach to resolving disputes, if and how partners can be bought out, and the steps that need to be taken to dissolve the partnership when the time comes.

Partnerships help raise more funds and pool ideas from multiple people. Partners share the stress and worries that come with running a business. However, partnerships bring together people with different backgrounds and different future aspirations, so it can sometimes be difficult to agree on decisions, big and small. Because the partners are jointly responsible for the liabilities of the business, if one partner is unable to pay the dues, the other partner is then liable for the full amount. Think carefully about who you want to partner with before you enter into a partnership! Generally speaking, partnerships should be reserved for when a partner is critical to success – say, when the prospective partner brings financial resources, connections, or vital skills you lack.

"So often, [individuals enter] business partnerships having not identified their motivation and common ground, sparking issues that are hard to resolve," says Charles Kerns, founder of consulting firm CorPerformance. For example, in a partnership, one partner may want to make investments outside the business to increase his or her personal net worth. The other may want to grow the business by reinvesting profits in the business rather than distributing them to the partners. When the partners have divergent motivations and goals for the business, it may be difficult to find common ground on which they can both agree.

9.1.3 Corporation: They Are People Too!

A **corporation** is a separate legal entity with an existence distinct from the people who started it. In other words, the corporation, not its owners, is legally liable for its actions. It is chartered by the state where it is headquartered. It can enter into contractual agreements and can be taxed. It does not dissolve when ownership changes. The corporation has a life of its own. Corporations, the U.S. Supreme Court has affirmed time and again, are people too!

Creating a corporation is a more complex and formal process than for a proprietorship or partnership. Yet it is not so complex that it is only for large, more established businesses with numerous employees. Room One Corp, for example, owns MoviE-Town, an eight-screen theater housed in what was once a car dealership, in Elizabethtown, PA.

Corporations were first recognized as a distinct legal entity around 1600 in England, the source of law in the United States. Some view the Catholic Church as the first corporation, as it could legally buy, hold, and sell property in its own name. Later, the U.S. Supreme Court defined a corporation as "an artificial being, invisible, intangible, and existing only in the contemplation of the law." In other words, it is a separate legal entity that exists at the pleasure of the law. As a legal entity, a corporation can own property, sue, and be sued. Corporations have transferable ownership, which means that they can issue stock to investors in exchange for capital. A corporation also has **continuous existence**, which means that it will survive the demise of its owners. The death of one or more shareholders does not affect its life.

One disadvantage of corporations is **double taxation**. The profits of a corporation are taxed twice – first on the profit the company makes and then on the **dividends** received by the shareholders. Dividend refers to the sum of money paid by a company to its shareholders from the profits it makes. If profits are retained to fund the growth of the company, then there are no dividends, and hence no tax on them. Furthermore, many companies make no profits in the early years, so that there are no taxes on losses.

The traditional form of the corporation is called a **C-Corporation** (sometimes known as *C-Corp*). To avoid double taxation and still get the benefits of a corporation, some owners may choose to form an **S-Corporation** (or *S-Corp*) instead. The stockholders of an S-Corp get special treatment for income tax purposes. As is the case for proprietorships and partnerships, the income and losses of S-Corps pass through to the tax returns of its owners and are then taxed at the individual rates. For companies expecting to lose money in the short term, S-Corp is an attractive option. The loss from the company can offset other incomes earned by the shareholders, serving as a sort of tax shelter. For all other purposes, an S-Corp is similar to a C-Corp.

In order to qualify for legal status as an S-Corp, the company must be a US domestic corporation and must have no more than 100 shareholders. The shareholders need to be individual US citizens or legal residents (so, not partnerships or other corporations), and all shareholders can own only one class of common stock. The restrictions on the number and types of shareholders an S-Corp can have cause many corporations to switch to C-Corp status after they have achieved some growth. Did you know that S-Corp is the most popular corporate structure in America? The IRS estimates that there are about five million S-Corp owners in the United States, twice the number of traditional corporations. Read more about S-Corps at www.s-corp.org.

After Jennifer Chu was laid off from an investment-bank job, she launched her business, Chu Shu, a maker of odor-absorbing liners for women's shoes. She wanted to form an S-Corp in part because the tax structure would be more beneficial to the company. However, she did not elect the S-Corp status in time to apply those benefits to her New York business tax returns for the year. "I didn't realize there was a deadline," she says. The IRS requires that businesses elect to become an S-Corp by March 15 of any given year to gain any tax benefits associated with that status for that year's tax returns. Overlooking the March 15 deadline "could cause a small-business owner to miss out on thousands in tax savings," says Brian Wendroff, managing partner for Wendroff & Associates, an Arlington, VA, accounting firm.

Many US states and the District of Columbia also recognize **benefit corporations** (also known as *benefit corp*), which are for-profit legal entities that allow for positive

TABLE 9.1

Why Operate as a Benefit Corporation?

OPERATING AS A BENEFIT CORPORATION MAKES ROOM FOR OTHER PRIORITIES

What is a 'benefit corporation'?
A company whose charter allows the board to consider social or environmental objectives ahead of profits.

What is the advantage?
Protection from investor allegations of not maximizing shareholder value.

Does that make it a nonprofit?
No, a benefit corporation isn't a nonprofit nor is it tax exempt.

How many states allow it? Seven. With bills introduced in four additional states.

What are the downsides? 'For an investor, this is a terrible idea' due to lack of accountability, says Charles Elson, who teaches corporate governance at the University of Delaware. If management makes a bad decision, 'there's very little you can do about it as a shareholder.'

Source: Adapted from When Profits Can Take a Back Seat to Doing Good, *The Wall Street Journal.*

societal impact in addition to profits as its legally defined goals. A firm may either choose to file as a benefit corporation or change its legal status to one simply by stating in its approved bylaws that it is a benefit corporation. Maryland was the first US state to pass legislation that allowed creation of benefit corporations, and since then several states have followed suit.

Jonathan Harrison, chief executive of a six-employee firm Emerge Workplace Solutions, sees the benefit corporation as a tool to help his business stand apart from other payday lenders that charge higher interest rates and fees for workers needing fast cash between paychecks. "It's really important for us to have a designation that we're the good guys," he says. His firm offers short-term emergency loans to hourly workers at annual interest rates from 9 to 19.99%, in contrast to the 400% typically charged by payday lenders. Emerge also provides financial coaching and other services to help the working poor, which payday lenders generally do not provide. Table 9.1 outlines some of the characteristics of a benefit corporation.

A **limited liability company** (LLC) is a legal structure that allows a business to combine the limited liability benefit of a corporation with the pass-through taxation aspect of a partnership or proprietorship. While an S-Corp also allows such a combination, an LLC can choose whether to be taxed as a partnership or as a corporation ("Check the box taxation"). As with a partnership, owners (called "members") of an LLC enter into an operating agreement specifying their rights and responsibilities. Many states allow perpetual existence for LLCs. As a result, LLCs are gaining in popularity, and may even be replacing S-Corps as the legal entity of choice for many startup ventures.

After getting laid off from a senior engineering job, Marc Karell launched a consulting business from his home in Mamaroneck, NY. Before he landed a single client, the unemployment benefits he had been relying on to make ends meet came to a sudden halt. The reason: He established his venture, Climate Change & Environmental Services, as an LLC. Had he known the move would mean an end to his layoff benefits, Marc says, he "probably would've held off on being an LLC for a little while."

There are also **professional corporations** (PCs), another form of a corporation, but reserved exclusively for licensed professionals who want to incorporate their practice.

A PC requires that all directors, officers, and shareholders must belong to the same profession. PCs are created by the state, with each state having its own list of professions

Do-It-Yourself Legal Websites

Small business owners frequently complain about how expensive legal help can be. DIY legal websites such as Legal Zoom and Rocket Lawyer promise to provide quality legal help without having to pay the big bucks. One Life Yoga is a boutique yoga studio in Pasadena, CA. The owner Reza Samadi used Legal Zoom to prepare and file the paperwork for the legal form for his business.

Watch the video online: https://www.youtube.com/watch?v=dxmvWOoSFyA

required by statute to incorporate a PC. Accountants, attorneys, doctors, and veterinarians are some professions that are generally required to form a PC. A PC offers the benefit that when a professional leaves or retires, ownership is transferable readily to others. It also allows multiple professionals to share management responsibilities and profits without having shared liability in case of malpractice.

Have you heard of B-Corps? **B-Corps** are different from benefit corporations discussed earlier, though their underlying logic is quite similar. B-Corps are firms that commit to balance profit and purpose, considering the impact of their decisions on their stakeholders, including customers, suppliers, workers, environment, and the community as a whole. Unlike Benefit Corps, a B-Corp certification is issued by a private organization B Lab, which is a nonprofit with offices around the world. As of this writing, more than 3200 firms across 150 industries and 71 countries had obtained B-Corp certification. In the United States, B-Corp-certified firms include Ben & Jerry's, Stonyfield, New Belgium Brewing, and Amalgamated Bank, to list a few. You can learn more about B-Corp certification at www.bcorporation.net. Table 9.2 showcases some B-Corps founded by women.

There are several other business structures present in the United States, including **limited liability partnerships** (LLP), **family limited partnerships** (FLP), **cooperatives** (association of independent producers, sellers, and consumers, who share in the profits of the group), and **nonprofit corporations** (organizations that

TABLE 9.2

Six Inspiring Women-Owned B-Corps

Business owner	Name of B-Corp	What is offered?
Rita Hogan and Lynn Higgins	Farm Dog Naturals	Sustainable and safe herbal remedies for dogs
Tracy Puhl	GladRags	Environmentally friendly feminine products that are comfortable and washable
Jill Robbins	Homefree	Baked treats free of gluten, peanuts, tree nuts, eggs, wheat, and dairy
Lisa Linhardt	Linhardt Design	Socially responsible jewelry that uses recycled previous metals and mine-to-market gemstones
Carolyn Coquilette	Luscious Garage	Ethical auto-repair services (paperless workflow, solar power, and hybrid taxicabs serviced by the night shift)
Maria Uspenski	The Tea Spot	Loose-leaf tea and modern steepware tools to create handcrafted tea that is flavorful and eco-friendly

enjoy tax-free status and limited personal liability in exchange for not paying out profits to their owners).

There is also a growing trend of **fractional ownership** in the United States and many other developed countries. In fractional ownership, ownership of a high-value tangible asset such as a jet or a yacht is shared by unrelated parties. You have probably heard of NetJets, the US-based airlines company that offers fractional ownership in airplanes. When it launched, NetJets offered the first aviation fractional ownership program.

Fractional ownership is sometimes confused with **timeshares** that have been popular in the real-estate industry for a long time. A key distinction between fractional ownership and timeshare is that with the former the buyer gets part ownership in an asset, but with the latter buyer gets only part use of the asset.

Deciding the appropriate legal form for your new business – and when to do it – may require more research and consideration than many other tasks business owners undertake. The costs associated with setting up the various types of entities vary by state, as do the rules regarding eligibility for unemployment benefits. Furthermore, each legal form has distinct tax and liability implications. "You have to understand the ramifications of choosing one form or another," says Matthew Gilman of Boston law firm Pepper Hamilton.

Comprehension Check

1. What are the common legal forms in the United States?
2. What is an S-Corp?
3. Distinguish between fractional ownership and timeshare.

Module 9.2 Fundamentals of Contracts

In everyday life, the vast majority of business law relates to contracts. At a basic level, contracts are legally enforced promises. Contract laws stipulate that the parties entering into an agreement comply with its provisions. When a party reneges on its commitments, other parties can take legal action. Thus, contracts are agreements in which the parties exchange promises within the constraints of the law.

The words "We have a contract" may be used in daily life quite casually. Say, your neighbor's son promises to mow your lawn for $25 through the summer. You agree to pay him in cash. You shake hands across the fence. He does it once and you pay him, but then he refuses to do it again. You may be upset or aggrieved, but without a recorded contract, enforcement is impossible. **Oral promises** (also called **handshake agreements**) are made and broken all the time, but they are not true contracts in the strict legal sense, they cannot be enforced if the two sides disagree.

Rob Johnson was a newspaper man in Florida when he saw an opportunity that no one else seemed to have noticed. Orlando resort hotels had tennis courts, but few of them employed full-time instructors. Rob's idea was to create an outcall service: The hotels would refer guests to him for lessons, and he would use their courts as classrooms. He wouldn't have to hunt down customers, or invest in his own facilities. He printed up business cards and invested $500 in 100 "Coach Rob" T-shirts for repeat customers. By the time he launched the business, he had handshake agreements with five lodgings. Rob launched his business on the bases of the five handshake agreements, and none of them reneged.

An agreement must have four basic elements – prerequisites – to be considered a valid contract:

1. **Capacity**. The law requires that a person need to possess the legal capacity to enter into a contract. Minors, people with diminished mental capacity, and intoxicated persons are not bound by contracts. Indeed, contracts signed by those who

fall into any of these categories are void. A party that does not understand the nature and consequences of an agreement is considered lacking in the mental capacity to enter into a contract. Ignorance of facts is usually not a reasonable ground for lack of capacity. Sean Belnick started selling furniture on his website www.bizchair.com when he was 14 and was generating millions of dollars in revenues within a short period. Of course, Sean is not the only minor to start a business. Yet, because the law does not consider minors to have the legal capacity to enter into a contract (unless they are emancipated), an adult needs to co-sign contracts for them.

2. **Legality**. Every contract must have a legal purpose. A contract for something illegal is not enforceable. For example, as child labor is illegal in the United States, two parties cannot enter into a contract for employing underage workers. When the U.S. Department of Labor barred farm hands younger than 16 years from jobs such as operating power equipment, branding and breeding farm animals, and working atop ladders at heights over 6 feet, many farmers protested that they would not be able to hire local kids to move hay or pull the grain cart at the harvest time. Lorinda Carlson, who owns a small orchard in Chelan County, Washington, D.C., says the law would make it harder to hire the five 13-to-15-year-old workers who usually help her load cherries during the harvest season, a job, she says, adults are rarely willing to do. As long as it is legal to hire children under 16 years for farming operations not owned and operated by their parents, farmers and farmhands can legally enter into a contract for the work.

3. **Acceptance**. A contract has two sides: an offer and an acceptance. When you accept an offer, you are consenting to its terms. Without proof of acceptance, there is no contract.

4. **Consideration**. A contract must include something of value for both parties. Without the provision of something valuable, the agreement is a gift, and not a contract. For example, if a parent promises to give their adult children a car for free (without any payment), it is a gift, and does not qualify as a contract. Of course, the car can be legally sold for a dollar, and then it's a contract.

Interactive Exercise

Check out the website of Child Abduction Recovery International (www.childabductionrecovery.com), a Sweden-based small business founded by an Australian veteran Adam Whittington. What business are they in? If a client signed a contract with them, would it be legally enforceable?

KEY TAKEAWAY

An agreement must have four basic elements to be considered a contract: capacity, legality, acceptance, and consideration.

Assuming that a valid contract is in place, what does one do if a party refuses to follow through on their end of the deal? For example, you sold someone your car for $2000, half of which is to be paid in one month, but no payment is forthcoming even though three months have passed. When someone does not hold up their end of a deal, it is called a **breach of contract**. Several remedies are available for the aggrieved party when the other side reneges on the contract. A judge or arbitrator may set a monetary award for breach of contract, also called **compensatory damages**. In some cases, particularly when the exchange involved in the contract is non-substitutable (that is, it is unique), money alone may not be sufficient to make the aggrieved party whole. In such situations, the party that is in breach of contract may be ordered to undertake a specific performance to ensure that justice is done. The party violating the contract may be required to do exactly what they agreed to do in the contract.

9.2.1 Types of Contracts

There are many different types of contracts pertaining to small businesses. Below are the common types.

Standard contracts. Contracts that are used over and over again, with minor changes that can be readily made, are called **standard contracts**. Anyone who bought a house has seen a standard contract, where the address of the property and buyer–seller names change, but the rest of the agreement remains largely the same.

Specialty contracts. Contracts with unique provisions or involving large payments are called **specialty contracts**. Not all contracts with large dollar amounts are specialty contracts. For example, in December 2019, the median sales price for a single-family home in Suffolk County (where Boston is located) was $595,000. For comparison, consider that the median household income in the United States is about $60,000. You could buy a historic house in Boston using a standard contract, but if you knew about the rotting wooden foundation causing many of the houses in the city to sink, you would want a specialty contract to account for that damage.

Interstate contracts. Contracts that involve businesses in more than one state are called **interstate contracts**. Given variations in laws across states, interstate contracts need to abide by laws of all states where they apply.

Noncompete contracts. Some contracts involve one party promising not to be in a situation that would put them into direct competition with the other party. This includes working for a competitor firm or starting a competitor business. Of course, no one can be kept out of their line of business forever, so **noncompete contracts** need to be reasonable. Ann Anderson, who started Nexus Staffing Specialists in Larchmont, NY, opted to wait one year to start a business filling temporary positions for clients, in order to avoid a potential lawsuit by the company for which two former employees had worked. She didn't want to delay building her business, but felt that waiting for the noncompete clause to lapse "was a better choice as a startup."

There is a growing concern that noncompete agreements are now ridiculously abused. Delaney Dunne of North Carolina found out firsthand how noncompete agreements can limit employment opportunities for young interns who sign them without understanding the nuances of the contract. In her case, during her junior year in college, she took an internship for class credit and $10 an hour at coworking company Tek Mountain in Wilmington, NC. On graduation day, she received a letter from Tek Mountain asking about her employment status and reminding her she had signed a noncompete agreement that restricted her employment options. While no solid information exists on how many interns are affected by noncompete agreements, around one in five workers in the American labor force overall are bound by such contracts.

When Rami Essaid launched his startup to protect websites from attacks by automated computer programs, he was sued by his former employer for violating

What Do You Think?

Jon Hirschtick is founder of Belmont Technology Inc. in Cambridge, MA, which makes product-design software. He says non-compete contracts have made it tougher for his firm to recruit software engineers. "We've had inquiries from many people we'd otherwise like to hire, that we cannot because of their non-compete agreements," he says. His lawyer is advising him to require new employees to sign non-competes "as a way of protecting some of the value" his company creates. Do you think Jon should ask new employees to sign non-competes when he doesn't like them himself?

a noncompete clause in his previous employment contract. He spent six months negotiating a settlement with his ex-employer. Noncompete agreements, he says, can be a significant impediment to people who aspire to start their own firms because they "limit your ability to grow and tap your networks."

Hold harmless agreements. A **hold harmless agreement** is a legal contract that stipulates that one party will not hold another party liable for risk (often physical risk) or damage. Such agreements can be one directional (unilateral) or bidirectional (reciprocal) and may be signed before or after the work has been performed. Firms in the construction industry rely quite extensively on hold harmless agreements to insure against work done by subcontractors.

A hold harmless agreement can be quite expansive (broad form) or constrained (limited form). The **broad form agreement** protects one party from all liability for accidents or negligence, whether it is their fault or that of the other party. For example, under this form of agreement, a subcontractor assumes all related liabilities for accidents, its own negligence, general contractor negligence, and the combined negligence of both the contractor and subcontractor. CoasterStone is a division of DSH Indiana, a family-owned firm with roots dating back to the 1800s. The company offers custom-made absorbent coasters. Their product packing includes a broad form hold harmless statement that insulates them from liability beyond replacement or repair of the product at no charge to the customer.

The **intermediate form agreement** protects one party from liability for accidents or negligence that are the other party's responsibility. For example, with this type of agreement, a subcontractor is responsible only for their related actions and cannot be held accountable for the general contractor's accidents or negligence. Such agreements are not dependent on whether the subcontractor is at fault; the issue is only who is responsible for the accident or who is acting negligently. If both parties are negligent, a subcontractor bears responsibility for his or her actions only and will be liable for his or her actions and omissions.

The **limited form agreement** constrains the liability of one party to the proportional part of what is their responsibility. For example, with such an agreement, the liability of a subcontractor is limited only to their responsibility and will include others, under their respective agreements, for their part of the accident or negligence.

Contracts may also have an **exculpatory clause** stipulating that one party will not be responsible for certain things. Such clauses are often included in agreements where one party to the contract comes into contact with things that relate to the personal property, possessions, or physical well-being of the other party. For example, when parking a vehicle in a paid spot, a patron may be informed that damages or theft are not the responsibility of the parking company. Some contracts may include special conditions when an exculpatory clause comes into effect. For example, if a passenger on an airport shuttle does not abide by the rules about safe behaviors and actions that are permitted on their journey, the operator of the vehicle might invoke the terms of their exculpatory clause if injuries occur.

CoasterStone®
Art that's truly absorbing

You hold in your hand the original absorbent stone coaster! Not only will CoasterStone's extraordinary designs flatter any home, but their remarkable surface absorbs moisture exceptionally well. Condensation sinks right in to protect your furniture. Beautiful design and exceptional function make CoasterStone the coaster of choice.

Be sure coasters are clean and dry before stacking.

Cleaning Instructions: If a coaster becomes stained, you can minimize discoloration by soaking it in hot water with a mild liquid detergent for 60 minutes, rinse thoroughly and let air dry. For a stubborn stain such as wine or coffee, pour one part household bleach and three parts hot water into a china or enamel bowl. Soak the coaster overnight. Remove, rinse thoroughly and let air dry. Repeat if necessary.

———————— Liability Limit: ————————

This product has been thoroughly inspected before shipment. In the unlikely event of a product defect (excluding breakage), the Company's only obligation and buyer's exclusive remedy is the replacement or repair of the product at no charge to the buyer. The Company shall not be liable for any direct, consequential, or incidental loss or damage.

© 2016 CoasterStone®
Div. of DSH Indiana, Inc.

All CoasterStone coasters are shipped with packaging that clearly presents the 'hold harmless' statement.

Comprehension Check

1. What are the prerequisites for a contract?
2. What is a noncompete agreement?
3. What is an exculpatory clause?

Module 9.3 Introduction to Intellectual Property

Could you upload the latest Harry Potter movie to the Internet for millions to watch? The technology may be there, but the law does not allow you to make a copy of someone else's work and share it with others. All intangible creations of human intelligence, including ideas, slogans, and expressions, are considered **intellectual property** (IP).

Laws protecting IP cover trademarks, copyright, trade secrets, and patents for physical and nonphysical products that result from original thought and can be owned by someone. The 1624 Statute of Monopolies and the 1710 Statute of Anne in England are considered to be the origins of patent law and copyright law, respectively. Today, many startups, across industries and around the world, are dependent on IP protection. Without IP protection, companies such as Apple and Google may have never gotten off the ground.

However, some believe that the term IP is vague and abstract, and IP laws generally overreach. Richard Stallman, founder of the Free Software Foundation, argues that the term IP "operates as a catch-all to lump together disparate laws that originated separately, evolved differently, cover different activities, have different rules, and raise different public policy issues." There is also considerable disagreement among experts and economists on whether strong IP laws encourage or deter innovation, with some claiming that many small firms face the demise at an early age because large, well-established companies sue them for IP infringement.

In the United States, the law covers four types of IP: trademark, trade secret, copyright, and patent. Let us look at each of them in turn.

KEY TAKEAWAY

The U.S. law covers four main types of intellectual property: trademark, trade secret, copyright, and patents.

9.3.1 Trademark (or Service Mark)

Any identification used to delineate and promote a certain product is a **trademark**. Trademarks, therefore, identify specific goods. A trademark can be a name or symbol. The clothing company Lacoste, for example, has the green crocodile logo as its trademark. When a shirt has the Lacoste trademark, it means it's a genuine Lacoste shirt as only the French company Lacoste (albeit Swiss-owned since 2012) has the legal right to use the trademark. When other companies use Lacoste's trademark, they are selling counterfeits. In case you are wondering what made Lacoste adopt the crocodile logo, the founder of the company, Rene Lacoste, was a tennis player who was fondly called "the crocodile" by his fans.

Lacoste's crocodile trademark is widely recognized around the world.

Friemann/Alamy Stock Photo

For service products, the related concept is called a **service mark**. Since services can be harder to define unambiguously compared to physical products, registering a service mark can require more rigorous evidence. An example for service marks comes from the aviation giant United Airlines. The tagline "Fly the Friendly Skies" is a service mark because United provides a service: airline flights around the world.

In practice, the term *mark* is used to include both trademarks and service marks. Once a mark is established as identifying a certain product, the owner has the legal right to prevent others from using a similar or identical mark for similar or identical goods or services. As is the case with all IP, anyone using the mark without permission is in violation of the law and is subject to legal action.

Trademarks, Copyright, and Patents

If you want to learn more about trademarks, copyright, and patents, as well as the differences between these three terms, you can watch the video at https://www.youtube.com/ watch?v=yMGTNCo-2ho. The video is brought to you by The Invention Laboratory, a trademarked podcast of KCharlton Industries, a Pennsylvania-based consulting firm.

9.3.2 Trade Secret

The term **trade secret** refers to confidential information known to only certain people within a company, such that it is not publicly known or accessible. This includes recipes, formulae, customer lists, patterns, or any other information that can provide the company with a competitive advantage but is not known or understood by people outside the company. The most famous example of a trade secret worldwide is the original formula for Coca Cola. From the beginning, Coca Cola treated the formula as a trade secret, and so it continues to have exclusive use of it even after so many years.

Accusations of stealing trade secrets are commonplace in the United States: Uber vs. Waymo (a Google company), Apple allegedly stealing from Qualcomm, and Huawei accused of stealing from T-Mobile. Chicago-based Garrett Popcorn (or CaramelCrisp) accused one of its employees of stealing information that "put its secret recipes at risk." The company's recipes were available to only three employees, each of whom had to verify their identity with a biometric thumbprint for access. One of the three employees was accused of stealing "information about recipes, batch pricing, product weights, production processes," and sharing them via email with the company's competitors.

9.3.3 Copyright

Expressions of ideas are covered by **copyright**. Thus, it is not the idea itself, but the tangible expression of the idea that is protected by copyright law. Copyright for new works lasts for the creator's life plus 70 years, during which the heirs of the creator have the legal right to the works he or she created. For "work for hire" bought from the creator, copyright protection lasts for 120 years after original creation or 95 years from first publication, whichever is earlier.

When someone creates a unique expression of ideas, they automatically own the copyright to it. You have probably seen the symbol © with the creator's name and year of creation on books, paintings, sculptures, or computer programs. Such a notation, though not required, is a clear message that materials cannot simply be copied without explicit permission of the creator (and copyright holder). The US government does not create copyright, but one can register copyrights on their works with the government (www.copyright.gov).

David Slater vs. PETA is probably one of the most famous copyright infringement cases in the world. At the heart of this case is the issue of "if a monkey takes a picture with your camera, does the picture belong to you or the monkey?" Naruto, an Indonesian macaque, took selfies with wildlife photographer David Slater's camera, which he (Slater, not Naruto!) then included in his book *Wildlife Personalities*. The photographs became popular, and the Wikipedia used them without Slater's permission under the assumption that "copyright cannot vest in non-human authors" and "when a work's copyright cannot vest in a human, it falls into the public domain." Slater countered that he put a lot of work into preparing the photos and was even holding the tripod when Naruto clicked them. On behalf of Naruto, People for the Ethical Treatment of Animals (PETA) sued Slater claiming the copyright for the photos belonged to the macaque for it was he who pressed the shutter. When the case was settled, Slater agreed to donate 25% of future revenue from the photos to groups that protect crested macaques and their habitat in Indonesia.

The selfies of the Indonesian macaque Naruto led to one of the most famous copyright infringement cases.

A common but mistaken belief is that when you ask or pay someone to produce a work for you, then you own the rights to it. For instance, business owners often hire graphic designers to create a logo for their company. Or couples may pay a photographer to take pictures of their wedding. Who owns the copyright in these situations? Not the business owner or the couple, but the graphic designer and the photographer. The creator of the work owns the copyrights unless the agreement is for a **work made for hire**. Per the Copyright Act, a work made for hire is (1) a work prepared by an employee within the scope of employment or (2) a work specially commissioned if the parties agree in writing that the work will be considered a work made for hire.

9.3.4 Patents

Patents grant someone the right to own an idea or invention. A **patent** cannot be issued for an idea in the head. The idea needs to be meaningfully described and communicated for it to be patentable. Once a patent is issued, everyone has access to the information covered by the patent, but the direct use of that information is not allowed without the explicit permission of the patent-holder.

To obtain a patent, one needs to apply to the country's government. The U.S. Patent Office (www.uspto.gov), for example, is responsible for issuing patents to those who want to retain the exclusive right to make, use, or sell their idea or invention for a specific time period. In order to obtain a patent, an applicant must show that the invention is nonobvious, provides a solution to some problem, and represents a new or novel way of doing something. In other words, the invention must be novel, nonobvious, and useful.

For patents in the United States, applicants have one year from the time the idea is disclosed to others to apply for a patent. In most other countries, one needs to apply for a patent before disclosing it publicly.

A **design patent** pertains to the look of an invention and the parts that are essential to the design. **Utility patents** are related to specific processes and functions. **Plant patents** are obtained for newly created strains of living matter. Generally, patents are valid for 20 years from the date of filing an application. Design patents last only 14 years from application filing.

Interactive Exercise

U.S. Patent Number 5878931 is for the Halloween Backpack, which is a backpack that dispenses Halloween candy. It was issued in March 1999 to Deborah Morphet of California. If you want to read some more examples of seemingly crazy patents, here is a good site to visit: http://www.freepatentsonline.com/crazy.html.

While it is advisable to get a patent if the product you have developed is eligible for it, patents offer far less protection than most people realize. For most small business owners, there is little they can do when someone copies their patented product, unless they are willing to spend considerable time and money pursuing legal options. Teri Mittelstadt is the cofounder of HiGear Design Inc. in California, a seller of patented Travelrest pillows, which attach to airline seats to prevent slipping. Her products were among the top-selling travel pillows on Amazon for seven years, until several foreign sellers started selling similar pillows on the site for a much lower price, making her patent essentially worthless. Kevin Williams, a Utah seller of patented water-powered cleaning brushes, found that his product had been copied without permission. While Kevin was selling his Brush Hero product for $34.99 apiece, copycats were listing it for as low as $9.99.

Some business owners find that their offerings get copied not by other small rival firms but also by large corporations selling at a cheaper price. Dalen Thomas, owner of Pirate Trading LLC, had a successful business (about $3.5 million in annual revenues) selling Ravelli-brand camera tripods on Amazon. Then, Amazon launched its own version of Pirate's top-selling tripods under the AmazonBasics label. Dalen ordered one of the Amazon tripods and found it had the same components and shared his product's design. Amazon even used the same manufacturer that supplied Dalen's products. Because Amazon was selling the clone tripod less than what Dalen paid his manufacturer to have Pirate's version made, sale of Ravelli tripods plunged drastically. Amazon claims that its tripods do not violate IP rights. "If a company is offering something that Amazon thinks it can do better, or can do less expensively, then they will try do it," says a former senior executive at Amazon.

The topic of IP remains divisive and controversial. For its advocates, IP protection is a fundamental prerequisite for innovation and entrepreneurship. For its critics, strong IP laws thwart innovation, making it difficult for new and small companies to compete effectively with large corporations. Some believe that the importance of IP laws cannot be overestimated, while others argue that IP protection is overhyped.

What Do You Think?

Fortem is a Brooklyn-based four-person company run by cofounders Yuriy Petriv and Oleg Maslakou. The company offers a car-trunk organizer, which is the No. 1 seller in the category on Amazon accounting for about 99.95% of the total sale over a 12-month period. Fortem spends as much as $60,000 a month on Amazon advertisements for its items to come up at the top of searches. When Amazon employees saw how well Fortem's car-trunk organizer was selling, it launched three similar trunks under its AmazonBasics private label brand. What do you think Foretm should do? Would it make a difference if Fortem's car-trunk organizer was patented?

Comprehension Check

1. What is a trademark? How does a trademark differ from a service mark?
2. What is a patent? Explain different types of patents.
3. Define copyright.

Module 9.4 Basics of Bankruptcy Laws

Any discussion of the laws and regulations that affect small businesses would be incomplete without covering bankruptcy laws. **Bankruptcy** is a legal process through which individuals, firms, or other entities who cannot repay debts may seek relief from some or all of what they owe. Bankruptcy is generally initiated by the debtor and imposed by a court order. The American Bankruptcy Institute estimates that, on average, about 26,000 businesses go bankrupt each year (based on the data from 2013 to 2017). More businesses go bankrupt during economic crisis, such as the Great Financial Crisis of 2008 or the global COVID-19 pandemic of 2020. Twisted Root Burger, a Texas-based burger chain, is an example. The company was a success story, expanding from one casual restaurant to 24 sites including restaurants, bars, a brewery, and a theater over a 14-year period. Twisted was forced to shut down its stores in March 2020 as the COVID-19 pandemic spread throughout the country. The company was already carrying debt from its fast expansion, and costs skyrocketed when stores closed. Some sites reopened a couple of months later only to be shut down again as the COVID-19 cases surged. "It'll never get back to normal business," says cofounder Jason Boso, who decided that bankruptcy was the best option for his company.

The Bankruptcy Reform Act of 1978 specified eight forms of bankruptcies, of which three are directly related to small business situations: Chapters 7, 11, and 13. Most small businesses are sole proprietorships, which are simply legal extensions of the owners. For sole proprietorships, the most common form of bankruptcy is Chapter 13. Chapters 7 and 11 bankruptcies are for partnerships and corporations.

> **KEY TAKEAWAY**
>
> The three types of bankruptcies most directly related to small businesses are Chapters 7, 11, and 13.

Jason Fyk of Philadelphia is founder of the humor website WTF Magazine (which, the homepage notes, stands for "Where's the Fun?"). One time, shortly after conducting an interview for his magazine, he saw some people fighting in a Baltimore street. He took a cellphone video – and the police arrested him. After 50 days in jail, all charges were dropped. He was left with tens of thousands of dollars of debt in attorney's fees, few career prospects, and a struggling business. Things were so bad at the time, he had to use his mother's ACCESS EBT card to purchase food for his four-year-old son. He decided to file for **Chapter 7 bankruptcy**.

Many people see bankruptcy as the end-of-the-line for a business. Jason proved them wrong. The bankruptcy was a turning point for him. Within a week after discharging his bankruptcy, Jason was able to negotiate $10,000 worth of affiliate marketing contracts for his Facebook pages. At the time, Facebook business pages were relatively new. Jason already had 10 Facebook pages, where he shared memes and other entertaining posts, and had about eight million "Likes." As his business grew, Jason's pages were making $350,000 per month. Soon, Jason became a millionaire, owning about 50 Facebook pages with about 30 million Facebook likes in total. Using Chapter 7 bankruptcy thoughtfully, Jason was able to turn around his business and become more successful after the bankruptcy than he was before it.

Chapter 11 bankruptcy is for firms that have a realistic chance to turn things around through reorganization. It provides a second chance for businesses in financial trouble but still have some path toward viability. Companies seeking Chapter 11 bankruptcy are required to file a detailed plan of reorganization outlining how they will deal with their creditors. The reorganization allows for terminating contracts and leases, recovering assets, and repaying a portion of the debts while discharging others to return to profitability. Creditors must approve the reorganization plan. If the plan is considered fair and equitable by the court, it is approved.

Borders Books was founded by brothers Tom and Louis Borders during their undergraduate and graduate years at University of Michigan, with the first bookstore on South State Street in Ann Arbor. Once the country's second-largest bookseller, the retailer was hit hard by the rise of Amazon and e-books. In February 2011, it filed for Chapter 11 bankruptcy protection. Management hoped for a buyout by a private equity firm, but the deal fell through, and in the absence of other buyers, the company shuttered its nearly 400 remaining stores, liquidating all assets. In the fire sale, Borders competitor Barnes & Noble bought all its intellectual property and a database of 48 million customers for $13.9 million.

Big companies like Borders have long used Chapter 11, but the law was too complicated and costly for most small firms. Smaller companies that did file for Chapter 11 bankruptcy often failed to survive. Small business owners often couldn't comply with the law's requirement that they either repay all debts to retain ownership or convince creditors to accept less. In August 2019, Congress passed the Small Business Reorganization Act of 2019, which allows applicants to file for Chapter 11 bankruptcy without having a reorganization plan approved by creditors. Two legal advisory groups, the National Bankruptcy Conference and the American Bankruptcy Institute, provided recommendations to congressional lawmakers. Under the new law, small firms do not need to pay Justice Department fees or file a formal disclosure statement, a legal document that can cost thousands of dollars in legal fees. It also gives small businesses access to a court-appointed financial expert to help fix their problems. Bankrupt firms are still required to fully repay taxes, loans, and other forms of secured debt. However, unsecured debt – money owed to suppliers, customers, and others – can be repaid through monthly payments without losing ownership.

Eric Brown, owner of Brown Bros Telecom & Utility in Dalton, GA, filed for Chapter 11 bankruptcy under the new law after collecting less money than expected on a completed project. "It's been an absolute game-changer," says Eric, "and so far, it's kept me working."

Small Business Bankruptcy

Is bankruptcy a tool to save yourself and your business a lot of trouble down the line? Jonathan Ginsberg, an Atlanta-based bankruptcy attorney, explains that bankruptcy may be a good option for a failed or failing business venture. Instead of using all their savings to save the business from failing, it may be better to file for bankruptcy for your business and move on to other options.

You can watch the video online at: https://www.youtube.com/watch?v=aPjPv7lwyq8.

Legal experts expect a surge in Chapter 11 bankruptcy filings by small firms in the aftermath of the COVID-19 pandemic. The new law, they believe, will make many business owners realize that filing for bankruptcy might be a better option than struggling for years to dig out of a financial hole, especially with the outlook being so unpredictable. Yet, and despite the many new provisions Congress enacted to make it easier for small businesses to organize in bankruptcy, the prospects for small firms filing for Chapter 11 bankruptcy are much bleaker than for large firms. Most small firms that enter bankruptcy will likely go under, as bankrupt businesses are obligated to dedicate all of their future profits to debt repayment, making it very difficult for owners to save up or invest.

What Do You Think?

A to Z Total Heating and Cooling in suburban Detroit was one of the first companies in the country to file for bankruptcy protection under the new Chapter 11 rules after the COVID-19 pandemic shut down the economy. The family-owned firm has been operating for nearly four decades, but business really took off in the past few years. If the firm had been growing well, what do you think could have led it to declare bankruptcy? A to Z wants to use bankruptcy to clean the slate, and start over. Do you think it will be possible for the company to come out stronger from bankruptcy than it was when it entered bankruptcy? What are some of the things that one needs to consider in such situations?

Keith Clark owned Waterford Receptions, a popular wedding and events venue operator with two locations in Northern Virginia. The business survived for 20 years, until COVID-19 happened. In April 2020, Keith received a $500,000 loan to pay 45 salaried employees over the summer while Waterford's two locations remained largely unused because of a statewide ban on large gatherings. Revenues fell by 90% to $567,000 in 2020 down from $6 million during the same period in 2019. Keith considered filing for Chapter 11 bankruptcy under the Small Business Reorganization Act, as it would have made it easier to quickly restructure operations and shed debt. However, as COVID-19 cases continued to climb over the summer, it became harder to envision a reopening for Waterford. Keith decided to put the company into Chapter 7 bankruptcy, to repay creditors by selling the company's assets. Making matters worse, Keith had personally guaranteed a $1.5 million SBA loan in 2019, which he would need to repay by filing for personal bankruptcy and selling his home to pay creditors.

Chapter 13 bankruptcy is for individuals, including small business owners, with regular income who want to adjust their debt repayment. Applicants should owe less than $250,000 in unsecured debts and less than $750,000 in secured debts and promise to pay back creditors over a three- to five-year period to qualify. The applicant must submit a repayment plan to a bankruptcy judge for approval. The court can reduce, or even eliminate, some types of debts.

Consider the Joneses – John and Jane – who owed $10,000 in income taxes from closing down a business that had struggled for several years. They also owed $7000 in the previous year's income taxes, plus $50,000 in a combination of medical and credit card debts. As the business struggled, the Joneses also fell behind $12,500 on their first mortgage and $5000 on property taxes. They also hadn't made payments on a second mortgage in months, so they were at risk of foreclosure there too. Their lawyer recommended Chapter 13 bankruptcy, charging them $4000 for filing it. In five years, John and Jane finished paying enough into their Chapter 13 plan for the bankruptcy judge to sign a discharge order. Nationwide, only 33% of Chapter 13 cases are discharged, and the Joneses are fortunate to have come out of bankruptcy without losing their house.

Comprehension Check

1. What is bankruptcy?
2. Explain Chapter 7 bankruptcy.
3. Differentiate between Chapter 11 and Chapter 13 bankruptcies.

Summary

Business and law are joined at the hip. Many small business owners complain that they are burdened with too many laws and regulations. Yet most business owners would not want to run their firms in a system without any laws or rules. Firms that do not follow rules will find themselves in trouble, with possible monetary fines and other legal sanctions.

It is therefore important for businesses to understand and follow the law. When you are running a small business, at some point, you are going to get to see the legal system in action. All businesses must deal with the never-ending challenge of keeping up with the laws and regulations they must honor. It is therefore very important for small business owners to have some understanding of the legal system. Understanding the legal system helps a business owner become prepared to deal with the law (and those accusing that business owner of violating it).

While business owners need the help of professional lawyers who can provide them appropriate legal help in the situation, it is always useful to have basic familiarity with the law. People who understand the legal fundamentals are able to have an intelligent conversation with their lawyers and are better positioned to make the right decisions even during difficult times. You may not always agree with the law, but you are expected to operate within it. It's like playing football. You may not agree with all the rules of football and their interpretations (they fill up 120 electronic pages on NFL.com), but if you want to be taken seriously when you play, you must follow the rules. If you do not follow the rules, you will not be allowed to play. It is the same for matters of the law. If you do not adhere to the law, you may be fined, sanctioned, or prosecuted.

World of Books

Legal Guide for Starting & Running a Small Business (16th ed.) by Fred S. Steingold and David Steingold

Law for Entrepreneurs and Small Business Owners by Robert Sprague

In the Movies

Robert Kearns is a happily married engineering professor. A wedding night accident left him with limited vision in his left eye, a condition that is exacerbated whenever he drives in rain. The constant motion of the windshield wipers of the time troubles him, and he decides to create a new wiper blade mechanism. He converts the basement of the family house into his laboratory and after several failed attempts develops a prototype that works well enough to be installed in his car. He patents his invention, and demonstrates it to researchers at the Ford Motor Co. who had been working on a similar project for some time without success. When Ford introduces the intermittent wiper in its new Mustang without Kearns's approval, he is heartbroken and files a lawsuit that leads to years of legal battle. *Flash of Genius* is a touching underdog story of a single guy fighting against a massive corporation for what he believes to be his IP.

Live Exercise

"Do you think our patent protects us from copycats?" Johnny asks you on the phone. Your parents had shared with him that you had been studying legal issues for small businesses in the class the past week. "To be honest, I understand that I should ask this question to a professional lawyer, but I am afraid I will end up spending a lot of money to get advice that may not even be in my best interest," Johnny continues. You are unsure if you have learned enough about legal issues in small firms to give practical advice to an experienced entrepreneur like Johnny, but you decide to give it a try. When you tell Johnny you are willing to try helping him on this issue, he asks if you can put together a two-page memo about the following issues:

1. The SoapStandle is patented (U.S. Patent No. 9307870). Does that give us enough protection from copycats?
2. As we come out with new designs, can they be patented? If yes, how much can we expect to spend on a patent application?

3. The company is currently run as a proprietorship firm. What legal form should we use? If we need to change our legal form, should we hire a lawyer or do it ourselves?

4. Any other legal issues that we need to consider at this stage of our business?

"This should be interesting!" you think to yourself as you sit down to work through the issues Johnny wants you to address.

Things to Remember

LO 9.1 **Distinguish between the various legal forms of small businesses**

- The type of legal structure affects various aspects of the way the business is managed.
- There are three general legal forms for businesses in the United States: proprietorships, partnerships, and corporations.
- For small businesses, the most popular form of legal structure is the sole proprietorship, perhaps because it is the most inexpensive and simplest to set up.
- A partnership is a voluntary association of two or more people who make a conscious decision to co-own a business together.
- A corporation is a separate legal entity with an existence distinct from the people who started it.
- Fractional ownership allows unrelated parties to share ownership of a high-value tangible asset such as a jet or a yacht.

LO 9.2 **Explain the basics of contracts**

- Contracts are legally enforced promises.
- When a party reneges on his or her commitments, other parties can take legal recourse.
- An agreement must have four basic elements – prerequisites – to be legally considered a valid contract: capacity, legality, acceptance, and consideration.
- When someone does not follow the terms of the contract, it is called a breach of contract.
- Contracts that are used over and over again, with minor changes that can be readily made, are called standard contracts.
- Contracts may also have an exculpatory clause stipulating that one party will not be responsible for certain things.

LO 9.3 **Identify the fundamentals of intellectual property**

- All intangible creations of human intelligence, including ideas, slogans, and expressions, are considered intellectual property.
- Any identification used to delineate and promote a certain product is a trademark.
- A service mark identifies specific services.
- The term *trade secret* refers to confidential information known to only certain people within a company, such that it is not publicly known or accessible.
- Expressions of ideas are covered by copyright.
- Patents grant someone the right to own an idea or invention.
- The topic of IP remains divisive and controversial.

LO 9.4 **Describe various types of bankruptcy laws**

- Bankruptcy is a legal process through which an individual, a firm, or another entity that cannot repay debts may seek relief from some or all of what is owed.
- Bankruptcy is generally initiated by the debtor and imposed by a court order.
- The Bankruptcy Reform Act of 1978 specified eight forms of bankruptcies, of which three are directly related to small business situations: Chapters 7, 11, and 13.
- Chapter 7 bankruptcy involves liquidation to pay off creditors.

- Chapter 11 bankruptcy is for firms that are in financial trouble but still have some path toward viability.
- Chapter 13 bankruptcy is for those with regular income who want their debt payment readjusted.

Key Terms

sole proprietorship	benefit corporations	acceptance	service mark
trade name	limited liability company	consideration	trade secret
assumed name	professional corporations	breach of contract	copyright
doing business as	B-Corps	compensatory damages	work made for hire
(DBA) name	limited liability	standard contracts	patent
pass-through taxation	partnerships	specialty contracts	design patent
partnership	family limited partnerships	interstate contracts	utility patents
general partnership	cooperatives	noncompete contracts	plant patents
limited partnership	nonprofit corporations	hold harmless agreements	bankruptcy
articles of copartnership	fractional ownership	broad form agreement	Chapter 7 bankruptcy
corporation	timeshares	intermediate	Chapter 11 bankruptcy
continuous existence	contracts	form agreement	Chapter 13 bankruptcy
double taxation	oral promises	limited form agreement	
dividends	handshake agreements	exculpatory clause	
C-Corporation	capacity	intellectual property	
S-Corporation	legality	trademark	

Experiential Exercise

Pick one topic of your choice that you may want to learn more about: *legal structures, contracts, intellectual property,* or *bankruptcy*. Using the appropriate keywords from that topic, find the website of three law firms that specialize in the area you have picked up. Carefully browse the websites of those law firms to understand what assistance they can provide to a small business owner. Prepare a one-page flyer for one law firm of your choice that they can send to prospective clients summarizing the services they offer.

As you browse the websites, ask yourself whether the law firm can readily offer other services that it currently does not provide within the topic area you have chosen. If yes, prepare a one-page memo advising the law firm of the services that they do not offer, but should offer based on your research. Explain clearly what those services are, why they should be offered, and how those services can be offered going forward.

Your client for this assignment is a law firm. It needs both deliverables: the one-page flyer and the one-page memo. The one-page flyer will help your client do a better job of reaching out to small firms. The one-page memo will help convince your client about the merits of expanding into a new line of business.

CHAPTER 10

Ethics and Social Responsibility

Free-enterprise capitalism must be grounded in an ethical system based on value creation for all stakeholders.

JOHN MACKEY,
Founder of Whole Foods

10.0 Introduction

It is hard to believe, but the issue of ethics and social responsibility of business attracts much debate and discussion in academic and popular media. Everyone agrees that a company should make a profit. Most people also recognize that a company should obey the law and play by the rules of the game. Whether a company also has a duty to behave ethically and contribute to the betterment of society is, however, very controversial. This chapter is about the importance of a firm doing the right thing. While it is important for businesses to make money and improve profits legally, this chapter discusses the importance of also being ethical and socially responsible. Do well *and* do good, as the saying goes! Bill George, author of the best-selling books *Authentic Leadership* and *True North*, says that well-run, values-centered businesses can contribute to humankind in more tangible ways than any other organization in society.

Module 10.1 Why Behave Ethically?

There are two popular reasons people give when they call upon businesses to be ethical and socially responsible. The first – **moral argument** – is that firms should behave ethically and be responsible toward society because it is the right thing to do. Do the right thing, it argues, simply because it is the right thing to do. You sleep well at night knowing

SPOTLIGHT | EO Products: People Before Profits

EO Products, a Bay Area maker of bath and body products, is owned by its founders Susan and Brad, a divorced couple who still work together. The company, with about 150 employees, sells the bulk of its products through retailers. Its products have been sold by Whole Foods for more than 20 years and now can be found at Walmart, Target, and Amazon. Until 2019, the company was doing roughly $100 million a year in sales.

Susan and Brad cofounded EO Products in their garage.

Total hand sanitizer sales in the United States were just below $200 million in 2019, a 4.5% decline from the previous year. The year 2020 was expected to be no different, but the landscape shifted drastically after the World Health Organization declared a global health emergency at the end of January. A month later, the state of Washington announced the first COVID-19-related death in the United States. Demand for items such as hand sanitizers suddenly spiked in March 2020 as people clamored to protect themselves from getting sick. Bath & Body Works, the scented bath product chain, reported a surge in demand for hand sanitizers. The websites of Amazon

and Walmart showed hand sanitizers were out of stock. Third parties were selling hand sanitizers at high prices. A pack of two 12-ounce bottles of Purell from a third-party seller sold for $49.99 (regular selling price $1 each); a generic bottle containing less than 2 ounces of hand sanitizer sold for $459. At the high prices, people still bought the products in quantity.

In response to heightened demand, EO Products quadrupled the production of hand sanitizer. The company ran extra shifts, speeded up production lines, hired temporary workers, and converted factory lines designed for other products to produce hand sanitizer instead. Ramping up the production for hand sanitizer is challenging because it is regulated by the Food and Drug Administration as an over-the-counter product and must meet the agency's safety and efficacy standards. Another problem: EO promises to use all-natural products and adhere to certain guidelines about employee pay and environmental impact, which limits which suppliers and third-party manufacturers the company can use to increase production. Hand sanitizer is not among EO's most profitable products, so switching production lines to produce hand sanitizer drags on margins.

Tom Feegel, President of EO Products, decided that even though there was a huge spike in demand, everything was selling out, and it was becoming more difficult to find supplies, the company would not increase prices. "Raising prices at this time would not be in alignment with our core values," Tom said. "All the business rules about profitability are off the table." Workers at the company, who get health insurance and paid sick time as well as free packages of sanitizer, "like the fact that they are contributing to something," says Rosa Prado, a senior supervisor on the factory floor.

Discussion Questions

1. Explain EO Product's business.

2. What issue did EO Products face when demand for hand sanitizer suddenly shot up?

3. Do you think EO Products made a good decision by not raising prices to as much as the market could bear?

that you did the right thing. The second – **business argument** – is that firms should behave ethically because doing so is good for business. Here, doing the right thing is financially beneficial for the firm as its customers, employees, or suppliers appreciate the ethical conduct of the firm. When firms behave unethically – say by doing what is prudent rather than what is right – it will pay the price, sooner or later.

KEY TAKEAWAY

Some believe that a firm should always do the right thing, whether it is financially beneficial or not.

Ethics is not just an issue for business owners but also for people who work in the business. As an employee, you may be asked to mislead a customer, or lie to a client. You could also be asked to take a shortcut you know would produce an inferior product or to spy on a fellow employee. If you go along with the unethical behavior, you become complicit. If you report it to a higher-up or outside organization, you could face retaliation. A National Business Ethics survey by the Ethics and Compliance Initiative revealed that about 53% employees in the United States who reported misconduct in their companies experienced some form of retaliation. That could include receiving worse evaluations and being passed up for promotions and raises. At the very least, whistleblowing has social costs, such as being uninvited from happy hours or given cold shoulders in the hallway. One person's whistleblower, they say, is another person's snitch. Table 10.1 shares some examples of situations where employees found themselves asked to deceive clients, hide

TABLE 10.1

Examples of Unethical Orders Some Employees Got at Small Firms

Name	Unethical orders	What was the outcome?
Ryan Kargel	I was asked to treat my female employees and male employees differently and likewise white and minority differently. These were explicit directives.	I explained why I couldn't legally do that and was left to go about my business. The outcome was correct, but the taste in my mouth was bitter.
Ella Lorenzo	I was asked not to serve the homeless man on the corner of the street even though he saved his pennies to come in and buy some coffee. The managers didn't want him stinking up the bakery.	During my shifts, I ushered him (the homeless man) and served him cookies, macarons, ice cream – whatever he wanted. I was fired shortly after.
Cindy Tayne	A former supervisor told me that I needed to hire more staff who "reflected the demographic of our clientele" and to "get rid of some staff" who had been working there for a while by "writing them up for every little thing." I was the director of a high-end child care center in a ritzy neighborhood.	When your boss tells you to do it, what options do you have?
David Brooks	I worked at an elevator/escalator company. I maintained the database of all the service calls. Some person was injured on one of the company's escalators, and my boss asked me to pull all the service call details for that specific escalator. One of the service logs described the escalator as "dangerous." My boss told me to delete the word "dangerous" from the log.	I was a kid just starting out. What could I do? I deleted it.
Olga Dmitrieva	We have been ordered to change stickers so the deodorants of our company would look like the famous ones. The whole office was doing it for two weeks or longer: ripping off actual stickers and sticking on the new ones.	For me it felt horrible! But it appeared to me they already had been doing that before. I was a newbie there at the time, and I needed money. I could not afford to quit. I feel ashamed even now, and it happened 16 years ago.

TABLE 10.1		
Continued		
Name	Unethical orders	What was the outcome?
Bethany Scott	I worked in a campus café in college. One day, my boss handed me a spreadsheet of refrigerator temperatures and asked me to fill it in for the past week "just random enough to make it look real."	I said yes at first, hemmed and hawed for a little while, then ultimately gave it back to him and said I couldn't live with it if someone ended up with food poisoning. He played it cool, but for a 20-year-old, it was nerve-racking.
Edwin Ortega	A company I used to work for forced me to install pirated copies of Microsoft Office and other productivity tools, circumventing the trial offers they had with key generators.	My hands were tied because they were sponsoring my J-1 visa, and I did not want to have to leave the country.
Carole Marmell	We had a hospice nurse who was pickpocketing patient meds. Our supervisor said she couldn't fire her because we didn't have enough nurses.	I threatened to turn them both in to the nursing board. Finally, she fired that nurse.
DyAnna Rose	A doctor asked me to keep a brain-dead 89-year-old alive even if I had to do CPR on her.	I refused and told him so. Then he told me I had to do whatever he ordered. I responded, "Um, no, I don't have to do anything illegal, immoral or unethical." I was removed from her care. I reported it, and within 10 minutes, she was declared a do-not-resuscitate.
Diedre Miller	One of my bosses asked me to spy on my co-workers.	I said, "if one of the higher-ups asked me to report on you, how would you feel about that?" She didn't like my answer. Sometimes you just have to stand your ground, no matter what the consequences are, and trust it will work out to your best interest.

Source: "My Hands Were Tied": How Readers Handled Unethical Workplace Requests, *New York Times*

misconduct, or engage in unethical behaviors. As you read the anecdotes employees shared, ask what you would do if you were in their shoes.

The Greek thinker Chilon is believed to have emphasized – in 560 BC – that a business owner does better to take a loss than to make a dishonest profit. In the United States, the American newspaperman Horace Greeley warned that "the darker hour in the history of any young man is when he sits down to study how to get money without honestly earning it." Sam Walton, who founded the retail giant Walmart, called upon his employees and managers to keep ethics front and center in everything they did. "Personal and moral integrity is one of our basic fundamentals and it has to start with each of us," he said.

To Blow Or Not To Blow

Imagine that you are fresh out of college and working at a company where the owner is a good friend of your grandfather. You are quite close to your grandfather, who has an impeccable reputation in the community. When you find out the company is engaging in fraudulent behavior, you mention your concerns to your grandfather, but he tells you not to worry. When you try to share your concerns with the company's owners, you are told to focus on your work. What do you do? This is the difficult situation that Tyler Shultz was in, who ultimately blew the whistle at Theranos, a high-growth venture with a charismatic founder.

Watch the video online at: https://www.youtube.com/watch?v=9wf_2KYRPWQ

Let us look at the brothers Matt and Noah Calvin of Tennessee to get a better sense of what it means to behave ethically in business. Matt Colvin is a former air force technical sergeant. In 2015, he started selling on Amazon, turning it into a six-figure career by selling Nike shoes and pet toys. In early February of 2020, after the World Health Organization declared a global health crisis, Matt spotted a chance to make some money. A nearby liquidation firm was selling 2000 "pandemic packs," leftovers from a defunct company. Each came with 50 face masks, four small bottles of hand sanitizer, and a thermometer. The price was $5 a pack. Matt haggled it to $3.50 and bought them all. He quickly sold all 2000 of the 50 packs of masks on eBay, pricing them from $40 to $50 each, and sometimes higher. The success stoked his appetite. When he saw the panicked American public starting to pounce on sanitizer and wipes, he and his brother Noah decided to stock up.

After the first COVID-19 death was announced in the United States, Matt and Noah drove around, buying up hand sanitizers and antibacterial wipes from Dollar Tree, Walmart, Staples and Home Depot. At each store, they cleaned out the shelves. Over the next three days, Noah took a 1300-mile road trip across Tennessee and into Kentucky, filling a U-Haul truck with thousands of bottles of hand sanitizer and thousands of packs of antibacterial wipes, mostly from "little hole-in-the-wall dollar stores in the backwoods," Matt said. Soon, they had stockpiled 17,700 bottles of hand sanitizer.

The Colvin brothers posted 300 sanitizer bottles on Amazon and immediately sold them all for between $8 and $70 each, multiples higher than what they had bought them for. To Matt, "it was crazy money." To many others, it was profiteering from a pandemic. Tennessee, where the brothers live, has a price-gouging law that bars people from charging "unreasonable prices for essential goods and services, including gasoline, in direct response to a disaster," according to a state website (https://www.nytimes.com/2020/03/14/technology/coronavirus-purell-wipes-amazon-sellers.html). Amazon soon pulled his items. *The New York Times* ran a story on the brothers, which quotes Matt as saying he was doing public service, helping drive out inefficiencies in the marketplace. He denied he was price-gouging, arguing that he was simply earning a fair profit.

After the *Times* ran the story, Tennessee attorney general's office sent investigators to the Colvin home, issued a cease-and-desist letter, and started an investigation. Under legal pressure, and facing strong vilification from the *Times* story, the brothers agreed to donate all the supplies to their church for distribution to local emergency responders. Under the terms of the settlement, the brothers agreed not to engage in any further price gouging during the COVID-19 health crisis. "Disrupting necessary supplies during an unprecedented pandemic is a serious offense," Tennessee's attorney general, said in a statement after the settlement was reached.

Interactive Exercise

Jonas Salk developed the first polio vaccine, but refused to earn any money from his discovery, preferring it to be distributed as widely as possible. Identify 10 friends, 7 family members, and 5 professors and ask them if they think the individual or company that makes a vaccine for the novel coronavirus should give it away at cost or should make money on it. Summarize the responses you get and share in the class.

Before moving ahead, it is useful to define two terms: business ethics and corporate social responsibility. **Business ethics** refers to the application of ethical principles and standards to the decisions and actions of firms, including the work-related conduct of their owners and employees. **Corporate social responsibility** (CSR) is the obligation that a business has toward its various stakeholders, including employees, customers, suppliers, and the community within which the firm operates.

Have you heard of the company This Bar Saves Life? Two American actors, Ryan Devlin and Todd Grinnell, started it after a humanitarian trip to Liberia where they saw children being treated for malnutrition – a preventable condition if there was enough food. After returning home, they got together with two other friends to start a granola bar company. Embracing the "buy one, give one" idea (so-called **giveback companies**), the four friends decided to donate a packet of Plumpy'Nut, a nutrient paste, to a child in need when someone buys a granola bar. "This Bar Saves Lives is a company that wants to help in malnutrition, and we happen to sell bars," says the company's chief executive. "We're not a bar company with a social mission." In a market filled with companies selling granola bars, This Bar stands out because of its strong sense of social responsibility for the underprivileged malnourished children. "Nowadays, people expect it," thinks Kevin Tighe II, founder and chief executive of Coastal Co., which sells surf apparel and donates a portion of sales to clean up beaches. "If you're not participating in a way to give back, it's almost frowned upon."

What Do You Think?

It is 2022 and the media is discussing the possibility of another public health crisis. The state of West Virginia has reported that high school students are being hospitalized with flu-like symptoms. There is no official advisory yet, but people are afraid of a return to the 2020 pandemic. Erica, who you know from college, shared with you that she has already gone around Ohio, buying 10,000 masks from stores. Using coupons, she was able to buy each 10-pack for about $15, which she then sold on Amazon for roughly $80 each, though she priced 2000 masks at $125. You quickly do the math, and the numbers are impressive. If a pandemic actually hits, the masks could probably sell for even higher, Erica shares. She is now asking you to join her by driving to Indiana, Kentucky, and Michigan to buy as many masks as possible. She will invest the money to buy the masks, and as you bring in new supplies, she will sell on Amazon and eBay. For your efforts, she is willing to give you a 25% share in the profits. This is an once-in-a-lifetime opportunity, she tells you, and can easily pay for next two semesters of college for both of you. You are not sure what to do. You've been working hard in a minimum-wage job in a local restaurant, but student loans are adding up. You could certainly use the money. Should you take the offer as-is? Should you try to negotiate a higher share of the profits? Should you decline Erica's offer? Should you report Erica to the local authorities? Erica has given you a short time to make a decision, and the clock is ticking.

Three-quarters of small business owners report donating a percentage of their profits to charity, with 5% of small firms donating more than 10%. In some cases, small business owners develop relationships with local nonprofits in ways that benefit both parties. Consider Norm and Mary Jo Lorentz, owners of three Cousins Subs sandwich franchises in Racine, WI. They reached out to schools and church groups in the Racine community that needed their help with fund-raising partnerships. The Lorentz's started offering a new product: a smaller Cousins sub sandwich called the Cup 'o Sub that nonprofits can purchase at a discount and then resell at a higher price at fund-raising events. This approach brings in more sales and new customers for the sub shop and the charities keep the proceeds. Cousins also provides nonprofits with promotional materials such as a banner and signs to publicize the event.

Comprehension Check

1. Define business ethics.
2. Differentiate between the moral argument and the business argument for ethical decisions.
3. Explain CSR.

Module 10.2 Legal and Moral Criteria for Ethical Behavior

Profit – the difference between what a company earns and what it spends – is at the heart of business. Making money is central to capitalism. However, the urge to make money and earn a profit needs to operate within some constraints set by society. Not everyone, however, agrees that businesses should look toward the criteria set by society to make ethical decisions. Some thinkers and philosophers believe that people should do what most advances their self-interest. From this perspective, **selfishness** is a virtue that guides human behavior in all spheres, including decisions made by small business owners.

KEY TAKEAWAY

The urge to make money and earn a profit needs to operate within some societal constraints.

Elite Fitness is a gym based in Frankfort, KY, that let customers enter through the back door and work out during the 2020 pandemic, despite an executive order issued by governor closing all nonessential businesses in the state, including gyms. While the decision to allow customers to work out may have been good for Elite Fitness, it had the potential to start an outbreak in the community. "Physical exercise is important to me," the governor said when he heard about the gym. "But if you run a gym where people will be in close proximity, all using the same equipment, spread the coronavirus and it is already killing people, with an order out there that you cannot operate and you would open up the back door?" The selfish decision of the owners of Elite Fitness could have led to a COVID outbreak in the community, potentially hurting hundreds or thousands of innocent people.

Interactive Exercise

Have you heard about Salon a la Mode of Dallas or Jackson's Blue River Pub in Milwaukee? Salon is owned by Shelley Luther and Jackson's by Dan Zierath. These are two business owners among many nationwide that reopened their premises in defiance of the lockdown in their area during the COVID-19 pandemic. When asked why they chose to remain open, the owners of these establishments gave some version of "I disagree with the stay-at-home orders." Identify 10 people who you can interview on whether they think following the law should be required or discretionary for small firms during a pandemic.

Most philosophers, thinkers, and educators refer to the **legal** and **moral** norms of society in making ethical decisions. A key consideration for business decisions is whether the action is allowed by the law. For example, in the United States, federal law prohibits selling tobacco products, including cigarettes, cigars, and e-cigarettes, to anyone under 21 years of age. If you run a convenience store and knowingly sell tobacco products to underage customers, you are in violation of the law. Every business is expected to adhere to the law. Milton Friedman, who won the Noble Prize in economics, famously encouraged businesses to maximize their profits, as long as they stayed within the limits of the law. The **Friedman doctrine** states that firms should use their resources and engage in activities designed to increase their profits so long as they play within the rules of the game, that is, abide by the law of the land.

A second consideration for a business decision rests on whether it is considered morally acceptable in society. Decisions or actions that violate the moral standards of a society are frowned upon and discouraged, even if they are not sanctioned by law. You have probably heard of the casting couch in Hollywood. The **casting couch** is practiced when someone in a position of power expects sexual favors from another person in order to advance that person's career. In Hollywood, some media moguls were known to ask aspiring and struggling actors to perform sexual acts with and for them before giving them a role. There is no law that bars sexual liaisons in exchange for access to desirable work, but our society finds it, by and large, morally repugnant. When the *Boston Globe* named several photographers – many of them famous powerbrokers in the multibillion fashion industry – who it said solicited sex for work from young models, including minors, many reputed magazines like *Condé Nast* terminated their relationships with the accused photographers.

Sex-for-work behavior is not limited to so-called **glamor industries** obsessed with good looks and sexual oomph. Charlie Thompson, CEO and cofounder of The Clean Collective, shared how she was propositioned when she was pitching her company to raise funds. When she informed other acquaintances of her experiences, she learned she's far from alone, with many relating similar experiences.

Charlie Thompson, cofounder and CEO of The Clean Collective, was propositioned when she was trying to raise funds for her business.

10.2.1 Law and Morality as Two Criteria in Making Business Decisions

When one considers legal and moral criteria, there are four types of business decisions (see Figure 10.1). The key question one needs to ask is if a decision is (a) legal or illegal, and (b) moral or immoral. Considering the law and morality as two distinct dimensions of ethical decisions help us better understand the dilemmas many business owners face.

	Yes	No
Yes	Decision is legal and moral	Decision is legal but not moral
No	Decision is illegal but moral	Decision is neither legal nor moral

Legal (vertical) / Moral (horizontal)

FIGURE 10.1 Ethics-focused Typology of Business Decisions

In the first group are business decisions that violate both legal and moral standards (Moral No, Legal No). Let's say there is a business opportunity that is not legal and widely considered immoral in the society where you live. Would you pursue it? Child pornography is about a $3 billion business in the United States. Few people, however, would be willing to start a business in this area as they will not only be in violation of federal laws in the country, but would also likely be sanctioned in their social circles for engaging in something that is widely considered repugnant in American society.

From an ethical standpoint, business decisions that meet both legal and moral standards (Moral Yes, Legal Yes) are perhaps the easiest to make. For example, the Egyptian Coffee Shop, a fixture in the Little Egypt area of New York City calls itself the "first hookah lounge in America." City law allows smoking within hookah cafés if the smoking mixture is tobacco free. As long as the hookah it offers does not have tobacco, the café's owner, Labib Salama, is in compliance. Without tobacco, hookah is just flavored water inhaled through a tall, ornate pipe that sits on the floor, so there are no moral or legal issues.

Of course, not all hookahs are tobacco free, and many places around the country sell hookahs with tobacco. Tobacco is considered a **sin industry** in the United States and is taxed heavily. Sin industries involve products or services that are considered immoral, such as alcohol, tobacco, gambling, and pornography. Decisions that involve something that is legal but not moral are quite challenging. These decisions are allowed under the law, but can attract intense social scrutiny because they violate the moral standards of society. Take the case of Ashley Madison, an online dating service targeted at married folks. The company's slogan: "Life is short. Have an affair." Trish McDermott, a consultant who helped found the online dating giant Match.com, accused Ashley Madison of being a "business built on the backs of broken hearts, ruined marriages, and damaged families." When the company wanted to file an initial public offering (IPO), the backlash was intense. "Lots of people gamble, lots of people drink and smoke, and I don't have any objection to that, but this is something different. There is no way my firm will touch this deal with a 10-foot barge pole," said the chief executive of a major stockbrokerage firm. Sam Smith, CEO of finnCap, noted that even though Ashley Madison seemed to have strong financials, his company was not going to support them. "When you bring businesses to the market, you need to believe in them and get behind them," he observed.

Scott Lizza, owner of Monroe's in West Palm Beach, FL, had always understood it was difficult to operate a business that adhered to the law but violated society's moral standards (Legal Yes, Moral No), yet he had never thought it could cause him to go bankrupt. Monroe's is a strip club with 125 employees. "My business isn't illegal," says Scott, who calls his establishment an "adult night club." When the COVID-19 pandemic hit, Monroe first saw a decline in revenue, and then patrons stopped coming. However, unlike most other small businesses in the country, Monroe's was not eligible for the government-guaranteed loans aimed at keeping employees on the job. Small Business Administration (SBA) programs that helped small firms, including independent contractors and sole proprietorships, weren't available to Monroe's because businesses that provide services or live performances of a "prurient sexual nature" are banned from receiving SBA loans under federal regulations (see Figure 10.2 for the types of businesses excluded from SBA mandates). Keep in mind that these businesses pay taxes and are expected to adhere to all relevant legal requirements.

The ban on such businesses isn't limited to new SBA loans introduced in the CARES Act; it applies to the SBA's existing business-loan programs as well. In 2019, strip clubs in

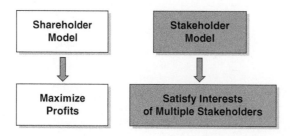

FIGURE 10.2 Shareholder Model Versus Stakeholder Model of Capitalism

TABLE 10.2

Types of Businesses Excluded for Ethical Reasons from SBA's Mandate

No.	Exclusion criteria	Example
1	Enterprises considered morally questionable by some	Strip clubs and marijuana stores
2	Businesses viewed as speculative	Oil wildcatting and finance companies
3	Companies that may be both morally questionable and speculative	Casinos
4	Miscellaneous	Lobbying firms

the United States generated a total of $8 billion in revenue, which was projected to grow at 4–5% before the coronavirus hit. Scott believes that though there was a time when his business was a place "you didn't want your wife to know you went," it now welcomed couples. "Proprietors within the strip clubs industry distanced themselves from the seedy past image associated with clubs," said a report by market research firm IBISWorld. "Instead, they marketed their establishments as high-class gentlemen's clubs and cocktail lounges that offer adult entertainment." SBA, however, doesn't see strip clubs as a business that federal money should support, in a time of crisis or outside of it (see Table 10.2).

There are also business decisions that may be moral, but are not legal (Moral Yes, Legal No). Like many bars in college towns around the country, Swamp Restaurant in Gainesville, FL, caters to college students. Though college drinking levels have declined slightly from peaks in the early 1980s, surveys find that more than 8 in 10 college students drink. This is a problem because minimum legal drinking age in all US states is 21 years, which means the majority of undergraduate college students are not legally allowed to drink. For many college-town bars, undergraduate students are a large part of their revenue. They require IDs from students, but fake IDs remain pervasive on campus. Possession of a fake or doctored driver's license is a felony. As a result, students have learned it is wiser to borrow – or buy – a driver's license from an older friend who bears a vague resemblance, as possession of another person's ID is only a misdemeanor. Bar owners know they are selling to underage drinkers, but they look the other way. "It's effortless to get a drink in a bar," says a former University of Florida undergraduate. "I had a fake ID and got turned away once in five years." Everyone, from parents and college presidents to cops and legislators, know there is rampant underage drinking in college towns. Alcohol "is a reality in the lives of 18-, 19- and 20-year-olds," as one college administrator put it, and college-town bars frequently lure students with two-for-one specials and Ladies Night promotions. Bar owners that have a business model predicated on selling alcoholic drinks to underage college kids are making a decision that is clearly illegal, even if it is not immoral by society's standards.

What Do You Think?

DNA Genetics Inc. is a marijuana producer in San Diego, CA. Like other marijuana producers, DNA found that pot sales soared during the early days of the 2020 COVID-19 shutdown. Cars inched for hours to reach the storefront as customers scrambled to stock up. However, as the pandemic dragged, sales cooled, and DNA saw fewer customers buying marijuana. The company laid off 12 of the 62 workers, and wanted a SBA-backed loan to help keep the rest employed. The SBA refused the company's loan application. Although marijuana is legal in about three dozen states – and deemed an essential service in some—it is illegal at the federal level. Do you think DNA should be eligible for federal help to stay afloat during the pandemic? What do you think are the issues with using public funds to help marijuana producers?

10.2.2 Ethics and the Role of Time and Place

Legal and moral standards may change with time or place, so that a business decision that is ethical in a particular situation may not be ethical in another time or place. For example, in the 1950s, many states allowed businesses to discriminate based on race, which is no longer allowed anywhere in the United States, as the legal and moral standards of the society underwent transformational change on this issue. Similarly, from the Industrial Revolution to the 1930s, American children routinely worked in a number of occupations, a practice that is now illegal in the United States and most other democratic countries. The fashion magazine *Cosmopolitan* once ran a story about an old Native American chieftain, who was given a tour of New York City in the early 1900s. On this excursion, he saw grand skyscrapers and the Brooklyn Bridge. He observed masses gathered in amusement at the circus and the poor huddled in tenements. Upon completion of the chieftain's journey, he was asked, "What is the most surprising thing you have seen?" The chieftain replied slowly with three words: "little children working." While child labor was once morally and legally accepted in the United States, it is no longer allowed in the country. Our legal and moral norms about child labor have undergone drastic change over the past century.

For some time during the 2020 pandemic, Pennsylvania closed all liquor stores considering as nonessential businesses, while other states – including many bordering Pennsylvania – considered liquor stores as essential businesses that were allowed to remain open. If a liquor store decided to open in Pennsylvania during the pandemic, it would be in violation of the state law, but the same would not be the case just across the state line in New York. Different places may have varying legal norms, as well as moral norms. As the seventeenth-century French scientist Blaise Pascal famously observed, "There are truths on this side of the Pyrenees that are falsehoods on the other."

The notion that an action may be ethically acceptable in one time and place, but not in another, is called **ethical relativism**. Variations in laws, social customs, traditions, or core values frequently give rise to different standards about right or wrong, fair or unfair. For example, Chinese and Japanese cultures prioritize collective good over individual benefits in a way that many Americans find either troubling or inconsistent with American norms. When Allan Guberski, who works for the Chinese company Haier in South Carolina, visited the company's factories in China, he was impressed by how each worker there was seen as an independent unit, rewarded for inventing ways to save the company money, and punished for wasting its resources. Gerald Reeves, Haier's human resources director in South Carolina, was impressed by how disciplined Chinese workers were. "When they had their end-of-day group meetings, they stood in nice straight lines. I'll never get my people here to stand in lines like that," he says.

Relativism does not mean that the views of an individual (or a small group) constitute sufficient justification for determining what is ethical (**naive relativism**). Instead, there must be a stable group reference point for reference (known as **cultural relativism**). Basing ethical decisions on an individual's whims and preferences risks collapsing the social order.

While ethical standards may change with time and place, there are also some universal ethical prescriptions. According to the notion of **ethical universalism**, the fundamental conceptions of right and wrong are universal and transcend social, religious, and cultural barriers. For example, all major world religions and cultures endorse the **golden rule**: Treat others as you want to be treated. Simon Blackburn, a modern English philosopher and the author of *Ethics: A Very Short Introduction*, observed that some form of the golden rule can be found in every major ethical tradition in the world.

Comprehension Check

1. Explain how the law helps make ethical decisions.
2. What is a sin industry?
3. Explain ethical relativism.

Module 10.3 Should Ethics Be Taught?

Is it useful to teach students, aspiring business owners, and others about ethical decision-making and socially responsible behaviors in small firms? It depends on who you ask. The different views on this topic can be organized into five major schools of thoughts (see Table 10.3). There are the **apologists**, who believe that all business is inherently moral. From this perspective, business – the activity of production and trade for profit – is, by definition, virtuous. The marketplace in which businesses operate is structured so that it's got built-in ethical correctors: If you do not treat your workers right or are not responsible about the products you're selling, people will stop buying from you. For apologists, the very act of producing and trading goods and services that help us survive and enjoy life is ethical. The pursuit of profits creates wealth that makes human life better. For this reason, apologists believe that business is always a force for good, and businesspeople are moral actors who should maximize their own returns without regard to others.

A second group comprises those who believe that once people have been told about the need to be ethical in their decisions and behaviors, they will always behave in a manner that is appropriate. This group – the **naivists** – sees ethical failures in business as stemming from a lack of ethics training during one's education. Raging social controversies and heightened public concerns over troubling events (e.g. Watergate) led colleges and universities to include the teaching of ethics in their curriculum. Today, it is a given that an undergraduate student – regardless of whether he or she is in literature or business or engineering – will come across some discussion of ethics during college. Where schools disagree is whether the teaching of ethics should be concentrated in a particular course or diffused throughout the curriculum. An ethics course, or two, should be a life-changing experience by helping students discover "new and fascinating intellectual incentives" to do the right thing, explained Andrew Daines, a graduate of Cornell University, in a letter to the *New York Times*.

Stand-alone ethics courses, however, risk "compartmentalizing" the issue for students, as if ethical questions are not applicable to all business disciplines. For this reason, many believe that most – if not all – college courses should include an ethics component to guide students in the workplace. When asked whether ethical lessons from college courses last 10 or 20 years out, some believe that they will because what you do then is based on what you learned and did now. Boston University's School of Management introduced a required ethics course for freshman business students, tasked instructors in other business classes to incorporate ethics into their lessons, and also overhauled a senior seminar to reinforce ethics topics. Their logic: Hit the students hard when they first get here, remind them of these principles throughout their core classes, and hit them once again before they leave.

TABLE 10.3

Five Major Schools of Thought on Teaching Business Ethics

School of thought	Main belief about ethics education
Apologists	All business is inherently moral.
Naivists	Ethical failures in business stem from a lack of ethics training during one's education.
Nihilists	There is no point in teaching ethics in college.
Purists	Business is inherently immoral.
Realists	Ethics can and should be emphasized throughout one's life, in college and outside.

KEY TAKEAWAY

Not everyone believes that business ethics can be or should be taught in college.

A third group – the **nihilists** – believes there is no point in teaching ethics. Nihilists believe that people set their ethical compass based on the messages they receive from parents and mass media. Schools and colleges have a negligible role to play in the development of ethics. George Rupp, President of Columbia University, argued that universities cannot be expected to "substitute for what the family has done or religious bodies have done." From this perspective, by the time, someone is in college or thinking of starting a business in their adult life, it's already too late to teach them about ethics. "To some extent, I'm a believer that everything you need to know you learned in kindergarten," says Kenneth Merchant, who teaches about corporate governance and ethics at University of South California.

Interactive Exercise

Identify seven professors who have taught you in college and pose them one question: "Should colleges and universities teach business ethics, and why?" Based on their response to this question, can you classify them into one of the five schools of thought identified here? Do you find answers that do not fit any of these five schools of thought?

For the **purists**, the very phrase "business ethics" or "ethical business" is an oxymoron, a contradiction in terms. In his book, *What They Teach You at Harvard Business School: My Two Years Inside the Cauldron of Capitalism*, the British-educated journalist Philip Delves Broughton writes that no matter how hard it tries, "business can never escape the fact that it is the practice of potentially thieving, treacherous, lying human beings." This is not an uncommon position. More than 50 years back, the *Harvard Business Review* published an article comparing business to poker, where bluffing – but not outright cheating – was perfectly legitimate and commonplace. Business was seen not as an arena for displays of high ethical standards but a game where the goal is to win by embracing all manners of tricks. The rough-and-tumble world of business, purists believe, is just not conducive to ivory tower aspirations of ethics and morality.

Realists are people who believe that ethics can and should be emphasized throughout one's life, in college and outside. From this perspective, young people deserve the most helpful readings and the most stimulating materials for ethical reflection that can be developed. In his book *Can Ethics Be Taught?*, Harvard professor Tom Piper emphasized that universities play an important role in developing the mental strength and cognitive sophistication necessary to recognize the presence of ethical dilemmas and to understand explicitly avoidable and unavoidable harms. Realists understand that students may not like being told what is considered virtuous, but they generally appreciate knowing about how others before them have successfully traversed complex ethical issues and learning about how to arrive at thoughtful judgments.

Regardless of which camp you find yourself to be in, the fact in American higher education today is that all colleges and universities emphasize ethics in their curriculum. The point of these courses, for the most part, is to think more deeply about practical ethical issues – about the reasons to be concerned, the arguments for and against alternative actions, and the possible consequences for other people.

What Do You Think?

A business student wrote on College Confidential, an online message board that "it's not like Johnny is going to be at the cusp of committing fraud and then think back to his b-school days and think, "gee, Professor Goody Two Shoes wouldn't approve." Implicit in this student's comment is that things we learn in college, including business ethics, should last us a lifetime and influence our decisions throughout life. Do you think it is reasonable to expect that what you study in college should last you a lifetime? If you were tasked with developing a plan to teach business ethics, what would you do differently from the way it is currently done at your school?

Comprehension Check

1. All business is inherently moral. Explain.
2. Some people believe that the term *business ethics* is an oxymoron. Explain.
3. What is the nihilist argument to teaching ethics?

Module 10.4 Corporate Social Responsibility

As discussed earlier, many people believe that the primary responsibility of a business is to make more money for its owners – the so-called **shareholder model** of capitalism. The famous Nobel laureate Milton Friedman was an emphatic proponent of this idea, which is why it is also called the **Friedman doctrine**. A contrarian idea that has gained popularity in recent years is the **stakeholder model**, which emphasizes that firms should balance the interests of all stakeholders, including owners, employees, customers, suppliers, communities, and society at large (see Figure 10.2). In 2019, the Business Roundtable, a national association of chief executives of America's leading companies, made a public declaration signed by 181 CEOs who committed to lead their companies to benefit all stakeholders. Since 1997, each version of the Business Roundtable had endorsed the idea that business exists principally to serve its owners, but with the 2019 declaration, there was a radical shift in the association's position (https://www.businessroundtable. org/business-roundtable-redefines-the-purpose-of-a-corporation-to-promote-an-economy-that-serves-all-americans):

> Each of our stakeholders is essential. We commit to deliver value to all of them, for the future success of our companies, our communities and our country.

When a firm specifically takes into account the impact of its decisions and actions on the well-being of its employees, local communities, the environment, and society at large, and the owners invoke a social conscience in operating the business, the firm is said to be socially responsible. Social responsibility, therefore, goes beyond participating in community service projects and donating money to charities and other worthy causes. It involves taking actions that earn the respect and trust of a wide range of shareholders by operating ethically and trying to make a difference in bettering society.

KEY TAKEAWAY

Modern firms operate in a world where they are expected to balance the interests of multiple stakeholders.

Firms that undertake CSR initiatives can direct them at the company's **triple bottom line**, which refers to focusing on three performance criteria: economic (*profits*), social (*people*), and environmental (*planet*). The **economic performance** of a firm is captured by the profits it earns for its owners. **Social performance** of a firm refers to the various initiatives targeted at internal and external stakeholders other than owners. This includes taking care of employees, community involvement, and going above and beyond its obligations to satisfy customers. **Environmental performance** pertains to the ecological footprint of a company, and the steps it takes to reduce its impact on the planet. When a company succeeds simultaneously in all three performance dimensions (see Figure 10.3), it is said to achieve truly high levels of CSR. Foodshed Investors NY is a band of 30 angel investors – including retired entrepreneurs and former Wall Streeters – who invest in "sustainable, small and local food and farm businesses." For investors in this group, social

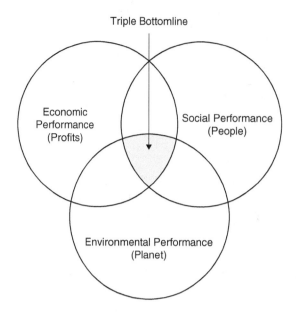

Triple Bottomline

Economic Performance (Profits)

Social Performance (People)

Environmental Performance (Planet)

FIGURE 10.3 Triple Bottom Line Involves Focusing on Profits, People, and Planet

good is as important as profit goals, which can be modest. Made by Lukas veggie burgers that already sell in 50 supermarkets – including Whole Foods – is the kind of ventures Foodshed wants to invest in.

Kirsten Dickerson is founder and CEO of Raven + Lily, a fashion and lifestyle brand that partners with artisans around the world to employ more than 1500 low-income and formerly enslaved women. She shares that she turned down investors if she did not feel that "they were committed to the triple bottom line concept" that is at the heart of her business.

Firms that exhibit a strong commitment to CSR may find themselves recognized on lists such as *Corporate Responsibility* magazine's "100 Best Corporate Citizens" or *Corporate Knights* magazine's "Global 100 most sustainable corporations." Some companies may also opt for **B-Corp certification**, which not only allows but legally obligates them to consider profits, people, and planet in their decision-making. Singlebrook Technology is a 12-person Web development B-Corp in Ithaca, NY. The company gets 35–40% of its business from other B-Corps – to whom it offers a 30% discount. Singlebrook also tries to buy from B-Corps. "It's in our employee handbook that if we are going to buy something, we first have to check to see whether there's a B-Corp offering that service," says CEO, Elisa Miller-Out. For example, when it needed postcards Singlebrook went to the B-Corp Greenprinter. Table 10.4 shares some of the experiences of B-Corp companies.

Interactive Exercise

Check out the website for the B-Corp certification: www. bcorporation.net. Click on the icon that says Directory. Search for B-Corp certified companies in your state. Are there companies in this list that you recognize? What do you think motivated them to choose B-Corp certification?

There are also companies that make false claims or provide misleading information about their CSR activities. For example, **greenwashing** refers to the use of deception in order to persuade others that a firm's products and goals are environmentally safe and thus more planet-friendly than they actually are. Some estimates suggest that as many as

TABLE 10.4

Some B-Corp Companies and Their Experiences

Company	Location	B-Corp experience
All Good Products	California	B-Corp folks came to our headquarters and did an extensive on-site audit of our business; they looked at numbers, including energy bills, inspected facilities and manufacturing practices, interviewed employees, and took it all into account for calculating our "score".
Opticos	California	We take the B-Corp assessment once or twice a year. Every time we take it we find new things we should be doing.
Cascade Engineering	Michigan	Triple bottom line has been in the company's DNA since the beginning.
IceStone	New York	There is long-term brand integrity around it. We were able to get into the marketplace quicker because of the story behind the company. If we were just another countertop material maybe we wouldn't have been received so well. I think it improves our bottom line.
Uncommon Goods	New York	The greatest upside is internal – you get people who want to work at a company that's sharing a mission.
Better World Books	Indiana	We were already a B-Corp. When B Lab negotiated discounts with salesforce.com, we jumped on it. We're such a big Salesforce user that we've saved hundreds of thousands of dollars just through that relationship alone.

TABLE 10.5

Seven Sins of Greenwashing

Sin	Meaning	Example
Hidden trade-off	A product may be green based on a narrow set of attributes without attention to other important environmental issues	Paper does not become environmentally preferable because it comes from a sustainably harvested forest. Other facets of the paper-making process, such as greenhouse gas emissions or chlorine use in bleaching, may be equally important
No proof	Claims not substantiated by easily accessible supporting information or by a reliable third-party certification	Many brands of facial tissues or toilet tissue products claim various percentages of postconsumer recycled content without providing evidence
Vagueness	Claim so poorly defined or broad that their real meaning is misunderstood by the consumer	All natural is not necessarily good. Mercury, arsenic, and formaldehyde are all naturally occurring, and poisonous
Worshiping fake certifications	Claims of third-party endorsement where no such endorsement exists	Truly Organic gave product samples to marketers and online influencers that had labels featuring false certifications. The company took a document issued to another company, erased that name, and added its own.
Irrelevance	Claims that may be truthful but are unimportant or unhelpful for consumers	CFCs (chlorofluorocarbons) are banned under the Montreal protocol, so claims of CFC-free are essentially meaningless
Lesser of two evils	Claims that may be true but distract from the overall adverse impact of the category as a whole	Organic cigarettes
Fibbing	Claims that are simply false	Many products falsely claim to be Energy Star certified

95% of the products marketed as eco-friendly had committed at least one of the "seven sins" of greenwashing, which include relatively benign acts like using weak data to more serious deceptions like inventing bogus certifications (see Table 10.5 for the list of seven greenwashing sins and their explanations). The apparel maker Lululemon Athletica, for example, marketed a line of clothes made partly out of seaweed that supposedly had health benefits, including releasing amino acids, minerals, and vitamins into the skin. An independent lab's analysis of the fabrics, however, found no meaningful difference in mineral content between the line of clothing and standard cotton T-shirts.

Growing concerns about greenwashing have motivated many small business owners to stop touting how their sustainable ingredients and production methods help the environment, and instead focus on the value their products deliver. Gunilla Eisenberg, founder of Gunilla Skin Alchemy, worked hard to source eco-friendly oils for her high-end beauty products and find a socially responsible manufacturer. Yet, she opted to focus her messaging on the efficacy and quality of the product. She has the sourcing and manufacturing information on the company's website, and each bottle notes the oil is "wild crafted" (that is, made from plants collected in the wild). Her reasoning: "I'm not pushing it as an eco-product because at the end of the day, I have to be able to charge a premium for my product in order to keep the level of quality I have—in order to be truly eco—and it's easier to do that with a luxury-branded product than an eco-branded product."

The *moral case* for CSR boils down to being the right thing to do. From this perspective, contributions to the well-being of society are expected of every business. Business owners are expected to recognize that their firms have an obligation to be a good citizen of society. There is also a school of thought – **implied social contract theory** – that stipulates that in return for the license to operate from society, a business assumes the obligation to do its fair share to promote societal welfare and avoid doing harm. The firm has a moral responsibility to operate honorably and display good citizenship because the society has allowed it to exist.

What Do You Think?

Your cousin George works in the evening and on the weekends at his family's small restaurant Nourish in Fargo, ND. George tells you that he is thinking about labeling a freshly squeezed orange juice they offer as "non-GMO" and then selling it at a premium price. Given increasing health awareness among young people, you think George has a good idea. When you mention it to your small business professor, she tells you that there are no GMO (genetically modified organism) oranges on the market. In other words, George would be making an "absence claim" – asserting a meaningless distinction between products in order to make theirs seem superior. What do you do now? Should you talk to George, his parents (your aunt and uncle), or just let it be?

The business case for CSR rests on the idea that there are several commercial reasons why companies should be good responsible citizens and devote time and resources to social responsibility initiatives. These reasons are given as follows:

1. *Greater buyer patronage.* When a company engages in socially responsible practices, it may increase its appeal to customers who prefer to do business with such companies. Higher Ground Roasters, based in Leeds, AL, specializes in 100% certified organic, fair trade, and shade-grown coffees. The coffee bean industry has the notoriety of being one of the largest sites of forced farm labor worldwide. The International Labor Organization estimates that 250 million child slaves are working to produce coffee beans around the world. The emphasis on **fair trade** coffee appeals to customers who favor ethical treatments of farm laborers and coffee growers. On its website (www.highergroundroasters.com), Higher Ground publicly affirms its commitment to "better beans by fairer means."

2. *Superior employee relations.* Companies with strong CSR commitment may be in a better position to attract and retain employees compared to those that are focused only on profit maximization. Many workers want to work in companies with a purpose. The paycheck is important, but they also care for purpose. Professor Amy Wrzesniewski, who teaches organizational behavior at Yale School of Management, believes that as many as one-third of employees see their work as a

calling and want to connect it to a higher purpose. Travelzoo, founded by journalist Ralph Bartel, emphasizes a shared sense of being part of something greater than themselves to motivate and unite its employees. "If we all traveled, there would be significantly more peace on Earth," Travelzoo Chief Executive Chris Loughlin tells his employees.

3. *Lower costs*. Doing the right thing can sometimes also result in significant cost savings for the company. It is commonplace today to see hotels give their customers the option to have their linens and towels washed daily or reuse them for two or more days. For many customers, it's an easy way to do their part for the environment. Less washing of towels and linens means less use of soap, water, and energy. At an average of 150,000 pounds of daily laundry at a large hotel, the savings can be considerable, both from a business point of view and an environmental perspective. Some hotels are now giving customers the option to completely opt out of housekeeping for the entire duration of their stay. As part of their "Make a Green Choice" program, Starwood Hotels and Resorts Worldwide offers hotel credits or points in its reward program. "I don't need my bed made every day and can certainly use the same towel three mornings in a row," shared Dr. Stuart Gitlow, a psychiatrist who travels for conferences. At the Marmara Manhattan, a luxury hotel and residence on New York's Upper East Side, guests who forgo housekeeping for three days receive a $20 discount for each night they stay without the service.

4. *Opportunities for revenue enhancements*. The drive toward social responsibility may lead companies to introduce new products and services that offer novel prospects for revenues. John Mackey grew up watching his mother fascinated by labor-saving devices like TV dinners and canned foods that one could just open up, pour out, and eat. She saw it as a revolution, a release from the kind of cooking bondage that housewives had endured for a long time. For John, however, it was inauthentic plastic food. John was attracted to natural food because he started believing what you ate affected your health and well-being, longevity, and how you felt. At 25, John and his then girlfriend borrowed $45,000 from family and friends to open a small vegetarian natural foods place called Saferway in Austin, TX, which in two years led to the first Whole Foods store. By some estimates, people are willing to pay as much as 50% more (and sometimes higher) for products labeled natural or organic.

5. *Superior reputation*. Companies that place a strong emphasis on operating in a socially responsible manner are able to earn a superior reputation for quality. Ben & Jerry's, a well-known ice-cream brand, has built a reputation for caring more about people than profit (making plenty of money in the process). "The more engaged in the community we've been, the more money we've made," says Ben Cohen, one half of the founding team. Companies that do the right thing protect themselves from the wrath of consumers, environmental and human rights activist groups who are quick to criticize firms they believe to be out of line. Instead, engaging in socially responsible practices can generate positive publicity for the company and influence like-minded or sympathetic buyers to give the company's products a try.

Did you know that 67% of all employees prefer to work for socially responsible companies, and 55% of consumers say they are willing to pay extra for products sold by companies committed to having a positive social impact? Of course, we know that "willing" is not the same as actually doing, but it does give us a sense of the interest employees and customers have in companies that behave responsibly toward their various stakeholders.

Comprehension Check

1. Explain triple bottom line.
2. Explain implied social contract theory.
3. What is the stakeholder model for CSR?

Module 10.5 Introduction to Ethical Frameworks

How does one do the right thing? This question has perplexed philosophers and thinkers for centuries. The ancient Greek philosopher, statesman Aristotle followed his predecessors Socrates and Plato in placing ethics (virtues) to be central to a well-lived life. For him, one's happiness was the highest goal and the end toward which all of one's efforts are to be directed.

KEY TAKEAWAY

Philosophers and thinkers have wondered for centuries about how one does the right thing.

Utilitarianism, generally associated with the nineteenth-century philosopher Jeremy Bentham, focuses on the consequences of a decision. Bentham described it as "greatest good for the greatest number of people." The standard utilitarianism process is to start by identifying all alternatives in a given situation, determine costs and benefits for various stakeholders (e.g. shareholders, employees, customers, suppliers, competitors, community) for each alternative, and selecting the alternative that results in (or tends to produce) the greatest net good (i.e. also referred to as benefit utility, happiness, pleasure, or absence of pain). The **human rights approach** arises from our existence as human beings. A decision is considered ethical if it respects the fundamental rights of affected individuals. Fundamental rights refer to one's right to life, health, and safety. The typical human rights process involves determining the human rights of each stakeholder and the duties owed to other stakeholders, weighing the relative significance of these rights and duties, and selecting an alternative that best respects the rights and duties of individual stakeholders. **Egoism** is concerned with maximizing the long-term self-interest of the decision-maker. Egoism (i.e. self-interest) is often attributed to the eighteenth-century economist Adam Smith (who was interested in **conditional egoism**: self-interest, but only when it leads to betterment of society). Most modern philosophers believe that self-interest can be a criterion for ethical decision-making, but only if it is not based on excessive forms of self-interest such as greed, selfishness, avarice, or hedonism, and does not lead to direct unnecessary harm to others.

When it comes to ethical decision-making, another major criterion is whether the actions can be considered just or fair, the **justice approach**. Seems simple, but fairness means different things to different people. **Distributive justice** pertains to equitable or fair distribution of the benefits and burdens imposed by a decision or action. **Procedural justice** refers to fairness in the procedures for decision-making. **Compensatory justice** relates to appropriately compensating people for a past harm or injustice (e.g. restitution) resulting from an intentional (as opposed to accidental) decision or action. **Retributive justice** focuses on punishing a decision-maker that has inflicted harm on others, as long as it is established that they were actually responsible for the harm, and the punishment is consistent with and proportionate to the harm inflicted on others.

A common framework for making ethical decisions is the *golden rule*, which refers to treating others as you would want to be treated yourself. Melissa Powell, COO of the Allure Group, advises business people to treat employees and customers as they would want to be treated themselves. The **extended golden rule** calls for treating others as you would want your family to be treated. Some small firms even try to create a family-like atmosphere at work. Decagon Devices, a Pullman, Washington, D.C., scientific instruments and sensor maker with about 70 employees, is one such company. CEO Tamsin Jolley believes treating employees like family involves trying to know the names of all employees, their spouses, and their children. It also involves providing great health-care coverage and other benefits, so that when they come to work they don't have to worry about those things. The company also does weekly lunch meetings with all employees at which employees prepare meal for their colleagues, a summer picnic and Christmas party, and offers activities like soccer and a slot track game that employees can enjoy together on their a breaks.

KEY TAKEAWAY

Almost all major cultural traditions of the world recognize some form of "treat others as you would want others to treat you or your family."

America's most famous investor, Warren Buffett emphasizes the **newspaper test** as a guide to making ethical decisions. Buffet advises decision-makers to consider how they would feel if the decision they made was discussed on the front page of a newspaper by an intelligent – though unfriendly – reporter. "It's pretty simple," the billionaire investor, sometimes called the Sage of Omaha, says, "if the decision passes that test, it's okay. If anything is too close to the lines, it's out."

Interactive Exercise

Interview a small business owner you know. Alternatively, you can interview a professor who teaches a course related to small business or entrepreneurship. Ask them how they make decisions when confronted with an ethical dilemma. Is their answer consistent with any of the ethical frameworks discussed in this section?

Another guide to ethical decision-making comes in the form of the **children test**, which suggests asking if you would want your child (or grandchild) to engage in the same behavior now or in the future. People generally have higher expectations for their children's or grandchildren's behavior than they do for their own. Consequently, they tend to behave more ethically when they consider that their children are observing, judging, and emulating their behavior. A former Israeli Prime Minister, after being convicted of receiving bribes from a businessman in exchange for favorable building approvals, shared with the judges: "The real punishment is the shame. What do I say to my grandchild?" Another version of the children test is the **mother test**, which asks the decision-maker to consider whether how they would feel if their mother found out what they had done.

Yet, another guide to ethical decision-making is the **sleep test**, which focuses on whether the decision will make you feel guilty and keep you awake at night. A businessman who had gone bust worked out a deal to pay back his debtors, even though he wasn't legally obligated to do so. When asked why he paid them back after liquidating all his assets, his response was "I've got to sleep at night." Whether you are able to sleep at night can be one measure gauging the ethicality of your decision. The sleep test is also sometimes described as the **mirror test**, which asks how you would feel looking in the mirror after making the decision. Dr. Jeffrey Wigand, who was the whistleblower at the tobacco firm Brown & Williamson for their use of a dangerous chemical additive in their cigarettes, when asked why he risked taking on his employer, said, "By this time I had a significant problem looking at myself in the mirror."

What Do You Think?

Breathe Easy manufacturers and sells high-end mouthwash. The couple who owns the company wants their daughter Emily to join them in growing the company after she graduates. One day when Emily is helping to promote the company on social media, she comes across a user's comment that Breathe Easy is being unethical because the mouthwash contained a cheap form of alcohol possibly deleterious to health. When she asks her father about this, he tells her that "We're in a highly competitive industry. If we're going to stay in business, we have to look for profit wherever the law permits. We don't make the laws. We obey them. Then why do we have to put up with this 'holier than thou' talk about ethics? It's sheer hypocrisy. We're not in business to promote ethics." Emily has been quite distraught ever since. As her best friend, what would you advise Emily to do?

A final framework is the **role-reversal test**, which urges the decision-maker to put themselves in the place of the person who would be affected by their decision and to view the decision through their eyes. In other words, how would you feel about being on the receiving end of the decision or behavior you are about to undertake? For example, when refusing to pay a subcontractor for a work they did for you, perhaps ask if you would be okay tomorrow if someone did the same to you.

The Newspaper Test

"It took us a lot of time to get here. We can lose it in a few minutes" if we behave unethically. This is Warren Buffett's message to all his employees. Buffett is widely considered among the most respected figures in Corporate America. One reason for his stellar public reputation: strong commitment to ethics.

Forbes.com

Watch the video online at: https://www.youtube.com/watch?v=GNF793Inghg

Comprehension Check

1. Explain egoism, and distinguish it from conditional egoism.
2. What is the newspaper test?
3. Explain the justice approach to ethical decision-making.

Summary

Warren Buffett, CEO and chairman of Berkshire Hathaway, says that "it takes 20 years to build a reputation and five minutes to ruin it. If you think about that, you'll do things differently." The overall message of this chapter is that ethics and CSR are important considerations for any business. Adhering to laws and regulations is a primary objective for any firm. Yet, good ethics is good business. Firms that behave unethically risk getting derailed, as employees, customers, and other stakeholders have increasingly become less tolerant of ethical violations. When firms behave ethically and act in a socially responsible manner, the company thrives in the long term. Information sharing across the Internet reveals there is growing appreciation of ethical firms.

World of Books

Intentional Integrity: How Smart Companies Can Lead an Ethical Revolution by Robert Chesnut

Better Business: How the B Corp Movement Is Remaking Capitalism by Christopher Marquis

The Triple Bottom Line: How Today's Best Run Companies Are Achieving Economic, Social, and Environmental Success by Andrew Savitz

In the Movies

Jerry Maguire is a slick sports agent who has a moral epiphany one day. He writes a heartfelt company-wide memo calling for sports agents to take care of their clients. When he is fired for expressing his views, Jerry starts his own management firm. Jerry finds himself alone in his crisis of conscience, except for one colleague (a single mother) and one client (an egomaniacal difficult football player). Starting his own business and running it based on his new moral philosophy of clients come first is more difficult than Jerry had imagined. A critic described the movie *Jerry Maguire* as "magic on celluloid – fresh, funny, romantic, and upbeat."

Live Exercise

One evening when you are out for drinks with friends, you share Johnny's story with them. When you tell them about SoapStandle sales on Amazon, your friends share some ideas that you had never considered before:

1. Join a Facebook group called "Amazon Reviews" and promise people a full refund if they did the following on the retailer's site: (a) Write a positive review for the SoapStandle, (b) post photos of the product, and (c) rate it five stars. Why would you do this? You are guaranteed five star reviews. As the number of items sold on Amazon has increased, items with five-star reviews are likely to sell much better than others.

2. Hire a company that will help SoapStandle get the "Amazon's Choice" badge. Amazon introduced the "Amazon's Choice" service as a way to suggest products to shoppers who make purchases using Alexa, its voice-controlled assistant. Amazon says the badge will appear next to select "highly rated, well-priced" items. The company you will hire will manipulate specific keywords to ensure the SoapStandle is included in the recommendation engine.

3. Pay a broker to boost your Amazon ratings. In exchange for payments ranging from about $80 to more than $2000, brokers for Amazon employees offer internal sales metrics and reviewers' email addresses, as well as a service to delete negative reviews.

You patiently hear out your friends, but are resistant to trying out their ideas. "Well, if you don't like our suggestions, at least mention to your friend Johnny and see what he thinks," they say. As the evening winds down and you walk home, you find yourself wondering if these ideas are worth taking to Johnny. You also wonder if your friends have a point when they say that everyone is doing these things. "Well, you can't run a successful business these days, without trying some new creative ideas," your friend Sam had said right before you left. What should you do?

Things to Remember

LO 10.1   Recognize the main reasons for businesses to behave ethically
- Firms should behave ethically and be responsible toward society because it is the right thing to do.
- Firms should behave ethically because customers, employees, or suppliers appreciate such behavior.
- Ethical principles and standards can be applied to the decisions and actions of firms, including the work-related conduct of their owners and employees.
- Firms have obligations toward their various stakeholders, including employees, customers, suppliers, and the community within which the firm operates.

LO 10.2   Distinguish between legal and moral standards for ethical behavior
- The urge to make money and earn a profit should operate within some constraints set by society.
- A key consideration for business decisions is whether the action is allowed by law.
- Business decisions should be made within what is considered morally acceptable in society.
- Business decisions that meet both legal and moral standards are perhaps the easiest to make.
- Sin industries involve products or services that are considered legal but immoral in society.
- Decisions that involve something that is legal but not moral are quite challenging.
- Some business decisions may be moral but not legal.
- Business decisions that are neither legal nor moral should be avoided, even if they can generate substantial profits.
- Legal and moral standards may change with time or place, so that a business decision that is ethical in a particular situation may not be ethical in another time or place.
- Variations in laws, social customs, traditions, and core values frequently give rise to different standards about right or wrong, fair or unfair, resulting in ethical relativism.

LO 10.3   **Outline the arguments in favor of and against teaching business ethics**
- Apologists believe all business is inherently moral.
- Naivists see ethical failures in business as stemming from a lack of ethics training during one's education.
- Nihilists believe there is no point in teaching ethics because people set their ethical compass based on the messages they receive from parents and mass media.
- Purists consider the very phrase "business ethics" or "ethical business" to be an oxymoron, a contradiction in terms.
- Realists believe that ethics can and should be emphasized throughout one's life, in college and outside.

LO 10.4   **Explain the importance of corporate social responsibility**
- The shareholder model of capitalism posits that the primary responsibility of a business is to make more money for its owners.
- The stakeholder model emphasizes that firms should balance the interests of all stakeholders, including owners, employees, customers, suppliers, communities, and society at large.
- The triple bottom-line approach focuses on three performance criteria: economic (profits), social (people), and environmental (planet).
- Economic performance of a firm is captured by the profits it earns for its owners.
- Social performance of a firm refers to the various initiatives targeted at internal and external stakeholders other than owners.
- Environmental performance pertains to the ecological footprint of the company.
- B-Corp certification legally obligates companies to consider profits, people, and the planet in their decision-making.
- Greenwashing involves the use of deception to persuade others that a firm's products and goals are environmentally safe and thus more planet-friendly than they actually are.
- The moral case for CSR boils down to "It's the right thing to do."
- Implied social contract theory stipulates that in return for a license to operate from society, a business assumes the obligation to do its fair share to promote societal welfare and avoid doing harm.

LO 10.5   **Describe basic frameworks to guide ethical behaviors**
- Utilitarianism is concerned with the greatest overall good for society.
- The human rights approach focuses on respect for the fundamental rights of affected individuals.
- Egoism pertains to maximizing the long-term self-interest of the decision-maker.
- The justice approach emphasizes that actions should be considered just or fair.
- The golden rule is about treating others as you would want to be treated yourself.
- The extended golden rule calls for treating others as you would want your family to be treated.
- The newspaper test focuses on how one would feel if the decision they made was discussed on the front page of a newspaper.
- Asking if you would want your child (or grandchild) to engage in the same behavior now or in future is part of the children test.
- The mother test asks the decision-maker to consider how they would feel sharing their decision or action with their mother.
- The sleep test focuses on whether the decision will make you feel guilty and keep you awake at night.
- The mirror test asks how you would feel looking in the mirror after making the decision.
- The role-reversal test urges the decision-maker to put themselves in the place of the person who would be affected by their decision and view the decision through their eyes.

Key Terms

moral argument
business argument
business ethics
corporate social
    responsibility
giveback companies
selfishness
legal standards
moral standards
Friedman doctrine
casting couch
glamor industries
sin industry

ethical relativism
naive relativism
cultural relativism
ethical universalism
golden rule
apologists
naivists
nihilists
purists
realists
shareholder model
Friedman doctrine
stakeholder model

social performance
environmental
    performance
implied social con-
    tract theory
triple bottom line
B-Corp certification
greenwashing
fair trade
utilitarianism
human rights approach
egoism
conditional egoism

justice approach
distributive justice
procedural justice
compensatory justice
retributive justice
extended golden rule
newspaper test
children test
mother test
sleep test
mirror test
role-reversal test

Experiential Exercise

For this exercise, pick one of three options based on your interest:

1. Draper James, Hollywood actor Reese Witherspoon's fashion business, announced that it would give away free dresses to teachers during the 2020 pandemic.

2. LuLaRoe, a multilevel marketing company, asks women to buy inventory at a wholesale price and then sell it for retail as independent salespeople.

3. Shelley Luther, owner of Salon a la Mode in Dallas, opened her hair salon in violation of her state's stay-at-home order during the Covid-19 pandemic.

If you need to do some preliminary research to decide which one you prefer, you can search about them on the Internet.

Once you have settled on the option for this exercise, you are asked to do the following:

1. Based on just the facts you find in your research, describe what happened so that someone who knows nothing about the particular issue gets to know the basics.

2. Consider the discussion of ethics in this chapter, and relate the principles and concepts you have learned to the facts of the option you researched.

3. Do you see an ethical problem in the option you researched?

Leadership and Its Challenges

The binding constraint on the growth of a business arises from the limited capacities of the person(s) running it.

EDITH PENROSE

11.0 Introduction

Courses on small business management and entrepreneurship generally focus on identifying and exploiting potentially profitable opportunities. Enterprising individuals need to become skilled at pursuing new opportunities, but they also need to gain the personal and professional skills needed to manage the business they operate; otherwise, it may all amount to naught. "It is shocking how often businesses fail because of the personality flaws and deep-seated traumas of their founders and execs," observes Garry Tan, managing partner at startup investor Initialized Capital.

Anyone who runs a business that employs one or more individuals is taking on the responsibilities of a leader – someone who influences others to work toward a goal. Unfortunately, business owners often do not see themselves as leaders, perhaps because they find themselves occupied with the day-to-day operational work associated with the smooth running of the business. Yet, unless a business wants to remain a tiny one-person firm forever, leadership is likely to play an important role in the growth trajectory of the business. This chapter examines leadership issues and challenges that small firms face as they grow and thrive. Our focus is on leading the firm well and fostering a healthy culture in one's firm, two key responsibilities of a business owner. These two entrepreneurial tasks unfortunately get little attention until something goes terribly wrong, and by then

SPOTLIGHT | Green Gables: The Short Life of a Bed-and-Breakfast

Frania Shelley-Grielen was a real-estate title closer in New York when she decided to run an inn surrounded by nature. She searched for places in travel magazines, eventually landing on a 100-year-old four-bedroom, four-bath house near Clearwater, FL, that had already been a bed-and-breakfast before. Frania loved the property. When she saw "the dock on the bayou and the bay on the corner with all their golden sunsets, the pelicans, egrets, ibises, herons and osprey, the century-old oaks dripping Spanish moss and trees covered with grapefruits and oranges", she thought, "I could do this, run this place. I can make it work."

Frania shares her cautionary tale of running the B&B in *Confessions of a Bed and Breakfast Diva*

Personal Communication, 2021

Frania moved with her husband to Florida, naming the B&B Green Gables. Managing Green Gables turned out to be overwhelming, stretching Frania in unexpected ways. Many guests violated her privacy, stepping into off-limits areas where she and her husband slept and watched television. Some guests wanted her to be friendlier than she

felt: "an artificial instant intimacy to be affected" for the pleasure of the guests. Frania turned inwards, and began to avoid guests. She would "retreat to the kitchen and close the door" behind her. Some guests still did not leave her alone. They would say things like "hope you'll be joining us," which Frania saw as a "command performance," from which there was no escape. No one who came there really wanted "the bedroom and a breakfast" in the morning, they wanted the "charm and romance" of not just relationship to the place but to the host, she feels.

Running a B&B can be a lot of work, much of it pedestrian. Guests checking out? Change linens and launder all towels as well as completely clean the room and the bath. Guests staying on? Make the bed, launder towels left on the floor, empty trash, and wipe down showers and toilets. For Frania, these routine chores started feeling unbearable. When laundering sheets and towels, she put on disposable gloves. "This is the part of the business I hated most," she says. Cleaning bedrooms and bathrooms made her feel "like the maid," she shares.

Guests didn't always appreciate Frania's culinary skills the way she had hoped. Her homemade frittata was mistaken for quiche. One guest didn't like eggs, so wasn't willing to try some of Frania's favorite dishes. "I felt almost personally offended and would insist on putting an unwanted 'eggy' concoction" for her breakfast," she says.

For almost four years, Frania – and her husband – tried to make the B&B work. They "drained their savings, plundered IRAs, and borrowed money," but could not turn a profit. Tired of the constant struggle, she sold the property and moved back to Manhattan where she got a graduate degree in animal behavior and now runs a business in that field.

Discussion Questions

1. What parts of running the B&B did Frania like and what parts did she dislike?

2. Could Frania have changed anything to manage the place better?

3. What expectations did Frania seem to have from the B&B before she started?

it is generally too late. Business owners would do well to think about these issues before, rather than after, problems arise. An ounce of prevention, as the popular saying goes, is better than a pound of cure.

Module 11.1 Qualities of Successful Entrepreneurs

The most common approach to understanding effective leadership is to focus on a set of characteristics and traits that distinguish leaders from non-leaders. The personal qualities that seem most important to successfully managing one's own business are discussed in the following sections.

11.1.1 Passion

A common advice given to young people is to *follow your passion*, which usually means do what you love. In his famous Stanford commencement speech (see the video at https://www.youtube.com/watch?v=UF8uR6Z6KLc), Steve Jobs encouraged the graduating class to do what they love, and if they didn't yet know what they liked doing, he encouraged them to keep looking until they found it. Good advice! And, as obvious from the 35 million-plus views of the speech on YouTube, the idea of doing what you love resonates with many people. But there is another side to passion that is equally important: Love what you do. No matter which profession you choose (or anything else in life for that matter), you will rarely do something where you love every aspect of it. There will always be some facets of the tasks you will not like, and for many people, this can be demotivating unless they also remember the need to love what they are doing. In other words, passion involves doing what you love and/or loving what you do.

Many business owners start a company because they have a passion for a particular product or service. Michel Verdure is the world's top photographer of cruise ships. His clients – some of the largest cruise-ship companies in the world – swear by him. "I won't use anyone else but him" for architectural and exterior shots, say many of his customers. People like Michel Verdure can be found in every business. They love to do something, and then build a business around it. The problem is that as soon as you start a business, you realize that there is a lot more to it than the one or two things that you love. Waiting on customers, keeping the books, dealing with rejections are all part of running a business. If you are like most people, you may never really love this part of your business, but you do need to learn to deal with the negatives in a way that helps you focus on the survival and growth of the business. If you do not learn to embrace the less glamorous (and more mundane) parts of running the business, you will get disillusioned and be tempted to quit.

That's the situation Josh Frey found himself in when he decided to pursue his passion. During his student days at University of Wisconsin, Josh started working at a bakery across the street from his dorm. He went on to launch a mail-order food company after graduating, making and selling muffins, cookies, breads, and other baked goods. Soon, Josh was frustrated with inventory management, order fulfillment, and hiring laborers. Josh realized a lot of what he had enjoyed about working in a bakery had nothing to do with baking, such as connecting with people. He refocused on an area that promised better and more reliable profits: promotional items and corporate gifts. He also began cherry-picking the parts of the job he liked and discarding the ones he did not.

When a business owner feels his or her passion begin to wane, he or she can reorient the business, acquire new skills more suited to the needs of the business, or try to find new aspects of the work that may rekindle the passion. This is what Barry Werner did when he bought Scarborough Fair, a six-bedroom, six-bath row house near Baltimore's Inner Harbor. Although Barry had never managed a bed-and-breakfast before, he found joy in running the place. Satisfying picky eaters, doing laundry, and preparing the place for Halloween, no work was too small for Barry. Once the B&B became moderately profitable, Barry decided to remodel the six bedrooms, each with the theme of a famous author (e.g. Edgar Allan Poe Suite). For Berry, managing the B&B well is the reward. As he says, "One thing that makes this job perfect is you're helping people have the perfect vacation, or business trip. You're the person who makes their lives everything they want them to be for a few days. The rewards of that are immeasurable."

Passion refers to a strong inclination toward an activity, task, or goal that people like, find it important, and in which they invest time and energy. When this passion – the intense emotion that channels your energy and fuels your motivation – is targeted to starting and running a business, it is called entrepreneurial passion. Many successful entrepreneurs have emphasized the role of passion in entrepreneurship: Anita Roddick of Body Shop asserted that "to succeed you have to believe in something with such a passion that it becomes a reality." Michael Dell suggested that "passion should be the fire that drives your life's work."

Psychologists distinguish between two forms of passion: harmonious and obsessive. **Harmonious passion** involves willed and controllable interest in one's work. Here, work is seen as important, but not all-consuming. **Obsessive passion** entails strong and uncontrollable affliction with one's work. The person is unable to regulate their engagement with work, so that they are frustrated or lost when they are not at work. Harmonious passion is consistent with work–family balance, whereas obsessive passion is not. While obsessive passion may produce superior outcomes in the short run, harmonious passion is desirable for winning in the long term.

The story of Daniel Thomas Hind, who, at 26, started his first business offering nutrition coaching, is quite telling. When Daniel started, he was determined to succeed but had no idea how to lead a business. Like many enterprising individuals just starting out, Daniel initially differentiated himself by telling clients he would "work harder than anyone you've ever worked with." He delivered on his promise, offering clients "around-the-clock support." His customer base grew rapidly. Daniel worked hard at the business, and the company was successful. Daniel, however, found that there was a limit to how much a person can handle before he breaks. Daniel shares:

> My body had been running on fumes for so long, it finally shut down. Stress hormones punch holes in the immune system. . . . I'd be in bed and wouldn't be able to move my body. I became incredibly lethargic and depressed, sleeping 12 hours a day.

Daniel was passionate about his business. In his quest to build his nascent business and make it a success, Daniel probably did not even realize that his passion for the business had become counterproductive. It was only when his body gave out and he was physically unable to work he realized the damage inflicted by the obsessive passion.

Compare Daniel's situation with Suzanne McMinn of Roane County in West Virginia. Suzanne wakes up at 2 am every day to bake in her kitchen, where she works up to 15 hours a day, 7 days a week. She makes cookies, scones, biscuits, breads, and muffins, which she sells to customers all around the country through the online retailer Etsy. Demand for Suzanne's products increased drastically during the COVID-19 pandemic. Searches for terms like "baked goods" and "brownies" on Etsy roughly doubled during the pandemic, and many bakers reported increases in orders of between 200% and 450% during the same period. As demand increased, competition also intensified. So far, Suzanne has done a good job of meeting demand and staving off rivals.

You can see that both Daniel and Suzanne invest considerable time and effort in their businesses. It is hard to invest so much effort on a regular basis without being passionate about what you are doing. The challenge is to make sure that your efforts toward the business are driven by harmonic passion, and not by obsessive passion. Yet, if the business owner is not careful, harmonic passion can and does become obsessive, which can be detrimental to both the company and its owner (as was the case with Daniel Hind).

Interactive Exercise

Interview five people to ask them what they think are essential qualities for those who run their business well. You can interview either professors or business owners. What qualities were common across your interviewees?

Richard Branson, the famed founder of the Virgin Group, says that as much as working on your business is important, you also need time away from work as a way to have harmony in your life. Branson advises entrepreneurs to "ditch any guilt you might feel about stopping work," and schedule relaxation time in your life. "I've found that it's not a good idea to dive straight into work when you wake up," Branson says, "so I dedicate my mornings to exercise and family time. It helps me clear my mind and energizes me for the day ahead." Taking time off from work, exercise, and spending time with family are all ways to prevent harmonic obsession from becoming obsessive.

Figure 11.1 presents some questions that business owners can ask themselves to examine if their passion is constructive or destructive for the business.

11.1.2 Perseverance

Most people are disappointed when they do not get something right the first time. If it happens a second or third time, they may even get frustrated. But what happens when you try repeatedly and still don't get it right? Many people become resigned, abandoning their efforts. A few, however, persevere and push through the frustration, no matter how difficult or daunting the task seems to be. Calvin Coolidge, the 30th President of the United States, was reportedly a firm believer in perseverance. The advice to press on, he believed, solves many of the problems we confront in life and work. Most dictionary definitions describe **perseverance** as "steadfastness in doing something despite difficulty, delay, or setbacks."

Legend has it that Colonel Sanders was reduced to living off of his Social Security check when he started the business that would later come to be known as Kentucky Fried Chicken. He supposedly made over 1000 calls to different restaurants asking people to try his fried chicken until he perfected the recipe. Imagine being rejected a thousand times, and yet maintaining the motivation to give it another try. That was the situation Angie Hicks found herself in when she cofounded a business providing crowdsourced reviews of Columbus, Ohio-based businesses. Most days she would spend hours walking around

Is Your Passion Blinding You? Do you...

- FEEL LIKE YOU'RE on a mission to change the world?

- GET INSULTED WHEN someone points out legitimate flaws in your idea or product?

- FIND IT HARD TO come up with pitfalls you might face or to detail a worst-case scenario for your venture?

- CHOOSE A CO-FOUNDER with a similar background to yours, increasing the chance of leaving holes in your team?

- RAISE MONEY FROM professional investors when your #1 goal is "to work for myself" or "to control my own destiny"?

- HIRE FRIENDS and family whom you may not be able to fire if they underperform or circumstances change, because you're confident you won't face those issues?

- NEGLECT TO RUN careful tests to assess consumer demand?

- ASSUME YOU WON'T need a financial cushion in case the venture takes longer than anticipated to generate income?

- RESIST TALKING HONESTLY with your significant other about the money and time you expect to commit to your venture, and about the potential pitfalls you face?

- FIGURE YOU DON'T need to address the holes in your skills or networks in advance of founding?

FIGURE 11.1 Signs Your Passion Is Destructive
Source: How an Entrepreneur's Passion Can Destroy a Startup, *The Wall Street Journal*

in various neighborhoods, and may be sign up one subscriber. To help cope with all of the rejection, she focused on the numbers and the idea that while they were moving slowly, they were at least moving. "I realized I had to make 20 calls to get one or two sales," she says. Her small business later became Angie's List, a company that went onto have a national footprint. She says entrepreneurs who are feeling frustrated should look for signs that they're making progress. Learning to celebrate "wins," even though they may be small, helped motivate her when she wanted to give up.

When you are serious about success, you persevere through all the criticisms and work toward the pot of gold at the end of the rainbow. Josh Turner, founder and CEO of LinkedSelling, has this to say about perseverance for business owners:

> While everyone has different talents and objectives, the underlying quality you need to have as an entrepreneur is perseverance. It's hard and there are a lot of challenges, but you can't give up. You need to be able to adapt, you need to be able to pick yourself up by the bootstraps, you need to learn how to figure things out, and you need to be able to persevere. Because you are going to fail, we fail all of the time. We've got a graveyard of products, services, and strategies that we've tried and failed with. But the key is to put you out there and to take action and constantly be moving forward. If you do . . . it's just a matter of time until you strike gold.[1]

A quality related to perseverance is **resilience**, the capacity to recover quickly from difficulties and setbacks. Brian Chesky, one of the Airbnb founders and the company's chief executive, believes that building a company takes resilience. Airbnb, he shares, launched four different times before success. Whenever times got tough, he would think about a metaphorical mountaintop and keep climbing in his head. At one point in its early years, when Airbnb wasn't generating enough revenue, Chesky and his cofounder Joe Gebbia made 1000 presidential-themed boxes of cereal by hand, which they hot-glued together and sold for $40 apiece. The out-of-the box idea got them on national TV, generated $30,000 in profits, and helped them get into the Silicon Valley startup accelerator program, Y Combinator. How did making cereal boxes with the images of John McCain and Barack Obama help them get into the YC? Well, YC cofounder Paul Graham was looking for **cockroaches** – startup firms that can survive nuclear winter, the tough times during the company's early years when revenues are less than expenses – to let into the accelerator program, and the cereal box idea impressed him very much.

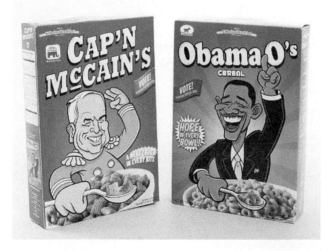

Cereal boxes with the pictures of Obama and McCain helped save Airbnb in its early days.

---

[1]*Source:* Growth Through Focus and Perseverance, Josh Turner (insightssuccess.com).

When thinking about perseverance, one needs to avoid the **sunk cost fallacy**. For economists, sunk costs are investments that can never be recovered. The sunk cost fallacy refers to the human tendency to continue an endeavor or behavior simply because they have already invested in it. Mark Doust, founder and CEO of Quiet Light Brokerage, an Internet business brokerage firm, believes that many entrepreneurs fall victim to the sunk cost fallacy because they are advised to trust themselves and carry on despite negative market feedback.

What Do You Think?

Brad Price quit his six-figure job to start a business that cleans up property damage such as mold and flooded basements. Brad considers himself very self-motivated and a good leader. An experienced business owner shared with Brad that he will also need to cold-call and strike deals, things that he never had to do in previous jobs. Brad is wondering what else he will need to do in his new business that he hadn't considered. Can you make a list of things that Brad needs to be prepared to do in his new business?

Table 11.1 shares the advice from successful entrepreneurs about perseverance and resilience in achieving success as a business owner.

11.1.3 Humility

Another important leadership quality for business owners is humility. In business, **humility** refers to an expressed developmental orientation associated with (a) willingness to view oneself accurately, (b) appreciation of others' strengths and contributions, and (c) openness to learning and self-improvement. The origins of humility can be traced back to the Latin word *humus*, which means "of the ground or earth." Humble leaders are, therefore, close to the ground – in other words, they are not secluded in their ivory tower, or so "high up" in the firm that it is difficult for employees or customers to engage with them. In his best-selling book *Good to Great*, the celebrated author Jim Collins talks about Level 5 leaders, who, he found, were the most effective at leading a firm, as iron-willed,

TABLE 11.1

Advice from Some Ambitious Entrepreneurs Who Succeeded Despite Obstacles

Name	Business	Advice
Angie Hicks	Angie's List	I think what it comes down to is really perseverance and just be willing to move the dirt.
Rebecca Minkoff	Rebecca Minkoff	Entrepreneurs who want to achieve success should keep trying and asking for support. If you knock on enough doors, something will happen.
Barbara Bradley Baekgaard	Vera Bradley	If it doesn't work out, don't be ashamed. Instead, try another idea.
Josie Natori	The Natori Company	To get through difficult times, entrepreneurs must be tenacious and work hard to persevere. Wallowing in a past defeat or setback isn't an option.
Rana El Kaliouby	Affectiva	Remember that one day you will look back on your obstacles and laugh.
Barbara Corcoran	The Corcoran Group	Declare war on the tapes in your head that tell you that you're not good enough.

humble CEOs who aspired to take their firms to new heights (they were ambitious, but their ambition was for the business and not for themselves).

Humility may be one of the important leadership traits for business owners, but it is not a common quality. Many people think "I own the business, why should I be humble?" Justin Seeley, cofounder and CEO of Seattle-based OmNom, an online food delivery search engine, encourages his fellow entrepreneurs to embrace the title of **cocky jerks**, by which he means being narcissistic, arrogant, and condescending. Not very humble, is he? Some confuse humility with humiliation, a lack of confidence, or the proverbial doormat – anyone can walk over you. Humility is not about having a low estimate of one's worth or merit. It is not the lack of self-assertion. Instead, it is about the absence of self-exaltation. In other words, humility is thinking less about yourself as opposed to thinking less of yourself. To quote Jim Collins, "the X-factor of great leadership is humility."

Being humble is not easy when you are succeeding in your business. For the vast majority of people, success fuels arrogance and increases hubris. "I have succeeded in the face of hardships and obstacles, so I must be good" is how many people think. For business owners, arrogance and hubris can alienate employees, suppliers, and customers (and sometimes even family members). Given that success can produce arrogance and hubris without conscious awareness, it is important to make a deliberate effort to stay grounded and remain humble. Michael Dermer, author of *The Lonely Entrepreneur*, writes that "there's a humility that comes with the fact that yes, I'm self-assured about my idea but it makes me actually better at being an entrepreneur by recognizing and embracing what I don't know."

Jay Elliot, who wrote the fascinating book *The Steve Jobs Way*, shares what happened when he left his job at chip-maker Intel to work for a new up-and-coming computer company that had been very successful and seemed to have a good future. As Elliot tells it:

> The day of the public offering, the CEO became an instant multimillionaire and celebrated by going out drinking with his cofounders. From there he drove right over to buy himself a Ferrari, took a car from the dealership for a happy test drive, and crashed. He died, the company died, and the job I had quit Intel to take was over before I had even reported for work.

Sad, isn't it? It gets even sadder: The deceased founder had a wife and three small kids (one son and two daughters) waiting for him at home when he crashed; the company had to make the unusual decision to rescind the initial public offering. Would things have been different for the company if its young founder had been humble about his success? Perhaps if the young entrepreneur had thought less about his rising wealth and more about his responsibility toward customers, employees, and family, he would not have behaved recklessly and met his untimely demise.

KEY TAKEAWAY

There are three key qualities for success as a business owner: passion, perseverance, and humility.

Comprehension Check

1. Define entrepreneurial passion and distinguish between positive and negative forms of passion.
2. Explain resilience and why it is an important quality for small business owners.
3. What is humility? Why is humility a useful quality for entrepreneurship?

An Authority On Transformational Leadership

Keith Krach was a cofounder of Ariba, a business-to-business e-commerce company. He was the inaugural recipient of the Life & News Transformational Leader of the Year Award.

In this interview, Krach explains what he thinks is transformational leadership.

Watch the video online at: https://www.youtube.com/watch?v=Ag3OINp-kSc

Module 11.2 Leadership Styles of Entrepreneurs

For several years, management scholars have been doing research on leadership style. Let us review some developments in the field of leadership style. The style many researchers identify as most desirable is **transformational leadership**, which involves challenging the status quo and motivating everyone to perform beyond expectations. Transformational leaders rely on four key qualities to influence employees and create incredible commitment to company goals. First, transformational leaders have **charisma** – the ability to attract, charm, and influence others. Second, transformational leaders show personal concern for the people who work for them, also called **individualized consideration**. During the Great Depression of the 1930s, when most of America was struggling, Walt Disney was paying his employees a relative fortune. Disney took great interest in his employees' personal lives and challenges. Third, transformational leaders inspire others to work for a higher purpose, **inspirational motivation**. Neal Gabler, author of *Walt Disney: The Triumph of the American Imagination*, writes that the Disney founder had an uncanny ability to make people feel that what he wanted done was an incredibly important thing to do. Steve Jobs, another transformational leader, was famous for his emphasis on "making a dent in the universe." Finally, transformational leaders believe in **intellectual stimulation**, which means they encourage employees to think creatively and work harder. Explore and innovate, Sam Walton would often tell his employees and managers.

Transformational leadership is most suitable for organizations that need to change. But sometimes firms need a calming leader who maintains the status quo and focuses on improving the operational efficiency of the company. This is called **steady-hand leadership**. Entrepreneurs who follow steady-hand leadership do not make unnecessary demands on their employees and stakeholders. Instead, they focus on ironing out operational inefficiencies in the business. It is worth considering that after Steve Jobs – a highly admired transformational leader – passed, Apple's next CEO was Tim Cook, who had served as Chief Operating Officer under Jobs and was virtually unknown outside the company before taking the highest position at Apple. His main job: Keep Apple on the track that Jobs had established.

Another popular leadership style is **authentic leadership**, the idea that leaders are most effective when they behave in ways consistent with their true, positive selves. Thus, authentic leadership is about being yourself. All of us have different backgrounds, different life experiences, and different aspirations for ourselves. Instead of trying to fit into common societal expectations about how a leader should behave, authentic leaders base their management style on their values and preferences. The key aspect of authentic leadership is therefore self-awareness. Instead of trying to imitate other successful leaders, authentic leaders hone their own style based on their personality and experiences. To do so, they need to be introspective, clearly understand where they are coming from, and have confidence in their own values and priorities.

Interactive Exercise

Do most people recognize their core values and preferences? Remember that recognizing one's core values and preferences is essential for authentic leadership. Interview seven people who you believe are well established in their careers to ask them what they see as their most important value or preference. What trends do you see?

The consequences of an inauthentic approach to leadership can be damaging for the firm. Employees who don't view their leaders as authentic are less engaged at work. Inauthentic owners may breach the trust that is so essential in new and small firms. When people feel that they see an incomplete or misleading picture, it inadvertently creates mistrust in working relationships among colleagues, suppliers, customers, and employees.

Bill George, author of *Discovering Your True North*, considers Oprah Winfrey, a media celebrity and serial entrepreneur, as an example of someone who is famously authentic. Then, there is Chick-fil-A. Since its founding, the company has been closed on Sundays, a practice established by the founder Truett Cathy to allow employees a day of rest and worship. Even after Truett's passing, his son Dan Cathy continues the practice. Employees see the Cathys as authentic leaders, who set a good example for the rest of the company to follow.

The business world is full of stories of leaders who abuse their powerful positions. Books are written about the wild and reckless life of business executives, many of which are bestsellers. The 2018 book *Brotopia*, for example, unmasks the secretive, orgiastic dark side of Silicon Valley, where exclusive, drug-fueled, sex-laced parties are a weekly affair. The best-selling author Michael Lewis chronicled the testosterone-fueled world of Wall Street in the now-classic book *Liar's Poker*. Concerned by the scandalous nature of business highlighted by these books, some experts are emphasizing the importance of prioritizing the interests of others over everything else. **Servant leadership** is an approach that directs the leader to serve the needs of others. Servant leaders see their primary mission as developing employees and helping them reach their goals. Servant leadership is about one's responsibilities to employees, customers, and the external community.

"Bit by bit, I came to understand that you lead best by serving the needs of your people," Ken Melrose, former CEO of lawnmower and equipment company Toro, wrote in *Making the Grass Greener on Your Side*. To better understand workers and learn about the challenges they faced, Melrose would sometimes spend days working alongside them in factories or call centers.

Gary Burrell cofounded Garmin Ltd., a maker of GPS products. His colleagues remember him as someone who put the concerns of employees at the center of operational decisions. Garmin was headquartered in Kansas, where Gary had grown up as a child. After founding Garmin, he lived the rest of his life only minutes away from the company's headquarters.

What Do You Think?

Kailey wants to start a restaurant in a college town. She knows that she will be hiring college students to work at the restaurant. Her customers will be mostly people affiliated with the university and living in the community. What leadership style do you think would work best for Kailey? Are there some leadership mistakes Kailey should avoid?

Servant leadership is a tough approach for many executives and business owners who have been socialized to prioritize their own needs first, be focused on succeeding at all costs, and telling people what to do. If you have a chance, read Mike Wilson's *The Difference Between God and Larry Ellison: God Doesn't Think He's Larry Ellison*. As you may know, Ellison is the founder of technology company Oracle, who started with $1200 and built a Silicon Valley giant. He is also a poster child for "jerk entrepreneurs," as Wilson described in his entertaining biography.

Some entrepreneurs will tell you that "You can't make an omelet without breaking a few eggs." Many bosses criticize, demean, and yell. Uber founder Travis Kalanick was one such entrepreneur. Under his leadership, the company listed "toe-stepping" and "hustling" as corporate values. He once joked in an interview that the company should be called "Boob-er" because of his ability to attract female companions, and he mocked customers online for complaining about pricing. He supported an internal Uber tool that let employees track movements of specific riders, including previous romantic interests and estranged spouses. Kalanick was what you may call an abusive leader. **Abusive leadership** involves repeated display of hostile, humiliating, or derogatory verbal and nonverbal behaviors toward employees, customers, or suppliers. Abusive leaders alienate stakeholders, generate unhappiness in the workplace, and increase stress for everyone.

KEY TAKEAWAY

Many business owners abuse their positions, which hurts their leadership effectiveness.

At Uber, Kalanick had managed to resist many calls to change his leadership style, until an online video appeared of him berating one of the ride-hailing service's drivers. Kalanick was then forced to leave the company he had founded and taken to stratospheric heights. In a note to employees, he vowed to grow up and shared that he was ashamed of the behavior captured on camera. "This is the first time I've been willing to admit that I need leadership help and I intend to get it," he said.

Some research show that workers at firms with 50 or fewer employees report more abuse from their supervisors than those at larger businesses. The abuse includes everything from forcing long hours on workers to yelling and behaving in a threatening way. Road Science LLC, a 110-employee technology company based in Tulsa, OK, pledges in its employee handbook to maintain a "jerk-free" culture. Over the years, many states have introduced legislation to curb workplace bullying, including at small firms, although none have become. Yet, many small business owners recognize that bullying is unhealthy and strive to maintain a nurturing workplace. Suzanne Miller, owner of SPM Communications LP, a public-relations company in Dallas with 18 employees, says she used to work for an abusive boss before she left to start her own business. Because of her own prior experience, Suzanne is committed to maintaining an abuse-free workplace and makes considerable effort to ensure she does not hire people with abusive tendencies.

Comprehension Check

1. What is transformational leadership? Is transformational leadership always a preferred approach for entrepreneurs?
2. Define and explain servant leadership.
3. Some entrepreneurs use abusive leadership to manage their business. Why is it wrong to rely on abusive leadership?

Module 11.3 Stress and Well-being

There is not much conversation about a very important aspect of being a small business owner: stress and emotional well-being. Popular media and academic writings focus on entrepreneurs as people who pursue their dreams to achieve independence, wealth, and work satisfaction. However, the dark side of many a business owner's lifestyle often goes unnoticed. Behind the veneer of multimillion-dollar income and fancy parties, many business owners are struggling with issues such as anxiety, binge eating, drug addiction, insomnia, and depression. Ben Tauber, a Silicon Valley executive coach at Velocity Group, says that when you talk with many entrepreneurial types, "they say they are killing it," but "inside many of them are dying."

Brandon Truaxe of Toronto-based DECIEM Inc. offers a cautionary tale. Brandon ran much of the beauty company himself, sleeping little and using ephedrine and caffeine. As the company grew, the pressure mounted. Brandon started using crystal methamphetamine, leading to increasingly erratic behavior. Estee Lauder Co., an investor in DECIEM, took legal action, alleging that Brandon had made hundreds of "disturbing posts" on social-media accounts, including threats, and further that he had leased a private plane and a new headquarters without consulting the board. Brandon was fired from the company he founded. Despondent and adrift, he was hospitalized three times as a result of hallucinations from heavy drug use, twice in London and once in Canada. Within a year of his firing from DECIEM, Brandon died after falling from his 32nd-floor condo.

Stress in the workplace refers to a condition wherein job-related factors influence someone to change (disrupt or enhance) his or her psychological or physiological condition in ways that deviate from normal functioning. Stress usually gets a bad name, but research has shown that there is an inverted U relationship between stress and performance. Stress initially improves performance as one starts to push beyond one's usual functioning. However, after a certain level, stress depresses performance and becomes counterproductive. The level at which stress ceases to be productive and starts having a destructive effect is one's **tipping point**. Before the tipping point, stress can propel you into "the zone," spurring higher performance and well-being. Too much stress, though, strains the heart, depletes memory and mental clarity, and amplifies the risk of chronic disease.

Different people have different tipping points for stress. As such, business owners need to avoid stress when it passes their tipping point, and they also need to refrain from working too close to the tipping point for extended periods of time. When stress becomes overbearing and unrelenting, it wears down the body's capacity to work. If stress can be managed constructively – below the tipping point with some highs and lows – it can increase a person's efficiency and improve performance.

Starting and managing a business often means taking on a massive workload. The message from media and other business owners is usually what some call **hustle porn**, the notion that working nonstop is a badge of honor. Hard work is good and productive, but working long hours without enough sleep and rest can be a recipe for disaster. The wear and tear of long hours, constantly buzzing phones (calls, texts, and messages), uncertain working conditions, and family demands create **allostatic load**, a condition where the stress switch is stuck in the half-on position. The result: fatigue, frustration, anger, and burnout. Add alcohol, drugs, and caffeine, and you have a disaster waiting to happen. Rebecca Jean Alonzi was busy building her farm-to-office foodservice company Nourish Inc., when she developed a dependence on sugary foods to fuel long work nights. Soon, she gained 30 pounds. She joined Overeaters Anonymous and got on track to lose weight. Then she found herself having trouble focusing. A psychiatrist diagnosed her with attention-deficit hyperactivity disorder and prescribed Adderall, a stimulant, which she says made her "skinny, bitchy and very productive." Within a year, she began having headaches and quit Adderall, concluding that while building a health-food company she was hurting her own body. "I cared so deeply about making a difference that I was willing to push myself past my limit," she says.

Troubled by the path she had taken, Alonzi decided to mend her working style. She groomed a new CEO who took over day-to-day work at the company, while Alonzi focused on new projects. She started incorporating into her routine "regenerative" activities like deep breathing, walks without a cellphone, and relaxed hikes. "What I later learned is there are ways to achieve super-humanity that didn't involve self-sacrifice," she says.

Research has identified six broad causes of the stress that business owners face: (a) financial, (b) interpersonal, (c) self-regulation, (d) nature of work, (e) uncertainty, and (f) work–life balance.

Interactive Exercise

You need to survey people to ask them (a) what stresses they feel at work? and (b) what do they do to help reduce the stress they face? Develop a short survey that people can quickly take online. What are your major findings?

11.3.1 Financial Stressors

Although the ranks of millionaires in American include a disproportionately large share of business owners (compared to other professions), running a business often involves taking on considerable financial responsibilities. This includes generating a positive cash flow, meeting payroll, and investing resources in business growth. A living salary for one's self is often the last thing on the entrepreneurs' mind.

When Jennifer Walzer was laid off from a $100,000 consulting job, she started Backup My Info! Inc., which sells online data-backup services to businesses. In its first year, the New York–based company brought in just $29,000 in gross revenue. Jennifer didn't get a salary until the third year, and even then it was just $30,000. She may have been able to draw a higher pay, but then she would not have much left to invest back into the business to keep it financially sustainable.

The effect of financial stressors is heightened during economic downturns and recessions. Kevin Smith, based in Miramar, FL, has a consulting business that makes enough money to provide for his family of seven and covers loans on three cars, including a BMW X5. The COVID-19 pandemic changed Kevin's economic situation as consulting assignments dried up. When his son lost his job and the daughter lost her part-time position, Kevin found himself unable to afford groceries, make car payments, and provide for his family.

11.3.2 Interpersonal Stressors

Running one's own business involves dealing with people, so it's common to think that business owners are good at managing people. The truth is that entrepreneurs frequently find themselves dealing with interpersonal stressors. For business owners, interpersonal issues take two forms: loneliness and people problems.

For many business owners, loneliness is a major problem. They are surrounded by people – employees, customers, and suppliers – yet struggle with finding people in whom they can confide. Kim Jordan, founder of New Belgium Brewing, thinks that "the hardest part of being an entrepreneur is feeling so much weight on your shoulders." Even when you have people around you who care for the company, "there's something very singular about being the founder. It can be very lonely."

People problems can involve conflicts with subordinates or customers, getting others to do the work they are expected to do, and finding motivated people to work with. An all-too familiar story in small businesses is that a team that seems a great combination on paper collapses – and takes down the firm with it – because the founders find themselves clashing over their goals, work styles, or basic personality differences. "Some business owners have unbelievable work ethics and some work for themselves because they think they don't have to work as hard as they did when they worked for others," says Peter Stanwyck, a small business attorney in Oakland, CA.

For Neil Blumenthal, cofounder of the online retailer Warby Parker, the most stressful aspect of running his own business is having realistic expectations of his employees. As he explains, "You worry: Was the hiring process as robust as it should have been? Was the role properly defined? Even when all of those things seem to have been done right, and you feel you've given someone every opportunity to succeed, it's really hard."

What Do You Think?

John and Emily are a married couple. Emily's cousin Tara is married to John's best friend from college, Brian. John, Emily, Tara, and Brian decided to open a restaurant together, and drew up an agreement that gave each couple a 50% ownership of the business. Each couple also contributed half of the start-up capital and decided to split the responsibilities of running the business in the middle: Tara and Brian handled the front end of the restaurant and John–Emily took responsibility for the back end. Both couples were hardworking, and the restaurant took off quickly. Reviewers praised both the food and customer service, rare in the restaurant business. Unfortunately, soon the two couples found themselves in conflict. Tara and Brian wanted to entertain and give drinks to their friends who came in. John and Emily ran a tight kitchen, which reduced waste but increased employee turnover. What would you advise the two feuding couples?

11.3.3 Self-regulation Problems

Entrepreneurs are often not good at managing their own time and feelings (though they should be). They may make good money but be too immersed in the business to be able to enjoy themselves. David Finkel, CEO of Maui Mastermind, has worked with thousands of business owners over the years, and for a large majority of them, a huge concern is lack of time off. They are married to their business, leaving them little time to pursue outside interests. Even when they can steal away some time, it's hard to find somebody who can fill in for the owner. Many entrepreneurs bring along their cellphone and laptop with them when they socialize so they can respond to questions from clients or employees.

Some entrepreneurs take the losses in the business personally, unable to deal effectively with their grief. Serial entrepreneur Kwiri Yang shares that she found herself in a "stress cage" as head of strategy at Fuhu, a children's tablet maker. After Fuhu was sold to Mattel Inc. in a bankruptcy auction, she says she fell physically ill and grew severely depressed, cycling through seven therapists and three executive coaches.

11.3.4 Nature of Work

Stressors related to the nature of business ownership include dealing with multiple aspects of running a business; taking on the responsibility for others; workload; and dealing with paperwork, regulations, and taxes. Building a successful business can take years filled with setbacks, long hours, and little tangible rewards for all the work. Those who were used to steady paychecks, four weeks' paid vacation, and employer-sponsored health benefits will not find that self-employment is a good fit for them. In the early stages of a business, owners are often expected to handle everything from billing customers to hiring employees to writing marketing materials. Some new founders become frustrated when they spend the majority of their time on administration rather than focusing on the work they enjoy.

Tim Brown, cofounder of sneaker company Allbirds, believes that "your business embeds itself 6 inches into your brain, and you can't shake it. You're in the shower, you're out to dinner, you're on vacation—you're always thinking about it, even when you don't want to be. Taking an idea out into the skeptical world and forcing them to believe that it might make sense and then delivering on it is just extraordinarily difficult and takes a tremendous amount of mental engagement. Building a business will take everything you give it."

11.3.5 Uncertainty

Managing your own business means dealing with uncertainty and ambiguity. In the early days of the business, there is uncertainty about whether the business will survive. Payal Kadakia, founder of ClassPass, explains that "building a company takes time, and there's no blueprint to guide you. It requires a lot of iterating and pivoting. Our initial product didn't take off, and it took three years for us to get it right. We were originally a search engine for classes with no membership offering; you would book a class and pay full price for it. In that original iteration, there were weeks when nobody made a reservation on the site. It wasn't until we found our current model – a subscription and a community – when the magic happened."

As the business grows, there is still uncertainty about the future trajectory of the business. Research has shown that of firms that make it onto the *Inc.* magazine's *Inc.* 500 list of rapidly growing firms each year, only one in three manages to return the next year. Growing a company to scale confronts the management team with unforeseen challenges that can strain them to the point where they become stressed and wish their companies had remained small. Rick Shelley is the founder of First Standard Freight, a New York–based firm that served as a customs broker and freight forwarder for firms shipping goods by land, sea, or air. Within a few years, annual revenues had grown to about $20 million, with a monthly payroll of $600,000. Shelley found himself feeling confused and anxious. When would the firm's position stabilize? What business strategy would make that happen? Where was the business headed? "I'm hearing stuff from customers, but I don't know where to direct resources – to a Web server, to outsourcing? That's the spooky thing. I'm telling you, it's hard to compete right now – really, really hard," Shelley says.

11.3.6 Work–Life Conflict

Working long hours, having difficulty relaxing and no real time off, and not spending time on kids' activities can produce work–life conflict for business owners. John Jordan, CEO of Sonoma County's Jordan Winery, a digital-wine-list entrepreneur and founder of the John Jordan Foundation, believes that "successful entrepreneurs derive so much of their satisfaction from their business that their work is their life." For him, a lifestyle where business is interwoven with vacations and diversions is the life of an entrepreneur.

One in five of the people Dr. Arlie Hochschild of University of California at Berkeley interviewed in the course of research for her book *The Time Bind* said the rewards of work could actually become stronger than the comforts of home, so "home became work, and work became home."

Decades of research have linked stress to everything from heart attacks and stroke to diabetes and a weakened immune system. People who report being stressed incur health-care costs that are 46% higher, or an average of $600 more per person, than others. Estimates by the American Institute of Stress in New York suggest that work-related stress costs the nation more than $300 billion each year in health care, missed work, and programs designed to help keep stress under control. The Japanese have termed work-induced stress as **karoshi**, which means "death from overwork," a growing concern worldwide.

KEY TAKEAWAY

Working long hours, having difficulty relaxing and no real time off, and not spending time on family activities can produce work–life conflict for business owners.

For business owners, stress is real. You now understand the causes of stress for business owners. Once entrepreneurs understand the cause(s) of their stress, they can work on taking actions to coping with stress. There are some specific ways that business owners can attempt to cope with their stress, which are discussed in the following sections:

11.3.6.1 Taking time off Most of us think that we get done more if we work seven days a week than if we work six days a week. Working longer hours, we think, is better than working fewer hours. While this idea is intuitively appealing, we are not considering the fatigue that comes from working long hours. When we are tired – mentally or physically – our efficiency and effectiveness at work decrease. One antidote to stress is taking time off from work. Not everyone can take days or weeks off from work (or even six months off in Africa as did Jack Dorsey of Twitter and Square), but short breaks are possible for everyone. When on break, it is helpful to avoid work as much as you can. You can carve out time from your weekly schedule where you do not check email or respond to work calls and avoid thinking about the business altogether.

11.3.6.2 Exercising Exercise is believed to be one of the best methods for reducing emotional tension, stress, and anxiety. Stress releases hormones, such as adrenaline and cortisol, that increase heart rate, which causes blood vessels to constrict, blood pressure to increase, and mental acuity to go up as a result of the fight-or-flight response. "Exercise stimulates the release of endorphins and neurotransmitters that help relieve the stress response and cardiovascular responses that modulate stress," says Brad Roy, the executive director of the Summit Medical Fitness Center in Kalispell, MT. Increased endorphin levels counteract the stress response that is so damaging to the immune system.

The type of exercise to do – running, weight lifting, or yoga – really depends on what each individual enjoys. Exercise is most useful when it is preventative, so that you exercise regularly and not just when you are stressed or upset. Regular exercise prepares the body and mind to better deal with stressful situations.

Working out reduces stress and anxiety, but exercise and drugs are a bad combination. Unfortunately, it seems there is a growing trend of mixing workouts with getting high. Pauline Nordin is a trainer, model, and licensed nutritionist. She also eats two cannabis cookies each night before going to bed, which she says helps her recover from the punishing workouts. While it may be helpful in the short term, drugs and exercise do not mix well. Drugs can contribute to injury and also encourage reckless behavior in the gym and at work.

Paul Solotaroff was a freshman at Stony Brook University on Long Island, and – as he describes it – the shameful owner of a concave chest and spindly arms. An asthmatic, insecure, frightfully skinny child, Paul longed to resemble the muscular comic-book heroes he idolized. With relentless training and regular steroid injections, he was able to achieve that goal, gaining 50 muscled pounds within six months. Paul's steroid use lasted two years, ending only when he began to experience serious health problems like heart arrhythmia and recurring asthma, as well as anxiety attacks. For entrepreneurs, who look toward exercise as a way to reduce stress and increase emotional well-being, it is best to stay away from drugs and steroids. Getting stoned is not a healthy way to get toned!

11.3.6.3 Personal board of advisors Some business owners put together an advisory board to bounce off ideas and share their concerns. You have probably heard the expression "it's lonely at the top." To help with the debilitating feeling that the weight of the world is on your shoulders, it can be helpful to have a personal advisory board of people you trust and respect. These people are not involved in your business in any way but have your best interest in mind and the life experience to give you some direction. Stefanie Strack, founder of VIS Holdings, a sports-advocacy business supporting female athletes aged 12–22, has her trusted advisory board that she turns to when she needs advice. Her advisors include Patty Ross, a director of two public companies and former vice president at Nike; A. K. Pradeep, founder of machineVantage; Genevieve Roth, founder of Invisible Hand; and Sade Greenidge, an African American track-and-field star.

Wall Street Journal

Stefanie Strack turns to her personal advisory board when she needs advice about her business and life.

Note that the personal advisory board is not a legal board of directors. A company's legally compliant board of directors is usually a paid role and is obligated to make decisions that are in the best interest of the firm. A personal board of advisors is always unpaid and looks out for you as an individual. When Debra Lee started Leading Women Defined to encourage women in business and host an annual summit for them, she relied on advice from her personal board of advisors comprising successful leaders she thought had much to offer her.

11.3.6.4 Consulting with a life coach Many business owners find help from life coaches. Denise Spatafora is one such life coach. Ali Riaz was a successful business owner, married, with two children and two homes, when he was advised to see if a life coach could help him deal with the stress of managing a fast-growing, cutting-edge company. "Kids getting bigger, parents getting older, business is growing – just using hard work and natural-born talents was getting hard. I wondered if there were techniques I could use," Ali shares. Reluctantly, Ali turned to Denise, who came highly recommended. Denise started by asking all the people around Ali, employees, executives, and his family, about his strengths and weaknesses, guaranteeing anonymity to the interviewees. She conducted a classic 360-degree assessment and held Ali accountable to change what people said made him difficult. She shared her assessment with Ali in a way that did not cause him to become defensive and reject it. He then had to come up with a "game plan" to change things, which Denise critically reviewed.

11.3.6.5 Involving the family For many entrepreneurs, work is seductive, and in spending much of their time at work, they ignore their family. To address this problem, one of the solutions some entrepreneurs offer is to involve the family in the business. Bob and Susan Birch, who own a clothing line and retail chain, have immersed their children in entrepreneurship for their whole lives. The couple used to bring work home so that the whole family could share in it – and then took their family to work so they could share in the process there also. They would take the children for "normal" family activities like trips to museums, restaurants, and the theater as well as to factories, construction sites, and design studios – before they'd lost their baby teeth. "Every day was 'bring your kid to work day,'" their oldest son Roby remembers. "We were constantly going to warehouses, showrooms and ranches. We were always looking at something and thinking, 'How can we build this into a greater vision?'" Dinner talk at home revolved around retail, fashion, and design. During those conversations, the children absorbed the business language and the strategies for growing a brand. "My dad was so good at mental math – you make it for this, you wholesale it for that, you retail it for this, you'll need to go out and raise this amount of money," daughter Chloe explains. "Pretty quickly we got to, 'Is it a financially viable concept?'"

Eating a healthy diet, exercising regularly, getting enough sleep, and finding time for pleasurable activities in our day are all activities that strengthen our physical immune system and also support us mentally. Having strong relationships and reminding ourselves what we are grateful for can also boost what mental health experts call the **psychological immune system**. Just as the **physiological immune system** aims to safeguard physical health, the psychological immune system encompasses emotional processes that help protect our mental health. Meditation, a basic mental fitness exercise that brings discipline to the mind and aims to keep it focused on one thing, can also be helpful in reducing stress and increasing well-being. In his book *Altered Traits: Science Reveals How Meditation Changes Your Mind, Brain and Body*, psychologist and author Daniel Goleman says that research shows meditation can decrease symptoms of depression and anxiety, boost compassion, and bring lasting positive changes to the brain.

Comprehension Check

1. Why do many business owners have work–life conflict and what can be done about it?
2. What is a personal board of advisors? How is it helpful for a business owner to have his or her own personal advisory board?
3. "I can outwork everyone." What do you think are the advantages and disadvantages of this approach to managing one's own business?

Module 11.4 Delegation and Professional Management

On a scale of 1–5, where 1 = not true at all and 5 = very true, how would you rate the statement "People who have their own business are very good at delegating work"? If you answered 3 or higher, you would be wrong. Business owners who delegate well are great managers and supportive bosses. As the famed American business tycoon Andrew Carnegie said, "No person will make a great business who wants to do it all himself or get all the credit." Yet 75% of the employer entrepreneurs Gallup studied have limited-to-low levels of delegator skills. Entrepreneurs who are not good delegators find that their company's growth is thwarted. When Gallup studied 143 CEOs included in the *Inc.* 500 list, an annual ranking of America's fastest-growing private companies, it was found that those that delegate well had an average three-year firm growth rate of 1751% – about 112 percentage points greater than those CEOs with limited or low delegation skills.

KEY TAKEAWAY

Business owners who want to grow their company need to be able to delegate well.

It is well known that entrepreneurs find it *very* difficult to delegate *even* the simplest of tasks. Why is this so? There are five major reasons that business owners find delegation difficult:

1. *Thinking only you can do it.* Managing a business, especially if it is one that you want to grow, requires a range of skills. Even if you can learn and do everything, you will find yourself running out of time to do all that needs to be done. You need to divide and conquer. To grow the venture, the owner not only needs to work in the business but also work on the business.
2. *Not making the time to explain and delegate work.* Many business owners lack the patience and forethought to explain what they need to get done. They think the employees should know what needs to be done and how it is to be done. Yet, even the most loyal and dedicated employees need guidance and direction. Also, delegation actually helps you to clarify and organize the requirements in your own mind. Of course, you need to hire people who have the training and experience to do the work you are expecting them to do.
3. *Not trusting others.* Many business owners are paranoid, assuming that everyone has some other agenda, or may steal their idea or customers. Trust must be earned, but it's also critical to do due diligence before hiring key employees. After due diligence, the best approach is to be vigilant but explicitly communicate your trust and confidence in others' abilities.
4. *Lack of clarity about what it takes to succeed.* Let's accept it: Many business owners do not delegate because they lack confidence in their own understanding of the work. Others simply find it hard to communicate the why and the how, or they are easily frustrated by team members who are struggling. Adrian Ghila, a serial entrepreneur and investor and the founder of Earth Car Wash LLC and CEO of Luxe RV Inc., shared that she was let down most of the time by the people to whom she delegated, which frustrated her. She also felt that delegating was more work than just doing the task herself.
5. *Fear of losing control.* Many business owners are afraid that if they delegate, they will lose control. Yet, delegation isn't about giving up the ultimate authority and responsibility for the business. Remember the famous Harry Truman quote, "the buck stops here." As the owner of the business, you will always be the face of the business. If something goes wrong, you are still the one in charge. The buck does stop with you, no matter to whom you delegate the work.

While most entrepreneurs have trouble delegating, there are some who dump work on others. **Dumping** work is usually not a good idea as the work often comes back to you. Entrepreneurs who dump work on others frequently suffer the boomerang effect of bad delegation. If you delegate more to employees who already have a full plate, tasks will not be completed. Assigning tasks to someone just because their skills are remotely related will also not help get the work done. Employees may not have the motivation or time to learn the new skills needed to complete the work given to them. Gail Angelo, a leadership coach in Charlotte, NC, says that those who just dump their work on others quickly find out that it doesn't work very well for them or the business.

How does an entrepreneur improve his or her chances of being successful at delegating work? There are certain steps that you can take to make delegation work for you.

1. *Hire well.* The first step to effective delegation is hiring well. You want to hire employees who have both the ability and motivation to perform the work you ask of them. If an employee doesn't have the ability or motivation to do the work you give them, there is not much you can do to get them to step up to the task. Hiring people with experience ensures your people will make great progress even when you are not around or when you do not give them an agenda. Hiring the right people also saves time for the entrepreneur in the follow-up process and/or if intervention is needed.

2. *Start small.* Like many other business owners, you may be new to delegation. In that case, start by delegating small specific tasks and monitoring how the tasks were done. As you get comfortable with your own ability to delegate, move to delegating more complex tasks. Break down complex tasks into smaller pieces, delegating individual pieces at a time.

3. *Experiment with different delegation techniques.* Be prepared to try out different ways of delegating work, especially when you are new to delegation. At this stage, you do not know what type of delegation works for you, the business, and your employees. It is possible that verbal delegation with a detailed explanation of tasks work well for your situation. Or delegating in writing is a good option, so that you and the employees are on the same page about what you expect from them. As the company's systems get more established, you may delegate with project management software to track the work done over time.

4. *Be realistic.* Many times when business owners delegate they think someone should be able to do things at least as good as, if not better than, they are able to do themselves. Well-meaning experts and consultants tell entrepreneurs to "hire people who are smarter than you and learn from them." Alex Tsepko, founder and CEO of Skylum Software, shares the story of hiring a person who was an expert in email marketing, automation, and after-purchase customer experiences. First day at work, the new hire redesigned the company's digital marketing processes so they were flawless. It sounds good, but you would be surprised at how rare such employees are. The advice to hire people smarter than you may work for a small group of entrepreneurs who are running growth firms with vast financial reserves to pay people, but it does not work for most business owners. Many business owners simply do not have the money or the cachet to attract employees who can hit the ground running and soon do things better than how they were already being done in the business. For most entrepreneurs, if their employees can do things about 75% as well as they were doing it themselves, it is a good outcome.

5. *Create structure.* Delegation works best when there is a structure to the work to be done. Unstructured, ambiguous work is more difficult to delegate. When employees know exactly how the task is to be done, when it should be completed, and who is responsible for doing it, delegation will work better.

Delegation is a first step toward managing the firm professionally. Here, business owners stop running the show and instead move to managing the show. The switch to professionally managed small business is important if the firm is to continue its growth trajectory. This is easier said than done because the skills or characteristics that are needed to establish and run the business in the startup phase are not always the same skills needed to manage a stable and established business. The shift from thinking like an owner to thinking like a manager starts with delegation, but also involves processes to hold individuals accountable and relying on numbers to allocate resources to different tasks. Some business owners understand that they do not have the skills needed to manage the firm, in which case they can bring a professional manager who runs the day-to-day work at the firm. Mark Zuckerberg, founder of Facebook, brought Sheryl Sandberg to be COO when the company was only four years old, in part to manage the chaos at the rapidly growing firm.

Comprehension Check

1. What do you think about the statement "Entrepreneurs are good delegators"?
2. Explain dumping and identify its pitfalls.
3. What can business owners do to be better delegators?

Summary

Many believe that the biggest constraint to the long-term survival and growth of a business is the leadership capabilities of its management, particularly the business owner and the founding team. Owners often run the business using a "seat-of-pants" approach, without much consideration to the latest knowledge about leadership qualities and styles. Business owners also report considerable stress in their work, with many entrepreneurs crashing and burning out from the strain of managing their business. Yet, there are specific steps that can be taken to manage stress and increase productivity. Entrepreneurs who delegate well and manage their business professionally will generally go further than those who try to do it all themselves.

World of Books

Shoe Dog: A Memoir by the Creator of Nike by Phil Knight
Dave's Way by R. David Thomas
Miss Jessie's: Creating a Successful Business from Scratch – Naturally by Miko Branch

In the Movies

The film '*Tucker: The Man and his Dream*' is about Preston Tucker, a Detroit engineer, who wants to build a car of the future. He starts the Tucker Corporation to manufacture cars with revolutionary safety designs. He faces tremendous resistance from some of his key employees, major competitors, and even the media. Tucker shows that he has convincingly delivered on the cars he promised, but he dies a broken man believing that small business owners are harmed by large corporations.

Live Exercise

"I am worried about Johnny, kiddo," your father says when you call him one evening after class. As you listen to your father describe his concerns, you see that he is not worrying unnecessarily. Here are some things your father tells you are worrying him about Johnny:

1. Johnny has been putting in very long hours at work. His time at home is now limited to sleeping there and getting ready for work. His wife says they haven't gone on a date-night together in months.
2. Johnny recently got into a verbal altercation with a reporter who questioned the usefulness of the SoapStandle. It wasn't a reporter from the *New York Times* or *Wall Street Journal* or anything like that, but still it resulted in negative coverage in the local paper.
3. Johnny has been talking about completing a certificate course that focuses on financial management, marketing, and customer service. The course will cost about $5000, which is not much money, but does Johnny really need to take college courses at this stage? His wife is worried that he is having a late mid-life crisis and the college is an excuse to meet younger women.
4. Johnny is talking about bringing on a partner who would help out with managing the growing company. While this seems like a good idea on the surface, can Johnny really find someone who is as devoted to this business as he is?

As you hear your Dad share his concerns, you think about some of the issues you have noticed with Johnny lately:

1. Johnny's updates on Facebook, LinkedIn, and Instagram have been showing up at odd hours, including really late at night or very early in the morning.
2. Johnny asked you about energy drinks, and when you asked him why he was so interested in the drinks that many college students were consuming, he evaded your question.
3. Johnny shared with you sometime back that he is troubled his supplier doesn't have the same enthusiasm for SoapStandle as he does. While Johnny wants to put out only the highest quality products on the market, his supplier has been more permissive about quality defects.

Based on what you know now, what advice would you give to Johnny? Your father and you know that Johnny cares about what you think. Lately, he's even hinted he wants you to call him Uncle Johnny. You have Johnny's ear the way few people do.

Things to Remember

LO 11.1 Explain the fundamental leadership qualities business owners need

- Passions means do what you love and love what you do.
- No matter which profession you choose, you will rarely do something where you love every aspect of it.
- When you start a business, you realize that there is a lot more to it than the one or two things you love.
- There are two forms of passion: harmonious and obsessive.
- Most people are disappointed when they do not get something right the first time.
- Resilience refers to the capacity to recover quickly from difficulties and setbacks.
- Sunk costs are investments that can never be recovered.
- Another important leadership quality for business owners is humility.
- Being humble is not easy when you are succeeding in your business.

LO 11.2 Distinguish between the various leadership styles for business owners

- Current research on leadership styles often focuses on transformational leadership.
- Employees working for transformational leaders focus on what is good for the company rather than what is best for them.
- Charisma refers to the rare ability to charm and persuade people in addition to being a good communicator.
- Sometimes firms need a calming leader who maintains the status quo and focuses on improving the operational efficiency of the company.
- Authentic leadership is about being your true self.
- Concerned by the scandals in business, some experts are emphasizing the importance of prioritizing the interests of others over everything else.

LO 11.3 Identify the causes and solutions for stress and emotional well-being for entrepreneurs

- Many business owners struggle with issues such as anxiety, binge eating, drug addiction, insomnia, or depression.
- There is an inverted U relationship between stress and performance. Stress initially improves performance as one starts to push beyond one's usual functioning, but after a certain level, stress depresses performance and becomes counterproductive.
- Starting and managing a business often means taking on a massive workload.
- The wear and tear of long hours, constantly buzzing phones (calls, texts, and messages), uncertain working conditions, and family demands can result in fatigue, frustration, anger, and burnout.
- Running a business often involves taking on considerable financial responsibilities.
- Entrepreneurs frequently find themselves dealing with interpersonal stressors.
- Entrepreneurs are often married to their business, leaving them little time to pursue outside interests.
- Building a successful business can take years filled with setbacks, long hours, and little tangible rewards.
- Growing a company to scale confronts the management team with unforeseen challenges that can strain them to the point where they become stressed and wish their companies had remained small.

- Working long hours, having difficulty relaxing and no real time off, and not spending time on kids' activities can produce work–life conflict for business owners.
- When we are tired – mentally or physically – our efficiency and effectiveness at work decrease.
- Some business owners put together an advisory board to bounce off ideas and share their concerns.

LO 11.4 **Discuss the challenges of delegation and professional management in small firms**

- Business owners who delegate well are great managers and supportive bosses.
- It is well known that entrepreneurs find it *very* difficult to delegate *even* the simplest of tasks.
- Even if you can learn and do everything, you will find yourself running out of time to do all that needs to be done.
- Many business owners lack the patience and forethought to explain what they need to get done.
- Many business owners are paranoid, assuming that everyone has some other agenda, or may steal their idea or customers.
- Many business owners are afraid that if they delegate, they will lose control.
- Many times when entrepreneurs delegate they think someone should be able to do things at least as good as, if not better than, they are able to do themselves.

Key Terms

passion	cocky jerks	steady-hand leadership	karoshi
harmonious passion	transformational	authentic leadership	psychological
obsessive passion	leadership	servant leadership	immune system
perseverance	charisma	abusive leadership	physiological
humility	individualized	stress	immune system
resilience	consideration	tipping point	dumping
cockroach	inspirational motivation	hustle porn	
sunk cost fallacy	intellectual stimulation	allostatic load	

Experiential Exercise

Toronto psychologist Kate Hays tells her patients to imagine a stress scale "ranging from 1, where you're practically asleep, to 10, where you're climbing off the ceiling." Then, she asks them to recall a past peak performance and figure out where their stress at that moment would have ranked. Many people say 4–6, but responses range from 2 to 8, says Dr. Hays, who specializes in sports and performance psychology. That becomes their personal stress management target.

Now think back to a past peak performance (when you performed the best work that you are proud of). What would you say your stress level was? Where would you say your own stress level currently is? Calculate the difference between your past peak stress level and your current stress level. What do you infer from this score?

Reach out to five business owners in your network. Ask them to rate their current stress level on the same scale as above (1 = you're practically asleep to 10 = you're climbing off the ceiling). Also, ask them to think back to a time in the past when they felt they performed at a very high level. What was their stress level at that point? For each of the business owners in your network, calculate the difference between their past peak stress level and the current stress level. What do you infer from this score?

Ask each of the five business owners in your network for advice on (a) the causes of the stress they face, and (b) how to manage the stress in their work. Prepare a memo that you can submit to your professor on stresses faced by business owners and the possible solutions for addressing their stress.

CHAPTER 12

Human Resources Management

LEARNING OBJECTIVES

This chapter will help you to:

LO 12.1 Outline the pros and cons of hiring workers for a small business

LO 12.2 Describe the various channels through which small firms find new employees

LO 12.3 Explain employee selection and training processes in small firms

LO 12.4 Explain how companies can discipline and reward employees

> *Nothing is achieved in organizations without people. Yet, what most employees experience in their organizations is that they are expendable "costs walking on legs".*

ANDREW MAYO

12.0 Introduction

Many small businesses never hire any employees. Indeed, for about 80% of the small businesses in the United States the owner single-handedly deals with all aspects of the business. The 20% or so of small firms that have one or more employees are often heralded as an important source of job creation for the economy. Why is the proportion of existing small businesses who hire employees so small? Hiring employees is expensive, not just in financial terms but also in terms of the time and effort you put into recruiting and training them.

This chapter discusses how small firms can manage employees in a way that is helpful for the business. When competent employees are recruited, trained, and incentivized to perform well on the job, they can boost a firm's performance and help take the firm to the next level. Consequently, hiring employees is one of the most important tasks of a small business.

SPOTLIGHT | Rose Pallet: Do Small Firms Need Recruiters?

Mia Allen founded Rose Pallet, partnering with her sister Amy Olson and uncle Alan Rose. Mia and Amy were veterans of the pallet industry, though they worked at competing firms. Because of their industry experience, Mia and Amy are quite knowledgeable about the functioning of the pallet business and have a rich network of buyers. The company offers a complete line of pallet management services and sells a wide variety of pallets and crates to customers in several different industries.

One major challenge that Allen faces is hiring salespeople for her 10-person company. "It's just extremely difficult to find somebody who wants to work and seems hungry to make money doing sales," she says. Low unemployment and rising wages create hiring challenges for companies of all sizes. The labor department reported 7.5 million unfilled jobs in the United States at the end of March 2019. The tight labor market is particularly problematic for small firms. "The smaller the company, the greater the challenge," notes Mark Zandi, chief economist at Moody's Analytics. As the labor market tightens, he says, "the problems are only going to intensify."

Rose Pallet's Mia Allen says finding someone who wants to work is very difficult.

For a recent hiring need, Allen pored over 300 résumés of salespeople – mostly nights and weekends – for more than two months. She interviewed more than 50 candidates by phone. When she still couldn't find someone who met her needs, she brought in a consultant to help her find a new salesperson.

Personnel recruitment consultancy is a crowded field, with thousands of firms competing to serve a somewhat limited market. The typical customer for recruitment firms is a large company that can afford to pay the consultant one-third of the first year's salary and bonus of the job candidate. There are just over a million establishments with more than 500 employees in the United States, according to the Census Bureau. There are about 5.2 million firms with 100 or fewer employees in the country. Though small firms have needs as acute as large companies to hire good people, they often lack the budgets and human resources capacity to fill those positions. "Small companies are not going to pay $15,000–$20,000 every time they hire somebody," says Daniel Solomon of Hyrian On Demand, which recruits personnel for small firms. Daniel's father had owned an electroplating plant and his grandparents had a food processing company that made pickled herrings and other products, which provided him his first lessons about the unique needs of small firms. The recruiting service "saves us the effort of canvassing résumés, interviewing candidates. It is very time consuming," says Christopher Campbell, president of Asset Smart Software, a Santa Monica, CA, company with about 20 employees.

The consultancy helped Allen land a new salesperson promptly. "When we found the person, it was a quicker process because we didn't want to dillydally and lose her." Now, Allen's concern is what happens if the new hire leaves soon or she has to hire for another position. While recruitment companies like Hyrian may have special low prices for small firms (as low as $1900 for junior positions like the salesperson Allen was seeking), the costs add up over time and eat into the company's profitability. Another problem: The consultancy fees were due at the time the hire was made and did not provide protection against hires that didn't work out or quit soon.

Discussion Questions

1. What do recruitment consultants bring to the table to help small firms with hiring?

2. Is Mia's concern about the sustainability of recruiting through recruitment consultants for her firm's needs justified?

3. Do you agree with Mia that it is difficult to find employees who are actually interested in working?

Module 12.1 Making the Decision to Hire

Hiring good people is difficult for firms of all sizes, but particularly onerous for small businesses that do not generally have the **slack** to deal with the problems and challenges associated with hiring. Consider the case of Torque Transmission, an Ohio-based manufacturer of mechanical power transmission components. The president of the family-run business John Rampe shares that the company has struggled to maintain a staff of three skilled machinists. "We have posted ads online. We have a sign out on the front lawn. We have a couple of temp agencies working on it. Being a small business, we definitely have it a bit tougher. We don't have the strong wage scale some other, larger companies do." On at least 10 occasions, the company has hired a machinist, but the new hire shows up late or not at all or turns out not to be a good fit.

You have probably heard managers and entrepreneurs say things like "our biggest assets walk out of the door every evening." The assets they are talking about are their employees. Such statements are very pleasing to the ear. Yet, the truth is that there is no company in the world that lists employees as an asset on its balance sheet. Employees are considered an expense (perhaps, even a liability!), a cost item that needs to be controlled, or better still, reduced to zero. As one experienced person frustratingly noted, "Being an employee of several different companies, I can honestly say that I've felt like nothing more than a line item on a spreadsheet somewhere that an accountant is desperately trying to eliminate."

Hiring an employee brings many benefits to the business and its owner. Having employees means that more work can be done, allowing the company to stay open longer hours, serving more customers, and producing more output. At the same time, employees also impose additional demands on the owner. The firm needs to do more sales to cover the employees' wages or salary. The employee needs to be provided adequate training for the job. Employees also need to be properly supervised to evaluate their performance. When a business is not able to provide the right support for its new employees, it hurts everyone. As a business owner lamented, "Probably the biggest mistake I made in my early hires was hiring too early. As a result, we were not as profitable as we might have been if I had been slower to hire." Some experts suggest waiting a year or two from startup before hiring the first employee(s). Joanna Kotz, coauthor of the Microsoft Small Business Kit, advises that "while every business has its own rhythm, it's usually wise to go through the first year without hiring. Get a feel for the sales cycle and the downturns. Measure the 'just right' temperature of income and outgo. Squirreling away at least a year's worth of expenses and overheads before hiring will help see you through rough patches."

Consider Christina Hale of Bows 4U & Gifts 2, an 800-sq.-ft. retail store in Culpeper, VA. She began making hair bows for her seven-year-old daughter. Before long, she was selling her creations at crafts festivals and had expanded her offerings to include jewelry, wooden signs, wreaths, and more. When COVID-19 forced her to cancel the family summer vacation, she decided to use the $4000 vacation fund to rent a storefront that was available at rock-bottom rent. Developing a clientele has been slow. "Some people will stop and look in the window, but don't want to enter," Christina shares. As the business becomes more established, and she has a better sense of the market she is able to capture, Christina may be able to afford to hire some help for the store.

KEY TAKEAWAY

While hiring employees can bring many benefits to the business and its owner, it also imposes additional demands that cost time and money to the owner.

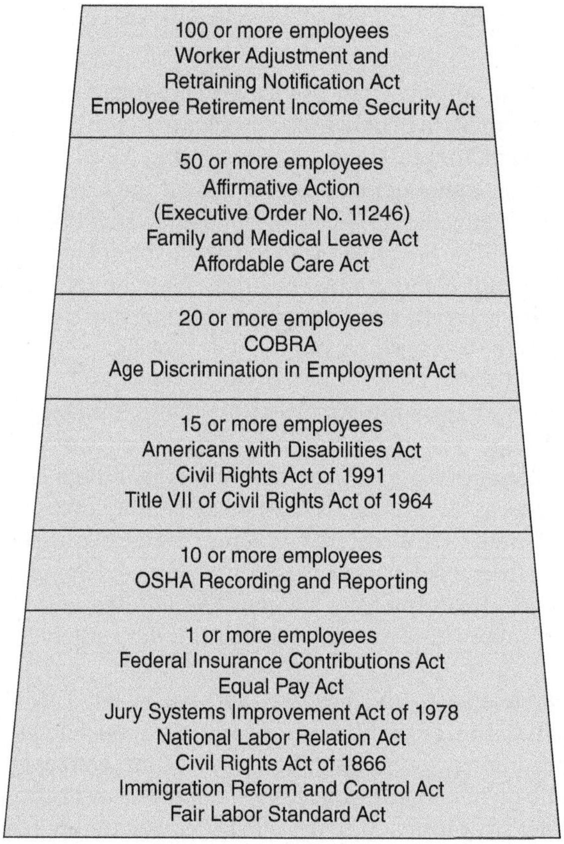

FIGURE 12.1 As a Small Business Grows, It Has to Comply with More Federal Laws

By hiring employees, businesses also take on legal responsibilities as an employer. Depending on the size of your firm, you may be subject to different regulatory requirements. Generally, as the number of employees in a firm increases, the laws governing compliance increase proportionally (see Figure 12.1). According to research released by the Small Business Administration's Office of Advocacy, it can cost about $2830 or more for firms with less than 20 employees than those with 500 or more employees to comply with government regulations on a per-employee basis. Firms that fail to meet their legal responsibilities toward employees may be penalized or sued. This is what happened to Madeira Restaurant Inc. in Rhone Island. The U.S. Labor Department filed suit against the restaurant accusing it of violating the Fair Labor Standard Act by withholding overtime pay from employees who worked more than 40 hours a week. A court ordered the restaurant to pay the employees $40,000 in back wages and damages.

Melinda Vetro, an immigrant from Hungary, is co-owner of Old Europe Pastries, a pastry shop in Asheville, NC. Her shop has been open for 25 years, with the last 10 in its current spot. When business plummeted in Spring 2020 due to COVID-19, Melinda was able to use a $62,500 Paycheck Protection Program loan to take care of payroll, rent, and a new mixer for the kitchen. She moved the pastry display case close to the front door and served a menu of coffee, croissants, cakes, and other drinks and pastries to go. She now employs 16 people, up from 13 before the pandemic (and is in the process of relocating to a larger facility). Based on what you just read about legal responsibilities that come with hiring employees, what new responsibilities do you think Melinda should consider when adding more people to her staff?

Melinda Vetro, and her son Bence, were able to expand their pastry business during the COVID-19 pandemic.

12.1.1 Using Independent Contractors

In weighing the pros and cons of hiring employees, some businesses decide to remain solo operated as long as they can. These businesses – **solo operators** – rely on contractors to do the work employees would have done, which allows them to benefit from additional labor, but without taking direct responsibility for the hiring of employees. Indeed, contract workers are now in fashion as thought leaders and companies extol the benefits of the **gig economy**, an economic system where the independent worker is paid by the "gig," or project. According to a 2017 report by Upwork, an online marketplace, some 57.3 million Americans, or 36% of the workforce, are now freelancing (that is, working outside the regular labor force). **Freelancers** are workers who sell their services by time or job to a variety of companies as opposed to working on a regular salary basis for one employer. While some believe the gig economy is the wave of the future, others argue that the gig economy has made it easier to exploit workers.

Interactive Exercise

The state of California recently passed a law, known as AB-5, that classifies many workers as employees instead of independent contractors. The law stipulates that if these workers perform tasks that are part of the normal course of a company's business, among other requirements, they will be eligible for health insurance, paid time off, and other benefits. The law has attracted much support and tons of criticism. Read as many articles as you can find to understand the benefits and drawbacks of AB-5. Do you understand enough to take a position about the usefulness of the law?

There are four major reasons for a small business to consider independent contractors rather than hiring employees:

Costs. Who is cheaper: contractors or employees? It is possible that for the work you have in mind contractors charge more than regular salaried workers. However, firms do not incur the cost of taxes, Social Security, or benefits when hiring contractors. When the service to be performed needs licensing or certification, contractors are responsible for having them, which is not usually the case for employees where the firm pays for them to obtain the necessary documentation. For these reasons, contract workers tend to be cheaper than employees.

Supervision. Contract workers, by definition, require less oversight than regular workers. Contractors are compensated based on measurable units (either time or amount of work), so they have an incentive to not shirk as regular employees may sometimes do.

Flexibility. For businesses where work is seasonal (e.g. agriculture), hiring a contractor means that the business is not obligated to keep paying them when the season ends or work doesn't come in. If worded appropriately, contracts are usually easier for the business to get out of it if work should dry up.

Consulting. When a business needs help or advice on a project, it is easier to use a contractor rather than regular workers. Even if the business is expanding into a new area and the same help may be needed regularly in the long run, starting out with a contractor could be good practice to see if it's a line of work the firm could benefit from. Also, contractors know that their work may not be ongoing, so there are no hard feelings when the company runs out of work to give to them.

Many small firms are taking advantage of a boom in service providers willing to handle functions such as human resources and marketing. Altraco, a contract manufacturer in Thousand Oaks, CA, first outsourced accounting and then shifted logistics and the creation of artwork and presentations to third parties. Scott Williams, co-owner of Altraco, which has 16 employees, says that "before we add people, we would look for an outsource opportunity because it's cheaper. It's a global economy. You have to be relentlessly pursuing efficiencies or you won't survive."

What Do You Think?

Ever heard of gun.io? It's a Nashville-based online startup that matches freelance software developers with business clients who want to outsource digital projects. Gun's overheads are very low. Three people, including its young CEO Teja Yenamandra, run the online platform. Office space is tiny and includes a few desks and some computer equipment. Amy Watters, 41, freelances for Gun. From a converted bedroom in her 1960s ranch house, she collaborates with developers across the world. Walters doesn't really need much to do her job: "a laptop, a phone, and an Internet connection," she says. Walters and her fellow freelancers are paid well, typically $100 an hour. But the work is part-time, and many of the workers either have other gigs or a spouse who works full-time. Gun doesn't pay benefits (so, no health insurance or Social Security), and any career development is up to the workers themselves. The lack of stability of her work doesn't concern Walters, who was once laid off from a full-time job – on 9/11 of all days and found the experience traumatizing. What do you think are the costs and benefits that workers like Walters should consider when deciding to work on contract? And, what do you think are the advantages and disadvantages for firms who rely on contractors like Walters?

12.1.2 Recruiting Employees

While using contract workers has a number of advantages, on the flip side, contract workers are independent, so the firm has less control over how and when they do the work assigned to them. To gain more control over the quality and delivery of their workers, firms may decide not to rely on contractors and hire regular workers instead. The process through which a firm hires new employees and brings them on-board is referred to as **recruitment**. When a firm decides it wants to hire an employee, it needs to (a) define the position(s) to be filled and (b) identify the qualifications needed to successfully complete the work in those positions. While it may seem difficult at first, the time and effort spent defining the job and determining the employees' abilities that are needed for that job are a good investment for business owners.

Many people start their own business because of the flexibility it offers. They do not like strict rules and red tape. As their own companies grow, they often realize they need to lay down the very rules that got on their nerves in the first place. Table 12.1 shares the experiences of five business owners who thought they could avoid structure in firms.

The goal of recruitment is to attract talented individuals to the firm. But does the firm always benefit from hiring the most talented individual available in the market? Consider the case of a small, five-employee marketing firm that advises clients on the use of digital ads, search engine optimization, and ways of increasing their Web traffic. Would such a firm necessarily benefit from hiring a PhD in Computer Science from Berkeley with work experience at Google? Moreover, would such an employee be happy working at a small firm with primarily local clients? Such issues are considered a part of **employee fit**, which is the match between the needs, expectations, and culture of the firm to the needs, expectations, and skills of the individual employees.

TABLE 12.1

What Causes Shift in Attitudes Toward Structure in Business?

Business owner	Business name	What they thought?	What happened to change their mind?
Nick Friedman	College Hunks Hauling Junk	Envisioned a real-life Never Never Land where work is always fun, and the culture is always stress-free	Client-service ratings decreased, employee morale was low, and profitability dwindled as excessive expenses skyrocketed. Also, we didn't have any alignment or positive company culture. We needed structure, we needed processes and systems.
Joe Apfelbaum	Ajax Union	Wanted a business that was free of corporate red tape—no meetings, no paperwork, just get the job done	Used to interview people without asking for an ID or asking them to fill out forms. Then things started going wrong. One potential hire, for instance, turned out to be a con artist who threatened one of the employees personally. Changed hiring to a detailed process that involves multiple interviews, personality tests, and background checks.
Paul Levering	FeatureTel	As a startup, we were "all in this together" and did not need a hierarchy or titles	As we grew the business and our new hires were more employees than they were adventurers like the group of founders, we needed more clarity . . . larger and more sophisticated customers also wanted to know we were a real business with clear lines of command and escalation paths to solve problems needing attention from higher-ups.
Sarah Schupp	UniversityParent	Will play things by the ear	An employee asked to be reimbursed for a family trip to see her family because she had stopped to see a potential client on the way. It turned into a big mess and misunderstanding because I hadn't clearly defined how we would reimburse.
R.J. Lewis	eHealthcare Solutions LLC	Didn't see a need for a policy manual	As the firm grew, things like unlimited sick days became unsustainable. One team member was "sick" about 20 times in the first half of a year, and one or two team members seemed to be sick only on Mondays and Fridays. The combinations of these abuses were enough to convince us that the unlimited policy was not fair to everyone.

There are three key steps in recruitment: job analysis, job description, and job specifications.

Job analysis. The first step in the recruitment process is to identify what is done in a particular job, how it is to be done, and who will do it. In formal terms, **job analysis** is the process of gathering and analyzing information about the content and requirements of jobs, as well as the context in which jobs are performed. It is the foundation for all subsequent human resource activities in the firm.

The courts and the Equal Employment Opportunity Commission (EEOC) generally consider information obtained from the job analysis as the basis to ensure whether firms are in compliance or violation of being an equal employment opportunity employer. At a basic level, job analysis involves collecting information about what the job is called, the responsibilities that are part of the job, the skills required to perform the job, the effort demanded from employees, and the working conditions in which employees will need to perform.

For firms with one or more employees already on the payroll, job analysis also involves gaining the cooperation and confidence of your existing employees for further hiring. Existing employees should also be consulted to determine what the job involves. Depending on the size of the existing workforce, firms may also need to identify an appropriate technique for job analysis. While questionnaires are the most commonly used technique for job analysis, firms may also use interviews or observations to understand the requirements of a job. **Interviews** involve one-on-one conversations with existing workers to obtain information about the work they do and the challenges they face. Interviews may be structured (that is, follow a predefined systematic approach) or unstructured (that is, no predefined specific questions) depending on the firm culture. **Observations** involve actually watching employees at work in their daily routines. The key benefit of the observation technique is that it yields first-hand knowledge of employees going about their daily tasks in their natural work environments.

Job description. The **job description** is a written statement describing the tasks, duties, and responsibilities of the position under consideration and the skills, knowledge, and abilities involved in performing that position. It is a snapshot of the job, so it is useful to identify the duties, qualifications, decision-making, interactions, supervision received/exercised, and impact of the position for each job in the firm. There is no standard format available for job description, but one must try to include the following elements:

The title of the job, where it is located within the company, and date of origin are all part of the introductory section. One may also include job code, salary range, pay classification, and the name of the analyst producing the job description.

The jobholder's responsibilities, scope of their authority, and who they report to (as well as who reports to them) should also be summarized.

Essential and nonessential duties should be clearly identified. The most important duties are listed first, followed by the less important ones. A good rule-of-thumb is that any duty that will take at least 5% of an employee's time should be included here.

The steps or activities needed to complete one's overall duties should be made explicit. The focus is on the outcomes or results rather than the manner in which they are performed (unless the manner is also critically important for the successful performance of the task). These task statements help to establish objective performance standards for the position.

Job description also includes travel requirements, working conditions, and any other stipulation that the workers must consider when performing the job. Employers may also include general-duty statements like "other duties as assigned" and indicate that the list is not comprehensive ("including, but not limited to"). Of course, job description should not include illegal or unethical conduct (e.g. "will need to be comfortable packaging venomous reptiles for shipment through USPS").

Job specifications. A **job specification** is a written statement capturing the knowledge, skills, abilities, experience, and other personal requirements – including, but not limited to, physical, emotional, technical, and communication attributes – required to perform a job. In writing the specification, firms need to carefully ensure that the stated requirements are truly necessary for successful performance of the job.

The information needed for the job specification comes from the job description. A job description is part of the job analysis. While the job description focuses on the duties and responsibilities of a job, the job specifications pertain to education, skills, and experience a prospective employee needs to have to be able to do the job well. At a minimum, a job specification statement should have three components:

Education. States what degrees, training, or certifications are required for the position. For example, a yoga studio may require that an instructor should have credentials that include study of poses, anatomy, and the history and philosophy of yoga. The studio may require instructors to have Yoga Alliance's 200-hour registered yoga-teacher credential, which has become the industry standard in the United States.

Experience. Includes the number of years of experience in the position and the overall work experience in the labor market. May also cover whether supervisory or managerial experience is needed.

Required skills and abilities. Identifies the qualities and attributes needed to successfully perform the job. For example, a day-care center may determine that "must enjoy spending time with children" is a necessary quality for all their customer-facing positions. Jess Sims, a fitness instructor with Peloton, shares that the key skill in her job is to be a good teacher.

What Do You Think?

Imagine your aunt is in the process of starting a day care for children. Kids will be hosted there from 8 am in the morning to 6 pm in the evening. Your aunt is now at the stage where she wants to hire some people to work in the day care. Can you identify what jobs need to be filled at the startup stage and what functions people will perform in those jobs? Can you conduct a job analysis, write a job description, and identify job specifications of the kind that providers of a day care may need to hire?

Comprehension Check

1. Describe the advantages and disadvantages of hiring employees for a small business.
2. What is the gig economy?
3. Define job analysis, job description, and job specifications.

Module 12.2 Finding New Employees

Let's say a small business is ready to recruit employees. The owners have thought about the help they need, they have done the job analysis, have prepared a job description, and have written up the job specification. Everything is now in place to recruit. However, where does one go to find new employees? There are a number of sources to recruit employees. As you can imagine, each recruitment source has its advantages and disadvantages that need to be considered.

> **KEY TAKEAWAY**
>
> Finding good employees is not easy for any company, but it is particularly difficult for small businesses.

12.2.1 Referrals

Would you like to hire someone who comes recommended by people you already know or have worked with before? For most small business owners, **referrals** are probably the best source of recruitment. Some even consider referrals the "holy grail" of recruitment.

Referrals may come from people officially connected with your business, such as suppliers, customers, or employees. Such references have the benefit of familiarity with the firm culture and some knowledge of the skills and abilities new employees may need to work there. Referrals may also come from people who know you personally – friends, acquaintances, and family members. Whether referrals come from professional or personal contacts, the challenge is that if the person referred is not hired or does not work out, the person who provided the referral may get upset.

According to the Society for Human Resource Management (SHRM), the largest organization of HR professionals worldwide, referrals from existing employees are the top source of new hires for employers. "Employee referrals have proven success," said Amber Hyatt, SHRM-SCP, vice president of product marketing for Chicago-based talent management software company SilkRoad. "Employee referrals have excellent conversion rates from interview to hire, as well as typically longer tenure with the organization." Indeed, employing workers who are related to one another is fairly common practice in small firms. For some owners, hiring through employee referrals helps boost team spirit and loyalty. However, in many cases, employing people from the network of your existing employees can create tension and expose the firm to potential fraud. Table 12.2 presents the experience three business owners had in hiring through their employees' networks.

TABLE 12.2

Experiences of Some Business Owners Who Hired Through Employees' Networks

Name	Business	What did they do?	What did they find out?
Mary Liz Curtin	Leon & Lulu LLC	Hired several of her existing employees' teenage kids to serve fresh coffee to shoppers – while wearing skates	When she reprimanded a staff member for sporting low-cut jeans and exposed bra straps on the job, the employee's mother, a cashier at Leon & Lulu, became defensive. "The lines got really blurred between who's the boss, who's the mother and who works for whom."
Sandy Jaffe	Booksource Inc.	Hired workers' relatives for decades. A worker's kin is "going to try and succeed if for no other reason to make their relative look good. They don't want to disappoint someone in their family"	One of his employees, who was close to being fired, once managed to retain his warehouse job thanks in part to his coworker spouse. Managers approached the wife about her husband's increasingly bad attitude after he failed to heed repeated warnings, and soon after, his behavior improved.
Denis Stepansky	ItsHot.com Inc.	Hired a top-notch employee's relative	That relative stopped showing up for work and a video camera appears to show him stealing at least $20,000 worth of jewelry from the small New York firm. "We trusted him blindly," which was a mistake.

Jeff Hyman, who runs the recruitment website recruitrockstars.com, is a firm believer in hiring through referrals. He says that "referrals deliver the highest quality candidates, in the least amount of time and for the lowest cost per hire. Plus, over the long term, referrals fit in better, outperform, and stay around longer than candidates hired through other sources."

The most challenging aspect of referrals is that the person who refers is also putting his or her reputation on the line when they recommend someone for a job. If the new hire works out, it can be a win–win for everyone. However, when the new hire falls short of the employer's expectation, the person referring them may find that his or her reputation also takes a hit.

12.2.2 Relatives and Friends

It is tempting to hire a family member or friend when there is a vacant position in the business. You will get to work with someone you already know well and you may also be helping them out in a time of need. When Kary Taylor started her own management consultancy company after several years of working for others, she employed two of her adult children in the business.

Perhaps, even better, some family members and friends may be willing to help in getting the new venture off the ground and work for free or for a reduced wage when you still have little or nothing to pay. Or, they just want to help you without expecting anything in return. Toshio Suzuki, chef and co-owner of the restaurant Sushi Zen in Midtown Manhattan, turned to his son Yuta Suzuki for help with getting the books in order. Yuta shares, his father "came to me with a serious face and said, 'I hear you're good at math. We have a small problem. We need your help.' When I looked at the books it wasn't healthy. I thought it was a great opportunity to try out what I could do. I stared at everything from auditing, to regular food purchases, to how consistently everyone was cutting the fish."

It does seem like hiring friends or relatives, especially if they need the job and truly want to help you, is a really good idea, right? Unfortunately, many family and friend hires do not work out well. Why is this the case? There are three major reasons:

Freedom. Family and friends who come to work for you may expect a sort of professional and personal freedom that is not available in normal work relationships. Coming in late, going home early, taking time off, and even acting as if they have more authority than generally associated with their position are some of the problems that come up.

Input. Remember that family dinner when your brother-in-law dispensed advice on every topic under the sun? From economic problems of the country to your kid's struggles in school, your brother-in-law has a solution for everything. He may be well-meaning, but would you want him offering unwanted advice all day about the business to you? Family members and friends who work for a small business may start offering unsolicited advice, which can be hard or rude to ignore. You may not be able to quiet them without offending them. Also, their input may not always be neutral or have your best interest in mind, so that it is unclear whether the advice they are offering is to help you or to advance their own agenda.

Commitments. When working for a family member or friend, many people may not appreciate the need to honor commitments and deadlines. As a result, the business may lose clients or jeopardize its relationship with important stakeholders. As a business owner, you want your employees to see you as the management authority in the firm. You may not always have all the answers to the problems that your business is dealing with, but you definitely want employees to follow your orders once you have made a decision. Unfortunately, when you have your family or friends working in the business, they may continue to consider the personal relationship over the professional. You want your nephew who also works for you to pick up a client's car at 9 am for engine work that needs to be done before the client leaves on a road trip, but your nephew decides that he wants to sleep in that day. Unfortunately, he does not tell you about it until you call him when the frantic client starts yelling at you. What does one do in such a situation?

TABLE **12.3**	
Advantages and Disadvantages of Hiring Friends and Family to Work for You	
Pros	**Cons**
Friends and family may already be familiar with your company and how it works. You wouldn't need to spend as much time training new employees with the aims of your company.	A friend or family member may take advantage of their status, knowing that it is more difficult to fire them.
Family members and close friends may be more willing to work longer hours (such as evenings or weekends) when necessary.	Other employees may feel jealous when you hire a friend or family member, thinking it is favoritism. This may especially be the case when a family member or friend is given a promotion over a nonrelative/friend.
You already know many of the capabilities of your relatives and close friends. This will let you assign just the right tasks to each person, based on their individual strengths and weaknesses.	Personal family problems or disagreements between friends may be brought to the workplace. Problems in the workplace may be brought home to the family or impact your relationship with your friends.

While the idea of recruiting from among family and friends is very appealing, it can be difficult to work with people who have a personal relationship with you. Table 12.3 summarizes the pros and cons of hiring friends and family to work for you.

12.2.3 Advertisements

Paid advertisements in newspapers, magazines, trade publications, or storefronts are a common method to generate leads for working in a small business. A key benefit of advertisements is that they reach a wider and more diverse audience compared to other techniques. Keep in mind that greater diversity in the applicant pool often comes with more heterogeneity in quality of applicants.

Advertisements can be a useful tool to reach prospective employees.
Source: Redrawn from Holimont, Inc.

12.2.4 Internet Job Sites

Recruiting on the Internet allows a business owner to post a job description on the Web or to search a database of résumés. There are many options for a business owner looking to recruit online, such as Monster.com and CareerBuilder.com. ZipRecruiter began as a tool for small businesses to post job listings affordably and has now expanded to become an online employment marketplace that uses artificial intelligence to connect businesses of all sizes with job seekers. The website Glassdoor started as a ratings platform with anonymous reviews about the company's work environment from current and former employees, but now also provides millions of job listings and a searchable dataset for employers. According to SHRM, the job site Indeed.com is the top external source of hiring for employers. Recruiting websites have increased the pace of hiring, as you can now post a job at midnight and expect to get responses within minutes. Employers who know exactly what they are looking for can use filters to search hundreds and thousands of résumés with high accuracy.

12.2.5 Social Media

The last few years have witnessed the increasing use of social media for hiring. Companies can pay firms like Appirio or Jobvite to mine the owner's social networking contacts for potential hires. "Appirio's matching engine comes up with a list of friends whose job titles, geographic location and other keywords match their company's available positions," says Ryan Nichols, Appirio's vice president of product management. The matching engine has access to the same information that a Facebook friend does. While the Appirio software can currently search Facebook contacts, the Jobvite tool can search Facebook, LinkedIn, and Twitter contacts. "And anyone who receives a Jobvite can search their own networks and pass it along again," shares Dan Finnigan, the chief executive of Jobvite. Total Attorneys, a Chicago-based company providing law firms with marketing services and administrative tasks such as preparing bankruptcy petitions, relies heavily on Jobvite for recruitment.

BranchOut Inc. is a startup with a Facebook app that invites anyone to sign up for its professional networking services. Users can allow the BranchOut app to access their work and education histories and contact information and those of their Facebook friends who choose to share such details on Facebook. Carolyn Betts, CEO of San Francisco–based Betts Recruiting LLC, says BranchOut lets her search for Facebook users based on where they work, years of experience, where they went to school, and their job title – all details that previously weren't searchable on Facebook.

Companies may also use social media to identify problems or issues with applicants that may not show up in the application process. Social Intelligence, based in Santa Barbara, CA, scrapes the Internet for everything prospective employees may have said or done online in the past seven years. It uses the information to assemble a dossier with examples of professional honors and charitable work, along with negative information that meets specific criteria: online evidence of racist remarks; references to drugs; sexually explicit photos, text messages, or videos; flagrant displays of weapons or bombs and clearly identifiable violent activity. Less than a third of the data surfaced by Social Intelligence comes from major social networking sites such as Facebook and Twitter, with the rest coming from deep Web searches that find comments on blogs and posts on smaller social sites, like Tumblr, the blogging site, as well as Yahoo user groups, e-commerce sites, bulletin boards, and even Craigslist. Despite of concerns about invasion of privacy, the use of social media for finding prospective employees and making hiring decisions is here to stay (see Figure 12.2).

12.2.6 Employment Agencies

An **employment agency** is an organization that matches employers to employees. Many countries, including the United States, have publicly funded employment agencies focusing primarily on helping junior-level employees find work locally. The first publicly funded employment agencies in the United States were set up under the New Deal. Over time, all 50 states and many large cities came to have employment agencies that match employers and employees at no cost.

Private employment agencies match employers and employees for a fee, usually paid by the employer. They are more useful than government agencies for businesses that

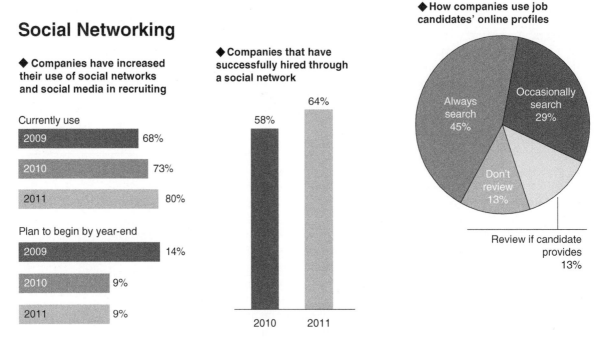

FIGURE 12.2 Increase in Use of Social Media in Recruiting
Source: Redrawn from Jobvite survey of U.S. Human Resources and Recruiting Professionals

need more skilled employees or senior-level executives. The first known private employment agency in the world, Gabbitas & Thring, was started in 1873 by John Gabbitas who recruited schoolmasters for public schools in England. In the United States, the first private employment agency was founded by Fred Winslow in 1893 for engineering talents. Private agencies that focus on upper echelon positions are also called **executive recruiters** or **headhunters**. Check out the Web for examples of executive headhunter firms. Here is one example: www.Pearlmeyer.com.

12.2.7 Company Websites

Your company website is another place to find new employees. Company websites give you full control over how your 'help-wanted' ad should look at only a small incremental cost (if any) to your website budget. This method is most effective when the site receives good traffic. If the website has little traffic, you won't receive many responses to your recruiting efforts.

12.2.8 Other Sources

The foregoing sources are not a comprehensive list of places where you can hope to find new employees. There are also other possible sources of potential employees, though they don't get used as much or are not as popular as the ones discussed above. There is always the option of a "help wanted" sign outside your premises or on the employee notice board.

Universities, at least in North America, generally have career services offices that operate job banks where companies can post openings to recruit undergraduate or graduate students for full-time positions or internships. An **internship** is a position in an organization, with or without pay, that a student or trainee takes up in order to gain work experience or satisfy the requirements of a degree or certificate. Internships are usually short term but may lead to full-time employment in the future. Services of career centers are usually available at no cost to companies and students.

Professional groups, job fairs, and trade association meetings can also be good sources for potential employees (and for employees looking for a new job). Many associations publish newsletters and post openings online on their websites or at their meeting locations.

Interactive Exercise

The growing trend of companies looking at social media to find new employees and obtain additional information to make hiring decisions is concerning for many people. Research online to identify the major concerns people have about the use of social media in hiring. Of the concerns your research reveals, which do you find the most problematic for you? How would you address this issue in your own career?

Finding good employees is not easy for any company, but it is particularly difficult for small businesses. There are several reasons why small businesses have difficulty in finding the employees they need. The biggest constraint is budget. Say you run a small technology company, where you want to hire engineers who are good with computer hardware or software, have programming skills, and are willing to work hard to meet the needs of your demanding clients. The problem is that behemoths like Amazon and Google (or Netflix, Microsoft, and Tesla) are also looking for the same kind of people. There is no way a small business can compete with these giant corporations in terms of either the money spent on recruiting or the salaries offered to new employees or the benefits (e.g. health care) they offer. Further, small firms lack the training and mentoring opportunities that are available for new employees in large companies. Finally, small firms also lack the name-brand recognition that comes with accepting an offer from a large, reputable company. For example, a job at Amazon today is much in demand among technology graduates or business majors in a way that is simply not possible for a small firm, even if the job entails similar work and requires similar qualifications.

Second Chances Inc.

When Progressive Coating LLC, a Chicago-based provider of custom-coating for products from shoe-dryer racks to industrial motor parts, had trouble finding employees, it turned to U-Turn Permitted, a job-training program for people with criminal records. Progressive is one of the growing number of companies giving ex-convicts a second chance. Richard Bronson started a platform 70 Million Jobs to match former felons with companies willing to hire them.

Watch the video online at: https://www.youtube.com/watch?v=W3RQUJIVTqU

Some mistakenly believe that smaller firms can outperform large businesses in attracting high-quality employees. While it is true that small firms offer a flatter organizational structure than large companies and may even be able to offer more flexibility in working hours, it may not be always enough to offset the **liability of smallness** that some firms face in hiring new employees. It is not uncommon to see news headlines such as "Tight U.S. Job Market Squeezes Smallest Businesses the Most" and "Smallest U.S.

Firms Struggle to Find Workers." Small business owners, therefore, need to be especially creative and diligent in recruiting new employees.

What Do You Think?

Consider two professions: yoga teacher and machinist. When it comes to yoga teachers, the supply of instructors (people with yoga teacher certification) is growing faster than demand for their services. For machinists, there seems to be a dearth of qualified personnel in the labor market. Assume that you have either started a new yoga studio or a machine shop and are now looking to hire an employee who can help you in the business either as a yoga instructor or as a machinist. How would you go about finding someone for your business? Would your approach vary depending on the business you are in?

Just as small business owners can benefit from learning how they can better attract and manage qualified workers, employees who work at small firms can also benefit from thinking about how they can be more effective in the work they do and add value to the firm. While appropriate academic qualifications, suitable training, and relevant experience are all important contributors to success, there are many things employees can do that require no prior talent, just a desire to perform well in their job.

10 things that require zero talent

1. Being on time
2. Work ethic
3. Effort
4. Body language
5. Energy
6. Attitude
7. Passion
8. Being coachable
9. Doing extra
10. Being prepared

Comprehension Check

1. What are some challenges associated with hiring friends and family for your small business?
2. Small businesses can outperform large firms in attracting quality employees. Do you agree or disagree with this statement? Why?
3. What are headhunters? Explain their role in employee recruitment.

Module 12.3 Selecting and Training Employees

If you are a lucky small business owner, you will have a pool of applicants from which to choose when looking for a new hire. If you are really lucky, your pool will be very competitive, so you will have many strong candidates with the right skills, experience, and temperament for the position you are trying to fill. Recall the idea of fit introduced earlier. You want to select employees who will be a good fit with your company (**P-O fit**) and the position (**P-J fit**) they are hired for.

At a basic level, P-O fit refers to the notion of compatibility between an individual and the organization hiring them. Similarly, P-J fit captures the match between an individual and the requirements of a specific job. Both P-O fit and P-J fit are specific manifestations of the more general idea that positive outcomes are more likely to occur when individuals fit or align well with the environment. Google likes to hire people who possess something it calls Googleyness, which includes things like enjoying fun and coping well with ambiguity. At Netflix, a big filter for hiring people used to be if they were "interested in our goal of making the customer happy?" says former Chief Talent Officer Patty McCord.

Interactive Exercise

Job interviews at Google involve questions that are strange enough to be parodied in popular culture. The film *The Internship* had this question from a Google interview: "You're shrunken down to the size of nickels and dropped to the bottom of a blender. What do you do?" How would you answer this question?

The notion of employee fit means that small businesses should not necessarily go for the most experienced employee or the person with the degree from the best school. Instead, business owners should think carefully about whom they want to hire. They should also think about who they will want to work with in the business. Small business owners, by definition, manage firms where employees and owners work closely together. If an applicant seems too arrogant or too disorganized for what you (the owner) are willing to work with, it should be factored into the selection decision. Fingerprint Marketing, an ad agency in Saratoga Springs, NY, looks for employees who are empathetic and at ease with his company's flat, no-titles, team-based culture. When founder Ed Mitzen interviews candidates, he explores whether they'll be kind to everyone regardless of status and pleasant to work with. He also relies on what can be called "The Driver Test": how candidates treat drivers for his company's car service en route to and from the interview. The logic is that how a person treats the driver provides a window into their true character. Once, he rejected an applicant in part because the applicant was curt with the driver and expected him to open the door for him. "Really? You're applying for a $150,000-a-year job," Ed says. "You're not applying to be ambassador to France. Take it easy."

Does the employee-fit idea assume that the employee or the organization has a certain profile, which is immutable? Elsewhere in this book, we learned about **growth mindset**, which means that our qualities and competencies are not fixed but can be changed through directed effort. There seems to be a contradiction between the notion of fit and the idea of a growth mindset, until one recognizes that while people and organizations can change, few actually make the investment necessary to bring about that change. Table 12.4 summarizes the idea of fit in hiring.

TABLE 12.4

Fit in Hiring

Fit	
What it is?	**What it's not?**
Shared enthusiasm about a company's mission or purpose	Sense of comfort and familiarity with coworkers
Common approach to working, together or individually	Shared enjoyment of such perks as ping pong and craft beer
Mutual understanding of how to make decisions and adapt to challenges	Common educational, cultural or career background

Source: https://www.nytimes.com/2015/05/31/opinion/sunday/guess-who-doesnt-fit-in-at-work.html, *New York Times*

12.3.1 Tools for Screening Applicants

There are several tools available to business owners that can be helpful in the selection stage. These are résumés and application forms, interview, testing, and others (e.g. handwriting analysis).

12.3.1.1 Résumés and application forms The most common tool used in employee selection is, undoubtedly, the **résumé**. A résumé contains information regarding the applicant's biographical information (name, address, valid email, telephone number), educational achievements (where did they went to college, what degree did they get), and work experience (where, how long, responsibilities). Sometimes, résumés may also contain hobbies and other nonwork interests.

While résumés are put together by candidates applying for a job (see Figure 12.3), application forms are prepared by companies to get essentially the same information as

---

Jane Roe
Business Development Manager

jane.roe@gmail.com ✉
202-555-0166 ▯
New York, USA ◉
linkedin.com/in/jane.roe in
jane.roe ⑤

Professional Business Developer with more than four years of experience in the business development processes. Involved in product testing, management, and development of new business opportunities.

SKILLS

SEO Public Speaking Negotiation Teamwork Decision Making Research & Strategy
Emotional Intelligence Outbound Marketing Email Marketing Google Analytics Sales & Marketing

WORK EXPERIENCE

○ **Business Development Manager**
AirState Solutions ☑
09/2014 – 06/2017   *New York, USA*

– Successfully managed $2 - 3 million budget projects and successfully achieved the project scheduled goals.
– Developed and implemented new marketing and sales plans and defined the strategy for the next 5 years.
– Reviewed constantly the customer feedback and then suggested ways to improve the processes and customer service levels which increased the satisfaction rate from 81% to 95%.
– Ensured that new clients will grow into a loyal customer base in a specialist niche market by implementing a new loyalty program.

○ **Business Development Assistant**
AirState Solutions
08/2012 – 09/2014   *Chicago, USA*

– Increased the customer satisfaction rate by 25% by improving the customer service.
– Planned, supervised, and coordinated daily activity of 3 junior business analysts.
– Improved the communication with the Marketing department to better understand the competitive position.
– Directed the creation and implementation of a Business Continuity Plan, and the management of audit programs.

EDUCATION

○ **MSc in Economics and Business Administration**
The University of Chicago
09/2008 – 06/2010

ORGANIZATIONS

American Management Association (2015 – Present)   Association of Private Enterprise Education (2014 – Present)

eBusiness Association (eBA) (2013 – Present)

FIGURE 12.3 A Sample Résumé
Source: Adapted from Resume Templates, Novaresume

in the résumé, but in a more standardized format. Candidates fill out the application form to answer questions about themselves in a way that allows them to stand out from the competition. Applications forms and résumés often also provide the names of potential references who can comment on the candidate's suitability for the job.

At some point, all business owners are faced with a difficult question: How much can you really trust the information a candidate shares in the résumé or application form? According to a 2018 CareerBuilder Survey, as many as 75% of hiring managers have caught applicants with fabrications on their résumés. Scott Samuels, CEO of Horizon Hospitality, an executive search firm, believes that lying on résumé "is endemic as more and more people feel like they can get away with lying because they think no one is going to check and verify. It's rampant."

Some falsehoods are quite outlandish, such as the applicant who claimed to be the assistant to the prime minister of a foreign country that does not have a prime minister, or shares being a babysitter to celebrities like Madonna and Tom Cruise, or report 25 years of work experience at the age of 32. Most résumé lies are, however, less outrageous and can easily go undetected for years.

According to Monster, the job search website, the three most common lies on applicant résumés are as follows:

1. *Embellishing education.* Applicants exaggerate the coursework they took to make it seem more impressive than it really was. One hiring manager reported, "We've had someone put down Cornell School of Hotel Management on their résumé, when they only took one class online. That person didn't graduate from there or even attend in person." Rather than embellish one's education, it may be more useful to add specific information in the résumé that demonstrates the depth or width of your education.

2. *Deceptive dates.* Many applicants try to cover up their employment gaps by expanding the time they worked somewhere or even making up a completely false interim job experience. Rather than deceive your employer on dates, it may be better to honestly admit that you took time off for other responsibilities (be as specific as you can be, without going into too many details), but that now you are full committed (if you truly are).

3. *Stretching skills.* It is not uncommon to see candidates claim proficiency on technical skills that they are just familiar with. Using Microsoft Excel a few times or speaking some words of French does not make someone an expert. One is better off being candid about things they are truly good at and skills they have only some familiarity with.

Have you heard of Ronald Zarrella, Marilee Jones, or Dave Edmondson? They were all in the news for lying on their résumés. Zarrella, who was CEO of Bausch & Lomb, claimed to have an MBA from the Stern School of Business at New York University, but in truth he never graduated there, though he did take classes. Jones, dean of admissions at MIT, made up degrees from Union College and Albany Medical College, neither of which had any record of her attendance. Edmondson, CEO of Radio Shack, reported psychology and theology degrees from the unaccredited Pacific Coast Baptist College in California, when the school doesn't even have a psychology program.

As a business owner, you may want to believe whatever people tell you, but it is better to view each applicant's résumé with some degree of healthy skepticism. Trust, but verify! Check out the facts listed on the résumé (e.g. by asking for a copy of the diploma) and contact previous employers or other references.

KEY TAKEAWAY

You may want to believe whatever a prospective employee tells you, but it is better to view each applicant's résumé with some degree of healthy skepticism.

George O'Leary was hired as head football coach at University of Notre Dame, but had to resign within the week when inaccuracies on his official biographical sketch came out. Coach O'Leary later released a statement saying, "In seeking employment I prepared a résumé that contained inaccuracies regarding my completion of course work for a master's degree and also my level of participation in football at my alma mater. These misstatements were never stricken from my résumé or biographical sketch in later years." If caught, **résumé padding**, which involves exaggerating on the résumé, can haunt you for a long time.

12.3.1.2 Interviews Personal interview is considered by many employers to be the most critical step in the selection process as it allows them to see and assess the applicant for themselves. This interview serves many purposes, including asking follow-up questions to gather more information or seek clarification on the résumé, confirm or reject initial impressions of the candidate that were based on the résumé, and also explain the finer details of the job and the position to the applicant. Think of the interview as a two-way street, with each side seeking information about the other with the goal of deciding if they can be happy with the other.

Effective interviews require that the business owner is well prepared to conduct the interview at a mutually agreed-upon time and place that is convenient to both parties. It is important that both parties stay professional throughout the interview and not make disparaging remarks about the other. It is helpful to keep good records of the interview, so you can go back to them later when needed.

Job interviews should involve a short set of questions that are asked of each candidate to make comparative assessments. This is not to say that an interviewer has to adhere strictly to a preset script. In fact, it is a good idea to have an unstructured component to

An Interview That Will Make You Cringe

Some business owners are horrible at interviewing people. Steve Jobs is now remembered as one of the most transformational entrepreneurs of our times. Early in his career, however, Steve was a young entrepreneur who had seen tremendous success with the business he started. He had little experience interviewing people, but that did not stop him from asserting himself. The way he treated prospective employees provides valuable lessons on how not to interview people who are interested in working for you.

Watch the video online at: https://www.youtube.com/watch?v=fwYy8R87JMA&t=62s

the interview, where the interviewer asks questions that arise from the conversation with the applicant.

A **job interview** is an opportunity to ask the applicant to behaviorally demonstrate that they have skills, knowledge, and abilities they claim and that you believe are crucial to the successful performance of the job. Do not just accept a candidate's claim that he or she possesses certain skills or knowledge. The **behavioral interview** is the technique of asking job aspirants to describe past behavior or perform a behavior in real time to determine their suitability for a position. For example, an applicant may be asked to describe how they behaved when they had a team member who was not contributing as expected to the group. Most behavioral interview questions start with "Give an example of when . . ." or "Tell us about a time when . . ."

No matter what side of the interview you are on, it is advisable to keep good notes for each interview.

12.3.1.3 Testing American businesses have long relied on tests to screen applicants. However, the legal environment around testing has evolved considerably over the years. Before the 1971 Supreme Court decision in Griggs vs. Duke Power Co., employers were for the most part free to do as they pleased with regard to the testing of job applicants. As the law has evolved around testing-based selection, employers can no longer do whatever they want in testing. At a minimum, the test should be a valid predictor of job performance and should not discriminate based on demographic attributes (e.g. gender).

Aqualon, a Virginia-based chemical company, was found by the Office of Federal Contract Compliance Programs (OFCCP) to use a discriminatory test as part of its selection process that negatively impacted Black applicants who applied for entry-level transition operator positions. The test was determined to be unrelated to the job and did not meet the requirements of the Uniform Guidelines (on Employee Selection Procedures, which apply to workers covered by Title VII of the Civil Rights Act of 1964 and federal contractors). Under the guidelines, companies are responsible for collecting gender and race data, save candidates' test results, calculate pass rate by race and gender, and provide a reasonable explanation for why a certain passing score was used. Tests are considered nondiscriminatory when the pass rates for each race and gender are nearly the same. If, however, the test rates of one social group are below 80% of the highest groups' pass rate, the enforcement agencies become involved.

For the most part, small businesses lack the resources to properly develop and statistically validate their own tests. Consequently, most business owners purchase tests already developed and validated by commercial vendors. A properly validated test is one that has been determined to predict performance in a specific job, says Jeffrey Ross, an attorney with Seyfarth Shaw in Chicago. "That usually means that the more successful an applicant is on the test, the more likely the employee will perform successfully on the job." Using a test that has been developed and validated by someone else is helpful, but the firm should also be able to show that the test is a sample or measure of the actual work employees perform on the job. "There are many types of employment tests, such as job sample tests, intelligence tests, cognitive ability tests, cognitive skills tests, physical agility tests, physical ability tests, and personality tests," Ross noted. "Any type of test can run afoul of the guidelines if it causes an adverse impact and is not job-related."

In the United States, the Equal Employment Opportunity Commission (EEOC) has approved three primary forms of test validity:

Criterion validity relates to the extent to which a test can predict how well a person performs on the job. Criterion validity can be established in two ways. Employers may test current employees and compare their test scores with job performance rating, so that the test scores and the job ratings are both available at the same time.

Alternatively, employers may compare applicants' test scores with their subsequent job performance. The former involves concurrent comparisons, while the latter predictive comparisons.

Construct validity pertains to the degree to which a selection instrument captures a specific construct (e.g. intelligence, honesty, comprehension) that is believed to underlie successful job performance. Note that one or more theoretical constructs are used as a predictor for establishing this form of validity.

Content validity refers to the way a test is designed to measure the specific knowledge, behaviors, and competencies that are considered important for successful performance in a job. If a test claims it is measuring something that is required to successfully perform a job, then it should actually measure what it claims.

There is a wide range of tests that companies can use for screening employees, but it is advisable to keep in mind that testing should be part of a broader approach to hiring. There is no single test or indicator that can provide complete guidance on hiring (or not) an applicant.

Firms are increasingly relying on **drug tests** to screen applicants. As the name suggests, the purpose of drug tests is to detect the presence of illegal drugs in the body. Drug-free employees are seen as more serious about coming to work, have greater productivity, and contribute to a safer workplace. The most common drug test used in employment settings is urine test, which is less invasive and relatively inexpensive compared to other tests such as saliva, hair, or blood. Unfortunately, urine tests also have high error rates (false positives or false negatives) and can also be easily tampered with.

Some firms conduct physical examinations to detect medical or physical limitations that may prevent the applicants from performing job duties. The Americans with Disabilities Act (ADA) stipulates that physical examination can be administered only after a conditional employment offer has been made and only if it is mandated for all employees in a particular job category.

12.3.1.4 Other screening procedures

12.3.1.4.1 Handwriting analysis Because of the difficulties involved in selecting good employees who will make a positive contribution to the firm, many companies have been searching for new ways to weed out potentially troublesome hires. One of the latest tactics is **handwriting analysis**, also called **graphology**. Some believe that graphology dates back to eleventh-century China, and Camillo Baldi, an Italian physician, was an early proponent who wrote a book on the subject in 1662. Today, handwriting analysis is widely used for screening applicants in many European countries, including France, Germany, and England. French employers in particular seem to favor the method, with some 75% reportedly using graphology as a part of their recruitment process. No hard data exists for the use of handwriting analysis in the United States, but the practice appears to be more common than generally realized.

Sheila Kurtz, chief executive and founder of the Graphology Consulting Group in New York, says her business has tripled over four years. Arlyn Imberman, another handwriting analyst in New York and coauthor of a book on handwriting analysis, saw her corporate business increase about 22% over three years. Howard Herzog, president of IJB Risk Services, a jewelry and fine arts consultancy in Manhattan, has relied on Arlyn Imberman's services. "The increase in employee theft made me do it," he said. "It's paid off very nicely in discovering who the potential stealers are and who's not."

Most employers are reluctant to admit they use the technique as handwriting analysis is often viewed with skepticism. Many scientists and doctors view graphology in disdain. Dr. Barry Beyerstein, professor of biological psychology at Simon Fraser University in British Columbia, places graphology in the same category as phrenology (using the shape of the skull to determine character) and physiognomy (judging character through body and facial features), which were both quite popular until the early twentieth century.

For its proponents, however, handwriting analysis can help gain new insights not readily available elsewhere. "When used correctly, graphology can give a good indication of a person's personality structure, their abilities, ability to grow and develop, and perhaps most importantly, their integrity," says graphologist Margaret White, who uses her skills to assess job applicants for recruiters.

12.3.1.4.2 Honesty and integrity tests Thousands of American firms use tests to try to screen which job applicants would be most likely to engage in theft or other counterproductive workplace behaviors, such as absenteeism or tardiness. The 1998 Employee Polygraph Protection Act made it illegal to use voice stress analyzers and other devices in employment screenings. The polygraph was a controversial tool used to obtain information on employees and anticipate behaviors on the job. Congress banned polygraph testing in employment contexts in response to concerns about privacy, reliability, and misuse of results. Numerous employers then turned to old-fashioned question-and-answer-based honesty tests that can be taken on the computer or via paper-and-pen questionnaires. These tests are designed to evaluate the applicant's propensity toward theft, honesty, and compatibility with others, based on the assumption that, in general, people's behaviors will reflect their stated tendencies or inclinations. Because applicants may be tempted to answer in socially desirable ways, questions may be overt (e.g. "How honest or prompt are you?") or more covert (e.g. "Do you make your bed?").

Firms that make good hiring decisions tend to have lower employee turnover and higher worker productivity, both of which positively impact the company's bottom line. Hiring the wrong people can dampen employee morale and waste valuable training and development dollars. Pre-employment testing with the right screening tools and procedures can help firms minimize hiring mistakes and select the individual most suited for the job.

What Do You Think?

Ronald Shaw, the chief executive of Pilot Pen Inc. in Trumbull, CT, observes, "People look great in an interview and then you don't recognize them when they come on board." He hired Sheila Kurtz, a New York–based graphologist, to provide another check against his own impressions. Her title is chief graphology officer. "It helps to find out if she thinks the person is trustworthy, creative, or resourceful, and able to work in our environment," he noted. In one case, before Sheila came on board, Ronald said he was looking for a regional sales manager, and was interested in one candidate in particular. The candidate, however, did not seem quite as aggressive as he needed to be. Ronald was not going to hire him but decided to show the application to a graphologist. The graphologist advised that the candidate could take the initiative, and Ronald took a chance on him. He has become one of the most productive employees at the company. What do you think are the pros and cons of using graphology in employment settings? Do you think small business owners should rely on handwriting analysis to better inform their hiring decisions?

12.3.2 Training Employees

It would be wonderful if all employees started their new job fully prepared and ready to take on the challenges that come their way. Unfortunately, most employees need at least some training in the new job, and many employees need a lot of training. The first step in the training process is employee orientation, where the new individual is introduced to the business and to the current employees in the firm. Orientation also includes some discussion of the core company values. Depending on the size of the company (in terms of the existing employees), orientation may involve anything from one-to-one meeting with the business owner to a formal, well-defined program that lasts several hours or days.

Beyond orientation programs, firms can choose from two broad types of training techniques: on-the-job and off-the-job. **On-the-job training** is delivered while employees perform their regular jobs. In this way, employees do not lose time learning and are able to readily see how their training can help them become better at their jobs. **Off-the-job training** is provided away from the employee's actual performance on the job, such as through lectures, role-playing, or laboratory training. It offers the benefit that the employee can be fully focused on learning the material provided to them without being distracted by the demands of the new job.

Many small business owners believe that one should not spend money in training employees. Why? Because employees will take the knowledge and skills they have acquired from the training and leave for a higher-paying job at another firm (perhaps even a competitor). So, should small firms invest in training employees? As with many other questions in business, the answer is "It depends." For academics, it is easy to advise business owners to think of training as an investment, and not an expense. After all, they are not the ones having to pay for it.

What Do You Think?

Loreta runs a small welding shop in Kearney, NE. She is good at what she does, but she hates the paperwork that comes with running her business. A business professor, with whom she is friends, advised her to hire someone to manage the office, which will leave her free to focus on the operations side of her business. The problem is that the two people she has hired over the last two years – Bill and Sammy – have both left after she spent hours training them. Bill was an eager 22-year-old, with an undergraduate degree in business and from the poor side of the town. He was hardworking and was willing to put in long hours at work without Loreta having to even ask him. However, he soon got married to a girl from Chicago, and they decided to move to be closer to her family. Sammy was an English major, who Loreta hired straight out of college. She was hardworking, and within six months she had learned the work so well that Loreta was even able to take a much-needed vacation with her family. However, Sammy wanted a higher salary, and when Loreta would not agree to it, Sammy left to join another firm in Kearney. Now, Loreta is wondering what she should do: Should she hire someone else, but then what if they too leave for another firm? Should she just put in longer hours at work and do the office work herself? Should she just wait for her son and daughter to get to high school, so she can have them manage the office part-time? Loreta wants to do what is best for the business and the family now, but she also wants to grow the business, so that her kids will have a reason to stay in Kearney after college. What advice would you offer Loreta?

For a business owner, the money, time, and energy spent in training a new employee can be considerable. When the employee leaves, the business owner has to start over again with another employee. If the training pertains to the work the employee has to do as part of his or her job, then the necessary training has to be provided. It is not fair to expect an employee to do well without the right training. Of course, not all employees want to learn (or are willing to put in the work to learn), so if the training efforts are not fruitful, you may want to reconsider the hiring choice you made. However, if the training is for the work the employee may do when she is promoted, such training can be considered discretionary. If you feel that the employee is someone who has a long-term future with the company, and the employee and you have an understanding about his or her future prospects, then you may invest in discretionary training.

Comprehension Check

1. What is résumé padding?
2. What are the different tests available to companies for recruitment?
3. Discuss the various forms of test validity.

Module 12.4 Rewarding and Disciplining Employees

All employees expect to be compensated fairly and equitably. The problem lies in determining what is fair and equitable compensation. Each of us would like to be paid more than we currently get, and there is nothing wrong with this feeling! What matters is whether we are getting paid our market value. Business owners should, therefore, strive to pay their employees based on their market value. If an employee leaves on friendly terms because they are receiving higher compensation elsewhere, then there is usually no reason for hard feelings on either side. After all, why hold a grudge against someone for leaving if they have better opportunities elsewhere!

KEY TAKEAWAY

All employees expect to be compensated fairly and equitably, but it is challenging to determine fair and equitable compensation.

Compensation has two components: wages and benefits. Let's first talk about wages and then about benefits. After all, when people think about how much they are paid, they are usually looking at wages.

12.4.1 Wages

The Fair Labor Standards Act (FLSA) classifies employees as exempt or nonexempt. The FLSA provisions, which specify minimum wage, overtime remuneration, and equal-pay-equal-work, do not apply to exempt employees. Exempt employees are usually paid a straight salary. The salary paid to exempt employees needs to be competitive and sustainable. **Competitive salary** refers to pay that is comparable to that paid by other companies in the same geographical area and industry. For example, if you want to hire a machinist in Chicago, you will need to pay her a salary comparable to that paid in other machine shops in Chicago. **Sustainable salary** is pay that the business can actually afford to give. When making hiring decisions, a business owner should think carefully about whether the firm can afford to pay the worker(s) it is hiring. Firms that fail to pay workers the salary they are promised may find themselves in violation of the Wage Theft Prevention and Wage Recovery Act. In the United States alone, workers lose a combined total of about $8.5 billion annually from wage theft. While wage theft is partly due to companies acting in bad faith (intentionally reneging on paying the employees their full due), companies hiring more workers at higher salaries than they can afford to pay are also responsible for the problem.

Nonexempt employees are paid a minimum wage set by Congress (or the state government, whichever is higher). Most firms pay nonexempt employees an hourly wage, which is a set rate of pay for each hour worked. At the time of this writing, the federal minimum wage was $7.25 per hour, though some states, cities, and counties have a higher minimum wage rate. When the state, city, or county minimum wage rate is higher than the federal rate, employers are required to pay workers the higher amount. As a result, the minimum wage across the country varies from the federally mandated minimum of $7.25 per hour in many states to as high as $13 per hour in California and $13.50 per hour in Washington, D.C. Employees covered under the federal Fair Labor Standards Act are subject to the federal minimum wage of $7.25, but those not covered under the FLSA may be paid the state minimum wage of $5.15 (e.g. Georgia).

Some companies may pay their workers based on **piecework rates**. Under piecework rate, the employee is paid a set amount for each unit produced. There may also be a premium for units produced above a predetermined level to incentivize the employee to produce more. For example, a firm making headlights for cars may pay workers $3 per unit, so that a worker who assembles 100 headline units in one day gets $300 for the day. Alternatively, there may be a minimum production quota for which a salary is paid, and then an incentive for higher production. For example, a firm may pay $3000 in salary with a stipulation of minimum 50 units per day, and then $1 for every additional unit above the minimum. Piecework rates are pay-for-performance.

Another **pay-for-performance** approach to compensation is **commissions**. In some jobs, such as sales, commissions are often the preferred approach. Commissions are usually based on sales volume, for example, if you sell $200,000 of equipment this month, you will make $4000 (for a 2% commission). A downside of commissions is that sales may also be affected by external factors beyond the employees' control. The rapid spread of COVID-19 resulted in canceled bookings for many companies in the travel business (e.g. cruise ships, hotels, resorts). For commission-based employees, such a situation is catastrophic. As a result, some employers and employees prefer compensation based on salary and commission.

What Do You Think?

As the COVID-19 pandemic spread through New York City, dog-walking service NYC Pooch suspended operations and laid off its staff of about 50 people. Employees there start at the City's $15 an hour minimum wage and earn commissions based on the volume of work they do. Some employees preferred to be laid off rather than have fewer walks as it allowed them to tap unemployment benefits. They figured they would be paid more in jobless benefits than they would earn with a few walks a week. Cofounder Shane McEvoy tried to find low-interest loans to keep the business afloat, but struggled to secure financing. Do you think business owners like McEvoy have any obligations to their employees during a crisis situation with no revenues coming in? If yes, what can McEvoy and other business owners do to help employees? If not, how do you think employees can pay rent and afford food?

12.4.2 Benefits

Benefits are supplements to wages. Typical benefits may include health and life insurance, vacation time, education plans, and discounts on company products. Employers are required to provide certain benefits; there are also optional benefits employers may choose to provide. The law requires employers to provide the following benefits:

1. Allow paid time off to vote, serve on a jury, or perform military service.
2. Withhold Social Security retirement and disability, as well as Medicaid and Medicare. Also, pay the employer's percentage. Presently, employees pay 6.2% of their earnings up to a cap, and employers pay a matching amount for a combined contribution of 12.4%.
3. Comply with the Federal Family and Medical Leave Act (FMLA), which provides employees temporary job security when faced with certain health-related care responsibilities that preclude them from working. Some states (e.g. California, Hawaii, Rhode Island, to name three) have enacted their own version of family and/or medical leave laws. FMLA is applicable for firms with 50 or more employees, but the bar is lower in some states (e.g. 15 or more in Maine and Maryland).
4. Contribute to state and federal unemployment programs by paying taxes so that unemployed people can be supported.

The following benefits are not required by the law, but companies may choose to provide them as inducements in a competitive market:

1. Maternity or paternity leave
2. Retirement plans
3. Child care
4. Product discounts
5. Paid vacations
6. Dental or vision plan
7. Educational assistance

As large companies alter their mix of benefits to better appeal to new hires, small firms find themselves under constant pressure to provide better benefits. The challenge for small firms is to offer a benefit package that is affordable to the employer and attractive to the employee.

Flexible benefits package. Because all employees do not have the same needs, many plans may allow employees to select the benefits that best suit their needs. Such plans are called **flexible benefit package** (or **cafeteria plans**) as they offer employees with a menu of benefits from which they can choose (as in a restaurant). Employees are often able to purchase benefits pretax, which allows them to reduce their taxable income and yet have enhanced benefits. There are also some downsides to flexible benefit plans. They have higher administrative costs related to maintaining records and complying with regulations as well as greater concern that employees may make suboptimal choices. Employees may be tempted to select benefits that are cheap for them in the short term but present a larger problem when there is a major illness or accident (penny wise, pound foolish!).

Incentive-pay programs. Incentive-pay programs reward employees based on performance. A common incentive pay program is **bonus reward**. In theory, a bonus is a one-time reward employees can get for high performance. It is usually paid at the end of the year to either an individual employee or a group of employees. Employees are not entitled to a bonus, so a good incentive program will tie bonus to a specific measure of performance.

Profit-sharing plans. **Profit-sharing plans** are another form of incentive-pay programs. In a profit-sharing plan, employers reward the workers according to the profits earned, so that the actual reward an employee receives will vary from year to year. **Stock options** or stock grants are also a form of incentive-pay programs. Based on their performance, employees may receive share in a company.

12.4.3 Disciplining Employees

Just as it is important to reward employees appropriately to obtain better performance from them, it is also crucial to discipline employees by taking appropriate action against those in violation of a company's rules and norms. Disciplining employees ensures that corporate guidelines and regulations are consistently followed to enhance the well-being of the firm and its employees. A fair disciplinary process should incorporate both **appraisal** and **appeal**. Appraisal refers to performance evaluation, preferably based on well-specified benchmarks tied to the job description. In addition, employees should be evaluated on their behaviors, particularly when certain behaviors interfere with performance on the job. Appeal allows employees to seek a review of their performance appraisal by a third party who is neither the appraiser nor the appraised. Appeal must result in a thorough and truly objective review of the facts of the case by someone other than the supervisor responsible for the initial review. Because a small firm usually has few people in managerial or supervisory roles, it may not always be possible for a more senior person to rule on the appeal.

Firing an employee is the most extreme disciplinary action a firm can take and should be done with care. While the owner may have a legitimate reason for dismissing an employee for unsatisfactory performance that does not meet expectations, or even a changing job description that renders a previously qualified employee unqualified, it is important to keep in mind that you are dealing with people with feelings and responsibilities. Be considerate when delivering the dismissal message and avoid making it personal. Employees may seek legal redress when fired by filing a lawsuit against the employer, so maintain good records of the person's conduct and performance at work, the conversation that occurred when the dismissal message was delivered, and evidence that the employee was treated in a manner consistent with past practices.

Comprehension Check

1. Define competitive salary.
2. What is piecework rate?
3. Explain flexible benefits package.

Summary

While it is commonly said that people are the most important resource for any business, it is also true that more people in the business means higher expenses and greater legal responsibility. Large firms have professional human resources managers who are responsible for employee-related issues and functions, but small business owners need to carry out many of these duties themselves. The responsibility to manage employees well is in addition to all the other duties and tasks the business owner has, but it is also one of the most important tasks. It is useful to remember that firms that are able to identify and hire good employees are more likely to succeed.

World of Books

Make It Matter: How Managers Can Motivate by Creating Meaning by Scott Mautz
The Essential HR Guide for Small Businesses and Startups by Marie Carasco and William Rothwell
Making the Grass Greener on Your Side by Ken Melrose

In the Movies

Office Christmas Party is a 2016 comedy film that satirizes the work culture in a struggling family-owned technology firm. The film portrays the tension between the brother and sister who inherit the firm from their father, but it also focuses on the lack of motivation among employees and highlights the issues related to white-collar employees and the workforce in general. While the movie's premise of saving a branch office of a technology firm from being closed down by hosting a wild office Christmas party with inappropriate behavior and endless drinking is essentially meaningless, it does successfully draw attention to the debauchery that had become commonplace at many new-age firms in the name of holiday work celebrations away from the office. Oh, and the employees are also under tremendous pressure from the CEO to come up with a new product to avoid layoffs.

Live Exercise

SoapStandle has been a one-person show so far. Johnny Gold started the company when no one believed that the idea had potential. He managed to get the company's product in scores of retail stores around the country. The product is selling and annual revenues are about $250,000 now. Johnny is now considering hiring people to help him expand the company. He thinks the company would benefit from someone taking care of the books. While he enjoys doing it himself, he feels that it is taking him away from things that he needs to do to grow the business. He also thinks the company needs a dedicated person in sales. Johnny has never liked the sales aspect of running his business; cold calling customers and the rejections that follow are emotionally draining for him. His wife thinks the business needs an office assistant. She has been Johnny's assistant over the last year, answering phones and responding to emails as they come in. She had hoped to enjoy retirement with her husband, and now she finds herself working an unpaid job that she didn't sign up for in the first place.

Can you help Johnny prioritize the hiring needs for his business? For each position that you think Johnny should hire, can you come up with a job description that Johnny can use? What advice would you give Johnny as his company moves to the next stage where he cannot do all the work for the business?

Things to Remember

LO 12.1 **Outline the pros and cons of hiring workers for a small business**
- Hiring an employee brings many benefits to the business and its owner. At the same time, employees also impose additional demands on the owner.
- By hiring employees, businesses also take on legal responsibilities as an employer.
- Some businesses decide to remain solo operated for as long as they can.
- Freelancers are workers who sell their services by time or job to a variety of companies as opposed to working on a regular salary basis for one employer.
- Firms do not incur the cost of taxes, Social Security, or benefits when hiring contractors.
- Contract workers are independent, so the firm has less control over how and when they do the work assigned to them.
- When a firm decides it wants to hire an employee, it needs to (a) define the position(s) to be filled and (b) identify the qualifications needed to successfully complete the work in those positions.
- **Employee fit** is the match between the needs, expectations, and culture of the firm with the needs, expectations, and skills of individual employees.

LO 12.2 **Describe the various channels through which small firms find new employees**
- For most small business owners, referrals are probably the best source of recruitment.
- Referrals may come from people officially connected with your business, such as suppliers, customers, or employees.
- It is tempting to hire a family member or friend when there is a vacant position in the business, but many family and friend hires do not work out well.
- Paid advertisements in newspaper, magazines, trade publications, or storefronts are a common method to generate leads for working in a small business.
- Recruiting on the Internet allows a business owner to post a job description to the Web or to search a database of résumés.
- Many countries, including the United States, have publicly funded employment agencies focusing primarily on helping junior-level employees find work locally.
- Your company website is another place to recruit new employees.

- A "help wanted" sign outside your premises or on the employee notice board is another way to reach out to prospective employees.
- An internship is a position in an organization, with or without pay, that a student or trainee takes in order to gain work experience or satisfy the requirements of a degree or certificate.
- Professional groups, job fairs, and trade association meetings can also be good sources for potential employees (and for employees looking for a new job).
- Finding good employees is not easy for any company, but it is particularly difficult for small businesses.

LO 12.3 **Explain employee selection and training processes in small firms**

- Employees who are a good fit with your company (P-O fit) and the position (P-J fit) they are hired for are desirable.
- Small businesses should not necessarily go for the most experienced employee or the person with the degree from the best school.
- A growth mindset means that our qualities and competencies are not fixed but can be changed through directed effort.
- The résumé is the most common tool used in employee selection.
- Falsehoods on résumés are fairly common.
- Personal interview is considered by many employers to be the most critical step in the selection process, as it allows them to see and assess the applicant for themselves.
- A behavioral interview is the technique of asking a job aspirant to describe past behavior or perform a behavior in real time to determine their suitability for a position.
- American businesses have long relied on tests to screen applicants, but the legal environment around the use of tests in hiring has evolved considerably over the years.
- Most small business owners purchase tests already developed and validated by commercial vendors.
- The purpose of drug tests is to detect the use of illegal drugs and their presence in the body.
- Handwriting analysis, or graphology, is widely used for screening applicants in many European countries.
- Firms that make good hiring decisions tend to have lower employee turnover and higher worker productivity, both of which positively impact the company's bottom line.
- Most employees need at least some training in the new job, and many employees need a lot of training.

LO 12.4 **Explain how companies can discipline and reward employees**

- Compensation has two components: wages and benefits.
- The Fair Labor Standards Act (FLSA) classifies employees as either exempt or nonexempt.
- The salary paid to exempt employees needs to be competitive and sustainable.
- Most firms pay nonexempt employees an hourly wage, which is a set rate of pay for each hour worked.
- Some companies may pay their workers based on piecework rates.
- Another pay-for-performance approach to compensation is commissions.
- Benefits are supplements to wages, and typically include health and life insurance, vacation time, education plans, and discounts on company products.
- Some benefits are not required by the law, but companies may still choose to provide them to be more attractive to employees in a competitive market.
- Flexible benefit packages (or cafeteria plans) offer employees a menu of benefits from which they can choose.
- A bonus is a one-time reward employees get for high performance.
- Profit-sharing plans reward workers according to the profits earned by the firm.

- Disciplining employees ensures that corporate guidelines and regulations are consistently followed to enhance the well-being of the firm and its employees.
- Appraisal refers to performance evaluation, preferably based on well-specified benchmarks tied to the job description.
- Appeal allows employees to seek a review of their performance appraisal by a third party who is neither the appraiser nor the appraised.
- Firing an employee is the most extreme disciplinary action a firm can take and should be done with care.

Key Terms

slack	internet job sites	behavioral interviews	piecework rates
solo operators	employment agencies	criterion validity	pay-for-performance
freelancers	executive recruiters	construct validity	commissions
gig economy	headhunters	content validity	flexible benefits package
recruitment	internship	drug tests	cafeteria plans
employee fit	liability of smallness	handwriting analysis	bonus reward
job analysis	P-O fit	graphology	profit-sharing plans
interviews	P-J fit	honesty and integrity tests	stock options
observations	growth mindset	on-the-job training	appraisal
job description	résumé	off-the-job training	appeal
job specifications	résumé padding	competitive salary	
referrals	job interview	sustainable salary	

Experiential Exercise

Use Google to search for Human Resources Tips for Small Business Owners. Based on the links you find on the first two pages of your Google search, make a list of 10 tips that you see come up most commonly for HR-related issues in small businesses.

Option A

Interview a small business owner who already employs at least one nonfamily employee in the business. Share your list of top 10 tips with them and ask what they think about the 10 tips based on their experience. Summarize their comments on each of the 10 tips in a two-page memo to your professor.

Option B

Prepare a survey to be administered to small business owners near your college or university. The survey should ask business owners to indicate how useful they find each of the top 10 tips for their business. Based on the responses you collect, rank the tips from 1 (most important) to 10 (least important).

CHAPTER 13

Operations and Supply Chain Management

> *Eighty-five percent of the reasons for failure are deficiencies in the systems and processes. The role of management is to change the processes to do better.*
>
> **W. EDWARDS DEMING**

LEARNING OBJECTIVES

This chapter will help you to:

LO 13.1 Describe the basics of managing operations

LO 13.2 Discuss the role of inventory management in business

LO 13.3 Explain the importance of scheduling

LO 13.4 Enumerate the reasons why quality control is important

13.0 Introduction

Walk into any store – the one around the corner, the gas station convenience store where you stop on your way to work or back home, the pharmacy where you pick up your refills – and you assume the store will have what you need. Beyond the physical world, many of us are now shopping online, where again we assume that what we want will be available as long as we can pay for it. When something we want is not available, as can happen sometimes, we expect it to be available soon. Of course, we know that the things we usually buy – from gasoline to clothes to groceries – do not exist in nature in the form we buy them. They have to be made and moved to get them to us. Even when we use something that is quite close to its natural state – for example, lumber – there is still some processing and movement involved in getting it to us. The management of resources required to produce the goods and services that an organization – whether it is a Subway store or the local credit union – is the domain of operations and supply chain management, the topic of this chapter. You will notice that there are a number of articles and books that focus on how to start, finance, or market your small business, but there is not much information about operating a small business. Yet, attention to the operational aspects of the business is imperative for those who want their firms to survive and grow.

SPOTLIGHT | The Surprising Saga of Toybox: Lots of Demand, No Supply

Toybox Labs Inc., founded by two former Microsoft engineers, Ben Baltes and Jenn Chin, sells 3D printers for kids. The printer connects to a mobile app that allows kids to print toys from a catalog. The app also has a creative space where kids can play "pretend designers" to create their own personal toys. Data analytics helps the company track which toys are more popular, and the catalog can be adjusted accordingly. The target market for the company is 6–9-year-olds, though some think the market potential for the company's 3D printers is even greater among 8–13-year-olds.

Toybox started in 2018, and by May 2019, Ben and Jenn were on the television show *Shark Tank* to ask for $150K in exchange for a 5% stake in the company, valuing the fledgling startup at $3 million. Toybox had already made $300,000 through Internet sales in a few months relying only on social media advertising. On *Shark Tank*, Ben and Jenn were more excited about the software than the hardware, enthusing over the uniqueness of their app and how easy it was for kids to select and design their own toys to be 3D printed from the app.

Toybox opted to make its 3D printers in China. The main attraction in sourcing from China was lower labor costs, short lead times, and a dense network of suppliers for printer parts. In 2020, the factory in Wuhu, Anhui Province, was shut down for the annual Lunar New Year holiday. As the COVID-19 epidemic worsened in China, the factory pushed back its reopening date several times. Efforts within China to slow the spread of the virus choked supplies, restricted travel, and limited the ability of employees to work. All across the country, thousands of factory workers were stuck at their family homes, hundreds of miles away from their factory.

By February 2020, Toybox had just 600 printers left in its inventory. When Ben asked the Wuhu-based supplier if they needed help, the factory asked for face masks, which were in short supply there. Ben spent nearly $1000 to ship hundreds of masks to China. He cut the company's advertising in the United States and expected to lose

Ben Baltes and Jenn Chin started Toybox Labs Inc.

about $5 million in revenue. "We pretty much have to slow down sales and wait it out," he said at the time.

By the end of March 2020, with huge swaths of the mainland United States under mandatory lockdown, and most Americans forced to remain home, Toybox found the demand growing, but the supply was still constrained. The material for 3D printing – Toybox calls it "printer food" – was already running low. Pineapple printer food: sold out. Blueberry printer food: no stock. Coffee printer food: sold out!

With the COVID-19 epidemic shutting down normal life in America, parents were with kids at home and needed something to keep the children occupied. Like many American companies, Toybox had bought extra inventory ahead of the Chinese Lunar New Year. Jenn had not, however, considered the possibility of businesses and factories coming to a halt in China because of the COVID-19 outbreak. He had also not anticipated the sudden growth in US demand for the 3D printers as millions of parents scrambled to take care of their children at home with schools around the country closed and babysitters unavailable.

As Ben and Jenn saw the COVID-19 epidemic spread throughout the United States and around the

(Continued)

world, they found themselves asking if they could have done more to prepare the company for the way things were: high demand, little to no supply. Perhaps, even more importantly, they wondered what they should do to better prepare the company going forward. If another such pandemic hit in the future, could Ben and Jenn do anything to have a supply chain better equipped to weather out the storm?

Discussion Questions

1. What problems is Toybox facing?
2. Why did Toybox decide to source its 3D printers from China?
3. What could Toybox have done to better prepare for the situation the company was facing?
4. What are the possible solutions to the inventory problems Toybox is facing?

Module 13.1 Basics of Managing Operations

Let's start with understanding two basic concepts. **Operations management** involves planning, organizing, and controlling the resources and activities that transform necessary inputs into desired products and services. Of course, no organization – no matter how big (yes, even as big as Walmart, Amazon, or Apple) – can do everything by itself. It needs to work with other firms, both upstream and downstream, to generate and deliver value for its customers. Walmart, for example, works with many businesses – large and small – to keep its aisles stocked with the goods you need. It also works with many companies – Instacart and FedEx, for example – to deliver your orders to your door. The integration of upstream and downstream perspectives in the planning of transforming raw materials into finished goods is called **supply chain management**. For a business to run well, it needs to pay attention to properly managing the operations within the firm, but also to focus on improving supply and demand management within and across the companies throughout its supply chain.

Klime and Anita Kovaceski, owners of Crust restaurant in Miami, say they are vigilant in purchasing food and enforcing standards with suppliers. "If a company delivers to you fish or produce that was good but not great, and you accept it, take a wild guess who it's going to happen to again." They also design the menu with a close watch on food costs (which for restaurants like them should be less than 28%). They encourage employees to see their work as "theater," coaching them to put aside personal concerns and focus on making guests happy. They answer every complaint, online and otherwise, to try to turn around the experience. "It doesn't mean the customer is always right. But you make them feel that they are right." Klime Kovaceski has been in the restaurant business for decades, seeing others make mistakes and making some himself. "The easiest thing is to open a restaurant," he says. "The hardest one is to make it work." The reality of the restaurant industry is consistent with Klime's sentiments. New restaurants are a great way to lose a lot of money – fast. The restaurant industry sees thousands of new entrants each year, and about 27% of them close their doors within 12 months, and 60% in the first three years.

The effective management of a firm's operations and its supply chain has the potential to change the lives of average people: how we bank, how we buy groceries, how we use parking garages, hospitals, public transportation, shopping malls, and many other amenities of modern life. Take the case of Stephenson National Bank and Trust, a seven-branch bank in Marinette, Wisconsin. Founded in 1874, the small community bank has seen it all: wars, panics, Great Depression, and epidemics. Community banks, often categorized as those with less than $10 billion in assets, controlled about 13% of US deposits at the end of 2019. Fifty years ago, a customer who wanted $20 at night from their account at Stephenson would need to wait until the next day. Today, you can visit one of their ATMs 24 hours a day, 7 days of the week. Even if you visited the bank during working hours, your trip back in the day would be very different from the one you may take today. In the good old days, you would go inside the bank and find a line behind a teller. A few minutes

Klime and Anita Kovaceski started Crust restaurant in Miami. They often work 12 or more hours a day six or seven days a week, trying to make it all seem effortless.

later, wondering why your line wasn't moving, you might change lines. When you did get to a teller, he would first need to manually locate and verify your identity against a signature card. He would then consult a binder to check the balance in your account. Only then would you get your money.

Nowadays, many young people have never been to a physical branch of a bank. Stephenson, like other banks, finds that most of its young customers have no appreciation for the banking of the past. Banking has moved online. You visit an ATM and get your money when you want it and where you want it. Technology changed, new solutions developed, and banks changed the way they managed their operations to meet their customers' expectations better. Those who did not adapt to the changing times found themselves irrelevant and were forced to close down. Over the past three decades, the number of community banks in the United States declined by more than 11,000. Within just one year, from 2018 to 2019, their ranks decreased from 4980 to 4750, according to Federal Deposit Insurance Co.

KEY TAKEAWAY

Every firm takes some materials, and using the owners' investment and the workers' time and effort, converts them into products or services that can be offered in the market.

Operations, one could say, is at the heart of any business. Every firm takes some materials, and using the owners' investment and the workers' time and effort, converts them into products or services that can be offered in the market. Of course, what is raw material for one business may be the product sold by another firm. Consider your neighborhood bakery that sells the whole-wheat bread you really like. The finished product of this bakery – the bread – is made using many ingredients: flour, honey, salt, and vegetable oil, at the minimum. The bakery buys all of these materials from suppliers. The bakery may sell its bread to you (the consumer) or to the neighborhood deli, who then uses it to make the sandwiches that you so desire for lunch. The bakery owner may choose to focus only on the operations within the bakery. The owner may also take a holistic perspective and look at the entire supply for its bread.

Five elements come together to form the operations of a business: input, output, transformative processes, feedback, and control system.

The **input** of a business includes all tangible and intangible resources that are needed to produce a good or service. Every business needs some combination of knowledge, skills, and money. The business may also need raw materials and natural resources. Good quality input is important to the quality of the finished product of the business. Let's say a bakery buys the cheapest flour in the market and hires the cheapest baker it can find. Do you think it will produce good-quality bread? Likely not. Because there is no alchemy that can turn lead into gold, it is important to pay close attention to the inputs of your business.

Does the quality of ingredients affect the quality of bread a baker makes?

Andrew Chisholm/Alamy Stock Photo

The **output** is what a business produces. Outputs may be tangible, such as the bread you buy from the bakery, or it can be intangible, such as a consultation with a therapist. Generally, output is the quality and quantity of things that produce revenues for a business. The output of a business may be consumed by individuals (for business-to-customers [B2C] enterprises), other businesses (business-to-business [B2B]), or governments (business-to-government [B2G]).

The methods through which inputs are converted into outputs are called **transformative processes**. This includes technologies and procedures that are combined with inputs to yield desired outputs. Consider, for example, a winery. It buys grapes from a supplier, but many other things need to happen before it has wine that it can sell for you to buy. Those other things that transform grapes into wines are the transformative processes for a winery.

Control systems are a means to monitor operations and fix problems or deviations when they occur. Ideally, controls should oversee all inputs, transformative processes, and outputs. When you buy honey, you want it to be consistent in quality and quantity every time. The company needs to have proper systems in place so that the quality and quantity of the honey you get every time is consistent and up to the standards the company has set.

Feedback is the link between control systems, on the one hand, and inputs, outputs, and transformative processes, on the other hand. It can be observational, verbal, written, or electronic in nature. For feedback to be useful not only in the present moment, but also in the future, it needs to be recorded in a way that it can be retrieved when needed.

Let us look at toilet paper to understand the different components of operations management. As you know, the toilet paper used to be an item thoughtlessly tossed into shopping carts. When Americans (unexpectedly) stocked up to hunker down during the COVID-19 pandemic, the humble roll of toilet paper became one of the hottest commodities at the supermarket and was hard to find.

The starting point for toilet paper is wood chips that are converted into pulp. A massive machine, a four-story-tall collection of intricately pieced-together parts, which costs billions of dollars and takes months to build, cleans the pulp and feeds it through massive rollers that soak out water. The pulp is then chemically whitened, spread on a screen, and put through a hot dryer, finishing up as a long sheet of paper that gets rotated into a spool. A single spool can hold about 50 miles of paper, which is then embossed for strength and aesthetics.

Another machine constructs cardboard into tubes roughly 5 feet long. Two sheets of the finished paper are combined to make two-ply tissue, which is then wrapped around the cardboard tubes. A machine seals the roll with a light glue and then a circular saw cuts the long roll into bathroom-sized rolls that are packaged and loaded for delivery (see Figure 13.1).

A big toilet paper facility is able to churn out a few million individual paper rolls a day, with that number varying significantly based on how many lines the factory devotes to toilet paper and the type and size of each roll, notes analyst Jonathan Rager of Fastmarkets RISI, an analytics firm specialized in the pulp and paper industry.

So, what is the basic input for a company making toilet paper? Wood chips. And, what's the output? Of course, toilet paper of different types and different sizes. The process is described above. Then, there is the control system to oversee that the whole process is working as it should. If the machine breaks down, it could take months to fix, as workers sit idle or are assigned to other tasks. At all times, managers have access to feedback information to make sure things are running smoothly.

And, if you are wondering about the thin, scratchy tissue found in public bathrooms and office restrooms, it is made at separate plants and has a different supply chain. You

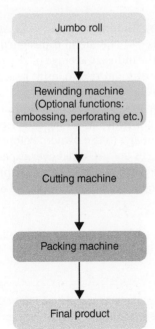

FIGURE 13.1 Making of a Roll of Toilet Paper
Source: Redrawn from Mayjoy Paper Machinery Co.

may recall the toilet paper shortages during the COVID-19 pandemic. Many argued that people were not actually using more toilet paper, they were just buying it at a faster rate, so that supply and demand would eventually balance out. The debate about toilet paper missed an important point related to our discussion in this chapter: The quantity of toilet paper used may not have increased, but the type of toilet paper being used changed as people spent much more time at home than at the office.

Interactive Exercise

Another casualty of the COVID-19 pandemic was paper towels. Use the Internet to find out how paper towels are made. What is the input, output, and transformative that bring us paper towels?

13.1.1 Productivity

Every business needs to know how efficiently it is using its inputs for the production of its output(s). The ratio of outputs to inputs is called **productivity**. That is,

$$\text{Productivity} = \text{Outputs} / \text{Inputs}$$

If the inputs for a bakery add up to $100 and the outputs add up to $500, then productivity is 5:1. If the bakery manages to reduce its input by half or doubles it output, then productivity is 10:1.

A major goal of operations management is improved productivity. Businesses that are serious about improving productivity can do so in two ways. First, a firm can increase its efficiency, so that it is producing more with less. Increasing output and decreasing input improves productivity. Second, a firm can increase the quality of its outputs, so that each output is now worth more in the market. There is also a third option – decrease the cost of the input – but that usually involves lowering the quality of the input, which will ultimately affect the prices for a firm's output.

Sometimes, the cost of the input can be reduced by running a tighter ship. At Crust, rent is about 5% of sales when the industry average is 6%. The menu is designed with a close watch on food costs, which are "a lot less than" the industry average of 28% of sales. There are several variations of the same item (e.g. mushroom risotto, mint risotto, basil risotto), which decreases spoilage and reduces costs. A lamb-chops entrée there is priced at $22.95, of which the cost of ingredients is more than 30%, but guests often order it with a bottle of wine, which typically is marked up 200–300% above its wholesale price. Controlling waste is also vital: Employees must show spoilage to the owners before throwing it out, so they can decide what went wrong. Novices are preferred over experienced workers as it saves on labor costs. Video-surveillance cameras throughout the premises help limit theft, and only the owners can void items or checks. The cumulative effect of all these small decisions is lower cost of inputs.

What Do You Think?

Kellcie has a small farm in rural Mississippi. She keeps some goats, using their milk to make goat milk soap that she sells in local farmer markets. Oxford, with its college kids and university employees with stable jobs, is a good market for Kellcie's goat milk soap. One day, on the prodding of one of her customers, Kellcie added up all the inputs that went into running her business. She also added up all the money she made from selling the goat milk soap. The math showed that total output per year was $55,000 and all the inputs added up to $40,000 yearly. What is Kellcie's productivity? What would you recommend Kellcie o improve her productivity?

A key decision for every business owner is how to source the ingredients that go into the recipe of their business: buy from outside suppliers or produce in-house? This is the classic **make-or-buy** decision in business. Every firm, large or small, faces this dilemma. The more specialized the needs or the more you need to safeguard the know-how that underlies your offering, the more likely it is that making it in-house is better for you. At the same time, it is generally easier to procure standardized parts and services from outside than to make them in-house.

A Bike Manufacturer's Dilemma

Let's consider the dilemma that Speedy Bike faces: Should they make the saddles in-house or buy from a supplier? They need to make similar decisions for other parts too: tires, paddles, and so on. How do they make the decision to make or buy in a thoughtful way that is based on rational analysis?

Africa Studio/Shutterstock.com

Watch this video online at: https://www.youtube.com/watch?v=vxZSaDtQgrs

On the surface, it seems make-or-buy decisions are only for manufacturing firms. Should we purchase the electric motor that goes into the lawnmowers we sell or should we make the motors in-house? Make-or-buy decisions are also relevant for service businesses. For example, if a cleaning services company gets more business than they can handle, they need to carefully think about whether they hire more staff to do it all themselves or contract part of the new business to other (smaller) companies. Similarly, retailers (or even professional services firms) need to consider if necessary functions such as janitorial and payroll services should be done in-house by their own employees or outsourced to independent companies and contractors.

Many business owners find themselves thinking they can do it cheaper and better than their suppliers and vendors. In other words, they lean toward making things in-house rather than buying from outside. Doing something in-house gives the business owner more control over how and when it is done. It also means that the business gets to retain the profitability that would have otherwise gone to the supplier. However, very often, the anticipated efficiency or profitability gains never materialize. Running a business well involves not only thinking about what to do but also carefully considering what *not* to do. Companies drift aimlessly when they try to do too much if the owners and managers fail to keep their eye on the ball.

Integrity Billing & Consulting LLC is a four-person firm founded and owned by Ginette Zuras-Hummel in Wilsonville, OR. The firm advises clients, which include chiropractors, naturopathic physicians, massage therapists, and acupuncturists, on billing and claims services. On its website (www.integritybillingconsulting.com), the company notes that it "specializes in keeping your practice/business on the right track while maximizing your profits so that you are paid accurately and efficiently." On average, the firm brings in about $12,000 per month in revenues. The firm's customers are small businesses who cannot afford to have in-house personnel to advise them on billing and other insurance claims. When a business cannot set up these services in-house (because it's too expensive or too difficult to find someone to do them in-house), they go outside to firms like Integrity to get the services they need at a cost.

Comprehension Check

1. What are the basic components of a firm's operations?
2. Define and explain productivity.
3. Explain make-or-buy decisions.

Module 13.2 The Fundamental Concept of Inventory

Let us now turn our attention to a key concept in operations and supply chain management: **inventory**. The word *inventory* may be used as a noun or a verb. When used as a noun, it refers to either the monetary value or the units of the goods in storage owned by a business at a given time. Car dealers in the United States, for example, had a total of 3.95 million vehicles in inventory in January 2019. Customers preferred cars with extra features and bigger trucks and SUVs, so that the average selling price of a new car in the country at the time was about $33,350. The total automobile inventory at the dealership was therefore about $1.3 billion. When used as a noun, inventory may refer to the total monetary value of goods in-stock (as is the case for $1.3 billion) or the number of units (3.95 million vehicles). Consider recent news from the *Wall Street Journal* (https://www.wsj.com/articles/dealers-dangle-deals-to-move-outgoing-models-11565874003):

> Dealers say they are sweetening incentives to purge their inventory, pressuring profit margins that have already been pinched by manufacturers

Purging inventory here may mean reducing either the number of units in stock or the total value of the cars in stock. Oftentimes, reducing one will also reduce the other.

The word *inventory* may also be used as a verb. You may have heard people ask "Have you have done your inventory yet?" The purpose of such a question is to know if the goods in stock have been measured or counted. How would a car dealership inventory what they have? Someone would be sent to physically count the cars in stock and then match their count against what the computer system says the company should have at the time.

A big challenge for companies is to figure out how much inventory to have at a given time. On the one hand, inventory is desirable. Firms need to have some goods in stock so that they do not lose business. Imagine having to close down a manufacturing plant because a critical part is not in stock, or losing sales because customers see empty shelves when they go to buy something. "Nobody wants stock-outs. If you go to a place, and they never have [what you want], pretty soon you just stop going there. That's very difficult revenue to recapture," said Brooks Bentz, president of supply chain consulting services at logistics company Transplace LLC. The small town of McLean, Texas, is home to The Devil's Rope Museum, a museum dedicated to barbed wire (slogan: "Get hooked on barbed wire"). The museum makes about $15,000 in sales a year, in part from selling books and T-shirts. Imagine, you go to the museum, and there are no books or T-shirts for you to buy. If you drive away without buying anything, do you think the museum can recoup that sale at a later time?

On the other hand, inventory can be a problem, as it represents idle money giving no immediate returns. For many businesses, inventory is the biggest part of their current assets. One entrepreneur who owned a brewpub in Grand Rapids, MI, reported having to discard thousands of dollars of perishable inventory when restaurants were asked to shut down by the state government in the face of the COVID-19 pandemic.

To complicate things, more inventory does not just mean money sitting idly on a shelf, it also means spending money to keep the inventory (or **inventory carrying cost**). "Get comfortable with days of inventory, not weeks," advocated Tom Shortt, Home Depot's senior vice president of supply chain. When Walmart's inventory rose more slowly than sales, it improved gross profit margins. "It's like oxygen in the store," Walmart CEO Doug McMillon observed at the company's annual meeting. "The weight of inventory has been relieved to an extent. And I think that bodes well for the future."

KEY TAKEAWAY

When it comes to inventory, both too little and too much are a problem for small business. Too little inventory risks stock-outs, too much inventory can be expensive to maintain.

There is no one formula that companies can use to determine the right amount of inventory they should keep. At a basic level, there are four factors that a company needs to consider:

1. The cost of maintaining the inventory
2. The cost of lost sales when you have a stock-out
3. The cost of ordering more goods from your suppliers
4. The time it takes to receive the goods from suppliers after they are ordered

To help a company figure out how much to order, consider the following formula:

> The cost of ordering inventory + The cost of buying the inventory +
> The cost of maintaining the inventory (storing it and securing it) –
> The cost of lost sales due to stock-outs.

When the formula returns a negative number, it means the company needs to stock up more; when the formula returns a positive number, the company may consider reducing inventory. The challenge, of course, is that some of these costs are difficult to determine in advance. For example, how does a company determine the cost of lost sales? In a similar vein, how does one truly determine the real cost of safeguarding one's inventory? Obtaining these costs is difficult, and especially so for new businesses. Oftentimes, business owners will estimate these numbers, knowing that it is simply an educated guess (albeit, not a random guess).

Guesstimation is the process of estimating using plausible assumptions and elementary arithmetic. At a basic level, we all guesstimate. Let's say it is 250 miles from Boston to New York. How long will it take to drive? For most people, the answer to this question easy: About four hours. You assume that the legal speed limit is 70 mph and there are no traffic jams. In reality, some may do it in 3.5 hours and others may take 4.5 hours, but almost no one would hesitate to venture a guess as to how long it may take. Once you have an estimate, you can now decide whether you want to drive from NYC to Boston (or not).

Say the question is how much domestic trash is collected each year in the United States. Can you venture a guess? Most people find it difficult to guesstimate here, because we are not used to thinking in this manner and we have no experience with trash collection (or so we think). Now, let's see how guesstimation can be helpful here. We know approximately how many people are in the United States (about 300 million at the time of this writing). How many times did your family empty the trash can in the kitchen every week when you were growing up? How many people were there in your household growing up? Assume that the answer to both questions is four: The trash is emptied four times in a typical week for a family of four people. A common trash bag holds 13 gallons. If a family of four empties four 13-gallon trash bags in a week, how many do they empty in a year: 52 × 4 equals 208 bags. So, that's 208 bags, 13 gallons each per year, which comes to 2704 gallons annually. If an average family size is 4 and there are 300 million Americans, how many families do we have in the country? About 75 million. Multiply 75 million by 2704 gallons, and you now have the total trash we produce as a country every year: about 202 billion gallons.

When deciding how much inventory to keep, firms and their managers guesstimate all the time. We all guesstimate in our daily life, like when we decide to drive somewhere. The same happens in business, just with different numbers and different assumptions. With experience, our ability to guesstimate improves. If you recently moved from Lincoln (NE) to the Northeast, your estimate of the driving time from Boston to NYC will be based on just numbers (250 miles or so, and 70 mph). Once you have lived in Boston for some time, and driven to NYC a few times, you will add other things to your estimate: time of day, day of week, weather conditions, and so on. Your guesstimate for the driving time will improve with experience. The same holds true for purchasing managers at the local supermarkets in your town who need to estimate how many trash bags to keep in stock or how much toilet paper they need to have on the shelves.

Let's look at the retail industry again. Inventory is one of retailers' highest costs. Go to any retail store, from a convenience store in your neighborhood to a furniture store in your town. You will see a lot of merchandise in the store. Money has been spent on producing and buying it, but the retailer will get that money back only when you buy an item. Reduction in the level of capital tied up in unsold goods will free up resources to invest elsewhere, such as covering wage increases or building out online operations. So, companies can choose to keep less stock. But destocking is not without risk. Bare shelves are an annoyance to shoppers who go into stores to buy something. If a customer cannot find the products she is looking for in a particular store, she will likely go to another store. The sale that the first store lost is likely never coming back. Too much inventory is a problem; too little inventory is also a problem.

13.2.1 Just-in-Time Inventory Management

There was a time when companies had lots of inventory. Producers and grocery stores such as Kroger Co. kept months of inventory on hand, and manufacturers piled up masses of parts and products. Then, in the 1980s, some US companies took a cue from their Japanese counterparts and began to adopt a **just-in-time** (JIT) approach to inventory. In the JIT system, the firm attempts to keep inventory levels to a minimum throughout the value chain from raw materials to finished goods. US companies were also drawn to other popular techniques prevalent in Japan at the time: **lean manufacturing** or **lean production**, for example. Lean manufacturing is ". . . a way to do more and more with less and less - less human effort, less equipment, less time, and less space - while coming closer and closer to providing customers exactly what they want."

Over time, JIT, and the lean approach, became widely adopted across entire industries such as automotive, electronics, apparel, and retailing. Companies were attracted to the idea that they could increase profits simply by reducing their inventory. Estimates suggested that in the US auto industry alone, major manufacturers saved more than $1 billion a year in inventory carrying costs by becoming lean using JIT methods.

Unfortunately, the emphasis on becoming lean may have made some companies anorexic. Supply chain experts believe companies can became so obsessed with reducing inventories that they squeeze out the cushioning needed to cope with business booms or interruptions. If supplies don't arrive as expected, whether because of a natural disaster, terrorist attack, or pandemic, companies can be left high and dry. "Just-in-time makes sense, but it's vulnerable to disruptions," says Ron DeFeo, CEO of heavy-equipment maker Terex Corp.

Interactive Exercise

During the COVID-19 pandemic, it was not uncommon to see that retailer shelves that were once stacked with paper towels were empty. Use the Internet to find out why paper towels were scarce during the pandemic. We all know that the demand for paper towels increased tremendously during the pandemic, but why couldn't supply keep pace with the growing demand. Hint: It has something to do with the concepts you studied in this section.

Concerns about the downside of being lean to the point of becoming anorexic have motivated some companies to begin stocking up more. Terex, for example, cut deals with its 15 biggest suppliers to guarantee it would buy fixed amounts of parts for three months in advance. Lawn-mower manufacturer AriensCo. opened new warehouses across North America to store finished mowers. Al-jon Manufacturing LLC, a family-owned maker of machines that crush metal waste, has taken to keeping a stash of hard-to-find parts at its factory in Iowa.

The events in the US grocery industry help illustrate the challenges associated with inventory management. In the 1990s, the grocery industry came under pressure from investors to improve profit margins. Companies embraced JIT systems that aimed to produce, ship, and stock as few goods as possible to meet demand. Retailers decreased capacity of their distribution centers, saving on rent, utilities, and labor. Distributors cut down on fuel and wages. Manufacturers reduced capital locked up in unsold inventory. Over time, the major companies in the industry went from having months of inventory on hand to holding only a four to six weeks' supply. Then the 2020 pandemic struck. Weeks of supplies sold out in days as customers made a run for essentials and other goods. Faced with a problem of too much (unanticipated) demand from people stocking up for weeks at home, companies began overriding the sophisticated algorithms that say how much of what products they should buy, after seeing how those models failed to account for this month's demand surge. Greg Lehmkuhl, CEO of Lineage Logistics LLC, a big refrigerated storage company, observed that similar spikes occurred regionally after disasters such as Hurricane Katrina but never across most of the world at once. Distributors that get perishables and other staples to supermarkets are straining under the demand, and truckers are working under challenging conditions because of the virus. "Just-in-time purchasing has been thrown out the window," noted Dave Hirz, chief executive of Smart & Final Stores Inc., which operates more than 300 stores in California, Arizona, and Nevada.

JIT is a finely balanced system that works well while goods are flowing steadily. When a major disruption occurs, the system crashes. When the disruption is severe, the whole system may fail. At the peak of the COVID-19 pandemic in the United States, Kraft Heinz Co. Chief Executive Miguel Patricio worried there was potential for the whole system to buckle under the pressure. "My biggest fear is that, what if the supply chain collapses?" he said.

What Do You Think?

Chet Morton is owner of Hardy Square Market. His store is located in North Carolina, the only one in a 15-mile radius. Chet's job is not easy. He runs a small-town grocery store with narrow margins, complex supply chains, and dozens of hourly employees. He has managed the store through the last recession, several hurricanes, and a flood, keeping the doors open in emergencies by stringing Christmas lights down the aisles, powered by a generator. His sales during the 2020 pandemic were up by at least a third, as were the accounts payable, with items costing much more in the crisis. Just the other day, Chet saw a woman and her son buy enough bottled water to fill two grocery carts. Even cookies are hard to keep in stock because all the kids are out of school. Bread is selling faster than he can buy it. He sells 9-packs of Charmin Ultra Soft at $15.19. The generic brand typically sells for half that but is unavailable. When the Purell dispensers ran dry, Chet decided against making his own sanitizer. "What if somebody comes in and claims it took the skin off their hands?" he says. Chet is 56, and he is already sleeping in the guest bedroom because he doesn't want to risk infecting his family if he becomes infected. His wife wants him to close down the store until the pandemic is over. Chet wants to order more inventory, but he is worried that if any of his workers got sick, he will have to ask the rest of his employees to self-quarantine for two weeks. In that situation, food would spoil and bills would go unpaid. He is trying to set up one-way traffic in store aisles and maintain 6 feet of distance between customers in the checkout line. What would you advise Chet to do? Should he close and wait for the storm to pass? Should he order more supplies, so that customers can buy enough? Should he limit the quantities his customers can buy? If yes, how do you suggest he do this? "I want to serve my people, and I want to do what's right for the customers and my family," he says, "and it makes it hard to do both those things at the same time."

13.2.2 No Inventory

What does a business owner do if there is no inventory to sell? This is the problem many small bike shop owners faced during the COVID-19 pandemic. Bike shops in the United States generally rely on Chinese suppliers for bikes and parts. When the pandemic made it difficult to get parts and bikes from China, many small bike shop owners realized that they were in a situation they had neither experienced before nor planned for: no inventory in the store. Jon Hughes is a third-generation bike shop owner in Ferndale, MI. The store ran out of the bikes to sell in May. By July, the store was running out of parts such as 26-inch tire tubes, a popular size that has never been out of stock since he opened the shop in 2010. Jon has no idea when bikes and parts will start coming in again, but he is not expecting it to become better until sometime in late 2021. Yet, the store is full with people waiting to get fix-it jobs done on bikes. While there is plenty of repair work to do for bike shop owners, the problem is that it does not pay as well. A mechanic may spend a full day on repair work to earn as much profit as a single high-end bicycle sale, for example. As people hunkered down during the pandemic, demand for bikes increased, but many bike shop owners had no inventory to sell.

It's not just bikes. Many sellers of arts supplies and jigsaw puzzles also found that demand skyrocketed during the pandemic. Lawrence Rosen, chairman of LaRose Industries LLC, had to increase production of jigsaw puzzles at a new Jacksonville, FL, factory to keep up with orders. Every other customer call to Sullivan's Toys & Art Supplies, Washington, D.C., is an inquiry about puzzles, and callers want puzzles that are going to take a while to finish. "They need something to keep the whole family occupied," shares Natalia Alcazar, the store's general manager. The problem: The store's stock of adult puzzles is depleted and fresh supplies are limited due to factory disruptions in China and shipping delays. The New Jersey–based family firm of LaRose Industries has seen similar demand spikes before when during the Great Depression puzzles were sold on street corners. "They're all key items to keep the family busy during the current situation," Lawrence said. There is, however, one key difference between then and now. The supply chain back then was local, and now it spans across the world, which means there is greater possibility of disruption due to unexpected events like the pandemic.

Comprehension Check

1. Explain JIT inventory management.
2. What is lean manufacturing?
3. What are the ways in which the word *inventory* is commonly used?

Module 13.3 Introduction to Scheduling

The dictionary definition of **scheduling** is "to arrange or plan an event to take place at a particular time." For manufacturing and services firms, scheduling is a fundamental part of operations management. Scheduling helps with efficient allocation of firm resources by fine-tuning the distribution of work across time, workers, and facilities. Crust is a restaurant in Miami that serves pizzas and pasta along with other fare. It is open 5 pm to 10 pm, with seating for 70 guests. If scheduling is done properly, Crust can use each table 2.5 times per night. What if each table is only used two or less times per night? Well, every year hundreds of similar restaurants close because they don't make enough money from the tables to cover expenses. Scheduling reservations at Crust is a juggling act. Most guests want reservations between 7 pm and 8 pm. Cofounder Anita Kovaceski often finds herself asking guests to push ahead or back a half-hour to smooth the flow during peak hours (and use each table enough times a night to make it financially viable).

Let's look at Frank's Auto Shop on University Avenue. Frank schedules one oil change every 20 minutes. Each oil change costs $41 and includes tire rotations. With four pits, the Auto Shop can accommodate four cars at one time. It's a good business, and it pays well for Frank's family and his five workers. Wednesdays are especially busy because Frank runs a $29 special for "lady drivers" (as he likes to say). If each oil change actually takes 15 minutes rather than the 20 minutes Frank plans for, the Auto Shop could do 16 oil changes an hour instead of the 12 it currently does. That's 32 more oil changes every day, for an 8-hour day. Doing less than what he could do means Frank is bringing in less revenue. He is losing money, though he may not realize it. If each oil change takes 30 minutes rather than 20, then Frank will be unable to complete on time the work he has taken on. He then has to either pay his employees overtime for the extra hours or risk the wrath of unhappy customers. For Frank, it is critical that he get the scheduling right.

Scheduling aims for the most efficient use of resources to complete a task within a stipulated time. Effective scheduling starts with a good understanding of the tasks that need to be done to complete the specified work and the time involved in each task. For work that is standard, scheduling is easier. For custom work, scheduling is more difficult. Changing motor oil is standard work, and Frank should be able to accurately measure how much time it takes to change oil in one car. However, if the oil changes are interrupted by clients who want custom work done on their cars, scheduling will be more difficult for Joe.

KEY TAKEAWAY

Scheduling aims for the most efficient use of resources to complete a task within a stipulated time.

There are two main types of scheduling practices: **forward scheduling** and **backward scheduling**. Forward scheduling starts the schedule as soon as the job requirements are known. Backward scheduling starts the scheduling from when the completed job has to be delivered. The starting point for forward scheduling is when the order comes in. For backward scheduling, the starting point is when the order must be completed. Forward scheduling is particularly useful for serial production, where the production order is fulfilled in the shortest possible time. Backward scheduling is appropriate for companies that make-to-order based on estimated sales forecast. The goal of "on time, on plan, and on budget" completion calls for a mix of forward and backward scheduling approaches.

Scheduling is done in conjunction with other practices. **Planning** involves making decisions about the future. Without a plan, scheduling cannot even begin or take place. **Routing** pertains to determining the path that must be followed from raw materials to a finished product. Good routing keeps the path short. **Dispatching** is about setting the various production activities in motion with the release of formal orders and instructions. It also provides a way to assess progress through the production process.

Joseph Ruggieri is the owner of Ruggieri & Sons Inc., a small family-owned fuel-oil delivery business based in Philadelphia. He has long struggled with routing and scheduling delivery vehicles in a way that little time is wasted, customers are happy, and costs are kept to a minimum. His five trucks make 30–40 stops every day within a 25-mile radius of his office. Moreover, "It's not the same route every day. You're not always doing the same stops in the same order." Historically, Ruggieri relied on "what's between my ears" to organize schedules and routes. More recently, he bought a computer system that uses built-in maps and mathematical algorithms to calculate each truck's daily schedule. The scheduling software also interacts with another computer system that tracks customers' fuel-oil usage rates to determine when each one needs a new supply. As a result, the company's trucks now travel 5–7% fewer miles, and make 5–7% more stops per hour.

Often, scheduling is affected by human factors that are unrelated to efficiency criteria. For example, Frank's schedule for his auto shop may be affected by one of his employees unexpectedly taking a day off, or one or two employees quitting, leaving Frank scrambling to get as much work done as he can with the workers he has left. When a new Crust employee, just two weeks on the job, called in sick on a Sunday, one of the busiest days for the restaurant, cofounder Klime Kovaceski told him that most of the time employees "call in Sunday because they're partying on Saturday." When the employee insisted that he was sick, Klime had to figure out how to manage tables with fewer employees, which increased service time.

Interactive Exercise

Identify a popular restaurant near your university or where you live. Does the restaurant have customers waiting to get a table for dinner? Talk to the owner to better understand how they schedule customers and employees in an efficient manner. Ask them what changes they have made in the last one year to their scheduling practices. What do you learn about scheduling after talking to the business owner?

Consider scheduling at universities. Most American universities have higher class occupancy during the day (from 11 am to 3 pm), with few classrooms filled in the early morning hours (say, 7–8 am) or in the evening (say, 6 pm). Classrooms are also largely empty on the weekends. At many universities, classrooms do not see much traffic on Fridays either. Scheduling here is not about efficiency, but about accommodating the specialized needs of the various stakeholders, primarily students, who do not like early morning classes, late evening classes, and weekend classes. If universities could use their facilities more efficiently, scheduling classes as and when the rooms are available, the cost of education would go down (less investment in expensive fixed assets).

What Do You Think?

Most college facilities are rarely used in the mornings, evenings, and on the weekends. Demand for college facilities is high during the peak-use hours, such as 11 am or 2 pm, and from Monday to Thursday. Do you think colleges should consider ways to spread the demand more evenly throughout the week? Do you think students would be receptive to lower tuition for courses during off-peak times? According to the Labor Department's College, tuition through the 1980s, 1990s, and aughts rose at double or triple the rate of overall inflation, according to the Labor Department's consumer price index. Do you think college tuition can be lowered with more judicious course scheduling?

Comprehension Check

1. What is scheduling?
2. Distinguish between forward and backward scheduling.
3. What is routing?

Module 13.4 Issues of Quality

In 1971, the Ford Motor Co. introduced the Pinto – a populist car that was to capture consumer hearts with its $2000 price tag. Within a few years, lawsuits alleged a structural design fault: The fuel tank was in proximity to the rear bumper and rear axle, so that rear-end collisions would elevate the risk of fires. Mark Dowie, an investigative journalist, revealed that the company was aware of the design flaw during production. Dowie published a cost–benefit analysis document that showed upper management at Ford comparing the cost of $11 per-vehicle repairs with the cost of settlements for deaths and injuries. Fearing reputational damage from the lawsuits, Ford recalled 1.5 million Ford Pintos in 1978, the largest recall in automotive history at the time. By 1980, Pinto was pulled from the market. In 2004, *Forbes* included the Pinto among its *Worst Cars of All Time*, saying "When people talk about how bad American small cars created an opportunity for the Japanese to come in and clean house in the 1970s and '80s, they are referring to vehicles like this." In 2009, *Time* magazine included the Pinto to its list of Top 10 product recalls, observing that the "Ford Pinto was a famously bad automobile, but worse still might be Ford's handling of the safety concerns."

Quality is important for every company, large or small. Large firms, of course, have more resources to invest in good quality control. Small firms, unfortunately, have fewer resources they can spend to ensure their products meet quality standards. Regardless of the company size, attention to quality is important. Firms that do not pay attention to quality do not survive very long. Laura-Jean Mallon is a former Wall Street executive-turned-stay-at-home mother who happily pays about $1000 for a haircut. One time she went to a top-tier haircutter who forgot to cut a section of hair in the back; she went home with a piece inches longer than the rest. "I had a tail," she says. If you paid $1000 for a haircut and the salon sent you home with a tail, would you want to go there again?

KEY TAKEAWAY

Quality is important for every company, large or small, but small companies have fewer resources to ensure their products meet quality standards.

What does quality really mean? There is considerable misunderstanding about what constitutes good quality. For some, ensuring quality means making the best product. That is not, however, what quality means here. BMW and Mercedes certainly have a strong reputation for high quality (and they charge a premium), but Toyota and Honda are also known for their quality (without the premium price). A basic Toyota Corolla and a top-of-the-line Mercedes-Benz are both quality cars. They each have specific engineering design standards to satisfy, and once those standards are met, then quality is delivered.

From a business perspective, quality involves three criteria: **functionality**, **safety**, and **consistency**. Functionality refers to a product meeting or exceeding its claims to customers and regulators. In 2015, the Environmental Protection Agency (EPA) found that many VW cars being sold in America had a "defeat device" in diesel engines that could detect when they were being tested and then altered the performance accordingly to improve results. The company's performance was lower than what it promised, a quality problem. Every year, more than 350,000 tons of olive oil is imported into the United States, primarily from European countries such as Italy and Spain. The *New York Times* warned that "much of the extra virgin olive oil flooding the world's market shelves is neither Italian nor virgin." Many companies are selling olive oil that does not meet the claims they are making to customers. Thus, the product falls short of the expectations customers have from it.

Safety means that risks associated with using a product are known to a reasonable customer (and certainly do not outweigh the benefits). The anti-nausea and sedative drug thalidomide, launched by German company Grunenthal, was sold from 1957 until 1962. The drug helped address the symptoms of morning sickness in pregnant women. Unfortunately, it also caused numerous birth defects in children, including malformation of limbs and internal organs. The drug's side effects outweighed its benefits to the consumer, a quality problem. The Italian eatery Delfina has long been considered one of the Bay Area's best restaurants. Yet, one night, when the restaurant was booked solely for a private party, about two dozen patrons were sickened by food poisoning. The staff determined that the most likely source of the food poisoning was tainted produce like salad greens, and reached out to their suppliers. Minimizing the chances of food poisoning is a top safety concern for most restaurants.

Consistency is about producing and delivering a product with low variance in quality. When variance is high, quality will vary drastically. Tesla has an enthusiastic following, but the cars it has delivered have not been consistent, including issues with its body hardware, as well as paint and trim. "While Teslas perform well in *Consumer Reports'* road tests and have excellent owner satisfaction, their reliability has not been consistent, according to our members," noted Jake Fisher, senior director of auto testing at *Consumer Reports*, when Tesla lost the CR recommendation. Tovala is a meal service, shipping ready-to-cook meal packages to be cooked in a special $400 steam oven connected to the Internet. The company has plenty of competition, such as Blue Apron and Hello Fresh, among others. Tovala's founders say their meal kits are for people who tried other options but gave up because they were too much work. What do you think do customers of meal delivery services look for other than cost? For many people, it is consistency of food quality. When customers open a meal package, they want to see consistency in the quality of foods they are getting. Would you like it if the meal packet you received had high-quality food one day, but poor quality food the next day? When the *Wall Street Journal's* personal technology columnist Geoffrey Fowler tried Tovala, he found the quality of food to be consistently high during the trial period.

The question "What is quality?" has many implications that flow across a business and throughout the lifetime of a company, its offerings, and its customers. When a company delivers a quality product, it brings success to the customer and, consequentially, to the business the customer buys from.

Total quality management (TQM) is the name for the philosophy of a systemic, organization-wide approach to managing quality in a firm. TQM emphasizes process measurement and controls as means of continuous improvement. In a TQM effort, all members of an organization are expected to participate in improving the processes and the culture within which they work with the goal of having superior products and services. The principles and processes that comprise TQM are specified in quality standards such as the ISO 9000 series and quality award programs such as the Deming Prize and the Malcolm Baldrige National Quality Award.

Six Sigma (6σ) is a quality management methodology that equips organizations with the tools to improve the capability of their business processes. It streamlines quality control in manufacturing or business processes in a way that minimizes variances throughout. The decrease in process variation helps to defect reduction and improvement in quality of products or services. The 6σ approach was originally introduced at Motorola, and the legendary CEO Jack Welch made it central to corporate strategy at GE in the 1990s. The term *Six Sigma* was registered in 1991 as a US Service Mark. 6σ focuses on reducing waste, eliminating defective products, and fixing inefficient services. When done well, it can help increase customer satisfaction, empower employees, and boost profitability.

The underlying philosophy of 6σ views all work as processes that can be defined, measured, analyzed, improved, and controlled (also called the **DMAIC** approach). Adequate training in statistical thinking is provided at all levels of the organization, with key people given extensive training in advanced statistics and project management. Teams throughout the firm are assigned well-defined projects that can have a direct impact on the organization's bottom line. Top management embraces quality improvement as part of the business strategy for the company.

6σ originated at a large corporation (Motorola) and was initially championed by other large corporations (e.g. General Electric). Over time, 6σ has also expanded to small firms, which generally lack the resources (money, time, qualified employees) necessary for such efforts to work. "It's really about breaking things down into steps, which is something most small companies don't do very well," says Rose Kasianiuk, president of Calgary, Alberta-based RK Business Solutions Inc., which provides marketing, process and project management services to small businesses. Kasianiuk, a former GE manager who holds a black belt in 6σ, says that small businesses without a process discipline are more likely to waste time and mismanage projects.

Interactive Exercise

Some say Six Sigma is not for small firms. Others say small firms can benefit tremendously from Six Sigma. Use the Internet to identify reasons that (a) support the case for Six Sigma in small firms and (b) oppose the use of Six Sigma in small businesses. After reading both sides of the argument, what do you think about implementing Six Sigma in small firms?

Quality circles (QCs), small groups of volunteer employees who meet regularly to identify, analyze, and solve quality and related problems in their area of responsibility, are another possible technique for improving quality in small firms. QCs are a Japanese invention that emerged after World War II. Instead of limiting quality control to just a select group of engineers, the Japanese made it the responsibility of all rank-and-file employees. The idea of QCs is based on motivational theory, which urges greater responsibility among employees for their own work quality. Each circle can select its own projects, as long as it pertains to the areas of expertise of circle members. For a while, hundreds of large American corporations like IBM, Honeywell, and Xerox embraced QCs as a way to improve quality. QCs are also touted as a possible way for small firms to adopt participatory management where employees come together to help solve problems related to their own jobs.

While there is no doubt that quality is an important concern for all firms, techniques such as TQM, 6σ, and QCs ebb and flow in popularity. The popularity of quality-enhancement techniques increases when evidence comes out about their success. The decline in popularity happens when companies realize how difficult it is to implement some of these seemingly simple ideas. Honeywell, for example, which formed 625 QCs but then, within 18 months, had abandoned almost all of them.

James Zimmerman and Jamie Weiss,[1] writing in *Quality*, sum the matter up as follows:

> "Quality and productivity initiatives have come and gone during the past few decades. The list of 'already rans' includes quality circles, statistical process control, total quality management, Baldrige protocol diagnostics, enterprise wide resource planning and lean manufacturing. Most have been sound in theory but inconsistent in implementation, not always delivering on their promises over the long run."

What Do You Think?

Your uncle Lonnie Thompson runs Perfect Aerosmith, a small manufacturer of test equipment for aviation maintenance. The 80-year-old company has engineering and manufacturing facilities in its East Grand Forks, MN, headquarters as well as in Phoenix, AZ. The company designs and manufactures motion simulators used to test various navigation systems and motion sensors. Perfect employs about 100 employees and is ISO 9001 certified. Its management team consists of six managers headed by Lonnie, the company's president. On a recent road trip with his family to South Dakota, Lonnie listened to an audiobook from former GE CEO Jack Welch (*Jack: Straight from the Gut*, Jack Welch and John A. Byrne, Warner Books, 2001; audio version published by Time Warner Audio Books). When he got back to the office, Lonnie wanted to give Six Sigma a try at Perfect. Lonnie has always been very proud of your achievements and wants your advice before he rolls out the latest initiative. What would you suggest to Uncle Lonnie and why? If Lonnie still decides to go ahead with the initiative, what do you think should be some things he should do to improve his chances of success?

TQM, 6σ, QCs, or any other quality improvement methodology is in itself a long-term effort. Results will not come tomorrow, or even next month. The idea is that regular commitment to quality improvement will pay off over time. "What you will get long-term in business results will more than outweigh your investment," Kasianiuk says.

Comprehension Check

1. What are the essential elements of quality?
2. What is total quality management?
3. Explain quality circles.

Summary

Operations and supply chain management is the nuts-and-bolts of a small business. It is also the unglamorous part of running a business, which is perhaps why the topic often gets less attention than it deserves. When a company excels at managing its operations and supply chain, it can create a competitive advantage that is hard for its rivals to duplicate. Companies that are unable to manage their operations and supply chain effectively will find themselves struggling and may eventually fail. What constitutes operations and supply chain management for a small firm will depend on the nature of the business it is in and the specific conditions of the business. The precise actions you will need to take to run things effectively will vary based on whether you are running a manufacturing plant, wholesale enterprise, retail firm, or service company, but you will need to keep a close eye on all the moving parts of the business to make sure everything is running smoothly.

---

[1]Zimmerman, James P., and Jamie Weiss. "Six sigma's seven deadly sins: while the seven sins can be deadly, redemption is possible." *Quality*, vol. 44, no. 1, January 2005, pp. 62–67.

World of Books

The Goal: A Process of Ongoing Improvement by Eliyahu Goldratt and Jeff Cox
The Checklist Manifesto: How to Get Things Right by Atul Gawande

In the Movies

Coffee shop seems like an easy business. Most of us can make coffee at home, and yet coffee shops charge us $4 or more for a latte. In the movie *Coffee Shop*, watch owner Donavan Turner run a hip neighborhood coffee shop in a quaint, scenic beach town. She enjoys her work and has the robust support of her family and the wonderful, eclectic group of her regulars. And yet, she faces foreclosure, with the bank threatening to close the shop Donavan started when she was 19. As you watch the film, look out for all the operational things a coffee shop owner has to manage on a daily basis. If you were a supplier, would you like to do business with Donavan's coffee shop?

Live Exercise

When Johnny started the SoapStandle business, he shaped modeling clay into a small oval, added some points that could enter a bar of soap and hold it in place, and baked the prototype in a cast-iron cooker (almost ruining the cooker). He took the idea to a company that helps develop inventions into products, but was turned down. He got some acquaintances to use their 3D printers for prototypes, and when that worked out well he bought his own printer. Johnny is now selling tens of thousands of SoapStandles a year, and finds himself confronting some difficult questions that need to be addressed. Let's see if you can help Johnny with the following issues:

1. Demand is exceeding Johnny's capacity to make the product on 3D printers. What he needs now is the capability to manufacture at an industrial scale. Should he outsource the production to a vendor or should he buy a factory to make the product himself?
2. As Johnny plans his future, do you envision him as a manufacturer selling his product or a trader buying from manufacturers and selling to buyers?
3. If Johnny decides to outsource production, should he make in the United States (where manufacturing costs are higher) or overseas in China or Vietnam (where costs are lower)?
4. In the beginning, Johnny made a few pieces at a time and then sold them before making more. As the product is now available at many national retail chains, and new colors and materials have been added, Johnny needs to maintain inventory. How should he make decisions about the inventory levels he needs to maintain?
5. Based on your consideration of Johnny's business, can you write an operations plan for Johnny? The plan should cover the major areas – labor, materials, facilities, equipment, and processes – and provide only major details – things critical to operations or that will give Johnny competitive advantage. The simplest way to treat operations is to think of it as a linear process that can be broken down into a sequence of tasks. Once the initial task listing is complete, turn your attention to who is needed to do which tasks. Keep this very simple and concentrate on major tasks such as producing a product or delivering a service.

Things to Remember

LO 13.1   **Describe the basics of managing operations**

- Five elements come together to form the operations of a business: input, output, transformative processes, feedback, and control system.
- Inputs include all tangible and intangible resources needed to produce a good or service.
- Output is what a business produces.
- The methods by which inputs are converted into outputs are called transformative processes.
- Control systems are a means of monitoring operations and fixing problems or deviations when they occur.
- Feedback is the link between control systems, on the one hand, and inputs, outputs, and transformative processes, on the other hand.
- The ratio of outputs to inputs is called productivity.
- A key decision for every business is whether to buy from outside suppliers or produce in-house.

LO 13.2   **Discuss the role of inventory management in business**

- Inventory refers to either the monetary value or the units of goods in storage owned by a business at a given time.
- The word *inventory* may also be used to describe the actual counting or measuring of the company's stock.
- Inventory carrying cost refers to the money a company spends on holding its inventory.
- Small firms often use plausible assumptions and elementary arithmetic to guesstimate future trends.
- Just-in-time (JIT) is an inventory management system in which firms attempt to keep inventory levels to a minimum.
- Lean manufacturing or lean production involves keeping minimal inventory in the production process.
- JIT is a finely balanced system that works well while goods are flowing steadily.

LO 13.3   **Explain the importance of scheduling**

- Scheduling helps with efficient allocation of firm resources by fine-tuning the distribution of work across time, workers, and facilities.
- Scheduling starts with a good understanding of the tasks that need to be done to complete the specified work and the time involved in each task.
- Forward scheduling starts the schedule as soon as the job requirements are known. It is particularly useful for serial production.
- Backward scheduling starts the scheduling from when the completed job has to be delivered. It is appropriate for companies that either make-to-order or based on estimated sales forecast.
- Routing pertains to determining the path that must be followed from raw materials to a finished product.
- Dispatching is about setting the various production activities in motion with the release of formal orders and instructions.

LO 13.4   **Enumerate the reasons quality control is important**

- Quality is important for every company, large or small.
- Quality resolves around three criteria: functionality, safety, and consistency.
- Functionality refers to the idea that a product should meet (or exceed) what it claims to customers and regulators.
- Safety means that the risks associated with using a product are known to a reasonable customer and do not outweigh the benefits.
- Consistency is about producing and delivering products with low variance.

- Total quality management (TQM) is the name for the philosophy of a systemic, organization-wide approach to managing quality in a firm.
- Six Sigma (6σ) is a quality management methodology that equips organizations with the tools to improve the capability of their business processes.
- Quality circles (QCs) refer to small groups of volunteer employees who meet regularly to identify, analyze, and solve quality and related problems in their area of responsibility.

Key Terms

operations management	productivity	lean production	functionality
supply chain management	make-or-buy	scheduling	safety
input	inventory	forward scheduling	consistency
output	inventory carrying cost	backward scheduling	total quality management
transformative processes	guesstimation	planning	Six Sigma
control systems	just-in-time	routing	DMAIC
feedback	lean manufacturing	dispatching	quality circles

Experiential Exercise

The Beer Game was developed in the late 1950s by Massachusetts Institute of Technology's Professor Jay Forrester. The team version, which is described here, is played with pen, paper, and poker chips. There is also a single-player digital version that students can play on their own without teammates.

Divide the class into teams of four students each. Within each team, there are four players: retailer, wholesaler, distributor, and brewer (manufacturer). If there is suitable space in the class, ask the students to sit next to each other, with the retailer at one end and the manufacturer at the other end. Customer demand (in kegs of beer) starts at the retailer, who replenishes the inventory from the wholesaler, the wholesaler from the distributor, and the distributor from the brewer. Material thus flows from upstream to downstream, information flows in the opposite direction through order placements.

In each period, every channel member must decide how much, if any, to order from their respective suppliers and the factory must decide how much, if any, to produce. There are penalties for having too much inventory (50 cents per case of beer per week) or unfilled back orders ($1 per case per week). Each link in the supply chain keeps track of its own costs, but a team's score is the sum of the four links. The lower the score, the better.

Each team is presented with consumer demand through cards, each of which has a number ranging from 1 to 10 written on it. The number on the card indicates consumer demand for beer. The first round begins with each retailer drawing a card indicating consumer demand for cases of beer (there will be a total of 10 rounds); at the same time, all the units send slips of paper with orders up the supply chain. In response, cases of beer – represented by poker chips – move in the opposite direction, from brewer to retailer. A small number of chips (let's say 5 each, although the teacher can decide to start with any number) are already at every station at the start of the game. To simulate the incomplete information every supply chain member has in real life, players cannot communicate across stations, apart from relaying orders (on pieces of paper).

Depending on how much time there is, the game may be played for 10 rounds or 20 rounds. At the end of the competition, the professor may choose to put up the details of every team's performance on the wall for everyone to see. The team with the lowest score wins.

A single-player virtual version of this game is available at www.beergame.transentis.com. If students have access to laptops and the Internet, the single-player digital game is a good option.

CHAPTER 14

Global Opportunities for Small Firms

If America – including American small businesses – wants to thrive in the 21st century, we must embrace globalization.

RHONDA ABRAMS

LEARNING OBJECTIVES

This chapter will help you to:

LO 14.1 Discuss the reasons for seeking business opportunities overseas

LO 14.2 Distinguish between the various modes of internationalization

LO 14.3 Explain how and why overseas expansion can be challenging for companies

LO 14.4 Identify the main strategic approaches for competing internationally

LO 14.5 Describe the reasons why internationalization attracts considerable opposition

14.0 Introduction

Looking overseas for trade opportunities has a long history. By the time of the First Dynasty of Egypt (c. 3150–c. 2890 BCE), there was already a thriving trade with neighboring lands, including the ancient regions of the Levant, Libya, and Nubia. Egyptian trading colonies existed in Canaan, Syria, and Nubia, with traders using both the sea-route and the overland route to buy and sell goods across borders. The ancient silk route stretched all the way from China and India in the East to Persia and Rome in the West, with traders moving in both directions to buy and sell items on the way. The advent of air travel, Internet, and mass media has hastened global trade, so that it is now commonplace for individuals and companies to do business with others outside the borders of their own country. The volume of goods, services, and investments crossing national borders has been expanding faster than world output for more than half a century.

For small businesses, global trade presents many opportunities and challenges. Small firms can expand their revenues by selling around the world and/or reduce costs by locating part or whole of their operations overseas. In this chapter, we take a look at the issues surrounding global opportunities for small businesses. We also discuss the challenges small firms face when they compete in global markets.

SPOTLIGHT | The Global Business of Hair Extensions

Sonia Seye is owner of the salon Hair Universal in Los Angeles, where she braids hair and turns multicolored hair extensions into intricate, fashionable coifs. She wants to supply salons across California with good-quality human-hair extensions. To make that happen, she decided to buy hair from India, where many firms sell local women's long, fine locks. These firms obtain much of their hair from Hindu temples – where, in a surrender of ego, men and women shave their heads in offerings to the gods. The temples then clean and prepare the hair for sale to the West.

When Sonia started her business, she bought hair from a local supplier in Los Angeles. Concerned about the quality and prices of the products she was buying, Sonia decided to try buying directly from India. She spent more than six months researching prospective suppliers online. The 12½-hour time difference made phone calls difficult, so she asked

Sonia Seye uses the hair she imports from India to make hair extensions for sale in her California salon.

them questions by email. She also checked their credentials with the Indian consulate.

Once Sonia identified three potential suppliers, she flew to Chennai, a major city on India's southern coast, where most of the country's hair suppliers are located. Chennai is near the Venkateshwara Temple at Tirupati, one of the richest shrines in the world, visited by more than 50,000 pilgrims every day. Sonia met the prospective suppliers and inspected their products. While Sonia didn't feel language was an obstacle (many suppliers spoke at least some English), she felt a little intimidated being alone in a new country. "A black woman in the middle of South India by herself, everywhere you go they are staring at you," she remembers.

Sonia was impressed with the hair stock at one firm, and placed an initial order of 22 pounds. When the monsoon downpour kept her freshly washed supplies from drying, she had to delay her departure two days, which strains her limited budget.

Buying directly from India helped Sonia halve the costs of the hair extensions, even as she held firm on her already low retail prices: $28 per ounce compared to $40 at competing salons. Encouraged by her initial success, Sonia asked current clients to tell their friends about the new extensions. Revenues went up by 60% to between $16,000 and $20,000 per month and her profits doubled. Sonia feels her trip to India, and buying directly from suppliers there, helped her get one step closer to building a successful business in hair extensions. "You don't have to be big to be global," says Sonia, who has an Indian hair piece sewn into her own hair.

Discussion Questions

1. What prompted Sonia to look overseas for her business?

2. What challenges did Sonia face when she traveled overseas for the business?

3. How did Sonia prepare for her maiden overseas business trip?

Module 14.1 Motivation for Competing Internationally

There is little doubt that businesses have more opportunities when they can trade across borders rather than when they are constrained to operate within the borders of a country. From a business perspective, **globalization** is the process by which firms operate across national boundaries. It is not, however, always clear that global opportunities also benefit small businesses. A common misconception is that small firms are hurt by globalization. American small businesses, the thinking goes, have lost customers or been driven out of business by competition from cheaper foreign manufacturers. The truth, however, is more nuanced. For some small firms, global trade is a boon; for others, it is a bane. Business owners who figured out how to compete in the face of globalization did well, but those who did not or could not find themselves unable to survive. Indeed, some experts believe that it's easier for entrepreneurs and small businesses to go global than large corporations because they tend to be more flexible and have fewer legal and bureaucratic constraints.

KEY TAKEAWAY

In general, businesses have more opportunities when they can trade across borders rather than when they are constrained to operate within the borders of a country.

There are a number of reasons why small firms look toward international markets (see Figure 14.1):

1. *Gain access to new customers.* Expanding into overseas markets provides access to new customers. For companies from small countries like Finland or Bahrain, the domestic market may not be large enough to provide good growth opportunities. Firms from larger countries like the United States or China expand overseas when growth opportunities are dwindling domestically or the company's products have a stronger market in other lands.

   Larry Lieberman is owner of Vision Quest Lighting, a small decorative lighting company in Long Island, NY. For Vision, during recession in the United States, sales to foreign markets including much of Europe, China, and Japan are a lifeline. "If we only had domestic sales we would have been in big trouble," Larry

FIGURE 14.1 Motivations for International Expansion

shares. Vision also plans to export solar-powered trailers to Haiti and South Africa, which is estimated to bring about $10–$20 million of revenue for the 30-employee company.

2. *Gain access to cheaper and better labor.* Foreign countries can also be a good source of cheaper or better labor than is available domestically. In the United States, for example, foreign workers dominate many economic sectors (e.g. farm labor), where domestic workers do not want to work. In some industries, a country may not have the skilled labor that it needs, forcing its businesses to look overseas. For example, in many Middle Eastern countries, skilled jobs tend to be occupied by foreign workers, as the domestic workers lack the education and training needed to perform those jobs. Bill Gates, cofounder and chairman of Microsoft, has long argued that technology-based American companies of all sizes struggle to find enough qualified domestic workers and should be allowed to hire more foreign workers.

Sumpraxis LLC of Delray Beach, FL, owns work centers in India and China, and provides overseas workers for small- and medium-sized companies in the United States. One of its customers is Subrogation Partners LLC of Connecticut, which is in the insurance claims business. Subrogation purchases and services claims that have been paid and then seeks to recover the money from other parties involved in the incidents. Sumpraxis provides Subrogation with 20–30 workers at a time, mostly in a partner center in India. The per-hour labor costs for Subrogation are about half what its US workers cost, even after it pays Sumpraxis for its services.

When small firms hire workers overseas, they need to carefully consider how the new employees will be managed (see Figure 14.2 for some expert advice on how to manage overseas employees).

3. *Lower costs.* Did you know that when adjusted for inflation median household income in the United States has barely budged over the last two decades? Yet we now have more of everything, including smartphones, smart TVs, and smart-watches. One reason that we can now buy more when personal earnings are flat is the relentless pursuit of our companies to lower costs by sourcing from cheaper places. Sourcing clothes from Bangladesh and sneakers from Thailand helps keep costs low, yielding higher profit margins for companies.

Reaching Out

Smaller companies increasingly look to tap offshore labor markets, as larger companies have for years. Consultants and executives offer these tips for managers at small firms thinking of expanding overseas.

- Locate overseas offices in regions that are home to bigger, multinational companies

- Monitor quality closely; errors can really hurt a small business

- Ensure that key executives visit frequently, and plan for the travel costs

- Offer consistent company-wide training so all workers use similar processes

- Track retention of overseas workers, as a few key departures could be crippling

FIGURE 14.2 Tips for Managing Overseas Employees
Source: Smaller Companies Join The Outsourcing Trend, WSJ

Becky Feinberg-Galvez is owner of Shop4ties, a nine-employee company that has been making custom-branded neckties, scarves, and Hawaiian shirts in China for years for sale stateside. Minnesota-based outdoor-fireplace maker Blue Rooster Co. imports cast-metal parts from China and then assembles them in stateside. Moving production to the United States will require building an aluminum foundry at a cost of up to $500,000, owner Blair Reuther shares. Greg Kerr is owner of Pin Game Strong, an online retailer that turns customers' artwork into enamel pins, patches, and stickers. The six-person company works with Chinese factories to cater to customers in the United States.

4. *Access to rare production inputs.* Companies in industries where natural resources (e.g. oil and gas, rubber) are not uniformly distributed across the world find it necessary to operate internationally. For some industries, raw material supplies and consumer demand may be located in different parts of the world. Consider the case of diamonds. The world's largest producers of natural diamonds are Russia, Democratic Republic of Congo (DRC), and Botswana, all together accounting over 60% of the global diamond production. Roughly 95% of the world's diamonds are cut and polished in India. The United States and China are the biggest consumer markets for diamonds. If you are in the diamond trade, globalization is the nature of business. New York's diamond district – the largest diamond market in the United States – is home to about 400 retailers occupying street-level storefronts, plus about 2000 other small businesses – wholesalers, diamond polishers, jewelry manufacturers – that occupy tiny offices in the space above the retailers. Dennis Marlow of Solitaire Creations and Richard Winick of Manny Winick & Son are examples of small business owners in the nation's largest diamond district serving the global diamonds market.

5. *Gain access to resources and capabilities located overseas.* Global management consulting is a trillion-dollar industry, dominated by American firms like Accenture, Deloitte, PwC, and McKinsey. When companies and governments in other countries need management consulting, they often turn to American firms. Access to cutting-edge resources and capabilities available overseas is another reason for looking beyond one's borders.

Joseph Boggs is owner of Boggs & Partners Architects Inc. of Annapolis, MD. He expects as much as 90% of the firm's revenues to come from outside the United States. Boggs & Partners had designed office buildings and museums in the United States, but had done little work overseas, until it landed big contracts in Qatar and India, where there was big demand for the kind of architectural services the company specialized in.

In addition, small companies may expand overseas to raise money for domestic expansion, to follow their large corporate customers who enter other markets, or to avoid intense competition in the domestic markets. There is truly no dearth of reasons for growth-minded companies to expand into foreign countries.

Interactive Exercise

Phil Knight, the founder of Nike, was a college student when he first came up with the idea of buying shoes from Japan to sell in the United States. If you could buy something from overseas and sale in the United States or buy in the United States to sell overseas, what would that be?

The various reasons for seeking global opportunities can be classified into three broad categories. **Factor market internationalization** (FMI) refers to looking overseas for improvements in a company's upstream supply chain, whether it is to access valuable natural resources, components, or labor needed to produce the goods offered by the market. Many Western apparel brands, for example, source their products from suppliers in Bangladesh (and other developing countries) to achieve lower costs. Consider the example of Phil Knight, a graduate of the University of Oregon and Stanford School of Business. On a short visit to Japan, Knight came across Tiger brand running shoes, which he liked so much that he ordered a shipment for sale in the western United States. A short while later, Knight started his own company Blue Ribbon Sports (now Nike) that relied on Japanese manufacturers to make shoes for sale in the United States. Since those initial days, Knight has come a long way, but every year thousands of business owners like him seek opportunities to import from other countries. American Scientific LLC, based in Columbus, Ohio, is one such company. The 10-employee firm sells scientific equipment for students, buying from Chinese suppliers and selling to schools districts in the United States.

Product market internationalization (PMI) involves overseas expansion of the downstream supply chain in search of new customers to buy the company's products. The popular media routinely discusses the experiences of companies like Walmart and Home Depot in opening new stores in foreign markets. Akio Morita cofounded Sony in war-ravaged Japan to make tape recorders. From the beginning, Morita knew that the company's growth was going to come from overseas, as Japan was still reeling from wartime shortages and cost cutting. The company's first branded product, the TR-55 transistor radio, was a hit among teens in the United States, making it a best-selling product and setting Sony on a path to successful global expansion.

Martha Montoya is a comic-strip artist in Santa Ana, CA. She sells her colorful cartoon characters for use on snack packages in China, Ecuador, Colombia, and other countries. She estimates that revenues at her company, Los Kitos Entertainment LLC, have grown between 30% and 40% since she started selling overseas. "You can grow your business much faster than if you keep trying to sell to the same customers here," Montoya believes.

Capital market internationalization (CMI) refers to raising money for the firm overseas, either through selling equity in the company or by tapping debt markets. BlaBlaCar is a French car share service that raised money from Passion Capital based in the United Kingdom. Magma Partners is a Chile-based venture capital firm that helps small Latin American firms raise money from US funds. Nathan Lustig, managing partner at Magma, observes that "some U.S. venture capitalists are starting to invest outside the U.S., but most non-U.S. founders still struggle to raise money from U.S. funds."

What Do You Think?

Blue Rooster Co. is a Minnesota-based seller of outdoor fireplaces. The company imports cast-metal parts from China and then assembles them stateside. During the 2020 COVID-19 pandemic, the company found that two of its three main suppliers in China were unable to operate because of local lockdowns where they were located. One advise the company got was to source most or all their production from within the United States. Another advice they got was to diversify their sourcing from China to Vietnam, Thailand, or Bangladesh. The company sells exclusively in the United States. They have also been advised to expand their sales overseas, including to North European countries, Australia and New Zealand, and Russia. What would you advise the company to do? Should they double down on the United States or hedge their bets through international expansion?

HaloSource, based in Seattle, makes water purification devices for use in American pools and spas, as well as for drinking water in countries like Brazil, China, and India. When the company wanted to raise money, it sought investors in the United Kingdom who were more sympathetic to growth opportunities in emerging markets.

FMI, PMI, and CMI are three distinct forms of internationalization that may be pursued one at a time or all at once, depending on the firm's needs. Companies make the decision based on their needs at the time. Given the challenges some businesses face to globalize, it is generally not advisable to pursue all three forms of internationalization at the same time. For most small firms, it is best to take one baby step at a time toward globalization.

Many small firms today are **born-global**, meaning that they operate across national boundaries from the very beginning. When the concept of born-global first appeared in a McKinsey report from Australia, it described a new type of company that was starting to operate globally in a short time after their creation (generally in six years). Over time, it became obvious that many companies operate internationally right from the start, and that is how the born-global concept is now used. Born-global firms can be found in many different industries, but the technology sector is considered a born-global haven. Quantilus Innovation Inc., a New York–based custom-software developer, is an example of a born-global firm, employing about 20 people in its China office to serve customers in the United States and Europe. Outside of the technology sector, Denver-based TerraSlate Paper, a small maker of waterproof paper and menus is another born-global firm, with about 20% of its revenues coming from Southeast Asia.

Some born-global firms are so successful; they are able to dominate their industry and compete with the largest firms worldwide. Have you heard of the phone manufacturer HTC, which at one time was second only to Apple in US smartphone sales (and, ahead of Apple in global smartphone sales)? Based in Taiwan, the company was founded by Myanmar-born Peter Chou as an original design manufacturer (ODM) for leading Western companies such as Verizon and Orange. It introduced the first smartphone powered by Microsoft software and the first smartphone running Google's Android operating system. For his visionary understanding of what makes a good product and the strong designs of the company's products, Chou is frequently compared to Apple cofounder Steve Jobs. Today, the company has a 2.5% market share of the global smartphone industry.

Comprehension Check

1. Define and explain factor market internationalization.
2. How does international expansion help companies achieve lower costs?
3. Define and explain capital market internationalization.

Module 14.2 Common Modes of International Expansion

Much of what we know about globalization is based on companies that sell their offerings overseas (or PMI as explained earlier). One study found that when asked why they wanted to expand overseas, the most common response from the owners of American small firms was about reaching new customers. More than 95% of the world's population lives outside the United States. As a result, successfully tapping into foreign markets can greatly increase the customer base of a US-based small firm. Similarly, firms in countries like Portugal, Japan, and Mexico have a small domestic customer base. If they can expand overseas, they can increase their market size considerably. This is what J. Moreira Ltd. of Portugal did when it faced heightened competition from a surge of low-cost Asia manufacturers. The company switched its focus from low-cost shoes to high-quality, expensive women's shoes under its own brand, Felmini. It bought new machinery, adopted new methods to treat leather, and created a commercial department to identify new fashion trends and untapped markets. Superior quality allowed the company to sell globally. The result: Sales more than doubled and the company increased wages even the workforce expanded from 170 to 200 employees. Exports of high-quality shoes by small- and medium-sized companies like J. Moreira have helped strengthen the Portuguese economy.

There are several strategies that a small firm can pursue to reach new customers. The most common path to internationalization involves **exporting** your products. Exporting is the sale of products produced in one country to customers in another country. It is often described as the first stage of globalization. A company that wants to expand overseas starts by looking at the possibility of exporting to another country. Some estimates suggest that 97% of all US exporters are small firms, and about one-third of American exports in economic terms come from small firms. Still, only about 1% of the country's nearly 30 million small firms sell overseas, according to US Census data. The majority (about 58%) of the small firms that export do so to only one country, typically Canada, Mexico, the United Kingdom, Germany, or China.

Exporting provides a low-cost way to expand into international markets without incurring the expense of starting costly operations overseas. The economic calculation here is simple: As long as you can sell overseas for more than the domestic sale price plus shipping costs and tariffs, exporting may be a viable option. Many economists see exporting by small firms as critical for economic growth and prosperity of the country. Former US Commerce Secretary Gary Locke declared that "for America to win the future, more small and medium-size businesses must export, because the more small businesses export, the more they produce; the more they produce, the more workers they need, and that means good-paying jobs here at home." Interested in exporting? Check out our five-step plan for prospective exporters (Figure 14.3).

In 2019, SBA recognized EarthQuaker Devices as the Small Business Exporter of the Year. The Akron, Ohio-based company builds guitar effects by hand. EarthQuaker started as a basement-based business and then moved to a renovated two-story, 15,000-sq.-ft. building where they build and distribute their products to 47 countries worldwide. David Glaccum, Associate Administrator for the Office of International Trade, noted that "EarthQuaker Devices is a great example of how a small business can flourish by entering

| **Step 1** |
| Take the Assessment for New Exporters at https://www.trade.gov/exporter-assessments-0 |
| **Step 2** |
| Browse the legal consideration section of Export.gov to research export requirements |
| **Step 3** |
| Talk to other exporters in your line of business or exporters in other lines of business exporting to countries you are interested in |
| **Step 4** |
| Contact the U.S. trade representative in your exporting destination and the trade representative of that country in the U.S. to learn about the business environment of that country. |
| **Step 5** |
| Are you prepared to make additional investments in your business to get export-ready? |

FIGURE 14.3 The Five Steps for Prospective Exporters

the international market. We are thrilled that the SBA was able to assist them as they grew into a global company."

Interactive Exercise

Check out the website of the Small Business Exporters Association (SBEA). On its website, SBEA profiles many successful small firms (https://sbea.org/category/export-profiles). If you could do an in-depth study on one of the exporters profiled by SBEA, which one captures your interest the most?

14.2.1 Types of Exporting

There are two modes that companies can use to export: **indirect exporting** and **direct exporting**. A company is said to engage in indirect export when it sells overseas through an intermediary. Indirect exporting involves considerably less exposure to the foreign market, which means less investment of time and money to expand overseas. On the flip side, the intermediary firm charges a fee or commission, which reduces the profit margin. Direct exporting involves doing business in another country without an intermediary. This allows the firm more control over the exporting process and direct contact with the customer, but also increases the risk to the company if something goes wrong.

To understand the difference between indirect and direct exporting, consider the case of Joe Alexander who started selling "green mattresses" for San Francisco mattress company Keetsa. Like all new businesses, Keetsa's first days were hard, says Joe, who was the company's first employee. Because there was little money for advertising, he paid local homeless people to hand out fliers on Market Street. Within a year, in response to inquiries from people overseas who had found Keetsa on the Web, the company began exporting its eco-friendly mattresses and other sleep products to Canada. This is direct exporting. If Keetsa was selling to foreign buyers through another company (say Amazon) without dealing with them directly, then it is indirect exporting.

When one talks of exporting, it is often for manufactured goods. However, exporting is also possible in the services sector. America already exports more services than any other country in the world. Yet many experts believe there is untapped potential to export more services. J. Bradford Jensen, author of *Global Trade in Services: Fear, Facts, and Offshoring*, believes that US companies are uniquely situated to provide **tradable services** to emerging economies. "There is this huge infrastructure boom where these big, fast-growing economies are going to need to build out their roads, sewers, telecommunications networks, factories, airports, harbors, you name it. All those projects require armies of architects, engineers, project managers, financial insurers" (see Figure 14.3). Tradable services are those that can be readily done at a distance, as opposed to work like cutting hair or doing nails. Tres Roeder, president of Roeder Consulting Inc., a Cleveland, OH, project management and training firm with less than a dozen employees, is interested in exporting his firm's services overseas. "The overall tide isn't rising here. But I look at foreign markets and they're growing," he says. While American corporate clients have been canceling training sessions, more international participants have joined the company's monthly webinars.

For US-based companies, the top five exporting destinations are Canada, Mexico, China, Japan, and United Kingdom. The United States is also a major export destination for companies from other countries. Five countries make up almost half of all importers into the United States: China, Canada, Mexico, Japan, and Germany. **Imports** refer to goods bought from another country. An import in the receiving country is an export for the sending country. Exports and imports are, therefore, two sides of the same coin.

Jenny Lefcourt is president and cofounder of Jenny & Francois Selections, a natural wine importer in New York. The United States imports over $4.25 billion a year in European wine, which is handled by thousands of importers, distributors, wine stores, and restaurants. There is a vast industry – comprising hundreds of small firms engaged in importing and selling billions of dollars of wine, whiskey, and other alcohol-based products from Europe. The wine industry is linked to other industries, such as hospitality. Importing companies sell to wholesalers (which together employ 100,000 people), which sell to retail shops and restaurants (three million employees). Trucking, warehouse, and shipping companies are also linked to the wine industry. Some of the winemakers in Jenny's portfolio are among the most sought after in the world, with limited capacity to expand. If the United States makes it difficult for American companies to import, these winemakers will then turn to booming markets like China or Russia, Jenny believes.

Exporting Basics: The Exporting Process Overview

Do you want to be among the tens of thousands of small firms that export successfully from the United States to other countries? If yes, you want to make sure you are as prepared as you can be when you start on the path to exporting. This means learning as much as you can about exporting, laws and regulations surrounding exporting, and the business conditions of the country that will be your export destination.

14.2.2 Licensing

Another popular path for small firms to internationalize is through **licensing**. In licensing, a firm sells the rights to manufacture and sell its product to a firm in another country. The firm selling the rights is called the **licensor** and the firm buying the rights is called the **licensee**. The licensor receives a fee paid for each unit produced for a specific time, also called royalties. An advantage to licensing is that it is a low-cost avenue for overseas expansion. A disadvantage is that the licensee may continue to use the know-how even after the contract expires without paying for it. Foreign licensing is now a common strategy in the US media business, where content is licensed to TV channels overseas as American companies are faced with a maturing pay-TV market at home (see Figure 14.4). Companies in the technology sector also use foreign licensing for overseas expansion. Advanced Micro Devices Inc., a Silicon Valley chip company, for example, licenses microprocessor technology to Chinese companies.

Husband-and-wife business partners Matt and Rene Greff own the 200-seat Arbor Brewing Company, a Michigan brewpub. They were approached by one of their regular customers about opening a brewpub in Bengaluru, India. Skeptical at first, the Greffs traveled to India, where they came to believe the idea was feasible: There was strong local beer-drinking culture, lots of US-educated professionals, including plenty of University of Michigan grads, and an untapped market for traditionally crafted microbrews like the ones they serve in Michigan. In exchange for providing their

Watching Overseas

Foreign pay-TV markets are less saturated than the U.S., and potential growth could fuel demand for content.

Percentage of TV households that have pay TV

U.S.	86.5%
France	80.1%
U.K.	59.6%
Germany	59.1%
Mexico	51.0%
Brazil	28.6%

FIGURE 14.4 Current Overseas Pay-TV Market Saturation *Source:* TV Studios Court Licensing Deals in Bustling Foreign Markets, *The Wall Street Journal*

know-how for making beer, the Greffs will be paid a licensing fees (plus a stake in the Bengaluru pub).

14.2.3 Franchising

Franchising is a variation of the licensing arrangement. As is the case with domestic franchising, international franchising involves a company – the franchisor – offering a standard package of systems and services to a company – the franchisee – that brings capital and operational management to the business. In terms of globalization, international franchising involves a franchisor and a franchisee from different countries. This approach is very popular with large US companies like McDonalds and Subway who have used it extensively to expand internationally. The tremendous success these large franchisors have achieved internationally has motivated smaller companies to also seek franchising opportunities overseas.

Steve Abrams is co-owner of Magnolia Bakery, the New York cupcake maker popularized by the TV show *Sex and the City*. Soon after receiving state approval to franchise, Abrams was fielding hundreds of queries from prospective franchisees across Asia, the Middle East, and South America. The company's first non-US store opened in Dubai. Within a few years, the company had franchisees in Abu Dhabi, Qatar, Jordan, South Korea, Philippines, Mexico, and India. Some years ago, "few smaller brands would have considered" international markets, says William Edwards, CEO of Edwards Global Services, an Irvine, CA, global franchise consulting firm. "The big challenge now is that in the US, it's very difficult for new franchisees to get financing. Money is not a problem in emerging markets, and there's a lot of demand" for American goods. A survey by the International Franchise Association (IFA) found that almost 85% of more than 150 US franchisers – including chains with fewer than 50 locations in the United States – reported planning to start or accelerate international operations in the near future. "Younger and smaller franchise companies are jumping into the global market," shares Scott Lehr, vice president of international development at the IFA. "They're looking at markets where it's possible to grow sales in double digits. That's pretty enticing."

What Do You Think?

Hye Kyung (Shelly) Hwang and Young Lee had an idea for a frozen yogurt shop in West Hollywood, CA. Shelly developed her own recipe for yogurt from whole milk, which could then be topped with fresh fruit toppings. Lee understood that aesthetics matter, and he painted the inside of the store in sherbet hues of peach, green and blue. Only two flavors of yogurt are available: plain and green tea. Within a month of opening, the store was turning a profit. Within six years, it had grown through franchising from a single location to more than 175 stores in 17 countries – including Bahrain, Jordan, and Peru. What can other frozen yogurt shops learn from Pinkberry's international success?

14.2.4 Foreign Partnerships

Foreign partnerships are formal interfirm relationships between companies from different countries. Such relationships can be classified into two broad types. **Strategic alliances** are non-equity partnerships where both companies retain their independence, but are expected to fulfill their contractual obligations toward each other. **Joint ventures** are partnerships that involve equity sharing. For example, an American firm may choose to enter into a joint venture with a Chinese firm where both companies own 50% each of the new business.

Consider the example of Kiva Container Corporation of Phoenix, AZ, which makes containers made of corrugated plastic – the material used in the letter-sorting containers you see at post offices. Kiva's containers are used for computer boards and chips and to ship fish packed in ice. Kiva entered into a strategic alliance with a British company, Team Tool Ltd. Kiva will distribute Team Tool's die-cutting equipment in the United States, and the British company will distribute Kiva containers in Europe. Kiva's plan was to use the strategic alliance to "test the waters" for a joint venture with Team Tool to eventually manufacture containers in Europe. "Eventually, we'll manufacture containers in Europe; that's more practical than shipping them from here," said Ruth Stafford, Kiva's vice president.

When establishing overseas partnerships, many small firms prefer to work with much larger foreign firms. A well-established foreign partner brings a strong brand reputation or deep pockets to the relationship, which may be very useful when trying to gain a foothold in a new country. Connie Mixon, CEO of MYCELX Technologies Corp. in Gainesville, GA, found that it was much easier to take her oil-removal technology to international markets after partnering with Siemens Water Technologies, a division of the German global giant Siemens AG. Connie believes "the partnership has been advantageous because we can enter a sales relationship with a potential customer at a level which would otherwise possibly take months or years to generate. They already have the existing infrastructure, sales team, and service personnel." For Connie, the benefit to a small firm from such a partnership is invaluable as the brand recognition of a well-known partner means "an automatic endorsement."

When the laws of the foreign country allow it, some small firms may choose to establish a foreign presence on their own without a relationship with an existing company. A firm with an existing customer base outside its home country may locate a production facility or sales office overseas. Some firms may choose to set up a **greenfield venture**, by starting from scratch a wholly owned subsidiary. Another possibility for overseas expansion is **cross-border acquisition**, which involves purchasing an existing foreign business. Both greenfield venturing and cross-border acquisition are go-it alone approaches to expanding in foreign markets, and as such expose the company to all the risks associated with operating in another country. Small firms should be careful when expanding overseas through such go-it alone strategies.

At four years old, the American online auction pioneer eBay was still in its infancy when it decided to expand its international footprint. At the time, eBay's registered users were drawn from 90 countries, but the site itself was designed and set up with only Americans in mind. Management believed that eBay had barely begun to tap the domestic market, so that there was no dearth of growth opportunities at home. However, other Internet startups like Amazon were starting to carve up the globe, and eBay did not want to be left behind. eBay decided to expand aggressively into new countries in the order of their Internet population. At the time, the United States, with its nearly 100 million users, was the world's leading Internet market, followed by Japan, the United Kingdom, Canada, and Germany. eBay expanded into Germany first, acquiring Alando.de, a highly successful German auction site founded by the Samwer brothers (and their three friends) just four months earlier. A month later, eBay launched its UK site by building its own platform. In Japan, eBay entered the online auction market by itself after turning down an offer from Softbank's Masayoshi Son to partner with Yahoo! eBay also acquired Paris-based iBazar, which helped eBay become the leading online auction site in France, Italy, Spain, Belgium, Portugal, and the Netherlands. eBay also bought a majority stake in Internet Auction Ltd., South Korea's largest online auction site.

The example of eBay illustrates how one company may choose to go alone in some international markets, by either starting their own operation from scratch (e.g. the United Kingdom and Japan) or acquiring a foreign player (e.g. Germany and France). In yet another market (South Korea), eBay formed a joint venture with a local dominant player. It is notable that even as the company established its global dominance, it regretted its decision to go-it alone in Japan. The company believes it should have partnered with a local player that was already well known in the Japanese market. "With 20/20 hindsight," said eBay CEO Meg Whitman, going alone in Japan "was probably one of the bigger strategic mistakes we made."

Comprehension Check

1. Differentiate between imports and exports.
2. Define and explain licensing as a way to expand internationally.
3. What are foreign partnerships?

Module 14.3 Challenges to Overseas Expansion

Even when a company has a strong commitment to international expansion, it may find its efforts derailed. Companies face many roadblocks when they try to go global. Large corporations like Walmart and Uber have had to shut down many of their overseas expansion plans due to the insurmountable problems they faced. The challenges are even greater for small firms because they generally lack the financial resources, brand recognition, and political influence that larger corporations have. When India passed tariffs on alcohol imports that tripled the price of Jack Daniels whiskey, the United States fought back. Jack Daniels, part of publicly owned Brown-Forman Corp's empire, has deep pockets and significant political influence. It was at the company's urging that Tennessee passed legislation requiring anything labeled "Tennessee Whiskey" not just to be made in the state, but also to be made from at least 51% corn, filtered through maple charcoal, and aged in new, charred oak barrels (which is exactly the recipe for Jack Daniels). Small craft whiskey distillers do not have the kind of resources and power needed to influence state and federal rules. Thus, while Jack Daniels was able to call on the US government to help reduce tariffs for its products in the Indian market, smaller firms lack such heft.

Consider the situation of Paul Wickberg, chief executive of SOL Inc., a Palm City, FL, manufacturer of solar-powered outdoor lighting. About 30% of his company's business, which involves supplying street and pathway lighting to local municipalities, comes from outside the United States, up from just 5% before the Great Recession of 2008. Given the economic headwinds in the United States, Paul says, the company has "got to find places where there's high demand and more money," such as South America, Africa, and Australia. The biggest obstacle his company faces, Paul believes, is taxes charged by foreign governments on imported products. Higher import duties can make it difficult for smaller US firms to be competitive in a regional market, he says.

Nancy Simmons of Orlando, FL, faced a different sort of challenge to international expansion. When contacted by customers in Brazil about buying refurbished aerospace parts from her company Aero Industries of the Space Coast Inc., she wasn't sure how to handle the language barrier. None of her eight employees spoke Portuguese, and she did not have the resources to pay for hiring in Brazil. She turned to a Portuguese-speaking neighbor to help negotiate the deal. After the deal was finalized, she enrolled her employees for a training program offered by Florida's Department of Commerce.

KEY TAKEAWAY

Small firms interested in expanding internationally face many challenges and problems.

14.3.1 Demographic and Cultural Factors

When making the decision to expand globally, you must think about the socioeconomic differences between your home country and the country you want to expand into. Consumer tastes and worker productivity may differ substantially across countries. In many Western countries, the week between Christmas and New Year's Day is typically a slow time for work as people spend time with their families. For retailers, the time between Thanksgiving and Christmas is a busy time, as shopping picks up for the holiday season. In China, it is the end of January, the time around Chinese New Year, when business sees a slow period as migrant workers all over the country go home for the holidays. In India, the slow period for most businesses, but high point for shopping, is the time around Diwali, the festival of lights that falls sometime in October or November depending on the lunar calendar. Islamic countries have Ramadan that lasts for 30 days, during which time work will slow down or even stop, as people fast from sunrise to sunset.

When doing business internationally, companies need to consider factors such as education level of the populace, religious beliefs, language, and social structure. Careful consideration of these factors will help a company determine how much it needs to adapt to the local conditions of the other country. Note that when it comes to doing business overseas, it is rarely the case that a company can continue to do business exactly as it has at home. Some level of adaptation is always required, so the key question is not if to adapt when expanding overseas, but how much to adapt.

It is said that Americans love breakfast. There is even an American adage "breakfast is the most important meal of the day" that many people embrace. If you've ever stopped at Starbucks or Dunkin Donuts on the way to work or school, you know that many Americans get their breakfast at restaurants, either drive-through or eat on-site.

The American breakfast market got a major impetus from women's entry into the workforce as both husband and wife now struggle to get ready for work in the morning after sending the kids to school. When both men and women work, there is no one with the time to make breakfast in the morning. However, an American business that drives much of its revenues from the breakfast market is unlikely to find similar traction in a market where women do not work, breakfast is considered a minor meal, or people stay at home with aged parents who can cook. Think about what you had for breakfast today. Would it surprise you to learn that Americans overwhelmingly eat sweet things for breakfast? The question that many food companies have to ask themselves is whether sweet breakfast food is a universal preference (in which case, what works in the United States can work elsewhere too) or savory is preferred for breakfast in some places (which would require substantive changes to the menu).

The online auction pioneer eBay struggled with many issues when it first expanded overseas. On the surface, the United States and the United Kingdom are very similar countries. Both are democratic, English-speaking, developed countries with shared heritage and history. The phrase "cousins across the pond" is often used to describe the relationship between the British and American people. After eBay entered the UK market, it found that Internet usage there was much behind than in the United States at the time because Web surfers had to pay British Telecom for their Internet connection by the minute. The United Kingdom also had no First Amendment on the books, and its defamation laws were far stricter than in the United States. As a result, British users who received negative feedback often threatened to sue the writer of the feedback and eBay, even when the criticism was trivial to American eyes. When eBay-UK sent out the company's standard responses to customer email, which had been drafted in the United States, British users complained that the exclamation-point-filled messages were insincere! The British, it seemed, were not used to being thanked profusely for complaining or filing a grievance. Then there was the problem of message boards. In the United States, eBay considered message boards to be critical to building community because buyers and sellers used them to chat about everything about their daily routine. In England, the company found that British users did not feel comfortable nattering on to strangers the way Americans did. Successfully working through these cultural challenges was the key to eBay's phenomenal success in the United Kingdom where, within a year of its launch, it pushed aside the homegrown QXL.

14.3.2 Government Policies and Regulatory Framework

Companies interested in doing business overseas need to be mindful of how government policies and regulations differ in their home country and in the places where they want to do business. Some governments welcome foreign business as a way to drive economic growth, provide customers with more options, create new jobs, and raise living standards for their workers. Some estimates suggest that foreign-owned companies in the United States have a workforce of more than 5.5 million, or some 3.5% of all workers, and are spread across all 50 states in sectors from manufacturing to publishing to retail. Mitch Daniels, the former governor of Indiana, observed that without foreign investment "we'd be a dust bowl."

At other times, governments enact policies and put up hurdles that make it difficult to do business there. This can be done through various means, including raising tariffs on foreign goods, providing subsidies to domestic players, and imposing burdensome customs inspection or regulatory reporting for foreign companies. Most of these restrictions apply to imports or foreign players taking their money out of the country. For example, China, which is estimated to surpass the United States as the world's largest movie market in 2021, currently allows only 34 Hollywood movies for release in the country on a revenue-sharing basis. In 2018, *Avengers: Endgame* and *Fast & Furious Presents: Hobbs & Shaw* were the top grossing Hollywood films in China. To bypass the quota, many US studios are seeking out Chinese investors. Films with Chinese investors now account for about 20% of US box-office ticket sales, with Hollywood movies increasingly playing to

Chinese tastes – with plot elements, actors, and scripts planned with Chinese viewers, and censors, in mind.

Sometimes, governments also put restrictions on exports. The United States, for example, has a **foreign direct product rule**, which restricts export of US products and technology for use in industries the government considers sensitive to military or national-security concerns. The export-control restrictions specify the list of US-made products and technology – including in semiconductor, aerospace, and other industry sectors – that need to be reviewed by national security experts before shipments can be sent overseas. During the COVID-19 pandemic of 2020, China imposed restrictions on the export of face masks, test kits, and other critical medical equipment as it struggled to deal with the rising numbers of cases domestically. Similar export restrictions were also imposed by other countries, including the United States, which restricted the export of certain face masks and gloves designed to slow the spread of the novel coronavirus as the demand for personal protective equipment soared in the United States along with the number of cases.

14.3.4 Political and Economic Risks

Companies interested in overseas expansion need to consider political and economic risks associated with operating in a foreign country. **Political risks** are associated with operating in countries with weak or unstable governments. Sometimes, a country's citizenry may revolt against dictatorial leaders (as happened in Libya), elections may produce corrupt or tyrannical government leaders (as is the case with Turkmenistan), or populist governments may impose greater restrictions on foreign companies (as happened in Venezuela). For years, legions of Indian outsourcing firms ran the digital engine rooms of American corporations with engineers in India. Tighter controls on skilled worker visas in the "Buy American, Hire American" executive order in response to growing protectionist sentiments in the country threatened their business model.

Economic risks are about the stability of a country's economy and monetary system. When inflation skyrockets or the country's monetary system breaks down because of reckless deficit spending by the government or risky bank lending practices, it could lead to prolonged economic distress. Greece is a prominent example of country that saw its economic risks skyrocket after the banking crisis in the country. Countries like Venezuela, Zimbabwe, and South Sudan have cripplingly high inflation rates that make it almost impossible for businesses to set the right prices and for customers to plan their spending.

James McDevitt is chief operating officer of Houston-based Applied Machinery Corp., which makes oil rigs. The company does about $70 million in business annually, with each oil rig costing between $14 million and $30 million. Political and economic risks are an important factor for Applied Machinery, as it sells the rigs from Africa to Latin America. Most Americans read about the collapse of the Venezuelan political and economic institutions in the newspaper or watched stories about it on TV. For McDevitt, the collapse hit close to home as it affected the company's business interests in that part of the world.

Interactive Exercise

For small firms interested in expanding abroad, much help is available, both from public organizations and private businesses. The Department of Commerce and Small Business Administration are among those that can help small businesses find contracts, screen foreign buyers, and learn the rules of financing in other countries. The Export-Import Bank of the United States provides financial support and credit insurance to small exporters. There are also private firms, such as Edwards Global Services, an Irvine, CA, global franchise consulting firm and Kepner-Tregoe of New Jersey that helps companies venture overseas. Check out the website of any one of these organizations and write a one-page memo about how they help small business owners expand internationally.

14.3.5 Adverse Exchange Rate Shifts

Exchange rate represents the value of one country's currency relative to that of another country. For example, the number of dollars that can be purchased with one euro or the number of Turkish Lira that be purchased with one dollar. When companies produce and sell goods across borders, they become vulnerable to the impact of favorable or unfavorable exchange rates. Sudden or unexpected changes in exchange rates can be a serious problem for small firms operating internationally, whether they sell overseas or source from there.

Jean-Paul Tennant is chief executive of a travel company, Geographic Expeditions, specializing in arranging ambitious trips to exotic lands. Based in San Francisco, the company books trips to Bhutan, Tibet, Central Asia, Patagonia, and the Galápagos Islands several months or even more than a year in advance. One time, Jean-Paul booked travel for eight clients who wanted to explore Northern India. Then the rupee began a double-digit climb against the dollar, prompting one Indian supplier to suddenly raise prices for hotel rooms, guides and drivers to raise prices. Suddenly a trip costing Geographic Expeditions $7500 per person was going to jump to $9000. "As soon as we commit to a price, we are heavily exposed if we don't know what our costs will be," Jean-Paul said. "It can totally kill a company like ours." For small companies like Geographic, changes in exchange rates can make financial transactions a challenge.

As more small companies expand overseas, owners are learning that exchange rate volatility can undermine profits. More small businesses are now using banks and international payment companies to create risk management strategies that mimic those of large corporations.

Business is affected, both when a country's currency gets stronger and when it gets weaker. Luxury retailers in Europe and the United States find more Chinese shoppers in the stores when the dollar or euro weakens compared to China's renminbi. Indeed, high-end retailers in places such as New York, Paris, and Milan are highly dependent on visitors from China, who often spend more than the typical tourist. On Milan's Via Monte Napoleone, almost every shop has hired a Chinese-speaking sales clerk in recent years. Chinese consumers buy nearly $110 billion worth of luxury goods annually, including clothes, leather goods, and jewelry – mostly outside China. Chinese represent 7% of all overseas visitors to the United States, and they spent roughly $34 billion on travel and transportation services in 2019, according to estimates by the research firm Tourism Economics. When the dollar rises in value compared to the renminbi, Chinese shopping in the United States decreases. Increasing dollar values are good for importers because they raise domestic buyer demand for foreign-made goods. Falling dollar values are good for exporters as now they are more price competitive compared to companies from other countries.

Ash Ashutosh, of Waltham, MA, shares that he found expansion into Europe to be quite challenging for his data-storage software company Actifio Inc. He feels that a hodgepodge of laws, languages, and cultures found on that continent, including unique

What Do You Think?

Sharon Doherty is cofounder of pet-care products manufacturer Vellus Products Inc. in Columbus, OH. When she decided to expand overseas, she established payment procedures up front as a way to protect her business, requiring customers to pay for the goods before they leave the warehouse as one safeguard against delinquent customers. She gives international customers her office, home, and mobile phone numbers so that they can reach her no matter where she is during their business hours. "People overseas like to know you care about them," she says, "because they're taking a chance with someone they don't know." What do you think are the benefits and pitfalls of sharing your personal contact information so openly with international business partners?

employment laws that are generally far stricter than what companies face in the United States, makes it difficult for foreigners to do business there. Regulations also differ from country to country with regard to where and how data can be stored.

Comprehension Check

1. What are some cultural obstacles that companies face when they expand overseas?
2. Explain how exchange rate fluctuation can thwart a company's internationalization efforts.
3. What are some political and economic risks that companies need to be mindful of when considering international expansion?

Module 14.4 Main Approaches to International Strategy

When companies mention **international strategy**, they are simply talking about the firm's strategy for competing in two or more countries – for example, an Indian or Chinese company doing business in the United States or a US company doing business in the Philippines or Japan. A company generally starts competing internationally by selecting one or more foreign markets, trying to identify a country where it can enter with the fewest obstacles. For US firms, China is often a first-choice destination when they think of sourcing their manufacturing needs internationally. Canada or the United Kingdom is the destination that most companies expand to first when they think of going international to sell their goods and services. These choices are partly based on what others in their industry are already doing, a process that sociologists refer to as **isomorphism**. In terms of internationalization, isomorphism means that a company's decision to enter a particular market is driven by peer or rival firms who are already in that market.

KEY TAKEAWAY

A company generally starts competing internationally by selecting one or more foreign markets, trying to identify a country where it can enter with the fewest obstacles.

Experts in international business talk about the notion of *cultural distance* as a helpful guide to make decisions about internationalization. **Culture**, in general, is the homogeneity of characteristics that separates one human group from another. At the national level, culture reflects a society's dominant norms, values, and beliefs. For example, you have probably heard that the United States is an individualistic or materialistic society. This does not mean that every person in the United States is individualistic or materialistic. Instead, this means that as a whole the United States tends to emphasize individualistic and materialistic values. The idea of **cultural distance** captures the differences between national cultures. For example, the United States and the United Kingdom tend to have low cultural distance, whereas the United States and Japan have high cultural distance. Underlying the use of the cultural distance construct in international business is the assumption that differences between foreign and home country cultures increase the cost of doing business in another country. When differences between countries are low, such as between Norway and Sweden or Spain and Portugal, it is easier for companies in one country to do business in the other country.

Using cultural distance to explain foreign expansion emerged from the observation that Swedish firms progressively expanded from their home base into countries that were less similar to them. For most Swedish firms, their first stop on the internationalization journey is another Scandinavian country like Norway or Denmark, so this is sometimes also described as the **Scandinavian model** for thinking about foreign expansion. To assess cultural distance, one needs to be able to measure culture in the first place. Hofstede's model of national culture as the composite of four dimensions – masculinity, uncertainty avoidance, power distance, and individualism (MUPI) – is often used to capture the national culture of a country. This model, proposed by the Dutch social scientist Geert Hofstede, emphasizes four specific cultural values: social preference for "tough" attributes, such as competition and achievement (**masculinity**), over "soft" attributes, such as nurturance and caring (**femininity**), lack of tolerance for ambiguity and absence of structure (**uncertainty avoidance**), acceptance of unequal distribution of authority and resources in society (**power distance**), and the elevation of the interests of the individual (**individualism**) over the family or community (**collectivism**).

Interactive Exercise

Visit the cultural insight page at https://www.hofstede-insights.com/country-comparison. Compare the United States with two other countries of your choice. Based on the cross-country comparison you see there, what do you learn about the culture of your selected countries compared to the United States?

Once a company has decided which countries it wants to expand into, it needs to make decisions about its strategy in the international markets. Every company that expands internationally faces two conflicting pressures: maintaining consistent offerings across markets (standardization) and responsiveness to local conditions (localization). Deciding on the balance between these competing forces is often the most strategic decision a company makes when it expands overseas. In making this decision, companies can choose from one of three options: Think Local, Act Local (TLAL; **multi-domestic strategy**), Think Global, Act Local (TGAL; **glocal strategy**), and Think Global, Act Global (TGAG; **transnational strategy**).

Consider what Steve Jobs of Apple told his biographer Walter Isaacson about visiting a Turkish bath in Istanbul, where a history professor had taken Jobs and his family when they visited Turkey: 'I had a real revelation. We were all in robes, and they made some Turkish coffee for us. The professor explained how the coffee was made very different from anywhere else, and I realized: "So what? Which kids in Turkey care about Turkish coffee? All day I looked at young people in Istanbul. They were all drinking what every other kid in the world drinks, and they were wearing clothes that look like they were bought at the Gap, and they are all using cell phones. They were like kids everywhere else. It hit me that, for young people, this whole world is the same now. When we are making products, there is no such thing as a Turkish phone, or a music player that young people in Turkey would want that's different from one young people elsewhere would want. We are just one world now."' Based on this experience, Jobs made a decision that was to guide Apple's international strategy for years to come: Make high-quality products and sell them worldwide (transnational strategy).

A multi-domestic strategy – think local, act local – is one in which a firm varies its competitive approach and product offerings from country to country in an effort to meet varied buyer needs and address differing local conditions. Such a strategy is most appropriate when (a) the need for local responsiveness is high because of significant cross-national differences and (b) efficiency gains from standardization are limited. To implement this strategy, firms need to decentralize decision-making to locals, who are most conversant with the market in which they operate. Despite its benefits, a multi-domestic strategy also has the drawback of higher overall costs (due to greater variety and shorter production runs of designs and components) and lower transference of the firm's capabilities and knowledge across borders (as the firm lacks integration or coordination across boundaries).

What Do You Think?

Peter Frykman was a graduate student at Stanford University when came up with a method for making drip irrigation systems inexpensively. After testing them in Ethiopia, "we saw that this could help farmers across the world," he says. He formed a company Driptech Inc. to install irrigation systems. Now, he is wondering where to try the first pilot project of the company. Can you offer some advice to Peter?

Consider the case of Azon USA Inc., a Kalamazoo, MI, supplier of machinery and chemicals used by makers of aluminum windows. As an exporter to Europe, Azon found it hard to match the prices of companies based in Europe, so it decided to set up distribution and manufacturing operations there. "You're a babe in the woods when you start out on these things," says James Dunstan, chairman of Azon. "If you're lucky, you don't get burned." In Wales, James set up a new sister company, Azon UK Ltd., and named as managing director a sales agent he had used before. He gave the executive a good deal of autonomy. Yet, James visits Wales annually, and the executive in-charge there also visits Kalamazoo every year. Between visits, James receives quarterly financial reports, but doesn't get very involved with the operations in Europe. "I've never written a check in Britain," he says. "I'm not even sure I have signature power at the bank. That gives you an idea of the kind of trust we have in our people there." The trust has been repaid, he says, with growing sales and profits. Azon is competing internationally, and gives substantial autonomy to the team it has in Wales.

Giving autonomy to local teams overseas does not always work out for firms. When Azon installed a sales manager in another European country, the man constantly traveled to five-star hotels but brought in little business. "I didn't have strong enough oversight," James says. "The autonomy that I gave the guy in Britain didn't work with the other guy." Despite the setback, James plans to continue international expansion. His thinking is that he will let local managers act autonomously in their respective region, but with oversight from Kalamazoo headquarters.

Comprehension Check

1. What is culture?
2. Define and explain **glocal strategy**.
3. Explain Hofstede's model of culture.

Module 14.5 Contemporary Issues in Globalization

Astute students will have noticed that so far the pursuit of global opportunities has been discussed as a choice that thoughtful business owners make. Some business owners may choose to pursue global opportunities; others may not choose. Global by choice is the mantra here. However, many experts believe that globalization may be a strategic imperative for small firms. This means that many small companies are forced to compete internationally just to stay alive. Notice the argument here is not that international expansion is required for companies to be successful, but that in many sectors of the economy, internationalization is essential to the very survival of the firm. "Nowadays, you don't really have much choice: You have to think globally," says Paul Griesse, chairman of Bry-Air Inc., a Sunbury, OH, maker of industrial dehumidifiers. Overseas customers accounted for more than 60% of the company's total sales, he says.

Look at Will-Burt Company of Ohio, which makes truck parts and mobile radio-transmission towers. While Will-Burt was already exporting its mobile radio towers to foreign markets, it also decided to manufacture them in Ireland with a partner that would provide the factory and sales force. The logic: Tap into the large European market without having to pay tariffs to sell there, and depending on the direction of the dollar, have the possibility of selling Irish-made towers in the United States for less than towers made in Ohio. Such a strategy, its chief executive Harry Featherstone believed, would protect the company from foreign rivals that might try to export towers to the United States when the dollar strengthens. This was not just "may happen someday" thinking. In the past, when the dollar had strengthened, Caterpillar Inc. canceled a million-dollar contract with Will-Burt for items such as cab doors and engine compartments, switching to lower-priced Belgian and Brazilian suppliers. "We realized then that we were operating in a worldwide market," said Harry about his company that had until then never had any foreign dealings. Will-Burt then cut costs in Ohio and expanded to China for castings and to Indonesia for welded parts, which helped it win back business from Caterpillar and also get new business from Volvo in Europe. "You can't protect your home market unless you are also in the fray overseas," said William Archey, former international vice president of the U.S. Chamber of Commerce. "If your first experience with foreign competitors is right here at home, you might not survive."

KEY TAKEAWAY

The tension between globalization and nationalism is present in every country throughout history.

The globalization of business is, however, just one part of the overall trend toward increasing interaction and integration among people, companies, and governments worldwide. The convergence of market preferences, declining trade barriers, and growing integration among different national economies is producing a global socioeconomic system. At the same time, during periods of crisis, such as the 2008 Great Financial Slowdown or the COVID-19 pandemic, interest in globalization decreases and affinity for nationalism increases. The tension between globalization and nationalism is present in every country throughout history. The ebb and flow of the economy influences the tension between globalization and nationalism. When the economy is rising and people see their quality of life improve, globalization trumps over nationalism in the minds of a country's populace. When the economy is in a downturn and people see themselves struggling to make ends meet, the preference for nationalism becomes stronger and interest in globalization decreases. The forces of globalization favor more engagement with the world beyond the country's borders; the forces of nationalization emphasize closing off borders and isolating from the rest of the world. Just as globalization has been a constant feature of societies throughout history, nationalization has also been with us across history.

Arguments against globalization and in favor of nationalization can be broadly divided into three categories: economic, technological, and cultural concerns. Let us look at these briefly. **Economic concerns** center around the financial troubles that come to some communities when they find themselves on the wrong side of globalization. For example, textile mills in Gaffney, SC – what one reporter described as "clangorous, dusty, productive engines of the Carolinas fabric trade" – fell one by one to the onslaught of foreign competitors. The closing of the mills resulted in fewer job opportunities locally, lower taxes for the city, and reduced investment in public facilities, all of which are undesirable outcomes. The local populace blames globalization for their troubles, which is understandable. They, however, forget that it was also globalization that brought the business to their community in the first place. For example, textile manufacturing migrated first from the Cottonopolises of England to the mill towns of New England and then to the Carolinas, where labor was even cheaper. As manufacturing became more expensive in the Carolinas, the textile industry mostly left the United States, and headed to Mexico, India, and China – wherever people were still willing to work for less.

What Do You Think?

For a thousand years, Persia (now Iran) enjoyed a virtual monopoly on cultivating the hardy yet demanding pistachio tree. Persian traders have exported pistachio since at least the seventh century, probably longer. Iran, however, has now lost its status as the world's top producer of pistachios to the United States, which started production only in the 1970s. Thanks to crippling sanctions against Iran, 47% of the global total pistachio production now comes from the United States, and 27% from Iran. About 99% of American pistachios are grown in California's San Joaquin Valley. More than half of pistachios produced in the United States are shipped abroad, with China and Hong Kong buying half the exports. The Chinese call the pistachios "happy nuts" because they look like they're smiling. Is globalization good or bad?

Technological concerns center around the absence or loss of technical know-how and expertise that befalls some communities because of globalization. This can take two forms: (a) communities realize that they lack the technical know-how that is needed to compete in the globalized world; and (b) the knowledge and expertise needed to perform critically important tasks does not exist domestically because businesses in some countries do a much better or cheaper job of providing it. Consider the concern that many Americans are losing white-collar jobs either to people overseas who are willing to do it for cheaper there or to immigrants who come from overseas to work here. Nowhere is this more visible than in the high-technology sector. Many companies like IBM and GE have relocated their research and development overseas to capitalize on the cheap and large pool of qualified workers. Other companies like Microsoft and Texas Instruments host hundreds of thousands of foreigners on their American campuses in large part because of the challenges in hiring qualified workers domestically. The replacement of domestic workers by foreign workers working in the United States or overseas fosters resentment among the local populace. It, however, goes unmentioned that one reason American companies like GE and Microsoft were able to grow spectacularly to get to where they are now is their domination of global markets. Whether you work in Japan or Brazil or Russia, Microsoft products, Dell laptops, and Google are ubiquitous.

Interactive Exercise

Interview seven working adults – professors, business owners, parents, siblings – on what they think are the benefits and costs (disadvantages) to the United States of competing internationally. Identify three to five most common benefits and costs you hear in your interviews.

Cultural concerns center around the anxiety and worry that ideas and practices from other countries are diluting, or even ruining, the culture of one's country. When businesses expand to other countries, people and ideas also travel overseas. The self-styled French philosopher Alain Finkielkraut, in his recent popular book *L'identité malheureuse* (The Unhappy Identity), laments that foreign influence is destroying French cultural identity. Many politicians and talk-show hosts in America proclaim themselves as champions of Western civilizations, which they believe is a superior civilization that should be shared with everybody. Many Indians believe that unbridled individualism and materialism from the West is destroying local communities and family relations. Those who voice cultural concerns about globalization often fail to understand that culture is, and has always been, dynamic and not static. The United States of the early 1900s with limited voting rights, legal slavery, and rampant child labor was very different from the country that we live in now (although some may certainly wish it was not). France of our times is much different from World War-II–era France, with its African colonies. Furthermore, international influences are commonplace in a country's culture at any given time in its historical evolution. This is the case for every country, from the United States and France to China and India.

Comprehension Check

1. Explain the tension between globalization and nationalization.
2. Explain economic concerns about the spread of globalization.
3. Explain cultural concerns about the spread of globalization.

Summary

The history of globalization goes as far back as recorded human history (and maybe more). Growth-minded traders have long sought new business opportunities outside their country's borders. While much is written and understood about how big businesses expand internationally, little attention has been paid to small firms who undertake international expansion. For many small firms, international expansion is not a choice, but a necessity for survival. Yet, business owners must think carefully before making the decision to expand overseas. Operating across national borders is inherently more complex than operating within a single country. Success in international markets rarely comes quickly or easily, so firms need to be patient and willing to adapt to new and unfamiliar ways of doing business.

World of Books

Small Company. Big World: You, Too, Can Take Your Small Business Global by William Frost

Exporting: The Definitive Guide to Selling Abroad Profitably by Laurel Delaney

Selling to China: A Guide for Small and Medium-Sized Businesses by Stanley Chao

In the Movies

The Kadam family runs a restaurant in Mumbai, but are forced to move to London after unexpected professional and personal tragedies. Finding London to be unreceptive to their venture, the family moves to France. On the way there, the car breaks down in a small town. The family decides to start an Indian restaurant in a small French town. The property they find for their restaurant is located opposite the town's popular Michelin-starred eatery. The Kadam family name their restaurant Maison Mumbai, and offer authentic Indian cuisine in small-town France. The existential question they now face – in the movie *The Hundred Foot Journey* – is whether there is a market for an authentic Indian restaurant in the small French town.

Live Exercise

Is internationalization a viable option for Johnny Gold? This is the question you find asking yourself after finishing the chapter on competing internationally in your small business entrepreneurship course. You are well aware that Johnny has been selling the SoapStandle only in the United States. He is also very proud of the "Designed and Made in the U.S.A." tagline. Yet, you find yourself wondering whether there is a market for the SoapStandle outside the United States too? Perhaps, in Europe or Asia, you think. After all, soap is used everywhere, and the problem that Johnny is trying to solve (preventing soap from falling when you are showering) seems like a universal human problem. If there is a market outside the United States, and Johnny is late in pursuing it, could it be that rivals will occupy that space and then make it difficult for Johnny to sell domestically? There is also the issue of sourcing the SoapStandle. Johnny took pride making it in the United States, but there may be much cost savings if it can be made overseas, perhaps in China. Should SoapStandle expand internationally, and if yes, what would such expansion look like?

Put together a PowerPoint presentation about the international potential of SoapStandle, taking a clear position either in favor of or in opposition to expanding internationally.

Things to Remember

LO 14.1 **Discuss the reasons for seeking business opportunities overseas**
- Expanding into overseas markets provides access to new customers.
- Foreign countries can also be a good source of cheaper or better labor than is available domestically.
- Sourcing from foreign countries helps firms keep costs low, yielding higher profit margins for companies.
- Companies in industries where natural resources (e.g. oil and gas, rubber) are not uniformly distributed across the world find it necessary to operate internationally.
- Access to cutting-edge resources and capabilities available overseas is another reason for looking beyond one's borders.
- Factor market internationalization (FMI) refers to looking overseas for improvements in a company's upstream supply chain.
- Product market internationalization (PMI) involves overseas expansion of the downstream supply chain in search of new customers to buy the company's products.
- Capital market internationalization (CMI) refers to raising money for the firm overseas, either through selling equity in the company or by tapping debt markets.

LO 14.2 **Distinguish between the various modes of internationalization**
- Exporting is the sale of products produced in one country to customers in another country.
- When one talks of exporting, it is often for manufactured goods. However, exporting is also possible in the services sector.
- *Imports* refer to goods bought from another country.
- Licensing involves a firm selling the rights to manufacture and sell its product to a firm in another country.

- Franchising involves a company – the franchisor – offering a standard package of systems and services to a company in another country – the franchisee – that brings capital and operational management to the business.
- Foreign partnerships are formal interfirm relationships between companies from different countries.

LO 14.3 **Explain how and why overseas expansion can be challenging for companies**

- Consumer tastes and worker productivity may differ substantially across countries.
- When doing business internationally, companies need to consider factors such as education level of the populace, religious beliefs, language, and social structure.
- Companies interested in doing business overseas need to be mindful of how government policies and regulations differ between their home country and the places where they want to do business.
- Companies interested in overseas expansion need to consider political and economic risks associated with operating in a country.
- Economics risks are about the stability of a country's economy and monetary system.
- When companies produce and sell goods across borders, they become vulnerable to exchange rate fluctuations.

LO 14.4 **Identify the main strategic approaches for competing internationally**

- A company's decision to enter a particular market may be driven by peer or rival firms who are already in that market.
- Differences between foreign and home country cultures increase the cost of doing business in another country.
- A multi-domestic strategy – think local, act local – is one in which a firm varies its competitive approach and product offerings from country to country in an effort to meet varied buyer needs and address differing local conditions.
- A global strategy – think global, act global – takes a standardized competitive approach to operating in international markets.
- A transnational strategy – think global, act local – seeks to strike a compromise between the extreme localization of multi-domestic strategy and global strategy.

LO 14.5 **Describe the reasons why internationalization attracts considerable opposition**

- Globalization may be a strategic imperative for small firms.
- All modern societies have to deal with the conflicting forces of globalization and nationalization.
- Economic concerns center around the financial troubles that come to some communities when they find themselves on the wrong side of globalization.
- Technological concerns center around the absence or loss of technical know-how and expertise that befalls some communities because of globalization.
- Cultural concerns center around the anxiety and worry that ideas and practices from other countries are diluting, or even ruining, the culture of one's country.

Key Terms

globalization	capital market	direct exporting	licensee
factor market	internationalization	tradable services	franchising
internationalization	born-global	imports	foreign partnerships
product market	exporting	licensing	strategic alliances
internationalization	indirect exporting	licensor	joint ventures

greenfield venture	international strategy	femininity	glocal strategy
cross-border acquisition	isomorphism	uncertainty avoidance	transnational strategy
foreign direct product rule	culture	power distance	economic concerns
political risks	cultural distance	individualism	technological concerns
economic risks	Scandinavian model	collectivism	cultural concerns
exchange rate	masculinity	multi-domestic strategy	

Experiential Exercise

Smashburger is an American fast-casual hamburger restaurant chain founded in Denver, CO. It was started in 2007 by two fast-food industry veterans to cater to consumers looking for a better burger. The name Smashburger, one of the founders later said, "had this really great hand-crafted connotation, which we do. It also kind of had this organic, earthy, commonly popular approach, and it had a little edginess to it, for younger, generational people." The classic Smashburger comes with American cheese – and the usual lettuce, tomato, onion, and pickle – along with its own "Smash sauce." The company also adds regional twists to its menu: In the Garden State, there is a New Jersey Burger with applewood-smoked bacon, blue cheese, grilled onions, and haystack onions (like shoestring fried onions) on a soft onion bun.

Visit the company's website and try to answer the following questions:

1. What are the different ways in which Smashburger is connected to the global world?
2. Which countries are part of Smashburger's international footprint?
3. Has globalization been good or bad for Smashburger?
4. Do Smashburger customers care about its international footprint?

Your employer has asked you to write a one-page memo about Smashburger's international footprint and your recommendations for its future. Draft a one-page memo and share it with your professor.

CHAPTER 15

Strategic Thinking for Small Firms

Without a strategy, the firm is like a ship without a rudder, going round in circles, or worse, getting lost at sea.

ANONYMOUS

LEARNING OBJECTIVES

This chapter will help you to:

LO 15.1 Explain the need for a small business to have a (good) strategy

LO 15.2 Describe what it means to think strategically in the small business context

LO 15.3 Explain how to conduct a SWOT analysis and what to do with it

LO 15.4 Identify generic strategies for small business managers

15.0 Introduction

Every business needs a strategy. A popular misconception is that strategy is only for large corporations. Small businesses, the thinking goes, do not need strategy. Contrary to such thinking, businesses of all sizes and shapes can benefit from having a good strategy (they can also be hurt by having a bad strategy). Without a sound strategy, it is very difficult, if not completely impossible, for the business to survive long, grow to its full potential, and become successful. Unfortunately, a good strategy is rarer than you would think. The absence of a good strategy makes a business more likely to fail, which may help to partly explain the high rate of failure in the small business world. According to *The Economist*, "In business, strategy is king. Leadership and hard work are all very well, and luck is mighty useful, but it is strategy that makes or breaks a firm."

This chapter lays the groundwork for the study of strategic thinking for small firms. It introduces some foundational ideas about strategy. Think of this chapter as the beginning of an exciting journey to understand how owners of small companies can think strategically about their business and the environment within which it operates.

SPOTLIGHT | RapidSOS and the Challenge of Strategy

RapidSOS is a young company, founded in 2013. Its youth, however, does not deter its founders Michael Martin, a Harvard Business School graduate, and Nicholas Horelik, an engineering grad from Massachusetts Institute of Technology, from having a grand vision: bringing 911 calls into the smartphone age. America has a pretty good emergency response system, but it was developed in the pre-mobile era. As a result, a major problem has been that it was difficult to identify the location of callers using cell phones, which increased response times and worsened medical outcomes. Martin personally experienced this problem when his father Charles fell from the roof of his rural Indiana house during a snowstorm, breaking his wrist and shattering his hip. For two hours, until his wife arrived from work, Charles lay in the freezing cold because the 911 call would not go through from his mobile phone. Martin and Horelik had managed to develop a way to transmit cell phone location to existing 911 systems that required little adaptation on the part of other players in the emergency services sector. After tasting initial success at new venture competitions, Martin and Horelik were at a crossroads: What was their strategy to be for the company going forward?

There were at least four different paths that RapidSOS could take: One option was to become a disruptor by initially targeting populations with limited access to the existing system, and then expanding to the broader market. Another was to replace the existing emergency response system altogether, developing a sort of Uber for ambulances. A third option involved helping established players modernize their operations, such as by working with 911 equipment suppliers such as Motorola. The final option was to partner with insurance companies who ultimately end up paying for ambulance services.

All four options seemed viable, making it difficult for the founders to select one. There might also be other, even better, options that they had not considered yet. Their problem was compounded by those who wanted them to do everything and those who told them to just go ahead and do it (no need to think too much). But Martin and Horelik had seen many startups fail by making wrong choices, so they wanted to make sure they had carefully considered what was the best course of action for their fledgling firm at this crucial juncture. A wrong step could mean the end of their company, whereas taking the right step could put them at the next level.

RapidSOS, based in New York, now employs more than 150 workers and helps protect more than 300 million people in the U.S.

Personal life-threatening emergencies motivated Michael Martin to start RapidSOS.

Discussion Questions

1. What are some important considerations to think about when making a strategy decision like the one Martin and Horelik were confronted with?

2. Two of Martin and Horelik's options were to challenge existing organizations, while their other two options required cooperation with existing organizations. What are the pros/cons of each approach?

3. RapidSOS has many stakeholders: customers, employees, suppliers, and investors, to name a few. How might each of these groups view RapidSOS's strategy decision?

4. If you were advising Martin and Horelik about their strategy, what would you tell them and why?

Module 15.1 Strategy of Small Business

In the context of small business, **strategy** is the set of actions that its owners-managers take to achieve superior profitability and/or outperform rivals. A well-crafted strategy yields success and profits that allow a small business to move to the next level. To be clear, the objective of a well-crafted strategy is not merely gaining competitive advantage, or even profits in the short run, but the kind of lasting success that can support the growth of the firm and secure its future over the long-term.

KEY TAKEAWAY

A well-crafted strategy yields success and profits that allow a small business to move to the next level

---

Having a good strategy entails making a strong commitment to a coherent array of well-considered choices about how to operate (see Figure 15.1). These include decisions about:

- *How* to position the company
- *How* to create products and services that attract new customers and retain existing ones
- *How* to operate the different areas of the firm (production, sales and marketing, finance)
- *How* to fund the existing operations and future expansion of the company
- *How* to achieve the company's performance goals

What makes strategy especially challenging for small firms is that often there is only one person at the helm who is responsible for formulating and implementing every move the company makes. This can be advantageous for a small business, but it can also be problematic. On the plus side, having a single person in charge allows for the kind of unified strategy with a clear chain of command in a small business that is very difficult to have in most large corporations. On the negative side, however, strategy in small businesses risks becoming a victim of unfavorable thinking and experiences of the person who may not (a) really understand the concept of strategy very well or (b) have the time or motivation to focus on strategy.

In most cases, managers of small businesses have considerable freedom in choosing the *hows* of strategy. Some small firms may compete by keeping costs lower costs than rivals, while others emphasize quality or personalization. Some small firms decide to

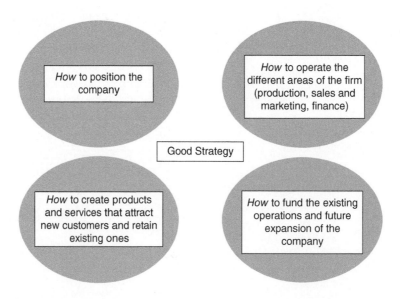

FIGURE 15.1 Components of a Good Business Strategy

operate in only one industry, while others operate in multiple industries. Some small companies position themselves in only one part of the industry's value chain, while others cover a broad spectrum of operations. The key is that the strategy must fit the company's particular situation as well as set it apart from rivals to produce a competitive advantage. This is the hallmark of a **good strategy**. When management is able to identify the critical factors in a situation and design a way of coordinating and focusing actions to deal with those factors, the business will have a good strategy.

Interactive Exercise

Interview five experts (either five business owners or five business professors) on what firm strategy means to them. Be prepared to explain to the class what you learn from these interviews.

Take the case of Georgetown Insurance Service Inc., a 30-person insurance agency in Silver Spring, MD. The company was selling complex policies to middle-market customers. The COVID-19 pandemic threatened the business of Georgetown. Decisions about complex property and casualty policies often involve in-person meetings and committee approvals, which was no longer possible during the pandemic. Some insurers also stopped sending out field inspectors to do safety reviews before they issue a quote, limiting the ability of agencies like Georgetown to bring in new customers. Georgetown decided to change its approach to align better with the new circumstances and avoid the fate of many other agencies. Instead of finding new clients by networking at Chamber of Commerce or association meetings or by knocking on doors, Georgetown agents started sending emails and picking up the telephone. The company moved away from large, complex policies for contractors, manufacturers, and wholesalers. It started emphasizing sales of smaller, commodity-type policies that it can close under its authority, such as one for a bridal shop, with decisions made by the business owner or a single executive, not a team.

Unfortunately, good strategy is far less common than bad strategy. Professor Richard Rumelt, one of the founding fathers of the academic field of strategy, observed that in most companies, bad strategy tends to crowd out good strategy.

So, what is a **bad strategy**? Here are a few defining characteristics of a bad strategy:

- *High on fluff.* Bad strategy often uses complex and inflated words to create the illusion of deep thinking.
- *Full of ambition.* It's good to be ambitious, but statements about ambition (e.g. We will soon be #1 in the business) are not strategy.
- *Emphasizes desire and ambition over everything else.* Ever heard slogans like "Strategy is never quitting until you win"? There is no strategy here, just a vague desire to do well.
- *Misstating goals for strategy.* Bad strategy equates goals (e.g. grow 10% annually with 10% profitability) with strategy. Strategy is what needs to happen to achieve those goals.
- *Failure to make choices.* Managing a business involves dealing with a variety of conflicting interests and demands. Should you take out money from the business to pay for a nice car for yourself or should you reinvest it in the firm? A good strategy is very much about what a manager decides to do as it is what he or she decides not to do.
- *Lacks coherence.* Strategy is an all-encompassing plan that directs the whole organization. As such, the various pieces of the plan should all fit together. Bad strategy tends to have misaligned parts because no one does the due diligence to hold them together. (See Figure 15.2 for a summary of these characteristics.)

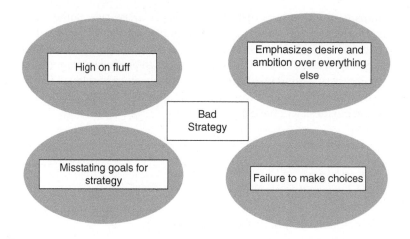

FIGURE 15.2 Characteristics of a Bad Business Strategy

Crimson Designs was a small graphic arts company, providing custom graphic services to small newspapers and magazines, book publishers, and local corporations. Its founder had recently died, leaving the company to his son Nick Gover, a college sports-hero-turned-graphic artist who had developed a strong taste for sales. One day Nick gathered his employees in a large meeting, and with much fanfare proceeded to announce his 20/20 Strategy. Revenues were to grow by 20% per year, and the profit margin was to be at least 20% or higher. He showed projections of revenues, costs, gross profit, and so on for the next five years, all of which showed that the company would do remarkably better than in the past few years when it had maintained its market share and kept its net profitability at about 10%. When asked why he thought the company would suddenly explode with unprecedented growth and profit, Logan quoted the successful business leader Jack Welch: By reaching for what appears to be the impossible, we often actually do the impossible. Notice that Nick does not have a real strategy for Crimson Designs. Nick has ambition and goals, but no strategy.

Comprehension Check

1. Define strategy. How does good strategy differ from bad strategy?
2. Why is bad strategy more common than good strategy?
3. What are some common elements of bad strategy?

Module 15.2 Thinking Strategically!

As any small business owner knows well, plenty of decisions are made every day in the business. These decisions can broadly be classified in one of two categories: (1) strategic and (2) operational. **Strategic decisions** involve issues that affect the whole organization, which include deciding the nature and direction of the firm, determining the scope of the firm, and figuring out how to compete effectively. **Operational decisions** involve issues that impact one or more aspects of the firm, but do not need strategic-level thinking. Such decisions help keep the business running by dealing with daily issues and problems. Ideally, operational decisions are shaped by strategic thinking that the top management has done for the entire organization. It is important to understand the distinction between strategic and operational decisions, but it is not always an easy distinction to make.

KEY TAKEAWAY

Strategic decisions involve issues that affect the whole organization, from deciding the nature and direction of the firm to figuring out how to compete effectively.

The typical way most people think about business is from an operational perspective. Indeed, focusing on strategic issues does not come naturally to most of us. Most students reading this text are unlikely to have been in situations that required them to think strategically about their organization. University education also prepares students to pursue specific courses of study that involve specialization in a particular function (e.g. marketing, finance, information systems), wherein they are operating mostly at the operational level. As a result, most students have never had to think deeply about strategic decisions.

Even when the conceptual distinction between strategic and operational decisions is clear, the line separating the two types of decisions is not always clear in reality. For example, the decision to hire two summer interns without pay seems to be a straightforward case of an operational decision, does it not? But, if the firm recruiting the two summer interns only has a total of five employees cramped in one garage-size space (like Apple in its early days), then does the decision to bring on summer interns suddenly become strategic in scope? In case you are wondering why, think about whether hiring two additional interns would require the firm to relocate to a bigger space or to move to a shift-based system for the employees, and perhaps even risk a change in the firm's culture as it adds two more to its present size of five employees. In a similar manner, payroll decisions that were once strategic for a nascent firm (e.g. Would bringing an additional employee on board risk the financial survival of the firm?) may become operational when the firms grows in size (say, it goes from 2 to 45 employees).

As with much else in business, deciding which decision is strategic and which is operational is a matter of judgment. Managers who control a broad range of decisions because they consider all of them strategic (when, in fact, many are not) risk getting lost in the woods and not fully seeing the forest. At Quibi, a streaming service for short-length videos, founder Jeffrey Katzenberg was criticized for being a micromanager who tried to be involved in various operational decisions. Conversely, managers who delegate much decision-making to subordinates are not giving the attention that important decisions need, which can create havoc in the firm by making them seem either distant and aloof or unknowledgeable about the company. At Twitter, CEO and cofounder Jack Dorsey is notorious for delegating most major decisions to subordinates, preferring instead to spend his time pursuing his personal passions.

Small business owners need to strike a balance between strategic and operational decisions. Tommy Lasorda, the former Los Angeles Dodgers' manager, captured this delicate balancing act well when he said, "I believe that managing is like holding a dove in your hand. If you hold it too tightly, you kill it. But if you hold it too loosely, you lose it."

To help clarify what should be viewed as strategic decision-making, the following issues need to be considered:

1. Does the decision affect the firm's chances of survival?
2. Does the decision alter the firm's competitive positioning?
3. Does the decision involve entering a new business?
4. Does the decision change the firm's significant relationships with its stakeholders, such as suppliers, customers, and debtholders, employees?
5. Does the decision have a significant impact on the financial condition of the firm?
6. Does the decision shift the image or reputation of the firm?
7. Does the decision change the ownership of the firm?

These questions are not a checklist to go through every time there is a decision to make. Instead, they should be used as a guide to think about the decision-making role of top management. Managers who spend adequate time and effort on strategic decisions will usually provide better stewardship of the firm. Unfortunately, too many mangers find themselves wasting time on decisions that not only can be delegated to other people but also keep them from growing the firm by distracting them from issues that *really* matter. Would you be surprised to learn that the biggest obstacle to small business growth is its management's inability to deal effectively with strategic issues? Small business managers who are able to deal with operational decisions as they arise and yet make time for thoughtful deliberation about strategic decisions are the ones who can grow the firm in a successful manner.

Interactive Exercise

Every business leader needs to judiciously differentiate between strategic and operational decisions. Ask a business leader you know about the strategic decisions they make in their work.

The benefit of thinking about strategic and operational decisions in the small business management course is that one begins to develop a type of *strategic thought process*. Managers who hone their ability to think strategically are then able to give more attention to strategic issues and less to operational issues (instead of the other way around). While effective small business management needs skillful handling of strategic and operational decisions, operational decisions help fight fires in the short term as opposed to strategic decisions that are useful for the long-term survival and growth of the firm.

What Do You Think?

Q Lodge, a small boutique hotel chain with nine properties in Arkansas, provides spacious and comfortable rooms in the economy segment. Properties are located next to well-trafficked shopping plazas, which avoids the need to have in-house restaurants and dining. Extra frills are avoided throughout the properties, but care is taken to provide guests with good value for money. When management asked property managers, employees, and guests for suggestions on how to make the hotels more competitive, ideas came flowing in: lower room prices, launch new advertising campaigns, offer discount coupons for first-time stays, increase customer service positions, incentivize employees with stock option plan, strengthen training for front-desk employees, revamp the company website, offer online booking, cater to more upscale customers, expand to other states, and merge with a national brand. Which of these, if any, involve strategic thinking?

Comprehension Check

1. How would you define strategic decisions? In what way(s), do strategic decisions differ from operational decisions?
2. Would the decision to change the name of the company be strategic or operational? Why?
3. Why is it that management's inability to give adequate attention to the right strategic decisions the single most important hurdle in the growth of small businesses?

Module 15.3 SWOT Analysis

At the heart of a good small business strategy is the ability to diagnose the situation, develop a guiding policy, and commit to a coherent action. An excellent tool for doing this is called a **SWOT** analysis. Stated simply, SWOT analysis is a diagnostic tool that considers a firm's strengths and weaknesses along with the opportunities and threats it faces. You are probably at least somewhat familiar with the SWOT framework: Strengths, Weaknesses, Opportunities, and Threats. If you are like most students, you see SWOT analysis as an old, overhyped tool that does not offer much help in a challenging situation. But, if that's what you think, you would be wrong! The problem with SWOT is that it is often used incorrectly. If one does not know how to drive a car properly and gets into an accident, the fault is not with the car (no matter how tempted we may be to blame the car). Instead, the blame lies with the driver who took to the road without the experience or training to drive. The best solution in such a situation is not to jettison the car forever or to start hitchhiking everywhere (which may be inconvenient or dangerous), but to learn how to drive well. The same goes for SWOT analysis. Just because SWOT is often used incorrectly does not mean it is a flawed tool in itself. For good or for bad, SWOT analysis is only as effective in a situation as the person wielding it.

KEY TAKEAWAY

SWOT analysis is a diagnostic tool that considers a firm's strengths and weaknesses along with the opportunities and threats it faces.

Two sets of factors go into a SWOT analysis: *internal* (strengths and weaknesses) and *external* (opportunities and threats). Internal factors occur within organizational boundaries. External factors occur outside organizational boundaries. For instance, experienced management is internal to the firm, while government (de)regulation is external to the firm. Strengths and weaknesses are internal to the firm, while opportunities and threats are external to the firm. You would not believe how many people get this simple distinction wrong, mistaking external factors for strengths or weaknesses, and confusing internal factors with opportunities and threats. The new salesperson the firm hired may be a strength or weakness. Similarly, rising demand for a company's products (say, because of unexpected government procurement) may be an opportunity.

Before we learn how to identify strengths, weaknesses, opportunities, and threats, it is useful to define them so that we know what we mean when we use these terms. A **strength** is something that a firm is good at doing or an attribute that enhances its competitiveness in the marketplace. A **weakness** is something that a company lacks or does more poorly than others or a condition that puts it at a disadvantage in the marketplace. **Opportunities** are events and trends that portend new avenues to improve the firm's competitiveness or performance. **Threats** are events or trends that can undermine a firm's competitiveness or performance (see Figure 15.3).

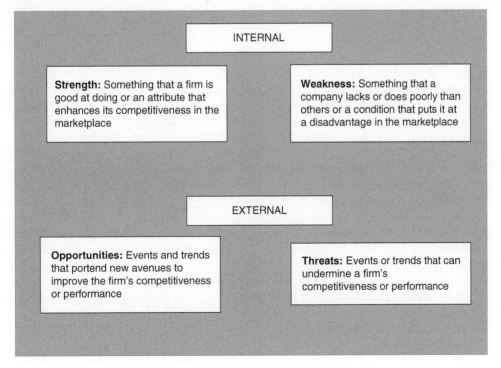

FIGURE 15.3 Internal and External Forces

15.3.1 Looking Outward

Where do opportunities and threats come from? The source of opportunities and threats is the **macro-environment** of the firm, the **industry** within which it operates, and the **competitors** it has. The macro-environment captures the broad environment context within which the firm and its industry are situated. For example, a firm in the marijuana business (about a $7 billion industry nationwide) would want to consider the macro-environment at both the state and the federal levels. An industry refers to a group of firms that offer similar products or services to meet specific customer needs. The athletic shoe industry, for example, has large corporations such as Nike, Under Armour, and Adidas, but also smaller players like New Balance, Brooks, Newton Running, and many others. Competitors are firms that compete for the same set of customers and have similar offerings. The energy drink industry is huge (about $50 billion worldwide in 2018), with companies like Red Bull, Hype, and Monster all jockeying for a larger share of the market (which comprises usually teenagers and young adults).

15.3.1.1 Analyzing the macro-environment in which the firm operates The macro-environment of the firm consists of all possible external influences that can affect managerial decisions and actions. Given the wide array of external influences, how do managers scan, let alone analyze, relevant conditions? The starting point is some sort of framework or system that can organize the myriad environmental influences in a meaningful way. A common technique is to consider environmental influences by source as in political, economic, social, technological, legal, and ecological factors (**PESTLE**). PESTLE is a popular framework for identifying relevant environmental forces because of its simple, yet systematic, approach to understand the critical factors that are likely to affect the opportunities and threats facing the firm. It is sometimes also referred to as STEEP (with legal and political factors merged into one) or PEST (merging legal with political, and ecological with social or technological).

The **political** segment captures the decisions and actions of government bodies that can influence firm behavior. This includes elements such as stability of governments, change in trade restrictions and tariffs, and tax policies. Currently, immigration policy is an aspect of the political dimension of the environment that holds important implications for many small businesses. The **economic** segment focuses on the conditions in the economy – federal, state, and local – within which small businesses operate. It includes elements such as growth rate, interest rate, inflation, rate of employment, and disposable income to name a few. During the Great Financial Crisis (GFC), for example, bank failures, and the associated tightening of bank lending criteria, for instance, were hard for many small businesses, as it became difficult for them to access credit. The **social** segment pertains to a society's norms, values, and culture. It includes factors such as demographic trends (population size, age, and ethnic mix), as well as cultural preferences (such as growing awareness about obesity and emphasis on health and fitness). Consider the growing number of yoga studios in cities nationwide, as more Americans turn toward yoga to counter the negative effects of their sedentary and stressful lifestyle.

The **technological** segment concentrates on scientific trends and breakthroughs that can affect small businesses. Relevant factors include increasing automation in our lives, Internet usage growth, progress in mobile computing, and development of new-age construction materials. Widespread access to high-speed Internet made it possible for companies such as Casper to sell online goods like mattresses that were previously sold only in brick-and-mortar stores. The **ecological** segment concerns issues related to the natural environment. It includes factors such as pollution levels, weather patterns, and natural disasters. The infamous BP oil spill in the Gulf of Mexico devastated fisheries and wildlife population, affecting local restaurants that could no longer rely on local sources of fish and seafood for the items they served. The **legal** segment centers on how the laws and judiciary influence business activity. It includes factors such as health and safety regulations, discrimination and equal opportunity laws, anti-trust rules, and the like. The federal Affordable Health Care Act enacted in 2009 mandated health insurance

TABLE 15.1	
Factors That Comprise the Macro-environment	
Political	Decisions and actions of government bodies that can influence firm behavior
Economic	Conditions in the economy – federal, state, and local – within which small businesses operate
Social	Society's norms, values, and culture
Technological	Scientific trends and breakthroughs that can affect small businesses
Legal	How the laws and judiciary influence business activity
Ecological	Issues related to the natural environment

for everyone. Its effects on small businesses continue to be discussed and debated, with many small firms reporting reduced hiring in order to keep health-care costs down. See Table 15.1 for a summary of macro-environment factors.

When applying PESTLE analysis, it is useful to keep in mind that merely listing a large number of external factors that can affect the firm is not particularly helpful. Instead, effective environmental analysis prioritizes environmental influences in order of importance and distinguishes the most critical from the barely relevant. In any situation, some PESTLE considerations will be more important than others, which will differ based on the business the firm operates in.

Small business owners must understand that virtually any environmental trend or event may create opportunities for some organizations and threats for others. This is true for everyday elements of the general environment, like the regulations governing interstate shipping of alcoholic beverages to consumers or even in extreme cases like Hurricane Maria that devastated life in Puerto Rico. While scores of people died directly or indirectly from the Category 5 hurricane that destroyed homes and local businesses, the tragic event also opened up significant opportunities for other businesses in rebuilding and construction.

What Do You Think?

Tesla Motor Co., run by the maverick entrepreneur Elon Musk, is in the electric car business. Tesla sold upward of 220,000 electric cars in 2018, according to LMC Automotive, about 70,000 more than its nearest competitor, the Chinese state–owned BAIC Group. While the electric car has a checkered past in the United States (General Motors' EV1 appeared on American roads in 1996, only to discontinued in 2003), there is growing consensus among auto industry executives and analysts that this time things are different. Estimates suggest that automakers will be able to sell fully electric cars for less than gasoline-powered cars by 2022 and that electric cars may outsell conventional cars by 2040. Established carmakers worldwide (e.g. Volkswagen and Renault-Nissan) and new players (e.g. Tesla and Rivian) are hoping to succeed in a new world in which electricity replaces gasoline and diesel. Does a PESTLE analysis of the electric car industry give you confidence in these predictions? Does this industry seem like a good arena for new players like Tesla?

Consider the impact of the most recent environmental shock: COVID-19 pandemic. At Sand & C Travel Inc., a Parkland, FL, travel agency specializing in cruises, revenue was down 85% in 2020 compared to 2019. Alan and Cathy Rosen, the owners of Sand & C, had to let go of all three of its part-time assistants. The Rosens had to give up the company office they had occupied for 8 of the 28 years the business had been in existence. At BioTech Partners Inc., a Charlotte, NC, boutique staffing agency specializing in life sciences, revenue was up 40% in 2020 compared to 2019. The company added three people, bringing head count up to 12. The company, which is getting a boost from its work with diagnostic test companies and vaccine makers, plans to hire five more employees as demand has swelled for the contract workers it provides. The CEO of BioTech Ross Petras shares that he is thankful for the "market we are in," a sentiment not shared by the Rosens who have been hit "very hard" by the pandemic.

15.3.1.2 Analyzing the firm's industry and competitors The term *industry* refers to a group of firms that cater to a particular market. In the context of small business, industry analysis starts with identifying the profitability of an industry. Some industries (e.g. agricultural insurance and commercial leasing) have very high profitability (50% or higher); others have much lower profitability (5% or less). Of course, even within highly profitable industries, some firms will not do well; within less profitable industries, there will still be firms that perform extraordinarily well. The point here is that industries matter, and so do firms (which we will discuss later in the chapter). Even the impact of external shocks such as COVID-19 may vary by industry. Performing-arts companies, travel agents, and bus operators were among the hardest-hit industries for small firms during the COVID-19 pandemic. Firms in highway construction, lawn and garden equipment retail, and scientific research saw employment and revenues increase in the pandemic. Figure 15.4 presents a visual summary of how small firms fared by industry relative to large firms during the 2020 pandemic.

Industries differ in their average profitability. For any organization, **profitability** is a function of two things: selling price and cost price. A firm makes profit when a customer is willing to pay for a product a price above the costs incurred by the firm to produce it.

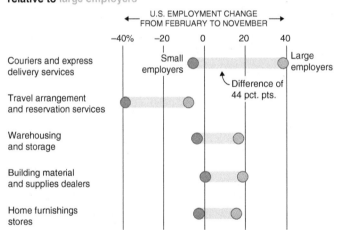

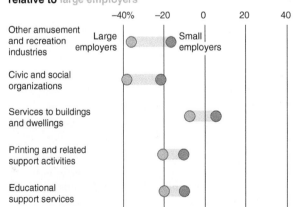

FIGURE 15.4 The Differential Impact of COVID-19 Pandemic for Big and Small Firms by Industry
Source: The Wall Street Journal

How much a customer is willing to pay depends on the forces of competition in the industry. How much it costs the firm to offer the product or service depends on the power of suppliers. Thus, the profits earned by firms in an industry are determined by three factors:

1. Value of the product to customers
2. Intensity of competition
3. Power of suppliers

Industry analysis brings all three factors into a holistic framework. As shown in Table 15.2, the strength of each of the three industry factors is in turn shaped by a number of key structural variables.

The precise boundaries of an industry are not always clear. For example, a Mexican restaurant in the town not only competes with other Mexican restaurants but also with other Latin restaurants locally (including Spanish and Brazilian eateries, for example) as well with all restaurants in general (which then includes Italian, Indian, Chinese food places). Thus, one could consider the industry as all Mexican restaurants, all Latin restaurants, or all restaurants. When the industry is narrowly defined, the number of direct competitors decreases and the number of indirect rivals increases. When an industry is defined broadly, the number of direct rivals increases and the number of indirect competitors decreases. Whether to define an industry narrowly or broadly will depend on how others – existing players in the industry, customers, and various stakeholders (e.g. resource providers) – see it.

Firms that serve similar consumer needs and preferences are rivals. Competitor analysis involves understanding the nature of rivalry in an industry. It involves identifying **direct** (or primary) and **indirect** (or secondary) rivals and their strategies. Direct competitors are rivals who provide the same product or service to the same target market. Indirect competitors are rivals who may not either provide the same offerings or may not focus on the same target segment. These are firms that people would turn to if they do not purchase your offerings. As an example, we can consider Sage Vegetarian Café in Chapel Hill, NC. Sage serves vegetarian Persian food, something that no other restaurant offers in the area. Sage's direct competitors would then include other restaurants serving either vegetarian or Persian food. All other restaurants in Chapel Hill, such as Mediterranean Deli and Al's Burger Shack, would be indirect competitors as they may cater to the same target market as Sage. A customer thinking about where to go for lunch or dinner may go to any restaurant in the town, be it Greek food or burger joint.

TABLE 15.2

Three Industry Factors

Value of product to customer	Intensity of competition	Power of suppliers
The product is more than just a commodity for the customer.	Numerous competitors exist or several competitors exist of similar sizes.	A few suppliers dominate the supply chain for the said product.
Customers find it difficult to replace the product with something else.	Competitor offerings are not readily distinguishable.	Each supplier has differentiated product offerings.
Has high importance for the customer.	Barriers to entry are low for new companies.	There is a lack of substitutes for the products bought from suppliers.
The worth of the product can be clearly signaled.	There is excess capacity available in the industry.	There is a high switching cost to changing suppliers.
The customer bears a high cost to making a wrong decision.	It is difficult for producers to keep large inventory.	There is a high possibility of forward integration among suppliers.

15.3.2 Looking Inward

So far, we have focused on the landscape in which the firm competes. The landscape – or the external environment – is a source of both opportunities and threats, which firms need to identify in order to craft a good strategy. But understanding opportunities and threats is only half the picture; the other half of the picture is analyzing strengths and weaknesses. As we mentioned earlier, strengths refer to things that a firm is good at doing or attributes that enhance its competitiveness in the marketplace. Weaknesses are things a company lacks or does more poorly than others or a condition that puts it at a disadvantage in the market. Understanding strengths and weaknesses requires businesses to look inward and focus on what they have that will help them compete.

The answer to the question "What are a firm's strengths?" is (deceptively) simple: resources and capabilities. **Resources** are the various assets and attributes controlled by a firm that enable it to conceive of and implement a strategy to improve its efficiency and/or effectiveness. Most resources are, or could be, quantified on a firm's balance sheet as assets, some tangible and others intangible. Tangible resources are those with physical presence, such as land, factories, machinery, equipment, or cash. Intangible resources are assets that do not have physical presence, such as patents, reputation, brand, and knowledge. Generally, four categories of resources are considered:

1. Physical resources, such as plant or equipment (e.g. a factory to manufacture the product)
2. Human resources, such as celebrity executives (e.g. Sheryl Sandberg at Facebook), management skills, and employee know-how
3. Financial resources, such as profits that can be ploughed back into the business
4. Intangible resources, such as copyrights, patents, and brands (e.g. the right to Mickey Mouse and other characters that Disney has)

Small businesses need to carefully consider their mix of the four types of resources and how the mix enables core operational and important administrative activities of the firm.

Capabilities are processes that the firm has developed over time to competently perform specific value creation activities. They are frequently the product of organizational learning and are reflected in the routines of the firm. Capabilities are therefore knowledge-based, reside in people (but not in any one particular person at the firm), in the intellectual capital of the firm, or in organizational processes and systems. For example, Netflix's capability to recommend movies relies on the extensive data it has collected on viewer watching habits and its complex algorithms.

Capabilities that are critical to a firm's mission are **core capabilities**. Focusing on these capabilities, and becoming even better at them, allows firms to satisfy their customers better. Capabilities that set a firm apart from rivals are **distinctive capabilities**. When a firm focuses on core capabilities that distinguish it from rivals, it helps the firm outcompete other companies in its industry.

Resources and capabilities that a company has are its strengths. Resources and capabilities that a company lacks (but should have because customers care about them or competitors have them) are its weaknesses (see Figure 15.5).

Resources
Tangible
  Physical
  Human
  Financial
Intangible

Capabilities
  Core capabilities
  Distinctive capabilities
Result from organizational learning over time

FIGURE 15.5 Resources and Capabilities

Interactive Exercise

Would you like to conduct a SWOT analysis for your organization? Let's do a SWOT analysis   for the business school where you study. What do you learn from this SWOT analysis?

15.3.3 Aligning Internal with External

Once the firm's strengths and weaknesses (within the firm) and the opportunities and threats (from its environment) have been identified, the next step is to ask a series of strategic questions that link the internal analysis with the external analysis:

1. How can the manager use strengths to take advantage of opportunities?
2. How can the manager use strengths to counter the likelihood and impact of threats?
3. How will weaknesses prevent the firm from taking advantage of these opportunities? What can management do in such a situation?
4. How will weaknesses exacerbate, or worsen, the likelihood and impact of threats? What can management do in such a situation?

The matching, or aligning, of key internal and external factors is the most difficult part of conducting a SWOT analysis. This is because it requires informed judgment, and there is no one BEST configuration of matching.

The SO match draws attention to how a firm's (internal) strengths can be used to take advantage of (external) opportunities. These are what can be called **leverage** points that firms need to build on in developing their strategy. It goes without saying that all small businesses would like to be in a position in which all internal strengths can be used to benefit from all relevant external events and trends. However, this is problematic because it can spread the available resources too thin. Consequently, astute managers need to carefully consider the most fruitful opportunities that can be met with the best strengths they have.

The ST match relates to how a firm's strengths can be used to avoid or reduce the impact of external threats. These capture the **vulnerability** points for the firm. A small business should not try to meet all threats in the external environment head-on. Some threats need to be avoided, but not all threats are avoidable. Managers need to make judgments about which threats they want to address with their strengths.

The WO match pertains to internal weaknesses that prevent a firm from taking advantage of external opportunities. These are sometimes referred to as points of **constraints** for the firm. Many small businesses find themselves in positions where key external opportunities exist, but internal weaknesses of the firm prevent it from benefitting from those opportunities.

The WT match focuses on internal weaknesses that can exacerbate the impact of external threats. These are what one may call **peril** points. Small businesses faced with numerous external threats that align very closely with internal weaknesses of the firm will be in a precarious position. Such firms may need to fight hard for their very survival, having to choose between options such as bankruptcy, retrenchment, getting acquired, or liquidation.

A schematic representation of the SWOT matrix is presented below. The four elemental cells, labeled S, W, O, and T are completed first. The match cells, labeled SO, ST, WO, and WT are completed next. The process can be summarized in eight steps:

1. List key strengths of the firm (at least three most important).
2. List key weaknesses of the firm (at least three most important).
3. List key opportunities available in the external environment (at least three most important).
4. List key threats from the external environment (at least three most important).

At this stage, some managers find that they do not have even three attributes in each of the four groups of SWOT. Why does this happen? Mostly, because they have not yet done adequate research on the company and its environment.

5. Match strengths with opportunities (SO match).
6. Match strengths with threats (ST match).
7. Match weaknesses with opportunities (WO match).
8. Match weaknesses with threats (WT match).

It is helpful to quantify both internal and external factors, so that the four elemental cells and the match cells should be stated, as much as possible, in quantitative terms (see Figure 15.6). The purpose of SWOT is to understand how the firm's strengths and weaknesses align with the opportunities and threats in its environment. What strategy a firm can develop based on this analysis is a matter of judgment. The manager needs to identify points of action based on the matching to come up with a strategy for the firm. Keep in mind that no firm has sufficient capital or resources to develop a strategy that can address every issue unearthed by SWOT analysis.

	STRENGTHS	WEAKNESSES
	Financial Resources	Inferior product quality
	Strong brand-name or company reputation	Weak management (one-person show)
	Distinctive and core competencies	Cost disadvantage vis-à-vis rivals
	Proprietary technology, superior skills, and useful patents	Narrow product line
	Superior product quality	Poor reputation or weak brand name
	Large footprint or wide geographic coverage	Obsolete facilities or internal operating problems
	Partnerships and alliances that can provide access to new technologies or markets	Weak balance sheet (low profitability, high debt)
	Visionary leadership	No clear or loyal customer base

OPPORTUNITIES	SO (Leverage)	WO (Constraints)
Rising buyer demand in the industry		
Strong economic growth		
New geographical markets coming up		
Falling trade barriers overseas		
New technologies emerging		

THREATS	ST (Vulnerability)	WT (Perils)
Economic recession		
Consolidation among suppliers or customers		
Adverse demographic changes that may curtail demand for the product		
Tight credit conditions		
Unfavorable government policies		
Rising prices on key inputs		
Change in buyer tastes		

FIGURE 15.6 A Sample SWOT Analysis

SWOT analysis has long been one of the most popular and widely used tools for strategists. It may be used fruitfully by organizations of all sizes and forms, ranging from small businesses to large corporations, and government agencies to nonprofits such as school and churches. Its popularity stems in part from the ease of use, but also from its ability to align internal factors with external issues. Despite its widespread usage, a word of caution about SWOT analysis is in order. A problem with this framework is that a strength for one firm can be a weakness for another, and an opportunity for someone can be a threat for another. For this reason, there is no generic SWOT analysis. SWOT analysis should be specific to a particular firm.

What Do You Think?

Dropbox, founded in 2007, is the brainchild of Drew Houston, a graduate of the computer engineering program of Massachusetts Institute of Technology. Drew was a student at the time he started the company, getting the idea for Dropbox when he found himself repeatedly forgetting the USB drive that held his college files and folders. Dropbox was officially launched in 2008, crossed the one million user mark in 2009, and went public in 2018. It had more than 500 million user accounts by 2018, of which only about 13 million are paid users. At the end of 2018, Dropbox had annual revenues of around $1.4 billion with a net loss of about $480 million. Can a SWOT analysis of Dropbox help Drew Houston figure out the future of his young company? How would this SWOT analysis be similar to, or differ from, the one for Box, another cloud-storage file-hosting site started in 2005 by then University of South California student Aaron Levie?

15.3.4 Common Mistakes in SWOT Analysis

Most professors who cover SWOT analysis in their class find that almost every cohort of students makes some common mistakes. To avoid making such mistakes, it is useful to briefly discuss the most common ones. First, and this has been mentioned earlier in this chapter, in identifying the four elements of SWOT, internal and external factors should not be confused with each other. Students will often mix up strengths with opportunities, and weaknesses with threats. This is problematic because strengths and weaknesses are internal factors that are expected to be under direct managerial influence, while opportunities and threats are external trends to which managers are responding. Thus, students should avoid listing strengths as opportunities (or vice versa), and weaknesses as threats (or vice versa). Second, it is a common tendency among students to present SWOT analysis without any numbers. Consider, a SWOT analysis for Dropbox listing high growth in cloud storage as an opportunity. Does high growth here mean 2%, 20%, or 200%? We have no idea from the analysis. Further, is it always high growth or is the current period one of high growth? Put some temporal boundaries around the SWOT elements you are discussing. Perhaps something like "20% growth in the US cloud storage industry in the last three years, which is likely to continue over the next five years." You may have heard of the humorous statement that expands on a well-known motto appearing on the US currency: *In God we trust, everyone else bring data*. Well, the same is true of SWOT analysis.

Third, no one can just get the SWOT elements from thin air. You should be able to identify credible sources for most, if not all, factors that are part of SWOT. Let's say you were doing a SWOT analysis for RadioShack and wanted to say that a major weakness of the company was low customer service. Well, what is your source for this information? Your experience? If yes, is your experience representative of the experience of a typical RadioShack customer? Perhaps you researched RadioShack and saw some third-party rankings of retailers. Good sourcing of the information you are using is important if you want to get it right. Fourth, you will find that SWOT analysis is often thin on weaknesses compared to strengths, low on threats compared to opportunities. This is especially true if you are doing a SWOT analysis for a company or organization that is doing well. You will even hear people say "They are doing so well, how can there be anything wrong here?" For such optimistic analysts, the former CEO of Intel Andy Grove had two words: Be Paranoid. When doing a SWOT analysis, it is crucial that you try to identify weaknesses or threats. Finally, think of SWOT analysis as one tool in the strategists' portfolio. It is not the final word on anything. The information produced during the SWOT analysis offers a starting point for the manager's effort to develop a strategy for their firms, and it would be a big mistake to think of it as the finish line.

Comprehension Check

1. What are the components of a SWOT analysis? What does a firm hope to achieve through a SWOT analysis?
2. Explain PESTLE analysis and describe the various components of PESTLE.
3. What are some common mistakes made in conducting a SWOT analysis? Can these mistakes be avoided?

Module 15.4 Generic Strategies for Small Firms

A SWOT analysis, done well, can serve as a good foundation for formulating a good strategy for small businesses. Entrepreneurs can use the SWOT analysis to position the new venture concept or startup for a well-defined strategy that will be more likely to become the basis for competitive advantage for the firm. Choosing a good strategy that makes sense for a particular business is a crucial early step toward superior performance in the long run. For most small businesses, a good strategy will increase both top-line and bottom-line performance (revenue and profits, respectively), both in the present and in the future.

> ### KEY TAKEAWAY
>
> Choosing a good strategy that makes sense for a particular business is a crucial early step toward superior performance in the long run.

To come up with a good strategy, firms need to make decisions about two important factors:

1. Do we want to be a low-cost player or a differentiated player? Low-cost players compete on the basis of keeping their overall costs low. In fact, they keep their costs so low that it is hard for any rival to match those costs, let alone beat them. A differentiated player, on the other hand, provides an offering that sets it apart in some way from rivals' products or services (perhaps, aesthetics or functionality) and allows the firm to charge a premium for the differentiated offering. Payless Shoes had a low-cost strategic orientation (even the name communicated its strategic choice); Victoria Secret aspires toward a differentiated orientation.
2. Do we want to be a mass-market player or focus on a particular niche? A mass-market player does not cater to a specific market segment in its industry, choosing to serve a **broad market**. Conversely, focus players identify a specific **niche** that they believe gives them enough market to thrive, at least for some time. General Motors targets the mass market (a car for every purse and purpose); Tesla Motors focuses only on electric cars (though it does hope to make electric cars the mass-market choice one day!).

Decisions about the source of competitive advantage (low cost versus differentiation) and the scope of competitive advantage (mass market versus differentiation) are not

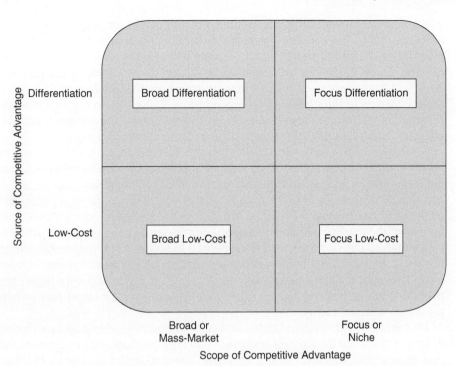

Differentiation

Broad Differentiation

Focus Differentiation

Low-Cost

Broad Low-Cost

Focus Low-Cost

Source of Competitive Advantage

Broad or
Mass-Market

Focus or
Niche

Scope of Competitive Advantage

FIGURE 15.7 Four Generic Strategies

set in stone, meaning that they are not immutable and forever. Firms can change these decisions as the circumstances around them change, the industry in which they compete evolves, and other growth-minded companies either imitate or outshine the firm's strategy. Figure 15.7 illustrates the four possible strategies using a 2 × 2 framework. We can understand this 2 × 2 framework by using the haircut salon industry. You can go to Great Clips, a low-cost player that charges $15 for an adult haircut, or to Valerie Joseph, where a haircut starts at $295. You could also go to Supercuts, a mass-market player or Sport Clips that promises a "championship experience" for boys and men.

Firms that chose a **low-cost** strategic emphasis must hold down their (overall) costs so that they can compete by charging lower prices for their products or services and still make a decent profit. Cost savings can come from multiple places, including labor cost, management overhead, and operational efficiency. To follow a low-cost strategy, a small business must start with a comprehensive survey of the competitors' offerings and prices and a realistic estimate of its own costs and profits. Larger competitors may be able to lower their costs by leveraging economies of scale in procurement and operations, while smaller rivals can lower costs by keeping their overheads to a minimum. It is therefore useful to remember that factors that can provide the basis of a cost advantage are quite numerous and diverse; the entrepreneur's challenge is in identifying ways to compete on costs and undercut smaller or larger competitors by keeping down both costs and prices. This is not easy and requires strict cost discipline on the entrepreneur's part. Features and services that buyers consider essential still need to be provided, and not all frills can be eliminated as buyers may consider some to be a given when buying the product. Of course, taking the low-cost path is not without risks, especially because it often triggers a price war with some rivals always willing to sell at a lower price (perhaps, at a lower quality too). This strategy also tends to attract customers who are always searching for the best deal and have little loyalty to any particular seller. Consequently, low-cost players may find it challenging to develop loyal customers.

A **differentiation-based** strategic orientation emphasizes unique features of the firm's products or services (in terms of attributes other than cost). For the strategy to be effective, the buyer must (a) be convinced of the uniqueness of the offering and (b) care about or value the differentiated feature. The differentiation may be real or perceived, as long as the buyer sees value in it. Firms that can create and sustain an attractive differentiating feature are usually able to attract and retain loyal customers who will pay a premium for their products. Successful differentiation requires careful study to understand what attributes buyers will find appealing, valuable, and worth paying for. Incorporating differentiated features in one's products or services often adds to the cost, which puts pressure on the profit margins, and so firms will often want to charge a premium for offering something that is differentiated. A differentiated strategic emphasis will fail if buyers do not believe there is something unique about the offerings or do not care about the uniqueness in their buying decision. Rivals will often try to match a company's differentiating features (if buyers value them), so the longer the company can protect its offerings from imitations, the more lasting its competitive advantage.

Some firms choose to have a **broad approach** that can appeal to the mass market. Such an approach works best when buyer needs and product uses are homogeneous across traditional market segments, and the firm is able to reach across various segments in a consistent manner. Other firms choose to have a **focus approach** targeting a particular market niche. Such an orientation helps the firm concentrate its effort on the needs of a limited portion of the market, which is very useful for resource-constrained companies entering a new market. Often, a focus strategy is helpful in avoiding competition with entrenched players if the firm can identify a niche that has previously been ignored or overlooked. Firms that want to appeal to the mass market usually need to allocate a bigger budget for marketing and advertising (as the message is diffused across a larger base) compared to those with a focus strategy.

Management's decision about the source of competitive advantage (cost based versus differentiation) and the scope of competitive advantage (mass market versus niche) yields four generic business-level strategies: broad low-cost, broad differentiation, focus low-cost, and focus differentiation. Understanding these four generic strategies is important because different generic strategies offer different value propositions to customers.

Broad low-cost is a competitive strategy based on low overall costs and satisfying the mass market. It requires aggressive pursuit of cost reductions from working closely with suppliers and customers, experience, and tight control on overhead expenses, rejections, and wastage. Because of its low costs, a firm pursuing a broad low-cost strategy will be able to charge a low price for its products and still make a profit. Targeting a broad market allows the firm to satisfy a wide range of customers, and in the process of doing so, have a large market share. The low-cost position allows the firm to earn profits even when rivals are vigorously competing on prices; the high market share gives it economies of scale, with respect to negotiating with suppliers, marketing and advertising expenses, and production costs. When firms are able to maintain a broad low-cost strategy over a sustained period of time, and it is reflected in low prices vis-à-vis competitors, they are also able to block new entrants from coming into the industry, as few nascent players will be able to match the firm's cost advantage.

Broad differentiation involves developing products or services that are unique in the minds of customers and aimed at the mass market. A company pursuing broad differentiation will often charge a premium for its offering (although it does not have to). Broad differentiation is a viable strategy for small businesses because the increased value that customers see in the firm's offerings reduces price sensitivity and increases customer loyalty, which then allows firms to have a high market share. Few firms are able to maintain a broad differentiation strategy for long periods as growth-minded rivals try to imitate the unique features of the company's offerings and customers grapple with the value they receive from buying the company's offerings.

A firm pursues a **focus low-cost** strategy when it concentrates on a particular buyer group (say, male or female, whites, blacks, or Hispanics) or geographic market or user needs and serves only this niche with low-cost offerings. Companies pursuing a focus low-cost strategy will need to match the quality of their rivals and their customers' minimum expectations of the product or service, as well as to identify a niche that is large enough for the company to be profitable. A firm pursues a **focus differentiation** strategy when it concentrates on a specific market segment and serves that niche with products that have unique features or services. Companies that takes this strategic approach need to offer something that customers perceive as differentiated and appeal to a large enough niche for it to be a viable player in the market. Whether low-cost or differentiated, any company with a focus strategy has to find a niche that is big enough to be profitable and offers some growth potential. It should, preferably, be a niche where large players are not competing, which helps a small business avoid a large player with a bigger and stronger war chest. The niche should also not be one in which rival companies are trying to establish themselves. Of course, if the niche grows over time and becomes attractive to large players, then it will become more difficult for small businesses to survive in the niche (unless they can find a smaller niche within it or a new niche to focus on). For example, in the late 1990s and early 2000s, Greek yogurt was a small niche in the US yogurt market (about 2% of the total market) and had only one prominent player (Fage), but over the last 20 years Greek yogurt has exploded (it is now about 40% of the total US yogurt market) and several players compete to become the preferred choice of the consumer.

Interactive Exercise

The husband-and-wife team, Bob and Yvonne Klein, started Ellenos as a small yogurt bar in Seattle, in partnership with father and son, Con and Alex Apostolopoulos, to bring the latter's family yogurt recipe to the United States. Read the story of Ellenos on the Internet. What do you find most interesting about the origin and rise of Ellenos?

Some firms fail to effectively pursue one of the four generic strategies, becoming **stuck-in-the-middle**. When a firm does not offer unique features that convince customers to buy its products or its costs are too high to compete effectively on price, it is said to have a stuck-in-the-middle strategy. Firms may get to this strategy by choice when they try to be everything to everyone or by accident when they end up there because of their oversight or outmaneuvering by rivals. Firms that are stuck-in-the middle generally perform poorly because they lack competitive pricing, unique value, or clear market. Very few firms are able to pull off trying to serve the varied needs of different segments of the market at prices that keep everyone satisfied, but when they do, they are said to have a **best-cost strategy**. When a company can incorporate points of differentiation into its product offerings at a lower cost than rivals, then it may have a best-cost strategy. Most firms who aspire for a best-cost strategy end up stuck-in-the-middle with nothing much to show for it, except a red bottom line. To have a profit-yielding best-cost strategy, a company must be able to incorporate differentiated features into its offerings without losing its low-cost advantage to competitors. It should also be able to appeal to a market larger than a conventional niche, though it may not be fully mass market. The target market for a best-cost strategy cuts across traditional segments: the status-conscious, value-hunting buyer who is looking for something extra without having to pay an arm and a leg for it. Once again, it is helpful to remember that the line separating stuck-in-the-middle from best cost is a very thin one, and firms often cross it to their disadvantage.

What Do You Think?

Pinterest, the online scrapbook that allows people to save images to virtual pin-boards, was launched in 2010 by Ben Silbermann, Paul Sciarria, and Evan Sharp. It is a unicorn, in that it is a tech startup valued at $1 billion or more. Soon after its launch, the company became "the digital scrapbook du jour for blushing brides, arts and crafts enthusiasts and home decorators hunting for ideas and inspiration." The Pinterest site gets about 70–80 million visitors a month. Estimates suggest that about 70% of Pinterest monthly visitors are women. In the United States alone, about 40% of online women use Pinterest as opposed to about 10–12% of online men. While Pinterest lags behind other social media sites in monthly visitors (e.g. Facebook at 200 million and LinkedIn at 90M), it is the most female-skewed social platform. Now management is faced with a problem: Should it broaden itself to become equally attractive to both men and women or should it focus more deeply to cater to its female clientele? The decision seems to become more complicated by the perception that it is more stigmatizing for a man to be on a woman's site than the reverse. But how does one change Pinterest's perception as a woman's world to a man's world or as gender-neutral territory? Or, does it not need to change?

Comprehension Check

1. Explain the benefits and pitfalls of a differentiation-based strategy?
2. What are some challenges faced by small businesses that want to emphasize a **cost-based strategic orientation?**
3. Explain why firms aspiring toward a best-cost strategy may end up stuck-in-the-middle.

Summary

This chapter discusses strategy for small businesses, an important topic that is often misunderstood. While many believe that strategy is only for large firms, and others publicly take pride in charging ahead without a clear strategy, our argument is that strategic thinking is very important for small businesses. The distinction between strategic and operational decisions is explained, and small business owners are advised to invest adequate time and effort in understanding the strategic issues facing their firms. Small business owners must remain informed about the trends and changes in the general environment, as well as the conditions of their specific industry, and the decisions and actions of their rivals. The PESTLE analysis provides a useful framework to understand the general environment of the firm, and strategic group mapping helps focus attention on close competitors that affect a firm more than other industry members. Small business owners should also actively manage their firm's resources to remain competitive. SWOT analysis is a valuable tool for consolidating the information gathered about internal and external factors with the goal of identifying key points of alignment and misalignment between the firm's resources and the changes and trends in the environment. Based on their analysis, small business owners can decide whether they want to emphasize a cost-based or differentiation orientation, and pursue a broad or niche market, which then yields a generic strategy for the company to adopt. When small business owners give strategy the importance it deserves, the chances of the firm becoming successful greatly increase.

World of Books

Good Strategy, Bad Strategy by Richard P. Rumelt
How I Built This by Guy Raz
Boss Life by Paul Downs

In the Movies

The film *You've Got Mail* tells the story of Kathleen Kelly, who owns a small profitable independent children's bookstore in New York, and finds herself in competition with a mega chain of bookstores. Kathleen's bookstore was founded by her mother, and the bookstore is now a labor of love for her. The large chain is owned by the Fox family, who sees books as just another product to be pushed and sold. Does the small bookstore have a chance against the large chain? What can a small bookstore do to compete against mega chains?

Live Exercise

"Do you think what you've learned about strategic thinking can help Johnny figure out how to take the company to the next level?" your Dad asks when you see him at Thanksgiving. "I think so, or at least that's what my professor said during class," you share. "I think we can do an external analysis, internal analysis, and SWOT analysis for SoapStandle quite readily."

"Well, then, perhaps you can use some of your time this weekend to do a preliminary analysis for SoapStandle. Johnny is coming for dinner next week and you can share your analysis with him," your father suggests. "That's a great idea," your mother speaks up, "it's a good way to put your learning from the class in practice in the real world."

After dinner, you walk up to your room and decide to write down the work you will need to do before you present your analysis to Johnny:

1. External Analysis: Environmental analysis (PESTEL) and competitor analysis
2. Internal Analysis: Resources and capabilities
3. SWOT Analysis: Identification of strengths, weaknesses, opportunities, and threats, and the alignment of internal with external factors

Things to Remember

LO 15.1 Explain the need for a small business to have a (good) strategy
- Strategy is useful for businesses of all sizes and forms.
- A well-crafted strategy yields competitive success and healthy profits that allow a small business to move to the next level.
- Strategy is especially challenging for small businesses because often there is only one person at the helm who is responsible for formulating and implementing the company's strategy.
- Small business owners have considerable leeway in deciding their firm's strategy.
- A good strategy fits the particular situation of a company and sets it apart from competitors.
- A bad strategy can hurt the firm, sometimes even wrecking it beyond repair.

LO 15.2 Describe what it means to think strategically in the small business context
- Small business owners make thousands of decisions every month, some of which are strategic, but the vast majority are operational in nature.
- Strategic decisions involve issues that affect the whole organization.
- Operational decisions involve issues that impact one or more aspects of the firm but do not need strategic-level thinking.
- The typical way most people think about business is from an operational perspective. Focusing on strategic issues does not come naturally to most of us.
- The distinction between operational and strategic decisions is not always as clear-cut as we would like it to be.
- Managers who spend adequate time and effort on strategic decisions will usually provide better stewardship of the firm.

LO 15.3 Explain how to conduct a SWOT analysis and what to do with it
- SWOT analysis is a diagnostic tool that considers a firm's strengths and weaknesses along with the opportunities and threats it faces.
- SWOT stands for strengths, weaknesses, opportunities, and threats. Strengths and weaknesses are internal to the firm; opportunities and threats are external to the firm.
- The source of strengths and weaknesses lies in the resources and capabilities that a small business has or can gain access to without much trouble. The source of opportunities and threats is the macro-environment of the firm, the industry within which it operates, and the competitors it has.
- A common framework to organize the myriad macro-environmental factors impacting a firm is PESTLE.
- The industry in which a firm operates has a significant influence on its survival and profitability.
- Direct competitors are rivals who provide the same product or service to the same target market. Indirect competitors are rivals who may not either provide the same offerings or may not focus on the same target segment.
- Firms can have tangible or intangible resources. A firm's capabilities are the result of organizational learning and experience.

- The matching, or aligning, of key internal and external factors is the most difficult part of conducting a SWOT analysis.

LO 15.4 **Identify generic strategies for small business managers**

- Firms need to decide whether they want to emphasize a cost-based or differentiation-based advantage.
- Firms need to decide whether they want to focus on the mass market or a niche market.
- There are four possible generic strategies: broad low-cost, broad differentiation, focus low-cost, and focus differentiation.
- Some firms are able to pursue a best-cost strategy, though most firms attempting to do so end up stuck-in-the middle.
- Firms that are unable to make up their mind about what generic strategy to pursue risk trying to be everything to everyone.

Key Terms

strategy	industry	indirect competition	low-cost
good strategy	competitors (or rivals)	resources	differentiation-based
bad strategy	PESTLE (or PEST, STEEP)	capabilities	broad approach
strategic decisions	political	core capabilities	focus approach
operational decisions	economic	distinctive capabilities	broad low-cost
SWOT	social	leverage	broad differentiation
strengths	technological	vulnerability	focus low-cost
weaknesses	ecological	constraints	focus differentiation
opportunities	legal	peril	stuck-in-the-middle
threats	profitability	broad market	best cost
macro-environment	direct competition	niche market	cost-based orientation

Experiential Exercise

This exercise can be done by an individual or people working in teams of two.

Identify a unicorn that recently went public. A unicorn is a startup with a market valuation of $1 billion. For example, Airbnb and Uber were both unicorns. Find a unicorn that appeals to you (perhaps because you have heard a lot about it and want to know more, or because the business they are in appeals to you). Visit the website of the company you identified, and go to its investor relations page. Download its latest annual report and read through it. Be prepared to answer the following basic questions:

1. When was this company founded and by whom?

2. What was the market valuation of this company when it went public? What is its market valuation now?

3. What industry is the company in? Who are the competitors? Information about industry and rivals is also provided in the annual report of the company.

Your assignment is to conduct a SWOT analysis on this unicorn, focusing on how things are presently. Follow all the SWOT guidelines provided in the chapter. Identify at least three to five elements for each of the SWOT cells. Align the internal factors with the external conditions, identifying at least two fit elements in each category (SO, SST, WO, and WT). Based on this SWOT analysis, can you make some recommendations for what strategy the company should follow?

Depending on how much time is available for this assignment, students may analyze either a specific subset of SWOT (e.g. only a PESTLE analysis or competitor analysis only) or they may cover the full scope of the SWOT analysis (including identifying leverage, vulnerability, constraint, and peril points).

Business Planning for Small Firms

When one fails to plan, they often end up planning to fail.

BENJAMIN FRANKLIN

16.0 Introduction

Starting a business is – in some ways – akin to going on a vacation. If you are like most people, you don't just get up one day and leave your house and work to go somewhere. Few of us are like the character *Juanita* from the 2019 movie of the same name, who took off on a vacation without any destination in mind (she ends up in Butte, Montana). Whether your vacation involves visiting Mount Rushmore in South Dakota, lazing on the beautiful beaches of Brazil, or taking a safari in South Africa, you need to make some plans and consider whether you have adequate resources to last the trip. You may not want to or need to make detailed plans for what you will be doing every day, but it is useful to have some sort of a roadmap for your vacation. In a similar manner, it is helpful to have some sort of plan for your business. Although everyone makes some sort of mental plans for the tasks they want to accomplish, writing down those thoughts can be very helpful for starting and growing a business.

It would not be an exaggeration to say that every business starts and grows with a plan. A business that starts and grows without any conscious plan on part of the entrepreneur is rare. Sometimes the initial planning is rudimentary, the kind that involves the back of a napkin, as was the case for Nora Herting and Heather Williams of ImageThink. At other times, the planning may be detailed and rigorous, as was the case for Jeff Bezos of Amazon, Phil Knight of Nike, and Fred Smith of FedEx. The purpose of this chapter is to understand how to think about planning for your business and put together a business plan that meets your needs at the time.

SPOTLIGHT | The Magic of Jeff

Jeff knew what he was going to name the company he was about to start: Cadabra Inc. He liked the way it sounded, a play on the magician's chant of "abracadabra." He also had a back-up name in mind – Makeitso.com – after Captain Jean-Luc Picard's frequent command from his favorite TV show *Star Trek: The Next Generation*. Jeff had already packed up the Manhattan apartment he shared with his wife Mackenzie. They had then flown to Fort Worth, TX, to pick up a 10-year-old Chevy Blazer his father had agreed to loan him. Jeff had decided to locate his new company in Seattle because it had gained a reputation as a technology hub, was close to a warehouse of one of the two big book distributors in the country at the time, and had a big university that produced computer science graduates. He knew the next step he needed to take was to write a business plan that could accurately capture the idea in his mind.

"What do you mean, you are going to sell books over the Internet?" Jeff's father asked when he called to share that he was leaving his well-paying Wall Street career to pursue an idea that sounded like utter madness. It was not even a very novel idea: There were already existing online bookstores, including Books.com, the website of a Cleveland-based bookstore. Now, having borrowed his Dad's old car, and Mackenzie driving them from Fort Worth to Seattle, Jeff took out his laptop and started working on the business plan. He did not need to raise money yet, but he needed to make sure his wife, parents, the employees he was looking to hire, and he himself actually understood the crazy idea he had in mind. By the time the couple got to Seattle,

Jeff had sketched out the basics of his idea in the form of a rough business plan and figured out some revenue projections in an Excel sheet – numbers that would later prove to be drastic underestimations.

Within three months of setting up shop in Seattle, Jeff changed the company's name to Amazon.com, after the biggest river on Earth. Cadabra, he had to come to realize, sounded too close to cadaver, and that was off-putting to many people. He then toyed with awake.com, browse.com, bookmall.com, and relentless.com, but then decided to name the company Amazon. At the time, website listings were alphabetized, so a name that started with "A" would appear at the top of the listing, making it more appealing to potential visitors. Soon, beta links of the new site went to family and friends, many of them initial investors in his project that still seemed like a crazy idea. The new company made its first sale on April 13, 1995. Two years later, Jeff was taking his business plan on the road to raise outside money. He was valuing the fledgling startup at $6 million. And, he cautioned potential investors, just as he had told his parents when they had first agreed to invest in his company, there was a 70% chance that the company could fail and they could lose all their investment. Yet, the truth was that the company was already doing much better than Jeff had estimated in his initial business plan.

Discussion Questions

1. Jeff drafted his business plan after he had an initial idea. He drafted the plan after it was already in motion, but before some of the major steps. What is the significance of the timing of when the business plan was drafted? In what ways did the timing of the business plan impact Amazon's success?

2. Many people, including Jeff's own father, questioned his idea to start his company. Even Jeff doubted his company's future during his presentations to investors. How do you think Amazon succeeded amidst this doubt? What parts of Jeff's plan do you think made the biggest difference?

3. What reasons led Jeff to decide to locate his company in Seattle?

Module 16.1 What Is a Business Plan?

Mention an idea for a new business to someone, and they are very likely to ask if you have a **business plan**. At a basic level, a business plan records your ideas and insights for the venture. During the formative stages of the venture, the focus of the plan is on the core concept underlying the business, including what problems will be solved and how the entrepreneur will solve them. You may be excited about your business idea and looking forward to starting the business, but actually documenting the various steps along the way can be daunting. For a business that already exists, the plan describes the relevant factors that will be influential in sustaining or growing the business. You may be passionate about the business you run, but synthesizing your thoughts and experiences in a coherent manner that provides some guidance about the future of the business is still challenging. Planning can be useful at every stage of the business, from startup to growth to exit, as it helps you think about the business in a logical and rigorous manner.

KEY TAKEAWAY

Having a plan will greatly increase the chances that you will successfully start or grow your business.

Countless well-intended books, websites, and friends will tell you that several successful entrepreneurs started their business without a plan (e.g. Steve Jobs). Faced with this message, you may even begin to wonder whether a business plan is really needed. The truth is that having a plan will greatly increase the chances that you will successfully start or grow your business. It is certainly possible to take a vacation without planning ahead (as Juanita did), but it is rarely advisable to do so. Once we agree that some planning is essential regardless of whether you are taking a vacation or starting a business, we are able to turn our attention to two fundamentally different approaches to planning (see Table 16.1): **goal-driven** (also called **causation**) and **means-driven** (also called **effectuation**). The former involves thinking about where you want to be and then considering the resources you will need to get there. The latter involves thinking about the resources you have and then considering where they can take you. Let us go back to the vacation example we used earlier. Say your idea of a vacation this year is to go on a safari in South Africa (we start with the goal here). To achieve this goal, you will research the expenses involved in getting to South Africa and staying there for the safari, and then calculating how much it will cost you in time and money. Then you will look at the calendar and the bank account to determine if you have the resources to go to South Africa. If you have the time and money, things are good and you can take your vacation. If you do not have the time and money at this point, you will start thinking about when you will have them and schedule your vacation for then. This is goal-driven planning or causation.

An alternative way to think about taking a vacation is to look at how much time and money you have now (the focus here is on the means you have), and where you can get with what you have. Perhaps you already have enough time and money to go to South Africa. Or, maybe you have much less than what a South African vacation will cost, but enough to get you to Costa Rica. Or, maybe you only have enough to take a safari domestically, perhaps in California's San Diego Zoo Safari Park or Georgia's Pine Mountain Safari. Either way, you need to decide which of the vacation options will give you the most satisfaction (and be a good investment of your time and money). This is means-driven planning or effectuation. Sometimes, the goals drive our plans, other times the means inform our plans, and sometimes it is a combination of means and goals that is the driver of our plans. As in life, so in business.

Imagine you have guests coming home for dinner. How do you make sure there is a nice, hot meal for them when they get there? One approach is to draw up a list of dishes you want to serve them, then identify the ingredients to make those dishes, get the ingredients either at home or buying them from the grocery store, and follow the recipe to prepare the dishes. Another approach is to look through your kitchen for items you already have at home (or maybe even ask your neighbor, if you really need it), then think of the possible dishes that you can prepare from those ingredients, and prepare some dishes based on your experimentation in the kitchen. Do you always prefer one of these

TABLE 16.1

Comparing Causation and Effectuation

Categories of differentiation	Causation (goal-driven)	Effectuation (means-driven)
Givens	Effect is given	Means are given
Decision-making selection criteria	Help choose between means to achieve the given effect	Help choose between possible effects that can be created with given means
	Selection criteria based on expected return	Selection criteria based on affordable loss or acceptable risk
	Effect dependent: Choice of means is driven by characteristics of the effect the decision maker wants to create and his or her knowledge of possible means	Actor dependent: Given specific means, choice of effect is driven by characteristics of the actor and his or her ability and use contingencies
Competencies employed	Excellent at exploiting knowledge	Excellent at exploiting contingencies
Context of relevance	More ubiquitous in nature	More ubiquitous in human action
	More useful in static, linear, and independent environments	Explicit assumption of dynamic, nonlinear, and ecological environments
Nature of unknowns	Focus on the predictable aspects of an uncertain future	Focus on the controllable aspects of an unpredictable future
Underlying logic	To the extent we can predict future, we can control it	To the extent we can control future, we do not need to predict it
Outcomes	Market share in existent markets through competitive strategies	New market created through alliances and other cooperative strategies

Source: Sarasvathy, S. D. (2001). Causation and effectuation: Toward a theoretical shift from economic inevitability to entrepreneurial contingency. *Academy of Management Review, 26*(2), 243–263.

approaches over the other? The first approach is goal-driven planning or causation, and the second one is means-driven planning or effectuation.

There are three primary reasons for putting together a business plan: to (a) provide direction for the business after it is up and running, (b) delve deeper into the feasibility of the business idea, and (c) attract capital and other resources to the nascent business. As with writing any report (or term paper), getting started with a business plan is often the hardest part.

16.1.1 To Provide Direction

When done well, a business plan should serve as a roadmap for the future. Anyone who has ever run a small business will tell you that it is easy to lose precious time in addressing day-to-day operational issues. After dealing with everyday problems, many business owners have little time or energy left to attend to the strategic issues that matter for the overall well-being of the business. Popular sayings like "you ain't gonna remember to swamp the drain when you're swimming with the alligators" and "missing the forest for the trees" speak to the challenges of staying on course when you are consumed with the everyday needs of the business. When there is a good roadmap to guide you for the long term, the business is more likely to stay the course.

16.1.2 To Determine Feasibility

There is something interesting about writing down your thoughts: it forces you to sift through the muddled, half-baked ideas in your head and make sense of what you really think. The cliché "all ideas seem good until you try to explain them to someone" applies well to business. Committing your business idea to paper forces you to look critically at the means, goals, and expectations you have. It is easy to get caught up in the excitement and emotions of the process. Unfortunately, business decisions that have not been carefully considered often prove to be problematic for the firm. Writing a business plan can soften, and perhaps even completely remove, strong personal emotions from the decision-making process.

16.1.3 To Attract Capital and Other Resources

There is probably no business in the world that did not have to look for support from others, whether it is capital from investors and bankers or material from suppliers without having to pay for it right away. When Steve Jobs booked the first order from the first retail customer, he also convinced the retailer to advance him money so he could buy the parts to assemble the computers. One of the first questions entrepreneurs are asked is "Where is your plan?" When bankers ask entrepreneurs for the business plan, they are not being unreasonable or difficult. Bankers tend to be financially conservative, so that before they provide capital, they want to be assured that the entrepreneur is knowledgeable about the business. A completed business plan shows that the entrepreneur knows what he or she is doing and has thought through the opportunities and problems that may come up. Business plans also reveal when the entrepreneur expects to break even, the anticipated profitability of the venture, and the realism of the financial projections.

It is worth remembering here that having a business plan does not mean that it is "set in stone" and cannot change at all. All plans change, and they should. There is no business owner for whom the business develops exactly as he or she had planned. In fact, if any one tells you that their business trajectory was exactly as described in their plan, they are either not being completely honest or they are misremembering their initial plan.

The way the world thinks about business plans has changed over the years. It used to be the case that entrepreneurs were expected to come up with a potentially very good idea, write detailed plans for what would take to get the idea to the market, go out to raise funds by pitching to various investors, and then start building products they would sell based on their market research in order to achieve profitability. Such thinking, which can be called the **strong logic** of business planning, has informed numerous classes and books on entrepreneurship. Of course, whether this kind of thinking was ever truly characteristic of entrepreneurship in the real world is debatable. The strong logic of business planning has certainly gone out of fashion, partly because it suggested that one could identify and solve all problems before a business is ever started. You have probably heard sayings like "A plan is only good until the first shot is fired" and "Everybody has a plan until they get punched in the mouth," which are used to ridicule the traditional emphasis on detailed business planning.

What Do You Think?

Let's say you wanted to start a new Web-based business where people could either offer or rent short-term lodging. Your company will not actually own any of the lodgings offered on the site; you will just be a broker that takes commission from each booking. Airbnb was a pioneer in such a business. What steps would you need to take if you followed the strong form of business planning? Did Airbnb take such steps when they were just starting out? What would you do if you were to follow the weak form of business planning?

A recent trend in business planning is **lean startup**. While the traditional business plan focused on what it would take to start your dream business, the lean startup is geared toward how you can start a business with the resources you can currently obtain. At the heart of lean startup approach is the philosophy of build–assess–learn, which is consistent with the **weak logic** of business planning. In this way of thinking, planning serves as a tool to figure out possible options and eliminate unviable ones. In the build–assess–learn framework, the emphasis is on pursuing an idea with the resources one can get to bring the idea to market quickly. Based on the market feedback about what works and what does not, the entrepreneur can then **pivot** or transform the characteristics or features of the offerings to something more sellable. While some firms pivot, others **morph** as they gradually change the business offerings to make themselves more appealing to the market. Learning about customer needs and wants during the formative years of the venture strengthens the feedback loop and increases the chances that the business will offer something for which there is good demand.

Interactive Exercise

Check out the lean startup website at www.theleanstartup .com. Take a look at the case studies provided there for companies that used lean startup to start. What are the most important learnings you get about lean startup from reading the case studies?

Comprehension Check

1. Differentiate between causation and effectuation logic in planning.
2. What is a lean startup and how is it helpful?
3. What do you understand by "pivot"?

Module 16.2 What Is a Business Model?

Every business starts with a hypothesis – a good guess. When a business is unsuccessful, the hypothesis is proven wrong. Of course, in the real world, things aren't always so simple, as some businesses may also fail even when the initial hypothesis was correct (due to what some call the implementation problem). A quick way of testing the entrepreneurial hypothesis underlying a new business idea is the **business model canvas**, developed by Alexander Osterwalder and Yves Pigneur from the University of Lausanne in Switzerland. The business model canvas is a template for articulating novel or existing business models and focuses on how the venture creates value for customers and the owners. Before we dig deeper into the business model canvas, let us first understand what is meant by a business model.

KEY TAKEAWAY

Every business starts with a hypothesis that needs to be tested in the market.

The term *business model* is quite ubiquitous, but few people understand well what it means. A straightforward definition of business model is that it explains in a clear and systematic manner how a business brings in revenue and how it spends money. You could call it the nuts and bolts of the business. A business model, therefore, assesses the anticipated financial situation of the company. Of course, no company operates in a vacuum, so that the eventual failure or success of any business model depends on how it (a) is viewed by others and (b) stacks up against competitors.

16.2.1 Coming Up with a Business Model

If you ask most people on the street, they will describe the business model in simple terms: A firm produces an offering and sells it to customers to make a profit. Such a business model is easy to understand. This is how companies like Ford, Chipotle, and Greyhound make their money.

But what about a company like Facebook? The users themselves do not pay anything, so the product is completely free for them. The advertisers pay for the product to be offered free to users. The business model of companies like Facebook is based on advertising revenue. Users, however, do not like to be loaded with advertisements when they use Facebook, so the company has found another source of revenue by selling user data to companies who will use it for marketing and analysis.

There are also companies like Dropbox that have a different sort of business model: **freemium**. It is a combination of "free" and "premium" and describes a business model that offers both free and premium services. Usually, the simple basic services are free for the user, while The advanced features are offered against payment.

Companies may also have a hybrid business model, combining elements from different models to have multiple streams of revenue. Case in point: LinkedIn. The basic product is free for everyone, but more advanced users can opt for the premium version (so, that's the freemium model). Notably, LinkedIn also makes money on advertising as well as selling user info to other companies. Take a look at the companies in Figure 16.1. Can you rank them from fully free for the user to nothing free for the user?

Startups are characterized by much uncertainty (this is something you will hear a lot in entrepreneurship courses). Thinking about the business model forces the entrepreneur to be disciplined and avoid wishful thinking about how the business will make money. The business model provides good evidence as to whether the idea can be translated into a viable, profitable business and the kind of investment required to make it happen.

Now that the business model for the venture has been worked out, it is time to broaden our attention to the business model canvas. The canvas is a useful tool to help think about creating, capturing, and delivering value in a structured manner. The canvas also helps

FIGURE 16.1 Companies Can Succeed with Different Business Models

identify answers to the most important questions that a business must confront. There are 10 building blocks in the canvas:

- Promoters

  Who are the people founding this business?
  What makes them (uniquely) suitable for starting this business?

- Offering

  What problem(s) does the business help the customers solve?
  Which customer needs is the business solving?

- Customer Segments

  Who are the most important customers of this business?
  For whom does this product create value?

- Channels

  What distribution, sales, or communication channels do the customers prefer?
  Which channels would be most efficient with regard to time and cost?

- Customer Relations

  How will the business attract new customers or retain existing ones?

- Key Resources

  What assets will the business need to bring the offering to the market?

- Key Activities

  What will the business need to do to bring the offering to the market?

- Key Partnerships

  Who will be the key partners and suppliers for the business?
  What will the partners do? Provide resources, perform key activities?

- Cost Structure

  What do key resources and activities cost?
  What other costs need to be considered?

- Revenue Stream

  What will customers be willing to pay for the company's offerings?
  What are the possible revenue streams for the business?

Figure 16.2 presents the canvas that you can use to identify the various elements of a firm's value proposition. Thinking through these 10 elements is nonlinear and iterative as one moves back and forth between them. It is unlikely that you can convincingly fill out the various elements of the canvas without testing at least of the some ideas by taking them "on the road." Prospective entrepreneurs should be willing to change their initial ideas as they work through the canvas to get the formula right for the business.

Interactive Exercise

The website https://canvanizer.com/home/new_canvas provides an online tool for putting together a canvas. Do you have a business idea that you can use to complete the online canvas? If not, find someone who has a business idea and help put together the canvas for them.

BUSINESS MODEL CANVAS	Prepared for:		Prepared by:		Date:	Version:
Promoters	Key Activities	Offerings	Key Partners		Customer Segments	
	Key Resources		Channels			
Cost Structure		Customer Relations		Revenue Stream(s)		

FIGURE 16.2 Template for Business Model Canvas

What Do You Think?

Lisa wants to start a new business "Eco-Scarf" that will sell face masks imprinted with original catchy designs by new artists. Lisa has an undergraduate degree from Carnegie Mellon School of Design and a graduate degree in entrepreneurship from Babson. During her education, she did not learn about the business model canvas. Do you think the business model canvas can be useful for her as she thinks about starting her business? If yes, how would it be used?

Comprehension Check

1. Define business model. Why is it important to understand the business model of a firm?
2. What are the different parts of a business model canvas?
3. What are some possible revenue streams for a firm?

Module 16.3 Writing a Business Plan

The written business plan is a formal planning tool that one can use to start, operate, and grow your own business. It is typically a comprehensive document that covers the various aspects of the business, ranging from articulating the underlying business model to examining the competitive environment within which the business is situated. The business plan should be detailed enough to give someone reading it a nuanced picture and understanding of the business. The process of writing the business plan should help the entrepreneur think through the nuances of the business.

> **KEY TAKEAWAY**
>
> The written business plan is a formal planning tool that one can use to start, operate, and grow one's own business.

Many entrepreneurs choose not to write a formal business plan, perhaps because they incorrectly estimate the length of the time that a plan will take to prepare. There is no doubt that writing a detailed plan can be daunting and time-consuming. However, not writing a plan can often be detrimental to the entrepreneur as it means they have not done the due diligence to clarify their thinking about the business.

The outline for a business plan is illustrated in Table 16.2. This outline is only a guide. Each business plan is different depending on the purpose of the plan and who will be reading it. Yet, items in this outline are critical elements in a general plan. Each of the items in the outline is detailed in the following text.

16.3.1 Cover Page

The cover page of a business plan presents the name of the business, its address and phone, and the date the plan was completed. The cover page may be the last thing you put to your business plan, but it is the first thing an investor or customer looks at when they get to your business plan. First impressions are important, so make sure your business plan has a well laid-out cover page that looks completely professional. The cover page should have at least the name, address, and contact details of the business as well as of the promoters.

Sometimes, the cover plan may also include a paragraph describing the company and the nature of the business. It may also include a statement of the confidentiality of the business plan. Some business plans may also mention the amount of financing needed and briefly describe the company and the nature of the business.

16.3.2 Table of Contents

Not everyone reads the business plans from page one all the way through the last page (to be honest, few do!). Many people like to turn directly to their preferred section of the business plan. Some prefer to start by looking at the financial projections, others focus on the background of the entrepreneur and the company, and yet others may start by first reading the customer section. To make the business plan easy to read for others, it helps to have a table of contents that will allow the reader to go straight to their desired section.

TABLE 16.2

Parts of the Business Plan

Business Plan Outline

Cover Page
1 Name and address of business
2 Name and address of promoters

Table of Contents

Executive Summary
One to two page summary of the complete business plan

Company Description
1 Venture Information
2 Management Team
3 Products and Services

Environmental and Industrial Analysis
1 Environmental Analysis
2 Industry Analysis
3 Competitor Analysis
4 Market Research

Manufacturing and Operations

Financial Analysis
1 Capital Structure
2 Income Statement
3 Balance Statement
4 Cash Flow Statement
5 Breakeven Analysis
6 Ratio Analysis

Critical Assumptions and Risks

Appendix
1 Resumes of Promoters
2 Promotional Materials
3 Product Catalogues
4 Possible Suppliers
5 Milestones

What Do You Think?

Suppose you had the opportunity to start a textbook reselling business. Not just reselling your own textbooks, but also the textbooks you can obtain from other students (and some faculty) on campus. Chances are that students on campus will agree to sell their books to you because it will save them the hassle of selling the books themselves online. Would you like to put together a business plan that you can use to pitch into a lender to secure a loan to get the business off the ground?

16.3.3 Executive Summary

An executive summary is a short overview of the entire plan, which is written in a way that enables readers to become familiar with the essential elements of the plan without having to read it all. It is typically one to two pages in length and helps readers avoid going through all 40–50 pages of the plan. The goal in writing the executive summary is to capture the reader's attention.

At the minimum, the executive summary of a business plan should include the following components:

 a. Company information: what products or services will be offered, the competitive advantage of the company when it is formed, and background of the founding team
 b. Market opportunity: expected size and growth rate of the target market, expected market share, and any relevant industry trends
 c. Financial data: forecasts or projections for first three to five years of operations, capital structure at startup, and investments that will be needed

It usually takes several drafts to get the executive summary ready for sharing. It is difficult to condense into one or two pages. If the entrepreneur truly understands the business he or she is launching, he or she can explain it clearly and succinctly. A good executive summary is a longer version of the one-minute "elevator pitch" – so named to describe the situation of finding yourself in an elevator with someone to whom you want to explain your business concept quickly and effectively.

Ideally, the executive summary is written after the rest of the business plan is complete. This is because you want to condense the plan into the summary, not expand the summary into a plan. One useful way to generate material for the executive summary is to go through each section of the business plan and highlight key sentences that you think are most important. Then collect all highlighted sentences and try to construct the executive summary around them.

16.3.4 Company Description

This section describes the background of the company, the legal business form chosen to start the company, and the rationale for launching the company. What will the company be doing and why? In other words, what is or will be the purpose of this company? Novices often think that the company's purpose is to make money. Sure, making money is important, but in this section we are talking about what it is that the company will be doing to make money.

A controversial issue pertaining to this section is whether one should also acknowledge setbacks or missteps that occurred on the journey so far. Some believe that it is important to be genuine and represent reality as it happened, while others caution about the dangers of writing the business plan as some sort of therapeutic exercise (and treating the reader as a personal shrink). It is useful to acknowledge major challenges and setbacks that have occurred so far but explain them so that the reader understands the lessons you learned from them.

16.3.4.1 Venture information Each company has the opportunity to identify its own unique mission, vision, and culture. In this section of the business plan, you can articulate the vision of the company (about 10–20 words), describing the "big picture" of what you want the organization to become. The mission statement will describe what the business is about for your customers and employees in a way that tries to concisely capture your passion for the business (about 40–50 words). You can also discuss the culture you want to have in your company, clearly identifying the beliefs, values, and norms that will guide how you want the company to be run.

For many businesses, their location may be vital to success. As a result, many business plans will emphasize the firm's location, with particular attention to issues such as access to customers, suppliers, and employees, relevant regulations or zoning laws, access to distribution and transportation facilities, and parking. You may also include an enlarged local map to help with the reader a visual summary of your location.

16.3.4.2 Management team This section discusses the background and abilities of the individuals launching the company. A good founding team is instrumental in transforming an abstract idea into a successful business. A business needs managers with three types of skills: general management skills, specific technical skills, and work experience. Who will bring these skills and abilities to the business? Assess the number of management positions needed to operate the business and how the business will afford these managers. You may also want to craft precise job descriptions for each position, and then think about where you will find these people.

Upon reading this section of the business plan, a reader should be able to answer the following questions:

1. Who are the founders of the business and where are they from?
2. What is the educational background of the founders? Does their background give them an edge in this business?
3. What work experience do the founders have, and is it relevant to the business?
4. What are the entrepreneur's prior accomplishments? What reputation does the entrepreneur have in the business community?
5. Who else needs to be on the team? Does the entrepreneur have access to these other people?
6. How will high-quality people be recruited for key positions?
7. How committed are the entrepreneurs to this business?
8. What motivated the entrepreneurs to start this business?

16.3.4.3 Products and services This section presents detailed information about your proposed products or service. What are potential uses or applications of the products or services you want to offer? Can the product line be expanded or developed over time? Are the offerings of your company different from the ones currently on the market? Keep in mind that every entrepreneur claims their offerings are superior to those of their competitors, so how will you convey to customers that your quality is indeed better (if it is)? If there are any patents or trademarks associated with the products, mention them too. Include drawings or pictures, where appropriate.

16.3.5 Environmental and Industrial Analysis

This section provides an opportunity to show how the business aligns with the broader context. It is important to put the new venture in an appropriate context by conducting an environmental and industrial analysis to identify external trends that may impact the new firm.

16.3.5.1 Environmental analysis The environmental analysis shows identified events and trends happening in the broader society that may influence the future of the small business. Discuss the political, economic, sociocultural, technological, ecological, and legal aspects of the macro-environment in which the firm operates (see Table 16.3 for PESTEL analysis). Understand and describe the evolving trends and future outlook within these categories. For example, regulatory changes in the three-tier automobile distribution system might be relevant to your business if you have a car dealership. Cultural trends toward organic healthy food may create new opportunities for your small local restaurant but may be problematic if you are a franchisee for a major fast-food corporation such as McDonalds. While small business owners generally do not have much influence on environmental factors, they can try to leverage the changes in the macro-environment

> **TABLE 16.3**
>
> **PESTEL Analysis – A Popular Framework for Organizing Key Factors in Broader Society and Isolating How They Influence Firms**
>
> | | |
> |---|---|
> | **P** | Political factors include things such as trade restrictions and tariffs, government stability, tax policies. |
> | **E** | Economics factors include things such as inflation, interest rates, gross domestic product, unemployment, and growth or decline in the broader economy. |
> | **S** | Social factors include demographic elements such as population size, age, religious-ethnic mix, and cultural trends such as participation of women in the workforce, child care, and consumer safety. |
> | **T** | Technological factors include things such as Internet connectivity, ecommerce, new product development, automation, and scientific advancements. |
> | **E** | Ecological factors encompass elements such as weather patterns, natural disasters, climate change, and pollution. |
> | **L** | Legal factors deal with rules and laws involving issues such as health and safety, employment, discrimination, and competition. |

for their benefit. The environmental analysis describes the entrepreneurs' understanding and assessment of the world in which they operate.

16.3.5.2 Industry analysis The industry analysis describes the industry within which the business operates. A question that often comes up here is how one decides the boundaries for the business. For example, let's say you want to start a small restaurant serving Middle Eastern food, like falafel and gyros. How do you decide whether you are part of the Middle Eastern food sector or the restaurant industry? How do you determine what other businesses or products should be included as part of your industry? Perhaps you can ask potential customers what they consider possible substitutes for a Middle Eastern restaurant. If customers believe that eating Chinese or Tex-Mex or hamburgers is a potential alternative to going for Middle Eastern food, then you may want to define your industry broadly. Once you have defined the industry, identify other major players in the same industry in your geographic coverage area. The geographic area covered by a small business depends on the nature of the business. A restaurant typically has a limited geographic coverage area, which tends to be much more constrained than a consultancy business. What competitive actions and industry-wide trends do you identify in this business?

16.3.5.3 Competitor analysis As part of the environmental and industrial analysis, it is also helpful to present a brief competitor analysis. How are the other players in this business competing? What are their weaknesses that you would be able to take advantage of? What can be done to outcompete other, more established businesses in the industry? Companies that do not pay attention to their rivals will have no inkling of what moves they will be making and will end up flying blind into the market. Gathering competitive intelligence allows a company to craft its own strategic moves with some confidence about what maneuvers to expect from rivals and prepare their own countermoves. A simple template for competitor analysis is presented in Table 16.4.

The environmental and industrial analysis section is quite challenging to write, but it helps you better understand the context within which you will be operating. You will need to cover broad issues and factors in this section but be concise in how you explain them to someone who may or may not know as much about your business. As a small business owner, you need to be knowledgeable about every pertinent factor that could influence your business, though the business plan is not to describe every possible development in detail. The analysis you present here is just the tip of the iceberg; your knowledge of the business should go way deeper than what can be presented in a business plan.

TABLE 16.4					
Template for Competitor Analysis					
Key Attributes	Rival 1	Rival 2	Rival 3	Rival 4	Rival 5
1 Promoters					
2 Product Offerings					
3 Capacity					
4 Pricing					
5 Average/Total Sales					
6 Target Customers					
7 Brochures/Advertising Material					
8 Unique Features					

16.3.5.4 Marketing research and assessment A key question for any small business is: Does a market exist? The section on marketing research and assessment provides information on the market segments you will be targeting and how you will be competitive in those segments. It is important to quantify the market size in units and dollars. Estimates sales by making an informed guess about the units and dollars worth of products you think you can sell. The sales forecast will become the basis for projecting many of your financial statements. Readers will want to know where you got your data from and the techniques you employed to estimate your sales.

Market segmentation and target customers. There are more than 300 million people in America. Are all of them potential customers for all businesses? The obvious answer in most cases is no. This is where market segmentation comes into play. Market segmentation is a marketing term that captures the aggregation of prospective buyers into groups (also called segments) on the basis of shared characteristics such as common needs or tastes. In what market segments are your target customers? Business owners need to figure out what the people who buy their products have in common? The common factor may be a demographic attribute such as age (18–25-year-olds, in college towns) or gender (male–female). It could also be a geographic variable (such as those who live within 5–7 miles of the campus) or a lifestyle marker (e.g. dual-earner families). Consider Hot Yoga Plus, a three-studio yoga business in the southeastern United States. Who do you think is their target market? Would all their locations have the same target market, or would the target customer vary by where the studio is located?

Market trends. There is no denying that consumer tastes change over time. Changes in tastes are more obvious in consumer-based products (or B2C markets) than in industrial products (B2B markets). Depending on what market you are in, you will need to understand how you will assess your customers' needs over time. The challenge with market segmentation is that target customers do not always want the same things. Explain your assessment of current market trends and how you will keep an eye on future trends.

Competition. Of all the possible rivals of your business, identify who you think you will be most concerned about. Who is the price leader or the quality leader? Who has the market cornered? Compare your offerings with the rivals' offerings on the basis of factors that customers consider when they are making decisions about how to buy.

Market share. If you estimate the size of the market and the competitors, you can also estimate the market share – the percentage of total industry sales – that you can realistically expect to gain. The pie chart is an effective visual tool to show market share estimates. For your estimate of market share to be considered realistic, you should also explain how you intend to achieve it. Pricing is, of course, a very important decision in achieving your desired market. The price should allow you to penetrate the market and make profits; right price for a particular product or service will depend on the owner. Most business owners decide on pricing based on either a cost-plus approach or a comparison-to-competitors approach, or a combination of both. The cost-plus approach involves figuring out your cost price, estimating a reasonable profit, and then determining the selling price accordingly. The comparison-to-competitors approach entails looking at competitors' pricing and using that information to decide one's selling price. In both cases, the goal is usually the same: Run a profitable business.

How will the business attract customers and communicate with them? The answer to this question shapes the promotion approach of the new business. Advertising and publicity for the new business can help you get the word out, but business owners also need to think about how they will distinguish themselves in a crowded marketplace. Business owners also need to determine the geographic coverage of the venture, which is the place part of the plan. A business can target local, regional, national, or even global customers, but the distribution channels to service those customers must also be considered (e.g. who will pitch to the customers and how much will it cost?).

16.3.6 Manufacturing and Operations

For most firms, the business plan will include a discussion of manufacturing and operations. This will include facilities, location, estimated space requirements, capital equipment, labor force, purchasing, and inventory control. What kind of facilities does your business need and where? Do you need office and/or warehouse space? Machinery? Are there options to rent, lease, or purchase these facilities? You may be able to buy things from someone who is exiting the business, which would lower your investment in the facilities. You will also need to decide what you will make in-house and what you will buy from others: make-or-buy decision. For example, if you are starting a coffee shop, will you roast your own coffee beans or will you buy roasted coffee beans from someone else? This section will also include a brief discussion of how quality and inventory will be managed in the firm. Do you need to hire skilled or unskilled employees for the venture? If yes, where will you find the employees and how will they be compensated?

16.3.7 Financial Analysis

The financial analysis demonstrates that all the information provided in the earlier parts of the business plan can come together to form a profitable and viable business. The financial section of the business plan is closely scrutinized by many to determine if the business seems financially viable. The projections presented in the **financial statements** should be your best estimates of future operations, and not your aspirations. The financial statements in the business plan should include the following sections:

1. Capital structure
2. Income statement
3. Balance sheet
4. Cash flow statement
5. Break-even analysis
6. Ratio analysis

Let us understand what these sections need to capture before we take a deep dive into how these documents are actually prepared in later chapters.

Capital structure statement. The statement of capital structure shows the various sources of funding for the new business. What part will be debt and what part will be equity? Who will provide this debt and equity?

Income statement. An **income statement**, also referred to as profit-and-loss (P&L) statement, summarizes income and expense activities over a specific period. For a business plan, one generally presents annual income statement, possibly over three years. If the business is already in existence, income statements should be based on actual operations of the firm. If the business is yet to be started, income statements are based on estimate for what the revenues and expenses will be once the business starts. It is helpful to estimate the best-case scenario, worst-case scenario, and most-likely scenario. The goal is to get to the most realistic projections for your business. The worst-case scenario assumes that everything goes as bad as it possibly can, and the best-case scenario assumes that everything will go as well as it possibly can. Your most realistic estimates will fall somewhere between the two extremes. Sales are broken down by product line (or type of service). If you have only one product line, then the income statement will become simplified. Conversely, if you have many products, the income statement will become more complicated. An example of a simple income statement is presented in Table 16.5.

Balance sheet. The **balance sheet** summarizes the various assets owned by the company and the liabilities owed by the company. The difference between assets and liabilities captures what the company has earned so far or the owner's equity in the business. The balance sheet allows readers to compute key financial ratios, such as debt-to-assets and quick ratio (discussed elsewhere in the book), which cast light on the financial condition of the business. It is advisable to have at least three years of balance sheets for the new business. An example of a simple balance sheet is presented in Table 16.6.

Cash flow statement. You have probably heard people say "cash is king." In business, cash flow is paramount. If a firm runs out of cash, it is in serious trouble. As a result, the most important financial statement for a small business is the **cash flow statement**. There are two parts to a cash flow statement: incoming and outgoing. The former adds all the money that comes into the business for a given time period (week, month, quarter) to the opening cash balance (which is the cash balance carried forward from previous financial year); the latter adds money the business spends in the same time period. At the end, you subtract outgoing cash from incoming cash to obtain the closing cash balance. This closing cash balance becomes the opening cash balance for the next time period. An example of a simple cash flow statement is presented in Table 16.7.

It is advisable to develop projected cash flow statements by month for first year of operations and by quarter for the second and third years. Cash flow shows you how

---

TABLE 16.5

Template for Income Statement

	Year 1	Year 2	Year 3
Net Sales Revenue (+)	$	$	$
Cost of Goods Sold (−)	$	$	$
Gross Profit (=)	$	$	$
Operating Expenses (−)	$	$	$
Operating Profit (=)	$	$	$
General Expenses (−)	$	$	$
Other Expenses (−)	$	$	$
Net Income Before Taxes (=)	$	$	$
Taxes (−)	$	$	$
Net Income (=)	$	$	$

TABLE 16.6

Template for Balance Sheet

Balance Sheet for ABC Company

As of Date (Month, Day, Year)

Assets	Year 1	Year 2	Year 3
Cash (+)	$	$	$
Accounts Receivables (+)	$	$	$
Inventory (+)	$	$	$
Capital Equipment (+)	$	$	$
Other Assets (+)	$	$	$
Total Assets (=)	$	$	$
Liabilities			
Short-term Liabilities (+)	$	$	$
Long-term Liabilities (+)	$	$	$
Total Liabilities (=)	$	$	$
Owner's Equity	$	$	$

TABLE 16.7

Template for Cash Flow Statement

Cash Flow Calculations	
Starting Cash	(+) $
Cash In from Sales	(+) $
Cash Out from Operations (COGS, Expenses, Taxes)	(_) $
Cash In from Investing (Equity, Earnings on Investment)	(+) $
Cash Out against Investing (Equipment Purchases, Investors Repayments)	(_) $
Cash In from Financing (Loans)	(+) $
Cash Out against Financing (Debt Repayment)	(_) $
Ending Cash Balance (Starting Balance for Next Period)	(=) $

much working capital the business will have at a given point. The cash flow is very important for businesses where sales are seasonal or cyclical.

Break-even analysis. The point at which gross sales exactly equals total costs is called the **break-even point**. As such, break-even analysis refers to the computation of how many units (or dollars worth) of the products or services will need to be sold to cover all costs. It gives an idea of how many units will need to be sold for the firm to not be in a loss. Calculating the break-even point will help demonstrate whether there is a viable market for your business. For example, Jasper, AR, is a small town with a population of about 460 people. If a firm needs to sell 500 units in this small town, one may need to reconsider the business plan. One calculates breakeven as follows:

$$\frac{\text{Fixed cost (\$)}}{\text{Gross profit per unit (S)}} = \text{Break-even units}$$

Ratio analysis. It is helpful to understand the business performance relative to industry peers based on standard ratios such as gross profit, net profit, return on assets

(ROA), return on equity (ROE), quick ratio, current ratio, debt-to-assets, and inventory turnover. By comparing the performance of your business over time and looking at others in the industry, you can assess how well the firm is doing. Such a comparison also helps you adjust the way the firm is managed. Table 16.8 provides a summary of the various ratios one can use for this part of the financial analysis.

16.3.8 Critical Assumptions and Risks

All business plans are based on certain assumptions. What assumptions does your business plan make? For Jeff Bezos of Amazon, a key assumption was the high growth rate in Internet penetration. Another key assumption he made was that people would be willing to buy on the Internet.

What are the risk factors in this business? Every business has some risk factors. The risk factors for your business could be related to personnel (severe health issues with the founder, maybe) or industry (e.g. federal regulation about toxicity of a key input), or any of the other 10,000 things that most people don't often think about.

Most of us do not like to think about the threats or weaknesses that can hold us back. But acknowledging these risk factors helps you prepare better for the future. Possible risk factors that you may consider are as follows:

1. *Price and quality.* Are the competitors likely to underprice you or offer a far superior product?
2. *Irregular supply of products or raw materials.* Do any of your raw materials or parts come from socially unstable or conflict-stricken areas? If yes, are you prepared for the possibility of disruption in your supplies?

TABLE 16.8

Common Ratios

Gross profit margin	$\dfrac{\text{Sales} - \text{cost of goods sold}}{\text{Sales}}$	Shows the percentage of revenues available to cover operating expenses and yield a profit. Higher is better, and the trend should be upward
Net profit margin	$\dfrac{\text{Profits after taxes}}{\text{Sales}}$	Shows after-tax profits per dollar of sales. Higher is better, and the trend should be upward
Return on assets	$\dfrac{\text{Profits after taxes} + \text{interest}}{\text{Total assets}}$	Captures return on total investment in the business. Interest is added to after-tax profits to form the numerator since total assets are financed by creditors, as well as by owners. Higher is better, and the trend should be upward
Return on equity	$\dfrac{\text{Profits after taxes}}{\text{Total owner's equity}}$	Shows the return owners are earning on their investment in the firm. Trend should be upward
Current ratio	$\dfrac{\text{Current assets}}{\text{Current liabilities}}$	Shows a firm's ability to pay current liabilities using assets that can be converted to cash in the near term. Ratio should definitely be higher than 1.0, ratios of 2 or higher are even better
Quick ratio (or acid-test ratio)	$\dfrac{\text{Current assets} - \text{inventory}}{\text{Current liabilities}}$	Shows a firm's ability to pay current liabilities without relying on the sale of its inventories
Debt-to-assets ratio	$\dfrac{\text{Total debt}}{\text{Total assets}}$	Measures the extent to which borrowed funds are used to finance the firm's operations. High fractions indicate the overuse of debt and greater risk of bankruptcy; low fractions or ratios are better
Inventory turnover	$\dfrac{\text{Cost of goods sold}}{\text{Inventory}}$	Measures the number of inventory turns per year. Higher is better
Average collection period	$\dfrac{\text{Accounts receivable}}{\text{Total sales} / 365}$	Indicates average length of time the firm must wait after making a sale to receive cash payment. Shorter collection time is better

3. *Unreliable sales forecasts.* What was the basis for your sales projections? Be prepared for the possibility that the market does not develop as quickly as you predict. You would be surprised at how many entrepreneurs overestimate the market for their products. There is a real possibility that no one is willing to buy your product in the beginning. Yet, what if the market develops faster than you expected? Growth slower than expected is a problem, and so is growth faster than expected. How prepared is the company to deal with sales forecasts that are way off the mark?

4. *Workers with the right training are not available.* Does your business require skilled personnel with specialized training? Have you considered the possibility that such workers may not be available at the price you are willing to pay?

Interactive Exercise

Visit the website https://www.bplans.com/sample_business_plans.php. Identify a sample business plan that is similar to the business you want to start. Based on your reading, can you identify three things that would help strengthen your own business plan?

16.3.9 Appendix

Business plans often have supplemental information and documents that are not crucial but may still be of interest to the reader. Such documents are included in the appendix. This includes resumes of owners and key executives, brochures, technical catalogs, samples, floor plan, and any related information. Different types of information should each be put in a separate appendix and labeled sequentially (e.g. Appendix I, Appendix II). Each appendix will be identified in the table of contents.

When a business plan is created, it must be thought of as a work in progress because things will often deviate from the plan. When things do not go according to the plan, there is no reason to despair. Yet, because things rarely go fully according to the plan, the formal business plan document has been replaced in some settings. There are four alternatives to business plan worth discussing here. The **business brief** is a three-to-four-page document outlining the most salient aspects of the venture, typically providing an overview of the company and discussing the value proposition, customers, and milestones. A key benefit of the business brief is that it gives you an at-a-glance understanding of the entrepreneur and the business. The **feasibility study** is an eight-to-ten-page document that focuses on the skills of the entrepreneur, the size of the market, and the main rivals, suppliers, and customers for the firm. The main objective of the feasibility study is to assess the viability of a business concept to determine whether your idea is workable and profitable. The **elevator pitch** (also called elevator speech) is a verbal explanation that should convey to the listener in an engaging way the essentials of what the entrepreneur is proposing. It is a brief persuasive spiel (usually one to two minutes) that explains the basic business concept in a way that the listener can understand it in a short period of time. The **pitch deck** is a presentation of the essential elements of a business plan in a way that seeks to excite your audience about the potential of the business. A pitch deck may be anywhere from 10 to 20 slides, or even longer depending on the audience you are targeting.

When writing a business plan, there are an almost unlimited number of resources that offer extensive guidance, including step-by-step instructions. An online search for "business plan software" will reveal many options, such as Bizplan (www.bizplan.com) and LivePlan (www.liveplan.com). There are also many books and websites that you can refer for ideas and insights on putting together a business plan or preparing an elevator pitch for your business. Despite all these resources, only the business owner really knows what should (or not) be in the plan. If you don't know, there is no need to panic. Start writing a business plan and work on learning about the various things you need to learn to prepare a good plan.

Comprehension Check

1. What are the reasons for writing a business plan?
2. What are the various parts of a business plan?
3. What are the different financial statements that should be included in a business plan?

Module 16.4 Customizing the Business Plan

A good business plan should be customized to match the company's situation. There are at least four situations in which it makes sense to write a plan with particular emphasis in mind.

> **KEY TAKEAWAY**
>
> A good business plan should be customized to match the company's situation.

A pioneering business. Some businesses have offerings that are truly new to the world. When your product or service is absolutely new to everyone, it is considered a **pioneering business**. For entrepreneurs launching such businesses, the challenges are how to: (a) explain their offerings to people, (b) show the usage of the product, (c) estimate the number of people willing to adopt the product, and (d) understand what people would be willing to pay for it. Anything that can be done to help people experience or see the product in action will help demystify it. Pilot tests, test marketing, or preselling are all essential to launching a pioneering business. Make sure the business plan explains the benefits customers will receive and shares some customers' personal experiences in using the product. Letters from manufacturers and competent technical people can be very useful in alleviating concerns that the proposed project cannot be viably manufactured.

A new entrant business. If the product or service already exists, but the company is a first of its kind in its specific market, it is considered a **new entrant business**. Entrepreneurs who launch new entrant businesses have trouble communicating the merit of their ventures to skeptical customers. This problem is exacerbated if another firm has failed previously trying to bring the same offering to the market. It will be useful to discuss how the product or service has done in other markets, especially markets similar to the ones where it is now being launched. Seeing that the product or service has worked elsewhere, but especially in a culturally similar market, can assuage some of the concerns about the viability of the business.

An existing business. Many times a business starts before the entrepreneur has put together a plan for it. Writing a business plan for an existing business has several benefits. The company already has a history, there is an existing market, and the firm has some financial track record. This information gives you a firm foundation for the business plan, and projections about future markets, sales, and profits can be built on historical information. At the same time, putting together a business plan for an existing business comes with its own challenges. Past performance, they say, is the best predictor of future performance. So, if the business has struggled so far, it becomes all the more difficult to put forth a convincing rationale for why it will do well in the future.

Businesses with significant regulations. Some entrepreneurs start businesses with offerings that are heavily regulated. Consider, for example, the following description of the US dairy industry:

> The U.S. dairy sector is also characterized by heavy government intervention. U.S. dairy policies center on four major areas: federal marketing orders, federal price supports, dairy compacts, and international trade policy. . . . U.S. trade measures restrict imports mainly through the imposition of TRQs. . . . TRQs apply to fluid milk as well as processed and high value-added products. High over-quota tariff rates restrict imports within quota levels, except under exceptional market conditions.[1]

You may be wondering what are TRQs. TRQ refers to **tariff-rate quota**, which means that a very small amount of the product can be imported at low or zero tariffs, but above that the rate is kept so high that for all practical purposes the imports cease (restricting imports is usually the primary purpose of high tariffs anyway). If you are in a dairy sector, you need to be aware of TRQs and other vocabulary that is used by dairy firms. The message here is that if your business is in a sector that is heavily regulated, the business plan should reflect a sound understanding of the regulations in that area. Further, if the business involves working with the government, such as is the case for business licensing, ecological impact, or zoning, one can expect things to take longer than expected. In such cases, the business plan needs to anticipate delays and explain how things will move if the government side of things does not come in time.

What Do You Think?

Alejandra Sanchez has an idea for a food truck that serves Korean barbecue-style tacos near your campus. Is there another eatery offering similar food in your town? If Alejandra was to put together a business plan, what are some specific issues that she needs to keep in mind in writing the business plan?

16.4.1 Things to Watch Out for in Business Plans

The philosopher-writer George Santayana is reported to have said that "those who do not learn from history are bound to repeat it." His point is that we should learn from the mistakes of others if we want to avoid making them ourselves. Writing business plans is no exception. People who read business plans for a living – bankers and investors, for example – assess hundreds of business plans each year looking for reasons to reject the proposals that come their way. By noticing common mistakes, they are able to weed out potentially risky investments and focus their attention on proposals that are most organized, focused, and realistic.

What can an entrepreneur do to stay out of the reject pile and make it to the one that says "accept"? How can one put together a business plan that conveys the owner's financial and professional knowledge in a positive light? Avoiding common mistakes is very helpful.

Overstated numbers. It is not uncommon for entrepreneurs to be overconfident and overoptimistic. As a result, they often see "blue skies and rainbows" even when it is overcast and cloudy. Inflated numbers in the financial statements that have no grounding in reality can make readers skeptical of all claims made in the business plans.

---

[1]Mother Jones, US Trade Policy on Dairy Is Simple: We Basically Allow No Imports at All.

Numbers that are plain wrong. It is quite common to see business plans where the numbers do not match in the different sections. This often happens when no one has taken the trouble to go back and read through the entire document to make sure things are consistent across the different parts of the business plan.

Outdated information. Be as current as you can be in the information you present in the business plan. A business plan presented in 2020 should not be using demand or supply numbers from 2010.

Avoid techno-jargon. People who really know their material are able to explain it so well that readers and listeners do not need to stress themselves to understand its meaning. If you have trouble expressing your thoughts in common language in the business plan, how will you eventually market your product?

Insufficient cushion. It is well known that new firms often spend themselves to death. It means that new firms usually run out of cash before they run out of ideas. Providing enough cash to survive the first six months will be very helpful in avoiding the risk of premature death.

Misunderstanding financial information. Entrepreneurs can always pay accountants to prepare financial statements, but understanding and accurately interpreting the statements is critical to the entrepreneurial function.

Thinking you are the only player in the game. Just because you are going to start this business does not mean customers will line up to buy your offerings and competitors will roll over without a fight. Think about how you would get customers to buy from you and not your rival. This is usually far more difficult than what most people believe.

Avoiding or disguising negative aspects. Most of us ignore or disguise potential problems. It is therefore not surprising that businesses find it difficult to think about potential weaknesses and threats. If the business plan does not mention possible problems, or whitewashes them, it gives the impression that the founding team is either ignorant or deceptive. Both perceptions are bad for nascent ventures.

No personal equity in the company. You did not invest any of your own money in the business? If you do not have the confidence to invest in your own venture, why should someone else have confidence in your business? It's hard to bank on someone who doesn't have any skin in the game. A vested interest in the business will help outsiders see that you will put your heart and soul into making the business succeed.

Still in the rough. When you present someone with a business plan, you are asking them to make a leap of faith that you can successfully run this business. As a result, business plans that do not look professional (e.g. have scratched-out words, loose sheets, or coffee stains) undermine the reader's confidence in your ability to succeed. If the business plan does not look professional, will the entrepreneur who put it together be able to run the venture professionally?

Experience deficits. When someone reads your business plan, do they see that you (or someone else in the team) has the experience to make this business successful? It is important that the entrepreneur has experience in either the line of business or the industry or in managing a business *per se*, or preferably some combination of both. It is a common misconception that one does not need experience to start a business. Without at least some experience, your chances of success decrease considerably and the chances of failure increase greatly.

Interactive Exercise

Google "mistakes in the business plan" and skim through as many Web pages as you are willing to read. Based on your reading, identify the top five most commonly discussed business plan mistakes. What does this reading exercise add to your knowledge of mistakes that people frequently make in business plans?

What does an investor think makes a "fantastic business plan"?

1. The plan is concise and accurate. It is considered by everyone daily. It is seen as a constant guide to high performance and corporate success.
2. The plan defines very precisely who the customers are, by the numbers, with specific, measurable demographics. Management knows everything about their buyers including what they watch, read, and hear. It knows what people will pay for their products or services. It knows why people need to buy; the emotional components as well as the utilitarian purposes.
3. Management knows the industry like the back of their hands. It knows everything about the competition and what they are doing.
4. Management understands industry trends and are forward thinking. It is able to forecast what people might purchase in the future even before the customer knows he or she will need it.
5. Management has conceived, developed and manufactured exactly what the customer needs. It has built products with features and benefits that differentiate themselves from competing product offerings.
6. Management has set specific priorities with key objectives they will achieve via the correct resources.
7. Management has developed sound, repeatable and time-tested processes that yield high efficiency and productivity.
8. Management has all the right people on the bus, with measurable tasks and rewards. Everyone has participated in developing their individual plans that are aligned to achieve their goals and the overall objectives of the organization.
9. The financial plan is defensible and accurate. There are backup plans in the event of unseen consequences.
10. Management meets regularly to evaluate their progress and the progress of each organization within the business. They report to all employees, often.
11. The company has a strong culture based on teamwork, innovation, client and employee satisfaction, integrity, results and hard work.

Source: From https://www.forbes.com/sites/alanhall/2012/08/26/how-to-build-a-billion-dollar-business-plan-10-top-points-2/#5520f2a512a2

EXHIBIT 16.1 Tips for Writing a Good Business Plan

It is highly advisable to have someone else review the plan before you start circulating it to others. Family members and friends are a good starting point to obtain some feedback on your business plans. There are also many outside resources that you can use to get some independent and critical eyes on the business plan. The free consultants from the Service Corps of Retired Executives (**SCORE**) is available via www.score.org. There is also the Small Business Development Center (SBDC), who can help you through their local chapter (www.sba.gov/sbdc). In addition, your entrepreneurship and small business professor may also be willing to give you feedback (especially, if you do well in their class). Exhibit 16.1 discusses the various elements that make a business plan attractive to an investor.

Comprehension Check

1. What are the different situations for which a business plan may be customized?
2. What are things to watch out for in writing a business plan?
3. What is SCORE and how does it help entrepreneurs?

Summary

Starting a business is like going on a vacation – you are unlikely to get anywhere worthwhile without some planning ahead of time. Planning is an essential ingredient of a successful business. Although we all create mental plans, those thoughts need to be documented or presented, preferably in a systematic manner, before starting a new business or undertaking growth efforts for a new business. In trying to document our thoughts, we are forced to clarify our thinking and better articulate our unstated assumptions. When our thoughts are clearer, we are able to better explain them, in writing and verbally. Many successful small business owners know that they must not only think deeply about their plans for the business, they also need to put it in writing and present before others as to make their thinking clearer and get feedback from others. A business plan can help the owners identify omissions and gaps in their thinking, which makes them better prepared for the future.

World of Books

The Lean Startup by Eric Ries
Business Model Generation: A Handbook for Visionaries, Game Changers, and Challengers by Alexander Osterwalder and Yves Pigneur
How to Write a Business Plan by Mike McKeever

In the Movies

Carl Casper is a head chef at a prestigious Los Angeles restaurant, where he finds himself in conflict with the owner. The reason: Carl wants to make innovative dishes, while the owner wants him to focus on classics. When Carl is pushed too far, he quits his job and travels with his ex-wife and estranged son to Miami, where he rediscovers his love for Cuban cuisine. He starts a food-truck business, driving across the country to Los Angeles, serving Cuban food. His son promotes the business on social media. The business is successful and Carl is invited to start a new restaurant where he will have complete creative control. After watching the movie *Chef*, you should be able to put together a business model canvas and a business plan for the food truck or the restaurant that Carl starts.

Live Exercise

Johnny Gold is ecstatic. He recently got a call from a leading venture capital (VC) firm that wants to hear about his business. If they like what he is doing, they may make a sizable investment in the company, which will help Johnny grow the company and earn a solid return on his investment. Johnny has asked you for help with putting together the material he will need to impress the potential financiers. Specifically, he wants to put together the following:

1. Business Model Canvas
2. Business Plan
3. Business Brief
4. Elevator Pitch
5. Pitch Deck

Can you put together these documents to help Johnny with impressing financiers in the work he is doing with SoapStandle? If there is anything else that you think will help Johnny, you can add those to the list too.

Things to Remember

LO 16.1 Explain what a business plan is and why it is helpful for a firm to have it

- A business plan is a written document that sets out your thinking about how enough products or services can be sold at a profit to form the bases for a viable enterprise.
- Starting a business is like going on a vacation. If you are like most people, you need to make some plans and consider whether you have adequate resources to last the trip.
- Causation involves thinking about where you want to be and then considering the resources you will need to get there. Those who subscribe to causation thinking are likely to start with a specific business idea.
- Effectuation involves thinking about the resources you have and where they can take you. Those who subscribe to causation thinking will usually start with the decision to have their own business.
- The way the world thinks about business plans has changed over the years.
- The strong logic of business planning stipulates that entrepreneurs come up with a potentially very good idea, write detailed plans for what would take to get the idea to the market, go out to raise funds by pitching to various investors, and only then start building products they would sell based on their market research in order to achieve profitability.
- The weak logic of business planning focuses on figuring out possible options to pursue based on the resources one has (or can access) and eliminate unviable ones.

LO 16.2 Recognize the importance of a (sound) business model

- Business model canvas is a template for articulating novel or existing business models and focuses on how the venture creates value for customers and the owners.
- A business model defines the nuts and bolts of the business. A business model explains in a clear and systematic manner how a business brings in revenue and how it spends money.
- Most people think of a company's business model as based on the user's paying for a company's product(s), but this is not always the case. Users do not always pay, as the company may make money from other sources.
- The business model provides good evidence as to whether the idea can be translated into a viable, profitable business and the kind of investment required to make it happen.
- The business model canvas comprises 10 building blocks: promoters, offering, customer segments, channels, customer relations, key resources, key activities, key partnerships, cost structure, and revenue stream.

LO 16.4 Outline the different parts of a business plan

- An executive summary is a short overview of the entire plan.
- At a minimum, the executive summary of a business plan should provide company information, market opportunity, and financial information.
- Ideally, the executive summary is written after the rest of the business plan is done.

- Company information includes the background of the company, the legal business form chosen to start the company, and the rationale for launching the company.
- The section on management team discusses the background and abilities of the individuals launching the company.
- Detailed information about your proposed products or service needs to be part of the business plan.
- The section on environmental and industrial analysis is an opportunity to show how the business aligns with the broader context.
- The section on marketing research and assessment provides information on the kind(s) of marketing you are targeting and how you will be competitive in that market.
- For most firms, the business plan will include a discussion of manufacturing and operations.
- A timeline for when major events and activities are expected to happen for the business should be generated.
- All business plans are based on certain assumptions, and those assumptions should be shared in the plan.
- Risk factors need to be identified and discussed in the business plan.
- Good business plans identify the value their business will create for the community and society.
- Financial statements demonstrate that all the information provided in the earlier parts of the business plan can come together to form a profitable and viable business.
- The appendix of a business plan presents supplemental information and documents that are not crucial but may still be of interest to the reader.

LO 16.4 Discuss how to make a business plan fit well with your needs
- Business plans need to be customized to match the company's situation.
- Depending on whether you are a pioneering business, a new entrant business, an existing business, or a business with significant regulations will influence how the business plan is written.
- Common mistakes in a business plan include overstated or incorrect numbers, outdated information, usage of techno-jargon, insufficient financial cushion, misunderstanding the financial information, avoiding or dismissing bad news, obvious experience deficits of the management team, and lack of editing and polishing the written document.
- It is useful to have someone else – friends and family, experienced executives, professionals, and advisors – review the plan before you start circulating it to others.

Key Terms

business plan	weak logic	income statement	elevator pitch
goal-driven or causation	pivot	balance sheet	pitch deck
means-driven or effectuation	morph	cash flow statement	pioneering business
strong logic	business model canvas	break-even point	new entrant business
lean startup	freemium	business brief	tariff-rate quotas
	financial statements	feasibility study	SCORE

Experiential Exercise

This exercise should be done by individuals working on their own. The professor may assign students to buddy up with someone else to get initial feedback on the idea they are developing.

Is there a business you have always wanted to start? If not, pick up the latest issue of the *Inc.* magazine and look through the new businesses they profile until you come to a business that you like. Is this a business someone like you can start? If not, keep looking until you come to something you can start.

Once you have an idea for a business you want to start or can start, discuss it with someone else in class. Tell them what the business is and why you want to start it. Listen carefully to their feedback and take notes on what their questions or concerns are. Now prepare a business model canvas that summarizes your business idea. Fill out all 10 cells of the business model canvas,

highlighting in green the cells you feel most confident about, in red the cells you believe are a weak point in your canvas, and in yellow the cells that you are unsure about. Get feedback from your professor on your canvas and improve as needed.

Prepare a one-minute pitch for your business idea. When outlining the pitch, keep in mind that it should explain what the business idea is, why it makes sense for you to pursue that idea, and how you are going to address that idea in a profitable manner.

At this stage, it would be a good exercise to put together a formal business plan for the venture that you want to start. Alternatively, if you already have your own business, you can put together a business plan that describes how you plan to grow the firm.

Harvesting the Business

Most entrepreneurs – perhaps the majority – initiate a business without much thought to how they will eventually exit it.

DAWN R. DETIENNE

17.0 Introduction

All business owners have one thing in common: They will one day leave the business. Some owners will sell the business, others may close it down, and some will die. Exit is a necessary aspect of business ownership. When it comes to the issue of exit, the question is not if, but when. Every owner must exit their business at some point in time. More than 40% of the 30.7 million small business owners in the United States are 55 or older. Many began with a dream and spent decades fulfilling it, raising children along the way, some of whom joined them at the counter or warehouse. Their businesses are often a part of the local community and provide jobs and gathering spots for neighbors. Yet each of these business owners will exit the business sooner or later.

The focus of this chapter is on a specific type of business exit: harvest. Once the firm is harvested, the business owner is usually no longer involved in it. Not every business can be successfully harvested. Some are loaded with debt or do not offer products or services of lasting value. Some experts say that it takes at least 10 years for a business to reach a point at which it can be harvested, although there is no hard and fast rule about how long it might take. With that in mind, let us now move to systematically studying when and how a business owner can harvest his or her firm.

SPOTLIGHT | A Win–Win Exit: The Shara Mendelson Story

Raised in a competitive school system where tracked career paths were the norm, Shara Mendelson wanted to go to an Ivy-league school, head to Wall Street, get an MBA, and live the dream. Instead, after graduating from Middlebury College in Vermont, Shara found herself working in the accounts department of a major advertising agency. It was a coveted job, but Shara was disappointed and miserable. There were no mentors, no simulating projects, and the work was dull and boring.

Bored with her accounting job, Shara ended up starting a business that she sold after building it.

Her father, who had recently become involved with a nonprofit theater company, asked if she would help them stuff envelopes on the weekend. There, she met struggling actors and playwrights, all working at least two jobs. Despite economic hardships, they seemed to be passionate about their work. They were working for something that they cared about, and at 23, Shara liked the idea of finding passion in work. Soon, she quit her job and devoted herself full-time to marketing theater and Broadway shows. The work was difficult because resources were limited and there was little awareness among potential audiences about theater, but Shara enjoyed it.

A desire to help passionate theater folks generate new streams of ticket sales was the genesis of the idea for Plum Benefits, which provides millions of corporate employees with discounts to live entertainment sales. The business grew, and 12 years later, Shubert Organization, America's oldest professional theater company and the largest theater owner on Broadway, wanted to buy her out. Shara was excited her company would now be able to tap into the resources of a much larger organization. Her employees saw the acquisition as offering better benefits, greater prospects for advancement, and more support to do their work.

There was one problem though. Shubert wanted Shara to stay at least a year to help with the acquisition and continue running her business. Her employees liked the idea of her staying through the acquisition. They thought if she stayed, it would help them integrate into the new operations. Her friends, who had sold companies in the past, told her that hanging around after the buyout can be a nightmare. "A lot of my friends said it was going to be the worst year of my life," she recalls. She would have to play by someone else's rules and would not have a say in management. Her own company would become a division of a large corporation, where decisions would take longer to make and require approval from senior managers. Perhaps she could stay for a few months and then leave. She could also negotiate revenue goals, and maybe even have hiring and firing authority.

The money Shara would receive from selling the business was good and enough for her to have a comfortable life. At the same time, Shara never really saw money as the primary motivating factor in her life. She needed to make some decisions soon, but it was unclear what path she should take.

Discussion Questions

1. What led Shara to start her own business?
2. Why did Shara think selling to Shubert would be a win–win for everyone?
3. What post-exit arrangements do you think Shara should make with Shubert?

Module 17.1 Approaches to Harvesting a Business

At a basic level, harvesting is a method to cash out of an ownership position in a company. Not all exits are harvests; all harvests are, however, exits. Consider two factors: (a) an owner can exit a business either by sale or by **liquidation**; (b) a business may be performing well or it may be performing poorly. Intersecting these two factors gives us four possible outcomes: harvest sale (high-performing firm, exit by sale), harvest liquidation (high-performance firm, exit by liquidation), distress sale (low-performance firm, exit by sale), and distress liquidation (low-performance sale, exit by liquidation) (see Figure 17.1). In firms performing poorly, owners exit under distress to salvage whatever they can from the business. In firms performing well, owners exit so as to reap a positive value from their investment.

Consider the case of David Karangu, a graduate of Morgan State University in Baltimore. During his college years, David interned at a Chevrolet dealership; after graduation, he began working for the Ford Motor Company at various dealerships located in Florida and Detroit. A few years later, and with the help of Ford's program to help minorities buy dealerships, David became the owner of his first dealership with a partner, a nonminority dealer in Augusta, GA, and a good friend. David and his partner bought one more dealership together, and David also grew his business aggressively by buying his own dealerships without a partner. Just after his 40th birthday, someone from a large, publicly traded holding company for car dealerships called David's office wanting to buy his entire portfolio of dealerships. Before this call, David had never thought about his exit and declared that he was not interested in selling. The caller countered with an offer of a very large amount of money. When David told his wife what had happened and the sum of money on the table, she immediately said, "Sell!" Negotiations went on for about six months, concluding with all-cash sale of David's business. At age 40, David was wealthier than he had ever dreamed.

The remainder of this chapter focuses on harvest sale and harvest liquidation. It does not include distress sale and distress liquidation, both of which are related to failure, since the business was not able to succeed, did not achieve its economic goals, and had to cease operations because it ran out of money.

		Firm performance	
		Good	**Poor**
Exit route	Exit by sale	Harvest sale	Distress sale
	Exit by liquidation	Harvest liquidation	Distress liquidation

FIGURE 17.1 Harvesting a Business

David Karangu built a small chain of car dealerships that he then sold to a large, publicly traded company.

Astute students will notice that the four-pronged classification of exit does not cover owners who hand over the business to the next generation (exit by succession), a topic which has already been covered in the chapter on family business. It also does not discuss the situation where the owner decides to simply stop reinvesting the profits to grow the business, and instead diverts all the cash flows to the owners. When owners exit by withdrawing as much cash as possible from the business and liquidating the remainder of the assets, they do not need to seek out a buyer or bear the expenses associated with selling the business. At the same time, the disadvantage of not investing in the business is that the firm gradually weakens until it is no longer able to compete in the market. The gradual weakening of the firm reduces its value and may be difficult to reverse if the owners change their mind at a later time.

What Do You Think?

Ajay Walia is owner of Pizza & Pipes in Redwood City, CA. He had bought the place for $200,000, but six years later was ready to sell it for $170,000 because sales were slumping. There were no buyers at that price, and another three years later, he had it back on the market for $75,000 and a soft loan to the buyer for 25% of the sale price. "There's a time when you have to bite the bullet and move on," he says. Of the four approaches to harvesting a business discussed here, which one do you think most fits Ajay's situation?

There are two distinct ways in which owners of private firms can harvest their investment: (a) sell the firm and (b) private equity recapitalization.

17.1.1 Harvest Through Sale of the Firm

A common harvest strategy for successful business owners is to sell the firm. When considering selling the business, the most important question to ask oneself is WHY. As in, why do you want to sell the business that took years of blood, sweat and tears to build? When answering this question, business owners need to be brutally honest. Many experts believe that if the only reason to sell is for money, then the entrepreneur may not be ready to sell the business yet. Netflix was only a year-old, and still an unprofitable firm searching for a repeatable and scalable business model, when Amazon offered to buy it for about $16–18 million, but Reed Hastings and Marc Randolph declined to sell it because "it didn't seem like the right moment to give up." When considering the sale of the company, the owners should carefully identify their reason for wanting to sell the company. If they are not convinced it's the right time or reason to sell, then they should continue working on the business.

Consider the case of John and Samantha, a married couple in their 60s. They run a small business that's more than 30 years old and makes about $4 million in sales annually. They earn a combined $200,000 a year in salary from the business. The company also pays for their health insurance, company cars, many restaurant meals, additional benefits that added up to another $150,000 yearly for them. If they sell, they need to either sell it for an amount that allows them to make about $350,000 annually or downsize to reduce their expenses. They also have the option not to sell, and instead try to run the business in a way that reduces their involvement as they get older and yet brings them the kind of money they need to sustain their upper middle-class lifestyle.

If you want to sell your business someday, you need to start the planning several years before you are ready to sell. Run the business as if a buyer will come along at any moment. "Whether it's now, 5 years or 10 years down the road, if you're not ready and that buyer comes, you may not get that price that you want," says Karen Reynolds Sharkey, national business owner strategy executive at U.S. Trust. Owners also need to regularly review how the business is doing relative to its competitors. Matt Matich, who ran a trucking distribution company, sold it when he felt the business was unable to provide the kinds of services that clients were expecting and other firms in the industry were already providing those services. Some owners scale back their businesses in anticipation of selling them. Such an approach can, however, greatly reduce the sales price. Buyers want potential, but they pay for history. A business that has been declining in client numbers will not get the right price or necessarily appeal to buyers. Businesses with formalized processes sell better than firms that are run in a more casual fashion. Many small business owners do not maintain good books, make sales off-the-books, or pay employees in cash, making it difficult for an outsider to accurately value the business.

KEY TAKEAWAY

If you want to sell your business someday, you should start the planning several years before you are ready to sell.

For business owners committed to sell, potential buyers can come from a number of places. When a business that is doing well is on the market, there are many potential buyers: suppliers, customers, competitors, employees, family, or friends. Businesses may sell through brokers, classified advertising, or direct to someone the owner already knows. A **business broker** is a professional intermediary who assists in the buying and selling of firms. The International Business Brokers Association (www.ibba.org) is a US-based community of commercial brokers who help buy and sell businesses. Of course, brokers can be expensive, as they charge a hefty commission (about 8–12%) when the sale is consummated. Also, not all brokers are equally honest, with some brokers bringing utmost sincerity and integrity to their work and others behaving unprofessionally, making false claims, and presenting misleading or false information. As is the case with buying a house, it is useful to inquire around about the broker before you sell through them.

Interactive Activity

Visit the website of International Business Brokers Association (www.ibba.org). Using the search option available on the main page, find business brokers in your area. Call a business broker to ask them about what kind of sellers they represent and if they can share with you some examples of businesses they have helped sell in recent years. Make sure to tell them you are a college student, so they feel more motivated to answer your questions.

When the owners of Ocean Liquors LLC in Boca Raton, FL, decided to sell, they selected Transworld Business Brokers LLC of Ft. Lauderdale to find them a buyer. The brokerage firm found them a buyer, Donna Merelli, who had lost her office-manager job at a mill when it went out of business. Donna was able to negotiate $50,000 less than the initial asking price, secure a $100,000 loan from the seller to be paid back within five years at 7% interest, and use her savings to cover the balance. Why did Donna want to buy the business? The alcohol industry is "somewhat recession-proof," she says. "When times are bad people drink, and when times are good people drink."

Many owners and brokers use classified advertisements in newspapers and magazines to sell businesses (see Figure 17.2).

When a business is sold, the owner makes money, but there's more to selling the business than just making the most money you can. Many business owners have a deep attachment to the company, so that when the business is sold, they feel lost and purposeless. For others, the buyer may have paid well but is not the right person to run the

FIGURE 17.2 Typical Classified Advertisements Selling Businesses

firm. Rick Spilde thought he was done with his green energy company, Essential Energy Services, when he and his partner sold it to an investment firm in Texas, where the company was based. "Our company was at a plateau," he said. "We needed more management or more sales staff. We were maxing out our capacity." He consulted for the investment group for two years and then moved to Florida to retire. But then the company began to fail. Rick and his partner bought back their company, paying far less than they sold it for, and put a professional management team in place. "The first time around, we were trying to build the company," he says. "The second time around, we're as busy, or busier, than before but we're letting our employees run the company. This time, if we go to sell it, we have some really key people in place who aren't owners and that means the company will survive."

17.1.2 Sales to Rivals

A possible buyer for a thriving existing business is its competitor. Competitors already know the market, are likely already qualified to buy the business, and will be more successful in securing financing when purchasing a company in an industry they know well. In most cases, the seller also already knows quite a bit about the potential buyer from prior interactions and mutual suppliers or customers. Competitors may want to buy the business for several reasons: increase market share, gain access to more and/or better equipment or facilities, acquire highly skilled and competent employees, and increase return on investment.

There are three types of competitors who may be interested in buying your business: **Direct rivals** who compete with you head to head on product, service, and price. **Indirect rivals** compete with you on some products or services, but not on your full line of products and services. **Near rivals** are companies that compete in a different territory and seldom operate in your area, so you rarely cross paths with them. Not all competitors are genuine buyers as many are simply looking to acquire the seller's knowledge (e.g. customer lists, profit margins), thereby gaining competitive advantage over someone who is thinking of selling his or her business.

Buying a competitor's business also poses challenges for the buyer. "The real issue is for the competitor buying the business," says Adam Scavone, managing attorney at Scavone Law. "The buyer needs to worry that the seller will go back into business as a competitor the next day. That situation can be disastrous for the buyer, who likely spent a lot of time, money and energy clearing the field of an existing competitor. Getting the seller's agreement not to compete is imperative. Any buyer who goes ahead with the sale of a business without getting a comprehensive agreement from the seller not to compete is playing with fire," he said.

17.1.3 Sales to Employees

For some business owners, selling to employees is one way to exit their business. Employees understand the business and industry well. Customers and suppliers also already know the employees, so there is greater post-sale continuity for the business. However, it's actually not very common for a business owner to sell the firm to one or more employees. There are three major reasons. First, employees rarely have the money to pay top dollar, or even a fair price, for the business. Second, employees will typically think that the firm is worth less than the business owner does because they privy to the weaknesses, dysfunctional aspects, and inner workings of the business. Third, it is generally not a good idea to share with employees that you are considering selling the business since such news may create fear that they will be losing their jobs soon.

Despite these concerns, many business owners prefer selling to employees because it means the business stays in good hands that are likely to care about it. John Clark and Alistair Miller were itching to sell their firm Novograf and get on with retirement. They were approached by a large firm, which offered to pay handsomely for their company. Clark and Miller were happy about how smoothly the selling process was going, when they learned that the buyer company planned to shut down their business after a year or so. Once the factory disappeared, so too would the jobs and the livelihoods of 60-odd workers and their families. "You'd be sitting back with your piles of cash," says Clark, "but at some point you're going to bump into those guys. Some of them have been there longer than me. I know their families." Eventually, Novograf was sold to its employees, who were willing to put in "the blood, sweat and tears" for the company.

There are two ways to selling a company to its employees: (a) one or more employees buy out the owners and (b) ownership in the company is transferred to a trust in exchange for the employees buying out the owners, also called **employee stock ownership plans** (ESOP). Established by the Congress in 1974, ESOP has now been adopted by more than 6000 American companies. In an ESOP, a company sets up a trust fund, into which it contributes new shares of its own stock or cash to buy existing shares. Alternatively, the ESOP can borrow money to buy new or existing shares, with the company making cash contributions to the plan to enable it to repay the loan. Regardless of how the plan acquires stock, company contributions to the trust are tax-deductible, within certain limits. Shares in the trust are allocated to individual employee accounts. Although there are some exceptions, generally all full-time employees over 21 participate in the plan. Allocations are made either on the basis of relative pay or some more equal formula. As employees accumulate seniority with the company, they acquire an increasing right to the shares in their account, a process known as vesting. When employees leave the company, they receive their stock, which the company must buy back from them at its fair market value (unless there is a public market for the shares). Private companies must have an annual outside valuation to determine the price of their shares.

Publix Supermarkets, an American supermarket chain headquartered in Lakeland, FL, first made stock available to its employees in 1959, and is now a prominent employee-owned company in the southeastern United States. Olum's, a major furniture retailer in the Binghamton–Syracuse area of New York, is also owned and operated by its employees. At Pennsylvania-based NCC Automated Systems, a full-service integrator specializing in automation, packaging, and material handling, the firm's owner, Kevin Mauger, assembled the employees to make a surprise announcement. After asking everyone to stand up, he declared that "if you are standing and you are an employee of NCC, you are now an owner." To the surprise of his employees, Kevin had decided that workers should be able to gain shares in the company over time.

When Clark and Miller announced their idea for selling Novograf to their employees, they reserved space in a local hotel, put on a fancy feast, and gave a great presentation. "The very first question we got was, 'Have we still got a job?'" remembers Clark. "Nobody had a clue what it meant," says a factory technician. "People assumed that everyone was going to have to get a mortgage to buy the company. It proved impossible for the employees to raise cash upfront for the purchase price. Not one of the major banks was interested. Not even our own," recalls Miller. So Clark and Miller turned themselves into a bank – handing over the company shares while allowing employees to pay them back over a few years, with interest. And with conditions: as long as the pair retains an interest in the firm it cannot relocate more than 200 miles away, "because that would defeat the entire purpose of the deal."

To learn more about ESOPs, you can visit the website of the National Center for Employee Ownership (https://www.nceo.org/articles/esop-employee-stock-ownership-plan), and browse the educational material there. Figure 17.3 provides a brief summary of ESOPs in the country. As you can see, ESOPs are a truly national phenomenon, with the Midwest having the highest proportions of ESOPs.

17.1.4 Sales to Other Buyers

Buyers for small businesses can be other firms looking to either enter into the seller's industry to diversify their own product line or to access the cash-generating potential of the seller's business. **Strategic buyers** are interested in buying a business because of the synergies they think can be created by combining the acquired firm with their existing business. **Financial buyers** focus on increasing future sales, reducing costs, or both, as their primary interest is in the firm's revenues and profits.

Facebook's acquisition of Instagram from its founders Kevin Systrom and Mike Krieger is an example of a strategic buyout. At the time of the sale, Instagram employed 13 people and was sold for $1 billion in cash and stock. Berkshire Hathaway, the investment company owned by Warren Buffett, is a famous financial buyer. Its portfolio includes well-performing companies like Precision Castparts Company, a manufacturer of industrial components, which it bought for about $37 billion.

Jeffrey E. Merry, founder of the Business House, a business brokerage firm in Gainesville, GA, says that the buyers he works with tend to fall into two categories: companies making strategic acquisitions to fill out their business portfolios and individual buyers leaving corporate careers.

Buyers can purchase a company in an all-cash deal, a combination of cash and stock, or by taking on debt. Some estimate that 60–90% of small business sales involve seller financing. The seller offers a loan to buyers that covers a portion (or all) of the total purchase price of their business. In turn, buyers repay the seller in installments, with interest. In effect, the seller of the business is essentially acting as a banker to the buyer. This method of financing offers benefits to both buyers and sellers. For the seller, such an arrangement can significantly expand the pool of potential buyers. For the buyer who doesn't have enough cash to buy a business outright, it can be a bridge to business ownership.

Founded in 1959, Bimac – a castings manufacturer – has nearly 70 employees at its headquarters and foundry location in Moraine, OH. Dan Bizzarro and Bill Jordan were still in college when they went to work at Bimac. After graduation, they joined full-time as manufacturing and engineering executives. And eventually they teamed with a third employee Roger Reedy to buy the business. They had a good ride. A few decades later, they were ready to sell. Working with a broker, they placed an online listing that drew the attention of Roberto Santos, a mechanical engineer from Ecuador, who was working at a family firm in Houston.

"The industry was taking a hit," he said. "I decided it was a good time to look for something of my own." During his seven-month hunt, Roberto gathered information on 10 potential acquisitions and visited 2 of the companies before finding Bimac. He bought the business and its assets, including its real estate, for $2.5 million. He put down 13% in cash,

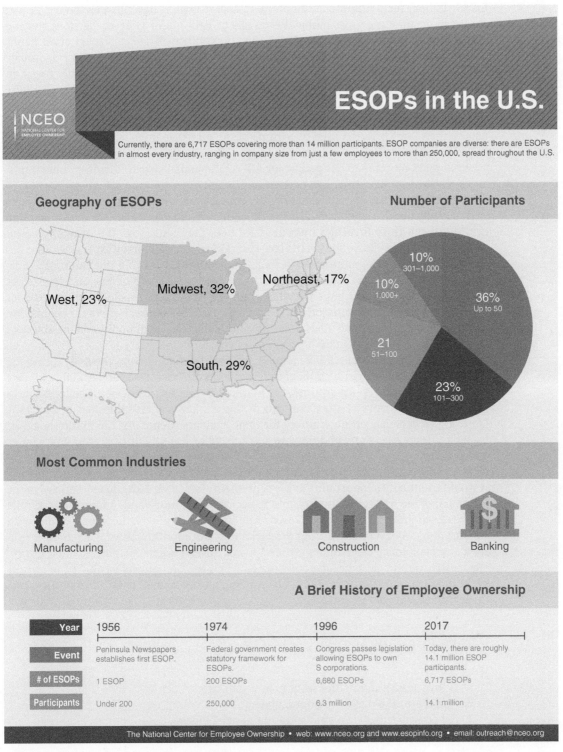

ESOPs in the U.S.

Currently, there are 6,717 ESOPs covering more than 14 million participants. ESOP companies are diverse: there are ESOPs in almost every industry, ranging in company size from just a few employees to more than 250,000, spread throughout the U.S.

Geography of ESOPs

West, 23%
Midwest, 32%
Northeast, 17%
South, 29%

Number of Participants

10% 301–1,000
10% 1,000+
36% Up to 50
21 51–100
23% 101–300

Most Common Industries

Manufacturing   Engineering   Construction   Banking

A Brief History of Employee Ownership

Year	1956	1974	1996	2017
Event	Peninsula Newspapers establishes first ESOP.	Federal government creates statutory framework for ESOPs.	Congress passes legislation allowing ESOPs to own S corporations.	Today, there are roughly 14.1 million ESOP participants.
# of ESOPs	1 ESOP	200 ESOPs	6,680 ESOPs	6,717 ESOPs
Participants	Under 200	250,000	6.3 million	14.1 million

The National Center for Employee Ownership • web: www.nceo.org and www.esopinfo.org • email: outreach@nceo.org

FIGURE 17.3 ESOPs in the United States, 1956–2017

and Bimac's previous owners financed another 12% through a seller's note. The balance of the sale price came from a bank loan guaranteed by the Small Business Administration.

Buyers who lack the financial resources to purchase a business may opt for **leveraged buyout** (LBO), where one can borrow on the company's assets. There was a time when LBOs were very popular in the United States. The famed investor Henry R. Kravis and his firm Kohlberg Kravis popularized the LBO in the 1980s. In *Barbarians at the Gate*, a best-selling book (later turned into a movie) focusing on the acquisition of RJR Nabisco for $31 billion, including the assumption of debt, Kravis is described as having "a war chest greater than the gross national products of Pakistan or Greece, his clout rivaling that of any in financial history." The success of Kohlberg Kravis attracted other firms, so that within a decade, it had to compete with hundreds of rivals competing vigorously in a shrinking market. Academic and popular discussions of LBOs generally focus on transactions between large firms and ignore entrepreneurial leveraged buyouts (E-LBO). In an E-LBO, majority investors are involved with active management of the company after acquisition, more than 50% of equity in the company is owned by single individuals or their family, and at least two-thirds of the purchase price is generated from borrowed funds.

What makes a company attractive for LBOs? Dependable cash flow from operations, an established product line, low current and long-term debt, and a high proportion of fixed assets (plant, equipment) that are fully depreciated. Most LBOs are asset-backed, so that they rely on the target firm having sufficient assets to loan against and take on more debt. For **cash-flow leverage buyout** (CF-LBO), the focus is on the company's cash receipts and positive cash flow as the basis for taking on debt. First Castle, a Manhattan-based investment firm, shares that it looks for companies making unglamorous, overlooked products like diamond-studded drill-bit inserts, airplane toilets, and class rings (dependable demand and huge installed customer base). First Castle does not consider companies in volatile sectors such as technology, fashion, and real estate for acquisition because their revenues and cash flows are unpredictable. Commodity businesses with large fixed costs (think airlines) are also out of consideration.

The prospects for selling a business are affected by market conditions. At times, the market is buyer friendly, which means many successful businesses are available for sale at an attractive price. At other times, the market for existing businesses is seller friendly, which means the pool of firms for sale in the market is small, the pool of buyers is large, and sellers can get good prices for their business. Generally, the market is buyer friendly during recessions and downturns, and seller friendly during economic booms and upturns.

Dennis Dreibelbis bought the G-Lodge Restaurant in eastern Pennsylvania, hoping it would eventually support him in his retirement. In March 2020, when Pennsylvania, like much of the rest of the country, told residents to stay home and ordered nonessential businesses to shut down, G-Lodge closed its doors. Dennis came to the Phoenixville-based restaurant nearly every day during the lockdown, but monthly bills for insurance, utilities, and bank loans were adding up, and it was unclear when customers would return. He doesn't want to close permanently or sell when the economy is weak. "I can't throw everything I worked for under the bridge," he says, from a small back office of the diner. "I'm sitting in my retirement."

Comprehension Check

1. Why would a competitor want to buy your firm?
2. What are employee stock-option plans?
3. Differentiate between strategic and financial buyers.

Module 17.2 Valuing a Firm

For a firm to sell, it needs to be valued. Facebook was barely two years old and had only eight to nine million users and about $20 million in revenue when Yahoo valued it at a billion dollars. Facebook's founder Mark Zuckerberg responded that Yahoo was undervaluing the fledgling business. There were all these things that Facebook was going to build, and Yahoo's valuation – Zuckerberg thought – did not consider the new features Facebook was planning to introduce.

KEY TAKEAWAY

The value of a business is based partly on formula, but also on experience, intuition, and industry trends.

There are various methods that can be used to calculate the value of a business. However, the decision of how to value a firm is based only partly on a formula; the rest of it is based on experience, intuition, and industry trends. This is because the quantified figures are calculated based on hidden values and costs such as personal expenses, goodwill, possible losses, and free family labor. Assumptions are made to arrive at projections that may (or not) turn out to be correct. Although one may say that coming up with a sale price for a business is partly science and partly art, the availability of a specific formula does give both the seller and buyer a common point at which to start.

Interactive Exercise

Professor Damodaran is among the world's foremost experts on valuation. You can watch his lecture on valuing private businesses (for sale or IPO) on YouTube (https://www. youtube.com/watch?v=NKR6XbUPNbE). Identify one or two things that stood out to you from his lecture and share with this class.

A common – and straightforward – method of valuing a business is to compute its net worth as the difference between total assets and total liabilities. **Book value** refers to the total amount a company would be worth if it liquidated its assets and paid back all its liabilities. Thus, the simplest approach to valuation is the book value of the firm. Imagine an athletics show manufacturer that has $406,359 in total assets and $99,039 in total liabilities (see Table 17.1). The book value of this company comes to $307,320.

TABLE 17.1

Assets and Liabilities of a Small Sneaker Manufacturer

Assets	In dollars
Cash on hand	18,852
Accounts receivables	90,610
Footwear inventories	8,873
Total current assets	118,335
Net plant investment	254,374
Construction work in progress	33,650
Total fixed assets	288,024
Total assets	406,359
Liabilities	
Accounts payable	18,619
Current portion of long-term loans	24,892
Total current liabilities	43,511
Long-term bank loans outstanding	55,528
Total liabilities	99,039

For many assets, the value on the books may not reflect their true economic worth as inflation and depreciation affect the market price for the asset. Consider a company that owns real estate, where the value of real estate has gone up considerably from the time it was bought. Alternatively, a company may own real estate in a market where the value has crashed. In **adjusted tangible book value**, the value of each asset reported on the balance sheet is adjusted upward or downward to reflect the fair market price for the asset. The assets considered in this approach include goodwill, patents, reputation, location, and so on. A popular hangout near a college campus may have assets worth only a hundred thousand, but if the students love it and keep it busy, the physical assets are worth only just a fraction of the total value of the business. Conversely, a daycare center accused of child abuse will take such a hit to its reputation that the market value of the business is likely much lower than the aggregate value of the physical assets.

Assume that the shoe company we looked at above has its warehouse flooded due to an unexpected storm. The flooding damaged their inventory, which was uninsured at the time. After the flooding, the inventory was appraised at 10% of its original value. This markdown in the valuation of the inventory will also affect the book value of the company. The inventory was originally valued at $8873, which was reduced to $887 after the flooding. As a result of this markdown, the total assets of the company decreased to $398,373. The new book value of the company (adjustable tangible market value) is $299,344.

The real value of most small businesses lies in their potential earning power. The **discounted earnings method** determines the firm's value based on the current and future earnings of the firm. To understand this method, one needs to first recognize the importance of the **time value of money** – money now is worth more than the identical sum in the future. In other words, the $100 you receive today is worth more than $100 you receive a year from now. For this reason, a firm's projected future earnings are worth less than the same amount of earnings today. Cash flow today is worth more than identical cash flow in the future because cash available today can be invested immediately and begin earning returns, while future cash flows cannot be invested until they occur. Future cash flows are therefore discounted to arrive at their present value, also described as **net present value** (NPV). The rate used to estimate future cash flows to the present value is called the **discount rate** (or **discount factor** or **interest rate**).

Let's look at a simple example to understand the concept of NPV. Suppose a business owner is offered $500,000 today or $550,000 in one year for her firm. If the interest rate is 5% per year, then $500,000 today is worth $525,000 in one year. Thus, the $550,000 she is being offered for the firm in one year well exceeds the $500,000 offered for the firm today.

There are four steps to value a firm using the discounted earnings method:

1. Estimate future cash flows. Given that the focus of this chapter is on well-established small firms that have been in business for a considerable length of time, historical data on cash flows is used to estimate cash flows for the future. Basic finance argues that the value of any business is the net present value of the future cash flows of that business. For most firms, past performance is a good predictor of future performance, though adjustments should be made when data suggest that future cash flows will change. For example, being near a subway station can be beneficial to many businesses, so if a new subway line comes up near a pizzeria or a station is built in the proximity, future cash flows may be higher. Further, a business owner selling a firm that is growing rapidly will want to estimate future cash flows differently than an owner selling a more mature firm with stable revenues and profits.

2. Determine the discount rate. The discount rate is often different for buyers and sellers, since each side looks differently at the risks of a deal. Whether the seller is in a rush to sell or is just exploring his or her options will affect the discount rate, as will the investment opportunities a buyer is considering at the time.

3. Consider reasonable lifespan of the business. Buyers and sellers need to arrive at a reasonable life expectancy of the firm. One considers the length of time a firm would survive if it was not sold now. The seller's age may also be a factor, as a

TABLE 17.2

Converting Future Value to Present Value of Juana's Food Truck

Year	Future value	Discount factor	Present value
1	$5000	$(1 + 0.12)$	4464.29
2	$6000	$(1 + 0.12)^2$	4783.16
3	$7500	$(1 + 0.12)^3$	5338.35
			14,585.80

75-year-old business owner may not be able to get away with claiming 25-year life expectancy for a firm in the same way that a 50-year-old business owner can.

4. Determine the firm's value by discounting the estimated cash flow using the appropriate discount rate over the expected remaining life of the business.

Let us look at the example of Juana's food truck to illustrate the use of discounted earnings method to calculate the value of her business. Suppose that Juana expects her food truck to yield $5000 one year from now, $6000 in two years, and then $7500 in three years. Say that Juana's interest rate is 12%. Table 17.2 illustrates how to convert each of these future values to present value so Juana can determine the total net present value of her business. According to our calculations, the total present value of future cash flows for Juana's business equals $14,585.80.

Another way to estimate the sale price is to consider a certain **multiple of earnings**, generally based on rules of thumb for the industry. For example, restaurants are usually valued between two and three times their annual profits. Table 20 is a popular farm-to-table restaurant in the working class community of Cartersville, GA, bringing in about $17,500 in weekly revenue serving lunch, dinner and craft cocktails, such as a limoncello basil martini with organic vodka and locally grown basil. Annual revenues at Table 20 come to nearly $910,000. At about 15% net profits, Table 20 makes about $182,000 per year. If Allie and Chris Lyons, owners of Table 20, wanted to sell the restaurant, they could expect the sale price to be between two and three times the annual net profit, which comes to about $364,000 (on the lower side) and $546,000 (on the higher side).

What Do You Think?

A business owner was testifying in a lawsuit when the lawyer asked him if he was familiar with the concept of net present value. "The concept of net present value to me would be the value of the business after debt," the owner responded. He continued, "Well, the word 'net' is an interesting word. It's really – the word 'value' is the important word. If you have an asset that you can do other things with but you don't choose to do them – I haven't chosen to do that." Do you think the business owner is describing the NPV concept accurately? If not, how would you answer it if you were asked the same question?

Another consideration is that your business is worth what someone will pay for it. The way to assess what someone will pay for your business is to search for **comparables**. In other words, what businesses similar to yours and located in the same area or a similar area have sold for recently is a good guide for the **market value** of your business. For example, say a restaurant doing a million dollars in sales in your neighborhood sold for $500,000. This price can then serve as a comparable for other restaurant sellers in the area, who can set the value of their dining establishments accordingly.

Yet another approach to determine the value of a business is **return on investment** (ROI), which is the ratio of net profit (or earnings before interest on taxes, depreciation, and amortization) to investment. The seller can combine ROI information with estimates of future earnings to determine the value for the business. If Jim invests $300,000 in a food truck and makes about $80,000 that year, his return on investment is 26.67% (which he gets by dividing investment by net profit). This ROI information and estimates for future earnings can then be used by Jim to figure out the worth of his food truck business.

When valuing a business, it is useful to consider that sellers and buyers will have different estimates for how much the business is worth. Sellers will usually value their business higher than the buyer does, so that there will be some negotiation during which the two parties go back and forth to arrive at a price acceptable to both parties. At this time, the negotiating skills of the respective parties will also come into play. For a successful harvest, one thing is certain: There must be a willing buyer. It doesn't matter who wants to sell and at what price; if someone is not willing to buy at a certain price, the harvest will not happen. Thus, in a way, the business is worth only what someone is willing to pay for it. The Govers, for example, owned a nursery located on 1500 acres of farmland. They wanted to sell it to someone who would continue to employ their 15 workers. Unfortunately, there was no buyer. The reason: The nursery was always in the red. The Govers put in $300,000 of their own money annually just to keep the business afloat. The Govers claimed the nursery was a business, but it really a hobby that never made any money for them. Eventually, they closed the nursery (after selling all the inventories), laid off the 15 employees on relatively generous terms, and then sold the land on which the nursery was located.

Once the buyer and seller agree on the valuation of the business, they also need to figure out the method of payment. A business owner has three options when selling the firm: sell all assets of the firm, sell equity in the firm as is, and combine the firm with another company. Buyers may prefer to procure the firm's assets as it relieves them of paying any debts or other liabilities of the firm. Sellers may prefer to sell equity in the firm as it counts for capital gain and saves them money in taxes. Very few owners will manage to sell their business for good money and still maintain full control. It may not even be in the interest of the owner to have the responsibility of running the business after selling it to the buyer.

When a business is sold, owners may be paid in cash or in the stock of the company. Generally, cash is preferred over stock. When the professional networking company LinkedIn was considering offers from Microsoft and Salesforce, both companies initially contemplated funding a portion of the deal with stock. LinkedIn ultimately accepted an all-cash deal from Microsoft. Entrepreneurs need to have tremendous confidence in the buying firm's performance to agree to payment in stock. Being paid in stock is definitely riskier than cash payments. Yet, some founders accept all-stock offers for selling their company. Matt Maloney, who cofounded Grubhub as a scrappy food-delivery startup in Chicago, sold his company to the European company Just Eat Takeaway in an all-stock deal.

Comprehension Check

1. Explain book value of a firm.
2. Explain the discounted earnings method for firm valuation.
3. What is market value of a firm?

Module 17.3 Challenges to Harvesting

All owners exit the business someday, but few actually manage to have successful exits. For many small businesses, a common outcome is closing the business one day with a "going out of business" sale sign. Owners who do manage to harvest the business are not always happy with the process and the outcome. This section discusses the steps business owners can take to increase the likelihood of a successful harvest someday.

17.3.1 Anticipating the Harvest

Many business owners do not consider the possibility that they will need to exit the business someday. As a result, they do not run the business in a manner that is amenable to a successful harvest. Could a business run if the owner fell sick for a week or longer? If the work of a business will come to a standstill in the absence of the owner, there is unlikely to be a successful harvest one day.

Another issue for many small firms is that they depend on the unpaid labor of family members. This model works when the business is in the family, but harvesting means bringing in new owners. If the way to profitability for a business is through labor from family members who work for free or below market wages, the likelihood that the owner can someday successfully sell the business to an outsider is low.

Owners who wish to harvest their business one day should run it as if a buyer may walk in any day. If a prospective buyer walked in today to make an offer on your business, what should she see? As you can imagine, buyers are willing to pay more for a well-run, organized business that follows appropriate systems and policies. Maintaining an accounting process that clearly separates the business from the owner's personal finances, keeping good books that properly document every financial transaction in the business, and managing a firm to produce a successful track record of consistent performance are all helpful in eventually harvesting the business.

KEY TAKEAWAY

Owners who wish to harvest their business one day should run it as if a buyer may walk in any day.

17.3.1.1 Don't stop running the business Harvesting takes a lot of time and energy on the part of the firm's owners and can distract them from day-to-day affairs of the business. You need to meet with prospective buyers, show them the inner workings of the business, and spend time discussing the business with them. There is also work involved in the valuation of the business and poring through offers from prospective buyers. Amid all this, many owners lose their focus and momentum, resulting in poor performance for the firm.

Selling the business creates high uncertainty for everyone, including employees, who may become anxious about the prospects of a new owner. Employee morale may go down as workers start worry about whether they will even have a job under new ownership. Maintaining employee morale during the time a business is on the market is not easy at all. Yet it is important to keep employees engaged and committed during this difficult time.

Interactive Exercise

Interview a broker who has successfully helped business owners sell their firms. Ask them about the common problems they see on the seller's end. Also, see if they can help you understand why many sellers report being unhappy with the process and outcomes of selling their firms.

Loyal customers are every firm's dream. However, customer loyalty cannot be taken for granted. Customers who feel neglected or cheated will rarely stay with the firm. News of the possible sale of a firm can be upsetting for its customers. It is therefore important to continue investing in customers to keep them happy. If one or two major customers abandon ship and begin purchasing from the firm's rivals, the market value of the firm will be affected.

17.3.1.2 Expect conflict

Negotiating the sale of a business can be rough, especially for the seller who is typically emotionally vested in the business. Buyers will search for and highlight each weakness and imperfection of the firm. Buyers may also visit the business premises and document each issue and shortcoming as if it was a serious problem that could irreparably damage the firm. The seller has emotional ties to the business, while the buyer can be detached and emotionally unencumbered. Conflicts about the value of the business, its imperfections, and its future trajectory are inevitable in the selling process and should not be taken personally.

In many harvest transactions, the entrepreneur is expected to remain with the firm for a period of time to help see the sale through. The purpose here is to ensure a smooth transition and reduce disruption. Unfortunately, after the harvest, the entrepreneur no longer owns the firm and does not usually have the same decision-making latitude they had earlier. When America's famed investor Warren Buffett buys a business to add to the portfolio of companies owned by his firm Berkshire Hathaway, he prefers to keep the owner to manage the business and asks them to follow two rules: (1) Never lose money, and (2) Never forget rule #1. Such hands-off buyers are rare in harvesting situations. In the vast majority of cases, the seller will need to buy into the vision and strategy of the buyer if they want to stay with the firm, or be ready to completely exit the business.

17.3.1.3 Seek advice

Harvesting is an once-in-a-lifetime transaction for most business owners. As such, learning the ins and outs of harvesting on the job can be stressful and financially problematic. Thus, there is a real need for good advice on the various facets of harvesting (how to value the firm, how to get paid for it, and so on). This advice may come from those who have previously been through a harvest or from experienced professionals who specialize in harvest-related matters. People who may have been good advisors during the time you were starting and building the business may not be very effective in guiding you through selling the business. So, carefully find competent and experienced advisors who can give you candid and constructive advice about selling the business.

Owners interested in selling their firms can seek professional advice from experts who specialize in helping with sale of businesses. They should also talk to other business owners who have successfully harvested their firms. Talking to those who have previously been there helps you anticipate what to expect both financially and emotionally during the harvest process.

17.3.2 Post-harvest Planning

Some owners are habitual sellers. They are serial entrepreneurs who build businesses with the goal of selling them one day. Consider Duke Rohlen, who planned to attend law school after graduating from Stanford University but became an entrepreneur after a chance meeting with Stanford business student Maurice Werdegar. Maurice asked Duke for help starting a restaurant business. With little enthusiasm for law school, Duke dropped his plans and joined Werdegar. Together, they started Blue Chalk Cafe Corp., opening a restaurant in Palo Alto, CA, to serve organic southern-style food. They went on to open eight California restaurants and grew the company to $20 million in sales before hiring a more experienced restaurateur as chief executive and departing from the company. "Duke worked long hours leading sales, marketing and expansion efforts while also bussing tables, greeting guests and helping in the kitchen as needed – always with a smile," Maurice later recalled. From there, Duke entered Harvard Business School with an eye toward moving into health care. In his second year there, he attended classes in Boston on Mondays, Tuesdays, and Wednesdays and flew the red eye to California on Wednesday nights to work the rest of the week at Redwood City–based medtech startup LuMend Inc. Over the years, he has sold four medical-device startups, each time providing quick returns to investors within four years of his taking the helm, about twice as fast as is normal in the industry.

For entrepreneurs like Duke Rohlen, the plan is clear: Get into a business, sell it at a profit, and find the next business. For most owners, however, selling a business can be a very emotional experience. The sale of a business may be accompanied by a loss of purpose. What does one do after the business is sold? Entrepreneurs should therefore carefully think about what they want to do after the business is sold and the money is in the bank. After Bimac was sold, two of the three partners, Dan Bizzarro and Bill Jordan, were not ready to retire yet. "If we retired, I think both of us would just go out and find another job," Dan shares. Roberto Santos, who bought the company from them, says he is happy to have the previous owners stick around. He is planning to make some changes at Bimac – he would like to invest more in automation and expand the company's export business – but he likes having their institutional knowledge to draw on. "I'm going to keep them as long as I can," he says. "They are teaching me a lot of things about the business."

Have You Thought About Exit?

Many business owners have no exit strategy for their business, perhaps because they are occupied with the day-to-day management of the company or they do not want to think about the business without them (or themselves without the business). Learn some practical tips on developing an "exit strategy" for your business. Watch the video online at: https://www.youtube.com/watch?v=JAH9T7cfDgQ.

A successful harvest provides liquidity and free time, but not all entrepreneurs who sell the business are able to figure out how to use them constructively. David Lonsdale sold his company and went on a vacation but found that the novelty quickly wore off. He became restless, bored, and somewhat cranky. He then set up shop in his home office, which led him to spend each day in the same house as his wife Kittie, an interior designer. The problem was Kittie was used to having the entire house to herself, working intensely in peace and quiet so that she could get into her "creative zone." Now she suddenly had an intruder wandering down the hall every five minutes, saying that perhaps she'd be more productive if she did her invoicing first. David was still unconsciously in CEO-mode, and assumed she needed him to give her direction. Two weeks later, Kittie walked into his home office, handed him the car keys, and said, "Honey, I do love you, but I need you to get out of the house. I don't care where you go, just find somewhere else to be."

What Do You Think?

David Morgan grew up seeing his father build the company Pac Paper Inc. in Vancouver, Washington, D.C. The company's main product: sleeves for coffee cups. When David came of age, he joined his father in the business, and after a few years, replaced his father as the owner of the company. Unfortunately, the next generation of Morgans or the other longtime co-owners had no interest in running the business. What do you think David should do? If he gets a good offer to sell the company to a rival, should he take it?

Bill Quish, senior managing director of Lyons Solutions LLC, shares that many business owners find selling and walking away from their business to be a difficult and emotionally charged decision. In such cases, **seller's remorse** is a common emotional reaction, and can occur immediately prior to or after the sale of a business. It is a frequent reason the sale fails to complete and can cause significant seller anxiety post-closing. The sale of a business may be accompanied by a sense of regret that one made a wrong and unnecessary decision. Owners who want to sell their business should have a clear idea of what they want to do after they exit the business. There is nothing wrong with having a good time in retirement, if you have earned enough to see you through the rest of your years and retiring is what you really want. When asked what she likes to do after selling Plum Benefits, Shara Mendelson responded, "travel, entertaining, taking random classes, running, hiking, anything that includes movement outdoors."

For many business owners, harvesting the business provides the money and time to give back to the world. Bill Gates, founder of Microsoft, has attracted a lot of attention for his philanthropic activities since he retired. One doesn't have to be Gates-rich to give back in retirement. Delores Kesler of Florida grew up on a chicken farm in Jacksonville as the daughter of a budding entrepreneur who always had something on the side, but chronic alcoholism kept him from achieving much. Years later, after her boss advised her to start her own company, Kesler took out a small loan and started her own staffing agency. She paid off the loan in six months, got a bigger loan, and gradually expanded the company. The business eventually merged with two other staffing companies and Kesler served as CEO of the company and on a four-person board that included three men ("unusual" at the time). By the time she retired after taking the company public, Kesler headed a business with an estimated $2 billion in annual revenue. Her retirement plan was to travel with her husband and spend more time with her family. Instead, she started her own foundation that provides scholarships to college students, in addition to providing additional funding to established mentorship programs. She also became involved with the Horatio Alger Association and helped develop young entrepreneurs through a venture capital fund she established for startup operations. "I have totally failed retirement," said Kesler. "It's easy to get caught up in the process of working with things that are measurable and not focusing on the personal side. I want to not fail and keep my life balanced."

Comprehension Check

1. Why is harvesting a problem for firms where several family members contribute free labor?
2. Explain seller's remorse.
3. Why do some business owners become despondent after selling the business?

Module 17.4 Harvesting by Going Public

There is one approach to harvesting a business that has not been discussed yet: initial public offering. Owners who want to monetize their investment in the firm can take the firm public, which refers to sale of a company's equity on the stock market. The first time a company's equity is offered for sale on the public market is referred to as **initial public offering** (IPO). The year 1999 was the most active for IPOs in the United States when 486 companies were taken public to raise nearly $108 billion. In 2019, 211 companies that went public raised $62.33 billion. Nine of the 2019 IPOs raised $1 billion each, among them Uber, Lyft, and SmileDirectClub. Only 39 firms went public in 2008, perhaps due to the Great Financial Crisis (GFC), which reduced the demand for stocks from investors. IPO activity varies annually, with economic conditions playing a large role in how many companies go public in a year.

> **KEY TAKEAWAY**
>
> When a firm talks about going public, it means offering the company's equity for sale on the stock market through an IPO.

There are several advantages to harvesting the firm through an IPO:

Reputation. Publicly traded firms often have a more positive reputation in the eyes of suppliers, customers, and financiers. Going public enhances the visibility of all firms, but especially small, regional or business-to-business firms that generally do not get the attention other firms get. Aneel Bhusri, CEO and cofounder of Workday, experienced a halo effect from the IPO as it brought in an array of new Workday customers, including those who may not have signed on before it was a public company. After the IPO, Workday could target a new set of customers in traditionally risk-averse verticals like financial services that only wanted to bet on a company they knew they could trust for the long run. These prospective customers viewed the IPO as the necessary "stamp of approval" to engage with Workday.

Value. IPOs put a value on the company, so that owners and investors are able to better understand how much their firm is worth. For example, investors value Airbnb at more than $31 billion. When a firm goes public, the market will put a value on it. In the first step, large banks that help take the company public (called underwriters) value the firm. In the second step, the investing public decides – through their buying and selling of the stock – if the firm is truly worth the price tag the underwriters put on it.

Liquidity. From a harvesting perspective, public markets allow owners to readily sell their stocks (with some conditions), providing them liquidity (that is, cash in their pocket). However, IPOs are not a harvesting option for mom-and-pop shops or the vast majority of small businesses that make up 99% of companies in the United States.

Large sums of capital. Going public is a fast way to raise large amounts of capital in a relatively short period of time. Facebook, for example, raised $16 billion in 2012, which instantly made Mark Zuckerberg a multibillionaire in the process.

What Do You Think?

Brian Chesky started Airbnb when he (and his cofounders) rented out an air mattress in their San Francisco apartment. Over the next few years, Brian built Airbnb into one of the most well-known private firms in the world. While the company continues to be unprofitable, it is valued at about $30 billion. For some time now, Brian has been toying with the idea of taking the company public. The COVID-19 pandemic brought Airbnb to the brink of collapse, as discretionary travel came to a halt. As the economy begins to come back to life, and travel is picking up again, Brian faces a dilemma: Should he try to take the company public soon or wait another couple of years? What would you advise Brian?

Going public is a formal process that needs to follow the guidelines laid out by the Securities and Exchange Commission (SEC). The SEC requires companies to file a registration statement that includes a complete prospectus of the company. The SEC then reviews the registration to determine whether the disclosure meets certain guidelines. If the company is determined to meet all the necessary guidelines, it is given permission to proceed. Complying with SEC regulations for IPOs can be costly and time-consuming. Julia Hartz, cofounder of Eventbrite, compares the amount of work that goes into an IPO process to the work that went into planning the wedding in "My Big Fat Greek Wedding." Just like that event, the journey to IPO is expensive, filled with conflicting opinions, and extremely time-consuming.

Interactive Exercise

The SEC provides several educational resources for companies interested in doing an IPO. You can find the SEC readings for IPOs by visiting the website https://www.sec.gov/ smallbusiness/goingpublic (or google SEC small business going public). What do you learn from those readings beyond what you already know about IPOs?

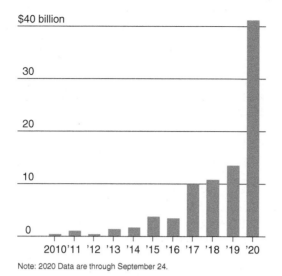

FIGURE 17.4 Money Raised in Blank-check Company IPOs in the United States
Note: 2020 Data are through September 24.
Source: Blank-Check Firms Offering IPO Alternative Are Under Regulatory Scrutiny, *The Wall Street Journal*

A growing trend in IPOs is special-purpose acquisition companies (**SPACs**), more commonly referred to as **blank-check** companies. Such firms have no assets or operating histories when they go public. They are essentially shell companies that go public to raise cash for future acquisitions. After a blank-check company goes public, its founders have a limited period of time, typically about two years, in which to find a private company to merge with or acquire. The private company then gains the SPAC's spot on the stock exchange, like a reverse merger. As Figure 17.4 shows, there is a boom in SPACs in the United States. The popularity of SPACs is also growing overseas (e.g. Europe).

Comprehension Check

1. What is an IPO?
2. What is the reputational benefit of going public?
3. Briefly explain the IPO process.

Summary

Every entrepreneur will exit the business someday. Some entrepreneurs will exit the business under distress. Other entrepreneurs will exit from the business profitably. Successful harvesting of the business requires owners to plan in advance. When owners want to harvest the firm, they need to be mindful of the challenges that make harvesting difficult. Owners also need to think about the several problems and difficulties that can come up post-harvesting. While some entrepreneurs start and sell multiple businesses, harvesting a business is a once-in-lifetime event for most people. A particularly attractive way to exit for many entrepreneurs is by going public. When firms sell their equity on the public markets, entrepreneurs are able to bring a large infusion of capital into the firm. Whichever way entrepreneurs choose to sell, a key challenge is to value the firm accurately.

World of Books

RIPE: Harvesting the Value of Your Business by Deborah Douglas
When Is the Right Time to Sell My business by Richard Mowrey
The IPO Playbook by Steve Cakebread

In the Movies

How do companies go public? What are some of the challenges enterprising individuals face when they decide to do an IPO? In the movie *Equity*, Cachet is a company with a social networking platform that is seeking to raise money from the public. The protagonist at the center of this film is a senior investment banker who has asked to handle Cachet's IPO after she faces some professional setbacks including major clients losing confidence in her work. Because of some issues with Naomi and her colleagues, Cachet loses a third of its value on the first day of trading on the stock market. Naomi is fired from her job.

Live Exercise

You look at your phone after class and see that Johnny has tried to reach you 11 times. You call him back on the way to your next class. Before you can say "hello," you hear Johnny's excited voice on the other end. "You will not believe what happened this morning," he says. Without waiting for your response, Johnny continues: "Bed, Bath & Beyond called today. They want to buy SoapStandle." You remind Johnny that BB&B already sells Soap-Standle, and it's been selling well there. "No, No, No! You misunderstood. BB&B wants to buy our company and roll it into their new private-label brand." You had always heard about companies getting bought by other, more established firms, but this was the first time someone you knew well was in a position to sell their company. You decide to take some time to write down a few things that you think Johnny needs to consider to make this important decision.

1. Is this the right time to sell? If Johnny can grow the company more for a few years, he could make more money selling it at a later time.
2. Should Johnny meet with the management from Bed Bath to discuss their offer? If he does, is he going in there to move the deal further or to discourage efforts to buy his firm?
3. What sort of price tag is appropriate for SoapStandle at this time? Six-figures or seven-figures? If BB&B offers high five figures or low six figures for SoapStandle, should Johnny agree to consider it? Or, should he decline anything under low eight figures? You recall reading somewhere that when a buyer says "low eight figures," it really means barely eight figures (about $12–$15 million).

As you are writing down things for Johnny to consider, a message pops up on your phone. It's Johnny again. "Would you like to come for the meeting with the BB&B folks? You can learn first-hand how these deals work." As soon as you read Johnny's message, you know you are going to be missing some classes soon. Meeting the BB&B CEO to hear out their offer to buy SoapStandle is not something you want to miss. It would be a good opportunity to see how owners think about the decision to exit the firm.

Things to Remember

LO 17.1 Distinguish between the various ways to harvest a successful business
- If the only reason to sell is for money, then the entrepreneur may not be ready to sell the business yet.
- When considering the sale of the company, owners should carefully identify their reason for wanting to sell the company.
- If you want to sell your business someday, you need to start the planning several years in advance of the sale.
- For business owners committed to sell, potential buyers can come from a number of places.
- Many business owners have a deep attachment to the company, so that when the business is sold, they feel lost and purposeless.

- A possible buyer for a thriving existing business is a competitor.
- For some business owners, selling to employees is one way to exit their business.
- Buyers for small businesses can be other firms looking to either enter into the seller's industry to diversify their own product line or to access the cash-generating potential of the seller's business.
- Buyers can purchase a company in an all-cash deal, a combination of cash and stock, or by taking on debt.
- The prospects for selling a business are affected by economic conditions.

LO 17.2 Identify the various approaches to value a firm

- For a firm to sell, it needs to be valued.
- Various methods can be used to calculate the value of a business, but firm valuation is based only partly on some formula, so that in large part valuation derives from experience, intuition, and industry trends.
- A common method of valuing a business is to compute its net worth as the difference between total assets and total liabilities.
- Firm valuation may involve adjusting upward or downward the value of each asset to reflect its fair market price.
- A firm may be valued by considering the current and future earnings of the firm.
- Another way to value a firm is as a multiple of annual earnings.
- A business is worth only what someone will pay for it.
- Sellers and buyers usually have different estimates for how much the business is worth.
- Once the buyer and the seller agree on the valuation of the business, they also need to figure out the method of payment.

LO 17.3 Identify the challenges that owners face in harvesting

- For many small businesses, a common outcome is closing the business one day with a "going out of business sale" sign.
- Many business owners do not consider the possibility that they will need to exit the business someday.
- An issue for many small firms is that they depend on the unpaid labor of family members.
- Owners who wish to harvest their business one day should run it as if a buyer may walk in any day.
- Amid all the work involved in harvesting a firm, many owners forget to run the business.
- Selling the business is a time of high uncertainty for everyone, including employees and customers, who are concerned about how the firm will operate under a new owner.
- Negotiating the sale of a business can be rough, especially for the seller who is typically emotionally invested in the business.
- Owners should identify competent and experienced advisors who can give candid and constructive advice about selling the business.
- Growing a company to scale confronts the management team with unforeseen challenges that can strain them to the point where they become stressed and wish their companies had remained small.
- Some entrepreneurs are habitual sellers, but for most business owners, selling the firm is a once-in-a-lifetime experience.
- Successful harvest provides liquidity and free time, but not all entrepreneurs who sell the business are able to figure out how to use them constructively.
- The sale of a business may be accompanied by a sense of regret that one made a wrong and unnecessary decision in selling the business.

LO 17.4 Explain harvesting by going public

- Owners who want to monetize their investment in the firm can take the firm public.
- The first time a company's equity is offered for sale on the public market is referred to as initial public offering (IPO).

- Publicly traded firms often have a more positive reputation in the eyes of suppliers, customers, and financiers.
- Public markets allow owners to readily sell their stocks (with some conditions), providing them liquidity.
- Going public is a fast way to raise large amounts of capital in a relatively short period of time.
- Firms interested in going public need to follow the guidelines laid out by the Securities and Exchange Commission (SEC).

Key Terms

liquidation	financial buyers	time value of money	return on investment
business broker	leveraged buyout	net present value	seller's remorse
direct rivals	cash-flow leverage buyout	discount rate	initial public offering
indirect rivals	book value	discount factor	SPAC
near rivals	adjusted tangible	interest rate	blank-check IPO
employee stock own-	book value	multiple of earnings	
ership plans	discounted earnings	comparables	
strategic buyers	method	market value	

Experiential Exercise

Use the Internet to identify the list of companies that went public in the last year. One place to find this list is at Dr. Jay Ritter's website: https://site.warrington.ufl.edu/ritter/files/2019/05/FoundingDates.pdf.

If you have trouble finding the list of all IPO firms from last year, you can just google top 10 IPO firms of last year.

Whether you are working with the full list of IPO firms or the list of top 10 firms, you should be able to successfully complete this exercise.

For each firm, identify the industry in which the firm competes and its valuation when the firm goes public. What are the most represented industries in your list? What valuations do you see for the firms in your list?

If you were asked to think about which firm(s) in your list are likely to be most successful going forward, what would be your best guess?

Once each student in class generates his or her list of IPO firm(s) most likely to succeed, the instructor can tabulate the results and share the summary information with the class.

Select one firm from your list. Try to find, using the Internet resources available to you, why this firm went public and what were some of the challenges it faced in going public. Based on the information you gathered, put together a memo for companies interested in going public. What are the opportunities and problems companies should consider when they are trying to go public?

INDEX